4TH Edition

INFANT AND TODDLER DEVELOPMENT AND RESPONSIVE PROGRAM PLANNING

A Relationship-Based Approach

Donna S. Wittmer
University of Colorado Denver

Sandra H. Petersen
ZERO TO THREE: The National Center for
Infants, Toddlers, and Families

330 Hudson Street, NY NY 10013

Editorial Director: Kevin Davis
Executive portfolio Manager: Julie Peters
Managing Content Producer: Megan Moffo
Portfolio Management Assistant: Maria Feliberty
Development Editor: Krista Slavicek
Executive Product Marketing Manager: Christopher Barry
Executive Field Marketing Manager: Krista Clark
Manufacturing Buyer: Carol Melville
Cover Design: Carie Keller, Cenveo
Cover Art: VadimGuzhva/Fotolia
Media Producer: Michael Goncalves
Editorial Production and Composition Services: SPi Global, Inc.
Full-Service Project Manager: Michelle Gardner
Printer/Binder: LSC Communications
Cover Printer: LSC Communications
Text Font: Meridien Com

Credits and acknowledgments for materials borrowed from other sources and reproduced, with permission, in this textbook appear on the appropriate page within the text.

Every effort has been made to provide accurate and current Internet information in this book. However, the Internet and information posted on it are constantly changing, so it is inevitable that some of the Internet addresses listed in this textbook will change.

Library of Congress Cataloging-in-Publication Data
Names: Wittmer, Donna Sasse, author. | Petersen, Sandra H., author.
Title: Infant and toddler development and responsive program planning : a
relationship-based approach / Donna S. Wittmer, University of Colorado
Denver Sandra H. Petersen, Zero To Three, The National Center for Infants,
Toddlers, and Families.
Description: Forth edition. | Boston : Pearson, [2016] | Includes
bibliographical references and index.
Identifiers: LCCN 2016027923| ISBN 9780134450094 | ISBN 0134450094
Subjects: LCSH: Child development—Study and teaching. |
Infants—Development—Study and teaching. | Toddlers—Development—Study
and teaching.
Classification: LCC RJ131 .W56 2016 | DDC 618.9200076—dc23
LC record available at https://lccn.loc.gov/2016027923

eText Package
ISBN 10:   0-13-429007-0
ISBN 13: 978-0-13-429007-2

Student Edition
ISBN 10:   0-13-445009-4
ISBN 13: 978-0-13-445009-4

eText
ISBN 10:   0-13-452072-6
ISBN 13: 978-0-13-452072-8

We would like to dedicate the fourth edition to our husbands
and children who support our work continuously and wholeheartedly
and to our grandchildren who teach us each day what it is like to be a child.
We appreciate them more than words can say.

Donna Wittmer
Sandy Petersen

Preface

This new edition of a comprehensive, applied text not only covers but *celebrates* infant and toddler development from birth through age 36 months, curriculum and program planning, and guidance using a relationship-based model. In addition, it focuses on the importance of families' and teachers' relationships and responsiveness in interactions with children; the latest developmental research; an emphasis on child-centered planning; strong coverage of infants and toddlers with special needs; and an emphasis on the effects of culture, families, and quality programs on infant-toddler development and interactions. It is research based and written so that the information is accessible and highly motivating to a wide range of readers.

What Is a Relationship-Based Approach?

Infants and toddlers have emotional and social needs to feel safe, valued, loved, and appreciated for their individuality and to be deeply connected with their family, culture, important adults, and peers. Supportive and positive relationships meet these needs and create the environment in which development proceeds.

Infant and Toddler Development and Responsive Program Planning uses a relationship-based model as a framework for understanding how infants and toddlers grow and learn with the support of their families and teachers. A relationship-based model respects the effects of an individual child's characteristics and the environment on the quality of the child's relationships. These relationships then become the filter and the catalyst for children's sense of well-being and development. As you use the relationship-based model to discover the importance of the infant and toddler years, we hope that you will gain a sense of enthusiasm and excitement about the influence that infant and toddler professionals can have on the quality of experiences and programs for young children and their families.

What This Book Provides for Our Readers

Our text provides a foundation in how infants and toddlers develop, in typical and atypical ways, and in program planning. See a detailed description on the next page.

Why and How of Developmental Practice

We present all aspects of development within the context of brain development and the foundational structure of emotional development and early relationships. We want students to understand *why*, according to the science of child development, certain practices support or hinder an infant's or toddler's optimal learning—and *how* to provide responsive, high-quality programs. This book integrates theory, research, and practice in usable language for teachers.

Program Planning

In addition to including developmental content, it also uniquely includes program planning, which highlights the following components:

- **D**eveloping the foundation of a program,
- **T**he teacher's roles,
- **T**he importance of relationships with families and how to provide culturally sensitive care,
- **A** responsive planning process,
- **C**onducting sensitive transitions and routines,
- **C**reating responsive and relationship-based environments,
- **P**roviding responsive experiences and opportunities for children, and
- **A** relationship-based approach to guidance.

An Emphasis on Culture and Children with Disabilities

To fully respect the impact of culture on early development, information on this and on the importance of inclusion of children with disabilities in early care and learning programs is included throughout the book. These topics are presented as they relate to the major content of each chapter, such as how disabilities may affect learning or how people from different cultures approach learning. Many of the scenarios in boxes are about children who develop atypically as well as on a more typical trajectory.

New to This Edition

1. **New video links have been embedded in this edition's Pearson eText.** Several videos relevant to the chapter content have been embedded in each chapter of this edition's Pearson eText, putting media-enhanced learning directly with students. Look for the "Play" button icon and click to observe infants, toddlers, teachers, and family members to learn about development, program planning, and professionalism.
2. The new **Observation Invitations** (in Chapters 6 through 10) invite readers to enter the world of a child or children to reflect on what a video or series of photos reveals about the child's development and goals. Reflection questions and possible answers guide the reader to think deeply about the meaning of children's thinking and behavior. This interactivity is available in the Pearson eText.
3. **Learning Outcomes** in each chapter identify the primary objectives for learning in the chapter. These assist the reader in focusing on, reflecting, self-assessing, and assimilating the knowledge base in each chapter.
4. **New to this edition of the Pearson eText are self-check quizzes**. These quizzes, called *Check Your Understanding*, are meant to help you, the student, assess how well you have mastered the chapter learning outcomes. These self-checks are made up of self-grading multiple-choice items that not only provide feedback on whether questions are answered correctly or incorrectly, but also provide rationales for correct answers.

5. **The writing style and reading level is more accessible.** We took special care this edition to keep our broad range of students in mind and your need to put information into practice as we revised this edition. Our writing style is more explanatory, direct, and has more focus on application than in previous editions.

6. The research information has been updated and new concepts are discussed. Each year, exciting, **innovative research on brain development, infants, toddlers, families, and culture** contributes to our understanding of young children's growth, development, and learning as well as family dynamics and teacher practices. This research has been integrated into this new edition.

7. Information on **children with special needs** is integrated into each chapter. There is also a separate chapter that focuses on children with special needs.

8. A new **Respect, Reflect, and Relate feature** is included which emphasizes the three ways to think about planning interactions and programs.

9. A **Program Practices** section in each of the development chapters highlights practices that have been proven to be effective.

SPECIAL PEDAGOGICAL FEATURES

Francisco has been exploring his own image. He watches himself giving his mirror image a kiss. Click on the icon to answer questions about the photo.

The special interactive digital features of this text include the following within the Pearson eText.

- **Videos**
- **Check Your Understanding**
- **Observation Invitations** in the development chapters (Chapters 6 through 10) invite readers to enter the world of a child to reflect on what a video or photo reveals about the child's development and learning.

Other useful pedagogical features in this text include the following:

- **Strategies to Support:** At the end of each development chapter, a Strategies to Support box summarizes specific strategies for teachers and other adults that facilitate the child's development in that domain.
- **Observation and planning forms** for individuals and groups in Chapters 12, 13, and Appendix D.
- Each development chapter presents a comprehensive chart, **Developmental Trends and Responsive Interactions,** which describes the capacities of the child as well as developmental milestones. It includes examples of development to help students connect theory with practice; lists teacher or parent interaction strategies to support development and learning; and provides a list of toys, materials, equipment, and other environmental supports that enhance development and learning. These tables also appear in Spanish in Appendix C.

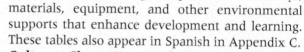

CULTURE CLOSE UP

Ms. Katika ran a quiet home family care, offering a rich assortment of experiences. Her assistant Patty loved working there—except for one thing. For example, 2-year-old Rosie chose a tub of large pegs and a board to stick them into. Ms. Katika at first observed and then encouraged her. She gently but firmly kept Rosie there until all 10 pegs were in. Her East Indian belief included building a strong work ethic. Patty believed infants and toddlers should be free to explore. What do you believe and why?

- **Culture Close Up:** Readers who care about infants and toddlers will experience close-up experiences with cultural and family beliefs and goals concerning how infants and toddlers are cared for and how they learn. This edition includes new Culture Close Up features that identify a real-life cultural opportunity that infant and toddler professionals encountered in their work with coworkers, families, and communities. The Culture Close Up includes creative thinking that contributes to relationship building and culturally sensitive practice and usually includes an inquiry that leads to group problem solving.

Other learning features:

- **Reflections and Resources for the Reader** at the end of each chapter provide follow-up questions and reinforcing material to correspond with the chapter's content. Relevant Web links are provided as well.
- **Vignettes** are woven throughout the chapters to illustrate how theories and concepts look in real settings where infants and toddlers learn and develop.
- **Glossary terms** are defined in the margin of the page where the term is used. Glossary definitions also appear when glossary terms are clicked on in the Pearson eText.
- **Quotes** from a variety of early childhood education and child development authors are highlighted throughout the text to illuminate specific points of interest.
- A complete **Summary** at the end of each chapter highlights the major points of that chapter.

Organization

Chapters 1 through 3 set the stage by focusing on early experiences, family relationships, and theoretical perspectives. Chapter 1 describes the current status of the infant and toddler field. Powerful research informs us that the early years matter. Science is establishing that the child's attitudes, knowledge, and skills developed during the first 3 years provide a foundation for a lifetime of learning and loving. Families, as the primary influence on their child's development, build this foundation, and the factors that influence how families function are explored in Chapter 2. Infant and toddler professionals also have a strong influence on whether babies thrive, and it is important that teachers build their practice on knowledge of theoretical perspectives. In Chapter 3, the theories that guide teachers to become purposeful about their work, understand how infants and toddlers develop, know what they need, and appreciate how they learn are described. The observation and documentation strategies highlighted in Chapter 4, provide methods for teachers to learn about children—how they develop and think and what they need to thrive.

The second section of this book describes the remarkable learning and development of children in the prenatal period (Chapter 5), and in the emotional (Chapter 6), social (Chapter 7), cognitive (Chapter 8), language (Chapter 9), and physical or motor (Chapter 10) domains. Each domain of learning and development is explored on several levels that relate to the relationship-based model presented in the first chapter. We describe the capacities that each child brings to that domain and then explore individual attributes such as gender or temperament. Early disabling conditions and intervention strategies are included in "Children with Special Needs." The development of the child within his or her family, culture, and an infant and toddler program is emphasized, along with strategies for supporting that aspect of development. At the end of these chapters, we describe components of programs that support and enhance the development of infants, toddlers, and their families.

The third section of the book (Chapters 11 through 16) takes you, the infant and toddler teacher, into the world of responsive program planning that happens day to day, the relationship way. Equipped with the knowledge of the importance of the early years, theoretical perspectives, and the impressive development of infants and toddlers, you will learn how to plan a program that meets their needs and supports them as they learn. This process includes *respecting* the child's experience, *reflecting* on his or her intentions and your own reactions, and *relating* to the child through your responsive interactions.

Nurturing and responsiveness are key elements of being an infant and toddler professional, and you will learn ways to promote the emotional development of young children within a program setting. With an emphasis on responsive interactions and relationships, you will discover how to set up an enriched environment full of learning opportunities (Chapter 13). The guidance strategies recommended (Chapter 14) respect the child's culture and individuality, require reflection on the part of the professional, and build infants' and toddlers' capacity to be in constructive relationships with others. Because programs include children with disabilities as well as children with diverse interests, needs, and abilities, Chapter 15 discusses how to individualize programs for children with special needs and how to work with the early intervention system.

The quest for quality experiences for very young children leads us to focus on what it means to be a professional who works with infants, toddlers, and their families. Chapter 16 describes the professional's journey toward developing an identity as an infant and toddler professional; becoming reflective; creating and nurturing relationships for professional development; and advocating for teachers, children, families, programs, and the community to move the profession forward.

We hope this book inspires you to promote the well-being, competence, and quality of life for infants and toddlers and their families. We also hope that it is the beginning of a new or renewed journey to develop a community of caring that recognizes the importance of the infant and toddler years. Infants and toddlers are depending on it.

Instructor Resources

The following ancillaries can be downloaded from www.pearsonhighered.com by instructors who adopt this text. Click on "Educators" and then "Download Instructor Resources."

Instructor's Resource Manual: An extensive *Instructor's Resource Manual* includes learning objectives, a multitude of active learning strategies, ideas for using the videos embedded in the text, and resources such as videos, DVDs, articles, and books to accompany each chapter of the text.

Test Bank: The Test Bank contains multiple-choice and essay items for every chapter.

PowerPoint Slides: These slides cover the major points and strategies of each chapter.

Test Generator Software: Known as TestGen, this test-generator software permits instructors to create and customize exams.

Course Management: The assessment items in the Test Bank are available in a variety of learning management system formats.

Acknowledgments

No book is written without affecting the lives of the friends and families of the authors. We especially want to thank our husbands, children, and sons-in-law for their never-ending support and encouragement. They, and our grandchildren, provide a secure and joyous base from which to explore this field.

We have shared numerous professional and personal experiences, and we have been influenced by many of the same individuals and programs. Together, we gratefully acknowledge and thank Dr. Ron Lally and Dr. Peter Mangione for their mentorship, friendship, and untiring leadership in their efforts to improve the quality of early care and learning programs for young children. Because they embrace their Fellows as family, we thank everyone at ZERO TO THREE who has led to the promotion of relationship-based practice. These people have deepened our understanding of the infant family field and have been a constant source of support for us.

To our friend Jo Koehn, we offer deep respect, affection, and gratitude. Her wisdom and fortitude have provided us with endless opportunities to deepen and refine our understanding of infant and toddler care through the Colorado Department of Education's statewide infant and toddler training, Expanding Quality for Infants and Toddlers. We offer our heartfelt appreciation to the faculty, community teachers, and participants across the state who are endlessly supporting quality care.

Special thanks to Julie Peters, our editor at Pearson, who strives for quality in all she does. She is insightful, knowledgeable, and wise. We definitely could not have completed this book without her positive regard, constructive support and constant encouragement. We sincerely and gratefully thank Michelle Gardner for her production work. They are key to the ongoing and finished project. Their humor, excellence, and guidance are indispensable.

We would also like to thank Carla Mestas, who took many of the excellent photos in the book that represent relationship-based care and education. We would like to thank Janelle, a wonderful family child care provider and all of the parents and teachers who provided the photographs of themselves and beautiful children throughout this text.

We would like to say a special thank you to Dr. Alice Honig, professor emeritus at Syracuse University, and a mentor and friend of Donna's since graduate school, for her continuous warm support and her infinite wisdom about infants and toddlers. For their influence on our visions of quality for infants, toddlers, and families, we also offer our gratitude and affection to Rose Bromwich, Jeree Pawl, Judith Pekarsky, Lillian Sugarman, Judie Jerrald, and Tammy Mann.

Finally, we would like to acknowledge the following fourth edition reviewers for their insight and comments: Sue Boyd, Central Carolina Community College; Anne Hanley, MiraCosta College; Barbara G. McWethy, Mercer University; and Glenda B. Patton, Somerset Community College. They greatly improve the content because of their experience with adult learners and their knowledge of infants, toddlers, and families.

Brief Contents

Contents

4 The Power of Observation: Learning About Infants and Toddlers   72

5 Genetics and Prenatal Development   94

Genes and Experiences Interact in the Womb   95

Language Learning and Development   206

Each Child Is Capable and Unique   208

Motor Learning and Development   240

Each Child is Capable and Unique   241

Including Infants and Toddlers with Disabilities in Child Care and Learning Programs   404

Respect, Reflect, and Relate: The 3 R Approach to Guidance   368

16 The Infant-Toddler Professional   428

1

The Importance of the Infant and Toddler Years: A Relationship-Based Approach

LEARNING OUTCOMES

After reading this chapter, you will be able to:

- Explain the importance of the prenatal, infancy, and toddler periods, including how infants and toddlers learn and how adults can support their learning and development

- Define a relationship-based model of thinking about children's development and programs for infants and toddlers and describe why it is important

- Describe the programs that serve infants, toddlers, and families, the importance of knowledgeable professionals, and how to apply the relationship-based approach

Pearson Education

It is easier to build a child than to rebuild an adult. (Author unknown)

Infants and toddlers are delightful and engaging human beings. They need healthy emotional connections with their responsive families, teachers, and peers to thrive. In this book we emphasize the capabilities of infants and toddlers to learn. We also emphasize how sensitive interactions and relationships influence infants' and toddlers' well-being.

Who are we talking about when we use terms like *infants* and *toddlers*?

> *The word infant derives from Latin words meaning "not yet speaking." It emphasizes what the child cannot do and reflects the baby's total dependence on adults. The word toddler, however, demonstrates our change in perspective, for it focuses on the child's increasing mobility and burgeoning independence. (Kutner)*

The general term *infants and toddlers* refers to children from birth to 36 months of age. An **infant** is a baby from birth to approximately 12 months of age. From age 12 to 36 months, infants become **toddlers**, walking and even running in a straight-legged manner that causes them to toddle—sometimes wobble, weave, and bobble—as their physical and mental abilities develop at lightning speed. At times we may refer to young toddlers from 12 to 18 months of age and older toddlers who are 18 to 36 months of age. In this textbook, the terms *babies, infants and toddlers*, and *infancy* are used to refer to children from birth to age 3. **Prenatal** development occurs prior to birth. From the prenatal period to age 3, babies grow from helpless dependency to children with a rich collection of relationships, skills, attitudes, and behaviors.

Who are the professionals who work with infants, toddlers, and their families? We use the term **infant and toddler professional** to refer to the broad range of specialists who teach or administer child learning and development programs, which include *center infant and toddler programs* and *family (home) child care* programs. *Infant and toddler professionals* also refers to professionals who support families in the care and education of their children through home visits, early intervention, and family support programs. These types of programs are defined and discussed later in the chapter and text.

The term **teacher** refers to a professional who has received specialized training to work with young children individually and in groups. He or she is in a position of responsibility with infants and toddlers in a classroom or home setting. We have chosen to use the word *teacher* rather than the more commonly used term *caregiver* because of the mistaken notion that caregivers give care but do not support children's education. The reality is that with infants and toddlers, *teaching* is

- taking care of infants' and toddlers' physical needs,
- interacting with them in responsive ways that meet their emotional and social needs and facilitate their development,
- setting up an environment that promotes learning in all domains, and
- working closely with the families of the children to build trusting relationships with them.

The term teacher is *not* used in this book for someone who imparts knowledge, but rather someone who provides caring, sensitive interactions and opportunities that support children's learning. These interactions and opportunities build on children's interests, strengths, and needs.

In this book when the term **caregiver** is used, it is in the context of any adult who takes care of and cares about young children. Caregivers include parents, teachers, grandparents, and others.

Our goal for this book is that you gain an appreciation for how vitally important the prenatal period and the first 3 years of life are. Our hope is that you will become knowledgeable about and gain a passion for promoting the well-being, competence, good developmental outcomes, and quality of life of infants and toddlers and their families. *Well-being* refers to "how a child feels and thinks about him- or herself and the joy and satisfaction that the child experiences in regard to his or her relationships and accomplishments" (1, p. 26). *Competence* refers to how effectively the child adjusts to day-to-day changes—how adaptable and flexible a child is. This is the outward manifestation of "*good developmental outcomes*" (p. 26, italics added). *Developmental outcomes* include the increasing abilities in learning, language, motor, emotional, and social skills. *Quality of life* refers to the child's feelings about the value, worth, living conditions, and relationships that he or she experiences. We hope that your enthusiasm and excitement about these four goals will grow and guide you in your interactions with, beliefs about, and support for infants and toddlers.

We promote a relationship-based model that fosters infants' and toddlers' optimal **mental health** in the context of the children's family, culture, community, and world. When toddlers reach age 3, they will be mentally healthy if they

- feel competent and confident,
- enjoy intimate and caring relationships,
- feel safe,
- have basic trust in others,
- regulate and express emotions in healthy ways,
- communicate and are understood,
- feel valued for their unique personalities,
- have the energy and curiosity to learn, and
- enjoy excellent health and nutrition.

The Importance of the Early Years

Recent science of brain development shows that experiences provided by parents and other early childhood caregivers have a greater influence over a child's positive self-identity, social development, and learning potential than any later interactions with classroom teachers or university professors. (Lally)

The new discoveries on the importance of the early years are exciting. We know now how much infants and toddlers are learning prenatally and through the first 3 years of life. The experiences that they have in the early years influence how well they grow, develop, and learn. The early years have a long-lasting effect on who the infant and toddler is and will become. Infants' and toddlers' early experiences will influence their ability to learn, feelings of self-worth, sense of competence, and capacity to love and care for others.

Caring adults are absolutely crucial for young children's optimal development.

 Watch the video on the amazing learning abilities of infants and toddlers. Why are the early years important?

(https://www.youtube.com/watch?v=DGls-Z4e6OI)

Some infants and toddlers are healthy, have enough to eat, feel safe and loved, are talked to in responsive ways, and feel like valued members of their families and cultures. Sadly, other infants and toddlers are hungry, fearful, surrounded by violence, or abused and neglected. Do these early experiences make a difference? Yes, without a doubt. *No other stage of human development requires as much learning and results in as many changes as the first 3 years of life.*

> *Early childhood is both the most critical and the most vulnerable time in any child's development.* (Brazelton & Greenspan)

Parents and professionals are learning more each day about how the kinds of environments in which an infant or toddler lives has a strong and lasting influence on that child's development.

> *Sammy, age 15 months, opens his eyes after a nap and cries out for his mother. As she comes to the side of the crib, she says soothingly, "Hello, you're awake? How are you feeling?" He wiggles around and then turns over and gradually stands up to see her better. His face relaxes and he smiles as she asks, "Are you ready to get out of your crib?" He answers by reaching up with his hands, getting ready for her to reach in the crib and pick him up.*

In this short but important interaction, Sammy is learning that he is important enough to be responded to quickly, that he can make things happen in this world, and that adults can be trusted to meet his needs most of the time. He is learning about who he is, how to be a generous partner in a relationship, and important concepts about the world in which he was born. These are the most important things for him to be learning at this time in his life, and these lessons will serve him well in years to come. If Sammy consistently receives this kind of responsive care, he will continue to thrive.

The infancy years do matter— and you can make a difference in promoting the health, wellness, quality of life, and happiness of children and families in these important years of development. Working with infants and toddlers is definitely not just babysitting! The work of parenting, caring for, and educating young children from birth to age 3, during this time of rapid growth and development, is among the most important work that exists.

The importance of the first 3 years of life cannot be disputed.

Pearson Education

Brains Are Building—Now Is the Time

It is easier to build a child than to rebuild an adult. (Author unknown)

 Watch this video on early learning and brain development. Which numbers explain brain development?

(https://www.youtube.com/watch?v=7Qb3DXY_7fU)

> *A ray of sunlight dances across 6-month-old Tamara's line of vision. Her dad talks warmly to her about the bright light, her eyes, and what she is seeing. We can't see inside of Tamara's head as new signals race along neural pathways in her brain. If we look closely, though, we can see it in her eyes, as they show curiosity, wonder, and joy.*
>
> *In another home, the stresses of life have caused Jo's parents to reach the end of their coping skills. As Jo, barely 1-year-old, reaches for a forbidden cookie, her hands are slapped hard, as they are, frequently. We can't see how hormones of fear surge in her brain, and how development is hindered by the constant fear and vigilance that Jo must maintain to protect herself, but if we look closely, we can see it in her eyes, as they show sadness, panic, anger, and pain.*

The discoveries about the brain development of Tamara, Jo, and other infants and toddlers have been remarkable. This knowledge has influenced parents' and professionals' beliefs about the importance of the early years. For Tamara everyday experiences evoke a healthy bath of hormones in her brain, helping build strong circuitry and creating a platform for learning. For Jo a bath of harmful, stress-induced hormones bathe her brain, which is being built to be vigilant to danger rather than other information around her.

As a mom, dad, or teacher talks to a baby, a song is sung, or the baby is positioned on the parent's body where he can see the playing dog, the baby reacts to these events, taking in information, processing it, and storing it. The synapses and the pathways formed actively create a web of learning in the brain. This is why early responsive experiences are so crucial: Those synapses that have been activated many times by virtue of repeated early experience tend to become permanent to ensure optimal emotional, social, language, and thinking development. The synapses that aren't activated disappear (2).

There is always one moment in childhood when the door opens and lets the future in. (Graham Greene)

Our understanding of **windows of opportunity** has made a difference in how we view the importance of the early years. There are windows of opportunity for learning that nature seems to fling open. These windows of opportunity are periods in the development of the brain when specific types of learning take place. Later, like windows stuck with age, they are more difficult to open and use. For example, the learning window for language is from birth to 10 years. However, circuits in the auditory section of the brain are wired by age 1, and the more words used in meaningful ways that a child hears by age 2, the larger her vocabulary will grow. Early-life windows of opportunity have been discovered for vision, hearing, math and logic, cognition, problem solving, and emotional development.

Now is the time to reduce infants' and toddlers' stress levels. The experiences that a child has can affect how the brain is structured. Scientists know that **toxic stress** changes the architecture of the child's brain and other organ systems and causes impairment. Toxic stress increases the risk for children (even into adulthood) to experience stress-related diseases and even impaired thinking abilities. Strong, positive adult-child relationships can buffer the effects of toxic stress on the child (3, 4). You will read more about the effects of stress in later chapters.

We must remember, however, that all is not lost if the infant, toddler, or preschooler has a less than optimal start. Many competent adults have overcome difficult and challenging starts in life. The human brain has a significant capacity to change, but timing is essential. Time and effort are often required to help older children or adults compensate for negative and damaging experiences in their lives. For example, a child whose world has been mostly silent during the first 2 years of life because of a hearing loss or lack of responsive language talk with an adult will likely be delayed in language development. This child will need intensive support to learn how to use language to communicate in a variety of ways. In the future, brain-imaging techniques may help unravel the mysteries of when **sensitive periods** occur and how intervention can remediate losses (5).

The brain power developed during the first 3 years is a foundation for the child to build on for learning and loving, just as a house must have a strong foundation to continue standing. Will the foundation be resilient and sturdy, upon which one can build solidly, or will the foundation crumble easily under the weight of future challenging times—the emotional windstorms, sleet, hail, and drought that may occur in a person's life? The exciting research on brain development in the early years has led to a better understanding of human development and the importance of the first 3 years of life. You will read much more about this exciting research in Chapter 5 of this book.

 Watch this video on brain architecture. How do experiences actually build brain structure?

(https://www.youtube.com/watch?v=VNNsN9IJkws)

They Are Competent Learners in the Early Years

> *While you have been reading this, a newborn baby has opened her eyes for the first time and sensed the closeness of her mother gazing lovingly into her eyes, and a toddler, seeking nurturing, has reached up for his father's hand. In this moment, a young toddler is learning to walk, falling down every 5 seconds but quickly getting up to master the task.*

Infants and toddlers are learning each moment of each day. We know that

- learning begins before the baby is born.
- learning is rapid and cumulative in the first 3 years—faster than at any other time in a person's life.
- learning prenatally and in the first 3 years of life provides the foundation for all later learning.
- early experience is built into our bodies (e.g. too much stress can create illness and loving relationships can create health).
- brain growth in the first 3 years determines how the brain is structured and affects all learning (6).

Infants and toddlers truly are remarkable learners. You will learn more about their amazing capabilities to learn in the chapters on emotional, social, cognitive, language, and physical development. Learning is also shaped by both genetics and the environment, children's active learning abilities, their ability to discern patterns, and their ability to learn through social interactions.

Learning Is Shaped by a Dynamic Interaction Between Genetics and the Environment

The impact of a child's experiences is dramatic and specific. It has often been asked which has more effect on a child's development: nature (genetic influences on growth and development) or nurture (environment, experiences, and educational influences on growth and development). This is no longer a controversy in the early childhood field. There is a complex interplay between these two in the development of infants and toddlers. Both play their parts in shaping whom the child will become. Genes provide the blueprint for learning and development. For example, we are genetically programmed to learn and use language. However, we need experiences with language for that learning to happen. When children experience rich language environments, their brain grows and is prepared for further language learning. When children don't hear as many words or aren't involved in infant and toddler "conversations," their brain is not as prepared for later learning. Experience makes the difference!

Experience actually affects whether some genes will be activated, as we know from the new science of **epigenetics** (7, 8).

Children Contribute to Their Own Development Through Active Exploration

Infants and toddlers don't need lessons to learn to walk, or drill practice to learn to talk. Rather, babies desire to walk and talk; they practice on their own and with responsive peers and adults. Infants and toddlers act on their environment; they put objects in containers to learn where they go. They shake, bang, roll, and stack objects to see what will happen. They make all kinds of funny sounds to get a response from a laughing sibling. They have goals, such as getting a favorite adult to look at them or opening a door. They experiment with different strategies to make these events happen. When all is going well, infants and toddlers are curious, energetic, and motivated to experiment and problem-solve. They are communication partners who need to take a turn in a conversation, even if the communication turn is a sneeze or a soft cooing sound. When given the opportunity (and this is how they learn best), they pursue their interests with adults who keep them safe, talk to them, nurture them, and support their learning. They are *motivated* to learn about themselves, others, and the world in which they live.

Children's thinking is "astonishingly competent, active, and insightful from a very early age" (Thompson)

Children Discern Patterns

Infants listen to language and are able to figure out where a word begins and where it ends when used in a sentence. They are figuring out statistical patterns in language (9). They learn which sounds are more likely to follow other sounds. They determine what causes a person or object to react. They learn how to solve problems. They watch and listen and create their own theories about how things work. For example, through experience they may theorize that one has to shake a box very hard to get the toys out. Through more experience they figure out that they can stick their fingers in the box to get the toys out. They make generalizations like, "only men can be doctors" and "women can be nurses." They generalize that things that are dropped go down and are surprised when a toy motorized airplane takes off into the air. Their brains are powerful learning tools (10).

Learning Is Social

Infants and toddlers use social cues to learn (11). Very early in the first year they watch trusted adults' faces to determine if another person or thing is safe. They pay attention to who is nice and who is not, who can be trusted and who can not. They look where an adult is looking or pointing to learn new words. They learn by imitating others. They are capable of learning through their interactions with others.

They Learn So Much in the Early Years

Emotional Skills—"Children's social and emotional well-being are as important to school readiness as are language and math skills." (Thompson).

How infants and toddlers learn amazes us. What they learn builds a foundation for all further learning.

They Learn in All Domains

The early years are important because infants and toddlers learn so much in emotional, social, language, cognitive, and physical/motor/perceptual **domains** of learning (See Figure 1.1). Children build on this knowledge as they grow. Future learning builds on past learning.

Infants and toddlers are emotional beings. Infants and toddlers express emotions and are ready to learn about their own and others' emotions. They learn who they are, where they belong, and whether they are loveable or not. They learn about their own self-worth and their capabilities. They learn who will protect them and whether adults can be trusted. They learn how to be in relationships based on the quality of their first relationships. They learn **self-regulation**.(12, 13)

Infants and toddlers are social beings. They need others. Infants are ready to interact with their special adults who take care of them. They learn through their shared experiences with others. They learn about peers and how to negotiate and cooperate. They are naturally prosocial—caring and helping—and with the right environment prosocial behavior grows. With adult help they learn how to channel aggressive feelings and enjoy others.

They are cognitive beings. They are thinking, seeing patterns in language, sensing regularities (e.g., objects usually fall when dropped), and building expectations for the physical and social environment based on their experiences. They grow in their ability to attend and remember. They gain knowledge about the physical and social world.

They are ready to communicate and learn languages. They learn how to listen and understand language. They learn to express themselves. They learn how to use language to tell people important things (e.g., that they are hungry). They learn to question, and get their needs met. Their vocabulary grows when adults are responsive and use descriptive and loving language with them.

FIGURE 1.1   **Domains of Development and Learning.**

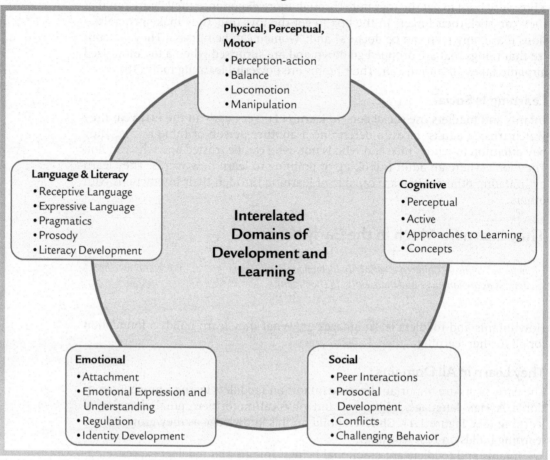

They are physical beings. They are ready to learn through touching, tasting, smelling, seeing, and hearing. They learn to move. They move to learn.

They are able and ready to learn when they are born. During the first 3 years they learn more than they will learn during any other time period in their lives. Special adults embrace infants' and toddlers' ability to learn and understand the importance of the early years for learning. Adults guide young children through a meaningful and momentous journey of development and acquisition of skills and knowledge.

 Watch the video on the importance of early child development. Why is development in the early years important?

(https://www.youtube.com/watch?v=M89VFIk4D-s)

They Learn the Values and Expectations of Their Family, Culture, and the Environment

All families and cultures have different backgrounds, experiences, and dreams for their children, as well as habits and customs that guide their thinking about raising children (14). All people see the world through the lens of their own culture (15). For example, by age 2, children's culture predicts children's attention to objects and actions. Children from China paid more attention to action, while children from the United States paid more attention to objects. The authors of this study stated that by age 2 infants are becoming "native lookers." They are learning their looking preferences from the adults in their culture (16).

 Watch the video on infants and toddlers as active learners. What are infants and toddlers learning, and what are the important roles of adults that support children's learning?

(https://www.youtube.com/watch?v=8db0Gcv3V10)

 Check Your Understanding 1.1
Click here to check your understanding of the concepts in this section.

A Relationship-Based Approach

A relationship-based approach to thinking about how to interact with children, what is important, and how to provide learning opportunities is the key to infants' and toddlers' well-being.

A Relationship-Based Model of Learning

Constructive, positive, caring relationships are fundamental to the human experience. A **relationship-based model** recognizes that positive relationships are vital for infants and toddlers (see Figure 1.2). Infants and toddlers learn through relationships. They need loving adults to protect them, nurture them, and help them learn. Responsive and caring relationships with the special adults in their lives are *essential* to infants' and toddlers' sense of security, self-worth, self-confidence, and motivation to learn. Infants' and toddlers' experience of healthy relationships is the foundation for their ability to love and learn (17).

Infants and toddlers exist within a network of relationships: mother–child, father–child, mother–father, mother–grandmother, father–neighbor, mother–employer, and many more that are influenced by and in turn influence infants' well-being (see Figure 1.2). A relationship-based model predicts that the quality of the relationship in one dyad (two people who interact with each other) affects the quality of relationships in other dyads (18). For example, a parent's positive relationship with the infant can affect the expectations that the infant has for a relationship with an infant teacher. Both of these relationships can then have an impact on the nature of the child's peer interactions. The array and quality of children's relationships exist within and throughout a web of interconnected circles, with each relationship influencing the other.

Both the *ecology* (environment), including culture, and the child's individual characteristics influence the features of the relationships that a child experiences.

FIGURE 1.2   **Relationship-based model for infant and toddler development and program planning.**

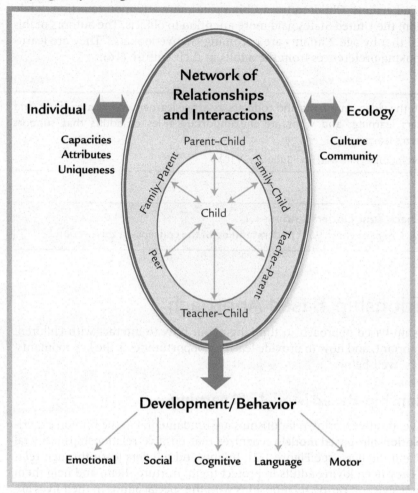

How the Ecology Affects Relationships

When infants and toddlers are physically, emotionally, and cognitively healthy and experiencing positive relationships, it is because of a support system that involves family, culture, the neighborhood, community, and a society that knows and cares deeply about the importance of the first 3 years of life. According to **bioecological systems theory** (19, 20, 21, 22), the ecology—the personal and physical environment—influences the nature of the relationships that the child experiences. These relationships are most influenced by the immediate settings: namely, family, community, and the early care and learning program that the child is experiencing (see Figure 1.2).

Families are also influenced by their **culture**—the values and beliefs about what is important in life, including traditions, celebrations, languages, and styles of interacting with others (23). Culture includes "the abstract values, beliefs, and perceptions of the world that lie behind people's behavior, and which are reflected in their behavior" (24). For example, a family's culture may value a child who is quiet, whereas other parents might encourage their child to be assertive and vocal. These values and beliefs guide the decisions about how to respond to the child's behavior. A **culturally competent** teacher learns and is respectful of children's and families' cultures. The importance of cultural perspectives, as a key part of the ecological model, is highlighted in this book.

National and international laws and policies are a part of the ecology that influences the quality of a child's relationships with parents, family, and teachers. For example, how a nation's citizens view families in poverty, welfare reform, or the importance of quality child care intensely affects life's possibilities for infants and toddlers.

In addition to being influenced by the environment, infants and toddlers influence the relationships they have with their parents and families. Infants and toddlers are born with unique characteristics that have an effect on how we, as adults, interact and relate to them.

How Children's Uniqueness Affects Relationships

Transactional theory highlights how the feelings and reactions of families and teachers are affected by their children's *uniqueness*—age, biological makeup, gender, temperament, appearance, and actions (25) (see Figure 1.2). These unique characteristics influence how the family or teacher treats the infant or toddler. Not all babies within the same family or program are treated the same. For example, a toddler who reminds the family of a favorite uncle has a different impact than a child who resembles a relative who isn't liked by the family.

How much a child's characteristics influence a family, however, may depend on the ecology of the particular family. A family under stress that has outside support from relatives, friends, or a community program may do well with a fussy baby. A family that is isolated from relatives or friends may have a difficult time with the same type of baby, who cries often and requires sensitive adult responses. When families perceive that they have social support from a shared community, the family and the children in that family are more likely to thrive (26). The families that have social support are better able to sooth and support a fussy baby and that baby, in turn, has less influence on the family's stress level.

Infants and toddlers come into this world with many capacities. They have the ability to express and interpret emotions, be social, learn, communicate, and move. These capacities blossom throughout the infant and

Beginning in infancy, create the child's capacity to love and nurture.

Pearson Education

toddler years within loving relationships with family members and other caring adults and peers. Each of these capacities and what caring adults can do to support them are covered in separate chapters in this book.

In a relationship-based model of infant and toddler development, there is a constant interplay between children's uniqueness and the ecology, and these—together and separately—influence the quality of children's relationships. The quality of the relationships then affects the experiences and development of the children.

Why A Relationship-Based Approach is Important

"Nurturing human relationships are the 'active' ingredients of healthy development." (Thompson)

The research on the importance of infants' and toddlers' positive, caring relationships with family members, teachers, and early interventionists (who work with children with special needs) is clear. Caring relationships help infants and toddlers feel safe and secure. Young infants and toddlers who feel safe and secure with their mother, father, other family members, and teachers

- feel less stressed (27).
- can express and control emotions in healthy ways (self-regulation) (28, 29) compared to young children who experience fearful or anxious relationships.
- experience higher levels of self-worth (30).
- have more reciprocal and diverse friendships (31, 32).
- expect less hostile responses from peers (33).
- are more cooperative and compliant and are less resistant with their special caregivers (34).
- demonstrate fewer behavior problems at 3 years of age (35, 36).
- experience improved relationships between parents and children (37).
- are better able to problem-solve (38).

Children feel secure when adults are

- responsive and affectionate (39).
- sensitive to children's needs and distress (40, 41, 42).
- emotionally available (43, 44).
- supportive of children's self-directed activities and autonomy (45).

Responsiveness is a key term that is used frequently in this book. Infants and toddlers communicate through their facial expressions, body postures, gestures, and words. **Responsiveness** refers to both how well the adult understands what the infant or toddler is trying to communicate (the child's cues) and how effectively (promptly, **contingently**, and appropriately) the adult acts in response to the child (46). Responsiveness occurs moment to moment in an interaction with the child and over time as the adult plans future interactions, an environment, and experiences that meet the child's needs and interests. Adult responsiveness influences how infants and toddlers expect others to treat them. For example, in one study mothers' warm and contingent (based on the child's cues) responsiveness influenced infants' expectations for positive social interactions and a sense of self-efficacy (a belief in their ability to interact effectively) (47). In another study, the authors found that toddlers' social-emotional competence was related to the contingent responsiveness of the mother (48).

Infants' and toddlers' secure relationships with teachers in infant and toddler programs also are vital for the children's development. When children feel secure within caring relationships with teachers, they are more socially competent (49), have better language development, can regulate their emotions, and participate more in problem-solving activities (50). Classic research found that young children feel secure to love and learn when teachers are highly involved with the children—hold them, hug them for comfort, and engage them in conversations. The more sensitive (warm, attentive, and engaged) the teacher is with children as compared to harsh (critical, threatening, and punitive) or detached (low levels of interaction), the more secure the child feels with the teacher (51).

Research shows that not only the quality of the teacher–child interactions is important, but also the quantity: "In center day care, children not only need sensitive caregivers but, more importantly, they need sensitive caregivers who find the *time* to display their sensitivity frequently enough to create a sense of confidence in their availability as a safe haven and a secure base" (52, p. 648). We need to ask, "how is the young child *experiencing* the sensitivity and responsiveness of the teacher? Does the child feel safe and secure with the teacher and in the setting?" A relationship-based program creates secure children.

Risk and Resiliency—How Relationships Make a Difference

Caring relationships with young children reduce risk and build resiliency.

Shana, a 1-year-old, has experienced much anguish in her short life: excessive hunger, hours of crying for someone to come to her crib to take her out, and bouts of severe diarrhea. She feels helpless and defenseless and open to further trauma. Yet, there are sources of **resilience** (ability to thrive despite risk factors) in Shana's and in many children's lives that contribute to **positive turnarounds** (53, 54). Resilience may come from the child's family—a loving grandfather or a mother who is at first neglectful of her child but then goes to school or gains support for new, positive ways of interacting with her baby. The source of competence for Shana could come later in life in the form of a caring circle of friends, counseling, or an adult mentor. Every person has sources of vulnerability and sources of resilience (55, 56).

Risks

"Risks to development can come both from direct threats and from the absence of normal, expectable opportunities" (57, p. 77). Risk conditions (see Figure 1.3) can influence current and later outcomes for children in learning, language, social, and emotional development. The most serious detrimental effects occur when multiple **risk factors** are present in a child's life (58, 59). Children who are **vulnerable** because of health, a challenging temperament, or physical conditions are more susceptible to the negative effects of risk factors (60).

Poverty is a risk factor. Poverty affects everyone either through experience or through the effects that it has on a nation. Poverty in the United States is defined by income. The 2013 federal poverty levels were $23,624 for a family of four with two children, $18,751 for a family of three with one child, and

Children can live in a state of fear and sadness.

Pearson Education

FIGURE 1.3   **Risk conditions.**

- Poor nutrition
- The child's own biological risks—such as injury, low birth weight, or health
- Living in poverty or near poverty
- Parents who are addicted to drugs or alcohol
- Parents who are depressed or have anxiety
- Parents who are in extreme distress
- Negative and abusive parenting
- Parents' use of harsh physical punishment
- Lack of social support for the family
- Living in a community with a high rate of violence
- Parents who are unemployed
- Low-wage jobs for parents
- Lack of quality child care
- Parents who have medical problems
- Lack of access to health and medical care
- Low parent-education levels
- Moving frequently (transience)
- Parent in jail or prison

Sources: Based on Werner, E. E. (2000). The power of protective factors in the early years. *Zero to Three, 20*(3), 3–5.; Weitzman, C., Edmonds, D., Davagnino, J., & Briggs-Gowan, M. (2014). Young child Socioemotional/behavioral problems and cumulative psychosocial risk John Wiley & Sons, Inc. doi:10.1002/imhj.21421.

$16,057 for a family of two with one child. The term "low income" is defined as at or above 200 percent of the federal poverty threshold (FPT), while the term, "poor" is defined as below 100 percent of FPT (61). According to the National Center for Children in Poverty (62), in 2013, 47 percent of children under the age of 3 years (5.3 million) lived in families experiencing low-income, including 25 percent (2.7 million) living in families who were classified as poor. Obviously, too many families in the United States are experiencing challenges in their attempt to meet their most basic needs.

Poverty is a global concern (63). From a basic needs approach to defining poverty, seven elements that children need have been identified: "drinking water, sanitation, nutrition, health, shelter, education, [and] information" (64). When a child lacks one of the seven elements in his life, he is considered as living in poverty. Delamonica and Minujim (65) report that in 46 developing countries, 1 billion children—one-half of the population—are deprived of at least one of these elements. An organization of the United Nations—the United Nations Children's Fund, or UNICEF (66) in its publication *The State of the World's Children 2008* reports that although vast improvements have been made in reducing the number of newborns who do not live to see their fifth birthday, an estimated almost 10 million children worldwide still do not as a result of the lack of one or more of the seven elements children need to survive.

Living in poverty, whether defined as low income or lack of basic rights, is difficult and challenging, to say the least, for families of infants and toddlers. Families that are in or near poverty face challenges that include the need for well-paying jobs, access to high-quality affordable child care and health care, adequate nutrition, decent housing, and basic services provided by the community (e.g., see the

FIGURE 1.4   **Reducing poverty.**

Reducing child poverty is one of the smartest investments that Americans can make in their nation's future. Fewer children in poverty will mean:

- More children entering school ready to learn
- More successful schools and fewer school dropouts
- Better child health and less strain on hospitals and public health systems
- Less stress on the juvenile justice system
- Less child hunger and malnutrition, and other important advances

Source: Based on National Center for Children in Poverty (2014). Child Poverty (2014). Information is available from the National Center for Children in Poverty Web site: http://www.nccp.org/topics/childpoverty.html.

National Center for Children in Poverty Web site www.nccp.org). These stresses for families in poverty can negatively affect children's academics, health, and social outcomes. The information in Figure 1.4 emphasizes how reducing child poverty is one of the smartest investments in the future that nations can make.

Resiliency

There are personal and environmental characteristics that contribute to resilience in children who are experiencing risk factors.

"Resilience is the ability to thrive, mature, and increase competence in the face of adverse circumstances" (67, p. 47). Resilient children have aspects within themselves or their environments that help them withstand more stress and cope better than many other children. Breslin (68) notes that it is not helpful to label a child "at risk," but rather to focus on the strengths and competencies in each child that can help him thrive—the resiliency factors. Resiliency factors (see Figure 1.5), or features that contribute to the resiliency in the child, can be divided into three groups: personal, environmental, and relationship based.

FIGURE 1.5   **Resiliency factors.**

1. *Personal factors*—characteristics of the infant or toddler
   - Energetic
   - Tolerant of frustration
   - Cooperative
   - Internal locus of control
   - Strong social skills
2. *Environmental factors*—characteristics of the environment
   - Social support for the mother
   - Social support for the family
   - Caregiver with education
   - A safe community
3. *Relationship factors*—characteristics of the child's relationships with others
   - Strong caregiver–child bond
   - Nurturing adults in the child's life
   - Responsive caregiver
   - Parents and teachers who allow ample exploration time within a safe environment
   - Peers
   - Adults who give positive feedback about strengths

Just as many threads woven tightly together hold up well against outside forces, the more threads of resiliency there are for a child, the more likely that they will create a durable tapestry that resonates strength and transformation despite risk and adversity. Werner demonstrated the importance of **protective factors** (factors that shield and protect the child) in forming resiliency in a study of 698 multiethnic children born into high-risk environments in 1955 (69). In a follow-up report when those children were 45 years old, Werner found that primarily positive caregiving during the first years of life is a protective factor that results in better adjusted adults. Also, the emotional support of close friends, spouses, adult mentors, and parent education classes contributed to the resiliency of the adults (70). Werner's work inspires us to think about the importance of personal, environmental, and relationship factors when planning policy and redesigning programs for infants, toddlers, and their families. When adults recognize risk and resiliency factors for young children and their families, then they can make important decisions in community and business practices that recognize the significance of loving, responsive adults for infants and toddlers.

 Watch the video on resilience. What is Resilience? How can parents and teachers help build children's resilience?

(https://www.youtube.com/watch?v=cqO7YoMsccU)

The importance of a responsive, caring environment during the first 3 years of life cannot be disputed. However, a wonderful infancy is not a magical immunization against later troubles in life. A 3-year-old may be bright, full of zip, caring, and engaging and yet face severe trauma as a 4-year-old or as a teenager. A result of stress and trauma could be an erosion of the child's trust in others and her own sense of self-worth. The developing child remains vulnerable to risks at all ages. Conversely, a child is still open to protective factors after age 3. For example, a child who has an emotionally difficult first 3 years and has challenging behaviors may respond beautifully to a loving adult who sincerely believes in the child's positive characteristics and supports the child by providing a consistent caring environment that promotes the child's competence (71, 72).

 Check Your Understanding 1.2:
Click here to check your understanding of the concepts in this section.

Infant and Toddler Programs and School Readiness

Infant and toddler care and learning programs are an important part of the lives of infants and toddlers and their families in the United States. Quality programs that support parents can reduce infants' and toddlers' exposure to risk factors and build resiliency and positive relationships. Quality programs support infants' and toddlers' learning and sense of well-being. There is great need for professionals who understand how to create relationship-based quality programs.

Types of Infant and Toddler Programs

Let's examine three types of infant and toddler programs available to families and a few of the issues related to these programs: (1) infant and toddler care and learning programs, (2) early intervention programs for children at risk, and (3) early intervention programs for children with disabilities. A community may provide each type of program separately or combine them into one program.

Infant/Toddler Care and Learning Programs

Infant/toddler care and learning programs offer varying hours of care for infants and toddlers, usually during the day while parents are at work. These programs are often referred to as just "child care" or even "day care." However, we think they should be named, **infant/toddler care and learning programs**. Too often the term "child care" is thought of as just babysitting. Rather, professionals who own, teach in, or provide child care and learning programs have an opportunity and an obligation to think of themselves as providing an enriched program where infants and toddlers learn.

The number of families utilizing infant/toddler care and learning programs is continually increasing. In 2011, more than 9 million mothers with children under age 3 were in the workforce, one-third of those with children under age 1 (73). As the need for infant and toddler care and learning programs increases, so does the urgent need for public and private resources to improve the quantity and quality of these programs. Parents often use an assortment of child services that may change and blend with one another to create an array of experience for infants and toddlers. These choices include infant and toddler care and learning programs provided in private homes (family child care) or in centers.

Family child care homes may be of the following types:

- Small, family child care programs (or a few children in the home of the care provider)
- Large, family, or group child care homes (typically no more than 7 to 12 children in the home of the care provider, who has a full-time assistant)
- In-home child care (by a nonrelative in the family home)
- Kith and kin care (provided by a relative, friend, or neighbor)

Center infant and toddler care and learning programs includes the following:

- Nonprofit (community or agency supported)
- Local for-profit (privately owned)
- National chain for-profit (centers found across a region or nationally or internationally owned by one company)
- Church supported (sponsored by and usually located in a church)
- On-site business (child care operated by a company, on-site for its employees)

National policies affect if and when parents use infant and toddler care and learning programs. For example, an employed mother in the United States usually must use her accumulated sick and personal days to stay home with her newborn baby for approximately 6 to 12 weeks and is still apt to go without pay for some of that time. In the United States, the Family and Medical Leave Act provides family members with 3 months of *unpaid* leave. However, in 128 other countries mothers are provided an average of 16 weeks *paid* and job-protected leave to be used before and after the birth of their baby with benefits provided by a combination of sources—government, employers, and health insurance.

For example, Sweden provides full parental leave at 80 percent of the previous salary for 18 months. Parental leave in some countries may be extended if the father stays home with the child for a period of time, as in Austria, where 3 years of extended leave are provided, but only if the father takes 6 months of the leave. Several countries—for example, the United Kingdom and Sweden—also provide parents with choices as to how the leave is spread out over the first 18 months after the birth of the child (74). Parents in the United States, because of work leave policies, may choose to use child care services much earlier than in other countries.

Parents want a setting where their children will be safe and where teachers show they care about their children. The challenge is to find infant-toddler care and learning programs that have adequately trained teachers, low child-to-teacher ratios, and small group sizes that make nurturing, relationship-based care possible. Unfortunately, parents have difficulty locating care for their children that is both affordable and excellent.

In a classic study concerning the availability of affordable and quality care of 400 child care centers located in four states, only 8 percent of infant classrooms were judged to be of good or excellent quality. An astonishing 40 percent of the centers observed were rated poor on the Infant/Toddler Environment Rating Scale (ITERS), a widely used measure of the physical and emotional characteristics of a child care environment (75). The other 52 percent were deemed mediocre.

More recently, the Early Child Care Research Network of the National Institute of Child Health and Human Development conducted a longitudinal study of more than 1,000 children to determine the characteristics and quality of infant and toddler care and learning programs for infants, toddlers, and preschoolers. Researchers conducting the study reported in 2000 that among infants and toddlers who attend care and learning programs, the ones who attend higher-quality facilities develop better language, intellectual, and social skills (76, 77). Higher-quality care emphasizes the importance of an adult's gentle and considerate responsive interactions, well-organized learning toys and materials, language development, and friendly and reciprocal program-family relationships. And, it has a positive effect on the development of infants and toddlers.

A Web site (childcareaware.org) has been created to bring together all of the federal agency resources concerning child care. Parents, professionals, and providers will benefit from information on this site on health, safety, family child care, staff training, regulations, and funding. The results of research studies, news, and publications are also included at the site. We devote five chapters (Chapters 11 through 16) to the development of programs for infants and toddlers that are responsive to infants', toddlers', and families' needs, promote learning, and are relationship based.

Early Intervention Programs for Children at Risk

Early intervention programs for children at risk comprise a second type of resource for families and children. One such program is Early Head Start (EHS), which has been said to mark "a turning point in America's commitment to our youngest children and their families" (78). An example of a nationally supported intervention program that provides support to families living in poverty, EHS reduces infants' and toddlers' risk factors, builds resiliency, and provides child and family development services. As Donna Shalala, former secretary of the Department of Health and Human Services, described it, "Early Head Start is about giving our youngest and most disadvantaged children a chance to grow up healthy, to learn, and to prepare for school" (79). The feder-ally funded program provides services to families that are expecting a child or have a child age 3 or younger and helps parents support their children's development. The program includes child development services, family involvement and parent education, health and nutrition, and prevention and early intervention. These services may take place as a home-based option, as family child care services, as center-based programs, or in some combination. The detailed and comprehensive Head Start Program Performance Standards (HSPPS), which EHS programs must meet, are often used as a basis of comparison as individual states develop their own program standards.

This center-based program offers inviting environments.

Each of the 1,007 EHS programs that exists across the United States emphasizes collaboration with community agencies to provide services. Specific services that EHS provides, in collaboration with its community partners, include prenatal and postpartum education, counseling services, infant and toddler child development programs, family education and engagement, health and nutrition education, medical and dental services, and referrals and assistance to families to access comprehensive prenatal and postpartum care. These services are also provided through home visits planned collaboratively with the family, infant and toddler group socialization experiences, family support groups, and a multitude of other creative initiatives.

The results of a comprehensive national study (80) of the effectiveness of EHS that included approximately 3,000 infants and toddlers from 17 sites demonstrate that EHS is making a difference for children and families. Half of the 3,000 children who participated in the study were enrolled in EHS (the experimental group) and half were not (the control group). EHS children scored higher than the control group on measures of cognition (thinking) and language (vocabulary and use of complex sentences), had better attention with play objects, were more emotionally engaged with their parents, and scored lower in aggressive behavior at age 3 (81). Only 50 percent of the EHS children moved into formal programs at age 3, and those who did had higher reading-related skills at age 5. At age 5, the EHS children had significantly fewer behavior problems and scored higher on approaches to learning.

The program is making a difference for families as well as children. When the EHS children were 3 years old, the EHS families were observed to have more supportive attitudes toward learning than the control group families; were more likely to read to their children; were more emotionally supportive of their children; and scored higher on measures of the quality of home environment, parenting behavior, and knowledge of infant-toddler development. Parents who attended EHS reported that they spanked their children less and were more likely to resolve problems by using distraction, explanation, or mild responses rather than physical punishment. EHS families reported lower levels of parenting stress and family conflict and were more likely to attend school or a job training program (82,83). When the EHS children were 5 years old, their parents read more to their children, provided a more enriched home environment, and were at lower risk for depression (84). This longitudinal study highlights the benefits of EHS as well as the importance of the EHS children attending a formal preschool, but unfortunately, because of limited federal funding, fewer than 4 percent (120,433) (85) of the poorest infants and toddlers in the United States attend EHS. The major Web site providing additional information and resources for families and professionals on Early Head Start is the Early Childhood Knowledge and Learning Center (ECLKC) at eclkc.ohs.acf.hhs.gov/.

Another major type of program for infants and toddlers at risk is home visiting. There are many home visiting programs across the country. Significant funding for these programs comes from the Maternal, Infant, and Early Childhood Home Visiting Program (MIECHV). Search for their Web site online for more information. MIECHV is covered in later chapters as well.

Early Intervention for Children with Disabilities

Early intervention services for children with disabilities and their families are the third type of early development and education program we will discuss. All infants and toddlers in the United States are entitled to a comprehensive assessment to determine whether or not they have a disability. A disability may include a developmental delay in how the child communicates and relates with others, moves, thinks, or perceives. This comprehensive assessment is provided by the school district in which the family lives. Or, a physician or child development specialist may refer the child for services. If a child qualifies for services, then the family and the professionals involved develop a plan for the child and family that builds on the family's strengths, priorities, concerns, and resources. The early intervention program may offer home visits and family support to "enhance the ability of families to work toward their own goals and deal effectively with their own concerns" about their child and family (86, p. 159). Infants and toddlers may also receive special help from professionals while attending an infant and toddler care and learning center or family child care home.

The Individuals with Disabilities Education Act (IDEA) provides federal funds, paired with a high proportion of state funds, for special education services for children with disabilities. Part C of IDEA provides funds and directives for providing early intervention services to infants and toddlers with disabilities. The act specifies which intervention services must be available for children but also sets policies that ensure that parents function as active members of the team and determine the goals for their own children. A high value is placed on the full inclusion of individuals with disabilities in their communities by specifying that early intervention services must be offered in natural settings, to the extent possible—homes, parks, child care programs, and other places where very young children without disabilities would be spending time. The final regulations of the current act were published in 2011 and are available at idea.ed.gov/.

The number of children identified with disabilities and served under Part C of IDEA has increased from a total of 165,351 in 1994 (the first year that state-reported data are considered reliable) to 342,821 in 2010 (87). Children's disabilities will be discussed in many of the following chapters and will receive special attention in Chapter 15. See ECTACenter (Early Childhood Technical Assistance Center) on the web for information on the importance of early intervention for infants and toddlers with disabilities and their families.

Infants and toddlers have irreducible needs for good health, belonging, and love.

Pearson Education

The Need for a Quality Workforce for Infants and Toddlers

As you read this book, you will begin to understand the knowledge and skills that teachers and other infant and toddler professionals need to support infants' and toddlers' development and learning, as well respectfully work with families and teams. There is a great need for professionals with specialized knowledge and skills to develop creative programs as they work with infants, toddlers, and families.

Using a Relationship-Based Approach in Infant and Toddler Programs

A relationship-based program applies our knowledge about the importance of teachers' secure, trusting, caring relationships with children. Children are then able to love and learn.

Responsive and Sensitive Interactions

Teachers observe infants and toddlers, read their engagement and distress cues, and respond in ways that meet the needs of the children. Teachers are thoughtful and intentional in their interactions. They are sympathetic to the struggles of young children. They provide affection, protection, and emotional connections. They follow children's lead for what they need. They talk with, not at, children. They model language, caring behaviors, and excitement about discoveries. They are day-to-day the relationship way.

 Watch the video on making a difference in children's lives. How can *you* make a difference in children's lives?

(https://www.youtube.com/watch?v=5EX9dMTsIXk)

Safe and Exciting Environment for Learning

Relationship-based programs emphasize the emotional availability of teachers. Teachers are available as infants and toddlers explore and play. Teachers create learning opportunities and observe the discoveries that infants and toddlers make each day. These discoveries then lead to teachers adapting the environment for individual children's interests and skills.

Small Groups

Small groups create more opportunities for stable and secure adult-child and peer relationships to develop. Language opportunities are possible in rooms with fewer children. Teachers are better able to meet children's individual interests and needs for emotional, social, language, cognitive, and physical development and learning.

Primary Care and Continuity of Care

Primary care and **continuity of care** in infant and toddler care and learning programs are important for young children's feelings of security. All teachers develop warm relationships with all of the children in the room. Babies develop trust with all teachers. However, with primary care each infant or toddler is assigned a teacher who establishes an affectionate connection (attachment relationship) with the child. This teacher tries to be the one to rock, feed, and tuck to sleep.

This teacher establishes a connection with the family to respect the family's culture and wishes. Continuity of care involves uninterrupted, continuous adult-child and peer relationships. A teacher(s) moves to a new room with a group of children as they age. Helen Raikes (88) observed infants and toddlers in child care centers and found that 91 percent of the children who stayed with a teacher more than 1 year felt secure, whereas only about 50 percent of those children who were with a teacher for a shorter period of time felt secure. A more recent study of more than 1,000 toddlers found that when at least one teacher "moves up" with the group or all teachers stay with the group as they age, the following occurs:

> Children and teachers develop close trusting affectionate relationships.
> Children are more positive with peers in the program.
> At home, children are less negative and less aggressive.
> Children have increased cognitive and language skills. (89)

When teachers do not move with the children and the children experience the loss, the results are not as positive. The more caregiver losses infants and toddlers have experienced by the time they are preschoolers, the more likely they are to be socially withdrawn and aggressive with peers (90). Infants and toddlers learn to trust adults and learn *how* to be in quality relationships with continuous care.

School Readiness? Yes, School Readiness

Only a few years ago, there was debate in the field as to whether we should be talking about school readiness for infants and toddlers. There was concern that we would pressure very young children to learn and then perform on assessments. However, in the last several years, we have understood that the connections made in the brain in the prenatal period and the first 3 years of life become the foundation of the brain that is used for the rest of the person's life.

"Birth to age 3 is a distinct developmental period that is the foundation for all later learning" (91, p. 3). The foundations for attention, memory, curiosity, problem-solving, and persistence are formed in the first three years and then refined and used over a lifetime. The child develops strength and stability in his trunk that allows him to sit and read and write later. He learns to understand and use language. He develops basic concepts about himself, other people, and the world. He learns about literacy and numbers. Most importantly, he learns about his own feelings and abilities and the intricacies of being with other people.

In order for children to be on the way to school readiness by age 3, they need responsive adults. They need adults who see the opportunities for learning in both short and long interactions. They need adults who can encourage learning with age-appropriate strategies. These strategies include play, exploration, and warm, encouraging interactions.

Meeting Young Children's Irreducible Needs

Meeting young children's irreducible needs is the thread that ties types of early development and education programs, the need for a quality workforce, and school readiness together. **Irreducible needs** are the needs of children that are absolutely necessary for them to survive and thrive (see Figure 1.6). Brazelton and Greenspan (92) emphasize that when these seven needs are met, a child will grow, learn, and flourish. We can think of these from the child's perspective and imagine what it must feel like to the infant or toddler whose irreducible needs are

FIGURE 1.6   **Infants' and toddlers' irreducible needs.**

1. Ongoing nurturing relationships

2. Physical protection, safety, and regulation

3. Experiences tailored to individual differences

4. Developmentally appropriate experiences

5. Limit setting, structure, and expectations

6. Stable communities and cultural continuity

7. Adults to protect the future

Source: Based on Brazelton, T. B., & Greenspan, S. I. (2000). *The irreducible needs of children: What every child must have to grow, learn, and flourish.* New York: Perseus.

met compared to the infant or toddler whose irreducible needs are not met. This text contains research and descriptions of practice that will provide strategies to meet children's irreducible needs. It is our hope that all adults, including those who read this book, can work together to meet infants' and toddlers' needs so that they can thrive—feel secure, be able to relate (feel warm and close) to others, communicate, solve problems, express feelings in culturally appropriate ways, appreciate their own and others' individuality, and have a sense of self-worth.

In this book, stories of children, families, and communities are shared to bring to life the uniqueness of each child, the relationships, and the ecology of infants and toddlers in the first 3 years of life. Our intention is to share these stories; the results of research; information on development and responsive care; ideas about relationship-based programs; and how to help infants love, laugh, and learn in such a way that you, too, will become an advocate for the importance of the early years.

Check Your Understanding 1.3
Click here to check your understanding of the concepts in this section.

Summary

The goal of this text is that you will become knowledge-able about and gain a passion for promoting the well-being, competence, and good developmental outcomes of infants and toddlers and their families.

- The prenatal period and the first 3 years of life are vitally important for children and for the adults they will become. Research on brain development has influenced the way parents and professionals view the significance of the first 3 years of life. Infants and toddlers learn in ways that we are just beginning to understand. They learn an inordinate amount in the first 3 years of life. You can make a significant difference in the lives of infants and toddlers.

- A relationship-based model of infant and toddler development informs and influences the content and organization of this book.

- □ The ecology of the child and the individual attributes and capacities of the child influence the quality of the relationships that the child experiences.
- □ The quality of the child's relationships influences the experiences and the development of the child.
- □ We can think about risk and resiliency in terms of the child's need for healthy relationships
- Infant and toddler programs are available for infants and toddlers.
  - □ There is a strong need for quality in early development and learning programs—programs that have adequately trained teachers, responsive and affectionate adult interactions with children, and mutually beneficial relationships with families.
  - □ School readiness is a part of the infant period because this age period builds a foundation for all later learning.

When we see the sparkle in an infant's eyes and the curiosity of a healthy toddler, then we know that the focus on healthy relationships and ecological factors that influence these relationships is a very worthwhile endeavor.

Key Terms

bioecological systems theory
caregiver
contingently
continuity of care
culturally competent
culture
domains
epigenetics
infant and toddler care and
    learning programs

infant and toddler professional
infants
irreducible needs
mental health
positive turnarounds
prenatal
primary care
protective factors
relationship-based model
resilience

responsiveness
risk factors
self-regulation
sensitive periods
teacher
toddlers
toxic stress
transactional theory
vulnerable
windows of opportunity

Reflections and Resources for the Reader

REFLECTIONS

1. Why do infants and toddlers need responsive, continuous caring relationships with parents, families, and teachers?
2. Create a list of why the first 3 years of life are so important for the well-being of infants and toddlers.
3. How are children's irreducible needs met in your community?
4. How has the research on brain development influenced the way parents and teachers think about the importance of the first 3 years of life?

OBSERVATION AND APPLICATION OPPORTUNITIES

1. Discuss how your uniqueness influences the relationships in your life.
2. Brianna lives in a family that is experiencing poverty. What are some of the risk and resiliency factors that may influence the quality of the relationships that she is experiencing?
3. Choose one of the irreducible needs of children and discuss what would happen to a child, from the child's perspective, if this need is or is not met.

SUPPLEMENTARY ARTICLES AND BOOKS TO READ

Gopnik, A. (2012). Nurturing brain development from birth to 3. *ZERO TO THREE, 32*(3), 12–17.

Lally, R. J. (2014). *The human brain's need for a "social womb" during infancy.* Retrieved from https://Forourbabies .org

Meltzoff, A. N., & Kuhl, P. K. (2016). Exploring the infant social brain: What's going on in there? *Zero to Three Journal, 36*(3), 2–9.

ZERO to THREE. (2016). Practical tips and tools: ZERO TO THREE critical competencies for infant-toddler educators . . . in brief. *Zero to Three Journal, 36*(3), 36–41.

INTERESTING LINKS

Better Brains for Babies: Recent Research on the Brain and Early Childhood Development Go to https://bbbgeorgia.org for many resources on brain development

Children's Defense Fund The mission of the CDF is to Leave No Child Behind® and to ensure every child a healthy start, a head start, a fair start, a safe start, and a moral start in life and successful passage to adulthood with the help of caring families and communities.

Child Trends Child Trends is an organization that seeks to impact policy decisions and programs that affect children through conducting and disseminating research, collecting and analyzing data, and sharing this information with those who set policy and provide services.

Child Care Aware of America (NACCRA) is a leading voice for child care. This organization works with resource and referral agencies nationwide to ensure that families have access to high-quality child care. It also leads projects that support professionals, conduct research, and advocate child care policies.

For Our Babies (forourbabies.org) Six brief and excellent videos on the state of child care in the United States.

Infant Brain Development Slide Show At slideshare .net, search for "Infant Brain Development: The Unfinished Brain."

The National Child Care Information Center (NCCIC) NCCIC a project of the Child Care Bureau, Administration for Children and Families (ACF), U.S. Department of Health and Human Services (HHS), is a national resource that links information and people to complement, enhance, and promote the child care delivery system, working to ensure that all children and families have access to high-quality comprehensive services.

National Center for Children in Poverty NCCP highlights 25 initiatives in the United States that improve the lives of infants and toddlers.

Parents Action

This Web site (I Am Your Child) has several articles on emotional development and some video clips, as well as a national public awareness and engagement campaign to make early childhood development a top priority for the country and show the importance of the first 3 years of life.

The Child Trauma Academy

Go to youtube and look for a free, 14 minute online video created and narrated by Bruce D. Perry. Core concepts regarding brain structure and function are introduced providing the basis for developmentally sensitive and trauma-informed caregiving, education and therapy.

The Child Trauma Academy Go to youtube and look for a 10 minute online video created and narrated by Bruce D. Perry. An introduction to the crucial role that patterns of stress response system activation play in pathology and healing is discussed.

UNICEF (United Nations Children's Fund) UNICEF was created by the United Nations after World War II. It works in 190 countries and focuses on children's rights to protection, education, health care, shelter, and good nutrition. Its work depends entirely on voluntary contributions of time and money. UNICEF published *The State of the World's Children 2016*, which can be accessed on its Web site.

ZERO TO THREE ZERO TO THREE is an organization that develops publications dedicated to advancing the healthy development of infants and toddlers. This Web site offers cutting-edge research, demonstrated best practices, parenting tips, publications, and conference information.

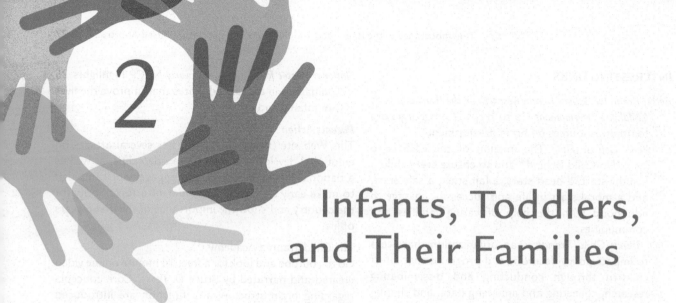

2

Infants, Toddlers, and Their Families

LEARNING OUTCOMES

After reading this chapter, you will be able to:

- Describe the effects of biology and culture on the family's experience of birth.

- Describe variations in the experience of becoming parents and parenting styles.

- Consider implications for families and teachers in the diversity of family structures.

- Explain aspects of programs that support parents.

Pearson Education

Looking around the room at the parent meeting, Sammie was impressed with the diversity of the group they served at the Metro Infant-Toddler Center. Some of the differences were racial. Some were cultural. Given their neighborhood, they tended to serve people of many backgrounds and religions. Nevertheless, there was more depth to the diversity. Susan was a single physician who had adopted a baby from Cambodia. Jewel was raising her grandbabies. Mare and Ernesto were adjusting from being a young married couple to becoming parents. Brooke and Tara were a lesbian couple raising Tara's baby. Each family seemed to have a unique situation regarding parenting, unique needs for support and information, and unique—and very strongly held—beliefs about parenting!

As Sammie understands, families come in all shapes and sizes. All kinds of families have happy, healthy, well-developing babies. All families are similar in some ways and each is unique in some ways. There are differences in size and structure. The roles of parents and children vary. The beliefs and values regarding infants and parents, even the rituals and processes surrounding birth itself differ. In this chapter, we also look beyond the immediate family to the support they receive as family members utilize infant and toddler programs, and other services. These services, in turn, are affected by policies and regulations made by state and federal legislators. Although these policies may seem far removed from any one family's daily life, they may have great effect on access to resources, services, and information, as reflected in bioecological theory (see Chapter 3).

Biological and Cultural Effects on the Family

All humans share common beginnings. The biology of conception, birth, and early development that will be described in Chapter 5 is much the same for all human babies. However, even within this basic model of early development, each beginning is different. Some mothers welcome the birth of their child. Some fear birth or don't want the child. Some biological fathers are present and active participants in the pregnancy and birth. Some are not. Like birth, parenting is an intensely personal experience. Each family creates its own, unique identity while incorporating its culture, current societal norms, personal history and characteristics, resources, stresses, and family structure.

Our Biology Affects Our Parenting

Biology and evolution have determined some of our parenting patterns. Because babies are born so dependent, parents around the world have developed ways to closely care for and protect their infants. Humans are born with large but not fully developed brains. The baby cannot stay in the mother's womb long enough for the brain to fully develop. Both the mother's body and the placenta can support the developing baby's needs only until the baby reaches a certain size. The baby's size is also an important factor in the birth process. Birth is now a long and arduous process for many mothers and babies. In most cultures the event is planned for and helpers attend the mother, whether they are medical professionals, doulas, midwives, or family members.

Human mothers and fathers react to newborns similarly across the world. Upon seeing their newborn for the first time, mothers and fathers hold the infant so that they can gaze into each other's eyes. They touch the baby's fingers, the palms, the arms and legs, and then the trunk (1). Babies, in turn, are born ready to participate in human interactions (2, 3).

The long gestation, difficult birth process, dependency of the infant, and predictable responses of the parents to the newborn are present across humanity. Together, they promote long-term, closely attentive, highly invested parenting. However, the exact nature of that parenting varies widely across cultures.

Cultural Effects on Parenting

Our parenting decisions today may be based in part on human biology. They are also based on cultural adaptations made by our ancestors. The following definition of *culture* can help clarify this idea:

> Each member of a group lives by a set of social rules, operates within a particular spiritual belief system, and adheres to an ideology that helps the society run smoothly. Each group can be described relative to the subsistence pattern, the production of goods and their distribution, the interpersonal interactions and social rules, and the history of its society (4, p. 74).

For example, consider a belief that *babies are godlike* versus a belief that *babies must be trained to be god-serving members of the community*. These cultural beliefs would result in very different parenting practices. The first parents might quickly meet every need expressed by the child. The latter parents might teach infants patience and generosity. Economics also affects our view of children and parenting. Imagine a society that depends on its children to watch the livestock on the farm or to care for the infants while the parents work. Then imagine an industrialized country where we generally see the *work life* beginning in adulthood. The expectations of the children, and the ways they are treated, will be very different.

Our own cultural beliefs are often invisible to us. We do not grow up hearing our mothers saying, "We're Italian and we believe this about babies." Or our grandfathers saying, "We're African-American and we believe this about babies." We grow up with a set of beliefs and values that are so rooted in culture that we believe we know the truth. The only truth. The way things are. It is only when we come across someone with different beliefs that we begin to recognize some of our *truths* may be culturally based. For example, a young couple struggled after the birth of their first child. The wife came from a Russian-Jewish upbringing where children were cherished above all others. The husband came from a Scandinavian background where elders dominated. The wife thought the new infant's schedule should be protected. The husband thought the infant should adjust to the couple's plans. For quite a while, neither recognized that cultural beliefs were at play.

Differing Cultural Values

Values concerning relationships differ by culture. The United States and Northern Europe are typically **individualist cultures**. They emphasize the importance of each person over the whole group. They value independence, competition, production, and personal responsibility. Latino, African, and Asian countries are typically **collectivist cultures**. They value cooperation, process (rather than production), and interdependent relationships. The individual is primarily responsible to the

---

 Watch this video to hear an anthropologist describe the approach of different cultures to childbirth. How does your culture see the transition to motherhood?

(https://www.youtube.com/watch?v=fVlklwmPptw)

---

harmony and well-being of the group, setting aside individual interests (5, 6).

Cultural beliefs about people are taught to babies through their earliest interactions with their caregivers. This is how infants and toddlers learn to become members of their family and community. One study looked at 214 families from nine cultural communities around the world. They described two major patterns of early interaction. The *proximal* style involves ongoing body contact. The proximal style is most often used by "traditional subsistence societies, in which socialization goals that embody relatedness, obedience, and hierarchy are preferred" (7). The *distal* style is characterized by face-to-face eye contact and object stimulation. The distal style is most often used by industrialized, educated societies that value "autonomy and separateness which have been demonstrated as precursors of independent agency" (8).

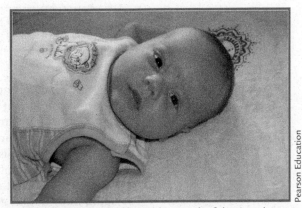

Wyatt's parents hold and carry him much of the time, but they also believe he needs time to experience his own body.

Parents who valued independence spent time showing their infants stimulating toys. However, they often held the infant while playing so there was also body contact. Parents who valued interdependence carried their babies against their bodies most of the time, providing a sense of closeness and shared responsibilities. Well-educated urban parents from highly interdependent cultures tended to use both styles of interaction (9).

Cultural Questions in Infant and Toddler Programs

Cultural differences create many questions for teachers and others who study child development. Teachers and parents may have different opinions on how they want to handle an infant or toddler in feeding, sleeping, being helped, developing language, or many other areas. When this happens, the differences may be grounded in each person's own invisible, cultural beliefs about babies. If so, respectful negotiations can lead to everyone agreeing on how these issues will be handled in care and learning. For example, consider a mother who always carried her baby son because, within her culture, carrying your baby signifies your love and protection of the baby. If the baby were allowed to play and crawl on the floor in the infant program, how would he know he was loved? The teacher believed just as strongly that floor time was good for physical development, and it was impossible for her to care for four infants when she was constantly carrying one. When the mother and teacher took time to discuss their positions, trying to respect and listen to each other, they were able to resolve their differences. The teacher assured the mother that she could play with the infant on a clean surface on the floor and help him feel protected by staying close. The teacher also agreed to more holding and carrying of the baby than she would do naturally, as a way of providing the kind of care the baby had come to expect.

CULTURE CLOSE UP

A New York City home visiting program served a growing community of Chinese immigrants, all from the same province. A home visitor had been working with a woman throughout her pregnancy. When the baby was born, the home visitor was looking forward to meeting him. She needed to see the mother within 2 weeks of birth–a protocol of her program and a rule of its funder. When the home visitor called to set a time, she was told that people from their province believe that a new mother and her baby should stay in bed and be cared for only by family for 100 days. How can the home visitor fulfill her funder's rules and respect the family's cultural beliefs?

Watch this video of Sue Bredekamp talk about the importance of working closely with parents. What are her main points?

Even when differences may be seen as cultural, some areas cannot be negotiated. An example that often arises is a parent who insists: "I was spanked as a child and I'm fine. I want you to spank my child if she gets out of line." Spanking, or any form of corporal punishment, may go against or be part of your cultural beliefs—but it is definitely not allowed under child care licensing regulations. No discussion of cultural differences is required with this one. A simple "our licensing does not allow us to spank children" should end that discussion. Providing information as to why licensing would have such a rule would be a useful parent education effort.

 Check Your Understanding 2.1
Click here to check your understanding of the concepts in this section.

Becoming Parents

Teachers meeting very young infants and toddlers in programs are often fascinated by the quick pace of change and development they are able to observe. Sometimes it seems as though an infant or toddler is changing before your very eyes. The huge changes the parents are experiencing within themselves are not always as obvious. However, they are equally profound. Teachers can be very helpful as people make the transition to parenthood.

Impacts on Parenting

So many factors affect parenting. Biology and culture are the beginning. An ecological approach to parenting describes many influences on how the family functions (10). These factors include early experiences and current circumstances.

The Impact of Childhood and Attachment Experience

Young women, who grew up in single-parent homes, are more likely to have a baby as a single parent. Young men, who grew up in unstable households with many transitions in their lives, are more likely to become a father early and less likely to live with the mother (11).

A person's early family structure sets some ideas about what a family will be like. The way family members act toward each other creates ideas about how all people will be with each other. Attachment theory (see Chapter 3) says that our first relationships create mental models of how people are together (12). Kind relationships teach us how to be kind people. Angry relationships teach us to be angry or fearful people. If an adult had a safe, caring family, the individual has a good model of relationships. The adult is more likely to handle upsetting marital problems in a constructive manner (13). If both adults had secure relationships as children, they are more positive about their marriage and more adept in parenting (14). They experience fewer divorces during their first six years of marriage, even if their parents were divorced (15).

The Influence of a Single Parent's Other Adult Relationships

Single parents and their children do better when the parents have other helpful adult relationships. Strong social groups of friends and/or family help single parents' ability to maintain strong, positive relationships with their children.

"Emotional support matters, even when you count family structure, income, gender, race/ethnicity, and child age" (16, p. 1). Mothers in poverty talked about the importance of emotional support. They said the children were less likely to act out, be depressed, or be retained a grade. They were more likely to be socially competent and engaged in school than children of mothers without emotional support.

Economics as a Factor Affecting Parent–Child Interactions

Economics also affects children's social and emotional development (17). Fathers who are employed and have good jobs tend to be more involved with their children. However, work schedules can interfere with consistent parenting opportunities (18). Flexible work schedules help increase time fathers spend with their children (19). Women's availability and work has not been studied as much. Women are still assumed to attend to both work and children.

Most women work before and after marrying. Women are more willing to marry if they see the man as raising her economic position. If her economic status seems more secure if she is single, she is more likely to want to live separately or cohabit, rather than marry (20).

The Imagined Baby and the Real Baby

Long before we become parents, long before we experience pregnancy, early in our own childhoods, we play at being parents. In our play, during teen years of babysitting, watching younger siblings or cousins growing up, we form ideas about what babies are like. During pregnancy, parents wonder about their baby and imagine what she will look like and how she will be. Mental health providers who specialize in the relationships between babies and their parents believe that expectant parents use the months of pregnancy to imagine the ideal child they hope to have (attractive, healthy, smart, athletic, happy), as well as deal with their fears of who the child might be (malformed, weak, ugly—or ultimately violent, alcoholic, or mean, like some disliked member of the family). Part of the process of becoming a parent after the birth is getting to know and accept the real baby (21). This may involve letting go of some imagined features while having the time to learn who this new baby really is. Infant and toddler teachers need to be aware that new parents are vulnerable to the thoughts and comments of others during the early infancy of their child. Their comments about each baby's character should be both true and positive.

Implications for Teachers

Joan Lombardi, a leader in early childhood policy, often says that the primary role of our field is to support the families of the children we serve. Understanding and appreciating the huge impact that becoming a parent has on the adults and on the couple can make the teacher a great source of support for the entire family.

In addition, giving parents a chance to meet other parents and explore personal and practical issues of parenting can be very valuable.

The Transition from Couples to Parents

There have been some recent game changers in parenting. Couples live together without marriage. They use contraception. Women earn as much or more than their husbands. Same sex marriage is legal and common. We have been through a recession and are in a slow recovery.

When marriage and living together are no longer tied to raising a family, the union is sometimes described as *expressive*. The couple feels stronger in expressing themselves as individuals and as a couple together (22). They value the romantic and sexual partnership but also the companionship, shared interests, and activities. When these couples do have a child, they share about having a baby and about the birth itself. However, the months following the birth often bring less satisfaction for the couple. Both partners miss time together, their roles become more gender bound, and they struggle with sleep deprivation and insecurity about handling the baby. For basically strong relationships, and when the infant settles in easily, this dissatisfaction begins to dissipate when the infant is around 6 months old (23, 24, 25).

Becoming a Mother

> *Nan woke up each morning feeling she could barely face the day. She had always wanted children and thought this should be the happiest time of her life. Her husband, Roy, had been increasingly distant since she announced her pregnancy and now he was out playing basketball almost every evening. Her family called and sent flowers when the baby was born, but they lived too far away to help. Friends from work seemed a lifetime away. She felt very much alone, and felt like a very bad mother for not just being grateful and happy that she had a baby. She was worried that she didn't know enough, or care enough, to ever be the kind of mother her baby deserved.*

Becoming a mother is both "a natural progression and a major transition" (26). It is a universal experience and a deeply personal, individual one. As a woman's body changes, as she sees the growth of the fetus in sonograms, and as she begins to think about herself caring for a baby, the process of becoming a mother is taking place. It can occur joyously or in despair. So much depends on the mother's health, her resources, her supports, and her relationship with the father and with her own mother.

A small group of pregnant women in Sweden shared their thoughts on many topics. Twelve women around the end of their first trimester talked about feeling that they had a secret only they and their partners knew. That felt good but it also felt lonely as they wanted to share this joyous news. The women talked about being happy to be able to give their parents a grandchild, but it also brought up memories of their own upbringing and parental losses (27). Conversations with pregnant women in New Zealand showed the more they felt they would be in charge of the birthing process, the better they felt about the birth itself (28). After the birth, women talked about marital dissatisfaction. Women felt worst about having less time alone with their partner and their sense of unfairness in the distribution of housework. They also struggled with exhaustion, loss of identity as a working person, a changed social life, and no time for themselves (29).

The term *high-intensity mothering* describes the high standards mothers expect of themselves. Social media is increasing the feeling they should do everything right—and believing there is a right way to do things. High-intensity mothering includes beliefs that mothers:

- are the most essential parent,
- should provide consistent intellectual stimulation,
- face challenges, and
- lives should totally revolve around their children.

These intensive beliefs were found to be associated with greater depression and feelings of stress (30).

Implications for Teachers

Teachers need to understand that becoming a mother—or becoming a mother again—affects a woman deeply. It may change her sense of herself, her satisfaction with her marriage, or her need for a social support network. Teachers can be sympathetic listeners and help mothers within the program get to know one another.

Becoming a Father

> Craig grew up thinking he wanted to have children someday, but he really believed that being a parent was something special between mothers and babies. Now he is the head-over-heels-in-love dad to 6-month-old Caitlin. When he picks up Caitlin from child care every day, her teacher always greets him saying, "Just look at how excited she is to see you. She just lights up when you enter the room!"

Teachers also have an important role in welcoming and valuing the child's father. The numbers about fathers are staggering. Twenty-four million children (one out of three) live without their biological father. At the same time, we know more about the importance of fathers for their unique contributions to positive development in their children (31).

> The guys who fear becoming fathers don't understand that fathering is not something perfect men do, but something that perfects the man. The end product of child raising is not the child but the parent. (Frank Pittman)

Men struggle with the changes in their lives. For many men, being a father has enormous meaning, through biology and culture. Fathers' images differ based on culture and social group. When fathers believe they have important roles to play, they are involved in caregiving activities, nurturing activities, physical care, and cognitive activities. They also show more paternal warmth (32).

Fathers are even important in prenatal health. If the father is involved, a woman is 40 percent more likely to get first trimester prenatal care. Fathers

This uncle and nephew clearly take great pleasure in each other's company.

Pearson Education

lower a pregnant woman's cigarette consumption by 36 percent. Expectant fathers can encourage a mother to breast-feed the newborn infant. Fathers who came with the mother on a prenatal visit were more likely to be part of father–child activities later in the child's life (33).

Holding education and income equal, fathers who are Caucasian, Latino, and African American, with college educations, used similar language with their infants. African American and Latino fathers played with and cared for their children more. African American fathers had a higher level of physical play. African American women suffering with postpartum depression reported that their children's fathers had more physical play with the child; this was not true for Caucasian women. This may reflect the collectivist African American culture that promotes closeness, with the fathers compensating for the mother's depression (34). Infants have secure attachments to the more sensitive fathers (35).

The mother's positive attitude toward the father and her support of the father's involvement are important for married and unmarried families (36). For fathers living outside out of the child's home, the parents' positive relationship was the strongest factor predicting the level of the father's involvement (37). Mothers draw fathers into involvement with their children by having child-centered conversations, encouraging fathers to take on caregiving tasks, and having a harmonious mother–father relationship (38).

Implications for Teachers

Infant-toddler teachers should make fathers feel welcome and appreciated for their relationship with the child. Teachers might hang posters of fathers with infants and toddlers, and offer information just for fathers. Having a few car or sports magazines in the foyer can help fathers feel welcome. It is also helpful for new fathers to hear from their child's teacher that they are doing a good job as a dad, that they have a wonderful child, and that it is clear that the infant or toddler loves them very much. Parent education for first-time fathers can be effective in teaching interaction skills if active learning strategies are used (39).

Parenting Styles

For each child, what matters is what it feels like to be with each parent. A parent may be present and engaged but if the child feels frightened, criticized, and blamed, the parenting is not helpful. Adults bring different beliefs, memories, and styles to their parenting.

The term *parenting styles* describes the normal variation in patterns of how parents try to guide and control their children (40). Parenting style includes both parent responsiveness and parent demands (41). Four parenting styles are commonly identified in the literature: *indulgent* (or *permissive*), *authoritarian, authoritative*, and *uninvolved*.

> **Indulgent (or permissive) parents** are highly responsive but seldom demand mature behavior from their child, depending instead on the child's self-regulation.
>
> **Authoritarian parents** are demanding but not responsive. They demand obedience to an extensive set of rules.
>
> **Authoritative parents** are demanding and responsive. They hold high standards for their children but are supportive in their discipline.
>
> **Uninvolved parents** are neither responsive nor demanding but not to the point of being neglectful (42).

In Western cultures, parenting styles are related to child outcomes, especially in adolescence. Children of indulgent parents have higher self-esteem but are more likely to have problems in school and in their behavior. Children from highly authoritarian families do well in school but tend toward poor self-esteem, depression, and poor social skills. Children whose parents are authoritative are rated more socially and intellectually competent than those of other parents. Children of uninvolved parents do most poorly in all areas (43).

However, parenting style is also related to culture. In America, with a predominant emphasis on individualism and freedom, authoritarian parents seem restrictive and constraining. However, children of Chinese families with highly authoritative styles develop very well, possibly reflecting the cultural attitude toward authority as serving the harmony of the group (44), and because strict and extensive rules are usually paired with great warmth and closeness, making the parenting style more of a mix between authoritative and authoritarian. The emphasis on effort and hard work over talent may seem authoritarian but really be authoritative (45).

Implications for Teachers

Infant-toddler teachers may find it helpful to share this information on parenting styles with the families they serve. However, this may also be useful information for self-reflection. As an infant-toddler teacher, you have a relationship with the children that is similar to that of a parent. Reflection on whether your style of relating to the children is permissive, authoritarian, authoritative, or uninvolved could be very enlightening.

 Check Your Understanding 2.2
Click here to check your understanding of the concepts in this section.

Family Structure

As we wrestle with the complexity of understanding families, one large task would be simply defining the word *family*. A **family** may meet the traditional image of two married, biological parents and their children. Or it may mean single parents, grandparents raising children, adoptive parents, blended families, or foster parents. Parents may be of the same or different religions and of the same or different races,

Pearson Education

Teachers may become part of a single parent's support network.

cultures, or sex. The changing composition of the family does not change what is important to the child about being a member of a family, however. A report from the American Academy of Pediatrics states, "Children's optimal development seems to be influenced more by the nature of the relationships and interactions within the family unit than by the particular structural form it takes" (46, p. 341).

We used to see only the two-biological-parent family as *normal*. Any other family structure was missing important elements. The many changes in the structure of families have caused us to look at this differently. We currently view all families as having both risk factors and protective factors (47). As defined in Chapter 1, *risk factors* are those life events or personal characteristics that threaten a child's or family's well-being. *Protective factors* are the events and characteristics that act against risk factors (48). For example, a calm, nurturing single-parent home would provide more protection than a two-biological-parent home affected by alcohol and violence.

Children can grow up happily, healthy, and without serious problems in all kinds of families. Children in two-parent households have some advantages. They are more likely to escape poverty, teenaged unmarried childbearing, and school and mental health issues (49). The majority of American children live in two-parent households. However, according to census reports, that percentage has been steadily decreasing since the 1960s. About 69 percent of children live with two parents (biological or stepparents), 24 percent live with only their mother, 4 percent live with only their father, and 4 percent live with neither parent (50). Teachers need skills for working with every kind of family. It is helpful to understand some of the issues that may be related to family structure. There are so many variations to the American family, and the issues surrounding them are so complex, that the following discussion should be considered a brief introduction to a topic worthy of deeper study.

Two-Biological-Parent Families

Of course, there is great variety within the group of two-biological-parent families. Both parents, one, or neither may work. Earning money and home-making may be shared tasks or held equally or more by one or the other partner. Making decisions concerning the infant or toddler may be shared or a responsibility owned more by one parent. Making major decisions may be the job of a grandparent—not even the parents! One parent may be more comfortable talking with you because of culture or personality.

Fathers and mothers bring different gifts to their infants. Mothers are more calming and nurturing. Their play is more social, preparing the child for future relationships. Fathers are more physical and play with novelty and excitement. Fathers are more likely to explain their own risk-taking, problem-solving, and managing frustration as they interact with the infant. All of these are important contributions to the child (51).

Implications for Teachers

Your work with families involves sharing general information about child development and specific information about your program and their child. While they are adjusting to diapers and burping, you will be helping them understand how to establish the foundations of healthy brain development and school readiness.

You need to learn from parents about their child, about their parenting beliefs, questions, struggles, and successes. Parent engagement is a real partnership between parents and teachers based on mutual respect. Parents must be in a position to make the decisions about their own child. At the same time, you are balancing the needs of the group and your own needs throughout the course of demanding days. You will need good listening skills, grounding in child development, and a desire to be flexible and find middle ground for effective parent engagement.

Divorce

Parents of infants and toddlers have special issues to consider when they divorce. Infants and toddlers may not understand the difficulties their parents are experiencing. However, they are very aware of the emotional tone of their environment. The sadness, tension, and anger of divorce can be stressful to even very young infants (52). The infant needs to develop a sense of trust in others. This depends on the adults' predictability and consistent emotional availability. Ex-husbands and wives are best at co-parenting when they are able to keep the child's well-being at the forefront.

Two developmental needs of infancy have been seen as conflicting. Each child benefits from a close, ongoing relationship with the father. Each child also needs at least one attachment relationship in which they feel safe, able to control anxiety, and share joy in being with someone special. These needs are not at odds but they often play out in divorce as a conflict. There is debate as to whether the child's attachment to the mother is primary or whether the attachment to both parents is of equal importance.

A major area of conflict is often the question of whether infants and young toddlers should have overnight visits with the noncustodial parent—usually the father. One concern is that overnight visits with fathers in divorced or separating families can be very stressful to young infants who are still establishing the rhythms of their days (53). However, infants may spend nights with friends or grandparents on occasion.

Two major problems arise. Infants and toddlers who are breastfed will need to be with the mother at night unless she is able to cooperate with providing breast milk to the father. In an age when many mothers use breast pumps to provide milk for care and education providers, this may not be a big problem. Still, mothers may need to nurse at night in order to keep their supply up.

It is attachment issues that make custody sharing so confusing for infants and toddlers. Much of the concern centers on the infant forming a secure attachment relationship with at least one adult. An attachment relationship is forming during the first 18 months. Some people believe that one primary attachment relationship must form first and that it must be protected. The sense of safety connected with a sleep routine, a place for sleep, and a wakening routine may be part of establishing that relationship.

Overall, the importance of the father's role and ongoing contact is clear. So is the attachment relationship—with both parents. These issues will not be resolved in the infant-toddler program. They will play out in mediation or courts or by negotiation. It is helpful to be knowledgeable about the potential for positive solutions.

Implications for Teachers

An infant-toddler teacher needs to be sure that she relates fairly to both divorced parents, supporting each parent's relationship with the child. The teacher must remain neutral in a situation that can be fraught with difficult feelings. In supporting the child's relationship with each parent, the teacher must keep both parents well informed about the child and find ways, when necessary, to describe the effect that the parents' relationship or the custody situation is having on the child.

Single Parents

There are many stresses and challenges facing single parents. The biggest challenge is poverty. The percentage of children born to women who have never married is increasing dramatically: In the early 1960s, less than 1 percent of children lived with a never-married parent. By 2000, nearly 1 in 10 children lived with a never-married parent. In 2009, 41 percent of all births occurred to unmarried women (54).

> Infants and toddlers in single parent families are more than twice as likely to be low-income as those in married couple families. Families are more than twice as likely to be low-income as those in married couple families. Overall, about 2.3 million infants and toddlers have at least one parent who works full-time, year round, whose wages still can't pull the family above the low-income level. Research shows that poverty at an early age can be especially harmful, affecting later achievement and employment (55, p. 1).

Single parents face other challenges as well. If they are employed or in school, they carry the weight of two full-time jobs. There is likely to be no one to share the joys or work of running a home and raising an infant or toddler. Single parents are often stressed and exhausted.

Implications for Teachers

Teachers need to be understanding. Your job is to support the parent–child relationship. Programs need to be sensitive to issues of poverty and stress. There is one more matter for infants and toddlers who are growing up with only one parent. These children need and long for safe, nurturing contact with adults of both sexes. Because care and education providers are predominantly female, it is easier to provide female experiences to children being raised by fathers than male experiences to children of single mothers.

Same-Sex Parents

Same-sex parents are estimated to be raising as many as 9 million of America's children, but accurate statistics are impossible to find. Gay and lesbian parents share the same concerns and worries of all parents but face additional issues unique to their situation. If the child was not originally conceived within an earlier heterosexual relationship, there are questions of adoption, artificial insemination, or surrogate mothers. In 2015, the Supreme Court ruling made same sex marriage legal in the United States. This has eased problems about full parental rights for both parents.

A study of the well-being of adult children raised by same-sex parents showed factors that seemed most influential in supporting their development. The adults with the best outcomes were raised in a community that had several similar families and a social climate that included voting Democratic, having more accepting religious beliefs, and school rules against bullying (56).

Many early childhood programs serve families through home visits, working with the parent and child together.

> More than two decades of research has failed to reveal important differences in the adjustment or development of children or adolescents reared by same-sex couples compared to those reared by other-sex couples. Results of the research suggest that qualities of family relationships are more tightly linked with child outcomes than is parental sexual orientation (57, p. 241).

Implications for Teachers

When same-sex couples bring an infant or toddler to a program, they may share the questions anyone brings to being a new parent. The teacher should, as always, be ready to share information on development and early parenting practices. However, same-sex parents may face more complicated questions about each person's new role. How does a baby have two mommies or two daddies? How does each person understand sharing this role? The teacher should listen to these questions with the same compassion and acceptance as she would with any other parent issues about adjusting to the role.

A bigger question for same-sex couples may be whether they and their child will be genuinely welcomed into the program. Staff or families may have negative feelings toward the couple based on religious or personal objections. These are issues that may also arise when families of a different race or religion enter an otherwise homogeneous program. As in dealing with any feelings of discomfort based on differences, the teacher should begin by examining her own feelings, perhaps in supervision or with the mental health consultant. The teacher may also want to practice with that person how to politely, but firmly, put a stop to cruel remarks from other parents. For example, "I can see you have strong feelings about Jami having two mommies, but this is not the time or place to talk about it. Our director will be happy to have a conversation with you, but we keep this room calm for the babies."

Although no one is free of bias toward others, each teacher is expected to behave in a professional manner. You always work to support the relationship between the child and his family. Many infant and toddler board books illustrate homes with two daddies or two mommies and will help the child from such a home feel represented.

Grandparents

Grandparents raising grandchildren is an increasing event in America (58). Parents may or may not live in the same household, but grandparents are increasingly providing primary care for grandchildren. According to the U.S. Census Bureau, in 2012, 2.7 million children were living in homes maintained by their grandparents (59). The steady increases are due to a variety of factors: substance abuse by parents, teen pregnancy, family violence, illness, and incarceration. Grandparents are sometimes able to offer a stable home to their grandchildren. However, they often care for their grandchildren without any legal rights. This leaves them in difficult conditions for accessing health care or other social supports for the children (60).

Implications for Teachers

Both the grandparents and the infant or toddler will need sensitive understanding from educators:

> While the home-school connection is critical for every young child, it is especially crucial in grandparent-headed households. Education professionals need unique insight and information about custodial grandparents' particular circumstances (61, p. 16).

The infants and toddlers may be grieving for the loss of a parent. Grandparents may be struggling with changing their role of a doting grandparent into one of a parent with many responsibilities for their grandchildren.

Adoptive Parents

Adoption is another subgroup of parenting with so many variables that it is tempting to say it can be understood only on a family-by-family basis. Given that in 2008, 135, 813 adoptions occurred in the United States and about 2.1 million children live with adoptive parents, there are endless differences (62). Infants may be adopted at birth from parents who relinquish their rights immediately. They may be adopted by a family member. Or they may be removed from their birth parents because of abuse or neglect and spend years in foster care without a permanent home. They may have been exposed to drugs or alcohol in the womb. Obviously, the circumstances leading up to the adoption will have considerable effect on the child's outcomes.

For infants and toddlers, the work of developing relationships and establishing trust is highly dependent on consistent, responsive caregiving. Achieving a balance between a secure attachment to a caregiver and a healthy ability to move out into the world to explore can be challenging for any baby. Infants and toddlers who have experienced many disruptions in early relationships may have particular difficulties in establishing trust and in feeling safe enough to explore the world.

Implications for Teachers

Teachers may need to support adoptive parents as they struggle with particular issues. In an earlier section of this chapter, we described some of the issues men and women work with as they become parents. The process of adoption may take years. Yet, many adoptive parents have only a few days between being notified that their child is available and actually receiving the child. In contrast to a 9-month pregnancy, this can leave little time for emotional preparation. In order to protect themselves from disappointment, the adoptive parents may not dream and fantasize about parenting as much as the pregnant couple. They may be afraid at first to become too attached to the baby. They may worry whether they will love the baby or whether the baby can love them, given the lack of genetic connection. They may also need help figuring out whether issues that arise are typical behavioral issues for infants and toddlers or whether they are related to the adoption.

Foster Parents

When children are abused or neglected, they enter the child welfare system and often are placed in foster homes. More than 43 percent of all children in foster care are under age 5. Almost 40 percent of the children who entered foster care in 2014 were under 5 years old (63). The largest single group of children entering foster care is children under the age of 3. These children are possibly the most vulnerable in our country. In order to be placed in foster care in the first months or years of life, they have already experienced great stress or dangerous parenting. Their mothers may not have received prenatal care, and they may have been poorly nourished and exposed to substances in utero.

Nearly 80 percent of these children are at risk for medical and developmental problems as a result of prenatal exposure to drugs or alcohol. They may have witnessed or been victims of physical or sexual violence. More than 40 percent of foster children were born prematurely or were of low birth weight. More than half have serious health problems and developmental delays—4 to 5 times the rate of children in the general population. They are highly unlikely to receive early intervention or mental health services because of fragmented systems and record keeping (64).

Implications for Teachers

Participation in high-quality early childhood programs is an important strategy to promote the healthy development of young children in foster care. These children have experienced trauma. High-quality early childhood programs provide stimulating, engaging, and nurturing environments that can be inherently supportive of development. Early childhood teachers can also provide information, strategies, ideas, and emotional support to foster parents.

Check Your Understanding 2.3
Click here to check your understanding of the concepts in this section.

Program Practices That Support Families

For some infant and toddler programs, the primary goal is supporting parents. Still, as repeated throughout this chapter, it is the responsibility of every program to support the parent–child relationship.

Family Engagement

Family engagement is defined as *positive and goal-oriented relationships* in which

> Parents and families observe, guide, promote, and participate in the everyday learning of their children at home, school, and in their communities (65).

The idea behind family engagement is that families need to be active in many ways to help their child be ready to succeed in school. The systems of the program such as hiring teachers, continuous improvement, leadership, and setting policies should all have parent input. The parents should influence the program services, as well. The programs should also attend to:

- family well-being.
- positive parent-child relationships.
- families as lifelong educators.
- families as learners.
- family engagement in transitions.
- family connections to peers and community.
- families as advocates and leaders.

We know we are helping to set the foundations in the infant's or toddler's brain for success in life and school. We should also recognize our ability to support the foundation of strong and healthy families. As families adjust to the entrance of a new life into their homes, they look to their child's teacher, family child care provider, or home visitor for information and support. Infancy is a critical time for a family and for parents to form a new image of themselves. Engaging parents in our services is a powerful intervention when we are well informed.

Parent Education

All programs that provide information to families might be called **parent education**. Some programs only work directly with parents to improve their knowledge and skills. Parent education includes a variety of services and supports. They range from resources and referrals, suggestions or strategies, informal community programs or groups, formal instruction through classes, to counseling and one-on-one support for parents (66). Because the home environment is so central to each child's development, programs often provide ideas for learning experiences for families to use at home. Families are encouraged to read to even the youngest infants for 15 minutes each day. Programs offer ideas for using rich, expansive language with young children. Most importantly, programs help parents respond to their young child with sensitive, accurate emotional responses.

All families need support at various stages of family life and at certain times. **Family support programs** provide and coordinate a variety of services and supports for families. They might include prenatal care for the mother, health services for children, quality infant and toddler care, and education options and subsidies for fees, assessment and services for special needs, education, and social services. Different agencies in a city, county, or state may collaborate to provide the services and supports in a coordinated way that creates a strong infrastructure to support families and children prenatally to age 5.

Home visiting is a very effective model for supporting vulnerable parents. It involves a consistent home visitor coming to a family's home, usually once a week.

 Watch this video to see a teacher prepare for a conference with a parent. Consider her thoughtfulness in preparation. What steps does she take?

The home visitor and family establish a close working relationship aimed at improving the parents' knowledge and skills in parenting. The overall goals tend to be similar to these:

- Improve health and development.
- Prevent child injuries, child abuse, neglect, or maltreatment, and reduce emergency department visits.
- Improve school readiness and achievement.
- Reduce crime, including domestic violence.
- Improve family economic self-sufficiency.
- Improve the coordination and referrals for other community resources and supports (67).

Parents of Children with Special Needs

A variety of education and support services are available to parents of children with disabilities. These parents represent every race, culture, economic status, and family structure. Programs provide information about legal, developmental, financial, and medical aspects of disabilities, as well as parent-to-parent connections and advocacy.

When infants or toddlers are identified with disabilities, parents may have any number of reactions. These are influenced by their personal history with disabilities, their religious or cultural beliefs about disability, the nature or severity of the particular disability, and their own capacity to be open to someone other than the wished-for perfect child.

Many people think that the discovery of a disability in one's child is a tragedy for the parent. However, parents describe many kinds of reactions. One study reported parents as describing themselves in a constant state of tension between feelings such as "joy and sorrow," "hope and no hope," and "defiance and despair." Parents also identified their own optimism and resourcefulness in meeting the ongoing challenges of their child's disability (68). Some parents have less positive experiences. Their reactions include fear over the child's future. Will she live a satisfying life? Some feel guilt over having possibly caused the disability through a physical or spiritual act. Some parents just feel confusion over the new situation. They are suddenly trying to understand complex medical information at a time when anxiety and lack of sleep make understanding anything difficult. Parents may feel powerless to control their own lives, may feel disappointed by the child they have produced, and even have feelings of rejection toward the child or the professionals who work with the child (69). Many parents describe themselves as having all of these feelings at different times—sometimes even having contradictory feelings at the same time!

The only disability is having no relationships. (Judith Snow)

Each state has at least one parent training and information center (PTIC) for families of children with disabilities. PTICs provide parents with training and information about disabilities, about parents' and children's rights under the relevant laws, and resources in the community, state, and nation (70). These centers are funded through the Individuals with Disabilities Education Act (IDEA), which provides special education services for children with disabilities. The parent center staff members are often parents of children with disabilities themselves. They provide information over the phone, through workshops, and through conferences. They help parents understand their own child's needs and learn about available services. They encourage parents to actively participate in making decisions about their child's services and in negotiating with providers and intervention systems to ensure that their child's legal rights to services are fulfilled.

Parent-to-Parent support programs are also available all over the country and through national clearinghouses. Parent-to-Parent is a program that matches parents of children with similar needs to provide support and information to each other. A parent whose child is newly identified as having a disability may contact a Parent-to-Parent program and be matched with an experienced parent trained to discuss the new parent's concerns. Parent-to-Parent may provide an understanding friend with whom the parent can share experiences of stress, confusion, or optimism. Strategies for utilizing resources, making decisions, and simply gaining confidence in trusting one's own feelings and understandings may be shared. Lifelong friendships sometimes begin in Parent-to-Parent matches (71).

Teachers should be considered part of the early intervention team serving an infant or toddler with disabilities. Teachers should have a good knowledge of the resources and programs in the local community. However, the role of the teacher or home visitor as a partner to the parent may be even more important in day-to-day life. Teachers can contribute ongoing observations and information about a child's new interests and accomplishments. They can help parents sort out what new behaviors may be related to the disability and what is typical toddler behavior. Most importantly, teachers can provide a genuine welcome to and true affection for a child whose acceptance in other settings may be of great concern to parents.

Check Your Understanding 2.4
Click here to check your understanding of the concepts in this section.

Summary

Many aspects of life affect how families form and function in their parenting:

- Human families all over the world share a common biology of reproduction that determines some aspects of their parenting—attending births, caring for vulnerable young infants, and valuing the bonds between parents and their children.

  □ Cultural beliefs about how people relate to each other and the role of children within the culture directly, if sometimes invisibly, determine the guidance parents offer their children.

- The transition to parenthood is a powerful and significant life change for the individual and for the couple, which can be supported or undermined by factors such as personal history, support from the partner, social support, and economic stability.

  □ Personality, culture, and the experiences of one's own childhood will influence the parenting styles each parent adopts—indulgent (or permissive), authoritarian, authoritative, or uninvolved.

- Families created through marriage, divorce, single parents, same-sex couples, grandparents raising grandchildren, adoption, and foster care may each provide different experiences for the family members. Nonetheless, the quality of caring, responsiveness, and relationship will have a greater impact on the child's mental health and overall developmental well-being than the configuration of the family.

- Many early childhood programs practices provide information and support to help parents do the best jobs they can with their children. These include parent engagement, parent education, family support programs, and early intervention parenting programs.

  ☐ Every early childhood program must respect the primacy of the family in the lives of infants and toddlers. Parents are our best partners, our best sources of information and guidance concerning their own children, and often our real reason for existence.

Key Terms

authoritarian parents
authoritative parents
collectivist cultures

family
family support programs
individualist cultures

indulgent (or permissive) parents
parent education
uninvolved parents

Reflections and Resources for the Reader

REFLECTIONS

1. In your own family, do you think your parents believed their job was basically to teach you to be independent and self-sufficient or to be interdependent? How did they communicate these messages to you?
2. In reading about different family structures, did you think that some kinds of families might be harder for you to accept than others? How would you manage that challenge, if it occurred? Discuss with a partner in class.

OBSERVATION AND APPLICATION OPPORTUNITIES

1. As you observe parents with their young children at an infant and toddler care and learning program, in a store, or on a bus, what do you see parents do that suggests to you that they might be authoritative, authoritarian, indulgent (or permissive), or uninvolved?
2. Children are able to grow and develop well in all sorts of families. What unique strengths have you seen in families of different structures such as grandparents raising children, single parents, divorced parents sharing custody, or others?
3. Visit a parenting class in your community. Evaluate how useful the class appears to be to the families.

SUPPLEMENTARY ARTICLES AND BOOKS TO READ

Fletcher, R., St. George, J., May, C., Hartman, D., & King, A. (2015). Father-inclusive practice in a family center: An Australian perspective. *Zero to Three Journal*, *35*(5), 60–67.

Lerner, C. (2015). Parenting in the 2000's: Learning from millennial moms and dads. *Zero to Three Journal*, *36*(2), 2–7.

McHale, J.P., & Phares, V. (2015). From dyads to family systems: A bold new direction for infant mental health practice. *Zero to Three Journal*, *35*(5), 2–10.

NAEYC (2014, Sept.). Engaging Families: Partnering in Meaningful Ways. *Young Child Journal*.

INTERESTING LINKS

Child Welfare Information Gateway This government Web site provides research briefs, statistics, and issue papers.

National Responsible Fatherhood Clearinghouse A resource of the U.S. Department of Health and Human Services Administration for Children and Families' (ACF) Office of Family Assistance (OFA).

National Parenting Education Network The National Parenting Education Network is a national organization that promotes parenting education. The Web site has many articles and resources on parenting education.

Parent Technical Assistance Center The Web site provides an array of data about parent training and information centers (PTICs) and community parent resource centers. PTICs are funded by the federal government to support parents of children with disabilities.

ZERO TO THREE website The Web site provides many resources on parenting, family systems, coparenting, and the influence of fathers.

3

Understanding and Using Theories

LEARNING OUTCOMES

After reading this chapter, you will be able to:

- Explain the meaning of *theories*, why they are important, and our theoretical framework.

- Describe the major points of emotional and social development theories.

- Describe the major points of cognitive, language, and motor development theories.

- Explain how theories would look applied in a program.

Pearson Education

It is not unusual for the new teacher or parent to discover contradictory information on child development. One book instructs adults to let babies cry themselves back to sleep if they awaken in the night; another tells them to respond with a comforting pat on the tummy. Women who are told by their mothers to keep babies on a strict feeding schedule—regardless of their cries of hunger, even during growth spurts—may be told by their pediatricians to feed their babies on demand. Parents and teachers alternately are seen as too strict or too lenient in guiding children's behavior. It is not surprising that people feel frustration in trying to sort out what, if anything, is really known about supporting development in children.

What Theories Are, Why They Are Important, and Our Theoretical Framework

From early in history, people have had a desire to understand how the world works. This is a desire we see reflected in even the youngest infants. In trying to make sense of human development, just as in trying to understand the changing seasons or the patterns of stars in the skies, people developed ideas about how and why things work. Some of those ideas may have been scoffed at and lost to history. Others were recognized, acknowledged, and adopted by thinking people of their day. These ideas were developed into theories.

What Are Theories?

Theories are explanations of information, observations, and life experiences. Bowlby's (1, 2, 3) and Ainsworth's attachment theory (4) explained how young children develop different qualities of attachment with their primary caregivers. These theorists made educated guesses (hypotheses) about the effects that the different qualities of attachment have on the children's behavior now and in the future. Attachment theory is an example of how theories attempt to provide continuity and meaning between past and present events. Theories also provide a way of thinking about, or anticipating, future events.

Theories are based on the thoughts and studies of one person or one group of people. Sometimes the theorist has been primarily interested in one area of development and proposes ideas about that area without trying to encompass every aspect of development. Piaget (5) is an example of this type of theorist. He concentrated on the stages that children go through in cognitive development as well as how they learn. He did not address emotional or social development.

Often, researchers will test the ideas of a theory. For attachment theory, researchers tried to discover if the effects differed for boys and girls. These researchers take the idea, add new information, examine it from new perspectives, and test its application to reality.

Why Theories Are Important

The benefit of a theory is that it helps us understand the possible relationship between separate events, for example, the quality of care that infants receive and their later behavior. The limitation of a theory is that reality is so complex that a single theory is unlikely to explain anything entirely.

As you will see, your theory of how children develop influences how you teach infants and toddlers and how you interact with families and communities. Will you believe that infants who cry are communicating their needs and thus require a response (attachment theory) or will you believe that infants who cry must be ignored so that their crying will decrease (behavioral theory)? It is important for you to think about which theories are most supported by research and then apply those theories to your work.

Our Theoretical Framework

Theories of child development have been proposed throughout all of recorded history. This chapter does not provide a history of theories or even an overview of recent theories. Instead, we introduce the theories that inform the beliefs and values expressed throughout this book. This theoretical framework derives from many important developmental theorists. Each of these theories is described here, but a major common theme among them is that infants and toddlers achieve their development within relationships with responsive, caring adults. This book is based on these beliefs:

- Optimal learning and development for children, families, and communities occurs within nurturing relationships.
- Children influence the relationships within their families, and families influence the children's relationships.
- Experiences prenatally and in the early years affect the course of development across the life span—the brain becomes wired to expect stress or to thrive within relationships, to learn or to be challenged by learning.
- Children are able to learn when they feel safe enough to explore, when they feel they can have a responsive effect on the people and objects in their environment, and when they have an adult partner who listens, talks, and reads to them.
- Children are active learners—constantly processing information, drawing conclusions, and experimenting—and children need nurturing responsive support to maximize their learning.
- Early developing attachment relationships may be disturbed by parental and other primary caregivers' histories or relationships such as unresolved losses and traumatic life events or current events that change the adults' circumstances.
- The relationships that parents have with other adults affect their ability to build positive, secure relationships with their children.
- A child is part of a family, which is part of a culture, which is part of a community, which is part of a country, and each of these elements affects the others.
- Service delivery models, community programs, and public policy can and should support strong relationships and reduce the risk of relationship failure.

The clear emphasis in this book on the importance of quality relationships for the well-being of infants and toddlers and their families reflects *relationship-based theory* of child development (6, 7), *transactional* (8, 9), and *unified (10) theories,* and *bioecological systems theory* (11). The neuroscience-based *ecobiodevelopmental theory* of development (12) also describes how the environment influences development and the quality of relationships. Each of these theories acknowledges the power of the cultural lens through which people make decisions, as well as the family and individual differences that exist within that person's particular culture (13).

Other theories of emotional, social, cognitive, language, and motor development also inform our thinking about the capabilities, competencies, and needs of infants and young children. Each of these complements and, to some extent, includes the others. Let's begin with the five major theories that emphasize the importance of relationships—relationship-based theory, transactional and unified theories, bioecological systems theory, and ecobiodevelopmental theory. We will then focus on other theories that inform your work with infants and toddlers. We will provide many examples of how these theories work when put into practice.

Relationship-Based Theory

When Tara, the infant-toddler teacher, welcomes Jaime into her arms in the morning, her warmth, the meeting of their eyes, and the sound of pleasure in her voice all make Jaime feel that Tara remembers him and is happy to see him. As Tara is welcoming Jaime, however, her words also address her relationship with his mother: "Have a good day. I'll take good care of Jaime today. We'll be fine, and then he'll be very happy when you come and get him after work."

Among these theories, the relationship-based theory most clearly describes the individual child's experience while also considering the social network in which he lives. Recall from Chapter 1 that relationship-based theory offers an understanding of development that is consistent with our current knowledge about brain development, our experience with the effects of adverse experiences such as abuse and neglect, and—perhaps most importantly—with our own personal experiences. We understand the power of a loving relationship to support us through difficulties.

Hinde (14) describes the relationship-based approach:

A relationships approach involves the recognition that children must be seen not as isolated entities, but as forming part of a network of social relationships; and requires a delicate balance between conceptions of the child as an individual and as a social being (p. 251–252).

Jeree Pawl (15), an infant-parent psychotherapist, wrote a wonderful description of the power of the infant's relationship with a trusted adult:

A two-month-old held facing outward will drop his head back to look at the holder from time to time, if he's well nurtured. By the time you are a sitting baby, with good enough ordinary experiences, your very back feels safe, held. You know you are watched—that is, that you exist, are held, in someone's mind. You feel secure, and secured. . . . But this only develops if you truly are consistently in the mind of someone, so that you are noted, noticed, spoken to over distance, rescued, protected, appreciated, and tethered across space and out of mutual sight. It is the teacher that creates and confirms this, by her continual surveillance and by holding the child in continual existence in her mind. This becomes a crucial part of a child's internal sense and experience (p. 5).

The infant-toddler teacher's relationship with each baby, holding the baby in her mind, is very important. Her relationship with each parent and other family members is also important because the adults' relationships may affect their relationships with the baby. So much of each infants' or toddlers' ability to develop well depends on the availability of responsive, meaningful relationships. Young children's ability to thrive also depends on the surrounding social and physical environments that support the adult in the relationship, and on the condition of the society in which they live. Holding a young child in your mind benefits the child, the child's family, and the child' community.

Care for your children as you wish them to care for your grandchildren. (Al Solnit & Sally Provence)

Relationship-based theory explicitly defines relationships. Within this construct, *relationship* is not a general word used to describe casual contacts or moments of interaction. Relationship-based theory says that relationships are effective as the organizing force of development, the element that gives an action or a feeling greater meaning and importance. According to this theory, relationships can differ depending on the following dimensions (16):

- *Content of the interactions.* The content of infant-adult interactions may include established routines, play, affection, guidance, and sharing interests and experiences. The content may have a predominantly positive or negative affective tone.
- *Diversity of the interactions.* Infant-adult interactions could be composed only of routine caregiving, such as diapering and feeding. Other adults and babies may share a wide range of interactions including conversation, singing, walks, play, and household activities.
- *Qualities of the interactions.* Relationships vary in how well the behavior of one partner coordinates with that of the other. A sensitive adult perceives the infant's signal, correctly interprets it, selects an appropriate response, and delivers the response in a timely, contingent fashion (17).
- *Qualities that emerge from the relative frequency and patterning of different types of interactions.* Behaviors are meaningful in a relationship not because they occur a certain number of times, but because the *pattern of frequency* of touching, smiling, and nuzzling amid the more neutral behaviors comes to have meaning. If touching occurs relatively often but only when the parent feels like it, it may be less satisfying to the infant or toddler than if it occurs less frequently but always in response to his signal that he desires contact.
- *Complementarity versus reciprocity of the interactions.* Complementary interactions are a negotiation of different behaviors in the two partners. Reciprocal interactions are characterized by both partners using similar behaviors. When parents cooperate with and facilitate the child's behavior, they establish the foundation of a reciprocal relationship whereby the adult partners can adjust their actions for the benefit of the infant or toddler in reaching his goal (comfort, food, a toy, a friend) (18).
- *Intimacy.* An intimate relationship provides a warm emotional tone, a desire for closeness, a sense of security in the close presence of the other, and a willingness to act on behalf of the well-being of the other.
- *Interpersonal perception.* Relationships are also characterized by how each partner feels the relationship affects

Teachers develop real affection for the children.

Pearson Education

him- or herself. This assessment of the effect of the relationship may depend on the emotional availability and cognitive understanding of self and of the other person.

- *Commitment.* The final dimension is the willingness to act on the other's behalf and work for the other's well-being, in a relationship that endures over time. It is this aspect of endurance that elevates another person's importance so that one would act supportively and empathically for the other person's good. Hinde (19) described the importance of endurance:

> At the behavioral level, a relationship involves a series of interactions between two individuals, each interaction being relatively limited in duration but affected by past interactions between the same individuals and affecting future ones. But a relationship can persist in the absence of interactions, and involves also subjective aspects—including especially memories of past interactions and expectations of future ones, which have both cognitive and affective aspects (p. 1).

Teachers utilizing the relationship-based theory of development commit to deep, meaningful relationships that endure over time with infants, toddlers, and families. They are capable of incorporating intimate relationships within their professional role.

Transactional and Unified Theories

> *A professional football player whose entire life is dedicated to rough physical contact becomes a father to a baby girl. This little girl is very sensitive about how she is handled and fusses unless treated gently. Her daddy does not want her to cry and he adjusts his handling of her so that she feels safe and comfortable in his arms. Over time, being close to her daddy becomes a high priority for this baby, and she learns to tolerate play that is more active because she feels his pleasure in it.*

These silent, instantaneous transactions are negotiated in each moment between infants and toddlers and those around them. As discussed in Chapter 1, *transactional theory*, as first proposed by Sameroff and Chandler (20), emphasizes characteristics of both the child and the environment, and their dynamic interplay over time. For example, the child has certain biological and genetic characteristics such as gender, temperament, physical health, behavior—or in the previous story a desire to be handled gently. The environmental influences include the resources and behaviors of the most important people in the child's life: parents, siblings, extended family, peers, friends, schools, and neighborhood communities. In the previous example, one influence was the dad's ability to be responsive but another was the dad's pleasure in active, physical sports. The child's characteristics and behavior interact with the child's environment. The dad is responsive to the child's need to be handled gently, so this child will most likely thrive. However, if the dad handled the child roughly to "get her ready for active, physical sports," the child will react negatively. This strategy will not succeed and the child will possibly withdraw from the dad and active sports.

Transactional theory was first developed as a way of understanding why children with similar biological risk factors at birth could have very different courses of development. Sameroff and Chandler (21) proposed that the child's biological status is only one contribution to development. The parent's understanding of the child and the appropriateness or helpfulness of the parent's response also have enormous impact.

> *Children affect their environment and environments affect children. Children are neither doomed nor protected by their characteristics or by the characteristics of their caregivers alone. (Sameroff and MacKenzie)*

The transactional theory identifies the "bi-directional, reciprocal relationships between infants and their caregivers" as providing several points as the basis for intervention (22, p. 19). (See Figure 3.1). Transaction is seen as a three-part sequence, offering three points at which to intervene. First, the infant or toddler stimulates the parents, either through his appearance or through his behavior. The parents then attribute some meaning to the child's message. Finally, the parents react with some form of caregiving. As seen in Figure 3.1, the dynamic between infant or toddler and parent (or teacher) could be changed at any of these three points. The child could be changed through **remediation**. The meaning of the child's behavior to the parents could be changed through **redefinition**. The parents' caregiving reaction could be changed through **reeducation** or increasing skills and knowledge (23).

Sameroff has also developed a unified theory of development (24). When we think of the word *unified* we think of integrated, joined together, and combined. Sameroff has combined personal *change over time* with the multiple environmental and cultural influences that affect personal development. He also considers how the child influences his or her environment and how adults influence the child in a dynamic, always changing process.

Teachers and parents who use a unified theory will understand child development and think about cultural and environmental influences on the child's development and behavior. They will understand how the personal traits and behavior of a child influence how the adult interacts with that child. They will understand that their role is to nurture children and provide opportunities for them to consider their own and others' well-being.

FIGURE 3.1 **Transactional theory of development and points of intervention**

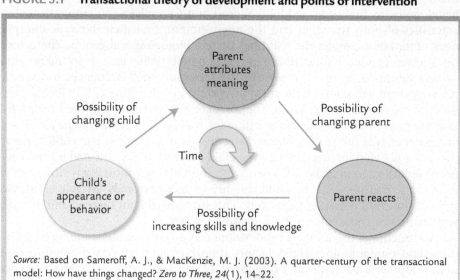

Source: Based on Sameroff, A. J., & MacKenzie, M. J. (2003). A quarter-century of the transactional model: How have things changed? *Zero to Three, 24*(1), 14–22.

Bioecological Systems Theory

> *Perry loved being a home family provider. She had close relationships with the children and their families. But her city council was putting new restrictions on home businesses, and she was worried about meeting the new requirements. Other providers were also concerned, and they were meeting with the state child care administrator, hoping for some help.*

The many levels that affect Perry's family child care home program are addressed within bioecological systems theory (25). Bioecological systems theory considers the effects of the family, community and society on the child. Bronfenbrenner begins with his belief that the primary relationship needs to be with someone who can provide a sense of caring for a lifetime. In fact, he emphasizes that each child needs someone who is crazy about him. Bronfenbrenner states that children need stable families that provide constant mutual interaction with their children. He then looks to the structure of society to determine whether society supports this level of relationship.

The bioecological systems model is usually portrayed as a series of concentric circles emanating from the child, as seen in Figure 3.2.

The innermost circle is the microsystem that describes the child's direct relationships with his family, and which relates most closely to relationship-based theory. In echoes of the transactional theory, the family members, friends, and teachers in the **microsystem** affect the child—but the child affects them as well. The next circle is the **mesosystem**; this includes relationships among the microsystems, also relating closely to transactional theory. For example, the infant-toddler teachers and parents have a relationship with each other that can affect the parent-child relationship or the teacher-child relationship.

The **exosystem** consists of settings that do not include children but that affect them. In Perry's case, it is the city council's new restrictions that are about to have an impact on her caregiving. She is hoping that the state administrator might be a more helpful part of this exosystem. Other exosystem examples would include the policies of the parent's workplace concerning flexible work hours or staying home with a sick child.

The next circle is the **macrosystem**, which refers to the values and laws of the society (26). A society that does not believe in women working will not support policies that give women equal wages and flexibility concerning their responsibilities to their children. In Perry's case, if the city values the service of home family providers and understands that the economics of this business are quite different from those of other businesses, the city council might exempt family child care homes from its new requirements.

CULTURE CLOSE UP

Delena, a toddler teacher in a large urban child care and learning center, couldn't wait to meet the new toddler coming with his mother to visit the center. The family members had recently come to the United States and the mother was working from her home and needed the toddler to be in the center in the mornings. After the children in the room had gone home, Delena greeted the mother and then bent her knees so she could greet the toddler. The mother seemed delighted to meet Delena and loved the possibilities for learning available in the toddler room. When talking about the child's eating, sleeping, and diapering, the mother said, "Oh, he is already toilet trained. When I see him make a certain face I know it is time to hold him over the toilet. Delena wasn't sure what to say. As primary caregiver of four toddlers and with eight toddlers in the room, she wasn't sure she and her teaching assistant could follow through on the mother's wishes. Delena also believed in following the child's lead physically and emotionally, making the toilet available, but not pushing the child. This difference between Delena and the mother seemed to be culturally based. What would you do?

FIGURE 3.2   **Bioecological systems theory of development, adapted to child care and learning programs**

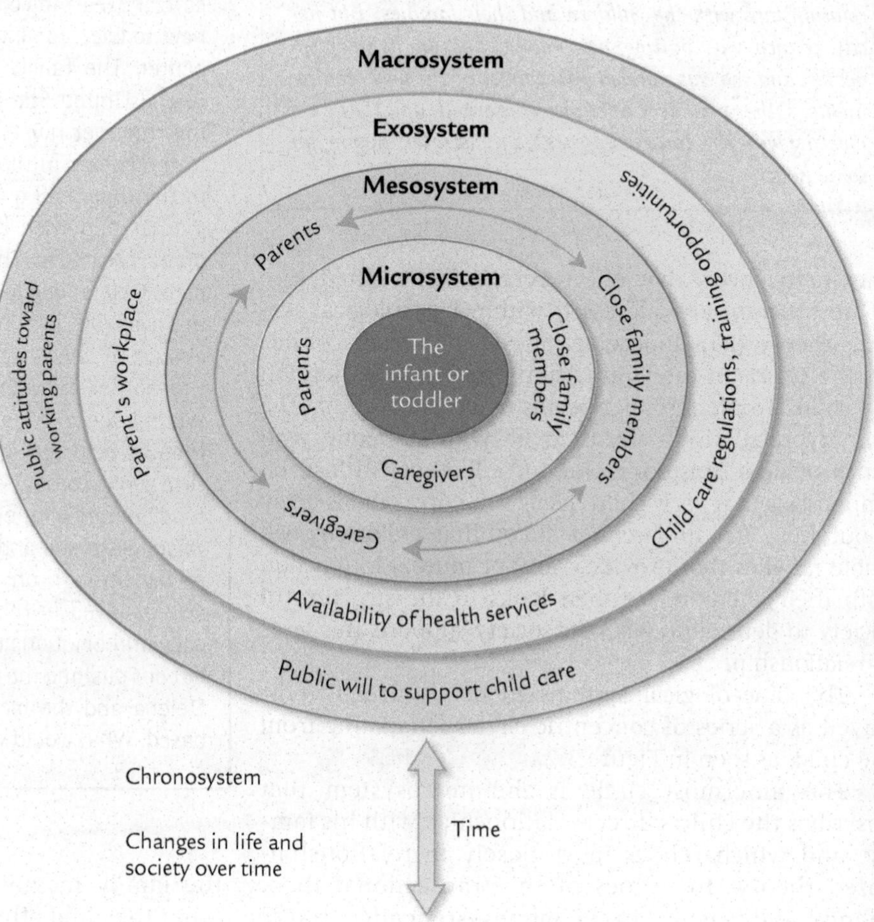

Source: Feldman, Robert S., *Child Development*, 4th Ed., ©2007. Reprinted and Electronically reproduced by permission of Pearson Education, Inc., Upper Saddle River, New Jersey.

The encompassing circle is the **chronosystem**, which addresses the element of time as it affects the child. Time elements might mark external events such as the parents' divorce or the birth of a sibling, or they may be internal, describing the growth and maturation of the child.

The well-being of any child depends on events and forces far beyond the child's own daily experiences. Teachers utilizing the bioecological systems theory will participate in professional organizations. Teachers might join the National Association for the Education of Young Children, Zero to Three, or the Family Child Care Association because these organizations advocate for increased quality in early childhood education. Programs will become aware of, for example, community resources for families and the impact of various laws.

Respect, Reflect, Relate

Respect: Respect the influence that the quality of relationships, culture and the environment have on children's well-being, beliefs, and behavior.

Reflect: Reflect on each child's unique personality and behavior that changes over time.

Relate: Interact with children to develop relationships with them and their families. Become knowledgeable about the influence of community resources, local and federal early childhood education policies. Become an advocate for each individual child and family as well as quality in early childhood education.

Ecobiodevelopmental Theory

> *Two days a week, Dr. Westmore worked in a public health clinic in the inner city. He was very familiar with the disparities between the children he saw there and the children he saw in his affluent, suburban practice. Too many of the inner-city children had little prenatal care, poor nutrition, and stressful home lives. The current science of neurobiology told him the children were at risk of challenges to their brain development.*

The American Academy of Pediatrics issued a paper (27) introducing a new theory of lifelong health. The **ecobiodevelopmental theory** puts together all aspects of health, an understanding of the effects of stressful environments and interventions to relieve them, and the new information from science about neurobiology and **epigenetics**. We now know that early experiences (prenatal and in the first years of life) actually affect the architecture of the brain—the way neural connections are made and strengthened or lost. This theory takes our current scientific knowledge and applies it to development.

The ecobiodevelopmental theory proposes that a new approach to providing health and intervention services could make a significant difference in the lives and health of children whose background has traditionally contributed to poor health, poor relationships, and poor performance in school and work. By concentrating on all aspects of health and providing parenting and learning supports, we could change the evolving structure of the brain within our children who are at-risk.

Check Your Understanding 3.1
Click here to check your understanding of the concepts in this section.

Theories of Emotional and Social Development: A Sense of Self and Relationships with Others

Other theories that guide a relationship-based approach to infant and toddler development and learning include emotional and social development theories.

Emotional Development Theories

Theories of emotional development tell us important information about how very young children develop a sense of self in relation to others. They include Erik Erikson's psychosocial theory (28, 29), Maslow's hierarchy of needs (30), attachment theory (31), and Stern's interpersonal development theory (32).

Emotional development includes our feelings, our loves, our motivations and desires, our fears and feelings of safety, and our ability to reflect on our experiences. These all develop within the context of our relationships. The theories of emotional development focus our attention on how we develop a sense of self and relationships with others. Although each of the following theories has a different focus, each has contributed to our understanding of how infants and toddlers discover and form an identity through a primary relationship with one or more adults.

Theory of Psychosocial Development

> *Cecil had worked with infants and toddlers for 15 years. When he had infants, he often thought, "This is my favorite stage!" Then he would have older toddlers and wonder at their competence, thinking, "This is my favorite stage!" Part of what Cecil likes is that at each stage, not only are the children different, but they seem to need different things from him.*

Cecil doesn't know it, but his thinking in terms of stages is very much like that of Erik Erikson, a psychologist who created a framework of stages to explain development from birth through adulthood, which he called the **theory of psychosocial development**. Erikson proposed that individuals go through *eight* distinct, predictable stages as they develop their sense of self and their relationships with others. The first three stages are critically important, as shown in Table 3.1 (33, 34). At each stage, as a child experiences different biological, social, and cognitive needs, a sort of developmental crisis provides an opportunity for that child to discover whether her family, society, and culture can meet those needs.

As you can see in Table 3.1, each stage is an opportunity for the child's increased, healthy development, and decreased vulnerability. Each stage's crisis reflects a child's struggle. In each stage we hope that the child will develop the first aspect of the crisis (trust versus mistrust) more than the second aspect of the crisis. However, children should also develop a healthy portion of the other half of the crisis (trust versus mistrust). For example, the infant should not feel that everyone could be trusted in every moment to meet every need. The toddler, while achieving increasing autonomy, must develop an understanding that his actions may have consequences that are hurtful or dangerous and that the feelings of shame and doubt can be good warning signals.

TABLE 3.1   **Erikson's psychosocial stages**

Age Range	Basic Conflicts	Developmental Tasks
Birth to 18 months	Trust vs. Mistrust	Infants learn that teachers can be trusted to meet their needs and that the world is a safe, pleasant place to grow up.
18 months to 3 years	Autonomy vs. Doubt, Shame	Toddlers discover that their actions are their own and enjoy independence, but they experience shame and doubt when corrected or criticized.
3 to 6 years	Initiative vs. Guilt	Children work hard to be responsible for their bodies, their toys, and their actions. When they are irresponsible or criticized, they may experience guilt.

Source: Based on Erikson, E. (1950). *Childhood and society*. New York: Norton.

The Hierarchy of Human Needs

> *Selma was a perceptive observer of the children in her care. She knew that trying to teach a crying 2-year-old was never a good idea. So when Joseph screamed over Cara taking a toy from his hand, she comforted him. Later, in a quiet moment, she talked to him about the words he could use when someone took a toy from him.*

Toddlers enjoy challenges they can master alone.

Selma is considering Joseph through the lens of **hierarchy of human needs** (35). In an explanation of development that is somewhat different from Erikson's (36, 37), Abraham Maslow looked at the research on human motivation. He suggested that people are motivated to further their development because of needs that arise and the desire for growth.

In the hierarchy of human needs, as shown in Figure 3.3, the needs that are lower in the figure, forming the foundation, must be met before the person

FIGURE 3.3   Maslow's hierarchy of human needs

Ensure that children reach their full potential.

Ensure children's desire to master skills and gain knowledge.

Ensure children's sense of belonging to family, peer group, & community.

Ensure children's feelings of safety at all times.

Ensure children's and families' physical needs are met in the classroom and through knowledge of community systems.

Teacher strategies to meet children's basic needs:
Based on Maslow's hierarchy of needs.

Source: Based on Maslow, Abraham H., Frager, Robert D., & Fadiman, James, *Motivation and Personality,* 3rd Edition, copyright 1987.

even experiences the needs that are higher in the figure. So Joseph, experiencing feelings of being unsafe and not belonging had to achieve comfort in those areas, which led him to feel safe again. Selma used her own ability to comfort him before she even began to appeal to his need for mastery—a way to consider using language when a peer took a toy. In one way, the hierarchy does follow a path of human development. Young infants must first regulate their physiological needs, and then they develop a sense of safety in the world. As that sense of safety evolves, they feel a sense of love and belonging with the adult who keeps them safe. During preschool and school years, children work on mastery, gaining the skills and knowledge they will need in life. As people mature, they find self-fulfillment in marital relationships, in work and productivity, and in passing on their legacy to another generation.

Attachment Theory

> *Aurelia was always fascinated by the differences among her little toddler group in how they played. Ethan was calm and played well alone or with others, as long as she checked in periodically. Meredith was clingy but also resisted being comforted. Alicia seemed to play very independently, rarely looking at Aurelia—but she was distraught if Aurelia ever moved out of her line of sight. What was so interesting to Aurelia was that when these children greeted their parents in the evening, she saw echoes of this behavior.*

Aurelia is seeing the three classic forms of behavior described in **attachment theory** (38, 39). These three children demonstrate how they use her presence to feel safe enough to play and explore. They also are showing her that they have had very different experiences with being kept safe by the adults in their lives. Attachment theory is described extensively in Chapter 6.

Teachers utilizing attachment theory in their work are responsive to infants and toddlers in ways that help them feel safe. They help young infants manage their own feelings and reactions to difficulties and help toddlers feel free to explore while gently assuring them of their safety.

Interpersonal Development Theory

> *At 6 months, Eli looks from his mother to his infant-toddler teacher, clearly knowing each of them. On some level, Eli has an ongoing sense of what it is to be Eli with these two people he knows so well.*

Stern (40), a psychoanalyst and developmental psychologist, offers a theory of emotional development based on the past several decades of infancy research. Stern asserts that infants experience themselves as separate beings from birth. However, they are also always working toward greater connection with others. He believes the child experiences moments in which he is aware of an internal and/or external experience. These moments become linked as memories or mental images. This *experience of being* occurs with a sense of self-agency (an ability to make things happen), a sense of self-coherence (awareness of being a complete, contained entity), and a sense of continuity (sensation of going-on-being). At the same time, the infant is aware of *being with other*—managing a sense of being a separate self with another person. Stern suggests that these are layered experiences that support one another. Rather than having stages of emotional development, he calls this *layered development.*

The infant-toddler teacher utilizing the interpersonal development theory would understand the importance of each moment's experience to the infant. She would be responsive to his cues and know that he is building his mental model of being with people, in part, from his moments with her (41).

 Watch this video and consider how the infant is aware of internal and external experiences. What is this baby learning about his own feelings? What is he experiencing?

Social Development Theory

Sociocultural theory, developed by Vygotsky (42, 43, 44) is useful when thinking about how children's social experiences and relationships affect their learning. His theory is used extensively today to plan and implement programs for young children.

Sociocultural Theory

> *Morris, at 7 months, enjoyed playing with trucks. He still sometimes mouthed them and threw them—but he also watched the older toddlers "driving" their trucks on a carpet with roads marked on it. Sophie, his teacher, talked with him about his trucks. "Look at all your trucks, Morris! Let's make sounds like trucks—rrrrr, rrrrr." After Morris finished playing with the trucks, Sophie took him to the window, "Oh, look out the window—there are trucks on the street!"*

While Vygotsky's sociocultural theory is sometimes thought of as a cognitive theory it is the social interactions that contribute to the child's ability to learn. Culture and social interactions influence what children learn and how they learn. The addition of the adult partner, or even the other children to watch, adds an important element to how children construct their knowledge about the world. Morris may be using schemas (making sounds and moving the truck) to learn about trucks, but he is also using the language of his teacher. Vygotsky believed that adults and more knowledgeable peers teach culture, language, beliefs, customs, and highly valued activities to younger children. In fact, full cognitive development could not occur without social interaction. He describes how learning happens when children get *just enough* help and information from adults to allow them to figure out solutions to problems that are just beyond their reach independently,

Children learn from their peers, as well as from adults.

Pearson Education

problems he describes as being in the **zone of proximal development**. For example, a 10-month-old infant who is playing with sounds becomes hungry and makes complaining noises to her teacher. Her teacher knows the baby is not ready to use words, but she is nearly ready. Word use is in her zone of proximal development. So the teacher supplies the word: "Bottle? You want a bottle?" The infant then makes a "Ba-ba" sound, demonstrating more skill in language with help (or **scaffolding**, to use Vygotsky's term) than she could do alone.

 Watch the video which demonstrates the zone of proximal development. While filmed with older children, this video demonstrates how scaffolding can support children's learning. How would you define the term *zone of proximal development*? Think of how you would consider the zone of proximal development when helping an infant begin to use a spoon.

https://www.youtube.com/watch?v=InzmZtHuZPY

A second important contribution from Vygotsky (45, 46) was attention to the role of language in learning. Young children use the language of others—parents, teachers, and peers—to help them develop new concepts. For example, by naming objects and using words such as *dog* the adult helps the child learn to classify and organize information.

A third, and perhaps most important, contribution from Vygotsky was his awareness of how knowledge is created. First, children experience their culture through interacting with their special adults and peers (**interpsychological** level). These social experiences then become a part of how the child thinks and acts (**intrapsychological**). A child's culture influences his beliefs, use of language, social attitudes and skills, and priorities.

The infant-toddler teacher who utilizes a sociocultural approach will study the cultures of the children in his program and discuss cultural beliefs with the families. He will observe children to determine the children's zone of proximal development and will scaffold children's learning to guide them to learn the tools for how to solve problems. He will use rich, descriptive language to support children's ability to communicate and to organize their world.

> ✓ **Check Your Understanding 3.2**
> Click here to check your understanding of the concepts in this section.

Theories of Cognitive, Language, and Motor Development

Certain cognitive language, and motor development theories also inform how we interact with infants, toddlers, parents, and communities that support young children.

Cognitive Development Theories

Many theories describe how children learn about the world. Many of these theories echo aspects of the theories of emotional development. They describe a developmental process of learning, some divide that process into stages, and most recognize the importance of interested, available adults in supporting learning. The learning theories most closely aligned with the theoretical basis of this book are constructivist theory, social learning theory, the new science theory of learning, and core knowledge theory, each of which is briefly described here.

Constructivist Theory of Learning

> *Over and over, 6-month-old Jeremiah would bang his little trucks together, suck on them, look at them, and toss them aside. He was always happy to see them on the play mat but didn't appear to look for them when his tossing landed them behind a larger toy and out of sight. At 9 months, however, if one of Jeremiah's trucks rolled out of his sight, he would crawl after it and retrieve it.*

Infant-toddler teachers have many opportunities to observe how very young children keep making new discoveries about how the world works. In his **constructivist theory**, Swiss developmental psychologist Jean Piaget depicted infants and children as actively constructing their understanding of the world through their play and exploration (47, 48, 49, 50). The child develops **schemas**, mental structures of his current understanding of the world.

Piaget suggested that children first try to use their existing schemas to understand new information and new experiences. He called this process **assimilation**. At 6 months, Jeremiah uses the schemas of sucking, shaking, and banging with almost every object. If the schemas are not adequate to explain the information, the child creates new schemas to use in a process called **accommodation**. For example, when a child who is using grasping and looking as a way of understanding the world is given a small drum and a rounded stick, he may decide to try banging as a new method of exploring the two items together. Piaget used the term **equilibrium** to describe the moments when the child's schemas and the information presented are in balance. When the current schemas are not adequate for exploring or explaining new information, the child's mental organization is thrown into **disequilibrium**. The child then modifies his mental structures to accommodate the new information (51, 52).

 Watch the video that summarizes Piaget's developmental theory. How did Piaget think children learn?

https://www.youtube.com/watch?v=QX6JxLwMJeQ

The impact of Piaget's work on American early childhood education cannot be overstated. Piaget's image of children busily constructing their knowledge of reality has been the driving force in early childhood programs creating learning environments to be explored. The assumption that children learn through exploration derives directly from his work. Interest in Piaget's basic theory of cognitive development has led researchers to more closely observe how children begin to think about themselves, how they think about relationships, and how they use different strategies to complete their goals.

As impressive as Piaget's contribution is to our understanding of children, his work is criticized on two points. First, research on learning and brain development in infancy suggests that Piaget greatly underestimated the young infant's ability to think—even to hypothesize about the possible outcomes of her actions. Second, the children Piaget writes about seem to discover all of their knowledge through their own exploration and construction. The role of culture and the impact of the other people in the children's lives are not identified within the learning process (53).

Despite these criticisms, constructivist theory continues to be a strong force in American education. Bruner (54, 55) extends Piaget's idea that learning is an active process in which learners construct new ideas or concepts based upon their current and past knowledge. Bruner's work incorporates the infancy research showing that the child selects and transforms information, constructs hypotheses, and makes decisions by relying on a cognitive structure to do so. The cognitive structure, whether called a schema or a **mental model**, provides meaning and organization to experiences and allows the individual to go beyond the information given. For Bruner, the role of the teacher is to provide opportunities for children to discover basic principles by themselves, although social and cultural influences are also at play. The teacher structures the information in ways that allow children to grasp it, understanding that they will continuously revisit the same information in greater depth as their capacity to understand deepens.

The infant-toddler teacher who utilizes the constructivist theory of learning will provide a variety of interesting materials for infants and toddlers to manipulate and explore. She will understand that the child is motivated to learn, actively building an understanding of how people relate, and figuring out how the objects in the world work. She will support these discoveries through her relationship with the child.

Social Learning/Cognitive Theory

Social learning theory (56) is now often referred to as social cognitive theory (57, 58) to recognize the importance of children's thinking abilities. Bandura (59) emphasizes self-efficacy, the ability of humans to set goals, problem solve, and reflect. He also emphasizes that what children believe about how effective they are influences how they act.

Imitation is a primary way that young children learn and cultures are transmitted from one generation to another. Bandura emphasized how children decide who and when to imitate, showing that imitation is not a rote action but rather a decision-making process. Children learn through imitation, with reasons for imitating some people over others or objects. For example, 18-month-olds will not imitate an adult's actions if that adult says "Oh, no" after completing the task, as this indicates to the infant that the behavior is not one to imitate.

This ability to make decisions about who and what to imitate is referred to as "rational imitation (60)." Infants and toddlers tune into the cues of an adult; for example, by 15 months, they can imitate what an adult intended to do but failed (for some reason) to do (61, 62). By 14 months, children choose to imitate someone who speaks their primary language over someone who speaks a language that is foreign to them (63). In other words, infants and toddlers are selective and make choices concerning who they will imitate.

An infant-toddler teacher who knows social cognitive theory will observe how and what the children in the program observe and imitate. The teacher will recognize that infants and toddlers can imitate adults' and peers' *goals* and *actions*. They will understand that a child's belief about his capabilities will influence how he behaves.

The New Science of Learning

A paper titled *Foundations for a New Science of Learning* (64) offers a theory of learning based on brain science.

1. *Learning is computational.* Infants attend to events that occur regularly and frequently around them. They know that events that occur more often are probably more important. Infants use this ability to compute to learn

about language and causal relationships. Long before they are able to talk, infants come to recognize the sounds and clusters of sounds of their own language(s) and the signals that separate words in a sentence. They also use the regularity of events to learn about cause and effect relationships in the world. They learn these things without adult instruction, but with adults' responsive interactions with them. It happens before infants can speak or effectively handle objects.

2. *Learning is social.* Infants want to attend to people and copy their actions. They are more likely to attend to and copy an action when it is performed by a human rather than a machine. Human interactions are also full of a variety of information. Social learning happens through imitation, shared attention, and empathy and shared emotions.

3. *Learning uses a network of mirror neurons.* Perception and action are linked in the brain. When infants (or adults) see someone lift their hand, the part of the baby's brain that sees (perceives) activates. And the part of the brain that would lift the baby's arm also activates, although the arm does not go up. A network of mirror neurons in the brain responds to others in a way that says, "You're like me! I can do that!" A newborn as young as 42 minutes reliably imitates a tongue thrust or mouth opening in an adult. The child has never seen a mirror. He has no idea what he looks like. But when an adult sticks out his tongue, the baby is able to imitate. The mechanism appears to be the mirror neuron network that links perception and action.

Core Knowledge Theory

Elizabeth Spelke, a cognitive psychologist, bases her core knowledge theory on the research on infant learning. This theory proposes that humans have evolved with inborn systems or brain structures ready to learn about those things necessary to survival. The four core knowledge systems address how infants learn about objects, agents, number, and geometry. The idea of separate knowledge systems refutes the belief that learning happens through one "general purpose device" (65, p. 91). Core knowledge also emphasizes the importance of social interactions that provide the content of what and how much children learn in the different systems.

The core system of *object representation* allows human infants to "perceive object boundaries, to represent the complete shapes of objects that move partly or fully out of view, and to predict when objects will move and where they will come to rest" (66, p. 89). For example, young babies (4 to 5 months old) will react as an object approaches, demonstrating an understanding that objects that move toward them may hit them (67). The core system of *agents* (persons and animals) allows infants to recognize goal-directed actions of living things. For example, at 10 to 11 months of age, an infant will follow an adult's head turning if the adult has her eyes open, but not if the adult's eyes are closed (68). The core system of *number* has its own limits and principles. An infant will look surprised if two objects move behind a curtain but only one object comes out the other side (69). 6- to 8-month-olds looked at a video with the number of adults that matched the number of voices they were hearing (70). The fourth system is *geometry of the environment*. It allows children and adults to orient themselves in relation to places in the environment. We've all seen infants who quickly learn how to crawl down a hallway, into the bedroom through one door and out the other, confidently orienting themselves in the environment.

The core knowledge theory suggests an inborn ability to learn about what is most important for survival. It suggests that different information is needed for different aspects of survival and that humans have developed structures in the brain to attend to that information.

Theories of Language Development

Theories of language development that emphasize the importance of relationships are Kuhl's perceptual mapping model and social interaction theory (71, 72, 73). These theories emphasize the importance of adult-child responsive language interactions with infants and toddlers.

Kuhl's Perceptual Mapping Model

Today, Patricia Kuhl, (74, 75, 76) a leading researcher in language acquisition, proposes a model of language acquisition called **perceptual mapping**. This theory is consistent with a constructionist theory of learning and a relationship-based theory of development. The basic premise of how infants learn language is that infants are able to figure out the structure of language in the first year of life before they can speak (77).

Kuhl emphasizes that in the first year of life, infants are more capable then many have thought. They can break down the language they hear to determine the critical aspects of that language and determine patterns. They are able to predict which sounds in their primary language generally follow each other. Infants are able to figure out the likelihood of when words will start and end by attending to how often certain combinations of sounds are likely to occur within words or between words. They learn which syllables in words in the language they are hearing are usually stressed and by 9 months prefer the patterns they hear in their language to patterns in other languages. They "map" the major components of language—sounds, words, intonation, and rules for how language is constructed.

According to Kuhl (78), experience with hearing language changes *how* infants hear language. Infants map the most commonly heard language sounds in their brain. When they hear similar sounds, these are drawn (as though by a magnet) to that same part of the brain to be stored. As infants, they are able to hear and discriminate the sounds (auditory processing) of every language in the world, but by 12 months they hear only the differences between sounds they have heard frequently.

Learning to speak a language requires hearing it spoken and hearing oneself making the sounds of the language (79). Many parents around the world use a high-pitched, exaggerated, simplified form of language called "parentese" in speaking directly to young infants. It includes using new words repeatedly and with many examples.

Infants and toddlers learn language through pleasant and interesting social interactions.

Dennis Wittmer

This exaggerated form of language is also called "child-directed speech" (80) because it is directed at the child and functions to help the child learn speech and language. Young children need this experience with responsive adults to learn to speak a language.

The infant-toddler teacher utilizing the perceptual mapping theory will recognize that for the infant, learning language is an active, reciprocal, relationship-based process. She will use parentese with young infants, speak to the infant or toddler frequently throughout the day, and read to the child, providing rich language experiences.

Social Interaction Theory

Social interaction language researchers emphasize how the social environment interacts with biology to influence language development rather than emphasizing specific innate language structures (81). *Social interaction theory* of language development incorporates Vygotsky's **sociocultural theory** (82, 83, 84) and emphasizes that infants and toddlers need (1) responsive interactions with adults to learn a language and (2) opportunities to communicate. This theory argues that it is important not only for a child to hear language but also that the adults speaking the language are responsive and engage infants and toddlers in conversations. Adult respond to sounds, wiggles, and words as an infant's contribution to a conversation. Adults imitate toddlers' language and add a word or two to their responses. This helps infants and toddlers learn *how* to engage in a conversation—with turn taking, pauses, and listening.

Teachers who emphasize *social interaction theory* will recognize that infants and toddlers are active learners who co-construct language with adults, as they adjust their language in order to be understood. Teachers will constantly listen for children's yawns, sounds, and words and respond in order to engage a young child in a conversation. They will give the child many opportunities to express herself, making mistakes but constantly learning how to engage in human communication.

A Theory of Motor Development: Learning to Move

> *Niko was a good crawler. He safely crawled around the room, up and down the three steps to the little climbing structure and even up and down the low slide. His teacher was surprised, when he first started walking, that he would step right off the 5-inch platform of the cozy area and fall on his nose! What happened to his good judgment about moving in space?*

The traditional theory of motor development proposes an ages and stages progression of locomotor abilities that flow as the child's neuromuscular system matures (85, 86). Today, however, movement is understood as a process of learning, or as Karen Adolph (87) puts it, "learning to learn to move" (p. 217). Movement requires the infant or toddler to overcome gravity, have the strength to support her own weight, and balance and coordinate body parts. It also requires the child to readjust to constantly changing skills, size, and environments. Adolph suggests that the skills and judgment needed moment to moment in movement require the child to "learn to learn" rather than to learn one particular solution. For instance, knowing how to maneuver down a small slope while *crawling* does not give the child the knowledge of how to *walk* down that same slope a month later. Niko, in the previous

Pearson Education

Find toys for young children that encourage a child to learn to learn.

vignette, cannot call upon his knowledge of crawling and slopes to keep him safe as a new walker. He has to take in new information, adjusting it to his current posture and mode of locomotion and learn how to solve the problem of walking down a slope. Adolph's *learn to learn* derives from Esther Thelen's dynamic systems theory (88).

Dynamic systems theory proposes that development moves forward as the young child finds the best solution to using his body to make something happen in his environment. The environment offers an opportunity for action, called an affordance. Let's say a toy is dangling above a 4-month-old lying on his back. The toy is an opportunity for reaching. The child organizes his body systems to reach for that toy in that moment. His visual system alerts him to the toy. His brain also perceives actions he can take with the toy. He then organizes his body, given his length, weight, proportions and factors such as the amount of support gravity is giving his trunk. Does he have enough muscle strength for his arm to resist gravity? Have his earlier experiences with reaching given him accuracy? As he reaches, he makes little adjustments in lifting his shoulder and reshaping his hand. With each attempt, his skills improve. With each day, his body changes. Motor skill development is a constant, dynamic system of learning.

The infant-toddler teacher who utilizes the learn to learn to move theory or the dynamic systems theory understands that each new posture requires new learning on the part of the infant or toddler as to how to move in the world. She would provide lots of opportunities for movement but understand that with each new posture, the child would need to learn again how to move in the environment. She would offer opportunities and encouragement but know that she needs to be vigilant about safety as infants and toddlers are constantly learning how their bodies work.

> ✓ **Check Your Understanding 3.3**
> Click here to check your understanding of the concepts in this section.

Applying Theories in Programs

Although most early childhood development and learning programs in America are based on the theoretical approaches described in this chapter, we are more likely to know them by names such as *developmentally based* or *relationship based*.

Child Development Programs

Most infant-toddler programs would identify themselves as being developmentally based and would reflect an understanding of attachment theory; of child development theories derived from Erikson, Piaget, and Vygotsky; and of the brain research of the past two decades. If you visited a high-quality, developmentally based program, you would see many things happening.

Attachment theory would be evident in that each teacher would have primary responsibility for a small group of infants and/or toddlers and would provide their care for a long period of time, preferably the first 3 years of life. The teacher and parents would have a close partnership in which each would support the other's understanding of and affection for the baby. Erikson's theory would be most evident in how teachers support the early development of a sense of self. With infants, the teachers would be highly responsive as they support the child's development of trust. With toddlers, teachers may consciously pull back, encouraging children to explore their environment and develop autonomy while still being physically and emotionally available to meet the toddlers' needs.

 Watch the video and notice how the teachers interact with the children to help them feel safe. Which theories are the teachers putting into practice?

Constructivism or Piaget's theory of cognitive development would be evident in how teachers follow the interests of the child and provide a variety of books, small toys, mirrors, and appropriate large motor experiences for the infant or toddler to explore. The materials would be likely to offer information on basic cognitive concepts such as object permanence or cause and effect. Vygotsky's theory of sociocultural development would be evident in the way the teacher interacts with the children and families and in the many symbols of the culture in the room. There would be posters showing "our community" and dramatic play materials that replicate the kitchen and workroom equipment used in the children's own households. Teachers would adjust the language they use and the type and amount of help they give children according to the child's ability to accomplish the task at hand.

Relationship-Based Programs

Although every early care and learning program probably values relationships, programs based on relationship theory would have some recognizable features. A relationship-based program would create a structure of teachers' schedules and group sizes that would provide opportunities for relationships to develop over time. A primary caregiver would be assigned to each child, and small groups of children would stay together with the same teacher from infancy to preschool. Friendships between children would be nurtured and honored (89). Adults would model caring, responsive, thoughtful relationships with children and with other adults (90). Teachers and families would communicate regularly to ensure a consistent caregiving experience for each child.

Care and attention would be given to the development of secure, affectionate attachment relationships and to the expression and understanding of emotional experiences.

 Check Your Understanding 3.4
Click here to check your understanding of the concepts in this section.

Summary

- Theories are explanations of information, observations, and life experiences. The theoretical foundation of this book encompasses, relationship-based theory, transactional and unified theory, bioecological systems theory and ecobiodevelopmental theory.

  - In Relationship-based theory infants and toddlers do not exist as separate entities but as part of social networks. Infants and toddlers require meaningful, supportive, enduring relationships. Relationships differ on a number of dimensions, and intimacy, reciprocity, and commitment are important factors in determining the quality and usefulness of a relationship.

  - In Transactional and Unified Theory relationships are bi-directional: Adults affect children and vice versa. Transactions include the child's behavior or appearance as a stimulus, the meaning given by the adult to the child's behavior, and the adult's response. Relationships that are troubled may be responsive to intervention at any of three points: the child by remediation, the meaning by redefinition, and the response by reeducation. Context, relationships, and time influence children's personal development.

  - In Bioecological systems theory development can be affected by many levels of relationships, from close family all the way to national policies. All systems affect one another.

  - In Ecobiodevelopmental theory early experiences affect the architecture of the brain. Chronic stress is damaging to the developing brain. Relationship-based interventions can support the developing brain.

- The theories of emotional and social development are constantly evolving. Some theories that are important today include the following:

  - Theory of psychosocial development: Erikson's stages of emotional development characterized by crises that need to be resolved.

  - The hierarchy of human needs: Maslow's description of human motivation.

  - Attachment theory: Bowlby's and Ainsworth's descriptions of organizational systems that allow us to explore and learn while remaining safe and protected.

  - Interpersonal development theory: Stern's description of how infants develop a sense of self and a sense of self with others.

  - Sociocultural theory: Vygotsky's processes of learning through exploration, relationships, and culture.

- Theories of cognitive, language, and motor development guide our thinking about how children learn:

  - Constructivism: Children actively construct their understanding of their world.

  - Social cognitive theory

  - The new science of learning

  - Core knowledge: Spelke's theory of four innate systems of knowledge that form a foundation for learning

  - Perceptual mapping: Kuhl's theory of language acquisition build on decoding the structure of language

  - Learning to move: Adolph's theory of movement as a learning process

- Teachers use different theories as they work with individual children, groups of children, and parents and families. It is important to think about the theories that you use in your practice.

Key Terms

accommodation
assimilation
attachment theory
chronosystem
constructivist theory
disequilibrium
ecobiodevelopmental
epigenetics
equilibrium

exosystem
hierarchy of human needs
interpsychological
intrapsychological
macrosystem
mental model
mesosystem
microsystem
perceptual mapping

redefinition
reeducation
remediation
scaffolding
schema
sociocultural theory
theory of psychosocial
   development
zone of proximal development

Reflections and Resources for the Reader

REFLECTIONS

1. In your own life, using Bronfenbrenner's bioecological systems theory, fill in the circles of the system. It is probably obvious to you that your family and closest friends, your teachers and your employers affect your life. However, you may see new connections between yourself and the people or groups in the exosystem and macrosystem of your own ecological system.

2. From your readings, observations, and experiences with infants and toddlers, can you describe your own unified theory of how children develop? Which theories will you try to utilize in your work with infants, toddlers, families, and the early childhood community?

OBSERVATION AND APPLICATION OPPORTUNITIES

1. Visit an infant-toddler program. From your observation of the environment and the interactions, how would you describe the theory of child development being practiced? What do the people in this program believe influences the development of a child?

2. In observing adults and children together, you may see one adult treating children differently from one another. Transactional theory suggests the child's characteristics are affecting the interaction. Are you able to observe differences in infants or toddlers that are influencing the responses of adults?

SUPPLEMENTARY ARTICLES AND BOOKS TO READ

Conboy, B. T., Brooks, R., Meltzoff, A. N., Patricia K. Kuhl, P. K. (2015). Social interaction in infants' learning of second-language phonetics: An exploration of brain-behavior relations. *Developmental Neuropsychology, 40*(4), 216–229.

Honig, A. S. (2015). *The best for babies: Expert advice for assessing infant-toddler programs.* Lewisville, NC: Gryphon House.

Mooney, C. G. (2013). *Theories of childhood: An introduction to Dewey, Montessori, Erikson, Piaget, and Vygotsky* (2nd ed.). St. Paul, MN: Redleaf.

INTERESTING LINKS

North Central Regional Educational Laboratory

Theories of Child Development and Learning The Web site of the North Central Regional Educational Laboratory includes a link to a short paper titled "Theories of Child Development and Learning," describing maturational, environmental, and developmental perspectives.

Early Childhood News

Theories of Child Development: Building Blocks of Developmentally Appropriate Practice. A Terri Jo Swim article in Early Childhood News describes the connection of theory and DAP.

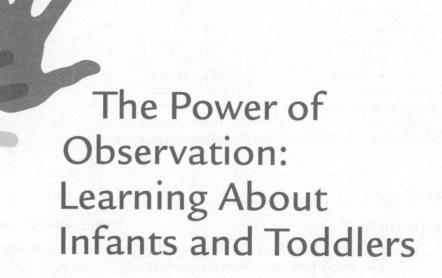

4

The Power of Observation: Learning About Infants and Toddlers

LEARNING OUTCOMES

After reading this chapter, you will be able to:

- Explain why conducting ethical observations is an important skill for early childhood professionals.

- Describe what a teacher might learn by observing an infant or toddler and methods for observing young children.

- Explain how observation is a part of assessment and the different types of assessment strategies.

- Explain what the observer brings to the observation.

Pearson Education

Patty thought to herself that if LaNita had one more tantrum she would throw herself on the floor and join her in the screaming! Patty felt as if LaNita had tantrums almost nonstop. When the behavior consultant from the Child Care Resource and Referral office came in to help, he began by observing and recording the tantrums. To Patty the day seemed like a typical one with LaNita having endless tantrums. To her amazement, there were only four tantrums. Patty realized that she spent the entire day dreading, tolerating, and recovering from the tantrums.

Sometimes our own reactions to events affect our ability to understand the meaning of the event for the child. Patty found LaNita's tantrums so upsetting that she felt they went on all day. An observation by the behavior consultant helped Patty see that LaNita had a limited number of tantrums. Each tantrum lasted less than 5 minutes. Together, Patty and the behavior consultant analyzed his notes and discovered that most of LaNita's tantrums occurred when both teachers in the room were busy responding to the immediate needs of other children. At these times the teachers couldn't help LaNita in the moment. When one of the teachers was on the floor where the children were playing, LaNita rarely lost control. Patty and the behavior consultant used the observation to make a plan to ensure that LaNita always had enough adult attention and to help her learn new ways of handling frustration.

Observing—A Powerful Skill

This chapter covers what is important to observe, the ethical considerations for observing, and many methods of observing and recording the observations. It also gives guidance on how to choose the best method for the purpose of the observation. We end the chapter with how effective observation also involves awareness of the observer's own reactions and **biases**. This chapter sets the stage for the use of strategies that readers can use as they move through the next 12 chapters. We hope that you will see children in new ways and be able to interpret their actions and reactions, the exciting ways they learn, their many emotions, and their individual interests. Throughout the chapter, we use the term teacher, however, the information applies to other infant-toddler professionals, including family child care providers who are also teachers of young children.

 Watch this video on how to stay positive while observing infants and toddlers. Explain why observation is important and how a teacher stays objective when observing.

https://www.youtube.com/watch?v=ghGxhrGI1MQ

Why Observation Is Important

Teachers use observation, a powerful skill, to learn more about infants and toddlers. Teachers learn about an individual child's interests, development, and perspectives and then plan curriculum that is responsive to each child's interests and goals. Families and home visitors use observation information to plan experiences at home. Both teachers and family members use observation information to make needed changes in the child's routines, guidance, and environment.

Teachers who observe deeply appreciate children's ongoing, meaningful learning. For example, a teacher could observe the many ways that one infant communicates with gestures, sounds, and facial expressions. This teacher may feel in awe of that infant's communication skills. The teacher then shares the information with other teachers and parents. The teachers and parents not only begin to see *a* child differently, but they may also see the capabilities of *all children* differently. This knowledge may change the way the adults value children's communication efforts and inspire them to respond to infants as budding communicators. Through observation, teachers understand and appreciate the capabilities of young children as well as how children may be challenged and when they need special support.

Most important, observing and documenting children's activities allow teachers and other professionals to build relationships with children and families: "Observing helps you build relationships by revealing the uniqueness of every child—including the child's temperament, strengths, personality, work style, and preferred mode of expression" (1, p. 11). When a child feels understood, the relationship grows. When family members know that a teacher understands their child, teacher-family relationships develop as well.

The Ethics of Observing

Adults who are with young children want to do the right thing by behaving ethically. Ethical considerations influence observation and documentation. The National Association for the Education of Young Children's (NAEYC) *Code of Ethical Conduct* and Division of Early Childhood's (DEC) Position Statement: *Code of Ethics* do not directly name observation, but specific statements should guide one's actions in doing observations. The overriding principle in NAEYC's *Code of Ethical Conduct* (2) states:

> P-1.1—Above all, we shall not harm children. We shall not participate in practices that are emotionally damaging, physically harmful, disrespectful, degrading, dangerous, exploitative, or intimidating to children. This principle has precedence over all others in this Code.

How could observations be harmful? Observation recordings may attribute unkind intentions to a child's actions or ridicule or demean the child, her family, or her culture. The purpose of observation should always be to achieve a deeper understanding of the child; never to prove there is something wrong with the child.

Teachers who conduct observations and share them with families can follow these principles from the NAEYC code:

> P-1.5—We shall use appropriate assessment systems, which include multiple sources of information, to provide information on children's learning and development.
>
> P-1.7—We shall strive to build individual relationships with each child; make individualized adaptations in teaching strategies, learning environments, and curricula; and consult with the family so that each child benefits from the program.

In addition, the DEC *Code of Ethics* (3) states:

> III. 7. We shall be responsible for protecting the confidentiality of the children and families we serve by protecting all forms of verbal, written, and electronic communication.

In summary, NAEYC and DEC emphasize respect for children, families, and other professionals. These considerations include:

- having permission to observe and record observations of a child,
- respecting the parent's right to see records,
- maintaining confidentiality, and
- writing and talking about children in respectful ways.

During a program's enrollment process, teachers should inform families that observations are part of the program and explain which recordings will be kept confidential and which might be shared publicly. For example, an observation method called *time sampling* to track biting would be kept confidential, but *photo panel documentations* with photos and captions are often posted on the wall for the children, families, and visitors to enjoy and appreciate what and how children are learning. The purpose of observation and documentation may be explained through a permission to observe form as seen in Figure 4.1.

FIGURE 4.1   Sample permission form

Observation Permission Form

Date: _____

Name of child: _____

*Name of Program, Agency, or Person Requesting Permission: _____

_____

Dear Parent or Guardian,
Please complete the remainder of this form and return it to

_____

I give permission for my child _____ to be observed for educational purposes. These observations can be written, photographic, or electronic (video or computer). I understand that these observations may be displayed or used in the program or in educational settings to provide insight to children, teachers, parents, family members, and the community concerning how children think and learn. My child's first name may be used unless I refuse by writing a note to that effect at the bottom of this page.

I understand that I may decide to refuse permission at any time and I understand that all observations will be available for me to review at any time.

Date Signed: _____

Name of Parent/Guardian (print): _____

Signature of Parent/Guardian: _____

Address: _____

City: _____

Zip code: _____

Phone (Home): _____ (Work or cell) _____

*Review the legality of this form with the program or agency for which you are doing the observation.

Check Your Understanding 4.1
Click here to check your understanding of the concepts in this section.

What We Can Learn and How We Observe to Learn

In this section, we will think about what is important to observe and the many methods you can use to observe infants and toddlers. Reflection on observations occurs as team members collaborate with each other and families to understand and wisely use the information gathered.

What We Can Learn

In the book *The Power of Observation*, Jablon and colleagues (4) define observation as "watching to learn." They go on to say, "We learn about children by watching them, listening to them, and studying their work. Watching and listening to children helps us understand what they are feeling, learning, and thinking" (p. 1).

What else can we learn by watching and listening to children? We can learn about how the child behaves and feels within different relationships. We learn about the stages of development (e.g., how a child coos before he says words), but we also learn about the *quality* of development (how a specific child uses communication, to whom he talks, the words he says, and the feelings expressed). We also learn the following:

- How infants and toddlers think and learn
- What they are feeling and how they regulate their emotions
- How they use their bodies
- Their interests and what they especially enjoy
- How they relate to others
- Their challenges
- Their many skills
- The strategies children use to accomplish their goals
- The interactions, materials, equipment, and toys to make available to children to encourage engagement, participation, and relationships

The observant teacher sees moments of kindness.

As can be seen from the list, you might choose to observe many areas. Sometimes it is helpful to try to capture everything that a child says and does for a time period, and at other times to choose a behavior, such as smiling, and record evidence of only that behavior. At other times, you may want to observe what the children in a group are learning from playing with certain materials such as water. As you observe, you will begin to see infants' and toddlers' behavior and interests in new ways.

Observers who study child development learn to observe the intricacies of infants' and toddlers' attitudes and behavior. For example, a classic study demonstrated how toddler hitting may have different meanings depending on how the toddler hits (5). An open or low-intensity hit or a swipe at the body of another toddler might mean "Leave me alone." When a toddler hits another child with an object in the hand in a low-intensity way, the behavior could mean "Hey, wanna play?" A hard hit, on the other hand, seems to mean "I don't like that" and is more likely than other hits to provoke a negative response from the other toddler. Once an observer knows that toddlers may understand hitting differently than adults do, the adults interpret toddler hitting differently.

How We Observe to Learn

There are many established methods of conducting and recording an observation. This section presents the steps for the use of anecdotal records and running records, event sampling, charts and diagrams, and documentation with infants and toddlers. Observation may also be used to create a portfolio for each child—a collection of teacher and family observations and the child's own creations such as scribbles on a piece of paper or a photo of a block structure.

With each of the following methods, you will want to begin recording the observation with a cover page that has space for

- The child's name
- Age
- Date of observation
- Setting
- Purpose of the observation
- Type of observation
- The name of the person conducting the observation

If the observations are placed in a portfolio, then families and other team members will appreciate the additional information.

Anecdotal Records and Running Records

Anecdotal records and running records are written accounts of children's actions and typically include comments that are written after reviewing a number of the observations.

Anecdotal records are short accounts of children's behavior written while or soon after the behavior occurs. They describe what happened in a factual way and include when and where it happened. They are usually brief descriptions that the teacher writes in an objective manner. Descriptions that are objective are factual and do not include the observer's opinions or feelings about the child's behavior. With practice, the adult captures the child's behavior with words that help someone who is reading the record visualize what the child was doing. Often, after capturing the child's actions objectively in the left-hand column of a page, the comments based on the observation, called interpretations or **inferences**, are written in the right-hand column.

Inferences are conclusions that the observer draws from the objective observation. For example, if a toddler was observed throwing dandelions into a stream and watching the current carry them away, the observer might infer that the child was learning about the properties of water and movement. She could objectively observe his motions, but she is inferring the intentions and mental processes that drive his motions. As a teacher records an observation, he may ask, "Is the child watching the current or is he just enjoying the movement of the flowers?" "Is he experimenting or are his actions random?" The teacher may write his questions and/or several possible inferences in the right-hand column. After several observations, the teacher might see a pattern in the child's behavior.

FIGURE 4.2   Sample anecdotal record

Name: Nicholas	Age: 33 months
Date: 6/1/16	Setting: Play yard
Purpose of Observation: Observe Nicholas's thinking	
Type of Observation: Anecdotal record	Observer: Candy

Sequence	Inference
Nicholas and the other toddlers in my group took off their socks and shoes to wade in our stream.	
Nicholas watched the water moving downstream in a little current.	Nicholas appeared to notice the movement of the water.
He dropped a dandelion from his hand into the stream and watched as the current took it away.	Dropping the dandelion looked accidental and he seemed surprised by the water carrying it away.
He picked a few more and threw them into the water that was carrying the dandelions.	He seemed to be trying to understand how the water carried the dandelions.
Picked up a plastic container and splashed water with it.	
Took container onto grass and half-filled it with dandelion flowers.	He seemed to be very purposeful in collecting the flowers.
Returned to stream and emptied dandelions into stream, watching current take them away. Smiled, pointed, and yelled, "Look. Look."	He seems to be testing his hypothesis about water, currents, and dandelions. His "Look" was a toddler "Eureka!"

 Watch this video on how to document a child's development through observation. What are the purposes of observation highlighted in the video? What are the methods that teachers can use to observe?

https://www.youtube.com/watch?v=GsXvbflrLu4

Anecdotal records may focus on behavior that represents the concepts explored by the child, such as how objects fit into containers; specific domains of development, such as the social domain; or behavior that is of special interest, such as challenging behavior. See Figure 4.2 for an example of an anecdotal record. Note how the actions in Figure 4.2 that are written in the left column are objective and the notes in the right column are interpretations of the records.

To use anecdotal records to focus on a particular area of development of a child, such as fine motor development, record a number of short observations over a time period, such as 4 months. See Figure 4.3 for an example of a series of anecdotal records of a toddler's ability to grasp that was observed during lunchtime once a month for 4 months and the inferences drawn from these observations. After sharing the information with the family, both the teacher and the mother expressed surprise at how LaDon's fine motor abilities had developed in such a short time.

FIGURE 4.3　**Sample anecdotal record of a child's fine motor development**

Name of child: LaDon　　　Age of child: See below	
Setting: Eating—several observations	
Purpose: To capture LaDon's fine motor development	
Type of observation: Anecdotal record	
Observer: Marvin	

Behavior	Inference
7/15/16 (7m) High chair Picks up softened cereal "O's" with raking motion–using all of her fingers without much help from the thumb.	She has an intent look as if she is really working hard.
8/14/16 (8m) High chair Picks up softened cereal "O's" with a scissors grasp–using her thumb with her fingers.	In one month she moved from using a raking grasp to a scissors grasp. She still looks very intent when she is accomplishing a task.
9/15/16 (9m) High chair Picks up cereal "O's" with a pincer grasp–using her thumb and first finger only.	In one month she has progressed to using a pincer grasp. She seems to like fine-motor and hand-eye coordination tasks.
10/15/16 (10m) High chair Picks up cereal "O's" with a pincer grasp. She picks up the cereal "O's" one by one and puts each one in her mouth.	She easily picks up the "O's" and as she picks them up, she often smiles as if she is really enjoying herself. We will need to provide safe eye-hand coordination activities each day as she really seems proud of herself and very interested.

Running Records

Running records are written observations that capture the details and sequence of children's behavior. They are typically longer than anecdotal records. Running records could be used, for example, if the observer wants to capture a child's behavior for 10 minutes on the playground. A teacher used the running record in Figure 4.4 to learn more about Paul's level of play, when he interacted with peers, and how he interacted with them.

When writing running records, try to write exactly what the children are doing and saying. Try to describe movements, facial expressions, and gestures. Describe exactly what the children say to each other without making inferences. Inferences are written after reviewing one or more running records.

Running records require practice to write a continuous stream of behavior. Immediately after the observation, the observer can review the record and add more details.

After reading several running records on Paul, the teachers recognized how important active play and movement are to him. They expanded the large motor area in the room and the time outdoors. The teachers also noticed that Paul had a great interest in Derrick (and Derrick in Paul), so the teachers sat them beside each other at lunch.

FIGURE 4.4   **Sample running record**

Name of child: Paul	**Age of child:** 20 months
Date: 12/17/15	**Setting:** Outdoors
Purpose: To observe Paul's play with peers	
Type of Observation: Running record	
Person observing: Mary	

Sequence	Inference
At outdoor time, Paul ran out the door to the play yard.	Paul seems intent on running the minute he is outside. He can hardly wait to get through the door.
For 3 minutes, Paul ran all around the yard, looking at his feet or just ahead of his feet as he ran.	He seems to need to run—he seems to feel good when he runs.

Paul looks content but serious as he is running. |
| Derrick (about 2 feet away) called "Paul" as Paul ran by him. Paul did not look at Derrick. After 3 minutes, with a smile on his face, Paul ran back to Derrick. He said "Trucks" to Derrick and sat on the hill, joining Derrick. Paul pushed a truck for approximately 2 feet using both hands while he knelt on the ground. He then turned to Derrick and said "Trucks go." Derrick looked at Paul and began pushing his truck. | He joins his friend after he runs, while still enjoying active play.

He seemed to enjoy interacting with Derrick and used one word and then two words to communicate with him.

We need to continue observing Paul to see whether active play helps him self-regulate and focus. |

 Watch the video of an infant playing with a stacking toy. Write an anecdotal record or running record, paying attention to how the child changes hands and strategies to accomplish his goal of placing the ring on the spool. Focus on being objective.

Teachers, early interventionists, and students have developed creative ways of observing with anecdotal and running records. They

- Use sticky notes or index cards kept in a pocket of an apron or clothing.
- Use a sheet of address labels on a clipboard, writing an anecdote on one or more labels. They can then attach these sticky labels to a page in the child's portfolio.
- Schedule times during the day when one teacher will observe while other teachers interact with the children.

FIGURE 4.5   Sample event sampling focusing on hitting events

Event Sampling					
Child's name: Grace			Child's age: 19 months		
Date of Observations: 2/18, 2/19, and 2/22			Settings: Varies		
Behavior to observe: Hitting			Type of Observation: Event Sampling		
Observer/teacher: Tom					
Define the behavior: Bringing a hand or tool in contact with someone in a way that causes harm or distress					
Date Time	Setting	What Happened Prior to the Event?	Event	What Happened Following the Event?	Dura-tion
2/18/16 9:10 a.m.	Breakfast	Sam pushed his chair close.	Grace hit him on arm.	Tom checked Sam's arm. Talked to Grace.	1 min
2/19/16 10:05 a.m.	Play time	Sarah sat on Grace's legs.	Grace hit Sarah's arm.	Tom checked Sarah. Talked firmly to Grace.	1.5 min
2/22/16 11:06 a.m.	Play time	Matt took Grace's toy.	Grace hit Matt's arm.	Tom took care of Matt's arm. Laura talked to Grace.	1 min

Event Sampling

Observers, such as teachers and parents, use **event sampling** to record and analyze the nature of certain events. The collection of information about events, such as hitting incidents, usually begins with a question, such as "When, where, and how does the child hit others?" (see Figure 4.5). Observers may also question the frequency, or how *often*, a child exhibits a particular behavior. Next, an observer decides when to observe the behavior. Perhaps the hitting behavior primarily occurs when the toddler is outside in a family child care setting. An observer might begin to observe in that setting. The observer then describes the incident as soon as possible after a hitting event with detailed information to answer the question (after responding to the situation of course).

After several of these events, the observer(s) might see a pattern of the child hitting when other children are moving in too closely to the child or when she is tired or before lunch when she is hungry. As shown in Figure 4.5, a teacher concluded that Grace, who doesn't have language yet, doesn't like it when another child moves in too closely to her and doesn't have words to tell the other child. A teacher stayed close to Grace for several days to try to support her to use sign language for STOP when another child came too close. The teacher continued conducting event sampling to see if the intervention worked to decrease hitting. Observing before, during, and after an intervention is planned and implemented gives adults valuable information about which intervention might be helpful to the child and would reduce the number of aggressive behaviors.

A second type of event sampling is shown in Figure 4.6. An observer may want to study a class of behaviors such as those that intentionally hurt others. These behaviors are often called aggressive behaviors. An event sampling can

FIGURE 4.6   Sample event sampling of aggressive behavior

Child's name: Melikia   Child's age: 22 months

Date: 9/10/15   Settings: Varies

Purpose of Observation: To observe behavior that seems to hurt others

Type of Observation: Event Sampling   Observer: Mia

Behavior/Time Event Occurs	Tally (Object of Behavior)
Hit with open hand	Peer: II
	Teacher:
Hit with closed fist	Peer: I
	Teacher:
Hit with an object	Peer: II
	Teacher:
Bite	Peer: II
	Teacher:
Push	Peer: I
	Teacher:

determine how often they occur (a frequency count). First, the observer (or observers) defines the term *aggressive behavior* in specific terms. An observer might discuss the following questions with teammates:

- Does *aggressive behavior* include hitting, biting, and yelling at another child?
- Does it include the child biting (or hurting) teachers as well as peers?
- Does the behavior need to seem intentional?

To obtain accurate observations, observers must be clear about these definitions.

The teachers who studied this event sampling learned that the child uses aggressive behaviors with peers rather than teachers (at this time). Melikia hits with an open hand, bites, hits with an object, pushes, and hits with a closed fist, which is more likely to cause the victim to retaliate. The next step would be to observe with the event sampling demonstrated in Figure 4.5 to learn what might be triggering the behaviors in the immediate context. The teacher can observe further and discuss the observations with the child's parents concerning

- the child's experience with trust and feelings of security (Erikson and Relationship-based theory),
- the child's thinking about how to interact with peers (Piaget),
- whom the child may be imitating (Bandura),
- the child's sociocultural experiences (Vygotsky), and
- what strategies scaffold the child's success in social situations (Vygotsky).

Teachers who use event sampling both before and after strategies are implemented can determine whether the strategies used were successful. Teachers will be able to see, for example, if prosocial behavior increased and aggressive behavior decreased. If not, then teachers and family members will need to revise the strategies.

Charts and Time Sampling

An interesting way to observe and document children's choice of activity and their behavior is the use of charts. Teachers and others interested in observing children often use **time sampling**.

Time sampling involves developing a chart that is used to observe children's behavior at designated times (see Figure 4.7). For example, a teacher might want to observe to determine how many children are using particular areas of the room. This chart could also reveal if there are any areas that are not being used by the children. The information will help the teacher develop an environment that infants and toddlers truly enjoy.

After studying the time sampling in Figure 4.7, the teachers could see that the housekeeping/dramatic play area was not used. A child or several children were wandering in four out of the seven observations. After several time samplings with similar results, the teachers began to watch for children who were wandering. The teachers then tried to help children make a choice of an activity or be with the teacher. The teachers added empty boxes of food and pretend grocery carts to the housekeeping area to see if that sparked any children's interest.

FIGURE 4.7   **Time sampling of toddlers: Eight toddlers/two teachers**

Name: Children in toddler room   Ages: 16-36 months   Date: 5/9/16
Setting: Toddler Room 1   Purpose of Observation: Observe where children play in the room
Type of Observation: Time Sampling   Name of Person Observing: Teacher Karlene

Activity/Time	9:00	9:05	9:10	9:15	9:20	9:25	9:30
Wandering—no obvious aim				1	1	1	1
Moving from one area/teacher to another	1	2		1			
Water			2	3	3	1	1
Painting	2	2	1	1	2	2	2
Housekeeping							
Manipulative	2	3	2		1	1	1
Construction				1			
Active area	2	1	2	1	1	3	2
With a teacher	1		1				1
Involved with game—such as, musical chairs—created by the children or teacher							

FIGURE 4.8   **Time sampling: Focus on a child**

Name: Josiah	Ages: 18 months		Date: 5/10/16			
Setting: Toddler Room 2		Purpose of Observation: Observe where Josiah plays in the room				
Type of Observation: Time Sampling		Name of Person Observing: Teacher Karlene				

Activity/Time	10:00	10:15	10:30	10:45	11:00	11:15	11:30
Playing beside another child	1						
Playing alone—no child within 3 feet			1	1		1	1
With a teacher—with other children		1					
With a teacher—without other children					1		

Teachers learned valuable information on children's patterns of behavior. These behaviors were not easily observed while the teachers were naturally very busy staying near or being with the toddlers. Figure 4.8 provides an example of time sampling with a focus on a child.

After reviewing Figure 4.8, the teachers realized how often Josiah is isolated from both peers and teachers. The teachers asked whether this behavior occurs because the child chooses to play away from others or because the child is being rejected by others. This led to further investigation with running records and event sampling. Note that the time sampling did not reveal how many minutes the child played beside another child or alone. It did reveal what Josiah was doing at the designated times he was observed.

Documentation

Documentation is more than record keeping. It is a special way of observing that records children's experiences through a variety of media. Teachers then use the observations to analyze and understand how children learn and to plan a child-centered curriculum based on children's interests and goals (6). Often documentation includes a series of photos, video recordings, and other *visual* means that are displayed to communicate the remarkable process of how infants and toddlers learn. Documentation frames your understanding of children and your work as a teacher. When photos or children's drawings are displayed, for example, the children's learning becomes visible to teachers and parents.

Our current interest in documentation has its origins in Reggio Emilia, an Italian approach to young children's care and learning. In the Reggio approach, respect for young children's ability to construct knowledge is central to the organization of the early childhood programs. The key tool used by teachers to understand the child's construction of knowledge is purposeful observation and documentation of the children's activities. This documentation process is not simply recording activities or accomplishments; it is a method of coming to thoughtful, reflective understanding of the children's activities and thinking. It is the basis of the teacher's planning for introducing new activities or materials into the program. The documentation process consists of observing and collecting supporting information (e.g., pictures and samples of a child's language), thinking about and talking with the other teachers and the families about the observations, and then planning and responding from one's understanding of the children's knowledge, goals and interests (7).

The documentation process usually begins with a question. It may be something general about many of the children in the group, such as "What are the children most interested in right now?" or "In what ways are children showing interest in mathematical concepts?" Or it may be quite specific and individual, such as "What is Mia learning as she takes her first steps?" or "What is Matt discovering when he plays with the blocks?" The question may be posed and one teacher in a center or several may choose to work together on the same question with the same or different children.

Observation within this model is not aiming at objective, detached recording of the children's activities. Teachers are actively involved with the children, trying to "construct a shared understanding of children's ways of interacting with the environment, of entering into relationships with other adults and other children, and of constructing that knowledge" (8, p. 125). The recording of observations, then, includes thoughtful choices concerning what to record and the medium to use for creating the record. Pen and paper, still cameras, video cameras, audio recordings, and the artwork of the children are all used. However, the intention is rarely to capture an event in just one photo. These documented observations record the series of moments that comprise an event—and related events over time.

Note that "The intent of documentation is to explain, not merely to display" (9, p. 241). The observations—as text, pictures, or artifacts—are reviewed and organized by the observer and shared with colleagues, parents, and the children themselves. The very act of reviewing the documentation and making choices regarding its organization provides the teacher an opportunity to reflect on the children's experience and on her own way of relating to the children. The observations then are shared with others to create a deeper and more complex understanding of the children's actions and ideas, as well as to plan which materials, environmental changes, and relationships could spark children's discoveries. Documentation also can be used to demonstrate how an infant or toddler with special needs is progressing on the goals that were developed by the family and recorded on an individualized family service plan (IFSP).

Example of Documentation

In Figure 4.9, Anthony is sitting down for a family-style meal. In the first picture, he is scooping carrots from a bowl. In the second, he is serving the carrots onto his plate. This documentation tells the teacher about his motor development, how he plans and works toward goals, and his ability to attend to a task. What are you learning about Anthony by looking at this documentation?

Documentation can be used to plan curriculum that meets the interests and needs of a number of infants or toddlers in a group. If a teacher provides opportunities for children to experience water and several children show an interest, the teacher will want to provide more opportunities related to water play. Further documentation can answer questions such as, "How do children communicate with each other during water play?" or "What are the goals, strategies, and theories that children use during play?"

Pearson Education

FIGURE 4.9   **Example of documentation**

Reflection with Team Members Including Families

Observation is only as good as the reflection that occurs on the meaning of the observations. Collaboration with team members including families is an important way to begin to understand what an experience means to a child, as well as the nature of the child's interests and skills. A team can brainstorm together to plan how to use the information for the benefit of the child.

Summary of Observation Methods

Teachers use anecdotal records, running records, event sampling, charts, and documentation strategies to increase their knowledge of individual children's development, thinking, and interests. Observing helps teachers discover how children relate to the enriched environments they create and the responsive interactions they use. Another way to gather information about children's development is through developmental profiles and screening instruments. In these methods, observation skills are critically important.

 Check Your Understanding 4.2
Click here to check your understanding of the concepts in this section.

Observation as Part of Assessment

Group care and learning programs and early intervention programs often use developmental profiles to observe and record children's development. These profiles also are used to *plan* for individual children and a group of children. As you read this book, you may want to observe children using the Developmental Trends and Responsive Interactions charts at the ends of Chapters 6 through 10 or a developmental profile discussed next.

Developmental Profiles

A **developmental profile** lists a sequence of behaviors in domains such as communication, emotional, social, thinking, and motor development.

A developmental profile outlines or profiles a child's development. Teachers and other observers watch a child over time in his home or program environment, using the information to learn about his development and, if in a program, to plan responsively for him.

Developmental profiles generally do not capture children's interests: for example, playing with water, dropping objects to see what will happen, fitting small bodies into small spaces, or making a friend. In addition, they often do not capture the nuances or qualities of a child's behavior—for example, the intensity with which a child expresses anger—although teachers' notes do. Nor do developmental profiles capture the variety of strategies that a child might use as he tries to fit objects into a container. These are all important aspects of a child's essence that adults want to observe and document to know a child well.

Developmental profiles do, however, provide valuable pieces of information about how the child is developing. If completed in concert with the family, they provide an excellent basis for conversations about the child. They also provide information that teachers can use to plan an individualized program for the child and that early interventionists might use with the family during a home visit. Developmental profiles help teachers and family members to discuss the strengths of the child and the next developmental steps. They also begin to give the family and teacher an idea of whether the child is developing as a typical child does.

Let's examine a few of the most commonly used developmental profiles, how they are used, and the information they provide.

The Ounce Scale

The Ounce Scale is an assessment from birth to age 3½. The *User's Guide* (10) emphasizes that "it can be used with children who are at risk, those living in poverty, those with known disabilities, and those who are thriving and developing as expected" (p. iii). Three elements make up the Ounce Scale: the observation record, a family album, and developmental profiles with associated learning standards. Each element is divided into eight age ranges: 0 to 4 months, 4 to 8 months, 8 to 12 months, 12 to 18 months, 18 to 24 months, 24 to 30 months, 30 to 36 months, and 36 to 42 months. For more information on the Ounce Scale, go to the following Web site: www.pearsonclinical.com/.

The Ounce Scale is organized around six meaningful areas of development:

- Personal connections—how children show trust
- Feelings about self—how children express who they are
- Relationships with other children—how children act around other children
- Understanding and communicating—how children understand and communicate
- Exploration and problem solving—how children explore and figure things out
- Movement and coordination—how children move their bodies and use their hands (11)

Pearson Education

Developmental profiles help teachers plan an individualized and group responsive curriculum.

The *observation record* provides a focus for center-based teachers, Early Head Start teachers, home visitors, parent support group leaders, visiting nurses, teen parenting program providers, early interventionist specialists, family home providers, or pediatricians and health aides to observe and document children's behaviors in programs or in the home (12).

The *family album* provides a means to learn about the child's development. It creates an opportunity for the teacher "to 'wonder' along with families so you [the teacher, early interventionists, etc.] can learn how they see or experience their child. This wondering and observing together is the foundation for building trusting relationships between professionals and parents" (13, p. 11).

Developmental profiles are organized by social and emotional, communication and language, cognitive development, and physical development and give the rater an opportunity to summarize growth and development and compare the development to expectations for that age. Summaries of the results for individuals and groups can be obtained from a Web database.

The authors emphasize that this is a relationship-based tool that improves the teacher-child relationship, family-child relationship, and teacher-family relationship. Families report how the Ounce Scale has helped them learn about typical child development as well as how they can support their children's learning at home.

High/Scope COR for Infants and Toddlers

The purpose of the Child Observation Record (COR) is to provide teachers a method for observing children's development and for determining "whether children are developing as they should be. They use the results to continue what is working and improve what is not; for example, to decide whether to provide more training to caregivers or to redesign infants' and toddlers' play areas" (14). (Go to www.highscope.org for more information.) The COR covers these developmental areas:

- Sense of self
- Social relations
- Creative representation
- Movement
- Music
- Communication and language
- Exploring objects
- Early quantity and number
- Space
- Time

With the COR, teachers write observations that describe children's behavior. The information can be entered into a Web database and summarized to plan for individual children and a group.

The Teaching Strategies GOLD for Infants, Toddlers, and Twos

This assessment provides sequential child behaviors in four areas: social/emotional, physical, cognitive, and language. The assessment system helps teachers observe children intentionally and use what they learn to respond to children's interests, strengths, and needs; share information

Pearson Education

What might teachers or parents from different cultures observe in this photo?

with families; and identify children's levels of development in reaction to 14 objectives in four goal areas (go to www.teachingstrategies.com and search for "Teaching Strategies GOLD"). The system is also designed to help teachers support the inclusion of children with disabilities.

These developmental continuum tools supplement the observation and documentation strategies discussed earlier in the chapter. In fact, the strategies described earlier are necessary in order to complete the developmental continuum tools in an accurate manner and to support the results with observations.

Screening Tools

Programs may also use screening instruments to find out if a discussion should occur between the teacher(s) and a child's family about referral to an assessment team for a more comprehensive evaluation to determine if the child has a disability. This referral process is described in Chapter 15 of this book. One screening tool that is frequently used is the *Ages & Stages Questionnaire (ASQ): A Parent Completed, Child Monitoring System*. The ASQ is a widely used system developed by Bricker and Squires (15). Parents answer questions at only one point in time or numerous times based on the age of their child. Because the measure is standardized, answers are scored and compared to cutoff scores to determine whether the child should be referred for more in-depth assessment. Chapter 15 describes the ASQ as well as the Denver Developmental Screening Test.

What method of observation would you use to capture this girl's joy in moving?

Pearson Education

 Check Your Understanding 4.3
Click here to check your understanding of the concepts in this section.

What the Observer Brings to Observations

Observers bring themselves to an observation—their past experiences, beliefs, values, culture, knowledge about children; their skills in observing; and their relationships with the children they are observing. They also bring their knowledge of which observation and assessment tools to use and how to interpret the information for the benefit of the child, family, and teacher.

Past Experiences, Beliefs, and Values

Past personal experiences, beliefs, and values about child rearing or culture may affect the observer's perspective. Teachers who believe that children should be heard and not just seen may focus on strategies that toddlers use to negotiate with adults. They may interpret a child saying no as a positive step in development, whereas others may see it as insubordination. To avoid this type of bias, observers can discuss their observations with team members and families before drawing conclusions from the behavior. Observers can give the objective piece of

CULTURE CLOSE UP

Assessments developed in one culture do not necessarily translate to another culture. One example is an American assessment that used the phrase "gets into everything." The exact translation into the Mandarin dialect was "wants to sort everything." The direct translation changed the meaning, connoting a thoughtful approach. The translators settled on the phrase "wants to participate in everything" (16, p. 8)

an observation to another person, ask for his or her interpretation, and then check to see how well the interpretations match (reliability).

Culture

Culture may provide a frame through which observers interpret behavior. A culture that promotes the independence of children will view a child's shy behavior differently than a culture that values interdependence or dependence of children. Awareness of all of the possible influences on an observer's choice of what, how, and when to observe; the interpretation of the observations; and the use of the observations are key to reducing bias, whether the observer is using more objective or subjective methods.

Presence

Observers try not to change the setting by their presence. If the observer knows the children, then observing is challenging because infants and toddlers have certain expectations for their teachers to respond to them as they typically do. If observing in a group setting, observe only if the ratio of teachers to toddlers is adequate without counting you. If observing a child or children who do not know you, introduce yourself, encourage the parent or teacher to smile at you to show the children that you are safe, and sit among the children for a period before observing. Once observation begins, however, it is important for the observer to try to remain unobtrusive.

TABLE 4.1   Sample questions and methods of observation

Sample Questions	Methods of Observation
What are the interests of each child and the children in the room?	Anecdotal records, running records, documentation
What concepts (space, time, object permanence, light, how to relate to peers) is a child or are the children exploring?	Anecdotal records, running records, documentation
When, where, and how frequently does a particular behavior occur, for example, biting?	Event sampling
How does each child spend his or her time when playing?	Time sampling, documentation
What does a child or what do the children in the group know about water, for example? What opportunities could be provided to help the children learn about the properties of water?	Anecdotal records of children's conversations, strategies, or concepts explored; documentation of children playing with water
How is a child or how are the children in the group developing?	Developmental checklists or series of documentations
How do we know if a child should be referred to an assessment team for a comprehensive evaluation to determine whether he or she is eligible for special support services?	Developmental screening

Remaining unobtrusive while observing is not easy. One of the authors thought she was being a low-profile observer of a toddler group when one of the toddlers speedily ran to her sitting in a low chair and hit her as hard as he could on the leg with a long block. Obviously, the child had been quite aware that a stranger was present and either he wanted the observer to know that he was not comfortable with her presence or he wanted to check to see if she was alive.

However, sitting back, staying low, and being quiet are still the best ways for an observer to create minimal changes in a setting. If a toddler approaches the observer, he can say, "I'm watching you play today" in an enthusiastic voice. After several observations with the same group, toddlers begin to ignore the observer.

What Method to Use

The observer decides which method of observation and assessment is important to use to gain the information needed. As we've discussed, there are many ways to observe and to record observations. These include anecdotal records, running records, event sampling, and time sampling. There are also a number of documentation strategies to use, for example, use of photos or video. Professionals and students of infant-toddler development also use developmental checklists and developmental screening tools. During assessments to determine whether a child has a disability, a team of professionals may use more formal assessments, but recommended practice advises using many of the described methods in this chapter to observe the child in familiar environments and involve families and teachers in the assessment process.

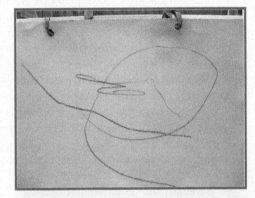

How does an observer know when to use a particular method of observing? The left-hand column of Table 4.1 lists sample questions that teachers and other professionals can ask themselves and discuss with team members and families. The right-hand column indicates methods that answer those questions. Each of these methods has been described in detail in this chapter.

How to Compile Information: Portfolios of Observations/Documentations

Teachers and others who are interested in learning about development may compile individual children's observations and creations into individual portfolios. Often a notebook is organized by information about the child, photos of the child, family photos, dated observations, child planning forms (see Chapter 12), documentation, photos of the child's interests and skills, artifacts such as scribbles, and results of assessments. Portfolios can be organized by age of child, by topic (drawing, playing blocks), or by domains (emotional, social, cognitive, language, and motor development) or placing artifacts in sequence throughout a certain time period. Portfolios support reflection by team members including families. They help observers understand the whole child.

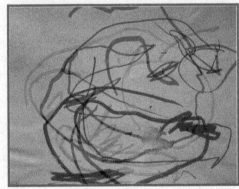

Deanna's early drawing and a later drawing can be placed in a portfolio to demonstrate changes in development.

Check Your Understanding 4.4
Click here to check your understanding of the concepts in this section.

Summary

- Parents, teachers, early interventionists, or students use skilled observing to learn more about child development, children's interests and needs, and how to plan responsively. Through observing, teachers understand the capabilities of young children as well as their special needs. Most important, observing and documenting children's activities allow teachers and other professionals to build relationships with children and families. Observers must follow ethical guidelines outlined in NAEYC and DEC's *Codes of Ethics*.

- By observing with various methods we learn how infants and toddlers think and learn, their interests, their skills, and their needs. We learn the meaning of experiences for the young children we care for and educate. There are many ways to observe including anecdotal and running records, event sampling, time sampling, and documentation. Reflection on the information obtained through observing is best analyzed by a team of professionals and family members.

- Professionals use good observation skills when completing developmental checklists and screening measures. Developmental checklists provide a sequence of development in different domains of development. These domains usually include emotional, social, language, cognitive, and motor development. Developmental checklists (profiles) provide valuable information about how children are developing. Teachers can use the information to plan responsive interactions, organize individualized activities, and provide appropriate materials and equipment that support the children. Teachers also use developmental checklists to determine if a child is developing in a typical way. The Ounce Scale, the COR, and the Teaching Strategies GOLD are examples of developmental checklists used by infant and toddler programs. Screening measures are used to decide if a child needs a referral for further evaluation by a professional team that determines if the child has special needs. Screening tools are usually administered by professionals who have been trained to use them appropriately.

- Observers bring their knowledge of child development, their skills in observing, their biases toward certain behaviors, and their culture to an observation. Past experiences, beliefs, and values influence not only what you will observe but also how you will observe and reflect on the information. Teachers and other professionals decide what methods to use to obtain the most accurate information that they are seeking. Observers also decide how to compile the information to benefit themselves, the children, and the families. Portfolios of observations/documentations are useful for compiling the information for further reflection. Portfolios support reflection by team members including families to understand the whole child.

Key Terms

anecdotal records
biases
developmental profile

documentation
event sampling
inferences

running records
time sampling

Reflections and Resources for the Reader

REFLECTIONS

1. What do you think is the most important aspect of a child to observe first to develop a positive relationship with the child?
2. Observation involves collaboration among you, the child, and the family. How will you improve your observation skills in a collaborative way? How will you build trust among the three participants?

OBSERVATION AND APPLICATION OPPORTUNITIES

1. Observe two children of approximately the same age usingthe Developmental Trends and Responsive Interactions charts at the end of Chapters 6 to 10 (or other observation technique). How are the two children alike? How are they different?
2. Observe two children of different ages using a running record; identify their interests and how they pursue those interests.

SUPPLEMENTAL ARTICLES AND BOOKS TO READ

Krechevsky, M., Mardell, B., Rivard, M., & Wilson, D. (2013). *Visible learners: promoting Reggio-Inspired approaches in all schools*. Jossey-Bass.

Mindes, G., & Jung, L.A. (2014). *Assessing young children* (5th ed.). Pearson.

Sunita, & Bilszta, J. L. C. (2013). Early identification of autism: A comparison of the checklist for autism in toddlers and the modified checklist for autism in toddlers. *Journal of Paediatrics & Child Health, 49*(6), 438–444. doi:10.1111/j.1440-1754.2012.02558.x

INTERESTING LINKS

Go to New Zealand's ECE on their education Web site. Click on the tab 0–6 years. Then click on Kei Tua o te Pae. Download Assessment for Infants and Toddlers.

This exquisite site sensitively discusses the meaning of documentation of infants and toddlers and provides specific examples of children's portfolio pages.

Go to Zero to Three's Web site and Look Up Multidisciplinary Consultant Modules

These modules were designed to complement training offered to early childhood consultants through the National Training Institute at the Department of Maternal and Child Health, University of North Carolina at Chapel Hill. They include: infant/toddler development, screening, and assessment. There are activities that help the reader practice compiling portfolios and comparing screening tools.

5

Genetics and Prenatal Development

LEARNING OUTCOMES

After reading this chapter, you will be able to:

- Describe the interactions of genetics and experiences, including nutrition, prenatal health care, toxins and teratogens, structural and metabolic birth defects, maternal infections, maternal anxiety and other factors, in prenatal development.

- Recount the development of the fetus through the three trimesters.

- Explain the prenatal and postnatal development of the brain.

- Describe the abilities of the newborn and the effects of premature birth.

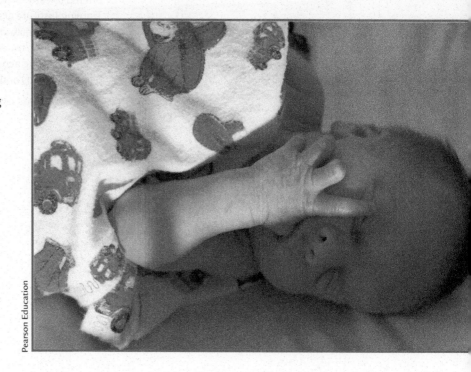

Pearson Education

LaShana smiled to herself as she remembered the morning. As a toddler teacher, she frequently was included in special moments in the lives of the children's families. This morning Alberto's mother was almost dancing as she brought him in. She pulled LaShana aside and whispered, "I'm pregnant!"

This really is beginning at the beginning.

You may wonder why a text on infant and toddler development and group care has a chapter on prenatal development. Development races forward from the moment the egg and sperm meet. The fetus's experience in the womb creates the physical foundation for all later learning. It helps us understand babies if we know about brain development, **conception**, **gestation**, and the first weeks after birth. The second reason is that infant-toddler teachers are often in a position to provide parent education on pregnancy. It may be through your role as a home visitor or as a toddler teacher when parents of your charges become pregnant. Parents recognize teachers as having knowledge and experience and see teachers as a source of personal support in parenting issues. Everyone benefits by the teacher being grounded in the details of healthy pregnancy and prenatal development.

Genes and Experiences Interact in the Womb

> As Peter entered the center to begin his shift as a toddler teacher, he passed by Trina, who seemed to be taking a minute in the doorway after dropping off her daughter for child care. Peter was surprised to see her smoking, as just a few weeks earlier she had happily announced that she was pregnant with her second child. Peter greeted her, paused, and said, "Trina, I'm a little startled to see you smoking. Do you know about the effects of smoking during pregnancy?" This time it was Trina's turn to be surprised. "No, is it a problem?" she asked. "I know not to drink beer or anything, but smoking . . . What's the problem?"

We used to think of the womb as a safe place for the developing fetus with the **placenta** as a barrier that kept dangerous things outside of the womb. Although the placenta is able to act as somewhat of a filter, we now know that the fetus can be compromised if the mother has inadequate nutrition. The fetus may be affected by many substances that can harm it. Genetic and other congenital factors can cause the formation to go astray. Maternal stress and anxiety may directly affect the baby's well-being. When infant-toddler teachers have ongoing contact with the expectant parents, they can provide information and resources that promote the best outcome for every pregnancy.

Genes provide directions to the cells in the developing **embryo** and **fetus** and throughout our lives. We know more about the composition of our bodies today than at any time in history, and more is being learned every day. For example, your body is composed of about 100 *trillion* cells. Your little toe is made of 2 or 3 billion cells. Each cell is smaller than the diameter of one strand of hair—and yet the material inside each cell makes us similar to all other human beings and, at the same time, our own, completely unique selves.

Watch this video to see how experiences build the architecture of the brain. How does this make the adult's interactions highly important?

https://www.youtube.com/watch?v=VNNsN9IJkws

Genetics

Our skin is made of skin cells, our liver made of liver cells. Around 200 kinds of cells are needed to create our bodies. Each cell contains genetic information that directs it to be a specific kind of cell doing the work it needs to do. (See Figure 5.1.)

Each cell is enclosed by a somewhat porous membrane. Within the cell membrane is a watery fluid called cytoplasm—a mixture of water, enzymes, amino acids, glucose, and other molecules. At the center of the cell is the nucleus. Protected by a nuclear membrane, the nucleus holds 6 feet of deoxyribonucleic acid (DNA) tightly packed into 46 chromosomes. Human beings inherit 23 chromosomes from their father and 23 from their mother. There are 22 pairs of autosomes and one pair of sex chromosomes, called the X chromosome and the Y chromosome, which determine gender. Females have two X chromosomes and males have one X and one Y chromosome. (See Figure 5.2.)

About 2 percent of the DNA provides genetic information. Each little section of the pattern of DNA is marked by a starting point and an ending point. The material between those points is a gene. Genes carry the general information on how to create and maintain the body. They also tell your body to have hair color like your mother's or a nose like your grandfather's (1). However, genes do not automatically express themselves as intended. Genes are affected by early

FIGURE 5.1   A cell.

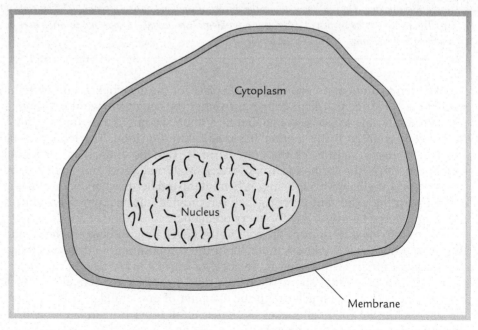

FIGURE 5.2   **A chromosome, genes, and DNA.**

Each chromosome is packed with long strands of DNA, carrying all of the body's genetic information.

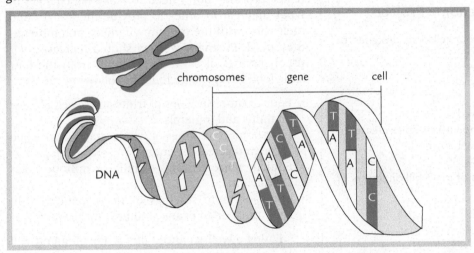

experiences. Hormones secreted in response to positive or negative experiences give genes directions about whether to turn on or express themselves. This process is called **epigenetics**. Toxic stress may also affect whether the genetic blueprint can be carried out (2).

There are around 25,000 genes in the human **genome**. The Human Genome Project, described in Box 5.1, has mapped out the entire human genome. At this point, we have identified more than 5,000 genes, any one of which, if damaged or missing, can cause drastic changes in the human being. Missing genes are known to cause a variety of diseases and disabling conditions including lactose intolerance, albinism, cystic fibrosis, Tay-Sachs disease, **sickle cell anemia**, hemophilia, and muscular dystrophy. Disabilities caused by genetic issues are described in Chapter 15.

 Watch this video to see 18 things you should know about genetics. How do genes, DNA, and chromosomes relate to one another?

https://www.youtube.com/watch?v=bVk0twJYL6Y

There is not necessarily a direct one-to-one, gene-to-disease correlation, however. Damage to one gene may cause a variety of problems, and many diseases are caused by damage to a set of genes. **Genetic counseling** can be helpful to families that have concerns about inherited diseases.

We are all complex and unique human beings—yet each of us is built of single cells that are predominantly exactly like the cells in all other human beings. Although the components and functioning of single cells are pretty impressive, when two cells meet and create a new human being, the following development is really thrilling!

BOX 5.1

The Human Genome Project

This study of the DNA in our cells was designed to tell us

- How many genes we have
- How cells work
- How living things evolved
- How single cells develop into complex creatures
- What happens when we become ill

The work includes

- Charting the sequence of the 3 billion letters of human DNA
- Mapping the human genes

Source: The Human Genome Project is funded by National Institutes of Health and the U.S. Department of Energy.

Nutrition

Women with a good nutritional diet before pregnancy probably don't need to make big changes in what they eat in order to provide themselves and their baby with the protein, vitamins, and minerals they need. Pregnant women should increase their usual servings of a variety of foods from the four basic food groups to include the following:

- Four or more servings of fruits and vegetables for vitamins and minerals
- Four or more servings of whole-grain or enriched bread and cereal for energy
- Four or more servings of milk or milk products for calcium
- Three or more servings of meat, poultry, fish, eggs, nuts, dried beans, and peas for protein

Eating a well-balanced diet while pregnant will help keep mother and baby healthy. Most physicians agree that the recommended daily allowances (RDAs), except those for iron, can be obtained through a proper diet (3).

There are some specific nutrients that pregnant women must be sure they are getting, either through diet or with supplements. Iron is needed in larger amounts, especially in the later stages of pregnancy, and it is difficult to consume enough of it through food. This mineral is essential to the formation of healthy red blood cells and will help the mother avoid anemia and being susceptible to infections.

A woman's need for folic acid doubles during pregnancy. Folic acid has been shown to be important in preventing neural tube defects, such as spina bifida and anencephaly, and is essential to the formation of red blood cells. Folic acid can be found in many foods, including kidney beans, leafy green vegetables, peas, and liver—or a doctor may prescribe a diet supplement.

Pregnant women need to increase their calcium and fluid intake. Pregnant and lactating adult women require an additional 40 percent of calcium a day (three extra servings of milk or dairy products). Almost all of the extra calcium goes into the baby's developing bones. Extra fluids, especially water, are needed to support pregnant women's increased blood volume. They should drink at least eight glasses of water each day to prevent dehydration and constipation (4). Table 5.1 shows how nutrients support fetal growth.

Casey benefitted from her mother's nutritional diet when Casey was in the womb.

Pearson Education

TABLE 5.1 **How nutrients support fetal growth.**

In addition to a well-rounded, healthy diet of low-fat proteins, dairy, vegetables, fruits, and whole-grained carbohydrates, healthy fats, there are three key nutrients the fetus needs.

Folic Acid to reduce the risk of birth defects that affect the spinal cord. Many grain-based foods have been fortified with folic acid.

Iron to reduce anemia. Foods with vitamin C help the body absorb the iron in red meats, dark, leafy vegetables, and other foods.

Calcium to support the healthy formation of a baby's teeth, bones, heart, nerves and muscles. Calcium comes from dairy products, dark, leafy greens, and calcium-fortified orange juice.

Culture and Nutrition

Many cultures around the world have certain beliefs about nutrition during pregnancy. In Egypt women knew that certain foods were not good during pregnancy but they misunderstood why.

> Junk food and caffeinated beverages as well as salty, pickled, and spicy foods are considered culturally taboo or "bad" during pregnancy. Intake of these foods is not always restricted, and their harm is generally misunderstood.
>
> Pregnant women said they recognize that junk foods (e.g., lunch meat, soda, prepackaged potato chips, biscuits, and locally made potato chips); salty foods; acidic foods (e.g., foods cooked with onions and tomatoes); and caffeinated beverages (e.g., tea and coffee) may adversely affect the mother and/or the child, for example, contributing to "high blood pressure" and "deformation of unborn children." Mothers mainly had misinformation about the harmful effects of these taboo foods. These effects included: "chips cause worms for the fetus," salty foods create "a burning sensation when delivering the child," and junk foods "cause cancer of the blood" (5, p. viii–ix).

Many Asian cultures also think generally about health, and particularly about food, in terms of being *hot* or *cold*. Not literally hot or cold in how they are served, but as in adding heat or cold to the balance of the body's temperatures. Pregnancy is thought of as adding heat, so cooling foods such as melons are increased to provide balance (6). Young mothers in Latin America avoid spicy foods during pregnancy but consume them in the postpartum period as a way of reestablishing heat lost in childbirth (7). Some cultures believe certain foods have specific effects on pregnancy. The Beng tribespeople in Africa avoid eating large bananas because they would create a fat baby. Meat from the striped antelope would create striped or patchy skin. Boiled yams would make for a difficult delivery (8). Middle Eastern Muslim customs include ensuring that the newly married woman eats foods that are rich in iron to ensure the baby is well nourished. These include a molasses-like grape drink and organ meats (9). An aboriginal group in Australia's desert believes it is important to avoid meat from animals with sharp, pointed parts to avoid miscarriage (10).

Cultural beliefs, habits, and access to healthy foods can all affect a woman's nutrition during pregnancy. Child care and learning programs often keep

The women of the Wind River Indian Reservation were very concerned about the poor pregnancy outcomes for their young mothers. American Indian/Alaska Native (AI/AN) women had the least access to prenatal care and the second highest infant mortality and prematurity rates in the country. Working with their Early Head Start program, the women wanted to support their young mothers in a more traditional manner. At the same time, the Cherokee Nation was surveying prenatal literature for the March of Dimes, looking for culturally relevant materials. They found 49 items out of 500 that were culturally appropriate.

The March of Dimes brought together a committee of women representing the Shoshone, Cherokee, Nez Perce, Choctaw, Mayan, Navajo, Dakota, Chickasaw, Blackfeet, and Athabascan Nations to determine what was needed to address the health care disparity. The committee ultimately created a prenatal information booklet called *The Coming of the Blessing*. This booklet told the story of a healthy pregnancy the way a mother would tell her daughter. The women created a medicine wheel on which the first trimester was called *the blessing has been planted*, the second *feel the blessing dance*, and the third *the blessing has arrived*. Traditional practices, information for the father, and the woman's circle of support accompany the medical information supplied by the March of Dimes.

The booklet was immensely successful and is now an ongoing part of the March of Dimes materials for Indian health educators (11).

pamphlets providing nutrition information in their parent information areas because they are helpful and of interest to pregnant women and future fathers. It is also helpful to keep information handy on what may be harmful to the developing fetus. Women like Trina, at the beginning of this section, may not always know what to avoid during pregnancy.

Prenatal Health Care

There are many reasons to get prenatal health care. In fact, if a woman is planning on becoming pregnant, she will want to start seeing a doctor in preparation.

Babies of mothers who do not get prenatal care are three times more likely to have a low birth weight and five times more likely to die than those born to mothers who do get care (12).

Prenatal health care promotes the health of mother and child. Nutrition information is supplied. The health professional will track the baby's growth and development. If there are any concerns, needed tests can be scheduled. Information about labor and delivery is shared. Expectant women are advised to avoid hot baths or hot tubs, smoking, alcohol, and street drugs. They are told to avoid cat litter, contact with rodents, and chemicals such as insecticides, solvents (like some cleaners or paint thinners), lead, mercury, and paint (including paint fumes). Women are advised to exercise, get enough sleep, and reduce stress in their lives.

Toxins and Teratogens

Many substances in the environment threaten the positive development and cause disabling conditions in the fetus. Some of these conditions and their effect on development are described more thoroughly in Chapter 15. This section contains information that infant-toddler teachers may want to share with expectant families. You may be a little uncomfortable bringing up the use of alcohol or drugs with a parent. However, general information about substances in the environment that may be harmful to a fetus or threatening to a pregnancy is important for expectant parents to know. Having this kind of information as part of ongoing parent education efforts is especially important because harm can occur before the mother even knows she's pregnant.

Because of the rapid division and replication of cells early in gestation, exposure to a toxic substance is likely to cause more damage the earlier it occurs in the pregnancy. Drinking alcohol during pregnancy can have severe effects on the child, including mental retardation, growth deficiency, and facial abnormalities (13). More than 40,000 babies a year are born with alcohol-related damage (14).

Cocaine use appears to be related to premature births and smaller babies (15). Determining the effects of cocaine is complicated because of pregnant women's use of multiple drugs and alcohol. A contributing factor to possible negative effects of cocaine use is that mothers who used cocaine prenatally show less sensitivity and more negative affect with infants and are angrier and aggressive with their toddlers (16).

An exhaustive review of studies of the effect of maternal smoking, looking at 12 million children including 173,000 with birth defects, showed that babies born to mothers who smoked had a

- Twenty to thirty percent increased risk of having shortened or missing arms and legs, cleft lips and cleft palates, and abnormally shaped heads or faces
- Twenty-seven percent increased risk of gastrointestinal abnormalities, including problems with the throat, esophagus, colon, intestine, bile ducts, gallbladder, and liver
- Fifty percent increased risk of being born with their intestines outside the body
- Twenty percent increased risk of being born with a blocked or closed anus
- Nine percent increased risk of heart defects
- Thirteen percent higher risk that baby boys would be born with undescended testes

Although researchers are not exactly sure how smoking damages the fetus, it is assumed that cigarette smoking limits the available oxygen. Nicotine causes blood vessels to constrict, and carbon monoxide binds to hemoglobin, which carries oxygen through the body. It is estimated that 20 percent of pregnant women younger than age 25 in the United States smoke (17).

Exposure during pregnancy to environmental toxins such as lead, mercury, arsenic, cleaning products, and chemical solvents may lead to miscarriage, premature birth, low birth weight, and developmental delays. Lead may be present in drinking water through old lead plumbing pipes or old paint. Mercury is stored in the fatty tissue of most fish. Arsenic exposure may occur through industrial workplaces and cleaning products and solvents often used in the home (18).

Pesticides pose similar hazards to the fetus; although unless women are in agricultural areas, the risk is not great. Some health care providers have voiced concerns about insect repellents containing DEET. However, in areas where there is the danger of West Nile virus or Lyme disease, it is suggested that a pregnant woman use small amounts of insect repellent on her clothing, socks, and shoes and that she wear gloves when applying it (19).

Child care providers may want to keep informative brochures on hand to help expectant families be aware of substances that could be harmful to their unborn child. Such materials can often be obtained from the March of Dimes or the local public health agency. A program's nurse consultant could be helpful in obtaining these materials.

Structural/Metabolic Birth Defects and Maternal Infections

Of course, many prenatal problems are not anticipated. Sometimes, for reasons we do not yet understand, malformations occur during gestation. Missing chromosomes, abnormal genes carried by one or both parents, and inaccurate migrations of cells can cause a variety of malformations in the fetus. **Cleft palate** may be caused by a combination of these factors. Metabolic disorders (1 in 3,500 babies) such as **Tay-Sachs** or **phenylketonuria (PKU)** are generally genetic diseases and can be harmful or even fatal.

Infectious agents also cause birth defects. The term TORCH syndrome—an acronym for Toxoplasmosis, Other agents, Rubella, Cytomegalovirus, and Herpes simplex—refers to a set of maternal infections that can cause harm to a fetus. Maternal infections such as rubella (rare, due to vaccinations) and cytomegalovirus (3,000 to 4,000 babies a year) occurring early in the pregnancy may result in mental retardation, blindness, or deafness. Sexually transmitted diseases (1 in 2,000 babies) may result in stillbirth, newborn death, or bone defects (20).

In late 2015 and 2016, a new mosquito-borne virus caught the world's attention. The Zika virus may have caused nearly 4000 babies to be born with small brains and heads (microencephely) in Brazil alone. The virus has been found in more than 20 Central and South American and other tropical countries. The World Health Organization has declared a world health emergency over concern for the birth defects (21). Some countries are suggesting women wait two more years after the outbreak before becoming pregnant—in countries where birth control is not easily available. The public health approach most widely promoted is containment of the mosquito. Women of child-bearing age should use DEET and wear long-sleeved and panted clothing outdoors.

Maternal Anxiety and Other Factors

Emotional experiences release hormones in the body. If the pregnant woman is struggling with stress, anxiety, or depression, the hormones floating in her body can be damaging to her unborn baby.

Anxiety

Pregnancy can be a joyful time if a family is stable and financially secure, has a good support system, and wants the child. When any of these components are missing—and sometimes even when they are all present—pregnant women can experience stress and anxiety. When the mother is anxious, the baby's heart rate may increase, less blood flows to the uterus, and the result can be a baby with decreased birth weight. When a mother has high levels of stress hormones—such as cortisol in her bloodstream—the baby is likely to have low birth weight, a small head, poor brain development, and low **APGAR** ratings in the minutes after birth. Certainly home visitors need to be aware of the impact of maternal stress on the developing fetus. Child care and learning providers would do well to attend to a mother's reports of stress and anxiety, as well as providing information and emotional support as they are able.

Stress

Human beings release the hormones cortisol and adrenalin in response to stress. These hormones sharpen our attention and help us respond quickly in an emergency. If the stress continues over time, these hormones can be harmful. Ongoing exposure to these hormones can cause health problems. In rodent studies, when pregnant rodents experience high levels of stress, their offspring are fearful and more reactive to stress. They have poorer memory and learning abilities. As they age, they have memory and cognitive problems (22).

Depression

Some situations during pregnancy are not well known but can be dangerous to the mother and the fetus (23). Although postpartum depression is familiar, the less well-known condition of prenatal depression is described here. Prenatal depression may be very difficult, even for professionals, to diagnose. Physical symptoms of pregnancy are so similar to symptoms of depression; poor appetite, fatigue, difficulty sleeping, and mood swings are certainly common to both depression and pregnancy. Home visitors, child care and learning providers, and health providers should pay particular attention to pregnant women who speak of feeling flat and hopeless. Depression during pregnancy is a strong predictor of postpartum depression. Women who are depressed during pregnancy should be referred for mental health evaluations and counseling.

Both men and women may become depressed following pregnancy. Each may also suffer from parenting distress in the first weeks after birth (24). Parents may be sleep deprived. Newborns may have colic. There are enormous adjustments being made within each person and each relationship.

Intimate Partner Violence

An even harder issue to think about during pregnancy is intimate partner violence and its impact on the fetus. In addition to the immediate physical dangers, the presence of domestic violence during a pregnancy may result in:

- Stress for the mother, with health implications for the baby.
- Delays in seeking prenatal care, with health implications for the baby.
- Unhappiness with being pregnant, with implications for the relationship between the mother and the child (25).

Home visitors may deal with these issues more directly than infant and toddler teachers. However, child care and learning programs could provide staff training on domestic violence, know about community resources, provide parent information brochures, and have a plan in place for helping move a woman and her children to safety if necessary.

Simply reading about some of these issues may feel heavy and difficult. It may seem far out of the realm of working in a pleasant child care and learning program and taking care of babies. Most teachers will never deal with these issues with pregnant mothers. Nonetheless, this is good information to tuck away. Simply being aware of these concerns, knowing your community resources, and keeping information available to parents could make a significant difference in the lives of children and their families.

Pregnancy is such a natural part of life that it's easy to take it for granted. Reading through all the potential dangers can be a little distressing, especially if you are of childbearing age yourself. So, it is important to remember that most pregnancies proceed without alarm and result in wonderful, healthy, and amazingly capable newborns.

Check Your Understanding 5.1
Click here to check your understanding of the concepts in this section.

Prenatal Development

The development of the baby from conception to birth takes about 40 weeks. In talking about gestation, or the period of pregnancy, we usually divide those weeks into three parts, or trimesters.

The First Trimester

Fetal development begins when the sperm cell from the father enters the ripe egg (ovum) of the mother. These two cells are different from all others in the human body. Where almost all cells have 46 chromosomes (23 pairs), the sperm and the ovum have only 23 each. This lets the genetic material from the mother and father pair up and begin to create a whole new person.

When the ovum and the sperm combine to create a new cell, this cell quickly multiplies. It travels down the fallopian tube to implant itself in the uterine wall on the 6th day after conception. The placenta develops to keep the fetus nourished and supply oxygen. In the first weeks following conception, the **amniotic sac** and placenta are developing. The amniotic sac will hold the developing fetus and the placenta in a bath of amniotic fluid. The embryo develops three layers of cells: (1) the ectoderm, which will become the brain, sensory organs, and nervous system; (2) the mesoderm, which will become the circulatory, skeletal, and muscular systems; and (3) the endoderm, which will become the digestive and glandular systems (see Figure 5.3).

During these first 3 months of development, the first trimester, the cells rapidly multiply but they also begin to differentiate into blood cells, liver cells, nerve cells, and so forth. As you can see in Figure 5.4, the external features such as eyes, ears, arms and legs, and the internal organs have begun to form. Although less than 3 inches long, the fetus can make a fist; spontaneously move their arms and

FIGURE 5.3   Early development of the human embryo.
The cells multiply and differentiate.

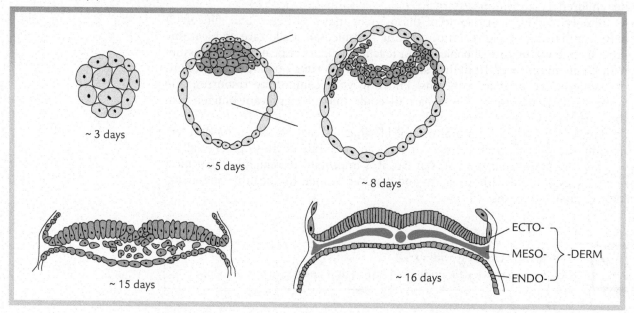

FIGURE 5.4   **First trimester of fetal development.**

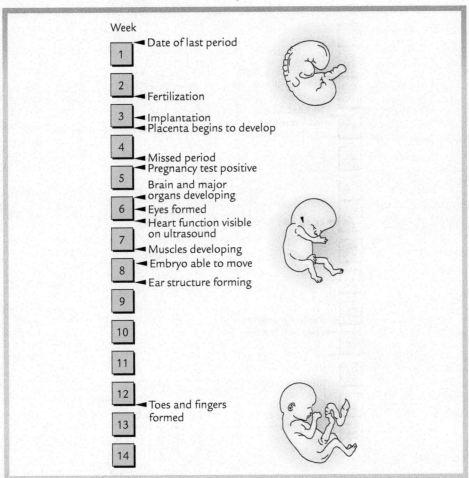

Week
1 — Date of last period
2 — Fertilization
3 — Implantation / Placenta begins to develop
4
5 — Missed period / Pregnancy test positive
Brain and major organs developing
6 — Eyes formed
Heart function visible on ultrasound
7 — Muscles developing
8 — Embryo able to move
Ear structure forming
9
10
11
12 — Toes and fingers formed
13
14

legs; begin a rudimentary sleep and waking cycle; and grasp, suck, and swallow (26). The embryo and then the fetus are especially vulnerable in the first weeks of gestation. The brain and the internal organs are forming. If one of the first cells is damaged, that damage will be replicated over and over as the cells divide and multiply.

 Watch this video to see a visualization of gestation. Why is it important for women of child-bearing age to behave as though they might be pregnant?

https://www.youtube.com/watch?v=fKyljukBE70

The Second Trimester

Months 4 through 6 of gestation are a time of growth and development. The fetus grows to about 15 inches and weighs about 2 pounds 11 ounces. (See Figure 5.5.) The fetus is active about half the time and the mother can sometimes

FIGURE 5.5   **Second trimester of fetal development.**

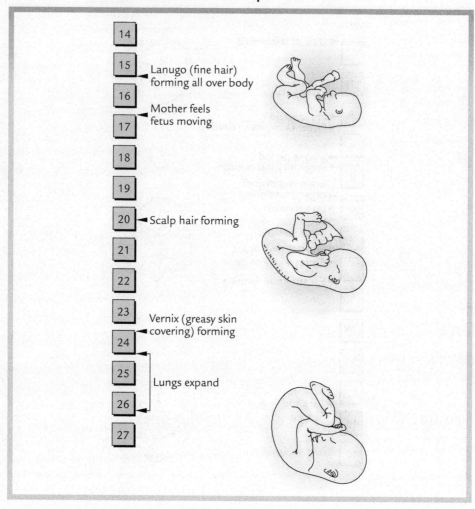

14

15   Lanugo (fine hair)
     forming all over body

16   Mother feels
     fetus moving

17

18

19

20 ◄ Scalp hair forming

21

22

23   Vernix (greasy skin
   ◄ covering) forming

24

25   Lungs expand

26

27

feel the movement. The heartbeat, and sometimes even crying, can be heard with a stethoscope.

The Third Trimester

By the beginning of the third trimester, the fetus could survive a premature birth, but the potential for complications is high. The brain is rapidly developing, perhaps in part stimulated by movement, light, temperature changes, and sounds. Listening through the noises of the womb to the voices of her family, she may be learning the sounds of her family's language. After birth, the baby will be able to recognize stories repeatedly read out loud during this gestational period. The fetus gains body fat and grows quickly to fill the entire uterus. (See Figure 5.6.)

Thus, the development of the human being is the work of the new cell formed by the egg and the sperm duplicating itself over and over. The genetic information encoded in the DNA tells each cell where to travel in the developing embryo and what sort of cell it should be. Over the course of 40 weeks, the human being grows from one cell into a complex, competent human being who is able to hear, react, and learn even while still inside the womb.

FIGURE 5.6   **Third trimester of fetal development.**

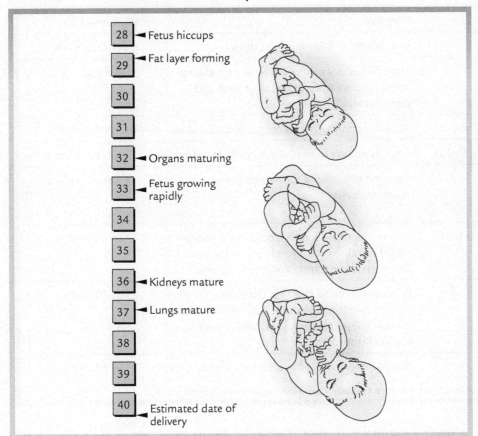

28 ◄ Fetus hiccups
29 ◄ Fat layer forming
30
31
32 ◄ Organs maturing
33 ◄ Fetus growing rapidly
34
35
36 ◄ Kidneys mature
37 ◄ Lungs mature
38
39
40 ◄ Estimated date of delivery

Prenatal Testing

Child care and learning programs are increasingly likely to serve infants and toddlers who are medically complex or have disabilities. Understanding both the normal progression of gestation and birth and the difficulties that can occur in the process will help you be a resource and support to expectant and new parents.

Many problems that occur during gestation can be diagnosed through prenatal testing. Doctors are able to test for specific conditions as well as the general well-being of the fetus. There are a variety of methods, from simple tests of the mother's blood to actually inserting a needle into the amniotic sac and removing fluid. The three-dimensional, moving

This mother was reassured by prenatal testing during her pregnancy.

Pearson Education

images of the fetus available through ultrasound are so fascinating that parents sometimes keep the still photographs or videos as their first pictures of their baby.

TABLE 5.2   Types of prenatal testing

Prenatal Test	Purpose	Performed at
Doppler device	Ultrasound to hear fetal heartbeat	6 weeks to birth
Ultrasound	High-frequency sound waves to provide live-action picture of fetus; track growth and development	5 weeks to birth
Chorionic villus sampling (CVS)	Needle sampling to test for genetic disorders	10.5 to 13 weeks
Magnetic resonance imaging (MRI)	Creates images of soft tissue, such as the brain	12 weeks to birth
Fetal echocardiography	Detailed ultrasound for babies at high risk for heart problems	14 weeks to birth
Alpha fetoprotein blood tests (AFP)	Part of the triple screen test. Screens mother's blood for alpha fetoprotein assessing risk of Down syndrome and neural tube defects	15 to 20 weeks
Triple screen test	A maternal blood test that that looks for AFP, human chorionic gonadotropin (hCG), and estriol. These tests assess potential genetic and physical disorders	15 to 20 weeks
Amniocentesis	Tests amniotic fluid for chromosomal disorders	16 to 20 weeks

Source: American Pregnancy Association. (2012). Retrieved from http://americanpregnancy.org/prenatal-testing/

Table 5.2 contains a short description of the most common prenatal tests. Nearly every pregnant woman hears her baby's heartbeat through the Doppler device during regular prenatal checkups. Medical offices sometimes use ultrasound to create a visual image of the developing fetus.

    Check Your Understanding 5.2
Click here to check your understanding of the concepts in this section.

The Developing Brain

The newborn responds to the feel of a nipple on his cheek with a reflex and begins to suck before the nipple even reaches his mouth. Five months later, the baby knows that when his caregiver moves from the cupboard to the sink, she is preparing a bottle for his snack. How much has been learned—and remembered—in these few months!

The development of the brain begins within the first days following conception. It continues to develop throughout our lifetimes. The course of brain development during gestation is generally predictable. It is affected by the mother's nutrition, her emotional condition, and her exposures to toxins. The nutrients available to the developing brain and the mother's experiences affect the structure of the brain.

The Structure of the Brain

By 4 weeks following conception, the embryo is about one-fourth-inch long. It is curled into a crescent with little nubs sticking off the sides. A heart tube forms and begins pulsating. The internal organs are beginning to develop. The future brain and nervous system become apparent as a spoon-shaped structure, only one cell thick, known as the neural plate. The neural groove runs the length of the neural plate, dividing it into right and left halves. This is a precursor of the future cerebral hemispheres.

Over the next several weeks, fetal brain cells, or neurons, are generated at about 200,000 per minute and the brain develops three areas: the forebrain, the midbrain, and the hindbrain (Figure 5.7). These become larger and more differentiated in the womb and form the sections of the adult nervous system. The forebrain becomes the cerebrum, controlling thinking and language; the midbrain becomes the thalamus and hypothalamus, controlling the passage of sensory information; and the hindbrain becomes the cerebellum and the brain stem, controlling heartbeat, respiration, and motor development (27).

At about 5 months of gestation, the brain is growing rapidly, but it is relatively smooth. In the last 3 months of gestation, the brain continues to grow quickly, limited by the containing force of the skull. As the surface of the brain continues to grow, the cerebral hemispheres fold in on themselves, packing themselves efficiently into the available space. By the time a baby is born, the brain looks as furled and gnarled as that of an older child or adult, with a visible crease down the middle separating the two hemispheres.

It is the large size and complexity of the human brain that make us different from every other species. Babies are born with about 100 billion brain cells—twice the number they will have as adults. This abundance of cells helps ensure that babies will be born with healthy brains and will be able to learn whatever they need to survive in their unique environment (28, p. 5).

FIGURE 5.7   **Prenatal brain development**

The cells rapidly multiply, the ball shape begins to flatten to a disk, and the embryo develops three layers of cells.

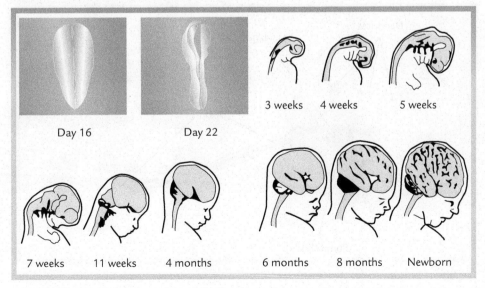

Day 16   Day 22

3 weeks   4 weeks   5 weeks

7 weeks   11 weeks   4 months   6 months   8 months   Newborn

Watch this video to see how the fetal brain develops. Watch for the process of multiplying and pruning.

https://www.youtube.com/watch?v=MS5HUDVNbGs

Creating Connections Between Neurons

The work of neurons is to make connections with other neurons, constantly exchanging information. The fetus's, and then the baby's, experiences provide the information that causes the connections to form. Experiences are creating the physical structure of the brain moment by moment. Each neuron has an axon (transmitter), a thin fiber that carries information in the form of electrical signals out from the neuron. The information is received by the dendrites (receivers) in other cells. Each neuron also has many dendrites, hairlike fibers that receive electrical information from other neurons (see Figure 5.8).

When an axon sends out information from one neuron, dendrites from one or more other neurons receive the information through a connection between axon and dendrite called a synapse. A neuron may connect to up to 15,000 other neurons, creating the phenomenon known as wiring the brain. In order for an electrical signal to be transmitted across the synapse, a neurotransmitter chemical such as serotonin, dopamine, or endorphins must be present (31). (See Figure 5.9.)

 Watch to the 6:41 mark on this video to see how synapses develop in the fetal brain. Which experiences does a fetus have that create learning?

https://www.youtube.com/watch?v=MS5HUDVNbGs

The synapses, or connections, that are used repeatedly in the infant's day-to-day life will be reinforced and strengthened. The synapses that form but are never

FIGURE 5.8   **The neuron**

A single neuron with one axon transmitting information and many dendrites receiving messages.

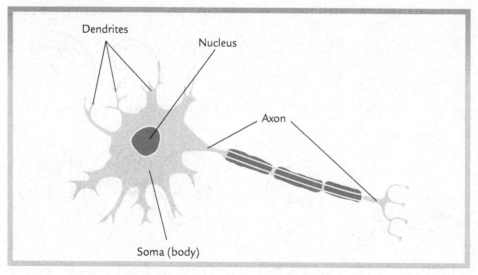

FIGURE 5.9   A synaptic connection

The axon and dendrite exchange information at a point of connection called a synapse, using chemical neurotransmitters.

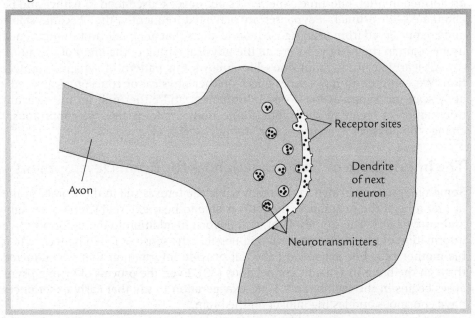

Receptor sites

Dendrite of next neuron

Axon

Neurotransmitters

reactivated will be eliminated in a process often called *pruning*. This profusion of synapses followed by weeding out of unused dendrites is a very efficient way of ensuring that the child learns what he or she needs to.

The genes are the bricks and mortar to build a brain. The environment is the architect. (Christine Hohmann)

For example, say a very young infant is hungry and crying. He sees a familiar shape moving toward him in a familiar way. The shape is wearing something soft and light blue. It has a familiar smell and it is making familiar sounds: "It's OK, honey, I'm here. Are you sooo hungry?" Synapses begin firing all over the baby's brain: "What do I know about that shape? Sometimes it's Aunt Sherri or a stranger, but it's usually Mommy. It looks like something Mommy often wears. It smells like Mommy, it sounds like Mommy's words and voice."

The infant has information about all of these aspects of "Mommy" stored in synapses in his brain. When he is near Mommy, or probably even just

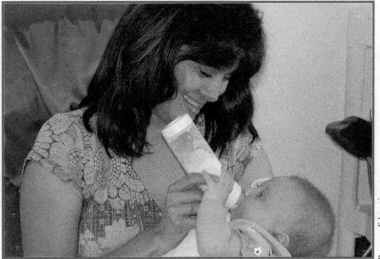

Amy's synapses are firing as she drinks her milk and gazes at her family child care provider.

Pearson Education

thinking about her, these synapses carrying familiar information are set off and become strengthened. On the other hand, if a stranger passes the infant in the grocery store, the baby registers information but never "reactivates" it. Synapses that are formed in brief, one-time experiences but never reused tend to wither and be eliminated—or pruned. If synapses are activated frequently, they become stable and are preserved from pruning. So, connections that are made and strengthened in the brain in the early years create the physical wiring of the brain of the adult.

All learning, throughout one's life, follows this pattern of synaptic connection. We continue to have experiences—either physical or conceptual, immediately scan our synapses for stored information, and either pull up the relevant information or create new synaptic connections. In doing this, we continuously change the physical structure of our brains.

The Importance of Early Experiences for Brain Development

Some synapses are created in the brain while the fetus is still in the womb. In the last months of the pregnancy, the fetus is able to hear external sounds, see light and taste flavors. The sounds, light, and flavors, in addition to the proprioceptive information of his own movement and possibly the sense of touch he feels when his mother rubs her expanded belly, all provide information that is conducted through the brain in synaptic connections (30). Even the process of pruning synapses begins in the womb. So it is no exaggeration to say that early experiences have enormous and lasting impact on the brain.

During the first year of life, an infant's brain grows to about 70 percent of its adult size; by age 3, the human brain develops to 90 percent of its full adult growth and establishes most of the structures that will guide all future emotional, behavioral, social, and psychological functioning later in life.

Newborns are dependent on adults for their survival and to help them have appropriate experiences with the world.

However, babies are not passive participants. They express their need for nourishment and comfort. They are interested in sensory experiences (sounds, smells, sights, touch) and relational experiences (hugging, cooing, smiling, comforting). These sensory and relational experiences occur at the same time. They influence the ongoing formation of the brain in positive ways. An infant's brain is most likely to keep the synapses formed through experiences that are repeated and occur within emotionally meaningful relationships.

Long before we knew the specifics of how our brains develop, we understood the importance of an emotionally available adult partner for babies. In studies of very young children in hospitals, orphanages, and other institutions in the 1930s, it was clear that food, clothing, and a bed to sleep in are not enough for young children. Between 25 and 30 percent of these infants and toddlers, receiving custodial care without human interaction, died. Many who survived were severely cognitively challenged (31, 32). Bruce Perry (33), a leading researcher in early brain development, puts it this way:

> The young child's undeveloped brain is trained in a "use dependent" way, mirroring the pattern, timing, nature, frequency, and quality of experiences and interactions. Think of it in terms of nutrition. If an infant or toddler is not fed consistent, predictable messages of love and communication, then those areas of the brain are shut down and the child's capacity to function later in life [is] compromised (p. 1).

The Effects of Stress and Violence on Brain Development

Of course, positive experiences are not the only ones that have an impact on brain development. Stressful experiences also occur. The National Scientific Council on the Developing Child (34) suggests that there are three levels of physical stress responses in young children—positive, tolerable, and toxic. Positive stress responses are mild and of short duration. Most importantly, a responsive adult with whom the child has a meaningful, ongoing relationship buffers the child's experience and helps calm him. Positive stress might occur with a vaccination or a loud, barking dog. Positive stress is helpful to the child's growing ability to deal with difficult situations. A tolerable stress response occurs when there is a drastic, life-changing event such as the death of a parent, divorce, a serious illness, or a natural disaster. The stress response will last longer but may not cause long-term damage to the brain if there is an adult helping the child through the experience.

Part of the biological response to stress is the increased secretion of the hormones cortisol and adrenalin. In situations of immediate threat, these hormones are useful in helping a person focus on survival. However, when these hormones are excessively high for long periods of time, they become toxic to the brain. As an evolutionary function of the brain, when survival is at stake people do not use the more thoughtful, reflective parts of their brain. Instead, cortisol, adrenalin, and other hormones activate the part of the brain that focuses on choosing a survival strategy: fight or flight, or in very young infants, freeze. As these neural connections are reinforced through use, they become the major pathways the brain uses to assess situations. Every event is perceived as a life-or-death situation. Even neutral situations are felt as threatening. Fetuses and very young children who live in homes with abuse, violence, mental illness, or substance abuse maintain their stress response much of the time. This chronic stress response is toxic to the developing brain and influences a child's ability to attend. Whether the fetus is exposed to these maternal hormones or the infant produces these hormones, the child builds a brain that is highly adaptive in abusive or neglectful situations, but it is inadequate for the work of healthy relationships (35).

The brain that is growing in an atmosphere of toxic stress actually develops a different physical structure: "The result may be a child who has great difficulty functioning when presented with the world of kindness, nurturing, and stimulation. It is an unfamiliar world to him; his brain has not developed the pathways and memories to adapt to this new world" (36). In a paper on stress (37, p.1), the authors state that "Excessive stress disrupts the architecture of the developing brain."

Children who experience toxic stress in infancy have brains that work differently later in life (38). They may be in a state of hyperarousal, always scanning the environment for signs of danger. These children may even evoke in others the abusive behavior that they fear, just to have some control over it. Therefore, a boy whose mother was raging and frightening may pick fights with other children, or a girl who was sexually abused may act seductively with a teacher. The opposite reaction to early frightening experiences is to feel so powerless that the child just freezes, or dissociates. Dissociation appears to be surrender to the situation, but the child feels as though she is not even present in the moment. During dissociation, the child may not even hear what is said to her, and so she does not attempt to respond. The child may have no memory of the experience. If children do not have reliable, responsive caregivers, they may not develop the neuronal pathways that would present adult assistance as a possible solution to problems. If children experience extreme deprivation in infancy, little contact with caregivers, and little stimulation from the environment, they will develop significantly smaller than normal brains (39). The brain may incorporate the effects of chronic frightening or neglectful early experiences for a lifetime.

Check Your Understanding 5.3
Click here to check your understanding of the concepts in this section.

The Newborn

The evidence that very young infants are active learners is compelling. They are born able to find the nipple and suck, thanks to inborn reflexes. They like to look at human faces and hear human voices. They use facial expressions that adults can easily understand, even though they have never seen their own faces. Newborns are ready to learn and ready to engage in relationships.

The first days and weeks after birth are a time of great adjustment for the new infant and the family, especially the mother. The baby is adjusting to life outside the womb, managing breathing, eating, digestion, elimination, and temperature regulation. The newborn infant is experiencing an array of new sensory experiences—touch, sound, light, odors, and tastes. The newborn can see about 8 to 12 inches and is most interested in human faces and human voices.

Adults help the newborn manage these sensations by reading their facial expressions, cries, and gestures to help determine what the infant needs. Adults help the baby learn to coordinate swallowing and sucking, keep diapers clean, and stay comfortably warm. Adults help the newborn fall asleep and maintain short periods of being awake and alert. During this time, mothers are going through hormonal changes as their bodies adjust to a postpregnancy condition. Mother and child may both be discovering the fine points of breast-feeding. Newborns may sleep for very short periods, needing to eat every few hours, so mothers are likely to be extremely fatigued during this postpartum stage.

At 6 weeks, just as mother and infant are each beginning to get their bearings, many mothers have to return to work. The baby may not have sleep patterns established yet. Breast-feeding babies may have little experience with the bottle, and their mothers may have difficulty expressing enough milk to send to child care. Babies often go through a growth spurt at 6 weeks, eating frequently and stimulating the production of more milk in the mother. Teachers need to be aware of how vulnerable these very young infants are when they enter group care.

This infant is being comforted by a pacifier during adult supervised "tummy time."

Pearson Education

Postnatal Brain Development

The food that is good for the heart is likely to be good for the brain. (Hippocrates)

The first 3 months of life are sometimes referred to as the fourth trimester of gestation. Human babies are born after 9 months in the womb, but they still have significant developmental tasks before them. Although the brain has been growing and becoming more complex, at birth it is only 25 percent of its adult weight. The lower parts of the brain (the spinal cord and cortex) are well developed, but the higher levels of the brain are quite immature. The lower brain controls much of the newborn's activity through reflexes.

The newborn brain has all of its neurons, but there are few connections among them in the cortex, the higher level of the brain. Over the course of the first year, these synaptic connections will begin to form at an astounding rate peaking at 2 million per second (40). Adults protect the newborn brain by maintaining a quiet and calm environment and being responsive to the baby's needs. The messages the baby receives and processes must be given in ways the baby can understand. Touch and language are two important ways adults communicate with newborns.

Touch

Touch is one of the most powerful sensory experiences for a young infant. In fact, Bruce Perry has said in conference presentations that touch is vital to an infant's ability to grow and develop: "Biologically, it is as critical for a baby to be touched and held as it is to be fed." Very young infants benefit from being held and carried much of the time they are awake. Teachers and home caregivers may want to use a commercially available infant carrier such as a Snuggly to keep the young infant against their own body while keeping hands free to be with other children.

Infants use touch to learn about the world—sucking on objects, feeling them with their hands, and kicking at them with their feet. They respond with strong cries to physical discomforts such as hunger or wet diapers and are comforted by being held close to their caregiver's body or snug swaddling.

Language

Long before infants are able to utter a single word, they are learning language by listening to the language around them. In order to acquire a specific language, the infant brain has to develop a structure that recognizes the distinctive sounds in the child's own language and ignores other sounds. A revealing, long-term, observational study (41) of infants and toddlers showed that children learn the language culture of their families. For example, some families' verbalizations to their children were composed of 80 percent negative comments. By age 3, the language used by these children was composed of about 80 percent negative comments to their parents and peers. Children also learn to talk about as much as their families talk. Children with the best verbal skills and highest intelligence scores were active partners in conversations with their parents. The parents were responsive, used a diverse vocabulary, had a positive tone, talked about the relationship between things and events, and often asked their children to do things rather than telling them what to do. Language learning, however, is a resilient process, meaning that even under adverse circumstances, children learn some communication strategies (42).

Abilities of the Newborn

In the first weeks of life, the newborn will move his arms and legs in small jerking movements or in wide flailing movements, but none of these actions appears to be intentional. Most babies will move their hands near their face. Those who sucked their thumbs in the womb may recover that skill. The newborn keeps his hands fisted and will hold an asymmetrical posture on his back, with one arm down to his side and the other raised near his head.

His hearing is good and, as described, he will recognize his mother's voice and the sound of her language. If he is lifted into an adult's arms, his head will fall backward because he does not have control of his head, neck, or trunk.

Most of his actions, including rooting for the nipple, moving his head from side to side, and grasping his daddy's finger, are actually reflexes. His reflexes are keyed to survival. They will help him latch onto the nipple and keep his head free to breathe.

In these first weeks, the infant depends entirely on responsive adults to help him regulate or manage his reactions to hunger, fatigue, and other discomfort. He needs help in learning how to suck and swallow and to burp up air from his tummy. He may need help to move from waking to sleeping, from sleeping to waking, and from crying to calm. Teachers and family child care providers who care for these very young infants will be helping with these basic tasks of regulation throughout the day.

As the baby reaches 4 months, he will use his arms to raise his head and chest when lying on his stomach. He can bring his hands together to his mouth and use his hands to hold and shake lightweight toys. He will recognize familiar people and grace them with a smile. His vision is improving and he may recognize his family at a small distance. He is likely to watch faces intently and enjoy playing with people.

At 4 months, infants are likely to be much better regulated and easier to serve in group care. They are likely to be accomplished at bottle feeding, interested in others, and communicate their needs clearly. They are able to play with an adult close by very short periods of time and may take longer naps. Mothers may be physically and emotionally better able to return to work.

Premature Birth

Not all babies remain in the womb for the full gestation of 40 weeks. Infants born before 37 weeks gestation are considered **premature**. There are many possible causes and outcomes of prematurity. However, medical intervention has improved so much that more than 90 percent of premature babies who weigh 800 grams or more (a little less than 2 pounds) survive. Those who weigh more than 500 grams (a little more than 1 pound) have a 40 to 50 percent chance of survival, although their chances of complications are greater (43). Infants closer to full term and weighing more usually have better outcomes.

The cause of a premature birth is not always known, but common causes include external threats to maternal and fetal health including the mother's use of drugs, alcohol consumption, cigarette smoking, poor nutrition and low weight gain, obesity, physical stress, and lack of prenatal health care. Medical conditions that can cause premature birth include maternal hormone imbalances, problems with the uterus, or various illnesses including high blood pressure and diabetes. Women carrying twins or triplets are also at increased risk for premature birth (44).

Premature births constitute about 12.5 percent of all births in the United States. About 25 percent of the more than half a million premature births are either induced or delivered by Caesarean (45).

Babies born prematurely are at risk for a variety of problems. The least mature babies, those born at less than 28 weeks gestation, need intensive medical intervention in specialized hospital wards called neonatal intensive care units (NICU). They may stay in the hospital for many months, even beyond the original due date, as they learn to suck, swallow, and breathe on their own. These infants are at high risk for significantly disabling conditions such as cerebral palsy and serious learning and communication disorders.

Premature infants are at risk for these issues:

- *Respiratory Distress Syndrome* (RDS). Babies born before 34 weeks gestation do not produce the protein **surfactant**, which helps the air sacs in the lungs stay open. Without the surfactant, these babies struggle to breathe. Now, mothers who are in premature labor are given medication to begin the production of surfactant in the baby. Artificial surfactant is then administered directly to the baby. Infants with RDS usually also require additional oxygen and, sometimes, a ventilator for breathing.
- *Apnea.* Apnea is a condition in which the brain is too immature to regulate breathing and the infant stops breathing. Most babies born at less than 30 weeks experience apnea. Babies may wear an apnea monitor in the hospital and at home. They may be given medication or use a device that blows a steady stream of air into their nostrils to keep the airways open.
- *Intraventricular hemorrage* (IVH). IVH occurs most often in infants born before 32 weeks gestation. This bleeding in the brain may resolve without damage or may cause severe damage resulting in cerebral palsy or other problems. IVH may be treated with medication or the insertion of a tube to relieve the buildup of fluid.
- *Retinopathy of prematurity* (ROP). ROP is the abnormal growth of blood vessels in the eye, which can result in vision disorders or blindness. Severe cases can be treated with a laser.
- *Jaundice (Hyperbilirubinemia).* Jaundice occurs when the liver is too immature to filter a waste product called bilirubin. Infants with jaundice are treated with special lights.
- *Chronic lung disease (Bronchopulmanory Displasia* [BPD]). BPD is a condition caused by extended use of oxygen, which causes a buildup of fluid, scarring, and lung damage. These children continue to suffer from a chronic lung disease that resembles asthma.

The following chapters will describe development in each of the domains in detail. The 9 months from conception to birth and the first 3 months of life are certainly a time of enormous growth and development. The next 3 years are even more exciting!

Check Your Understanding 5.4
Click here to check your understanding of the concepts in this section.

Summary

- Describe the interactions of genetics and experiences, including nutrition, prenatal health care, toxins and teratogens, structural and metabolic birth defects, maternal infections, maternal anxiety and other factors in prenatal development.
    - Genes provide directions to the cells in the developing embryo and fetus and throughout our lives.
    - Genes live on DNA which is found in each chromosome.
    - Chromosomes exist in each cell in the body.
    - The mother's diet provides all of the fetus's nutrition.
    - Prenatal health care protects the mother and the child with ongoing screening and information.
    - Birth defects and malformations may be caused by genes, diet or maternal infections or by, as yet, unknown causes.
    - Maternal stress during pregnancy can affect the fetus's health and brain development.
- Recount the development of the fetus through the three trimesters.
    - The first trimester of gestation is marked by rapid cell division and differentiation as cells become skin cells, muscle cells, brain cells, and so forth. Internal organs and external features are formed.
    - The second trimester is a period of growth and development. The mother can feel movement and, with a Doppler device, hear the baby's heartbeat.
    - The third trimester is a period of rapid growth and the formation of synapses in the brain as the baby experiences movement, light, and sound.
- Describe the prenatal and postnatal development of the brain.
    - The brain begins development within days of conception.
    - Rapid cell division follows from the moment of conception.
    - At 4 weeks, the neural groove appears, establishing the two cerebral hemispheres.
    - Over the next weeks, thousands of neurons are generated, creating the forebrain, the midbrain, and the hindbrain.
    - Neurons experience sensory information, transmitting that experience through an axon to dendrites on other neurons at a connection called a synapse.
    - A human infant is born with more than 100 billion neurons, twice the number he will have as an adult.
    - Synaptic connections develop rapidly in the first 3 months of life.
    - Hormones associated with stress and violence change the structure of the brain, creating a brain that is attentive to danger but not to affection.
- Describe the postnatal brain development, the abilities of the newborn, and the effects of premature birth.
    - The first days and weeks after birth are a time of great adjustment for the new infant and the family, especially the mother.
    - The baby is adjusting to life outside the womb, managing breathing, eating, digestion, elimination, temperature regulation, and an array of new sensory experiences.
    - Over the course of the first year, synaptic connections will begin to form at an astounding rate peaking at 2 million per second
    - Interactions with others including touch and language as well as the child's own movements stimulate synaptic connections.
    - The newborn's senses are working well.
    - The infant depends entirely on responsive adults to help him regulate or manage his reactions to hunger, fatigue, and other discomfort.
    - Premature birth creates many challenges for the developing newborn.

Key Terms

APGAR
amniotic sac
cleft palate
conception
embryo
epigenetics

fetus
genetic counseling
genome
gestation
phenylketonuria (PKU)
placenta

premature
sickle-cell anemia
surfactant
Tay-Sachs

Reflections and Resources for the Reader

REFLECTIONS

1. The emphasis on the impact of early experiences on brain development has changed some ways we think about being with infants. What would you try to be aware of in a baby's environment because of your knowledge of brain development?
2. The womb is not as safe a place as we once thought. What might you do as an infant-toddler teacher to support parents in having healthy pregnancies?

OBSERVATION AND APPLICATION OPPORTUNITIES

1. Visit an infant-toddler program. What, if any, information is available for parents on healthy pregnancies? Find three good resources on the internet.
2. Can you find information in newspapers and magazines that is readily available on having a healthy pregnancy?
3. Observe an infant-toddler program. In what ways are the environment and interactions supporting brain development? What would you change?

SUPPLEMENTARY ARTICLES AND BOOKS TO READ

Harvard Center for the Developing Child. (n.d.) InBrief: The Science of Early Childhood Development. Retrieved from: http://developingchild.harvard.edu/resources/inbrief-science-of-ecd/
Hurley, D. (2015) Grandma's experiences leave a mark on your genes. *Discover.* Retrieved from: http://www.urbanchildinstitute.org/why-0-3/baby-and-brain

Marshall, J. (2011). Infant neurosensory development: Considerations for infant child care. *Early Childhood Education Journal, 39*(3), 175–181.
Urban Child Institute. (2016). Baby's brain begins now: Conception to age 3. Urban Child Institute Web site. Retrieved from: http://www.urbanchildinstitute.org/why-0-3/baby-and-brain
WebMD. (2014) Slideshow: Fetal Development Month by Month. Retrieved from: http://www.webmd.com/baby/ss/slideshow-fetal-development

INTERESTING LINKS

Pregnancy on the *Parents* Web site. The links on this site provide a week-by-week description of prenatal development and information on a vast variety of other pregnancy topics.
The Secret Life of the Brain on the PBS Web site. This must-see series of video clips and text is taken from a PBS television series on the brain. Features include a 3-D brain anatomy and episodes titled "The Baby's Brain" and "The Child's Brain."
Life's Greatest Miracle on the PBS Web site. This film originally aired on the PBS series *Nova* and is available for viewing online. It shows the development of a fetus from the moment of conception through birth and provides a wonderful overview of the information covered in this chapter.
Brain Development on the ZERO TO THREE Web site. This long article describes many aspects of brain development.

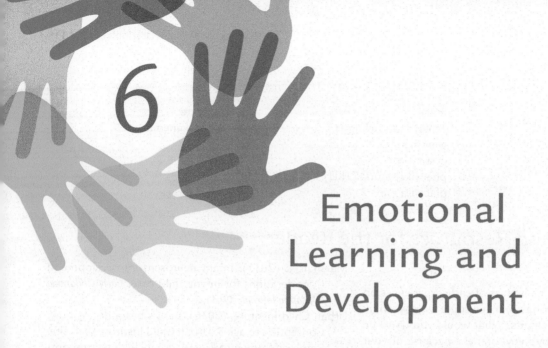

6

Emotional Learning and Development

LEARNING OUTCOMES

After reading this chapter, you will be able to:

- Identify the effects of temperament and gender on early emotional expression.
- Describe the role of relationships in regulation and forming an identity.
- Explain the history and importance of attachment relationship and emotional learning, and the effects of maternal depression.
- Describe the processes of promotion, prevention, and intervention in infant mental health.

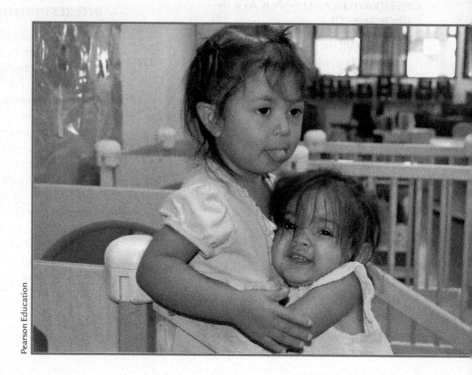

Pearson Education

Nora had midwifed hundreds of births. As she watches babies, even in their first minutes out of the womb, she reacts to them as though she believes they have feelings. As the newborn cries out, feeling room temperature air and flailing in space, Nora is sure to say, "Oh, you don't like this, do you? You want to be warm."

We react this way because from the first moments of life, babies are using the language of emotional expression to communicate with us. They don't need to be taught that quivering lips, a grimacing face, and a cry are ways to communicate. They are born as emotional communicators. We watch them and believe that we can understand their feelings from their expressions. We want to help them be calm and comfortable. Infants and toddlers use our responses to keep them feeling safe.

"Infants are born highly vulnerable and somewhat competent," said Ron Lally at a conference (1), adding, "And over the next few years, the balance changes and they become much less vulnerable and highly competent." Using their natural abilities for nonverbal communication, infants move quickly toward remarkable competence in emotional development. The major areas of emotional learning and development are

- Learning to regulate one's reactions to the environment.
- Learning to express emotions and understand the expression of emotions.
- Developing an attachment relationship with a caring adult.
- Developing a firm sense of self or identity.

Each Child Is Capable and Unique

The emotional system is primitive at birth but even newborns are truly feeling comfort or distress. Feelings become refined. They become complicated. They are always real, honest, and deeply felt.

A baby's cry is precisely as serious as it sounds. (Jean Liedloff)

Emotional learning and development describe the way the child reacts to and understands herself in the world. It is the feelings a child has and her ability to manage those feelings. Some aspects are genetic and biological. Some are learned from the way adults treat children. Temperament and gender are two important, biologically based aspects of personality that make emotional learning and development unique within each child.

Temperament

The following example illustrates how three children might react to a parent saying good-bye:

On entering the toddler room in the morning, Kevin sobs as though his heart is broken as his father leaves. After a moment of comforting, and full of energy, he enthusiastically plays with the rocking horse, leaps off, and runs to the easel. Faron enters the room quietly, kisses her mother good-bye, and settles into the housekeeping area. Terra clings to her mother's skirt, preventing her from leaving in the morning. When her mother finally is able to leave, Terra hangs back and watches the other children play while she sucks her thumb and holds her teddy bear.

Each child is entering school, greeting the infant and toddler teacher and watching a parent leave. The adult's actions matter but the children bring unique qualities to the situation as well.

Since the pioneering work of Thomas, Chess, Birch, Hertzig, and Korn (2), these differences have been known as **temperament**, or **temperament style**. Temperament is how a child relates to the world, given certain biological features. Thomas and colleagues identified nine *temperament traits*, defined in Figure 6.1: activity level, biological rhythms, approach/withdrawal, adaptability, intensity of reaction, mood, persistence, distractibility, and sensitivity. In children, these traits tend to appear in groups called *temperament types:* easy, difficult, and slow-to-warm-up. The "easy" or **flexible** child tends to eat, sleep and eliminate on a predictable schedule, have a pleasant mood, easily enters new experiences, has moderate emotional reactions, and is not too sensitive to sensory information. The **slow-to-warm-up** or shy child tends to withdraw from new situations and adjust to them slowly. The *difficult* or **feisty** child is very active, emotional expressions are intense, and attention is easily distracted. These children are very sensitive to changes in light or sound; they tend to eat and sleep without regular patterns; and their moods can change frequently (3).

Temperament makes sense to most people. We see these traits in ourselves. They can cause conflict or ease in our relationships. It's annoying when someone plays music louder than you like it. It is comfortable when the lighting in a room is just as you like it. You're frustrated when your boyfriend is shy around your friends when he has been so personable around you.

Some temperament traits may be more helpful than others to successful development. Intensity of reaction, sometimes called emotional reactivity or vitality, is one trait that may have enormous impact on a child's life (4). Emotional vitality or reactivity is the lively expression of emotion that is shared with others (5). Toddlers with high emotional vitality are more expressive. They are enjoyable playmates. They are also more likely to draw an adult into whatever interests them. These moments of interaction are opportunities for toddlers to develop a relationship with the adult during which the children may think, "I know you are interested in me—and you will help me when I need it. I know how to call on you for help."

FIGURE 6.1   Temperament traits

- *Activity level:* Amount of physical movement
- *Biological rhythms:* Regularity of eating, sleeping, elimination
- *Approach/withdrawal:* Comfort in new situations
- *Mood:* Amount of time in a pleasant, cheerful mood as opposed to fussing, crying, or resisting others
- *Intensity of reaction:* Energy level of emotional expressions
- *Sensitivity:* Response to sensory information, including light, sounds, textures, smells, tastes
- *Adaptability:* Ability to manage changes in routine or recover from being upset
- *Distractibility:* How easily the child's attention is distracted
- *Persistence:* How long a child will stay with a difficult activity before giving up

Source: Thomas, A., Chess, S., Birch, H. G., Hertzig, M. E., & Korn, S. (1963). *Behavioral individuality in early childhood.* New York: New York University Press.

Reactivity can also be harmful to the child. The more highly reactive child may have more negative reactions. For example, researchers sometimes restrain an infant's hands to produce a stressful situation. In a study looking at possible physical aspects of reactivity, researchers found that some 6-month-old infants briefly experienced slowing of the heart rate at the beginning of the restraint. These infants also cried louder and longer, tried more often to escape, and looked less at their mothers than the other infants. Imagine the difference, over a lifetime, of having a more intense biological reaction to stressful situations. There is clearly a physical component to reactivity (6).

Temperament may make some children ill suited for child care. All children have better outcomes when they are in higher-quality care and learning programs. However, children who are more reactive—either more easily upset or shyer— may be physically unable to handle a level of stress other children in group care can manage (7). These children may be even more at risk when in lower quality programs than their more flexible peers.

In a relationship-based model, we think about the effect of the child's temperament on the adult and on the relationship. Thomas et. al. (8) proposed the idea of "goodness of fit" between child and parents. No one temperament is better than others. Success in parenting children of different temperaments depends on how well matched the parent and child are on certain temperamental traits. For example, the highly active and emotionally expressive child would have a goodness of fit with a parent who was also active and expressive. That same child might be difficult for a very quiet, subdued parent. Or, it might not be the parent's own personality but his expectations about children derived from his own history or culture that would apply to the goodness of fit.

Gender

Boys and girls, as groups, are different in emotional learning and development. These qualities are probably a result of both biology and social expectations. In the womb, genes are expressed (turned on) and hormones are released. These create differences in boy's and girl's bodies and brains. In infancy, there are not a lot of major differences. As toddlers, boys are more active and have less language ability and less ability to control their reactions than girls. For example, boys show more anger than girls. We do not know if these differences begin to show up with age because of basic physical differences or because their experiences are different—or both (9).

Adults do treat boys and girls differently. Parents and other adults may not want boys to express feelings because of cultural expectations or because they are already more emotional and active. Adults talk more to girls about feelings and girls use more words about feelings. Adults may also prompt girls to stay within gender roles of being comforting, caring and having close friendships. This may encourage girls to be more expressive about happy feelings and keep feelings of shame, guilt, sadness, fear, and anxiety to themselves. Boys, in turn, may be encouraged to show anger and contempt. These feelings can be a source of strength in overcoming obstacles. These feelings are in line with society's gender roles for men to protect their families and face down dangers (10).

Children also choose their own gender roles. By 18 months, children are noticing gender roles in their culture. By watching how boys and men and girls and women act, they create an image of behaviors that belong to a gender. As they grow, they choose to act like the people of the gender they identify with most strongly. Gender differences in emotion become stronger as children have more cultural experiences.

Attachment is one of the most important aspects of emotional development in the first three years. It is discussed in detail later in this chapter. Here, we will look at some gender influences on attachment. Attachment is the child's sense of safety with an adult. Children with secure attachments have sensitive adults who can comfort them and help them explore. Children with insecure attachments may be fearful (ambivalent) or dismissive (avoidant). The attachment style or classification grows out of the child's experiences with the adult. Adults treat boys and girls differently even before birth. If adults believe that boys need to be strong, they may respond less to infant boys' cries of distress. These boys could grow up with a coldness toward relationships that is culturally correct but is an insecure attachment. If adults see girls as fragile, they may not give them enough opportunities to cope on their own and thus create fearful attachments (11).

Gender seems to affect the actions of children whose mothers have mental health issues. Some women are unable to respond well to their children. Some mothers withdraw from their toddlers and some become frightening. Eighteen-month-old boys and girls tended to approach their withdrawn mothers. When mothers became somewhat frightening, 18-month-old girls still came to their mothers in actions called *tend and befriend*. Boys did not. If mothers became highly frightening, girls would be fearful as they approached their mother. Boys would avoid or actively be in conflict with their mother in actions sometimes called a *flight or fight* response (12).

Check Your Understanding 6.1
Click here to check your understanding of the concepts in this section.

Knowing the Child

In the first years of life, all emotional learning and development occurs within relationships with adults. However, two of the important processes become very much a part of the child's mind. These two internal processes are regulation and forming an identity.

Regulation

Regulation is part of every area of development. For many years, emotional regulation was the main area we thought about. It is the young child's ability to manage her reactions to her feelings. Over the first 3 years of life, this includes being able to soothe herself to sleep, to stop crying, and be calm and alert much of the time. Regulation is also part of the child's ability to pay attention to the world. Over the first 3 years of life, the child begins to learn to regulate his reactions and attend to the most important information.

The newborn has to adjust to life outside of the womb. The baby must learn to breathe, manage body temperature, to eat and digest, eliminate, be awake and be asleep. Later, the infant learns to regulate reactions to both physical and emotional life experiences. Emotional regulation describes the activities used by the child "to tolerate frustration, curb aggressive impulses, delay gratification, and express emotions in socially acceptable ways" (13). Infants may turn away their gaze or suck their fingers. Adults may soothe, rock, or swaddle infants to reduce distress. Regulation helps the infants be calm and alert. Regulation is part of emotional learning and development. It is part of social competence, conscience, resiliency, and secure attachments. Poor regulation in infancy is linked to later behavior and mental health problems (14). The ability to regulate is probably a combination of the infant's biology and experiences. The goal of regulation is to manage one's own reactions to physical, emotional, social, and internal experiences. At best, regulation keeps the child in a state of attention that involves energy, excitement, and attention in learning without overwhelming the child.

It is easier to build strong children than to repair broken men. (Frederick Douglass)

Regulation and attention develop together at the same time, in the same part of the brain. The infant's ability to pay attention is basic to all further learning. The child's ability for regulation and attention depends greatly on a responsive adult who mediates the child's experiences. It is also influenced by the child's own temperament and physiology (15). In short, the development of regulation is pretty complex!

Hierarchy of Human Organization

A good way to understand regulation is to look at how the body maintains control of different systems. Many years ago, researchers saw an order in which an infant's body kept control. The relationship between the body's systems regarding regulation is well illustrated by the image of the hierarchy of human behavioral systems (16). (See Figure 6.2.) Although the construct has been around for a long time, it continues to provide guidance for neonatal nurseries. It can also help us understand when toddlers are beginning to fall apart.

OBSERVATION INVITATION **6.1**

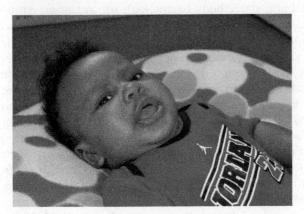

Pearson Education

(?) **Alijah is getting distressed alone on the blanket. Then a few minutes later, he is calm and peaceful. Click the icon to answer a question about the photo.**

FIGURE 6.2   **Hierarchy of behavioral organization**

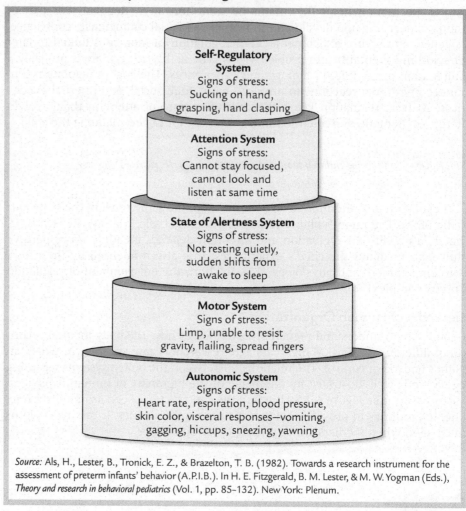

Self-Regulatory System
Signs of stress:
Sucking on hand, grasping, hand clasping

Attention System
Signs of stress:
Cannot stay focused, cannot look and listen at same time

State of Alertness System
Signs of stress:
Not resting quietly, sudden shifts from awake to sleep

Motor System
Signs of stress:
Limp, unable to resist gravity, flailing, spread fingers

Autonomic System
Signs of stress:
Heart rate, respiration, blood pressure, skin color, visceral responses—vomiting, gagging, hiccups, sneezing, yawning

Source: Als, H., Lester, B., Tronick, E. Z., & Brazelton, T. B. (1982). Towards a research instrument for the assessment of preterm infants' behavior (A.P.I.B.). In H. E. Fitzgerald, B. M. Lester, & M. W. Yogman (Eds.), *Theory and research in behavioral pediatrics* (Vol. 1, pp. 85–132). New York: Plenum.

Als et al. (18) observed that a stable body begins with the *autonomic system*: body temperature, digestion, and breathing. If that system is not regulated, no other system will work smoothly. If that is stable, the *motor system* involving muscle tone; the ability to resist gravity; and the capacity for graceful, controlled movement may function well. The next system is the *state of alertness system*, where the infant can achieve a deep restful sleep, an active REM sleep, and quiet and active alert states. The state system allows the baby's *attention system* to focus and attend to information, be excited, to calm and rest—and to move between these states without too much difficulty. At the top of the hierarchy is the *self-regulatory system*.

Babies lose their sense of organization system by system. First they lose their ability to self-comfort. They forget to suck on their fingers or rub their hair. Then they cry or seem unfocused. Their movements become jerky and disorganized. Finally, they lose the organization of their autonomic system by hiccupping, drooling, or gasping for breath. A sensitive adult can respond when the infant is struggling with self-comforting rather than waiting until the baby has completely fallen apart. The sensitive infant and toddler teacher can quickly help the mildly disorganized baby recover, calm, and attend to the world.

The hierarchy is just as helpful with toddlers. A good observer may catch little signs that a toddler is having trouble coping long before a tantrum starts. Is the toddler having trouble paying attention to play? Is he becoming clumsy? Is language being replaced by whining? These may be signals that regulation is breaking down and the child needs support.

Regulation and Relationships

Moments of distress may give parents opportunities to experience and understand the child's emotional cues. Infants who self-comfort too quickly may not give adults many chances to provide help and become their partners in understanding the world.

Regulation comes from both biology and adult actions. Some infants may be naturally better at regulating emotions than others. However, an infant and toddler teacher who sensitively meets an infant's emotional needs helps the baby develop regulation skills. A disinterested or rejecting infant and toddler teacher may leave the infant struggling to find ways to self-comfort (19). At 4 months, some infants with easy-going temperaments who experience a less sensitive mother may hold back their emotions and their own reactions. Other infants respond differently. They become highly emotionally reactive with less responsive mothers—perhaps reflecting more sensitive temperaments unable to tolerate distress. Their coping styles are aimed at drawing in less responsive mothers (20).

The adult helps the infant regulate her body by keeping her warm, dry, well fed, rested, and in a comfortable position. If a baby is crying, the adult soothes the baby by holding her upright against the shoulder, rocking, swaddling, or moving into another room or outdoors. When the baby is calm and awake, the adult can provide opportunities and support for the infant to focus her attention on interesting things. The quiet, alert infant is able to be an active partner in relationships. The calm toddler is a good playmate and active learner.

Respect, Reflect, Relate

Respect: The newborn's inability to manage reactions and how that skill grows with the help of an adult. For example, a young infant looks fretful and is trying to get her fist into her mouth.

Reflect: On what the child seems to be trying to figure out or accomplish. In this case, it looks like she is trying to respond to her hunger by getting something into her mouth.

Relate: Relate to support learning by

- picking her up.
- telling her, "You look so hungry. You're trying to get your whole fist into your mouth. Let's get your bottle ready.
- cuddling her while waiting for the bottle.

Identity Development

An identity, or sense of self, is the feeling or knowledge that *I was here before this, I am here in this moment, and I will be here in another moment.* One researcher (21) defined three parts to self-awareness:

1. Knowing one is separate and different from others.
2. Knowing one can control some things but not others.
3. Having a sense of existing over time.

He also wrote that infants are born with these abilities. For evidence, he pointed out that:

1. Infants cry harder when they hear others cry but not because of their own cry.
2. Infants delight in getting adults to respond or in their early handling of toys.
3. Infant mouths anticipate the arrival of a hand or a nipple from memory of earlier experiences.

The physical experience of being alive tells you that you are a separate being. Touching yourself feels different from having someone else touch you. Closing your eyes is different from someone turning off the lights. Hearing your own sounds is different from hearing someone else talk. Infants experience this from birth.

A baby feels every experience in his body and his emotions as information. As the child stores memories of experiences, he begins to develop a sense of himself, an internal picture of self, and an identity: "This is me when I am happy and playing with my infant and toddler teacher—my body is active, my face is smiling, I am comfortable and safe." "This is me throwing." "This is me walking." "This is me with my friend." "This is me really tired." Developing an identity is a complex mixture of the baby's own temperament; physical, sensory, and processing abilities; and the physical, social, and emotional environment surrounding him.

In infancy research, the development of a sense of self is understood to occur during interactions with others, through moment-by-moment experiences of emotional communication. Young children learn about themselves as they learn about the feelings of others.

▶▶▶ OBSERVATION INVITATION **6.2**

Pearson Education

? Francisco has been exploring his own image. He watches himself giving his mirror image a kiss. Click on the icon to answer questions about the photo.

Children have never been very good at listening to their elders, but they have never failed to imitate them. (James Baldwin)

Some theorists used to believe that in early infancy babies exist in a state of **self-fusion**. They did not know that they are separate beings from their mothers (22). Today we believe that from the moment of birth, babies experience themselves as separate beings contained in a boundary of skin. From the first moments, the experience of being held by another person is different from being swaddled in a crib. Seeing your own hand and feeling the movement of that hand are different from seeing another person's hand. As described in Chapter 3 (23), the infant's greatest task in emotional development is not learning that she is separate from others but learning to make connections with others.

A classic study of self-recognition or self-awareness is called the *mirror-mark test*. An adult puts a mark on a toddler's nose or forehead without the child noticing. Then the child is placed in front of a mirror. Under 18 months, most children just look in the mirror. After 18 months, most children seem to recognize that the image in the mirror is them and they touch the mark on their own bodies. For decades this was interpreted to mean that at 18 months, children are developing a sense of self. Because we now believe that children have some sense of self from much younger, people suggest that it means children recognize their image in the mirror at 18 months (24).

 Watch this video to see the mirror-mark test for self-recognition. Do you think the recognition of the mark signifies the beginning of a sense of self?

https://www.youtube.com/watch?v=cTP01Wbsh0E

A basic sense of self is beginning in the first year of life. Over the years, one's identity grows in depth and changes through experiences. However, the child always brings his sense of self into each experience. "I know I am friendly and likable as I go into the grocery store." Or, "Oh no, here is that place I don't like with all the noise and colors, and lights, and people." In the third year identity becomes even more important. There are so many ways the child learns about himself. The child begins to use language well. People around him think it is important to listen to his words and ideas. Or not. He has more time to play with friends. He is liked or bullied. He sees more of the world. He tries and succeeds or fails at so many things. Each experience adds to his idea of who he is, who he is with others, and who he is in the world.

Children with Special Needs

The emotional system is basic to the human body. The areas for pleasure and pain exist in the same part of the brain that regulates breathing and heart rate (25). This may explain why infants and toddlers with even the most significant disabilities are usually able to show us when they are happy or sad. They often show us that they know and prefer family members.

Emotions are felt within the brain. Conditions that affect the brain may also affect emotional development. **Autism spectrum disorder (ASD)** is an important set of conditions that are identified in the first three years. ASD is a developmental disability. A child may have difficulty understanding other people's thoughts or feelings. The child may not use language. She may repeat an action over and over such as flicking her fingers. She may be interested in one thing such as keys but have no other interests.

ASD occurs in about 1 of 68 children. Boys are five times more likely than girls to have ASD. Most children are identified between 3 and 4 years, although many can be diagnosed by 18 months or younger (26). One early sign is a child does not respond to her name by her first birthday. Other early signs in infancy include:

1. **Unusual visual fixations.** Unusually strong and persistent examination of objects.
2. **Abnormal repetitive behaviors.** Spending unusually long periods of time repeating an action, such as looking at their hands or rolling an object.
3. **Lack of age appropriate sound development.** Delayed development of vowel sounds, such as "ma ma, da da, ta ta."
4. **Delayed intentional communication.** Neutral facial tones and decreased efforts to gesture and gain parent attention.
5. **Decreased interest in interaction.** Greater interest in objects than people and difficult to sustain face-to-face interactions. (27)

It may be hard for an infant with autism to play in ways that help them learn. They may not listen to or use much language. Young children with autism may not display many emotions. They may not try to share joy or excitement with others. In fact, the areas of the brain that are active in feeling emotions are less active in children and adults with autism (28). Coping with anger can be very difficult for people with autism. Maybe that is because it is more of an internal feeling than a social one.

The most promising information on autism is about early identification, usually in the second or third year of life. Hopefully, that leads to early treatment and better outcomes. Identification and treatment for autism in the first year of life does not have a strong evidence base, yet. Between six and nine months, infants are considered at high risk of developing ASD if they show the target signs or have a sibling with autism. A small pilot study (29) taught parents how to coach their infants in each of the target areas listed above throughout their day of play, reading, and routines. The interventions were one hour every week for 12 weeks. There were also a series of follow-up meetings. Six out of seven infants had caught up developmentally by the end of the study. The children continued on a good track. The parents continued to be sensitive and support development. Early identification may be a very important tool with autism.

It is important to remember that emotional development must always be understood within the context of relationships. Adults are expected to provide safety, to see and respond accurately to communication cues, and to be sensitive and responsive. Even when infants or toddlers bring very real challenges, it is important to promote parenting relationships that can help the child achieve the best possible development. Further information about the progression of emotional development and how adults can create strong relationships is available in a chart called Developmental Trends and Responsive Interactions later in this chapter.

> ✓ **Check Your Understanding 6.2**
> Click here to check your understanding of the concepts in this section.

Learning Through the Adult-Child Relationship

Most emotional learning and development happens in relationships with adults in the first three years of life. The three areas in this section need adult interaction to develop. They are the attachment relationship, a sense of identity, and emotions within a cultural context.

> *Lyssa is playing on a blanket when the infant and toddler teacher, Tinnaka, walks past. Lyssa feels pleasure at seeing Tinnaka and smiles at her. To Lyssa, Tinnaka's smile looks somehow similar to the way her own smile feels and assures her about the accuracy of her emotional response to this experience. Tinnaka adds language to the experience by saying, "Lyssa, are you happy to see me? I'm sooo happy to see you today!" as she picks her up and snuggles her. Lyssa's sense of self, in this moment, is of a well-loved, easily understood, and welcomed human being.*

The Attachment Relationship

The attachment relationship between the infant and the parents becomes the way the child understands how people are with each other. It may be the most important factor in how we think about ourselves and what we expect of other people. It is not about love as much as how the infant feels safe, understood, and cared for with a specific adult.

Bowlby's Theory

The concept of attachment was introduced by the English psychiatrist, John Bowlby (30). Bowlby described infant's having various mental systems for understanding the world. An exploratory system forwards the child's goal of learning about the world. However, the young, vulnerable child also has the goal of survival. The attachment system drives the child to stay close to an adult who gives the child a sense of safety and security. The exploratory and attachment systems operate as balance to each other. Infants use the **attachment relationship** as a secure base from which to explore. As infants play and explore, they carefully stay close enough to see their important adult. The current, casual use of the term *attachment* often refers to feelings of love and affection. Attachment really addresses basic feelings of trust, safety, and security.

Bowlby and others describe infants as creating an image in their minds of what relationships look and feel like. As they grow, they bring that picture into other relationships. They will act in ways they learned in the first relationship. For example, if a parent is sensitive and responsive, the infant will grow up thinking that she will be understood and cared for. If a parent is cold, the infant will not bring warm feelings into later relationships.

Mary Ainsworth's Patterns of Attachment

Mary Ainsworth was Bowlby's student and went on to develop the science of attachment. She observed mothers and infants for the first year, in their homes. The goal of the baby in the first year of life seemed to be to have a feeling of safety and security. Physical closeness to the mother seemed to be the most effective way of achieving this. However, Ainsworth saw babies going about this task with three basic, but differing, strategies. Each one was a response to the mother's usual pattern of being with the baby. These strategies were eventually described as three patterns of attachment: **secure attachment**, **anxious-ambivalent attachment**, and

TABLE 6.1   **Patterns of attachment**

Attachment Classification	Maternal Behaviors	Infant Behaviors
Secure	Sensitively reads child's cues for comfort and responds effectively	Can signal distress, be comforted, resume play and exploration
Anxious-ambivalent	Attends to infant when it serves her own needs; may ignore infant's signals of distress	Find it difficult to allow themselves to be comforted; usually anxious during play
Anxious-avoidant	Ignores or feels anger toward infant much of the time	Appears to be unusually independent in play but maintains closeness to mother without engaging her

anxious-avoidant attachment (31). These patterns of attachment are described in Table 6.1.

The Strange Situation

After studying infants in their homes, Ainsworth created a research protocol called the *Strange Situation*. The Strange Situation takes place in a laboratory room. The older infant or young toddler is first alone in a room with their parent. It becomes increasingly stressful for the baby as a stranger enters; the parent leaves and returns, until finally the baby is momentarily alone in a room. The behavior of the infant upon reunion with his mother most clearly illustrates the attachment category of the child. Securely attached children run to their mothers and allow themselves to be comforted. Children with anxious-ambivalent attachment run to their mothers but resist being comforted. Children with anxious-avoidant attachments will appear to ignore the mother's return while backing up to get close to the mother (32).

 Watch the video on the Strange Situation and the 1-year-olds' reactions. What differences did you see between the two infants and the two mothers?

https://www.youtube.com/watch?v=s608077NtNl

Some children did not fit into any of the three patterns. Although the three categories were not the same in terms of healthy attachment, each allowed the child to engage the adult to provide enough care and attention for the child to feel secure. Main and Cassidy (33) call these the *organized* categories. However, not all attempts to elicit care work. They introduced a fourth pattern—one in which the children couldn't seem to come up with or settle on a strategy to help them feel secure. They labeled this one **disorganized attachment**. Children with disorganized attachment are more likely to have poor social and behavioral outcomes.

Children who demonstrated the disorganized pattern had parents whose behavior was violent, frightening, or frightened. Their own childhoods had been violent and frightening. Or they had experienced an unresolved loss. These parents responded to their children's attachment cues in very confusing ways. The children simply could not come up with a strategy that would consistently work to give them a feeling of safety and security. There was no way for the children to develop any feeling of control over a distressing situation.

Multiple Attachment Figures

The child's attachment classification comes, for the most part, from the adult's actions in responding and comforting. Children may have many adults close to them during infancy and the toddler years. A mother, a father, aunts, uncles, and grandparents may live close by or even together. An infant and toddler teacher may have that child for several years. Each adult will have his or her own ways of being with the child. The child may have a warm secure mental model of her mother and an anxious-ambivalent model with her mother's live-in boyfriend. Later in life, the child may draw on the model that feels most comfortable in the situation. This is an important way in which a responsive, relationship-based infant and toddler teacher can play a critical role in the life of a child. The infant and toddler teacher can be a secure attachment figure, especially if she is able to stay with the child for a long period of time.

. . . the emotional quality of our earliest attachment experience is perhaps the single most important influence on human development. (Alan Sroufe & Dan Siegel)

Current Attachment Research

Allan Schore (34) describes how the attachment relationship affects the development of the right hemisphere of the brain in the infant. There are two main mechanisms at work. Hormones are released in the brain and a network of mirror neurons or brain cells understand and reflect the emotional experience. The moments that pass back and forth between the infant and the caregiver are full of feelings. When the adult and child share joy, hormones such as oxytocin are released into the child's limbic system (the emotional center of the brain). The hormones tell the genes to express themselves in ways that build a healthy brain. The same hormones are released in the adult's limbic system. If the moments between adult and infant are frightening or disconnected, stress hormones like cortisol are released and they damage the new connections the brain is trying to make.

As the child watches the adult's expressions of interest and joy, he both takes in the information (perceives) and with the system of mirror neurons in his brain he also experiences interest and joy. Every emotional experience has both perception and action in the child's brain. So every moment of interaction is creating a hormone bath and firing mirror neurons. All of this activity is building a network of connections in the brain. These connections are building the child's basic understanding of relationships. This is called the working mental model of relationships.

Scientists have watched the brains of mothers and infants interacting in nice, responsive, back-and-forth moments. They see the same areas of the brain are firing in the infant and the mother at the same time. It is as though the right hemispheres of the two brains are communicating. The emotional tone of early interactions actually create the connections and the structure of the brain.

 Watch the video on the neurobiology of secure attachments. Describe the connection between the child's experiences and the construction of the brain.

https://www.youtube.com/watch?v=WVuJ5KhpL34

Schore helps answer how the attachment experience becomes the mental image the child holds of relationships. It becomes part of the structure of the brain. It becomes the only way an infant knows how to be with other people. The infant (or child or adult) may behave in ways that inspire the other person also to behave within the expectations of the attachment relationship. In fact, the child learns both parts of the attachment relationship and may play out either role as they grow older.

For example, Sherri, an infant and toddler teacher, has a history of secure relationships. She cares for little Ben, who has a history of anxious-ambivalent attachment. She responds to his distress by picking him up and comforting him. Ben, not believing that this comforting will really be available when he needs it, does not trust this moment and arches away from her, crying harder. Sherri reads his cues and puts him back down. She believes that is what he wants. Sherri is reenacting her mother's sensitive role as a caregiver in their attachment relationship. Ben's idea that people are not there for you when you need them is reinforced by being put down when he is distressed. Ben's behavior creates behavior in other people that tell him that he is right to be ambivalent about his relationships with others.

Attachment categories may change over time if life events change the family. For the most part, attachment predicts how the child will relate to others. One study showed that children with secure attachments had good self-regulation. This helped them manage the social and learning challenges of school. In fifth grade, they were very engaged in learning (35). Secure infants are liked by their preschool peers and teachers. They are neither victims nor bullies. Avoidant infants are sometimes bullies in preschool and often rejected by their teachers. Anxious-ambivalent infants tend to be babied by their preschool teachers, being treated as younger than they are. They are often the victims of bullies (36).

Adult Attachment

Mary Main (37) looked at how the mother's working model of relationships may direct her actions with her children. She created a scale to measure the parent's mental image of attachment. She found three organized classifications for adults. They are very similar to the three for infant attachment. Secure/autonomous adults value caring relationships and attachment experiences. They were parents of securely attached babies. Parents of avoidant babies dismissed the importance of attachment relationships. Insecure/preoccupied adults are always thinking about their own early relationships with their parents. This is like their own insecure/ambivalent babies who are always trying to keep track of their mothers. They cannot settle their attention on play (38). However, if adults had life events that helped them create new and healthier internal mental images of relationships, they were capable of creating secure relationships with their partners and children.

Cultural Differences and Emotional Expression

All five major elements of emotional development discussed in this chapter—regulation, attachment, temperament, identity formation, and emotional expression—must be considered within a cultural context. A number of studies suggest that infants around the world use the same facial expressions, with potentially the same meanings, in the same situation. However, they may express emotion more or less quickly and more or less heartily.

For example, one study looked at emotion regulation, expression, and attachment in two very different societies. One was an urban, middle-class, German group. The families were well educated, individualistic, lived in a money-driven society, and organized by autonomy. Their patterns of attachment and emotional expression were assessed with the Strange Situation and found to be similar to those in American studies. The other group members were the Cameroonian Nso tribe. They were subsistence farmers living in a highly interdependent society and organized by relatedness. Their children were never separated from their mothers. The Strange Situation was not considered culturally appropriate. Instead, an Nso female stranger came to the home, greeted the family, and picked up the child.

The three response patterns that emerged for the Nso had parallels to the Western secure, anxious-ambivalent, and anxious-avoidant patterns. One group of 1-year-olds was quiet and kept the same sober expressions throughout the interaction. The second group did not react to the stranger's entry but became distressed by physical contact. The third group became distressed at the woman's entry and remained distressed. Saliva tests of cortisol before and after the encounter showed the first group to have no change in cortisol, the second group to have increased cortisol demonstrating increased stress, and the third group had high levels of cortisol before and after the encounter. These children were distressed even before the woman arrived. The three sets of sober, nonreactive infants were already well socialized to a society that valued hiding individual emotions to contribute to the harmony of the group. The other two groups would be characterized as anxious-avoidant and anxious-ambivalent in our classifications (39).

CULTURE CLOSE UP

A Japanese family moved to Minneapolis for the father to spend a semester as a visiting professor at the university. After several weeks in an apartment, alone all day with her 2- and 4-year-old daughters, the mother enrolled them in a neighborhood infant-toddler program. Although the girls spoke no English, they enjoyed playing when they visited with their mother. After a few visits, the mother decided to leave them. They had never been away from her before. Together, they ran to the big glass door of the church, sobbing and looking down the sidewalk where their mother had disappeared. The 4-year-old kept repeating some words in Japanese. The director looked them up in a phonetic dictionary: "My mother is dead! My mother is dead!"

What do you feel for these two little girls who are separated from their mother for the first time and left with people who do not understand their language?

Emotional Expression and Understanding

Infants and toddlers communicate through emotions. Infants show their thoughts and feelings through expressing emotions. They learn about other's feelings through the hormonal and mirror neuron exchange described earlier while watching others express emotions. Young infants around the world use similar facial expressions for fear, happiness, sadness, surprise, anger, disgust, and pain. Even as they begin to use language, their communication is filled with emotions.

Progression of Emotional Expression

Babies show universal expressions in the first months of life. They are also learning through their interactions with others. Infants begin to respond to others with big, genuine social smiles and to anticipate how their favorite adults will behave. They learn to expect certain patterns of interaction and are surprised when things go differently. They will coo and smile at toys that respond contingently to their actions. Emotions become more specific as joy becomes different from contentment. Anger and sadness emerge as separate experiences from general distress. Active games such as "I'm going to get you!" followed by blowing on the baby's tummy can bring chortles at 4 months, especially when little variations create the sense of suspense and surprise. These social interactions also help the baby regulate and stay interested without getting overwhelmed.

OBSERVATION INVITATION **6.3**

Click the play button to watch the video and answer questions about social referencing.

?   **How does the little girl show that she is using social referencing to determine the safety of the situation?**

In the period from about 4 months through 7 months, there is a shift in emotional development, as infants begin to demonstrate that they are "falling in love" (40). They will brighten, smile, and reach for the beloved adult when they see her. A parent or consistent infant and toddler teacher gets the feeling that the baby recognizes her, enjoys her, and calms and feels safe when she is near.

At 9 to 12 months, infants go through a second shift in emotional development. They discover that others can know their own thoughts and feelings and that they can understand the thoughts and feelings of others (41). They are looking at eye gaze, facial expression, tone of voice, gestures, and actions. They begin to use the emotional tone of others as a way to interpret the meaning of events in their environment. This process, called **social referencing**, allows the baby to use a trusted adult to judge whether a stranger or a new experience is safe. The baby literally looks to the adult to see how to react.

This visual checking in with an adult to judge events can be easily observed in everyday situations. Researchers have also found creative ways to watch babies use social referencing. One group used a special table to show babies understand that an adult's emotional expression has meaning tied to an object or an event. They created a smooth surface for a baby to crawl over, with the mother waiting on the other side. The middle of the surface, however, appeared to have a sudden drop-off; it was a *visual cliff*. When the new crawler approached this apparent cliff edge, he would look to his mother for information. If she smiled and nodded reassuringly, the baby would continue crawling across the seemingly empty space. If she looked fearful, the baby would stay on his side of the cliff (42). (See Figure 6.3.)

FIGURE 6.3   **The visual cliff paradigm**

In the visual cliff study, an infant is seated on a table. In order to reach her mother, she must cross what appears to be a drop of more than 2 feet–although, in reality, the table is covered in a clear plastic. The mother either encourages the crossing with an inviting expression or discourages it with a terrified facial expression.

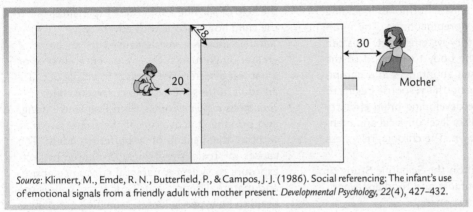

Source: Klinnert, M., Emde, R. N., Butterfield, P., & Campos, J. J. (1986). Social referencing: The infant's use of emotional signals from a friendly adult with mother present. *Developmental Psychology, 22*(4), 427–432.

Other researchers have shown that 14- and 18-month-old toddlers will watch a researcher's reactions to a toy or to the contents of two boxes. They willingly explored the objects that were targets of positive adult reactions and avoided the objects that adults treated with disgust (44). Children understand that the adult's facial expressions are related to what is in the box. In another study, 16-month-old children were shown how to push a button on a toy to make a sound. An adult came into the room. She sat down to read a magazine. The experimenter said to the adult, "Look at this" and pressed the buzzer. The adult angrily said, "That's annoying!" The experimenter said, "I thought it was interesting." The adult said, "It's not. It's irritating" with an angry voice. The experimenter gave the toy to the toddler. Most toddlers would not push the button if the angry adult was in the room. They would push the button if the adult closed her eyes or turned her chair to the wall. The toddlers understood the adult would be angry if they pushed the button. They did not understand that she would know about the buzzer if her eyes were closed (45).

During this period, infants also use information from adults to learn which emotions can be expressed and how and when they can be expressed. These **emotional display rules** may be specific to a culture, a family, or even a member of a family. One parent may encourage the child to experience the full range of human emotions. Another may be uncomfortable with displays of love and intimacy and react in very restrained ways in comforting or showing approval to his baby. Another family may be extremely uncomfortable with the expression of sadness or anger and may teach the child to minimize or avoid expression of these emotions (46).

Infants are constantly watching how adults express emotions and what events inspire them. In fact, when infants are taught to suppress negative emotions they may become anxious and have a physical response. They may store the negative emotion and the poor response in their memory to be used in future, similar situations. Infants and toddlers who live in fear have brains that are built to detect danger. Then, even neutral situations can be seen as frightening and bring about an aggressive response (47). (See Box 6.1.)

BOX 6.1

Toxic Stress

Stress causes the body to release hormones including cortisol, adrenaline, and norepinephrine. The internal organs and inflammatory systems react. This can be helpful in preparing the body to respond to the cause of the fear; but when an infant is in a chronically frightening environment, this response begins to wear the body down. The developing brain circuitry is disrupted, and the seeds of later physical and mental health problems are sown. The chronic, relentless stress is *toxic*.

The National Council on the Scientific Study of the Child proposes that infants and toddlers experience three kinds of stress responses:

- *Positive stress response* is brief and mild; a caring and responsive adult helps the child cope with the stressor. These are common life events such as frustration or getting an immunization. With the help of a loving adult, these experiences teach the child how to cope with adversity.
- *Tolerable stress response* is caused by an event of greater magnitude such as a parental divorce or a natural disaster. The stress is tolerable because an adult buffers the experience for the child.
- *Toxic stress response* comes from frequent, strong, and prolonged activation of the stress response without the benefit of a buffering adult. The causes of toxic stress include abuse, neglect, exposure to violence, parental substance abuse, and maternal depression. Toxic stress causes the brain to be hypervigilant in searching out danger and restricts the ability to learn.

Source: National Scientific Council on the Developing Child (2005/2014). Excessive Stress Disrupts the Architecture of the Developing Brain: Working Paper No. 3. Updated Edition. Retrieved from www.developingchild.harvard.edu.

The third major shift in emotional expression occurs as the infant becomes a toddler, between 18 and 20 months. As symbolic thinking becomes established, children are able to use language to organize their thinking. They remember past events and form ideas of repeated events that help them anticipate what future events might be like. This is particularly true of the representations they form of what it is like to be in a relationship.

The increased ability to symbolize is part of a more fully developed sense of self. Children begin to recognize themselves in a mirror, use personal pronouns to refer to themselves, and identify themselves as boys or girls. They express self-conscious emotions such as guilt, shame, embarrassment, and empathy. They are also beginning to control their own behavior in the service of maintaining relationships.

Impact of Maternal Depression

Brooke has just given birth to her third child. She took a leave from her job but is having trouble returning to it. She has always felt good about her life, her marriage, her children, and her work. Since this last birth, however, she can't seem to feel interested in anything. She is tired and bored. She can see her baby trying to have a relationship with her but just can't respond the way she wants to.

In the past several years, postpartum depression has been recognized as a major problem for a mother's ability to care for her new baby and as having lasting effects on the baby's abilities.

The *baby blues* is a friendly name for a very serious problem. There are three levels of postpartum maternal depression. The baby blues affects a majority (50%–80%) of new mothers. This may include a few days of mild feelings of sadness, fatigue, tearfulness, and feeling overwhelmed. Most women begin to feel better before long. About 19 percent of new mothers have a more moderate to severe depression. This will interfere with the woman's life and her ability to bond with her baby. The mother has a low mood, sleep and appetite changes, and lack of pleasure in daily life, poor concentration, fatigue, irritability, feelings of worthlessness, despair, and thoughts about harming herself or her child. A very small number of women experience postpartum psychosis, delusions, agitation, paranoia, and thoughts about suicide or infanticide. We see mothers suffering from postpartum psychosis on the news. Early Head Start national research reports that as many as 52 percent of women enrolling in EHS were depressed. For 12 percent of women, that depression was chronic and lasted through their child's third birthday (48).

Postpartum depression is a problem for both mother and infant. Maternal depression occurs in all income groups. Still, it often occurs with other risk factors such as low income, marital problems, earlier episodes of depression, and mothers' feeling badly about their neighborhoods. Colic in the baby and maternal depression may be related. Infant colic might cause maternal depression or depression might lead to infant colic.

Maternal depression has negative effects even on newborns. They may have been exposed to a biochemical imbalance in the mother's body. Clinically depressed mothers have babies who are poorly regulated. Depressed mothers seem to respond in one of two styles. They withdraw or they become very intrusive. Each of these styles has poor effects on the infant's ability to regulate, to interact, and to be responsive. Maternal depression is generally treatable, through medicine and therapy. When mothers were treated with antidepressants and cognitive therapy, many had remission from their depression. The earlier the remission, the better the infant's outcomes will be (49). Home visiting programs have been identified as particularly effective for helping depressed mothers get treatment.

Check Your Understanding 6.3
Click here to check your understanding of the concepts in this section.

Program Practices That Enhance Emotional Learning and Development

The approach to emotional wellness in young children includes promotion, prevention, and intervention. Promotion is infant and toddler teachers providing nurturing, responsive relationships to all young children. It is reaching out to parents with messages about playing with and talking to their child. Prevention services work with families under stress to provide information and support so they can help their child's emotional development. Intervention programs work with children who are having difficulties in emotions and relationships.

"Infant mental health" is defined as the healthy social and emotional development of a child from birth to 3 years; and a growing field of research and practice devoted to the:

Promotion of healthy social and emotional development;
Prevention of mental health problems; and
Treatment of the mental health problems of very young children in the context of their families.

(ZERO TO THREE Infant Mental Health Task Force)

Promotion

Warm, nurturing, responsive moments, shared with an infant or toddler, promote good emotional development. Infants and toddlers and parents have opportunities for promotion all day long. From the first day of life, an infant is ready to stare

STRATEGIES TO SUPPORT EMOTIONAL DEVELOPMENT AND LEARNING

1. Comfort young babies who are stressed or unhappy by swaddling, holding them close to you, rocking them, and speaking or singing quietly.

2. Help young babies learn to regulate themselves by letting them suck on their hands, feeding them on demand, and helping them fall asleep and awaken calmly.

3. Be available for interaction when babies are awake and alert; talk quietly and gaze into their eyes when they are interested; allow them to turn away and collect themselves when they need a break.

4. Mirror a baby's facial expressions, adding words that describe the feeling with a congruent tone of voice.

5. Express your own feelings honestly and clearly.

6. Allow infants and toddlers to express the full range of emotions. There are no *bad* feelings. Very young children need to learn socially acceptable ways to express their feelings.

7. Use your facial expressions and language to let infants and toddlers know whether or not a situation is safe from a small distance.

8. Be responsive and reassuring when infants and toddlers are fearful about exploring. Let them know you are watching them and will keep them safe.

9. Encourage infants and toddlers to explore and play, while you remain available when they return to you for moments of contact.

into your eyes as you stare back into his. From then on, if the child is rested and comfortable, he likes being with a caring adult better than anything.

A program for supporting social and emotional development lists six important ways a parent or infant and toddler teacher can promote mental wellness (50).

1. *Be engaged and engaging.* With young infants, answer their cooing with words as though you are having a conversation. Sing and read books often. Express interest and joy. Respond when an infant reaches, moves toward something, or shows you something. Toddlers who know you care will happily say, "Look at me!" as they do something wonderful.

2. *Be sensitive.* Respond quickly and accurately to an infant's needs. Be patient if you are unable to comfort the baby. Respect the child's temperament. Support the toddler through frustration.

3. *Be consistent.* Set up (flexible) routines for eating, napping, changing. Keep a pleasant tone during routines. Help toddlers learn simple rules and limits.

4. *Be responsive.* Comfort baby when distressed. Answer when she makes sounds. Smile when she smiles. Continue to comfort toddlers and keep them safe. Mirror their emotional experiences.

5. *Be enjoyable to be with.* Show pleasure in being with the child at every age. Joke and laugh. Show your pride in him.

6. *Be baby's voice.* Use words to name the child's feelings as you understand them. Help toddlers find the words they need to tell you about themselves and their discoveries.

Prevention

Prevention of mental health issues involves practices for families under stresses that challenge emotional development. When a family lives in poverty, they face daily struggles that may limit their ability to support their child. Threats such as mental illness, substance abuse, alcohol, and close partner violence put the child at risk.

Home visiting programs are especially effective in helping these families to support their infants' and toddlers' emotional health and learning. The Maternal, Infant, and Child Health Home Visiting (MIECHV) program funds voluntary, evidenced based models throughout the country. Home visitors build partnerships with parents to:

- Improve health and development.
- Prevent child injuries, child abuse, neglect, or maltreatment, and reduce emergency department visits.
- Improve school readiness and achievement.
- Reduce crime, including domestic violence.
- Improve family economic self-sufficiency.
- Improve the coordination and referrals for other community resources and supports (51).

The programs that qualify for MIECHV funding have proven to be effective. The families choose to be in them and can leave at any time. A consistent home visitor visits regularly. She develops an ongoing, caring partnership with the family. There is a curriculum to follow. The home visitors are well trained and supervised.

Intervention

Infant mental health professionals provide intervention for infants and families with identified emotional health issues. Sadly, even in the first 3 years of life, these include abuse or neglect, failure to thrive, or signs of depression or anxiety in the young child.

As should be clear from the rest of this chapter, in infants and toddlers, good mental health requires a partner who helps the baby regulate his reactions, express and understand expressions of emotions, and develop a secure base of attachment balanced by an autonomous sense of self. Unfortunately, for some babies that relationship is not available. Some parents do not recognize the message sent by the baby's expressions and actions. Instead the parent gives meanings and motivations to the baby that really generate from the parent's own life experiences (52). For example, a woman who has been physically abused, first by her father and then by her husband, sees her baby son as physically threatening to her. When adults are unable to "see" the infant, situations become confusing for the baby. Adults behave in ways that do not make sense and the child's development can be thrown off course.

 Watch the video on infant mental health. How might infants and toddlers struggle in the first year?

https://www.youtube.com/watch?v=rDSQIkrw0Jg

Infant mental health intervenes in the relationship between parent and infant when there are relationship challenges. The therapist supports the parent in giving accurate, responsive care. By compassionately understanding and caring about the parent's immediate or earlier experiences, the therapist may provide a kind of relationship never before experienced by the parent. The actual therapeutic work includes seeing the parent and infant together. Although the parent's conversation and actions may dominate the session, the therapist is always watching and sometimes commenting on the relationship between the parent and the baby. If a mother is revealing a particularly sad and painful story from her own childhood, the therapist might acknowledge the mother with a comment such as, "I'm sorry, that is really more than such a little girl should have to experience," but she may then add, "I'm really taken with how your baby watched you as you talked about this. She can't understand your words but she seems very concerned about whether you are all right." A while later, the therapist might point out, "Your

DEVELOPMENTAL TRENDS AND RESPONSIVE INTERACTIONS

EMOTIONAL LEARNING AND DEVELOPMENT

Infants and toddlers develop a strong sense of who they are through increasing self-regulation, learning about effective emotional expression, and developing attachment relationships.

Development	Example
0–4 months (infant)	
<ul><li>Infants are taking in a lot of information about the world.</li><li>Infants can get overwhelmed and begin to yawn, look away, or fuss.</li><li>Infants begin to calm themselves by sucking on their hands or listening to an adult talk quietly to them.</li><li>Infants gaze into their infant and toddler teacher's eyes as she feeds them.</li><li>Infants turn their heads toward a familiar voice.</li><li>Infants relax and allow themselves to be comforted by familiar people.</li><li>Infants cry when they are hungry, tired, or uncomfortable.</li></ul>	Carlos followed Karen with his eyes whenever she entered the room. When she came close to him, he looked at her as though he wanted her to join him. Accepting his invitation to play, she sat with him on the floor. As he began to tire and fuss, she swaddled him in a blanket, held him close, and spoke softly to him.
4–8 months (infant)	
<ul><li>Infants like to look at their hands and feet.</li><li>Infants wave their arms and kick in excitement when they see a familiar person.</li><li>Infants will smile at a infant and toddler teacher, expecting her to smile back.</li><li>Infants use their faces and bodies to express many feelings: everything from frowning and crying to laughing out loud.</li><li>Infants express their feelings more clearly to familiar people and are more reserved with strangers.</li></ul>	Deborah loves being carried in her teacher's arms as they move around the room "talking" about the things they see. Her eyes are wide and bright, she smiles, and she makes cooing sounds as though taking her turn in the conversation. When a visitor enters the room, Deborah gets very quiet and serious and holds tightly to her infant and toddler teacher's shoulder as she looks at the visitor.
8–12 months (infant)	
<ul><li>Infants may be fearful with strangers.</li><li>Infants will call upon familiar adults to help them when they are upset.</li><li>Infants will look at a familiar adult to determine whether a situation is safe or dangerous.</li><li>Infants will cling to a familiar adult when they are in a strange situation.</li><li>Infants will find humor in silly games and adults making big facial expressions.</li></ul>	Jamie is enjoying his new ability to quickly crawl anywhere he wants to go. He loves the little climber that lets him look out the window. But when another child joins him, he likes to look back at his infant and toddler teacher, Fred–just making sure he's still safe.
12–18 months (young toddler)	
<ul><li>Toddlers will imitate the actions of familiar adults, such as using the phone or caring for a baby doll.</li><li>Toddlers will seek an adult's attention by pulling on their leg or taking their hand.</li><li>Toddlers will use a favorite blanket or stuffed animal to help calm themselves.</li><li>Toddlers will protest loudly when their parents leave them.</li><li>Toddlers will relax and be comforted by cuddling with a familiar adult.</li><li>Toddlers will let their likes and dislikes be clearly known.</li></ul>	Amelia carries her teddy bear around all morning. Sometimes she copies her infant and toddler teacher Sophia's actions, patting its back or "feeding it a bottle." When she gets tired, she rubs the teddy against her ear and sucks her thumb.

Infant and Toddler Teacher or Parent–Child Interaction	Environment
0–4 months (infant)	

• Keep young infants close to you, in your arms, in a snuggly, or on a blanket nearby.	• Being close to a familiar infant and toddler teacher is best.
• Recognize the signals that indicate an infant wants to be with you—intent gazing, reaching, a happy look—and respond with quiet, verbal and nonverbal turn taking.	• A serene, quiet space with gentle lighting limits the information an infant needs to take in.
	• Avoid playing background music all day.
• Recognize the signals that indicate an infant needs a break—yawning, drooling, looking away—and sit back quietly and wait while the baby regroups.	• Limit the number of objects, sounds, and/or movements around a young infant.
	• The infant and toddler teacher is the most interesting thing for a baby to watch, but other babies, mirrors, and toys within the infant's visual range of focus are also interesting.
• Comfort infants whenever they cry.	

4–8 months (infant)	
• Provide opportunities for infants to look in mirrors as they play.	• Mount unbreakable mirrors on walls.
• Mirror the emotional expressions of the infant and add appropriate words: "I'm so excited to see you today!"	• Provide floor time when infants can play with their feet while on their backs, or move around on the ground.
• Respond to infants in a way that helps them be calm and active. If infants are crying, soothe them.	• Books and posters of photographs of real faces with different emotional expressions are very interesting to infants.

8–12 months (infant)	
• Encourage infants to move off and explore by reassuring them that you are watching and keeping them safe.	• Play peek-a-boo.
	• Read stories about mothers and fathers who go away and come back.
• Understand that infants may become afraid of new situations that wouldn't have been frightening a few months ago. Be comforting and reassuring.	• Read books with flaps to lift to find things.
	• Keep room arrangements and routines predictable.

12–18 months (young toddler)	
• Demonstrate your interest in toddlers' activities.	• Provide child-size copies of tools adults use: telephones, dishes, keys, etc.
• Show your pride in toddlers' accomplishments.	
• Let toddlers use you as a secure base from which to explore the world.	• Post photographs of the toddlers with their family on the wall.
	• Laminate photos of the toddlers with their family for carrying around.
• Let toddlers know you understand their feelings and respond with respect.	• Make photo albums of the children at your program and talk about the pictures.
• These are still very young children who need lots of cuddling and holding.	• Have adult chairs and quiet, comfortable spaces for holding children.

DEVELOPMENTAL TRENDS AND RESPONSIVE INTERACTIONS (Continued)

Development	Example
18–24 months (toddler)	
• Toddlers begin to control some impulses, saying "no, no, no" as they begin to throw blocks. • Toddlers may stop their actions when told to by a infant and toddler teacher. • Toddlers may not want to stop playing when their parent comes to pick them up. • Toddlers may cry when they are unable to master what they are trying to do. • Toddlers know their own names and may use "me" and "mine."	Frankie climbs up onto the table, looking his disapproving infant and toddler teacher right in the eye, and says "no, no, no."
24–36 months (toddler)	
• Toddlers can sometimes be independent, but they like to know the infant and toddler teacher is close by. • Toddlers like to study pictures of themselves, their friends, and their families. • Toddlers listen to your words and the tone of your voice when you talk about them. They want you to be interested in them and proud of their accomplishments. • Toddlers need clear and consistent limits. They will forget rules, or test rules, but feel secure when you remind them and help them follow the rules. • Toddlers may use words to express their feelings, or they may hit or bite. • Toddlers care about the feelings of others and will comfort someone who is sad or bring a Band-Aid to someone who is hurt.	Kiki carried her baby doll over to the photos of her own family on the wall. She crooned to her baby while looking at her own mother's face.

Infant and Toddler Teacher or Parent–Child Interaction	Environment
18–24 months (toddler)	
• Keep your sense of humor. Understand that sometimes toddlers can stop themselves from doing things but other times they cannot. • Respect the strong feelings of toddlers. Taking turns and sharing come later—now "me" and "mine" are an important part of developing a strong sense of self.	• Provide spaces that allow children to explore without ever being out of sight. • Have enough copies of the same toy for several children to each have one without sharing or taking turns. • Let children bring comfort items like blankets or stuffed animals to your program. Provide a quiet place where they can comfort themselves.
24–36 months (toddler)	
• Establish clear and consistent rules. Be prepared to remind the toddlers frequently of how to follow the rules: "We don't bite. Biting hurts." • Give toddlers enough of your time and attention so that they feel understood. • Echo the enthusiasm toddlers can bring to their play. • Notice and comment on the interactions that toddlers are watching and thinking about.	• Provide many photographs of the children with their family: on the walls, in little books, and laminated to carry around. • Provide protected spaces for quiet play. • Maintain predictable routines and room arrangement. • Provide books that tell simple stories of coming and going, of families, and of friendship. • Sing songs about feelings such as "When you're happy and you know it" and "When you're sad, angry . . . "

baby seems to watch you a lot. She's so interested in everything you do. And she really reacts to your feelings." The ability of the therapist to genuinely ally herself with a parent while still standing up for the baby may provide an entirely new kind of relational experience for the parent.

Respectful and consistent, the practitioner remains attentive to each parent's strengths and needs. Within the safety of this relationship, parents feel well cared for and secure, held by the therapist's words and in her mind (53). The practitioner listens carefully, follows the parent's lead, remains attuned, sets limits, and responds with empathy. Within the working relationship, the parent experiences possibilities for growth and change through the relationship with her own infant (54).

The therapy emerges from exposure to the parent and infant together, as the therapist becomes aware of particularly conflicted moments. The therapist may ask the parent how she feels when her baby cries. Does she remember how someone comforted her when she was little and crying? Questions designed to help parents remember and reflect on their own childhoods or their immediate feelings in this moment help them become aware of the discrepancy between their response and the baby's real needs.

Always be aware that you may also have issues in your relationship history that may play out in your caregiving relationships. Or a child's behavior may be so confusing that you will need support in understanding and responding to the child.

Check Your Understanding 6.4
Click here to check your understanding of the concepts in this section.

Summary

Self-regulation, emotional expression, and an attachment relationship create the core of the healthy development of a sense of self and a sense of oneself with others. Early emotional learning and development provides the basis for later relationships, learning, and motor development.

- Each infant and toddler teacher must find a balance between reacting to his experiences and regulating his reactions so that he can be relaxed, alert, and attentive. Adults help babies learn to self-regulate first with swaddling, rocking, and sucking, but later by helping them control their own reactions.

  □ Responsive adults build their relationship with infants through moments of regulation. Whether they take the opportunity to comfort a baby's distress or engage in interaction when a baby is alert, this sensitivity to regulation is an opportunity for the relationship.

  □ Temperament traits are inborn characteristics influencing how a child responds to the world.

There are nine traits: activity level, biological rhythms, approach/withdrawal, mood, intensity of reaction, sensitivity, adaptability, distractibility, and persistence. Temperament traits are often found in groupings called difficult or feisty; slow-to-warm-up, shy, or fearful; and easy or flexible.

- Over time, through repeated interactions, infants develop an attachment relationship with the important adults in their life. They use the adult as a source of safety and security as they venture out to explore their world.

  □ In the first three years, a child begins to develop an internal idea of who he is and how he is seen by others.

  □ Aspects of the level of security a child feels in the attachment relationship (secure, anxious-ambivalent, anxious-avoidant, or disorganized) may provide the mental model for later relationships in the child's life.

- ☐ Within the first year of life, infants learn their cultural norms regarding how intensely people express emotions and the nature of the attachment in infant-parent relationships.

- ☐ Infants and toddlers have active emotional lives. They express emotions in similar ways around the world and generally understand emotional expressions, although their ability to interpret expressions is influenced by their early experiences.

- ☐ Infants and toddlers use the facial expressions of those they trust to help them judge the safety of a situation through a process called social referencing.

- ☐ Infants and toddlers can tolerate and even grow from stressful experiences if an adult helps to buffer the situation. Toxic stress comes from situations that are frightening, chaotic, and chronic and can destroy parts of the brain.

- ☐ Many women experience postpartum depression to the extent that they are emotionally unavailable to their babies. Postpartum depression is often not identified, and it can have serious effects on the baby and on the mother-child relationship.

- ☐ Some parents are unable to establish a relationship with their infants because they have never had close relationships or because of traumatic losses or experiences in their own past. Infant mental health professionals can be effective during the early years of a child's life.

- • The emotional health of young children may require promotion, prevention, or intervention services from early childhood care and learning professionals.

Key Terms

anxious-ambivalent attachment
anxious-avoidant attachment
attachment relationship
autism spectrum disorder (ASD)
disorganized attachment
emotional display rules

feisty temperament
flexible temperament
infant mental health
regulation
secure attachment
self-fusion

slow-to-warm-up
social referencing
temperament
temperament style

Reflections and Resources for the Reader

REFLECTIONS

1. How do you see self-regulation as being a foundation of healthy development?
2. How could you meet the emotional needs of three or four infants and toddlers in your care at one time?

OBSERVATION AND APPLICATION OPPORTUNITIES

1. Observe a young baby with an adult. Do the baby's facial expressions become part of his or her language?
2. Visit a library or bookstore and look at some picture books for infants and toddlers. Can you find books that teach babies about emotional expression and about how adults keep them safe in attachment relationships? Share these books in class.

SUPPLEMENTARY ARTICLES AND BOOKS TO READ

Blair, C. & Raver, C. (2015). *School readiness and self-regulation: a developmental psychobiological approach*. Retrieved from ncbi.nlm.nih.gov/pmc/articles/PMC4682347/

Dewar, G.(2014) *Is your child securely attached? The Strange Situation test*. Retrieved from:parentingscience.com/strange-situation.html#sthash.X8EohHkx.dpuf

I-LABS. (2015) Training module 5: Understanding emotions. Retrieved from: modules.ilabs.uw.edu/outreach-modules/

Melmed, M. (2015) Infant mental health: Promotion, prevention, and treatment. Retrieved from: zerotothree.org/resources/series/infant-and-early-childhood-mental-health-promotion-prevention-and-treatment

INTERESTING LINKS

YouTube. Strange Situation. Use the key words *strange situation*

YouTube. Visual cliff experiment. Use key words *visual cliff*

YouTube. Alexander Thomas and Stella Chess talking about temperament: Use key words *Thomas and Chess*

Whole Child has charts from PBS: The ABCs of Child Development, Developmental Milestones for Your Child's First Five Years, as well as articles on emotional health. Use key words *Whole Child PBS*

ZERO TO THREE On this Web site, click on *Parents*. There are many interesting articles on emotional development under social emotional development. Use key words *zero to three parenting resources*

7

Social Learning and Development with Peers

Pearson Education

In his infant-toddler program, 9-month-old LeBron pulls himself up to stand, holding tight to a bar fastened securely on the wall. He sees another child nearby and reaches out to pat him on the head. They smile at each other, but then one, with awkward emerging motor skills, falls into the other and they both start crying.

An 18-month-old runs to her teacher to dump all kinds of little toys in the teacher's lap. Another toddler notices and soon is imitating the first toddler. Quickly, four toddlers join the others, running back and forth, following each other around the room. They squeal with delight as they move in and out of the group, communicating their joy with the toddler version of follow-the-leader.

For adults, relationships are a source of joy. They are at the core of being human. Relationships are important to young children, too. Infants and toddlers are active social partners with adults and peers. They enjoy social interactions—the moment to moment back and forth of sounds, gestures, expressions, and actions. Infants and toddlers thrive in positive social relationships imbued with affection. They develop a desire to be with others and experience warm feelings for each other. In this chapter we are focusing on child-to-child interactions and relationships (1), as well as how important responsive adult-child relationships and program practices are for peer development.

Learning about peer relationships for infants and toddlers is important for these reasons.

- Peer experiences add to infant and toddler social learning and development. They learn about their own and other's culture. They learn things from their peers that they do not learn from adults.
- With peers young children create ideas about how to play, how to cooperate, and how to deal with conflict.
- More than 65 percent of infants and toddlers are in out-of-home care. Being with other infants and toddlers is a part of their daily lives and we want them to enjoy their peers.
- Adults can help set a path for good social development, or not. Healthy adult-child relationships help children learn to be **prosocial** and control aggression. Unhealthy adult-child relationships affect young children, too. For example, young children with challenging temperaments (irritable, difficult to sooth) are more likely to act out and use aggressive behaviors when caregivers use harsh discipline, have higher rates of depression, or have lower rates of sensitivity. Relationship-based theory helps us understand how a child's first relationships with adults influences how the child will experience peers.
- Peer relationships are the foundation for later social skills. Positive early social relationships lead to better later social skills.

Infants and toddlers are capable of building strong, positive relationships with adults and peers. The major areas of social learning and development with peers discussed in this chapter are

- Communicating with peers,
- Playing with peers in increasingly complex ways,
- Developing prosocial behaviors, and
- Managing negative feelings and conflict with peers.

Each Child Is Capable and Unique

Each child is capable and unique. These capacities and uniqueness influence a child's relationships with peers. Both temperament and gender seem to have a great influence on how young children interact with their peers.

Interaction among children is a fundamental experience during the first years of life. (Malaguzzi)

Temperament

Each child's temperament affects his play with others. (See Chapter 6 for an in-depth look at temperament.) There are three dimensions of temperament that most impact social development (See Figure 7.1). *Self-regulation* includes focusing attention, controlling one's actions, and expressing strong feelings in a socially accept-able way. The range of emotions is the usual tone of the *child's mood*. The range from *shy to extroverted* describes the child's interest and skills in being with others.

The real issue may not be whether children are shy and anxious or overwhelmingly outgoing, but how they learn to regulate how they express who they are. (Shonkoff & Phillips)

Carlos approaches Jenny with a light touch on the head.

Pearson Education

Self-regulation may affect the quality of social interactions if, for example, a child has a difficult time controlling her emotions. Poor self-regulation can result in more aggression. It is challenging for toddlers to always control their emotions, though, and adults cannot expect that they will. However, adults can support infants' and toddlers' self-regulation skills by helping them learn to wait (a bit), learn words for their emotions, and comfort them when they are distressed.

Most children express a variety of moods, but some children are generally more negative or positive. If a toddler has a negative mood much of the time, especially if she doesn't want others near her, she may have fewer

FIGURE 7.1   Dimensions of temperament that affect social development.

Dimension 1: Self-regulation

Dimension 2: Negative to positive emotions

Dimension 3: Shy to extroverted

Source: Rothbart and Bates (1998). Temperament. In W. Damon (Series Ed.) & N. Einsenberg (Vol. Ed.), *Handbook of child psychology: Vol.3, Social, emotional, and personality development* (5th ed., pp. 105–176). New York: Wiley.

opportunities to learn how to interact with other toddlers. If a child has a positive mood much of the time, peers often will want to be near her.

The range from shy to **extroverted** describes whether children want to be with others. The **exuberant** children—the Tiggers of the world—are outgoing and demonstrative. Can't you just picture these enthusiastic, happy children bouncing through a room? Their excitement is contagious. They are highly social but they also can be overwhelming to other children. These children may actually be slightly more aggressive than others (2). Happy toddlers attract a group, are having fun, and are in the *middle of everything*. When a child is in the middle of everything, the chances are higher that the child will bump into other children or excitedly grab a toy from another toddler. Again, self-regulation is important. If these exuberant children control their negative emotions, then they are more likely to attract positive attention from peers. However, we must emphasize that we can't expect toddlers to control their emotions at all times—they are just learning how—and they need understanding adults to help them express their emotions with words and to help them calm down when they become too active or upset.

A contrasting temperament to exuberance is *inhibition*. Some young children are very busy and often like to explore and play alone. These busy toddlers who sometimes play by themselves would not be considered inhibited. **Inhibited** children are those who seem very shy, hesitant to interact with peers, anxious, and fearful of peers. They may also actively withdraw from other children or be rejected (3). Harsh parenting or overprotective parenting adds to a child's social withdrawal and inhibition, while gentle encouragement can help children become less inhibited (4, 5).

Inhibited toddlers are likely to be inhibited preschool children, unless they receive support and encouragement to enter the social world. It is easy to overlook inhibited children because they are quiet. Do not ignore them or expect them to change quickly. They may not be interacting with other children because of the fear of rejection.

New infant and toddler social skills develop through the assistance of helpful, but not intrusive, adults. When adults are critical or harsh with these children, they are more likely to continue to be withdrawn (6). If adults are overprotective and do not encourage peer interactions with kindness, these children may be more likely to continue to think that the world is a scary place. You can go with a hesitant child to a block area and engage the child with one other child. Or, encourage the child to go with you for a story with several other children. As these infants and toddlers gain experience, they have opportunities to imitate more **elaborate play schemes** and try them out within a safe environment.

Gender

Gender can also affect social learning and development. The behavior associated with gender may have biological roots, may be influenced by the environment, or may be influenced by a combination of both.

Pearson Education

Exuberant children often attract positive attention from peers.

FIGURE 7.2   **Three theories that explain children's desire to play with their own gender.**

(1) **Cognitive Consonance Theory**
When children learn to identify their own gender as male or female, they highly value anything associated with their gender category.

(2) **Gender-Types Toy Preference Theory**
Children segregate according to their toy and activity preferences, and the activities chosen bring children into contact with other peers who also prefer that activity.

(3) **Behavior Compatibility Theory**
Gender segregation develops out of toddlers' attraction to peers who exhibit play styles that are compatible.

Source: Moller, L., & Serbin, L. (1996). Antecedents of toddler gender segregation: Cognitive consonance, gender-typed toy preferences, and behavioral compatibility. *Sex Roles: A Journal of Research, 34*(7–8), 445–461.

Often, boys prefer to play with boys and girls with other girls. We can ask, "is that a problem?" Why do many toddlers seem to prefer **gender segregation**? Three theories that explain why young children might want to play with children of their own gender are presented in Figure 7.2.

The compatible play style explanation seems most likely. Children of the same sex with similar play styles prefer to play with each other. As children develop, their interest in **same-gender-play** increases. By the time children enter preschool, they prefer to spend time with same-gender peers. This preference increases throughout the elementary years. This choice occurs across cultures and may be a strong influence on children learning gender-specific roles in their culture (7).

OBSERVATION INVITATION **7.1**

Click the play button to watch the video of two boys playing together and answer related questions. Which theory does this video clip support? Support your answer with examples from the video clip.

Several researchers who observed children found that preschool boys' play was often rougher and more active than girls. There was more physical contact and taunting. Boys tended to play away from the teacher, engage in less structured play, follow peer direction, and engage in what could be considered math and science activities more than girls. Girls were more likely to emphasize cooperation and use forms of communication that promoted harmony. Girls played more often in the presence of a teacher and received more adult attention and direction from the teacher. They had more opportunities to regulate and control their behavior and emotions. Boys' and girls' different compatible play styles were fostering different behavioral norms and interaction styles. These play styles were contributing to very different learning experiences for boys and girls in the preschool classroom (8, 9).

You can observe toddlers during their play to see if this type of gender segregation is occurring. If so, consider whether the behaviors exhibited are of concern. You should be concerned with same-gender (and mixed-gender) play *if*

- the behaviors limit the opportunities for learning a variety of skills,
- the children in a particular group become more aggressive when they are with one another,
- a group frequently does not like to have an adult present, or
- a child hardly ever wants to play with a child of the other sex.

"Although it is important for children to develop a strong sense of self and incorporate what it means to be a girl or a boy, adults must help children see that neither girls nor boys should be limited by gender roles" (10).

Also, watch to see if boys and girls are beginning to develop the idea that certain toys are only for boys and other toys only for girls. For example, Carlini was likely to deny boys a chance to play with her doll because she mistakenly thought that only girls could play with dolls. If this happens, you could tell Carlini that both boys and girls like to play with the dolls. Then give both boys and girls opportunities and encouragement to do so. Another strategy to encourage children to play with all types of toys is to display pictures of both boys and girls playing with many types of materials and toys. Also, choose and read books that challenge gender stereotypes by showing girls and boys playing quietly with their toys *and* playing actively on the playground. However, it may be difficult to find children's books that show girls as the main character. When researchers examined 21st-century children's books, they found that "males are represented nearly twice as often in titles and 1.6 times as often as central characters" (11).

 Check Your Understanding 7.1
Click here to check your understanding of the concepts in this section.

Knowing the Child

Letta reached out to touch the nose of her 9-month-old playmate, Carla. Carla, sitting quietly let Letta softly stroke her nose and then reached out as to offer a hug. Letta and Carla, ever so gently, touched noses, laughed, and then crawled away to play with some toys next to them.

If you watch young children closely, you will see the many ways they interact. From birth to age 3, they grow in their desire and their skills to play with peers. They become more **socially competent**—taking part in social interactions that are satisfying to both partners. They learn to communicate. Toddlers become friends and share moments of glee with other toddlers. As they grow, they learn to use many social skills such as:

- offering,
- playing beside,
- approaching,
- playing with,
- initiating play or contact,
- being friendly,
- forming friendships,
- comforting,
- helping,
- giving,
- showing a toy,
- hugging,
- showing empathy, and
- defending favorite adults and peers.

Interacting and playing with other children facilitates development of language, self-concept, and sensorimotor thinking. (Bodrova & Leong)

First, we look at infants' and toddlers' social development with peers and then the children who may have special needs in social development.

Social Development with Peers

Infants and toddlers go through many stages of social development as they learn how to be socially competent. You will observe, at times, that these very young children are interested in trying to learn how to be social with peers. At other times, the challenges of learning how to negotiate the "me" with the "other" is difficult, and conflicts between peers often seem to erupt.

An infant or toddler might reach out to comfort another child; 5 minutes later, she might bite that same friend, either out of sheer emotional exuberance for the joy of the moment or out of anger because her friend took her toy. However, as they grow from birth to age 3, young children learn many skills for social interactions.

The Developmental Trends chart at the end of this chapter presents a sequence of peer development. Let's take a closer look at many of the milestones highlighted in the chart by examining the development of four capacities of infants and toddlers. Infants and toddlers, over the first 3 years of life, become increasingly able to

- Communicate with peers
- Play with peers in increasingly complex ways
- Develop prosocial behaviors
- Manage negative feelings and conflict with peers

At the end of their first 3 years of life, children still have much to learn and discover in the social domain. With adults who know that infants and toddlers desire and are able to learn to be good social partners, children gain a strong foundation of social skills.

Communication with Peers

Toddlers have a variety of communication skills that they use to begin and maintain relationships with other children. They inform; direct; and use sounds, words, and laughter to keep other children involved in play with them.

Gestural language.   Before they can talk, toddlers use a **gestural language**. Montagner, a French researcher found "Each child spoke a gestural language other children could read clearly, even if adults couldn't" (12, p. 60).

Pines (13) reported that Montagner discovered five major styles of nonverbal communication among children that begin as early as 9 to 12 months of age:

1. *Actions that pacify others or produce attachment:* offering another child toys, lightly touching or caressing the other child, jumping in place, clapping one's hands, smiling, extending one's hand as if begging, taking the other child's chin in one hand, cocking one's head over one's shoulder, leaning sideways, rocking from left to right, or vocalizing in a nonthreatening way.
2. *Threatening actions:* generally producing fear, flight, or tears in the target child, using loud vocalizations, frowning, showing clenched teeth, opening one's mouth wide, pointing one's index finger toward the other child, clenching one's fist, raising one's arm, leaning one's head forward, leaning one's whole trunk forward, or shadow boxing.
3. *Aggressive actions:* hitting with hands or feet, scratching, pinching, biting, pulling the other child's hair or clothes, shaking the other child, knocking the other child down, grabbing something that belongs to the other child, or throwing something at the other child.
4. *Gestures of fear and retreat:* widening one's eyes, blinking, protecting one's face with bent arms, moving one's head backward, moving one's trunk or one's whole body backward, running away, or crying after an encounter with another child.
5. *Actions that produce isolation:* thumb sucking, tugging at one's hair or ear, sucking on a toy or a blanket, standing or sitting somewhat apart from the other children, lying down, lying curled into the fetal position, or crying alone (p. 63).

The magical sequence: head tilted over one shoulder, a smile and outstretched hand. (Pines)

The young children differed greatly in the combinations of gestures that they used. The secret to a child's peer success (in fact, becoming a leader among peers) seems to be the use of as many of the pacifying gestures as possible. Also, peer leaders defend themselves with threatening behaviors only when necessary. Toddlers learn to "read" other children's behavior quickly, avoiding children who are often aggressive. Our understanding of this remarkable ability opens a window to a fresh view of infants' and toddlers' abilities to communicate nonverbally.

Conversations between and among peers.   It is often difficult for toddlers to know when to take a turn in a conversation, when to use a soft or loud voice, and how to use language to request, demand, offer, and question. They do not, it seems, have a problem with what to say to peers. Watching mealtime

With teacher support, mealtime is a great time for peer conversations.

conversations in a Norwegian preschool, one scientist found "two-year-olds trying to come to grips with the problems of life" (14). They talked about problems and expressed feelings such as anger, fear, loss, and desire. For example, one young child engaged his peers in a conversation about a scary event as he related a story about Santa Claus by saying, "Gloomy Santa Claus was there" (at the center of town). These young children also struggled with one another over who would control a story. An almost 3-year-old Ane raised her fist in the air and shouted to another child, "Me talk." Soon the other child responded to Ane with stifled anger, "Ah, me talk." This conflict between the two children at mealtime continued into their play. These peer conversations with or without adults add greatly to children's learning.

Children develop and adapt the meaning of their words as their conversations continue. Conversations or stories are built together with the teacher and peers, often in a group discussion. Through thoughtful questions and comments, a teacher often helps a child move from talking about the "here and now" (events and objects that are present) to the "there and then" (events and objects not present). Through reflection on children's words and conversations with their peers, the teacher can learn about children's cultures and the relationship experiences with the adults and peers in their lives. When you are with older infants, toddlers, and 2-year-olds you will find it fascinating to listen in on their "conversations" to learn more about young children's social interests and skills.

Play with Peers

Learning to play with others is another important set of skills. As young children develop, they participate in more complex interactions. Researchers have tried to capture these developmental experiences by creating scales that identify the important characteristics of each stage of development. In 1932, Mildred Parten (15) identified stages of young children's play that included solitary play, parallel play, associate play, and cooperative play.

Carolee Howes expanded on Parten's work by developing a peer play scale in 1980 (see Figure 7.3) and found more sophisticated play at earlier ages. Howes's social sequence, as Parten's did, identified a stage of parallel play. She added a stage of "parallel aware play" (a stage that captures the awareness that one child has for another when they play). The third stage, "simple social play," describes how young children take turns during play (as in run-chase games). When children work together on a common plan they are involved in "complementary and reciprocal play with mutual awareness."

"Complementary and reciprocal social play" occurs when children clearly are both leaders and followers (16). Using a revised Howe's scale, Howes and her colleague observed 48 children from infancy through preschool. They found that "more than half the children engaged in complementary and reciprocal social play by 13 to 15 months and nearly all had achieved this type of play by 19 to 23

FIGURE 7.3   Howes's peer play scale.

I. **12–15 Months: Parallel Play**
    Parallel play (playing beside) often includes eye contact and/or exchanges of social behavior (A vocalizes, B smiles).

II. **15–20 Months: Parallel Play with Mutual Regard**
    Engagement in similar activities is accompanied with turn taking social exchanges (while digging in the sandbox, A smiles to B and B vocalizes back).

III. **20–24 Months: Simple Social Play**
    Social exchange is marked by each partner taking turns at reversing the actions of the other (run-chase game, rolling a ball back and forth).

IV. **24–30 Months: Complementary and Reciprocal Play with Mutual Awareness**
    Joint activity has a common plan and the pair's actions are integrated (conversation during joint building of a block structure shows that both intend it for trucks to drive underneath).

V. **30–36 Months: Complementary and Reciprocal Social Play**
    The social play activity shows differentiation of leader and follower roles (while jointly building a block structure, A directs building construction and B delivers blocks)

Source: Based on Howes, C. (1988). Peer interaction in young children. *Monographs of the Society for Research in Child Development,* *53* (1), (Serial No. 217).

▶▶▶ OBSERVATION INVITATION **7.2**

Click the play button to watch the video of 3- and 4-year-olds demonstrating Parten's categories of parallel play, associative play, and cooperative play. What are the major differences in how children play in each category? Why is each type of play important for children's social development? Answer questions about the video in the Pearson eText.

months. More than half the children engaged in cooperative social pretend play by 30 to 35 months" (17). This type of play involves children having complementary roles (one child pretends to be the dog and the other a cat). These results tell us that teachers can offer and expect different types of play, even at young ages.

Prosocial Development in Infants and Toddlers

> *Marissa, 2, runs to Minnie, 18 months, when she cries, patting her cheek as her own mother does to her. When Sam or Mark yells "Help," the other one runs to help move blocks or somehow resolve the crisis. Lenny, only 15-months-old, lovingly tries to feed his teacher some of his applesauce. When Jo gets her finger stuck between some blocks and lets out a loud cry, Allison looks concerned, runs to pull on the teacher's leg, and looks back at Jo, as if to say, "Hurry—come help Jo."*

We know that infants and toddlers are just learning how to be social—so there can be biting, hitting, grabbing, and pushing when they are together in groups. However, young children can be prosocial. Prosocial behavior includes giving, defending, offering, helping, and showing empathy through facial expressions, words, or gestures. Infants and toddlers hug, pat, look concerned, and often want to give their food to others. You can observe many prosocial moments if you know they exist and if you are watching for them and encouraging them. There are two studies that began to help teachers and parents see "toddlers with new eyes" and observe their prosocial behaviors.

One researcher studied sympathy in 1936 and observed sympathetic behavior among 2-year-olds, including patting, hugging, kissing, picking up another child who fell, or pushing a swing when a child could not make it go (18). Another important work, conducted in the 70s, focused on the capacity of very young children for compassion and other prosocial behaviors (18). With observations in the homes of children between the ages of 10 months and 2½ years, and after reading the records that parents faithfully kept for 9 months, the researchers noted many examples of infants showing empathy for the feelings of others. To their great surprise, as early as 1 year of age, some babies tried to comfort people who were crying or in pain. Infants used gentle touches, snuggles, and hugs to try to make an unhappy person feel better. In a few cases, they offered their own bottle or food to an exhausted dad or a sad mom. One baby even tried to defend his mother against a force much larger than himself. When the mother was having her throat swabbed at the doctor's office, her infant, not quite a year old, reached out and tried to knock the throat swab from the doctor's hand when his mother made a strangling noise.

As the children moved toward 18 months, some toddlers became more inventive at figuring out how to comfort another child. They gave toys and food

 This video shows experiments that assess whether young children help and cooperate. Do you think that children are born with an inclination to be altruistic or do they need to be taught (or both)?

https://www.youtube.com/watch?v=Z-eU5xZW7cU

to the crying child and urgently pulled an adult over to help the child in distress. Infants' and toddlers' prosocial acts, however, did not always comfort the other person because the offer from the young child often mirrored their own needs rather than the needs of the other person. A sticky pacifier, chewed-up food, or an already used baby bottle may not be exactly what the adult or other child wants for consolation. However, these gifts represent a supreme sacrifice on the part of the toddler making such an offer and will ideally be appreciated as such by the receiving party. Figure 7.4 identifies ways that parents in Zahn-Waxler's, Radke-Yarrow's, and King's study (20) facilitated prosocial tendencies that could be useful for teachers.

We hear the term, "terrible twos" used to describe toddlers. However, fascinating and ground-breaking research also concludes that toddlers are capable of being prosocial. They are also capable of choosing others who are prosocial.

Infants choose prosocial others. Infants need to be able to distinguish between people who will be nice to them and those who are not so nice. Very creative researchers (21, 22) had 3-, 6-, and 10-month-olds watch a puppet show. One puppet (puppet 2) was helpful to a puppet trying to open a box (puppet 1) while another puppet (puppet 3) jumped on the box and was not at all helpful. In fact, that puppet hindered puppet 1 from opening the box. After watching the show, the infants were given an opportunity to choose to hold the helpful or hindering puppet. To everyone's surprise the infants were able to make social judgments. The majority of 6- and 10-month-olds reached out for the prosocial puppet and even 3-month-olds showed their preference for the prosocial puppet by looking at it longer. The conclusion was that infants prefer prosocial others to antisocial others, even at a very young age. You may have noticed infants who avoid adults who are not as nice to them as others.

By 8 months of age, though, infants were demonstrating even more sophisticated social judgments. Infants chose to hold puppets that were *not helpful* to an *antisocial* puppet. They seem to be demonstrating a willingness to punish puppets that were not helpful. As children become toddlers they become even more sophisticated social judges. After watching a similar puppet show, 14-month-olds

FIGURE 7.4   **Strategies used by parents of toddlers who were most prosocial.**

Parents of toddlers who were most prosocial...

- Helped their children see the connection between what they did and how it affected the other child. For instance, "You poked him. That hurt him."
- Gave explanations for why the child should or should not behave in a particular way. Just saying "No" or "Stop" without giving any additional information did not help children be kind. Instead it taught them to stop any activity when confronted with another's distress
- Taught their children what to do instead of biting, hitting, etc. A parent might say, "You can say 'Stop,'" or "Pat gently—it feels good when you pat gently."
- Were kind and loving toward their own children. They gave hugs and kisses, soothing words, Band-Aids, and tissues for gently wiping runny noses. The children modeled after their parents and used the same prosocial behaviors with their peers.
- Helped others when they saw that they were in distress. If the parent couldn't help—for example, if another child cried in the grocery store and that child's mom was already comforting her—then the parent talked to her own child about the event: "Yes, she's crying. She's feeling sad because she hurt herself on the cart. Her mom is making her feel better."

chose puppets that were nice to a puppet that liked the same food as they did (green beans or graham crackers). They were not nice to the puppet who liked the food different than what the toddler chose. This ability has value because infants and toddlers need to recognize those who are similar to them. It also reminds us that very young children are making social judgments about who is like them or not and who is prosocial or not. As children grow they begin to understand and appreciate that others may have preferences different from them and we hope will be nice to others who may like different things from them.

 Watch this video on research with young infants. What are the major themes of the video? What do infants feel towards the adults who are helpful or not helpful? What do their feelings towards the helpful and not helpful adults mean?

https://www.youtube.com/watch?v=FRvVFW85IcU

Toddlers help others, show empathic concern and comfort others. It seems that children naturally want to help others. Rewards actually undermine these kind impulses in 20-month-old infants (23). Prosocial behaviors increase during the second year of life because of toddlers' understanding of other children's and adults' emotions and perspectives.

Empathic concern for another's distress also appears during the second year of life. This happens as toddlers begin to develop a **theory of mind**, the ability to know that other people have feelings, thoughts, and desires that are different from your own. Toddlers in programs can comfort each other as well. A toddler teacher told us the following story: When 26-month-old Lonnie was sad, she grabbed her favorite stuffed bunny, sat on the floor, and hugged it tightly. Lukas and two other children saw that Lonnie was sad and sat beside her on the floor—reaching out to touch her gently. One toddler commented, "She sad," while another moved in closer and with a tilt of her head asked Lonnie, "What wrong—you OK?" The third toddler jumped up stating, "She like a sticker," as he ran off to get Lonnie a sticker to make her feel better. These children were growing in their ability to "think of the other" as they struggled to figure out what might make Lonnie feel better. After getting the sticker, Lonnie exclaimed, "All better now." These toddlers had found a way to comfort their friend in distress.

Toddlers learn to cooperate. Infants' and toddlers' ability to cooperate with each other on a task improves as they get older. It is a remarkable achievement of toddlers. For example, researchers presented a toy that required two children to pull handles from opposite sides of the toy to make it work. The majority of 27-month-old children could cooperate to activate the toy. However, 19- to 23-months-olds could not make the toy work by cooperating, even though the adults modeled how to cooperate and reminded the children about the goal of the task (24). We can wonder, though, and observe how infants and toddlers can cooperate if they know each other well in a program and if they are motivated to do a task such as fill a water table by cooperating to carry a bucket of water.

Toddlers experience glee. What fun it is to watch toddlers who burst into gales of laughter when with each other. They are experiencing glee (25). This delight, happiness, and laughter may occur during play or at less convenient times such as when eating. Yet, we can appreciate the joy and excitement that young children feel when experiencing another person their size and feel delight ourselves at the children's pleasure and amusement. They are making friends and enjoying each other.

Toddlers develop friendships Infants and toddlers develop friendships. Friendships occur "when two people bring out qualities in one another that are neither exhibited nor elicited in their other relationships" (26). Toddlers demonstrate their friendships in a number of ways (see Figure 7.5). A 15-month-old's face lights up each time she sees her friend arrive in the infant-toddler program. An 18-month-old runs to the other side of the living room to greet a friend who has come to visit.

An observer of two toddlers (13- and 14-months-old) concluded that, "In sum, infant friends displayed a strong preference for each other as well as reciprocal affection and a high level of intensity and enjoyment. Infant friends express their joy and affection toward each other through their whole body reciprocally" (27). The author of this observational study shared the following vignettes that demonstrate how friends greet each other and respond to the feelings of the other.

> *Emily greeted Katie with hugs and kisses. Emily comes to Katie, sitting on the floor, and sits down right in front of her. Emily faces Katie's face and says "hi." Katie also says "hi" to Emily and then both laugh. Emily gives Katie a big hug and holds her tightly, calling her name repeatedly all afternoon.*
>
> *On the way back to the classroom from the park, Katie starts fussing. Emily points to Katie who is sitting across from her in the cart and gently touches her body. Emily reaches into the backpack and takes out a tissue. Emily tries to help Katie wipe her running nose. (Observation)*

Toddlers who are friends may even grieve for each other if one child leaves a program or moves to another room.

> *Maria and Lisa had been together in the Boulder Journey School since they were babies. As toddlers they greeted each other, played together often, and obviously enjoyed each other very much. When Lisa's mother changed her work schedule, Lisa started attending the school on opposite days from Maria. Maria seemed to grieve for her friend. She would often go to the shelf with the "All About Me" books, choose Lisa's book, and lay on the floor looking at pictures of Lisa as a baby, of her first birthday, and as a toddler.*

FIGURE 7.5   A relationship is a friendship when . . .

The relationship is considered a friendship when these conditions are met:

- Toddlers choose to play with each other often
- Toddlers frequently play games such as "peek-a-boo" and "run and chase"
- Toddlers are affectionate with each other and look forward to seeing each other
- Toddlers miss each other when they can't see the other.

Friendships have been observed as early as 1 year of age.

Source: Howes, C. (2000). Social development, family, and attachment relationships. In D. Cryer & T. Harms (Eds.), *Infants and toddlers in out-of-home care* (pp. 103). Baltimore, MD: Brookes.

Teachers modeled these prosocial strategies with the children. The children were able to use the same loving strategies with their peers. It is gratifying to an adult who patiently and gently uses prosocial strategies with young children to see these types of peer-to-peer scenes that mirror the adult responses young children see and receive each day from their favorite adults.

Conflicts in Peer Relationships

Charissa toddled up to Ben, her favorite friend in the toddler room, and wrapped her arms around his head in a sweet, comforting way. Ben protested and tried to wriggle out of Charissa's head wrap. Later, Charissa clutched tightly to two toy telephones as Ben tried with all of his might to wrestle one from her grasp. Even later that day, Charissa handed Ben her special doll to hold and then quickly tried to take it back from him.

Of course, we also know that when very young children are together in groups, conflict will occur. Young children are learning to manage their emotions, to gain an understanding of "mine" and "yours," to use language to express their needs, and to understand the meaning of "share" and "take turns." Infants and toddlers can make great progress in their journey toward managing negative emotions and conflict with peers with the support of understanding adults.

Conflict scenes happen many times a day at home or in programs where there are two or more infants and toddlers. Older infants who are crawling and cruising and toddlers who are toddling sometimes give and sometimes take away. They often are very good at sharing their teachers, toys, food, and time. At other times, toddlers do not intend to share anyone or anything. Words like "mine" and "no" ring out from toddlers. They cling to their special teacher and push other children away. They hang on for dear life to toys that just a moment ago they discarded in a corner. They are learning about social interactions, but they seem to be following the "Toddler Property Laws":

Toddler Property Laws

If I like it, it's mine.
If it's in my hand, it's mine.
If I can take it from you, it's mine.
If I had it a little while ago, it's mine.
If it's mine, it must never appear to be yours in any way.
If I'm doing or building something, all the pieces are mine.
If it looks just like mine, it is mine.
(*Author unknown*)

Conflict may be related to social competence.   While infants and toddlers are learning to socialize, conflict happens. Conflict and aggression initially increase as children try to play together, peaking between ages 2 and 3 before they decline. However, conflict may actually be related to peer competence. In fact, research indicates that socially competent children may be involved in more conflicts than their less competent peers.

Conflict is different from mean-spirited aggression. It may be related to social competence in two ways. The first is that socially competent children are not withdrawn or aggressive, but can be rather assertive in their play. They are full of confidence and often right in the middle of the play action. This gives them

OBSERVATION INVITATION **7.3**

Click the play button to watch the video and describe what the young children learn during conflict.

more opportunities for conflict with peers. Second, young children learn valuable skills during conflict with their peers. They learn negotiation and self-regulation skills that prevent the conflict from escalating and interfering with play. These skills improve as these children gain experience in the art of disagreeing, resisting, or competing. Thus, involvement in conflict may actually play a positive role in peer development. The nature of young children's conflicts and teacher strategies for supporting children's problem solving are shared in Chapter 14.

You may have observed toddlers and noticed that some toddlers seem more **dominant** than other toddlers. They can take toys and the other children will not protest. Dominant children often seem to be the leaders in play. A basic quality of dominant children is that they interact with the environment easily, while peers that are subordinate do not, at least while dominant peers are present. Researchers have found that toddlers who are physically stronger, more mature, more cognitively advanced, and more goal directed seem to be more dominant than other toddlers. This is also true of toddlers who have more physical and social experience in a particular group setting. Girls were dominant more often than boys. Among the children who were observed, who ranged in age from 1.4 to 3.2 years, the toddler's developmental maturity was the highest predictor of whether a toddler was or was not dominant (28).

It is fascinating that a toddler might be dominant with one partner and not dominant with a different partner. The behavior of a particular toddler, then, may change based on his partner's behavior. Toddlers do not act the same way with all children and can adjust their behavior according to the behavior of a peer.

Dominant behavior has been observed in children as early as 19 months and may prevent aggression. As a teacher, you can help a toddler who is almost always dominant become an assertive *and* kind leader by using the strategies listed earlier in this chapter, in the section on prosocial development. You can also advocate for and aid a toddler who almost always is **subordinate** and can help the child become more self-confident in peer relationships. Look for these children's strengths and help them use them during play with dominant children.

Understanding the Richness of Peer Learning and Development

The teacher will understand and appreciate the richness of peer learning and development through use of observation, documentation, and reflection. Adults carefully observe each child to understand what the child is trying to accomplish—her goals, her strategies, and how she is thinking about her experiences—her theories.

Several researchers understood the meaning of toddler activities through their observations of six toddlers (18- to 36-months-old) one time a month for 6 months (29). The toddlers' social goal was to be with one another. The strategies they used were to move together. They made and kept contact with one another through moving their bodies in space, coming together, leaving, moving around the room together, and establishing contact through physical movement and imitation. They were holding a conversation with the body rather than with words. The young children's theory may have been "If I follow you, I can continue to be with you." In this example, the researchers gained an understanding of what leading and following mean to the growth of toddler social relationships.

Documentation of children's moment-to-moment social actions helps create an appreciation for the social competency of toddlers and their needs. Before playing with objects together, toddlers may need to move around the room together, experiencing and conversing kinesthetically. This social dance is so much more than parallel play. As children take turns being the leader and the followers, they demonstrate complementary and reciprocal interactions with awareness and great enjoyment of one another.

We all learn from these types of observations. Rather than trying to keep toddlers from moving, wise parents and teachers will provide safe opportunities for toddlers to hold their kinesthetic conversations.

Another detailed observation revealed further abilities of toddlers. When toddlers from ages 2½ to 3 were observed in a child care and learning center, they were able to develop expectations for the actions of other toddlers. The following vignette shows that some toddlers expect that a peer, Michael, will be hurtful in their play:

> *Michael, a 2-year-old in an infant-toddler center program, picked up a small hammer that accompanied a xylophone. In the small room of approximately 12 toddlers, Michael started swinging the hammer back and forth as he moved quickly around the room. As other toddlers noticed, they scattered to get away from their hammer swinging peer. Michael headed for the wooden lockers that held the toddlers' coats and sat down on the bottom of the locker between two toddlers who were using the lockers as sitting spots as well. As soon as he sat down, the other two toddlers took off, obviously running away from Michael.*

At 2 years of age, Michael already had a reputation for being rough, and the other children had learned to stay out of his way. The peers' theory of relationships with Michael seemed to be "Move away fast or get hurt." Michael had learned one way to try to be with peers. Perhaps this was his theory of relationships, his notion of how to be with others. Unfortunately, this theory won't help Michael make friends and have rewarding peer relationships. He needs an adult's help to learn better skills for getting along with peers. Otherwise, he will continue to frighten his peers.

Another observation of toddlers highlighted an example of how documenting and reflecting on these documentations of peer interaction illuminate the goals of young children:

> *Jason, after clutching three plastic bottles filled with colored water, gives them to his peers; after a few minutes, he insists on collecting them. Of course, the toddlers who now possess these coveted, colorful bottles do not want to return them. Jason begins to cry as he reaches for a bottle and turns to his teacher for help. The teacher says to Jason, "That was nice of you to share the bottles with your friends; sharing makes your friends happy."*
> *(30, p. 27)*

After documenting this example through written observation notes, the teachers decided that Jason wasn't sharing—at least in the same way that adults share. Rather, he was *distributing* items to others for them to hold for a moment, but expected them to give the bottles back to him when he wanted them.

Teachers and parents who observe this type of situation might come to the same conclusion through reflecting: What was Jason's goal? What were the strategies he was using to achieve his goal? What theories did he have about how relationships work? His goal seemed to be to have his peers hold the bottles for a moment and then give them back. His strategies were to give or distribute the bottles among his peers and then let them know that it was time to give the bottles back to him. His theory about relationships may be that when you give others something, they should give it back if you still want it. This may have happened often in a give-and-take game with his parents who are more willing than peers to give a toy back to him when he wants it.

These examples demonstrate how documenting the richness of peer interaction and then reflecting on these observations lead to adults "seeing" behaviors with new eyes. Infant and toddler development is fascinating when viewed through the lens of the child's perspective. Young children's behaviors that may have been seen through a negative filter are now wisely understood as progressive developmental steps toward the infant or toddler becoming socially competent. There can be a richness of peer interaction between children with special needs and their typically developing peers as well.

Children with Special Needs

Infants and toddlers with identified special needs often display delays in social interactions and the development of relationships. Parents and infant-toddler teachers can play a significant role in supporting and encouraging these children's social interactions with peers.

> Trevor was the first child with a disability to attend the child care center. Trevor had cerebral palsy. At the age of 18 months he crawled, and he used sounds, but not words, to communicate.
>
> Because of their own ideas about his disability, Trevor's teachers perceived him as fragile and in need of protection from everyone and everything in the environment. They kept him away from the other toddlers, strapped him into an infant seat at mealtimes, and held him on their laps during play times.
>
> Trevor was very lonely in child care. The toddlers in the classroom did interesting things nonstop. They ran from one side of the room to the other, challenging each other with a look to join in or keep up. They copied each other's table banging and joyful sounds, making them louder with each imitation.
>
> As Trevor watched the other children playing, moving, and singing, he became increasingly frustrated by the teachers' failure to move him along with the group. Sometimes he would join in the imitative play from a distance. He began to pounce on any opportunity when he was not physically constrained to crawl, and then walk, to where the other children were. His movements became faster and more purposeful. Trevor's moment-by-moment goal seemed to be to get close to the other children and do what they were doing. This interest in watching and imitating proved to be a powerful motivating force for him to try activities he'd refused before (31).

Adults can encourage social interactions between children with disabilities and children without disabilities. Teachers can do the following:

- Document how a child with disabilities likes to be touched or interact with peers so that the teacher can encourage those types of interactions.
- Place infants beside each other on the floor. Infants like to watch each other.
- Provide duplicates of toys to encourage children to play beside and with each other.
- Offer toys and activities that promote social interaction rather than isolated play. Some favorites among toddlers are a large bin full of balls (make sure they are not small enough for toddlers to put in their mouths and choke), water, sand, and coloring or painting on a huge piece of paper that everyone shares.
- Give children with disabilities toys that attract peers to their side, such as a new toy. Then support the child who has disabilities to show typical peers how to use the toy.
- Build on toddlers' inherent desires to imitate others by focusing the attention of the child with disabilities on the behavior of the other children. If other toddlers are patting a table, say "pat, pat, pat" as you show the child how to pat her hand on the table.
- Find a way for the child with disabilities to communicate with words, sign language, or a communication device and interpret the child's subtle cues to the other children. For example, say to the child without disabilities, "He said, 'Hi.' Say 'Hi' back," or, "She's really looking at the doll. Can you give her the doll?"
- Comment on how children are alike rather than different: "Look, Sarah likes shape boxes, just like you."
- Encourage toddlers to help by pulling another child in a wagon, turning on the faucet for a child with disabilities as the teacher holds her, or bringing toys to a child who has difficulty moving. Then point out how happy that makes the child being helped.

Your use of these strategies builds a harmonious environment where young children learn to see others for what they can do, not what they can't do.

Check Your Understanding 7.2
Click here to check your understanding of the concepts in this section.

Learning Through the Adult-Child Relationship

The importance of parent-child relationships for children's emotional development was discussed in Chapter 6. Adult-child relationships also have an effect on how infants and toddlers are with their peers. Young children develop ideas in their first relationships about how to interact with others and how others will treat them. Infants and toddlers then wisely apply this information to peer relationships.

Culture influences how both parents and children view the value of social interactions and how to relate to peers.

Culture: Learning in Relationships

It is principally through interacting with others that children find out what the culture is about and how it conceives their view of the world. (Bruner)

Children's social interactions differ according to their cultural experiences. In Letta's and Carla's culture, adults value peer interaction at an early age. This belief influenced their parents, who are friends, to find a child care home where Letta and Carla could be together during the day. The parents and the family child care provider believe strongly that young children need early peer interactions to learn how to play together. Parents in their culture encourage children to "not be shy" and are concerned when infants and toddlers are socially inhibited.

Many families in Italy also believe in the value of early friendships. Infant and toddler centers "are viewed as daily-life contexts with the potential to facilitate the growth and development of all children" (32). Parents want early social experiences for their children and they want teachers who will support young children's relationship skills.

There may be families, however, in which shyness and social inhibition are seen as beneficial. These families may want their children to spend time with family members rather than peers, especially during the infant-toddler years. It is important to talk with family members to discover what is important to them.

Respect, Reflect, and Relate

Respect: The families' vision and goals for the child. Respect the child's cultural and temperamental way of interacting with the world.

Reflect: Reflect on how to communicate effectively with the family and how to meet the child's needs, interests, and strengths.

Relate: Relate in responsive ways that benefit the child, family, and yourself by

- sharing information with the family,
- asking families about their culture, preferences, and both the parents' and child's daily needs
- building positive relationships with the child and family by conversing often, talking positively about their child, and sharing information about their child's day
- creating a personal and physical environment that supports the child's culture and personality.

CULTURE CLOSE UP

Graciele, an Early Head Start teacher, was worried about two older toddlers who were in her multiage classroom of 8 children. One boy, Keelan, hardly ever wanted to be close to other toddlers and he preferred to play by himself. He seemed embarrassed or shy when another toddler approached him. Yet, he was focused on his play and could engage with toys for long periods of time, even putting together a 10-piece puzzle by himself. The other child, Eiseo, was quite physical. When bumped by another child or when he wanted a toy that another child had he raised his fists in a threatening manner and sometimes pushed other children. If another child took Eiseo's toy, Eiseo would take the toy right back. Eiseo had started to grab Keelan's toys, push Keelan, and then run away with the toy. Keelan responded by looking sad, but then getting another toy. Graciele decided to talk with the boys' parents.

Keelan's parents reported that they want their children to be self-sufficient, but also peaceful and kind. They weren't concerned that Keelan played alone and didn't initiate play with other children. They wanted him to show self-control and not hurt anyone, even when another child hurt him. Eiseo's parents, one of whom had been a victim of bullying when young, reported that they did not want their child to be a victim of bullying. They wanted him to be assertive and be able to defend himself. Eiseo's parents were concerned that Eiseo was taking other children's toys; however, they were glad that Eiseo stood up for himself when another child took his toy. Graciele realized that the parents' views of child rearing reflected family cultural beliefs about individualism and collectivism. What would you do?

Relationships with Adults

Children's relationships with their families, teachers, other adults, and peers provide support for children's interacting with peers, play, prosocial behavior, and managing conflicts. Familiar adults demonstrate the emotional tone for interactions. They provide comfort or share joy during toddler-to-toddler moments. Adults coach toddlers to "touch gently" or "say, 'I want to play with you.'" They provide opportunities for toddlers to play and move and learn about each other.

The children with secure, sensitive, warm, and encouraging relationships with parents are more competent and more attractive as playmates. They also expect their peers to be emotionally and physically available to them. These young children know the basics of turn-taking in relationships, and feel good about themselves. They feel safe to explore the environment and interact with peers. They build on their experiences to become even more skilled at peer interactions. They know that relationships with other adults and peers are rewarding and worth pursuing.

On the other hand, infants and toddlers with negative and rejecting families also carry these expectations to their peer relationships. For example, when parents are aggressive toward their toddlers, the toddlers are more aggressive with peers (33).

Remember that many factors influence parent-child interactions. A child's temperament or fussiness may be hard for a parent (transactional theory). Family members may be under stress from other relationships or challenges (bioecological theory). Family support can help parents become more sensitive and this improves children's outcomes. For example, when insecurely attached children at 15 months began to receive highly sensitive mothering, they had better social, behavior, and language outcomes at age 3 (34).

Learning Through Caring Relationships

There are many ideas that parents and teachers can use to help children's peer social skills. Using these ideas at home or in a program will develop the adult-child relationship and peer relationships. Here we elaborate on several strategies that you will see in the box, Summary of Strategies to Support Social Learning with Peers.

1. *Provide continuity of care and groups.* Keeping groups of children together from infancy through toddlerhood promotes friendships. Peers who are familiar with each other are more likely to initiate play, be more positive, and engage in more complex interactions than children who are unfamiliar with each other (35). **Continuity of care** (when one or more caregivers move to a different room *with* a group of children as they age from birth to 3) is important for learning social skills. It enables teachers and children to develop more

trusting relationships. When there is continuity of care children are more positive with their peers, are less aggressive and negative at home, and have increased cognitive and language skills (36).

2. *Give children time together in an enriched environment.* If infants and toddlers can choose their activities, then they often choose to be near each other while learning how to help, comfort, and solve problems together. If teachers move children from activity to activity or if they offer only teacher-led activities, then children have a more difficult time interacting with others.

3. *Support positive social behaviors, comment on them, and cheer infants and toddlers on to continue caring behaviors.* Use clear approving words when an infant or toddler offers a toy or pats another child to comfort them. Teachers may talk about sharing, caring, giving, helping, comforting, loving, and being generous. Infants and toddlers begin to learn these words and to think about how the other child feels. As children begin to understand that positive behaviors are important to adults, those behaviors increase dramatically.

STRATEGIES TO SUPPORT SOCIAL DEVELOPMENT AND LEARNING

1. Model kindness with infants and toddlers. They learn from adults whether to be calm, exuberant, friendly, and kind or whether they need to be on guard, angry, sad, and aggressive with others.

2. Observe the temperament of each child. Help each child self-regulate his or her emotions with others. Individualize care based on a child's temperament.

   a. Realize that exuberant children may be slightly more aggressive than others just because they are often in the middle of the action.

   b. Help inhibited children by being understanding and supportive—do not attempt to over-control, scold, or be critical to get them to be involved with other children, as this undermines their social competence. Support their language and cognitive development and their interactions with peers.

3. Infants and toddlers learn social competence with peers in the company of "expert adults" who are helpful and not intrusive, and who support elaborate play schemes.

4. Help infants and toddlers get off to a good start in peer relationships. Help toddlers who are aggressive to feel loved and learn new behaviors.

5. Recognize and support prosocial behaviors.

6. Expect conflict as an important part of social development, and support children in learning how to resolve conflict with language and negotiation skills.

7. Infants and toddlers with disabilities may need adult encouragement and skills to play with children without disabilities, and vice versa.

8. Set up an environment that encourages peer interaction.

9. Include several peers in conversations. Comment on what other children are doing or saying.

10. Provide quality care.

11. Provide primary care.

12. Ensure continuity of peer groups.

13. Maintain appropriate ratios and group sizes.

14. Develop strong, positive adult-child relationships and sensitive, responsive care.

4. *Young children need to feel what it is like to have an adult be social and prosocial with them.* Give them food and toys in a generous way and comfort them when they are distressed. Children need to feel that their own emotional and physical needs are met before they can show empathy to another child. As adults offer warmth and kindness to children, these qualities become a part of how the children act with others. Teachers may provide positive models of prosocial behavior at many times during the day. Children see adults being kind to each other and, more importantly, they feel the prosocial atmosphere of the room or family child care home.

5. *Emphasize how being prosocial makes others feel.* Say things like, "Oh, Ian likes it when you pat him gently. Look, he's smiling." This type of comment helps infants and toddlers begin to take the perspective of others.

Check Your Understanding 7.3
Click here to check your understanding of the concepts in this section.

Program Practices That Enhance Social Learning and Development

For an infant or toddler, attending an infant-toddler program may be a wonderful experience or it may take all of the child's efforts to cope. Higher-quality infant-toddler programs do result in more competent peer relationships. In fact, the higher the program quality, the more positive the peer interactions will be.

Continuity of Peer Groups

Carolee Howes noted that children who remain together with the same peers over the infant-toddler years in an infant-toddler center or family home are more likely to maintain their friendships and increase their social skills. However, that doesn't often happen in a center program, while it occurs naturally in a family child care home. The author of an article titled *There's Elly, It must be Tuesday: Discontinuity in Child Care Programs and Its Impact on the Development of Peer Relationships in Young Children,* noted that Elly, who attended an infant-toddler center part time, took 6 months to develop a meaningful relationship with a peer. However, programs often move one child at a time to a new group based on their development or space available, rather than with their friends. Elly soon had to start over to develop a new friend.

The author noted that, "Importantly, the child care center's policies and practices for transitioning children in and out of classrooms seem to be at odds with current research on attachment, continuity, and the development of peer relationships" (37).

Relationship with the Infant-Toddler Teacher

A teacher's relationship with a young child is strongly related to that child's skills with peers. This adult-child relationship can be classified as secure or insecure (see Chapter 6 for a detailed description of these concepts). In a secure attachment

Pearson Education

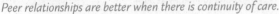
Peer relationships are better when there is continuity of care.

relationship, the teacher is sensitive and responsive to infant cues for food, attention, and play. The infant or toddler feels safe and confident and expects relationships to be emotionally satisfying. Infants who have a secure attachment relationship with their teacher are more likely to participate in complex peer play and are more sociable and expressive, less hostile, and less withdrawn at age 4 (38). Secure, warm relationships with teachers help infants start on a path of positive feelings of self-worth, trust in others, and peer competence.

In a study of more than 500 children, researchers summarized the importance of a positive, responsive teacher for a child's development of social competence: "The most consistent finding for child care experience [for 24- to 36-month-old children] was that more sensitive and responsive behavior by caregivers was associated with less negative, more positive play with other children" (39, p. 1492).

Socialization Strategies of the Teacher

Teachers can support peer skills and relationships. Take a shy child's hand as you join a group of toddlers playing with blocks. Show a child how to "touch gently." If an infant starts pulling other children's hair, provide an alternative like a doll with hair for the infant. The strategies for supporting prosocial development for children with disabilities are useful for all children, with or without disabilities. These strategies will result in more infant and toddler complex play and fewer behavior problems.

Negative strategies hurt social competence. Interrupting peer play, scolding or punishing peer contact, or separating children are harmful. When teachers use negative strategies, children participate in less complex peer play and teachers rate children as more difficult.

Check Your Understanding 7.4
Click here to check your understanding of the concepts in this section.

DEVELOPMENTAL TRENDS AND RESPONSIVE INTERACTIONS

SOCIAL LEARNING AND DEVELOPMENT WITH PEERS

Capacities: To communicate with peers, be prosocial, play with peers, and manage negative emotions and conflict in peer interaction.

Development	Example
0–4 months (infant)	
• Infants like to look at each other (visual regard). • Infants prefer to look at faces, especially the edges and the eyes. • Infants may cry when they hear other babies cry (contagion).	• After the teacher put Tamika near Sam on a blanket on the floor, Tamika stared intently at Sam.
4–8 months (infant)	
• Infants touch a peer, vocalize to each other, get excited, approach other babies, smile and laugh at each other. • Babies may treat other babies like objects–crawling over them, licking or sucking on them, or sitting on them. They are just learning the difference between people and objects. Infants may poke, push, or pat another baby to see what that other infant will do. They often look very surprised at the reaction they get.	• Amna crawled over to Nadia who was lying on the floor. Touching Nadia's hair, Amna laughed out loud.
8–12 months (infant)	
• Infants may show a peer an object, sit by each other, crawl after and around each other, play chase-and-retrieve games. • Infants smile and laugh at each other. • Infants make sounds to and with each other–may say first words with peers. • Peek-a-boo is a favorite game as infants explore separation: coming and going, in sight and out of sight. • Infants can learn to touch each other gently. • Because infants become more goal oriented at this age, they may push another baby's hand away from a toy or crawl over another baby to get a toy.	• Shamaine peeked around the low toy shelf and saw Carla crawling toward her. Shamaine quickly turned around and crawled away with Carla close behind. • Kai crawled over Bridger's legs to get a toy on the other side of Bridger.
12–18 months (young toddler)	
• Imitation (motor) and interactive turns begin. Toddlers may copy each other–if one gives a toy to another child, the other may imitate. • Toddlers begin to talk to each other. • Toddlers may show concern when other babies are distressed. • Toddlers may take a toy from another child, say "no," push away the other child, clutch toy to self and say "mine." • Toddlers are little scientists at this age, experimenting to see how things work. This affects how they get along with peers. They are constantly doing things to other children to see what response they will get. • Biting may appear as toddlers bite others "to see what happens," to get the toy they want, or to express frustration. Toddlers are on the cusp of communicating well; they may communicate through their mouths in the form of a bite.	• Rashida banged her spoon on the table and soon two others tried it. They seemed to be physically following one another's lead (as in a conversation). • First, Carmen tried pushing Toby away from her rocking horse. When that didn't work, she leaned over and took a bite out of his arm.

Teacher- or Parent-Child Interaction	Environment

0–4 months (infant)

- Hold two babies so they can look at each other.
- Place a few babies on a blanket on the floor so that they can look at and touch each other.

- The arms of teachers provide the best environment.
- Blankets on the floor—put two babies beside each other or so that their toes are touching.

4–8 months (infant)

- Move to music with a baby in each arm.
- While holding one baby in your lap, point out and talk about what another baby is doing.
- Place two babies on their tummies facing a mirror.
- Instead of saying "Don't" or "Stop that" to exploring babies, say "Touch gently." Tell children what you want them to do–model it for them.

- Hang a safety mirror horizontally on the wall, so the bottom is touching the floor.
- Cover an inner tube with soft cloth. Sit two babies in the inner tube so that their feet are touching.

8–12 months (infant)

- Name parts of infants' bodies as two infants sit close to each other:
  Here is baby's eyes
  Here is baby's nose
  Touch the part that sees
  Touch the part that blows
- Place an infant with one other infant (pairs), because more frequent, complex, and intense peer interaction occurs than when a child is near peers.
- Understand that infants are not being "naughty" when they push another child's hand away. Say "Jenny was holding that toy. Let's find you a different toy."

- While feeding, place high chairs so children can see each other.
- Set up cozy corners in the room where infants can "disappear" (but adults can still see them).
- Hang a long wide cloth (so infants won't get tangled in it) from the ceiling. Infants love to crawl around it.
- Place containers with different sizes of blocks in them between two infants. Sit beside them as they begin to explore the materials. Talk about what each one is doing.

12–18 months (young toddler)

- Show young toddlers how to roll down a small hill together.
- Help young toddlers learn each other's names by singing greeting and good-bye songs with the children's names in them: "Here is Tanya, how are you?" and "Here is Henry, how are you?" as you point or touch each child who comes by you or is sitting in your lap.
- Comment on prosocial behavior. Say "You gave him the doll. He likes that!" Toddlers may not understand your words, but they will be able to tell by your tone of voice that you are pleased with them.
- Toddlers will enjoy looking at books together by forming an informal group (this means they move in and out of the group) around the legs, lap, and arms of a favorite parent or teacher.

- Provide a large cardboard box, open on each end. Encourage toddlers to crawl in and out of the box with each other. Windows on the side encourage toddlers to peek at each other through the windows.
- Dolls, trucks, cars, and other play materials encourage interactions among peers.
- They love sand and water and playing with different sizes of safe bottles and balls. When each has his own bin or tub of water or sand, play goes more smoothly.
- Outside, large sandboxes or push toys encourage interactive play.

DEVELOPMENTAL TRENDS AND RESPONSIVE INTERACTIONS (Continued)

Development	Example

18–24 months (toddler)

- Friendships can develop early. Friends are more likely to touch, lean on each other, and smile at each other than are children who are not friends.
- Toddlers imitate each other's sounds and words and talk to each other and begin to communicate with others across more space.
- Toddlers give or offer a toy or food to another toddler.
- Toddlers may get or pull an adult to help another child or will help another child by getting a tissue, for example.
- Toddlers can show kindness for other babies who are feeling distressed. A toddler, however, may assume that what will comfort him will also comfort the distressed child.
- Children take turns, for example, with a ball or jumping up. They may have toddler kinesthetic conversations as they follow a leader in moving around the room—moving in and out of the group, taking turns as leader and follower—as if in a conversation of listening and talking, learning valuable turn-taking skills.
- Pushing, shoving, grabbing, and hitting may occur as children struggle over "mine for as long as I want it" and "yours, but I want it, too." Toddlers may fight over small toys more than large, nonmovable objects.

Paulie looked as if he was waiting by the door for Jamie to appear at the beginning of the day. When Jamie and his mom came in the door, Paulie toddled over and took Jamie's hand, a big smile on his face.

Tanya jumped (half fell) off a board several inches off the ground. Soon three toddlers were standing on the board and half jumping, half stepping off and on the board, enjoying the activity immensely.

24–36 months (toddler)

- Toddler friendship is "proximity seeking," wanting to be close and to show affection, such as smiling, laughing, and hugging. Friends prefer each other as interaction partners. Friendships continue to develop and deepen.
- Toddlers exchange information and can imitate past actions of others.
- Toddlers may congregate and cluster together. When a teacher begins playing with an interesting activity with one child, children often come running from the corners of the room.
- Some toddlers are capable of inventing a variety of ways to help others who are hurt or sad. Some may have an impressive repertoire of altruistic behavior, and if one thing doesn't work, they will try another way.
- Peers work together toward a common goal, with one the leader and one the follower.
- Object, personal space, and verbal struggles can occur. Toddlers also engage in playful exchanges—rough and tumble, run and chase, and verbal games.
- Some children may gain a reputation with peers for aggressive or kind behavior.
- Children become more positive and less negative in their social play between 24 and 36 months.
- Dominance of one child over another can occur.

Maria and Sally played on opposite sides of the small shelf of toys for 30 minutes, peeking over at each other every few minutes, and telling each other, "boat," "my boat," "hi," "want juice," "look at me," and saying each other's names over and over.

When a fire truck went by outside, several toddlers rushed to the window to look.

Josh and Mike pushed, pulled, rolled, and grunted as they worked hard to roll the huge pumpkin from inside to the playground where the toddlers and their teachers were going to cut it open and scoop out all of the seeds.

Teacher- or Parent-Child Interaction	Environment
18–24 months (toddler)	
When inside or outside, nurture toddlers as they come and go to "refuel" emotionally with a special teacher, encouraging several toddlers to sit together beside you or in your lap. Allow toddlers to touch each other gently.	Inside and outside: Provide sand areas large enough for several toddlers and expect them to sit right in the middle of the area.
Encourage several toddlers to make animal sounds together and imitate each other as you show them the pictures in a book.	Blankets on the floor or ground or over a table provide a spot for peers to play.
Ask one child to help another child by getting a tissue, turning the faucet on, opening a door, and so on.	Provide wagons: Pulling or pushing a friend in a wagon will result in squeals of delight.
Encourage kindness with one another. If one toddler cries, ask another what "we" could do to help.	Provide balls and pull-toys that encourage interactive play. Places to jump safely encourage social exchanges.
Encourage two peers to set a table together or sponge it off together after eating. Watch them imitate each other.	Provide musical toys, several of each kind, so children can make beautiful music together. Sometimes one will lead another follow, or vice-versa.
Sing songs, encouraging toddlers to take turns with the actions.	
24–36 months (toddler)	
Create situations where two toddlers need to work together–for example, to roll a pumpkin from one place to another or carry a bucket of "heavy" blocks from inside to outside.	Place hats and easy-to-put-on dress-up clothes in a cozy corner with a big mirror.
Put a Band-Aid on a doll's arm or leg and encourage toddlers to take care of the baby.	Toddlers will enjoy each other as their friends change appearances under a floppy hat or wearing big shoes.
Ask the toddlers, "How can we help Joey—he's sad—he's crying."	Spaces on or under a short loft encourage peer interaction.
Try to change the image of a child who is gaining a reputation for aggression. Keep the child close, show her how to touch gently, and comment on her helpful behavior. Give her an interesting toy that might interest other children to engage with her. Stay close and teach her how to play	Provide several types of dolls as well as safe feeding utensils, blankets, and small beds. Sit close and watch as toddlers pretend to care for their babies.
	Provide open-ended materials such as blocks, and activities that require cooperation such as painting with big brushes and water on outside walls or filling a big bucket with water from smaller containers.
	Large motor equipment such as climbers or rocking boats encourages toddlers to work together toward a common goal: everyone moving to the top of the climber or rocking the boat with everyone in it.

Summary

Infants and toddlers have the capacity to learn to enjoy peers, to play and communicate, to become prosocial, to become friends who enjoy each other's company, and to negotiate conflicts with peers. They become increasingly skilled during the first 3 years of life with parents and teachers who use sensitive, responsive strategies to promote these capacities and children's development.

- Children's unique attributes of temperament and gender influence peer relationships. There are three dimensions of temperament that most impact social development (See Figure 7.1). *Self-regulation* includes focusing attention, controlling one's actions, and expressing strong feelings in a socially acceptable way. The range of emotions is the usual tone of the *child's mood*. The range from *shy to extroverted* describes the child's interest and skills in being with others. Children with an inhibited temperament will need support from parents and teachers to develop confidence and skills to play with peers. Exuberant children, the Tiggers of the world, may be engaged in more joyous as well as conflictual peer interactions. Toddlers' preference to play with children of the same sex may be explained by the "compatible play styles" theory.

- Social development is complex and interesting. Infants and toddlers, during the first 3 years of life, have the capacity to learn to communicate with peers, increase their play skills, develop prosocial behaviors and attitudes, and manage conflict and negative feelings with peers. Children with special needs can gain social skills with typical peers. Toddlers have a variety of communication skills that they use to begin and maintain relationships with other children. They inform; direct; and use sounds, words, and laughter to keep other children involved in play with them. Toddlers often use a gestural language to communicate to each other. Carolee Howes expanded on Parten's work by developing a peer play scale in 1980 and found more sophisticated play at earlier ages. Older infants and toddlers are capable of helping, showing empathy, sharing, and comforting other children. They choose to be with those who are helpful.

- Children learn through responsive, caring relationships with adults. Adults can use many strategies to support peer development. Culture plays a part in whether early peer interactions are valued by adults.

- Program practices can enhance peer development. Peer competence is associated with higher-quality care in programs, smaller group size, lower child-to-teacher ratios, the nature of the child's relationship with the teacher, and the specific strategies used.

Key Terms

continuity of care
dominant
elaborate play schemes
extroverted
exuberant

gender segregation
gestural language
inhibited
prosocial

same-gender play
socially competent
subordinate
theory of mind

Reflections and Resources for the Reader

REFLECTIONS

1. Jaheed and Michael often play with each other in the Early Head Start center-based program. They are becoming increasingly aggressive and try to play away from where teachers are in the room. What would you do if you were a teacher in this room?
2. As a teacher in a center or family child care home, how would you implement a program that emphasizes prosocial development?
3. How can you promote positive social interactions between children who do have special needs and those who do not? Why is this so important to the children, families, teachers, and program?
4. How does your culture influence how you interact with your peer group?

OBSERVATION AND APPLICATION OPPORTUNITIES

1. Use the Developmental Trends and Responsive Interactions chart at the end of this chapter and observe infants and toddlers in a center program. What social behaviors do you see at what age?
2. Observe an infant or toddler with a special need who attends a center or family program. What strategies does the teacher use to encourage peer interactions? What else could she do to promote positive peer interactions?

SUPPLEMENTAL ARTICLES AND BOOKS TO READ

Ashby, N., & Neilsen-Hewett, C. (2012). Approaches to conflict and conflict resolution in toddler relationships. *Journal of Early Childhood Research, 10*(2), 145–161.

Clarke-Stewart, A., & Parke, R. D. (2014). *Social development* (2nd ed.). Hoboken, NJ: Wiley

Gloeckler, L., & Cassell, J. (2012). Teacher practices with toddlers during social problem solving opportunities. *Early Childhood Education Journal, 40*(4), 251–257.

Sloane, S., Baillargeon, R., & Premack, D. (2012). Do infants have a sense of fairness? *Psychological Science, 23*(2), 196–204.

Wittmer, D. S. (2012). The wonder and complexity of infant and toddler peer relationships. *Young Children, 67*(4), 16–25.

Y.-j. Choi, Y. Luo. (2015). 13-Month-Olds' understanding of social interactions. *Psychological Science, 26*(3), 274–283. doi:10.1177/0956797614562452

OTHER RESOURCES

NAEYC: Search for the NAEYC Web site's store and look for the following videos for sale: Social and Emotional Development of Infants and Toddlers DVD. Three videos include *Communication and Learning, Making Friends and Getting Along with Peers*, and *Acquiring Self-Regulation*.

ZERO TO THREE: Go to the ZERO TO THREE Web site and look for information on how to order the Video Series *The Magic of Everyday Moments: Seeing is believing*. Look for the video title: *From Feelings to Friendships*

INTERESTING LINKS

Educarer, Inc. Social Relationships of Infants in Daycare. Phyllis Porter highlights examples of how very young infants interact.

The National Network for Child Care NNCC provides access to articles on a variety of topics including children's social development.

ZERO TO THREE Links to documents on the development of social-emotional skills from birth to 12 months, 12 to 24 months, and 24 to 36 months.

8

Cognitive Learning and Development

LEARNING OUTCOMES

After reading this chapter, you will be able to:

- Identify the unique abilities of infants and toddlers to learn, including current theories

- Describe how infants and toddlers develop and learn, the role of regulation and attachment, approaches to learning, the role of the senses, and special learning needs

- Explain how infants and toddlers develop cognitively within relationships, including cultural influences, the approaches to learning, the concepts they learn, and strategies to support learning

- Describe the qualities of infant-toddler care and learning programs that have an effect on cognitive development

Pearson Education

The newborn, hours after birth, quietly studies her mother's face.

The 1-year-old repeatedly empties little blocks from a plastic container and then drops them back in. Sometimes he concentrates on the blocks, looking at shapes or colors; sometimes he looks to his infant--toddler teacher for her approval.

Bryan, Sherod, and Mikey take the container of musical instruments off the shelf. Each 2-year-old reaches in and takes out a favorite rhythm instrument. Bryan starts to shake his bells. Mikey sings, "Twinkle, Twinkle, Little Star," a song they sometimes sing with their infant--toddler teacher. Within moments the three are parading through the room, playing their instruments and singing.

The child is a unique and capable learner because of her senses and her active brain. As relationship-based theory points out, an adult partner can help the child's interests be deep and wide. The adult helps the child attend, discover, and explore. This chapter describes these important aspects of learning:

- How the brain and senses work.
- The processes of learning.
- The concepts of early learning.
- Engaging environments and responsive interactions.

Infants and toddlers have amazing abilities to learn. They are able to scan the world in a moment and make sense of the mass of information before them. They actively seek information and build their knowledge. Current science and theory suggest that there are several driving forces to learning. First, we are genetically programmed to learn. Our early sensory and social experiences trigger our genes to set in motion attention and organization of information. Our brains take shape as **neurons** connect with each other to create **neural networks** to hold and connect information. Second, the theory of Core Knowledge (1) says we are primed to pay attention to the things in the environment that are most important for survival. Third, infants' and toddlers' learning involves computing the order and frequency of the events around them, social interaction, and the mirroring neuronal system dedicated to learning the most important information (2). Fourth, emotional learning and development build the foundation for learning. We need to admire these early abilities without confusing them with the ways adults learn.

Each Child Is Capable and Unique

We once had an image of infants doing nothing but eating and sleeping. Now, the word we most often hear used in describing newborns is "Amazing!" Thanks to research on early learning, we know that babies are born with knowledge gained in the womb and that they are actively working to build an understanding of their world in every waking moment. Their sleeping moments are busy, too. Thanks to our ability to look at young brains in action, we know a lot about how the brain is taking in information, working with it, and storing it. Theory and science are coming together in today's studies.

In this section, we usually discuss the properties of gender and temperament that apply to the domain. In the infant and toddler years, gender and temperament do not have a significant effect on learning. Instead, we focus on the senses. The senses are the remarkable entry point for information to reach the child's brain.

The brain perceives all information through the senses. The senses are sight, touch, hearing, taste, smell, **proprioception**, and **vestibular**. Proprioception and vestibular senses will be covered in Chapter 10. In milliseconds, the brain takes in sensory information to the hippocampus near the brain stem. It is quickly sent to the limbic system to be scanned for danger. It is then immediately sent to be stored in the area of the brain that is devoted to that kind of information. It makes connections with similar information already stored in the brain.

To a great degree, a baby's ability to learn depends on her ability to perceive sensory information, then to process it, and make sense of and remember it. In fact, Piaget (3) named the first, newborn stage of learning the *sensorimotor* period, describing the active perceptual work infants do to study faces, to remember smells, and to touch and taste everything they can bring to their lips.

Even in the womb, infants are taking in sensory information such as sounds and light. The synapses in the brain capture and transmit this sensory informa-tion—the muffled sound of their parents' voices, the specific taste of amniotic fluid, and the shifting pressures of their mother's moving body—so that they are born with surprisingly well-organized perceptual systems.

Seeing

The very young infant may gaze with surprising seriousness and intensity. Watch-ing the eyes of very young babies, you can see that they are intent on drinking in all the information the world has to offer and putting the information together to make sense.

Newborns are able to visually follow movement within a distance of 9 to 12 inches, although the focus is a little fuzzy. This provides the newborn with the wonderful ability to look into his mother's eyes as she is feeding him from the breast or another family member's eyes as he cuddles him with a bottle.

In the first months, the baby sees best out of the corner of his eye, using periph-eral vision. He will be most interested in objects that offer high contrasts of light and dark and images that resemble the human face (4, 5). By 3 months of age, infants are looking straight ahead and showing interest in their own hands. They enjoy the movement of mobiles twirling slowly above them as they practice using their two eyes together, learning to focus on an object and fuse the images entering each eye. If the eyes are not aligned–some people call them "crossed"—the baby will have "double vision" and will stop using one eye to clear up the image. If one or both eyes do not work properly, the connections between the eye and the brain may not develop. By 6 months of age, the infant's range of vision has stretched to focus on greater distances; by 9 months, he can see as well as an adult at both close range and distances (6). The sequence of visual development is illustrated in Figure 8.1.

Edges and Lines

Although infants are highly interested in other human beings, they also spend quite a lot of time sorting out the pieces of the environment. Infants are sur-rounded by an endless number of colors, shapes, and noises. In order to learn, they must figure out which of these deserve their attention and which can be ignored. One of their first tasks is to organize the images they see and the sounds they hear into a recognizable and understandable order. Using their vision, very young infants study images with high contrasts between light and dark areas, and their eyes travel along the edges of objects as they learn where one object ends and one begins (8, 9).

FIGURE 8.1 **Vision milestones.**

Age	Visual Ability
Birth to 2 months	Sees best at 9 to 12 inches Sees best out of the corner of the eye Loves to look at your face Likes objects with strong contrasts in light and dark Can follow slow movement Eyes are sometimes uncoordinated
2 to 6 months	Begins to recognize objects as one image Looks at own hands Uses vision to reach for objects May stare at anything interesting Looks in mirror Recognizes bottle
6 to 8 months	Sees all colors Sees as well as a teenager May touch self in mirror Turns head to see object Likes certain colors
9 to 12 months	Can see small objects such as cereal pieces Is developing depth perception Can follow fast movements
12 to 18 months	Can do simple shape puzzles Interested in pictures and books Recognizes own face in mirror
18 to 36 months	Can focus near and far Points and gestures for certain objects Scribbles, sometimes in imitation

Based on: Morgan Stanley Children's Hospital of New York–Presbyterian. (n.d.). Age appropriate vision milestones. Retrieved from http://childrensnyp.org/

Moving Objects

Babies combine their interest in edges and lines with an interest in movement to figure out what makes up a single object. They quickly learn that an object that appears to be one single entity—given its visual edges—should move in space in one piece. The movement may be an important part of figuring out what makes a single object. For example, the cover of a book may have a title on a banner (with edges of its own) and a picture of a teddy bear (with its own defining edges). However, when the book is lifted and carried, the edges of the whole book move together. Here, the movement helps define the object (10).

Hearing

Infants are able to hear even before they are born. Newborns recognize sounds that are already familiar to them. Using particular patterns of sucking on specially designed pacifiers, newborn babies will suck harder and longer to hear voices similar to their mother's voice, which they hear in the last few months of gestation through the walls of the womb. Newborns demonstrate through their sucking on special pacifiers that they prefer to listen to the language that they heard prenatally. They even prefer to hear familiar passages of stories that their mothers had repeatedly read aloud during the pregnancy (11, 12).

Hearing milestones, as shown in Figure 8.2, are observed in relation to the baby's attention to language. Beginning at birth, babies turn toward a sound. They pay attention to sounds in the environment, such as caregivers talking quietly to them. Between 4 and 8 months of age, infants understand a few words such as "bye-bye" or "no." They will coo, babble and imitate sounds. Between 8 and 12 months, they begin to intentionally use simple words such as "mama" or "dada."

FIGURE 8.2 Hearing milestones.

Age	Hearing Ability
Birth to 2 months	Can hear many sounds Prefers human speech Startles at loud sounds Can be soothed by soft sounds Turns head toward familiar voice
2 to 6 months	Looks toward new sounds Responds to different tones of voice Enjoys toys that make sounds May babble repeated sounds "ba-ba-ba" Frightened by loud noises
6 to 8 months	Is very interested in human voices Looks for the source of a sound Babbles Responds to own name Recognizes simple, common words
9 to 12 months	Shows interest in telephone Understands many words Looks at pictures as adult describes them Points to pictures when named Sometimes follows one-step directions
12 to 18 months	Enjoys playing with sounds Uses a few words, maybe a few words in a sentence Points to body parts when asked Follows directions without being shown
18 to 24 months	Understands yes/no questions Understands simple phrases Enjoys hearing stories Will understand your use of color words
24 to 36 months	Understands size words Understands action words

Based on: Spectrum Health. (2009). *Hearing milestones.* Retrieved from https://www.spectrumhealth. org.

Touch

The skin is the largest organ in the body and infants are very sensitive to touch. Infants use touch for comfort, for stimulation, and to learn about the world. They suck on objects, feel them with their hands, and kick at them with their feet. Early studies of babies in institutions demonstrated that although babies may be fed adequate nutritional matter, if they are not held and touched they may actually die (13). Lack of experience with being touched is identified as one of the factors that cause the brains of maltreated children to be underdeveloped (14).

Touch has many beneficial effects. A massage of moderate pressure can reduce heart rate, increase attention, and help premature infants gain weight. It affects hormones, too. Massage lowers cortisol and adrenalin, and increases oxytocin (15). Some intensive care nurseries use touch with premature infants. In a practice called *kangaroo care*, parents hold their premature infant in skin-to-skin contact on their chests for several hours a day. Studies show these babies regulate their heart rate and breathing sooner, sleep longer, grow faster, and maintain their body temperature. Their brain activity seems to show contentment and the creation of synapses (16). They score higher on developmental tests at 6 months. Earlier studies showed that premature infants given gentle massage for 10 days, while still in the neonatal care intensive unit, increased their weight gain by nearly 50 percent more than babies not receiving massage (17). Mothers and fathers who are taught to give baby massages benefit as well. They are more sensitive to their baby's cues and at 3 months provide a better home environment.

▶▶▶ OBSERVATION INVITATION **8.1**

Pearson Education

❓ **Think about the effects of touch in this picture. Click on the icon to answer a question about the photo.**

Smelling and Tasting

The sense of smell develops quickly in the newborn and seems to be used to help the baby recognize his mother. In a series of studies, 2-day-old babies could not differentiate a pad soaked with their mother's breast milk from a clean pad or one soaked with another mother's milk. By 5 days, babies show significantly more interest in the pad with their mother's milk than in the clean pad. On the sixth day of life, babies turned their heads to keep their faces near their mother's milk-soaked pad rather than that of another new mother (18). It is possible that smell has some role in the development of attachment in both the baby's and the adult's experience. Babies quickly learn the shampoo or cologne scents of their parents and are more easily comforted by blankets or stuffed animals that carry familiar smells. The combination of smell and other senses used together probably help us develop a more accurate understanding of the world around us, a sort of sensory redundancy. This means we are able to take in different sensory information about the same experience and the extra information helps pull together a more accurate mental image.

At birth, babies are able to taste sweet, sour, and bitter. They prefer sweet tastes and will bring their hands to their mouths when given something sweet in the first weeks of life. Some cultures—such as those in Egypt, Mexico, Jamaica, and India—give newborns sweet-tasting liquids to help them stay calm and sleep. Breast milk is also very sweet. Although most babies do not taste salt until about 4 months, studies show that babies with a family history of hypertension are able to taste salt at 2 days—and they prefer it to other tastes. These studies suggest that salt sensitivity may be related to a predisposition to hypertension.

Babies show highly individual differences in their taste preferences. Some infants welcome the introduction of new foods at about 6 months of age; others demonstrate very clearly their preference for staying with the familiar. It is unclear if these differences are related to how babies taste differences, or whether it has more to do with their temperament and a desire to take risks versus keep everything pretty much the same.

Amodal Learning

Babies use their senses together. Despite this, we tend to think about them as individual modes of getting information. Babies are capable of this amodal or multimodal learning from birth. They are able to take in information through one sense and translate it into usable information for another sense. This happens even when the second sense had never been exposed to the object. They are also able to combine information from two or more senses.

Meltzoff and Moore (19) found evidence that infants can translate or transfer information from one sensory mode to another. They gave babies a rubber nipple to suck without letting the baby see the nipple. Some babies were given a smooth nipple; some were bumpy. After a few minutes of sucking, the baby was shown both the smooth and bumpy nipples. The babies consistently chose to look at the nipple that they had just felt in their mouth, as though recognizing it, although they had never seen it.

Babies also have expectations that their senses will provide them with coherent information. They want the information from their eyes to match the information from their ears. At 3 months, babies will look with interest at a video of their mother speaking while they hear her voice. However, they are distressed at the sight of their mother's face with someone else's voice coming from it or a picture of another woman with their mother's voice coming from it (20). This coordinated use of senses has not been well studied, but it may be one of the most powerful tools babies use as they explore and master their environment.

Check Your Understanding 8.1
Click here to check your understanding of the concepts in this section.

Knowing the Child

The senses are the gateway for learning. The young brain is prepared to work quickly and effectively with the sensory information. This section describes how the brain does the work of cognition. Core Knowledge is a theory that suggests that our genes have evolved to direct our attention to the most important parts of the environment. Young brains compute how often and in what order events occur. They have special mirror brain cells or neurons that create neuronal networks dedicated to learning about people, language, and their own bodies. These mental mechanisms begin to develop processes for thinking such as executive function and the approaches to learning.

Core Knowledge

Core Knowledge (21) is a theory that says as infants we are most likely to learn the things that are important for our survival and evolution as a species. Our genes seem to store some basic knowledge about the world—and what is important to know. Core Knowledge is about what we learn. Any environment is a display of lights, sounds, and shapes for a young infant. How do infants focus on what is important and filter out all the other information? Knowledge of how the most basic aspects of their world works serves their survival. Early childhood professionals build that knowledge with language and experiences supporting the child's inborn interest. For infants, (in the language of Core Knowledge) the most important elements of their environment are **objects**, **agency**, **spatial information**, **number**, and **social groups**. We'll discuss each of these in the following sections.

Objects

Infants have an idea about how objects behave. They know within months that objects stay in one piece and move as a whole. They are surprised in scientific studies if a solid object breaks into pieces and the pieces travel in different directions. They expect objects to obey gravity and are surprised if an object seen sitting on a table stays in the air if the table is removed. They know objects travel in a smooth arc in space. Objects can't travel through solid boundaries or occupy the same space as other objects. Infants and toddlers learn more about objects by having many opportunities to handle and explore a variety of materials.

Agency

Toddlers understand that people act with a sense of agency, an intention to achieve goals. In a variety of studies, toddlers would observe an adult trying to do something intentionally and also accidentally. For example, a young man with his hands full of books tries unsuccessfully to open a cupboard. One of the books falls. The toddler watching from nearby picks up the book and gives it to the man. He understands the man's intentions. Another toddler watches the man throw a book on the ground and the child leaves it there. He also understands the intention of that action. Infants and toddlers will be more interested in what the people around them are doing than in anything else.

Spatial Information

Toddlers will use spatial information to orient themselves in a room. For example, they will remember that a toy was hidden by the long wall rather than the square wall long before they are able to use what seem to be more obvious cues such as the color of the wall.

Number

Infants and toddlers seem to have an inherent understanding of number. At five months, infants watch two dolls being placed behind a screen. They watch one being removed. The screen is removed and two dolls are still there! The infants are surprised. They can tell the difference between larger and smaller amounts when the ratio is 2:1 at around 9 months. Build on their interest in numbers by counting up to three or five and using mathematical words such as more/less, big/small, and long, short.

 Watch this video to see how a study is conducted on an infant's early awareness of number. What are the researchers observing in the young infants?

https://www.youtube.com/watch?v=7uh8FkR_4OU

Social Group

Finally, even very young infants prefer to look at people who are "like them" in skin color or language. At only a few weeks, American infants prefer to hear English spoken with their regional accent. This serves survival in helping vulnerable young infants to turn to those most invested in their survival. If infants live in a multi-racial society, they will be equally interested in people of each race in their daily lives.

Learning is Computational and Social and Uses a Network of Mirror Neurons

Infants and toddlers are able to notice the frequency and patterns of events in their environment. This is most noticeable in how they decode language. They are also able to use this skill to predict the sequence of events (Papa keeps saying, "I'm gonna getcha." Then he tickles my tummy. Or when Mama puts me in the high chair and puts on my bib, I'm going to eat.) Infants use social interactions with adults to direct their attention. Imagine an adult showing a 2-year-old a friend's new baby. "Look, Mia. Jorge is so tiny. Feel how soft his hand is. Be very gentle. We'll use quiet voices so we don't startle him." The adult is using his voice and body to show Mia how to act around a newborn. His words and voice keep Mia's attention focused and her behavior contained. Finally, learning happens through a network of mirror neurons. Mirror neurons are brain cells that work in sets. As some cells perceive an action, the area in the brain that would perform the action also fires. It is as though these cells are able to make the body feel like an active mirror. When an infant sees his mother smile, his neurons perceive that smile. An additional part of the network experiences what it would feel like to smile himself. The brain works with an ongoing awareness of self and other. We are always connected. This is how the brain manages to learn through observation and imitation (22).

Regulation, Attention and Executive Function

In Chapter 6, we described regulation as part of emotional and cognitive learning and development. Regulation is the ability to manage one's physical and emotional reactions to internal and external events. In infancy, regulation relies on the help of an adult. The child's ability to self-regulate grows during the first three years and we are still working on it as adults. Regulation serves learning through attention. By managing her reactions, the child can be alert and focused. Three attention systems work together for learning. One helps the young child stay alert, a second will orient to sensory information, and the third keeps focused on an experience despite distractions (23).

Together, these growing abilities in regulation and attention develop into the most important brain activity for learning, **executive function (EF)**. Executive function is the brain's ability to use memory, plan, stay focused, process information, and filter out distractions. The basic processes of EF are built in the first 3 years of life. They grow and mature during preschool and childhood. You may not see a lot of higher level thinking in toddlers but you will see parts of EF. These are **working memory**, **self control**, and **mental flexibility** (24).

Working memory: the ability to hold information and use it. For example, a 2-year-old is trying to stuff a long string of beads into a canister. He is very focused. His friend comes by and shows him a photograph of her new dog. He looks at it and says, "Pretty goggie." Then, he turns back to his bead and canister project because he held it in his memory.

Self control: enables us to set priorities and resist impulsive actions or responses. For example, a toddler accidentally knocks down a friend by running past. They both go down. The downed girls raises her hand to hit the runner, stops herself, and says, "You bumped me!"

Mental flexibility: helps us to sustain or shift attention in response to different demands or to apply different rules in different settings. For example, as a group of 2-year-olds enters the classroom from the play yard, they start using their "indoor voices."

Approaches to Learning

As infants and toddlers are developing EF, they are also evolving other cognitive skills. These skills are often called *Approaches to Learning*. They describe how children learn. Approaches to Learning are defined in many ways. In this text, we include attention, memory, curiosity, information gathering, problem solving, and persistence through frustration. Attention and memory have already been discussed but are included here as part of the approaches to learning.

Attention

Attention is the ability to focus on one interaction or experience without being easily distracted. Self-regulation helps the infant use executive function and effortful control (25). Attention is the first step in learning.

Memory

Working memory describes the ability to take in new information while holding known information in mind. It seems that younger infants use several signals such as place, context, and other connections to "chunk" information in order to use it at a later time. For example, 20-month-old infants were exposed to a novel, three-step sequence in one of three ways—watching, imitating, or learning—and tested for recall in 15 minutes. Then they were retested in 1, 2, and 3 days or 1, 2, and 3 months. The more in-depth the exposure to the task, the better the recall over time (26). Even very young babies show the ability to remember actions from a week before. Infant and toddler teachers will begin to notice that young infants remember how they played with a toy earlier in the day. Older infants and toddlers may remember where a favorite toy is kept.

Curiosity

Curiosity is the infant's and toddler's desire to explore and understand himself, the people around him, and his world. Bowlby (27) described it as the balancing system to the attachment relationship. Infants have a huge, inborn desire to explore. As they become mobile, that could be dangerous. Imagine an infant crawling off into the jungle or busy traffic! The attachment relationship balances the desire to explore. The infant has an equally strong desire to be near her attachment figure. This stops her from moving out of visual contact with the person most likely to keep her safe. The infant and toddler teacher promotes curiosity by having a safe environment, interesting and responsive materials. She follows the child's interests and adds rich language.

 Watch this video to see an older 2-year-old follow his curiosity about a toy, water, and air. Note your observations of the boy's actions driven by curiosity.

Information Gathering

Infants and toddlers gather information through their senses and their magnetic neuronal networks. Magnetic neural networks are areas of the brain that are dedicated to finding, storing, and organizing information on a certain interest. For example, a magnetic, neural network is dedicated to learning about communication, another to movement. Infants and toddlers gather information guided by inherited interest of Core Knowledge, their experiences, and their interactions. They gather information about themselves, others, and the world. They learn about their bodies, movement and sound. They learn about the rules and values of their culture, their language, how emotions are expressed and daily routines. They learn about how the objects in their world work, about weather and time. Each bit of information is stored in a dedicated brain cell and connected to hundreds or thousands of other neurons.

Problem Solving

Infants and toddlers are constantly solving problems. How do I roll over if my arm won't move? How do I use this spoon to eat? How do I get the toy I want, now? The world seems to provide many opportunities to try and think, maybe get help, and solve problems. Adults support problem solving by providing encouragement, helping just enough without solving the problem itself, and sometimes just by staying nearby and interested.

Some of the most frequent and natural problem-solving opportunities occur during social interactions. Toddlers are naturally social, but they aren't equipped with all the social skills they need. Moments of conflict can be opportunities to teach problem-solving skills (28): "You can tell Bahn you're hurt"; "Bahn, you can tell her she can have the car when you're done." Infant-toddler teachers, family child care providers, and home visitors can all support this intersocial problem solving.

Persisting Through Small Frustrations

In many ways persistence brings us back full circle to regulation. When a toy becomes too predictable, it is no longer fun. If a parent comes every time the infant makes a sound, calling the parent would require no effort. What engages learners best is a challenge whose solution is possible but not simple. In order to see such a challenge through to solution, the infant or toddler must be able to tolerate some frustration. The adult partner assists in this by helping the child stay focused and excited as well as able to pause and gather more information. In an intriguing twist, researchers wondered whether the child's competence affected the mother's investment and satisfaction in supporting her child. They looked at children at 6 and 18 months to measure their ability to complete physical and social tasks through some frustration. They also measured the mother's satisfaction and sense of competence as a parent. Competent infants had confident

OBSERVATION INVITATION **8.2**

Click the play button to watch the video of a young toddler putting blocks into a shape box and answer related questions. What problems does this task present to the child? Which strategies does the child use?

mothers. Less competent infants had less satisfied mothers. This might have been because the mothers had expectations that were too high or fewer skills to support their children's efforts. Either way, it suggests the possibility of a transactional nature to this approach to learning (29).

Special Needs

Infants have great capacities for learning, but there are also great challenges. Developmental disabilities and environmental risks can have wide variation in their effect on development.

Insults to the brain, before or after birth, may delay or impair learning, social relationships, communication, or motor development. Some infants have biological risks from exposure to drugs, alcohol, or maternal stress hormones in utero. Sensory impairments may challenge a child's ability to perceive information from the world. Established conditions such as Down syndrome, cerebral palsy, autism, premature birth, or low birth weight may affect the child's ability to process or use the information in the environment.

Very young children are particularly vulnerable to the effects of environmental difficulties such as exposure to violence, a parent's mental illness, poor nutrition, and low educational achievement in the home. Large numbers of young children in our society are subject to abuse and neglect, are born to adolescents, or experience family disruption and/or foster care placement. Lead exposure through toys and foods from other countries may have harmful effects on infants. In the United States, lead has been restricted from paint and gasoline for decades.

These children may be particularly well served by early intervention. Infant/toddler care and learning programs deliver carefully designed interventions with well-defined goals. Parenting behavior and the child development can improve. Programs that combine child-focused educational activities with explicit attention to parent-child interaction patterns and relationship building appear to have the greatest impacts (30).

> *People's beliefs about their abilities have a profound effect on those abilities. Ability is not a fixed property; there is a huge variability in how you perform. People who have a sense of self-efficacy bounce back from failures; they approach things in terms of how to handle them rather than worrying about what can go wrong. (Albert Bandura)*

Infant-toddler teachers are able to provide rich learning environments for each child. You individualize the way experiences are offered. Strong observation skills help the teacher understand how the child perceives and processes information. Most important are your own interactions and relationship with the child. Here are some additional considerations for planning how to individualize learning activities for each infant or toddler:

- Which materials best meet the needs and interests of each child?
- How can I arrange the materials and equipment to encourage each child's participation?
- How can the activity be more accessible to each child?
- What can I do so children can come and go from the activity at their own pace? (31)

A more detailed description of what infants and toddlers learn, and what adults can do to support that learning, can be found in the Developmental Trends and Responsive Interactions chart.

Check Your Understanding 8.2
Click here to check your understanding of the concepts in this section.

Learning Through Adult-Child Relationships

Very young children learn almost everything within their relationship with an adult. They have the mental model of an adult keeping them safe even when they explore on their own. In this section, we will describe two theories of how children learn with adults. The first is learning through imitation. The theory is called *action representation* (32). The second is the idea that we learn through the lens of our culture because we learn through adults and older children. This is called *the socio-cultural theory* (33). Then we will describe some of the concepts that infants and toddlers master with their active minds.

Action Representation

Imitation is the primary way infants and toddlers learn. As described earlier, there is a neuronal network in the child's brain that perceives the action of another person. At the same time, the parts of the brain that would produce those same actions are activated in the child's brain. This gives the child the ability to imitate, if she has the muscle control to do this. Newborns, only one hour old, imitated a scientist sticking out his tongue in a classic, early study of imitation (34).

 Watch this video to see an infant, only ten minutes old, imitate his father's tongue thrust. Explain how this is action representation.

https://www.youtube.com/watch?v=l0N6mIpoN3M

Imitation, through the neuronal mirroring network, is how very young infants are wired to imitate. Imitation is the most powerful process for connecting with others and for learning. The brain is absorbing information. The infant stores memories of these sensations of actions. The action becomes a representation in the brain. These memories become refined as the child actually performs the actions and alters the mental models.

Adults model for very young children all the time. It comes naturally to us. And very young children imitate almost everything we do. In thinking about strategies, we have two ideas. First, be a good observer of when young children are imitating. Set good examples for healthy habits, kindness, reading, and all activities related to well-being. Second, do not overuse modeling. When toddlers are figuring out how to do puzzles, stack blocks, or dress themselves, give them time to struggle. They will learn so much from the process of trying.

Socio-Cultural Theory

Lev Vygotsky (35) was a Russian psychologist in the early twentieth century. His work did not become well known in the United States until the 1970s, forty years after his death. However, his theories of learning continue to influence our understanding today. These include the **tools of the mind**, the **zone of proximal** development (ZPD), and the critical role of learning from adults and older children through **scaffolding**.

Tools of the Mind

Vygotsky's tools of the mind are basically what we now call approaches to learning. He called attention, memory, and perception the elementary tools. A very important contribution is the idea that these tools, in fact everything we see and learn, is social and influenced by our culture. One example is the way we ask questions even of babies. "Where is your nose? Where are your eyes?" We live in a question asking culture. We use direct questions as a way to teach. A study in North Africa found children unwilling to answer direct questions, because in their culture people do not ask questions to which they know the answers. This kind of question would be seen as a challenge or a trick. In some cultures, although a 1-year-old might well know where her nose is, she would not be asked such a question because the role of children is to listen and obey adults, not to converse with them (36).

Zone of Proximal Development and Scaffolding

The ZPD is the set of information or skills that is beyond what the child knows but within what a child could learn and understand with support from a more knowledgeable person. For example, as an American 2-year-old is fiercely dressing himself, he may become frustrated when both legs go into the same pant leg. The infant and toddler teacher may offer the trick of starting out with the pants laid out and putting a foot into each pant leg. With that one bit of assistance, the child can successfully get any pair of pants on at any time. To return to the idea of learning being influenced by culture, some cultures would not value that independence. The adult may offer a lesson in being more cooperative in being dressed by an adult.

 Watch this video to see Sue Bredekamp discuss the importance of learning about culture for children and for the people who work with them. How does she describe socio-cultural theory?

Scaffolding is the way the adult structures their contributions to give the child just enough help for the child to solve the problem or take the next step alone. For example, say a young toddler is struggling with a puzzle piece. The adult could take the piece and show the child how it fits but that would be solving the problem for the child. Instead, the adult could say, "Try turning the piece around" and gesturing turning something with her hands at the same time. That could provide just enough information for the child to try a new strategy. He might even try it again on the next challenging puzzle piece.

Learning Concepts

> Arman yelled "In!" as he pushed hard to make a large puzzle piece fit in the hole in the puzzle. He first tried a strategy that had worked many times in the past: After tasting the piece, he placed it near the hole and pounded it with his fist. He then turned the piece one way and then another until it finally dropped in the hole. With a big sigh of contentment, he looked at his great accomplishment. Then he pulled out the piece and started all over again.

This little moment of activity is filled with learning. Arman is using and learning language, practicing cause and effect in pushing the puzzle piece, working on spatial relationships between the puzzle piece and the hole, hypothesizing and trying strategies to make the piece fit, and demonstrating how his curiosity and his image of himself as a learner contribute to his ability to persist in the task even when it is hard. The major discoveries of infancy discussed here are object permanence, cause and effect, use of tools, use of space, learning language and literacy, developing mental concepts and categories, and beginning to understand numbers. Other important discoveries include the natural world, symbolic thinking and play, theory of mind, and learning about their own culture.

Object Permanence

Babies discover that people and things continue to exist whether or not you are with them and can see them. They are making discoveries about the permanence of objects and persons. Infants have many experiences with their parents and infant and toddler teachers coming and going but always reappearing. This helps babies develop an understanding of the permanence of the existence of these people. The classic demonstration of object permanence involves hiding a toy under a cloth as the infant is watching. Very young babies behave as though the toy has disappeared and make no attempt to retrieve the toy. Somewhere around 8 months, however, the infant will lift the cloth with every expectation that the toy will be waiting (37). We now know that infants as young as three months have a sense of object permanence.

 Watch the video of a 3½-month-old infant demonstrating object permanence in scientist Rene Baillargeon's lab. What do you observe the infant doing that demonstrates object permanence?

https://www.youtube.com/watch?v=hwgo2O5Vk_g

Cause and Effect

Infants learn that people cause things to happen and that they can cause people to do things. Infants have numerous intrapersonal and interpersonal experiences with cause and effect. For example, an empty tummy makes a baby cry. The cry brings a caregiver with a loving cuddle and a warm bottle. Sucking the milk in the bottle causes the baby to feel comfortable and happy again. One event follows another in such a predictable way that the baby begins to have a sense of one event causing another to happen.

Materials and experiences provide many opportunities for infants and toddlers to discover and practice cause and effect. Babies need materials that respond to their actions. They need to be able to make things happen. Paper can be crumpled or torn. Toy pianos play notes when a key is pushed or a pad is kicked, jack-in-the-box toys that pop up when a button is pushed or a lever flipped, balls that roll away when pushed, blocks that make sounds when squeaked all teach the baby about cause and effect. And give her a sense that she is someone who can make things happen! Many of the new electronic toys are not responsive—once turned on, they provide a light and sound show to a passive baby. It might be entertaining, but infants and toddlers will not be learning about their own efficacy in the world from that kind of toy.

People's beliefs about their abilities have a profound effect on those abilities. Ability is not a fixed property; there is a huge variability in how you perform. People who have a sense of self-efficacy bounce back from failures; they approach things in terms of how to handle them rather than worrying about what can go wrong. (Albert Bandura)

Use of Tools

Infants learn some things about the use of tools through their interactions with people. They watch people use tools and see that people can be used as tools. If you cry, someone will come and comfort and feed you. If you point, someone will reach the stacking rings for you. Toddlers learn to ask adults for help in tasks they find frustrating by pointing, looking from the person to the object and back again, and using sounds and language.

Toddlers use tools when they use forks and spoons to feed themselves, when they climb on a chair to reach a shelf, or when they use paintbrushes or markers to create pictures. They use tools when they use a wooden spoon to bang on a pot or use a push toy to help them take their first steps.

Use of Space

Infants and toddlers learn that people have spatial relationships with each other and with the things in the world. People move through space in predictable ways, their bodies exist as a single entity, and they appear bigger when they are close and smaller when they are far away. Babies also have many opportunities to watch adults move objects around in space, put wallets in purses, cups in cupboards, and milk cartons in refrigerators. Babies bring this experience of watching adults to their own explorations of the world. The process of putting one thing into another can be endlessly fascinating to babies. Any collection of objects can become interesting when they are put into and dumped out of a bucket. Shape boxes that allow infants or toddlers to put a toy through a hole shaped like the toy will keep them trying over and over. For infants and toddlers, crawling, walking, and climbing are constant lessons in spatial relationships.

Language and Literacy

Language and literacy learning are such important aspects of development that they have their own chapter in this text. However, in any list of what infants learn from and about others, it is essential to include language and literacy. As mentioned earlier, babies hear the sounds of language even before they are born. Infants quickly learn to use the sounds of language in turn-taking interactions with adults. They recognize and begin to understand words by listening to all of the exchanges around them—but best of all, by their parents and teachers responding personally to them in little one-on-one, face-to-face conversations.

Numbers

Core Knowledge theory says that number is of basic interest to infants. The National Council of Teachers of Mathematics (38) includes references to infants in its standards for pre-K to grade 2. It points out that the foundation for mathematical learning is established in the earliest years, through ordinary experiences such as a parent counting crackers or cutting a sandwich into squares or triangles. Everyday life can provide infants and toddlers with many casual, offhand opportunities to understand the basics of mathematics.

In addition to the study of hiding one or two dolls described earlier, infants have further demonstrated their understanding of numbers. Researchers showed a baby a ball and then put it in a box, out of sight. They added a second ball and told the baby, "Get the ball." Babies would reach into the box two times and retrieve both balls. They never reached in just once, never more than twice (39).

Could a lot of this just be memory? Some researchers think that infants are not really counting but are using perceived information such as overall size and surface area to understand differences in numbers. Nonetheless, infants do demonstrate a variety of early mathematical skills. Six-month-olds can pick out one set of many items from another if they have a 2-to-1 ratio. Eleven-month-old infants can tell the difference between visual displays of items that increase or decrease in number. See Chapter 13 for ideas for promoting children's understanding of numbers.

Categories

Categories are groups of objects, people or experiences that share some characteristics. Categorizing is a way to organize and manage information in the brain. If every piece of information had to be filed separately in the brain, the world would be chaotic. Young toddlers beginning to use language categorize. For example, a 10-month-old had a pet dog. She echoed its bark and called it "va-va." Soon, all four-legged animals were "va-va."

Adults can help young children categorize by using grouping language. "This applesauce is good. You like this food." "Let's stack the blocks." "This color is blue." "Look at all these colors." "This dog is an animal. This cat is an animal, too."

The Natural World

Infants and toddlers are very interested in the natural world. They watch insects and play with sticks, stones and dirt. Streams, ponds, oceans and even water tables teach them about the properties of liquids. They watch plants grow over time. They watch the colors of leaves change and then jump in piles of fallen leaves. They learn about weather and seasons. There is more information about the importance and benefits of being outdoors in Chapter 10 and the curriculum chapters.

Symbolic Play

During the first 3 years of life, infants and toddlers have countless day-to-day experiences with language, with family photographs and picture books, with television, and with toy replicas of houses and cars and other real-life objects. They are constantly exposed to symbols of objects (and people and feelings) being used by adults and older children as meaningfully as they use real objects. By the age of 3, most children have mastered the use of symbols themselves. They use language fluently and creatively. They follow stories told in pictures and they can incorporate models of household objects into their pretend play. It is our use of symbols that allows human beings to communicate, learn, and create.

Stanley Greenspan (40) describes infants as initially being in a *behavior mode*, where being hugged by Mom or actually eating dinner are sources of contentment. As infants become toddlers and move into a *symbolic mode*, they can begin to feel satisfaction from the *knowledge* that "Mom loves me" or *knowing* that dinner is being prepared. As with every aspect of development, the key is in the relationship between the baby and the caregiver:

The shift in modes therefore requires the long-term participation of someone who promotes interaction, who supports ever greater use of signals, who joins in the child's pretend play, who helps the child link the pleasures of relating to the skills of communicating symbolically. The sheer enjoyment of being listened to, the satisfaction of gaining attention through the use of images, motivates the first step in this epochal move. The child delights not only in getting what he wants or having his expectations confirmed, but in letting others know what they are (p. 77).

Researchers have tracked how infants move from interest in looking at a picture to understanding that a picture represents a real thing and, yet, is different from that thing. Five-month-olds were given time to study a doll. They were then shown pictures of that doll and of a new doll. As in other **habituation** studies described in this chapter, the babies demonstrated their familiarity with the real doll by losing interest in its picture. They treated the picture of the real doll exactly as they would have treated the doll itself; they looked longer at the new doll (41). Nine-month-olds, presented with realistic picture books of objects, tried to touch and pick up the object, as though not recognizing that this was a *symbol* of the object. However, by 15 months, American infants with lots of experience with picture books would point to pictures and name the objects, demonstrating some idea of the representation (42).

Within a study of the development of social play, solitary pretend play, and social pretend play in toddlers, Carolee Howes et al. (43) describe a progression of increasingly complex use of symbolization. From about 12 to 15 months, toddlers will use auto-symbolic schemes in which they perform a pretend act aimed at themselves, such as pretending to drink from a cup. Toddlers love to pretend to sleep, smiling and looking at the teacher much of the time, while the teacher says, "Goodnight. Shhhh. Quiet everyone. Jacob's sleeping." Then Jacob jumps up laughing and the teacher says, "Jacob, you're up! Good morning!"—at which Jacob is likely to immediately repeat the routine, over and over. It is easy to see how a responsive adult can support this play and this desire to learn in a young child.

The important thing is not so much that every child should be taught, as that every child should be given the wish to learn. (John Lubbock)

OBSERVATION INVITATION **8.3**

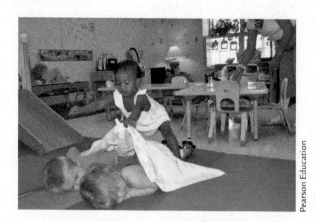

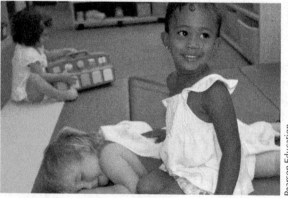

Pearson Education

? Think about symbolic play as you look at this little girl helping her friend prepare for a nap. Click on the icon to answer a question about the photo.

At around 15 to 20 months, in decentered symbolic play, the toddler directs the pretend action to a toy. However, the toy doesn't have it's own intentions in the play (feeds the doll but doesn't say the doll is hungry). At 20 to 25 months, toddlers begin sequencing pretend actions such as waking the doll, feeding her, and bathing her. They play repetitions of familiar routines, such as preparing a meal, eating it, and cleaning up afterward using realistic replications of household objects (44). At 24 to 30 months, toddlers engage in internally directed symbolic play whereby they ascribe agency or intention to the toys (the doll is hungry) and then interact with the toy through a sequence of pretend actions. Over the next several months, the child is increasingly able to simply pretend—to use an object such as a block or a stick to be first a coffee cup and then a set of keys. Less familiar and frequent events may also appear within the stories of pretend play. At 30 to 36 months, in behavioral role-play, toddlers assign roles to their dolls and toys such as being the father or the dog, and the play incorporates the roles.

As toddlers achieve greater use of language, the play becomes more filled with detail and the children have greater capacity to share their interests. Mastery of language and other symbols frees the child to think beyond the concrete experience of the moment.

Respect, Reflect, Relate

Respect: The child's active attempts to understand himself, others, and his environment.

Reflect: On what the child seems to be trying to figure out or accomplish.

Relate: Relate to support learning by

- Providing responsive, meaningful interactions with rich language.
- Providing interesting materials and experiences that respond to the child's actions.
- Expanding on the child's interests and skills.

Theory of Mind

At around 18 months, children begin to understand that other people have thoughts, feelings and desires that are different from their own. Many people believe this coincides with a growing sense of self. In numerous studies, toddlers show they are aware of the intentions of others. In one, the researcher tries to open a cupboard while his hands are full of books. One of the books drops. A toddler playing nearby will almost always pick up the book and hand it to the researcher. However, if the researcher enters a room and throws a book down, the watching toddler will leave it on the floor. In another study, an inept researcher cannot hang a ring of keys on a hook. They keep slipping and falling. A watching toddler will come over and hang the keys for the researcher. The classic theory of mind study involves a toddler coming to believe that the researcher would actually prefer broccoli to crackers.

 Watch this video to see a classic study of theory of mind with researcher Allison Gopnik. How do the children's facial expressions illuminate the thinking behind their actions?

https://www.youtube.com/watch?v=voq590su3m8

STRATEGIES TO SUPPORT COGNITIVE DEVELOPMENT AND LEARNING

Infants and toddlers will learn about themselves, about being in relationships with other people, and many of the basic concepts they need to understand the world. You can assist them with the following strategies:

1. Help infants maintain a quiet, alert state of attention by keeping them in comfortable positions, talking quietly, and looking at or manipulating things together.

2. Help toddlers keep focused and attentive by limiting distractions and interruptions. Express interest in their activities and try to observe and reflect on what you believe they are trying to accomplish.

3. Spark curiosity by offering materials in new ways, such as setting the dolls up in the book corner "reading" books, or the farm animals on a green cloth over blocks creating a gentle hill.

4. Spark curiosity by noticing things and suggesting, "Let's go see what that is!"

5. Support persistence through frustration by offering materials that are challenging enough to be interesting but not impossible, by offering a few choices, by expressing your interest and encouragement, and by sharing the joy children feel as they show you their accomplishments.

6. Support sensorimotor learning by offering play and exploration experiences that provide a variety of sensory modes: sand, water, cornstarch, smelling bottles, and so forth.

7. Help children develop memories by keeping the routine and room arrangement predictable; keep toys where children know to find them. Talk with children about what they did earlier in the day or the day before.

8. Provide many opportunities to categorize, match, sort, compare, and contrast with toys and activities.

9. Encourage problem solving by not stepping in immediately when a problem occurs—for example, if a child can't reach the ball that has rolled behind the slide, ask, "What can we do?" and let the child try to figure it out.

10. Play games like peek-a-boo, read stories about mommies and daddies being gone and coming back, read books with pictures hidden under flaps to encourage the development of object permanence.

11. Provide toys that respond contingently to a child's actions, such as balls, busy boxes, or push lights to encourage the understanding of cause and effect.

12. Provide toys and materials such as stacking cups, rings on a post, little houses, or tunnels to crawl through to encourage understanding of use of space.

13. Provide markers, paint, water, replicas of household tools, play telephones, keys, and so forth, to promote understanding of use of tools.

14. Provide language, ideas, and materials in ways that make the child's play just a little more elaborate and complex, scaffolding the child's play to become richer or more symbolic.

15. Provide toys and language to introduce awareness of shapes, comparative sizes, amounts, numbers, and one-to-one correspondence. Talk about concepts of time such as today, now, later, before, and after.

Consider Culture

The fetus begins learning about his family's culture in the womb. He hears the sounds and rhythms of their language(s). He tastes the flavors of their foods in the amniotic fluid he swallows. He feels the cycles of active and quiet times of his mother's days and nights.

Almost from birth, he is primed to attend to social cues. He will learn how people behave toward family members, children, elders and strangers. He will learn about turn-taking. He will learn what, when and how people eat. He will learn how people express emotions. For the most part, no one will teach him these things. His family might not even be able to describe them. Much of our cultural beliefs, values and rules are invisible to us. Yet infants and toddlers seek them out and learn them.

CULTURE CLOSE UP

Ms. Katika ran a quiet family child care home, offering a rich assortment of experiences. Her assistant Patty loved working there—except for one thing. For example, 2-year-old Rosie chose a tub of large pegs and a board to stick them into. Ms. Katika at first observed and then encouraged her. She gently but firmly kept Rosie there until all 10 pegs were in. Her East Indian belief included building a strong work ethic. Patty believed infants and toddlers should be free to explore. What do you believe and why?

Check Your Understanding 8.3
Click here to check your understanding of the concepts in this section.

Program Practices that Enhance Cognitive Learning and Development

Interest in early learning is greater now than any time in history. Policies and practices are being created by government agencies, school systems, and universities. This is vitally important because policies and funding are needed to bring the best practices to all children. Infant-toddler teachers need training. Infant/toddler care and learning programs need funding to guarantee that staff is qualified, ratios are low, and primary caregiving and continuity of care are in place.

Early Learning Guidelines for Infants and Toddlers

In 2002, President George W. Bush created an initiative for early childhood, *Good Start, Grow Smart.* It required the states to write early learning guidelines for infants and toddlers (ELG/ITs) describing what preschoolers should know and be able to do in language, literacy, and mathematics. Most states chose to write ELGs for each domain including approaches to learning. Many states found both the process of development and the documents so beneficial that they chose to create guidelines articulating what infants and toddlers are learning as well.

ELG/ITs help parents and teachers understand what infants and toddlers should know and be able to do during specific age ranges. Adults need to understand and appreciate what infants and toddlers are learning. Then, they can better support the children's natural curiosity, exploration, and discoveries. ELG/ITs are becoming a basic element of professional development systems.

In 2015, the Office of Head Start published the *Head Start Early Learning Outcome Framework: Ages Birth to Five* (HSELOF) (45). These were developed over the course of several years with a rigorous writing and review process that included many experts in the field. The HSELOF provides goals and learning progressions for approaches to learning, social and emotional development, language and literacy, cognition, and perceptual, motor, and physical development domains. For infants and toddlers the developmental progression is shown for the age ranges of birth to 9 months, 8 to 18 months, and 16 to 36 months.

These guidelines bring what infants and toddlers are learning to life. As an early childhood professional, they are a good addition to your basic training in learning and development. They are helpful for understanding what children are learning and for planning experiences and interactions. It is important to remember that these are just guidelines. They are not a curriculum or an assessment tool.

Curriculum

The curriculum is a written plan that defines what infants and toddlers experience and what they will learn from the experience (46).

> The adult's role is not to teach, but to observe and reflect on what infants/toddlers are experiencing and how they learn—and then to support the process through interactions, their relationship with the child, and provision of experiences in an environment that contributes to the child's success. In high-quality infant/toddler programs, the interests of the child and the belief that each child has a curriculum are what drive practice. The adult role is to discover the infant's curriculum and support its implementation (47).

As part of the effort to make quality part of policies and practices, there is a new focus on curriculum. Some government funded infant-toddler programs and many private programs want to adopt a curriculum that has been proven to be effective. There are many infant and toddler curricula available commercially. Some are tied to a preschool curriculum that has been proven to be effective. For the most part, the infant/toddler curricula do not have the same evidence base. However, we have a rich literature on the best practices for infants and toddlers. We also know a great deal about what they should know and be able to do. A program should review the available curricula and make sure it offers what you need. If it comes with an assessment, that can be helpful. However, the tool will assess what the curriculum teaches or vice versa. You might want to compare the children's goals to a good set of ELGs.

> *Our image is of a child who is competent, active, and critical; therefore a child who may be seen as a challenge and, sometimes, as troublesome . . . To us, the child is a producer of culture, values, and rights, competent in learning and competent in communicating . . . We have to try to organize a school, an infant-toddler center for this child (Carlina Rinaldi).*

Engaging Environments and Responsive Relationships

High-quality infant-toddler programs actively promote children's learning. The results of the National Institute of Child Health and Human Development (NICHD) study on child care demonstrated that child care quality matters (48).

High-quality care for young children is eloquently described by Carlina Rinaldi about Reggio Emilia:

> The infant-toddler care and learning program that meets that child's needs is characterized by engaging environments and responsive relationships. Infants and toddlers need experiences with materials that encourage exploration and discovery. One way to think about materials is to consider what information is offered. Is there something the child can make happen? Can the young infant

handle, look at and mouth the material? Does the material stack, roll, crush, tear, stick, move or somehow give information about any of the concepts described earlier in the chapter? (49)

We also want to think about the adult's responsive interactions. Is the adult helping the child to be alert and attentive? Is the adult using language that adds vocabulary and expands the uses of the material? Is the adult sharing the joy of discovery? Is the adult scaffolding the learning?

Check Your Understanding 8.4
Click here to check your understanding of the concepts in this section.

Summary

- Building a strong foundation for learning occurs in the first 3 years of life. Core Knowledge is a theory that says infants are genetically inclined to attend to the aspects of the environment most likely to be important for survival. Infants and toddlers are able to compute the frequency and order of some events to help them make sense of them. Networks of mirror neurons (brain cells) have infants perceive (use the senses) for an event and at the same time activate the parts of the brain that would be firing if the baby were performing the action.

- All information comes to the brain through the senses. It is then quickly scanned for danger and then sorted into the areas committed to that information. Thousands of connections can be made to similar information. A very important set of processes work together to help children achieve increasingly higher-level thinking by the age 3. These are regulation, attention, and executive function. The higher level thinking skills of executive function include working memory, self-control and mental flexibility. The approaches to learning are a set of cognitive processes that help children learn in all domains. They are attention, memory, curiosity, information gathering, problem solving, and persistence through frustration. Infants and toddlers with special needs may have challenges in learning. Infant--toddler teachers should work with families and early interventionists to find the best strategies to help each child learn.

- Action representation, essentially the mirroring neuronal network, explains how imitation works. Imitation is the most powerful learning tool an infant has. Socio-cultural theory emphasizes the importance of the older partner in a child's learning. The most important elements of this theory are the zone of proximal development, scaffolding, and the tools of the mind. Infants and toddlers create a wealth of knowledge during the first three years of life. Some of the concepts they develop include object permanence, cause and effect, use of tools, use of space, language and literacy, numbers, categories, the natural world, symbolic play, theory of mind, and the rules, beliefs and values of their culture.

- Early Learning Guidelines for Infants and Toddlers (ELG/IT) describe what children should know and be able to do within certain age ranges. They have become an important tool for teachers in understanding learning and planning for individual children. The curriculum is a written plan that defines what infants and toddlers experience and what they will learn from the experience. It is important to choose or develop a curriculum based on a strong understanding of the science of learning and development. The most significant element in a child's learning is a responsive, committed adult partner. The adult engages emotionally with the child and expands on their exploration and discovery. Engaging environments invite the child to move, touch, taste, toss, handle, build, pretend and follow all of their questions and wonder.

DEVELOPMENTAL TRENDS AND RESPONSIVE INTERACTIONS

COGNITIVE LEARNING AND DEVELOPMENT

Infants and toddlers learn about themselves, others, and the world through their own unique abilities, by utilizing the cognitive tools of learning.

Development	Example
0–4 months (infant)	
• Infants follow a moving object visually. • Infants cry to bring an adult to comfort or feed them. • Infants will look around the room with interest. • Infants begin to reach for a toy. • Infants notice that their arms or legs made something happen and will repeat the movement. • Infants recognize familiar people and objects. • Infants begin to bring objects to mouth.	Megan lifted her head, resting on her arms as she lay on the blanket. With a serious expression on her face, she watched the teachers and children around her. Willie kicked the mobile hanging over him and made it wiggle. He stopped, looked at it, and then kicked some more, watching the mobile to see if anything might happen.
4–8 months (infant)	
• Infants like to examine toys. • Infants like to make toys do something—make a sound, put one inside another. • Infants imitate adult expressions and gestures. • Infants turn toward a sound to see where it came from. • Infants look for toys they dropped.	Angela is interested in everything. She watches her friends and then looks at the teacher and smiles. Roger reaches out to touch a dangling toy. When it swings, making a sound, he reaches out to do it again.
8–12 months (infant)	
• Infants like to take the pieces of a toy apart and put them back together. • Infants like toys that do something when you touch them, pull them, bang them. • Infants begin very simple pretend play, such as lifting a cup to their mouth. • Infants like to find small toys hidden under a cloth or cup. • Infants like to pick up and examine a tiny item like a Cheerio. • Infants point to objects, knowing you can also see them.	Charlie loves to take each plastic animal out of the bucket and look at it. When the bucket is empty, he tosses it aside. Aliya likes the push button and the swinging doors on the busy box but can't work all the mechanisms yet. Her teacher expresses surprise with Aliya when the doors pop open and every once in a while shows her how to work another of the knobs.
12–18 months (young toddler)	
• Young toddlers like to use their mobility to explore—crawling, walking, climbing, and running. • Young toddlers enjoy playing with sand, water, and dough with different kinds of tools. • Young toddlers are interested in spatial relationships in puzzles and pegboards. • Young toddlers use tools such as keys or telephones in their pretend play. • Young toddlers enjoy looking at books and naming objects, animals, or body parts.	Alexis and Dan are gleeful about being on two feet. They follow each other around, one daringly balancing his way up the sloping surface with the other right behind. Sometimes they both try to squeeze into the area under the slide. Meredith loves to cuddle on her teacher's lap, pointing at pictures in books while her teacher names the animals or asks her to find a certain animal.

Teacher- or Parent-Child Interaction	Environment

0–4 months (infant)

- Slowly move a small toy from one side to another while the infant follows it with his gaze.
- Respond quickly to the baby's cries.
- Provide quiet time for infants to look at what is happening around them. Talk about what they see.
- React to infants' expressions with clear, even exaggerated facial expressions and language.

- Arrange the space so that infants can see some activity but still be protected.
- Provide a few interesting things to look at—small toys on the floor during tummy time, dangling toys when infants are on their backs.
- Provide nonbreakable mirrors.

4–8 months (infant)

- Hold the infant in your arms as you walk around, looking at things and talking about them.
- Sit nearby and talk to the baby about the toys she is looking at.
- Call the baby by name from a short distance to reassure her you are nearby.

- Provide a variety of small toys to handle and examine.
- Provide toys that make sounds when an infant moves them, fit inside each other, or dangle and move when touched.
- Offer board books.

8–12 months (infant)

- Help the infant focus on what is interesting to him, using your presence, your interest, and your enthusiasm to support his attention and exploration.
- Use your emotional expressions and words to show the infant that you delight in his discoveries.
- Use words to describe the child's activity: "Look, you found a Cheerio. You're picking it up with your fingers."

- Provide toys like stacking cups, rings on a post, pop-beads, and tubs full of small, interesting objects such as toy animals.
- Provide child-size replicas of dishes or household tools.
- Provide toys that respond to children's actions—busy boxes and water-filled pads.
- Provide sensory materials such as water and sand with a variety of tools.
- Provide board books with photographs.

12–18 months (young toddler)

- Allow toddlers protected time and space to explore.
- Stay nearby to express interest, provide words, and make the activity more elaborate and complex.
- Help oddlers express their interest in each other gently.
- Express enthusiasm for the things that interest toddlers.

- Provide simple puzzles, pegboards, shape forms, wooden beads with thick strings.
- Provide small climbers, tunnels, and interesting pathways.
- Provide toys that respond to winding and turning on and off.
- Provide simple props for pretend play.

DEVELOPMENTAL TRENDS AND RESPONSIVE INTERACTIONS (Continued)

Development	Example
18–24 months (toddler)	
• Toddlers enjoy the ease of their movement and like to use their hands to carry things around. • Toddlers understand they can cause things to happen. • Toddlers understand and remember the details of routines. • Toddlers use objects as substitutes for other objects in their pretend play. • Toddlers enjoy increasingly challenging materials that suggest activities such as building, sorting, matching shapes.	Lynn and Matt build little towers of blocks and then drive play trucks into them and knock them down. Before breakfast, Chris puts out his hands for the little song of thanks. When a child arrives and joins the table late, he reaches out for everyone to sing again. Fran takes out the box of 1-inch blocks and makes one pile of red blocks, one pile of blue blocks.
24–36 months (toddler)	
• Toddlers begin to understand concepts such as color, size, shape, time, size, and weight. • Toddlers toddlers are interested in the story and pictures in storybooks. • Toddlers toddlers create new stories in pretend play or new structures in block building, becoming more imaginative and creative. • Assign roles to toys and other children in pretend play; use chairs, blankets, and bookcases as substitutes for items in pretend play.	Eric is feeling a little sad and carries a picture of his mommy around with him, saying, "After nap." Sara takes charge of the dramatic play corner, handing out dolls and stuffed animals. She puts on a hat and says, "Mommy going shopping."

Key Terms

agency
executive functioning (EF)
habituation
mental flexibility
neural network
neurons

number
objects
proprioception
scaffolding
self-control
social group

spatial information
tools of the mind
vestibular
working memory
zone of proximal
    development (ZPD)

Reflections and Resources for the Reader

REFLECTIONS

1. Read the quotation from Rinaldi on page 203. What is your image of the child?
2. If infants and toddlers need to be able to have an effect on toys, what qualities would you look for in toys and which would you avoid?
3. If an infant had all the interesting toys in the world, do you think the infant would learn without an interested, engaged, and helpful adult?

OBSERVATION AND APPLICATION OPPORTUNITIES

1. Visit an infant-toddler care and learning program. How does the teacher set up an engaging, responsive learning environment that facilitates cognitive development? What would you change?
2. How does the teacher use herself to support the learning? Does she seem to understand and

Teacher- or Parent-Child Interaction	Environment
18–24 months (toddler)	
• Maintain predictable routines, reminding children of the order with questions like, "It's time to eat. What do we do?" • Keep materials in orderly and predictable places. • Provide scaffolding as toddlers think about their activities, with questions such as "What will you do next?" or "What will you buy at the store?"	• Have toys and materials arranged so that toddlers can make choices, reach them, and put them away (with reminders). • Frequently review the materials you have available to ensure that you are keeping a balance between what is familiar and what is a little challenging.
24–36 months (toddler)	
• Ask children how they might solve problems that occur and let them figure out answers. • Support children working together with materials to share ideas. • Use language that describes time (now, later, before nap, after lunch), weight (heavy, light), and size (bigger, smaller). • Count things during the day.	• Provide play opportunities that promote comparison of sizes, weights, colors, shapes, and quantities. • Have books available in all areas of the program. Have several copies of old favorites and bring in new books. • Allow children to combine materials from different areas in creative ways. • Present new materials or new combinations of materials.

anticipate that the infant or toddler is making new discoveries in his play?

3. What kinds of experiences might encourage a toddler's learning of object permanence, cause and effect, use of tools, or use of space?

SUPPLEMENTARY ARTICLES AND BOOKS TO READ

Dean, A., & Gillespie, L. (2015). Why teaching infants and toddlers is important. *Young Children, 70*(5), 94–95.

Maguire-Fong, M.J. (2015). *Teaching and learning with infants and toddlers. Where meaning-making begins.* New York: Teachers College Press.

Petersen, S. (2012). School readiness for infants and toddlers? Really? Yes, really! *Young Children, 67*(4), 10–15.

ZERO TO THREE. (2014). Early cognitive development. *Zero to Three Journal, 35*(2). The issue is devoted to early cognitive development in infants and toddlers. The articles in this issue describe how parents and caregivers play an important role in supporting the development of self-regulation and executive functions.

INTERESTING LINKS

Search the words *infant cognition laboratories*. A number of university programs that study infant learning will be listed—and the Web sites are worth visiting.

Center on the Developing Child This site includes publications and videos describing how young brains develop and children learn. Search using the words "Center for the Developing Child."

Institute for Learning and Brain Sciences This Web site has a series of 6 modules on infant development and learning from one of the premier infant research labs, the University of Washington. Search using the word "I-LABS."

Insights from the youngest minds A *New York Times* article profiling Elizabeth Spelke and the theory of core knowledge. Search using the words "Insights from the youngest minds."

ZERO TO THREE The section "School Readiness: Birth to 3" provides information and video clips on thinking skills as well as other areas of development. Search using the words "Zero to Three."

9

Language Learning and Development

LEARNING OUTCOMES

After reading this chapter, you will be able to:

- Explain the language capabilities of infants and toddlers and the influence of the unique characteristics of the child, including temperament and gender, on language learning and development in infancy.

- Identify aspects of knowing the child in language development: receptive, expressive, pragmatic, and the effects of hearing impairment and other special needs.

- Describe how infants and toddlers grow in language through relationships, including the influence of culture, key research concerning children's acquisition of two or more languages, and strategies to promote language development.

- Describe characteristics of program practices that enhance language learning and development.

Pearson Education

Kareem danced around, half hopping and half jumping, as he chanted, "oo, me jump, me dance." His dad, who knew that Kareem was communicating his joy through sounds and words, chimed in, too: "You're jumping, you're a jumper." Kareem danced and jumped higher and higher, around and around, saying, "Me jumping." This young boy and his wise father were engaged in a language dance, learning from each other as they took turns with the chant.

When the father modeled the word *jumping*, Kareem immediately said, "Me jumping." Infants and toddlers engage in a remarkable process of learning to listen, talk, and communicate their needs to others. In addition, they learn to make marks and scribbles on paper, and enjoy books—all aspects of language and literacy development.

Infants and toddlers desire human connection, and language is a primary way for them to make that connection. Language is power for young children—the power to get their needs met, comfort others, make others laugh, and engage in human relationships.

As relationship-based theory would predict, Kareem and other young children need

Language is acquired through social interactions.

adults as interactive partners. With responsive language partners, infants and toddlers make spectacular progress from producing soft cooing sounds (sustained production of single vowel sounds such as "ooo" and "aaa" that sound like a pigeon's coos) as newborns, to using single words by 1 year. They then progress to fairly complex sentences by age 3. Young children learn the joy of communicating with interactive language partners.

To study language development and relationships, it is important to know the definitions of common terms used. **Communication** is the giving of information through talk, signs, cues, gestures, or writing. An infant may communicate with eye gaze ("I'm interested in you"), arching the back ("Let me out of this situation"), sounds, or words. **Language** is "the ability to use words (or signs, if the language is one of the sign languages of the deaf) and to combine them in sentences so that thoughts in our minds can be transmitted to other people. We also consider the opposite: how we comprehend words spoken by others and turn them into concepts in our own mind" (1, p. 29). The word *language* can also describe the particular way in which a group of people form words through sounds and convey messages to others. English and Spanish are languages.

In this chapter, we explore how children have unique language learning capabilities. We also explore how their gender and temperament influence their language development. We take you on a journey investigating infants' and toddlers' remarkable growth in the major areas of language development:

- receptive language (hearing and understanding),
- expressive language (communicating to others),
- pragmatics (how language is used), and
- prosody (the rhythm and stresses on sounds and words that create meaning.

You will leave this chapter knowing many strategies that adults can use to support children's growth and the program practices that facilitate language development.

Each Child Is Capable and Unique

"Daddy, come here," a young child yells to her daddy, who has wandered from the grocery cart where the 2-year-old sits, "You getting losted." As children learn to speak, they create wonderfully unique and creative words and sentences based on their understanding of the principles of language. In this section we will explore young children's capacities to learn language as well as how gender and temperament influence language development.

 Watch this video of Dr. Patricia Kuhl, who you will read about in this chapter. Summarize two major points that she makes in the video.

https://www.youtube.com/watch?v=G2XBIkHW954&list=PLfoJWSBAwZAxpXAHjV6blIEBJWNSuvZv5

Language Capacities

Infants are born with the capacity to be communicators. The Developmental Trends and Responsive Interactions chart at the end of this chapter lists abilities that infants and toddlers have. Refer to this chart often as you read the chapter. From birth, they can hear the differences in speech sounds, such as "m" and "n"; are motivated to listen to the sounds of language; strive to communicate through body movements and vocalizations; and thrive when listened to by caring adults. Throughout the first 3 years, infants and toddlers learn to make the sounds of the language spoken to them; combine sounds into words and then combine words into sentences. They learn the syntax (grammar), pragmatics (use of language), and prosody (intonation) of language. They discover the meaning of an astonishing number of words; and communicate in a variety of ways—the furrowing of a brow, a loud screech, whining, pointing, talking, and shouting. While children progress through similar stages in their development, the content and their creativity with language can be unique.

The Brain Learning Language

Infants' brains are designed to learn a language with responsive adults. The brain develops when an adult names objects ("That's your cup"), describes what the adult is doing ("I'm changing your diaper"), sings songs, responds to an infant's sounds by repeating them, teaches a baby how to say "bye-bye," or talks about what the baby is doing ("You're playing"). Researchers describe what happens between the young brain and

Barbara Melinkovich

Language experiences are essential for the development of the language capable brain.

language experience that actually affects the capacity of a person to learn languages throughout life. In the first year of life, as infants hear adults talking with them, a cluster of neurons begins to fire. When pleasant language experiences are repeated—a song is sung over and over, a book is read many times to a delighted 8-month-old, or a word is used in a variety of ways (e.g., "a *cup*, where's the *cup*, you've got a *cup*")—the connections or paths between neurons are made stronger. An infant needs to hear adults talking *with* her and have an opportunity to *respond* about what is happening in the moment in order for the language capable brain to develop.

Gender

Just as adult responsiveness affects the quality of young children's language development, so does the gender of the child. Girls gesture, talk earlier, combine words earlier, and have larger vocabularies than boys. However, girls are only slightly ahead of boys (2, 3). Researchers who studied girl and boy language differences in 10 different countries found that girl toddlers were about 3 months ahead of boys in development. The girls also used more two-word combinations earlier than boys (4). The exception was in Sweden, a country that emphasizes equal rights for women. Researchers in Sweden, who gathered parental language reports on 336 children ages 16 to 28 months, did not find any significant gender differences in vocabulary, pragmatic skills, grammar skills, and the maximum length of utterance (5).

There are a variety of reasons for why girls may talk earlier than boys. There may be biological differences. Because girls talk earlier, they may be involved in more language opportunities than boys. Differences in experiences also influence girl and boy differences in the rate of language development. Parents have been found to talk less to boys than to girls even though the 3-to 11-month-old boys responded to their mother's language as often as did girls (6).

Parents and teachers will want to focus on providing equal language opportunities for boys and girls. However, infant boys may need higher levels of language encouragement than girls. It seems important for adults to pay particular attention to whether boys are using gestures and speech and building a strong vocabulary (7).

Temperament

"I no like dat (that)!!!" yelled a two-year-old to a peer when the peer grabbed his swing.

As we have described in earlier chapters, infants and toddlers differ in how they express emotions. Some children express more feelings of distress, frustration, and even anger. Other children express more feelings of joy, excitement, and pleasure. Earlier talkers express more positive feelings while later talkers express more negative feelings (8). Later talkers may be frustrated with fewer words to use. Or, their more difficult temperament may elicit different reactions from caregivers. We know, based on transactional theory (discussed in Chapter 3), that a child with a more challenging temperament may have fewer time sharing enjoyable language interactions with adults (9, 10). Parents and teachers who have children with temperaments that are challenging may need to intentionally provide rich language models and loving interactions with the children. They will have to take advantage of those times when the infants and toddlers are quietly alert, even when it is for a few minutes. Using soothing words of comfort and singing lullabies can both comfort and provide opportunities for language interactions with a child who is often irritable.

Home visitors and mentors can provide extra support to parents and teachers of young children who are struggling. All parents will need extra support to encourage language development if the family is experiencing stress. Even infants with an easy temperament at one year of age had lower language scores at three if they were experiencing a high-risk environment (11).

Another child temperament trait may contribute to the child experiencing fewer language interactions. A toddler who is fearful, socially wary, and socially anxious often will avoid adults and peers (12). These children need time alone with adults they trust to feel comfortable enough to communicate. When familiar adults read stories and talk gently while the children play, they will be providing rich language models.

It is easy to see how children's and adults' affect influences language development (13). Infants who hear a warm, loving voice will want to be with that adult. A child who is engaging and generally positive will attract people who will talk with him. When we are aware that a child who has a fussier, negative temperament may be involved in fewer language interactions, then we can go to work to provide those interactions.

Check Your Understanding 9.1
Click here to check your understanding of the concepts in this section.

Knowing the Child

What a remarkable journey we take with infants and toddlers who so seriously and competently listen to sounds, words, and sentences, figuring out the complex rules of language (Kuhl, 2007).

Think about how you learned your first language. You probably can't remember, because it happened so early in your life, and it now seems that the process was effortless. In reality, infants and toddlers are using a number of strategies to become a conversational partner with others, such as recognizing the voices of the special people in their lives, learning to predict when one word ends and another begins, or learning to use words in the correct order to convey meaning. As we still do as adults, infants and toddlers learn to use nonverbal gestures and facial expressions to communicate their thoughts and feelings. Let's travel with infants and toddlers as they move through their language-learning journey.

Receptive Language—Listening and Understanding

When Damion, an active two-year-old, heard his mother say, "We are going outside now," he ran to get his coat. He both heard and understood the words and the intent of the language. He knew that his mother was telling him something important. He demonstrated remarkable receptive language. Children often develop receptive language before they learn to express language. Language development changes in fairly predictable ways during the early years.

Prior to Birth

Infants are practicing listening to sounds while still snug inside their mothers' wombs. More than 30 years ago, some ingenious researchers found that newborns can distinguish between their mother's voice and another female's voice, almost immediately after birth. The infants, at 3 days old, were asked to do something they could already do very well: to suck on a pacifier-like nipple. The nipple was connected through wires to a tape recorder. If a baby sucked on the nipple at a fast rate, for example, she could hear her mother's voice; if the baby sucked the nipple at a slower rate, she would hear a stranger's voice. The babies quickly learned which rate of sucking would produce their mother's voice and consistently produced the rate of sucking to generate that sound (14). How did the infants know how to do this incredible feat? Did they immediately learn their mother's voice after birth or were they eavesdropping prior to birth?

To answer this question, researchers tried a different variation on the first research study (15). They asked pregnant women to read a particular children's story (such as Dr. Seuss's *Cat in the Hat*) aloud each day for the final 6 weeks of pregnancy. After the infants were born, the researchers played recordings of the mother reading this same story or a previously unheard story. The newborns again used sucking patterns to demonstrate that they clearly preferred the sound of the story they heard in utero. Infants are paying attention and discriminating between complex patterns of sounds even before birth. They want to hear the familiar story again!

Receptive Language: Birth to 4 Months

"Infants are 'citizens of the world' at birth and early in life they can hear the differences between all the consonants and vowels used in any language" (16). They can hear the differences in the sounds in words and are ready to begin to learn any language in the world. By 1 month of age, and probably earlier, infants prefer to hear talk that is directed toward them (higher pitch, sounds more articulated, simplified, repetitions in sounds and words) rather than adult-directed talk (17).

From 2 to 4 months of age, infants engage in a *language dance* with their parents and other important adults in their lives. For example, Josh, 3-months-old, looks into his language partner's eyes (his dad). As he makes soft cooing sounds, his dad patiently waits and then coos or sings or speaks softly to Josh. The partners, adult and infant, share the magic moment when a language connection is made and they are also emotionally connected.

Watch this video which shows the language dance that occurs when adults take "conversational" turns with an infant. How can you tell that the mother and child are emotionally connected? What is the mother doing that is responsive to the infant's sounds, body movements, etc.?

https://www.youtube.com/watch?v=9FeTK7ZXmVI

Receptive Language: 4 to 8 Months

At 6 months, babies are ready to speak any language that they hear frequently, as they can distinguish and make all sounds used in all languages (18). What a wonderful skill they have! After several months, though, they lose this ability and can only distinguish the sounds in the language(s) they are hearing.

By the young age of 7 to 12 months, infants are beginning to lose the ability to hear the differences between all of the sounds of the languages in the world. This is because they are listening to and practicing the sounds of the familiar language spoken to them. For example, the English language distinguishes *R* from *L*, and the Japanese language does not. So, Japanese children lose their ability to hear the differences in the sounds of *R* and *L*.

Something remarkable, though, happened when 8- to 12-month-old children, who usually lose their ability to hear sounds in a foreign language at this age, were exposed to a second language. If infants interacted with an adult speaking a foreign language for a total of 5 hours, they could distinguish the sounds of that language at 12 months. When infants looked at and heard a DVD or listened to a second language on a tape, though, they did *not* retain their ability to distinguish the sounds of the second language. It takes interacting with adults in a social context to "keep the brain open to sounds" (19).

Seven-month-olds can remember Mozart music passages and can still recall these passages after 2 weeks of not hearing them (20). Remarkably, they prefer to listen to passages that they've heard before and that are played in the same sequence. What a wonderful way for the infants to demonstrate their long-term memory as well as their receptive skills. Infants, during this age period, also begin to turn their heads when someone speaks their name–again demonstrating their recognition of the sound of their own name.

Receptive Language: 8 to 12 Months

During this stage infants have added listening abilities that contribute to learning a language well. Eight-month-olds show some ability to divide a continuous stream of speech sounds that they hear into individual words (21). For example, they can begin to divide "Hereisthemilk" into "Here is the milk." Demonstrating their receptive skills, mobile infants can perceive common sequences of sounds that form words. By 1 year of age, most American infants are learning that certain sounds go together to form words in English, and that other sequences of sounds are not combined in English, based on the language patterns they are hearing from adults (22). Infants are learning that certain sounds are likely to follow other sounds—such as in the word "baby," the "by" is more likely to follow the "ba" than are other sequences of sounds. They are using both tone and length of words to determine when a word begins and ends (23).

Many 10-month-olds understand a new word after an adult names it 5 times (24). However, these infants may apply the new word to an interesting object that they see, not a boring one, even though the adult looked at and named the boring object. The interesting object attracts infants' attention and they ignore the adult's eye gaze. By 12, 18, and 24 months, infants tune into the adult's social cue of looking at an object and understand that the label the adult uses is for that object (25). It is helpful to infants if adults also point to or hold up the object they are naming. Adults can watch where the infant is looking when they label or talk about an object. Otherwise, an infant may think that the word, "cup" is used for that interesting car that goes by in the street.

If a friend has their eyes closed, we usually don't follow when they turn their head toward an object. We do follow where they are looking when their eyes are open. Even many 9-, 10-, and 11-month-old infants are more likely to turn and follow the gaze of an adult when the adult's eyes are open rather than closed (26). These infants have learned an incredible amount about language in their first year of life.

Additional receptive (listening and understanding) skills that appear around the child's first birthday include beginning to understand simple directions and the language in games. An adult or sibling might give a direction such as "Wave bye-bye" or "Give Mommy a kiss." Again, these social infants love it when adults play familiar games such as peek-a-boo, pat-a-cake, or "How big are you?"

All of this information about the capabilities of infants demonstrates how important it is to talk *with* babies during their first year and definitely not wait until they say their first words to talk with them. If adults wait to talk with little babies, their language development will be compromised. Infants need to engage in the language dance with a responsive language partner beginning in their first weeks and months of life.

Receptive Language: 12 to 18 Months

Young toddlers this age can follow simple directions, such as "Go get your coat" and can correctly point to their nose, eyes, hair, foot, tummy, and other body parts when a parent or teacher playfully asks "Where's your nose?" and "Where's your tummy?"

You may want to think about how many ways you could say the word "ball" to a young toddler. You could say, "Here's a ball," "Roll the ball," and "The ball is yellow." You may get bored saying the word, "ball," but toddlers won't get bored. They will be listening carefully and may try to say the word, "ball" very soon. Clearly, young toddlers can comprehend the meaning of words quickly during this age period.

Receptive Language: 18 to 36 Months

Toddlers are accomplished at what is called **fast mapping**, quickly attaching a name to an object. Toddlers learn words faster when adults provide many examples of the word. When you place a yellow cup in front of the toddler and say, "cup" and later place a blue cup in front of the toddler and say, "cup," toddlers will learn the word, "cup" more easily. When you use the word, "yellow" when you say, "That's a yellow ball," and again when you say, "There's a yellow bus," toddlers are more likely to learn the word, "yellow." These are examples of providing multiple instances of the same word (27).

Toddlers also learn new words best when a gesture is used with a word. Again, pointing to an object or saying the word for an object the child is using will help the toddler learn new words. This is an example of **multimodal input** (28).

Another reason for a **language explosion** is that toddlers from 24 to 30 months of age are better at guessing the meanings of new words (29). If you said, "There's a dog and a cat" and the child knows the word, "dog," but not "cat," the toddler will guess that the other animal with the dog is the "cat." Toddlers who don't know the word, "orange" will figure out that the word, "orange" refers to the fruit when you say, "Tomar is eating an orange." Toddlers are figuring out what a word means from the context. This happens, though, only when a child's favorite adults use many descriptive words and the names of objects with the child. The adult is the provider of rich, language opportunities for young children and the child is the listening, active, and eager learner of language.

Infants and toddlers are more likely to behave better and succeed academically when they can understand and say more words. Children's vocabulary definitely influences their behavior. When two-year-olds can understand the words, "Please touch gently" they will be better able to control their actions (30). A two-year old who was upset because her parents left her with a baby sitter told her

Children learn how to communicate by listening to stories, listening to adults talk, and by interacting as conversational partners with adults and peers.

Pearson Education

parents the next day, "Me so sad and me so mad." She didn't have a tantrum because she was able to say how she felt. Toddlers who have larger vocabularies at 24 months also do better in school and have better behavior in kindergarten (31). You help infants and toddlers get a great head start when you help them learn many new words.

Very young children need language partners who make learning new words fun and rewarding. Adults must limit TV and interact more with children if they want infants and toddlers to learn new words. Several researchers found that *increases* in the number of hours that children at 29 months watched television predicted *decreases* in receptive vocabulary at kindergarten age (32).

OBSERVATION INVITATION **9.1**

Click the play button to watch the video and notice how the toddler plays with language and demonstrates the joy of communication. Listen to what Ariel says after her mother says, "Twinkle twinkle." You can hear Ariel add new sounds and possibly a word to her babbling. How is this a demonstration of receptive language? Answer questions related to the video in your Pearson eText.

Contingent interactions hold the key to young children learning new words. When 24 to 30 month olds Skyped with adults who used novel words while *contingently* responding to the children's actions and words, the toddlers learned new words (33).

Expressive Language—Communicating with Gestures, Sounds, and Words

There is a joy that infants and toddlers experience when they are able to express meaning through gestures, sounds, and words.

Expressive Language: Birth to 4 Months

Babies communicate in a variety of ways, one of which is to cry when they are in pain, hungry, or distressed. They yawn, scrunch up their faces, turn away, look peaceful and calm, and communicate in myriad ways. The adult pays attention to all of the verbal and nonverbal signals of the infant. Important caregivers in infants' lives begin to interpret the burps, quieting, and looking as forms of communication (see BOX 9.1). By 2 months of age, infants begin to have different cries for hunger and pain, and a wise parent can hear these differences and respond accordingly. Parents then can meet the infants' needs and help them begin to communicate successfully in different ways. Infants' language grows when the infant's language dance partner imitates the infant's sounds, both coos and babbles, and then waits for the infant to coo or babble again.

Expressive Language: 4 to 8 Months

Expressively, infants begin to demonstrate through their movements and facial expressions that they anticipate that their sounds and nonverbal communication (such as reaching up with their arms to be picked up) will get a reaction from an adult. They make sounds to get adults' valued attention. Can't you just hear an infant making sounds as he looks at a favorite adult, as if to say, "Look at me." Infants are learning how to communicate before they learn words. "Children engage in conversation with adults and with each other before they have acquired their first conventional word" (34, p. 53).

In addition to communicating nonverbally and cooing vowel sounds, they also begin to babble (repetition of consonant-vowel sounds, such as "ma" or "da"). At first they babble "ba" or "da" (one syllable) and toward the end of this age group are babbling more sounds together ("bababa" "dadada"). The sounds for mother and father, in many cultures, are babbling sounds that the infant first makes, such as "pa-pa," "ma-ma," and "da-da." That's why you may hear a parent say, "He said 'da-da'. He knows my name." In several months, the infant will say, "Ma-ma" or "Pa-pa" just for a special person, but for right now, they are probably just enjoying making the sounds.

The quality and type of babbling, however, depends on what infants are hearing and what they are trying to express. Infants will repeat sounds in their babbling that they hear when adults speak directly to them. For example, infants learning Korean may babble different sounds than infants learning only English (35). Recent research has even demonstrated that the intonation of babbling differs based on the intent of the child at the moment. Listen for babies to make a wider range of sounds when expressing unhappiness than when they seem to be

BOX 9.1

Babies' Nonverbal Communication

Mom to baby: "Oh, you're feeling tired. I can tell by those yawns. Oops, your tummy is growling. Are you telling me you're hungry?"

When adults treat infants' nonverbal behavior as forms of communication, babies begin to understand what it is like to be an interactive partner in a conversation.

telling you something (with babbling) (36). Thus, babbling differs based on the language the child is hearing and the child's intention when babbling.

Amazingly, when adults imitate infant's babbling, but also add a few different sounds than the infants used, infants immediately restructure their babbling to add the new sounds that they hear. This happened only if the adult babbling models were contingent on the infants' babbling. The adults quickly took their babbling turn, made the sounds that they heard the infants make, and added the new sounds (or a word). The adults who added more vowel sounds heard their infants make more vowel sounds. When adults added a word to their babbling back to the infants, they heard more consonant-vowel babbling syllables from their infants (37). A responsive adult encourages **phonological** learning.

Expressive Language: 8 to 12 Months

Infants this age want to communicate with you. They shake their heads "no," hold up their hands to be picked up, wave bye-bye, make many different sounds, and use first words to communicate their needs and desires. A responsive communication partner teaches an infant that gestures, sounds, and words get results, so that the infant does not need to cry to get his needs met. As described in the following example, when adults respond, infants enjoy communicating with a language partner:

> *Mika, 9-months-old, sat in the bathtub with her mother on the floor beside the tub. Playing with the sound of her voice, Mika said "da-da." Her mother imitated her and then said "da-da" in a different tone. Mika said "da-da" in a still different tone, putting emphasis on the second syllable. Her mother said "da-da" in a higher tone. On they went, taking turns with different sounds bouncing off the wall of the bathroom, until many turns had been taken and "da-da" had been exclaimed in as many melodies as possible.*

Mika was learning that communicating is fun. She was also learning that language has prosodic features (pitch, tempo, pauses, and emphatic stress on parts of a word) and that she could *initiate* a "conversation" (about "da-da"). She also could *sustain* a conversation by continuing to take her turn. She was learning that she could be an important and effective conversational partner.

Babbling continues to develop with combined syllables such as "dada," "mama," "nana," and "tutu." However, now the infant may be using these sounds

Infants often communicate with gestures.
Pearson Education

Pearson Education

to name the mother or father. These words are music to the ears of parents who feel special when their infant repeats these sounds primarily for them. Imitating the infants' babbling and adding new patterns continues to be very important to infants' language learning. Parents who responded to their 11-month-old infants' vocalizations while the infants were holding or pointing to an object had infants whose vocabulary was larger (than infants not responded to) at 15 months (38). The infants' object-directed vocalizations (ODVs) were a signal that they were ready to learn a new word.

Expressive Language: 12 to 18 Months

Infants are likely to begin to point to objects and people with their tiny index finger by the time they are 12-months-old, although some children begin earlier. In their attempt to *share attention*, infants may intentionally point at a person or object with a squeal of delight to direct another person's attention toward that object.

When infants point, they are aware that they can direct an adult's attention to some event or object. They are often very excited when adults actually look. The infants are now sharing experiences with others as they "tune into others and get others to tune into them" (39, p. 108). Pointing is an observable and exciting step forward in infants' cognitive, language, motor, social, and emotional development. Also, infants point to gain information (40). It is as if the infant is saying, "What is that?" When caregivers tune in to the infant's pointing and respond with, for example, "You see a ball, don't you?" or "Ooh—a ball—I see it," infants learn new words.

You can still expect to see many gestures because in the 12- to 18-month age period, 85 percent of infants continue to use gestures as well as words to request and label objects and people (41).

The growth of a young toddler's vocabulary is amazing during this age period. Through joint attention conversations with adults, mobile infants learn that every action and object has a name and they can use these wonderful new words. When adults respond to toddler's pointing, they are moving children toward a language explosion.

This rapid word learning when children near 18 months is often referred to as a *language explosion* or *productive naming explosion*. This is a very surprising increase in language development that demonstrates a toddler's desire to learn to label people, places, and things in a social context. Just as fireworks explode with a variety of colors and in many surprising directions, the language explosion delights adults who are in awe of the sudden increase and variety of words spoken by the toddler. The adult may wonder how these words can suddenly appear, but most infants and toddlers have been participating in a rich language dialogue since birth. Toddlers at 18 months have been found to be using as many as nine

FIGURE 9.1   **Language characteristics of a 16-month-old.**

Lamar, at 16 months, was very busy learning language.
"Sirt" (shirt) he exclaimed, while also pointing to a shirt his mom was holding.
"Kitty," he said, as he looked at the kitty.
"Buses teeth," as he pointed to his father who was brushing his teeth.
"Mama, mama, porch," Lamar called out.
Lamar joyfully practiced a new word: "Back, back, back," as he ran through the kitchen.
The next day he said "juice" when his dad took the juice container out of the refrigerator.
Other words that Lamar used over the next few days included "feet," "eye," "boke-boke" (broke) after breaking a plastic cup, "sut" (shut), and "pease" (please).

new words a day (42). You can hear phrases with two or more words at the end of this age period, such as "more mik" (milk), "more juice," and "Mama, bush (brush) teeth." Figure 9.1 lists some words and phrases that a 16-month-old boy used and that are characteristic of that age. Notice that Lamar says many words and is beginning to put two words together ("buses teeth").

Expressive Language: 18 to 36 Months

Toddlers use mostly words—not gestures. These impressive toddlers focus on learning words rather than gestures, simply because they *observe* that people around them use mostly words. Most toddlers delight in being around others so focusing on learning words to name people, places, and objects supports toddlers' social success.

From saying sounds to saying words to putting words together, infants and toddlers try to communicate with others. Toddlers make language mistakes, but they are developmentally appropriate mistakes. These mistakes tell us that toddlers are not just imitating what they hear, but are also applying some rules that they've discovered all by themselves. They may think that the word "dog" applies to all four-legged creatures, so the next cat, horse, or pig they see will enthusiastically be called "dog." They may also *undergeneralize* a word and not use it for all of the cases to which it applies. For example, to them, a cat is only a cat if it is a black cat. So, when they see a white cat, they think that it is named something else. After all, objects that they drink out of are strangely called cups, glasses, thermos,

OBSERVATION INVITATION **9.2**

Click the play button to watch the video on a toddler (Kai) who just turned two and is communicating with his grandfather. How many words is the child putting together in his utterances? Watch his eyes–he is telling a little joke–as he names the "juice" as "milk." How does his positive relationship with his grandfather influence the toddler's language development? How is the grandfather expanding and elaborating Kai's utterances? Answer questions related to the video in your Pearson eText.

or bottles, so shouldn't there be different names for a black, white, spotted, gray, or furless cat? During this age period, as before, toddlers work very hard to figure out all of the names of things, the characteristics that differentiate them, and how to talk about them. We can help them by engaging them in conversations about all of the exciting things in their environment, such as their red shoes, the large refrigerator, cheddar cheese, and how a puppy is different from a kitty, as well as talking with them about their emotions—anger, sadness, worry, fear, and joy.

> *At 18 months, Carmen could say the words "up," "meow," "open," "down," "door," "diaper," "pretzel," and "neck." She also could use sentences such as, "go kitty," "go car," and "go Mommy"—open-pivot sentences, so labeled because different words pivot around one word, such as "go."*

Toddlers progress from saying mostly one-word and some two-word sentences at 18 months to multiword sentences at 36 months. As noted in the previous example, they begin to use *open-pivot* sentences. They also use *telegraphic speech*. Spoken sentences such as "Kitty eat food" are called telegraphic because, just as a telegram leaves out words for the sake of brevity, the toddler leaves out words and uses the essential parts of speech that communicate meaning. Soon, Carmen was saying "Dada, dada, I boke (broke) eggs," adding the "s" on words to indicate that they are plural. Next, she added "ing" to say "I jumping" rather than "I jump." Again, mistakes are made because of a toddler's active mind. Applying the "s" rule to indicate plurals, some exceptions in the English language such as "deer" may be called "deers" by the learning toddler (43). By 3 years of age, Carmen was saying wonderfully creative sentences, such as "People pee in the potty and puppies pee in the now (snow)," "Why you are crying?" and "It's too louder" (the music was playing at a high volume).

Pragmatics—the Purposes of Language

You may have heard a toddler say, "No" quite loudly. Depending on the context, "No" may mean she is rejecting, refusing, or informing the adult or peer. Toddlers from 12 to 18 months use gestures, sounds, and words to reject, request, question, comment, refuse, demand, and inform. They will protest (shake their head "no"), request objects with an open or closed hand, request actions by pointing, take the hand of the adult, give an object, comment by pointing, and use gestures such has hugging and clapping (44).

Young toddlers may, at times, be difficult to understand. You will hear young toddlers *jargoning*—a sequence of sounds with intonation of an adult, such as "ba bad a da tu le?." They may sound as if they are asking a question. Or, they may seem to be telling you a piece of very important information with a great deal of emphasis on different sounds. Parents and teachers often have to be mind readers in order to understand toddlers who are intent on communicating something quite important, and who may get frustrated when adults don't understand them. Encouraging a young child to take your hand and show you can often help you understand what they are trying to communicate.

 Watch this video that shows how mobile infants' and toddlers' jargoning has meaning. Listen to the twins jargoning with each other and watch their gestures. They are definitely sharing information and it seems as if they are commenting and describing. What other functions of language do you hear and see?

https://www.youtube.com/watch?v=_JmA2ClUvUY

Listening to toddlers from 18 to 36 months talk is a joy because they try so hard to communicate their excitement about all of the new things that they are learning. They want to tell their special adults what's bothering them, where to look, what to feed them, and how to dress them. They want to share what they've found with you and want you to share in the moment with them—to really be there emotionally and linguistically. As they develop autonomy, they demand, request, inform, and describe their world. Their language is a window into what they are thinking, what they need, and what they want.

Prosody—The Music of Language

If a parents says, "Come here" in a tone that means, "I have something special for you" she is probably using a pleasant, warm tone. She is probably stressing the word "here" as well. If the same parent says, "Come here" emphatically she may have a firm tone to her voice. She may also be stressing the word, "Come." These examples show how the prosody or intonations, rhythm, and emphasis on words create different meanings. There is so much that infants and toddlers have to learn and that prosody creates meaning is one of them. Soon parents also will hear their toddlers say, "No" in many different tones.

Children with Special Needs

Individual infants and toddlers differ in how they develop and use language. You will notice that some children talk continuously and others are quieter; some talk to themselves as they are playing and others talk mostly with other people. As you observe infants and toddlers, you will also see differences in the ages at which infants and toddlers begin to speak. Most developmental charts indicate that typically developing infants will say their first word around 12 months, some two-word sentences by 18 months, and *many* single words and two-word sentences by 2 years. The average number of words that infants speak at 14 months is 10. Identifying a child's **language delay** will require discussions between parents and teachers to determine how many total words an infant understands and speaks. You will want to refer the child for a hearing test if that hasn't been completed yet. It is very important to identify language delay early because language delay at an early age may predict later language and reading challenges. Preschool children who were delayed in oral language had difficulty with reading in elementary grade (45). It is very important, then, to identify language delay early in a child's life, so that the child and family receive support in developing language skills.

Differences may occur for a variety of reasons, including biological and environmental. One primary reason is that there are differences in how much children are exposed to language. Some children hear many words from adults and some do not. Usually, the more descriptive and kind words that infants and toddlers hear, the more words they will use. When parents were taught how to take language-turns with their toddlers who had delayed language, the toddlers' receptive language improved (46). We know that receptive language preceeds expressive language, so increasing toddlers' receptive language is important.

Another reason for language delay may be hearing impairment. Children with hearing challenges may develop receptive and expressive language in a different way from other children. The pronunciation of sounds, as well as a child's vocabulary and syntax development, will all be affected by hearing challenges.

Hearing Impairment

Hearing loss is one of the most common abnormalities present at birth. Significant hearing loss is present in an estimated 1–3 per 1,000 newborn infants in the healthy nursery population. Hearing screening (Early Hearing Detection Intervention [EHDI] programs) now occurs in the hospital before babies are discharged from the hospital in 38 states (47). The American Academy of Pediatrics recommends that infants start treatments before 6 month of age to avoid permanent impairments in speech, language, and cognitive abilities (48). Infants, who are diagnosed before 6 months of age are likely to develop better language skills than children diagnosed after 6 months of age (49).

It is sometimes difficult for parents and teachers to read the subtle signs of hearing loss in their infant, especially if the hearing loss is mild. Following are a list of symptoms that may be observed in children with hearing loss.

- An infant who is hearing impaired may not turn her head toward a voice or look around when her own name is called (by 5 months of age).
- Older infants may babble, but the quality is different from typically developing children and babbling may diminish between 8 and 12 months, when hearing infants begin to practice just those sounds in the language that they are hearing.
- Infants and toddlers with hearing impairment may watch adults' gestures carefully and have a hard time following simple directions from words alone, without the additional information from the gestures.
- Infants may also be delayed in saying their first words and sentences.

Infants and toddlers with hearing impairment need language support during the early years—the sensitive period for language development. Young children with hearing impairment who learn a communication system, such as sign language, improve both their communication and cognitive abilities—thinking, problem solving, and categorizing.

The language-learning journey continues for many years, but what incredible progress children make from birth to age 3. It is through caring relationships that language development thrives.

 Watch the video to hear Dr. Lisa Shulman summarize infant and toddler communication milestones in social engagement, attention to language (receptive), and communicative (expressive) intent.

https://www.youtube.com/watch?v=pZSjm0drIGM

 Check Your Understanding 9.2
Click here to check your understanding of the concepts in this section.

Learning Through the Adult-Child Relationship

Infants and toddlers learn language through the key relationships that they have with adults and peers. Culture is a part of those relationships that makes a difference in how children learn and use language.

Learning Language Within Relationships

> The teacher's voice was warm and caring as she soothed Katrina after a fall. Katrina, 9-months-old, crying intensely, stopped and looked up at the teacher. The teacher continued comforting Katrina with calm words. The teacher then stopped and waited expectantly for Katrina to take a turn in the conversation. Katrina started babbling, as if telling the teacher all about the nasty fall. This communication exchange seemed emotionally satisfying to both Katrina and the teacher, as Katrina stopped crying, gave a big sigh, and began babbling excitedly.

The teacher in this example is using responsive language. She is empathic and waits for Katrina to take a turn in the conversation. Just like Katrina's teacher, parents and teachers use many of the following 12 strategies to support children learning to express themselves, to hear and understand language, and to become competent communicators.

(1) Build Relationships—Be an Empathic Language Partner

When a person cares about another person, he or she usually wants to communicate with that person. An infant or toddler will want to communicate with you when she feels safe and cared for in loving ways. Infants and toddlers communicate when it is pleasant to communicate, when the affect or feeling of the communication is warm and loving, and when they understand that their communication attempts will get a response.

(2) Respond and Take Turns—Be an Interactive Language Partner

Through your interactions with the infant or toddler you are helping the child learn to use language to communicate. When a toddler asks for a drink and a parent or teacher responds, then the toddler learns that communication is an effective way to get his needs met. Responsiveness, "supports infants' growing pragmatic understanding that language is a tool that enables intents to be shared socially" (50, p. 121). When an infant makes sounds or a toddler uses words, respond and then wait for the child to take a turn with sounds, words, or sentences. This **conversational dance** with each partner taking a turn helps the child learn the purposes (pragmatics) of conversation. They learn that people take turns exchanging ideas in a social context. These adult-child conversations build young children's skills in becoming a *conversational* partner and a *capable communicator.* Try not to dominate the conversation with an infant or toddler by taking more turns than the child or bombarding the child with language. Instead, focus on reciprocal and responsive interactions with equal give-and-take conversations.

(3) Respond to Nonverbal Communication

Infants' and toddlers' nonverbal body movements, gestures, and facial expressions have meaning. A yawn can mean the baby is tired or bored. Snuggling into an adult's body tells you that the infant feels safe and relaxed. A toddler running to you tells you she wants to connect with you. Kicking feet say, "I'm uncomfortable." When babies turn away, they may be communicating that they need a break from the interaction. When infants or toddlers use a strong communication cue, such as arching their back, it means "that hurts," or "stop what you are doing." When adults understand and respond to infants' and toddlers' nonverbal communication, they let children know that they are communication partners. With responsive adults, infants and toddlers are soon using sounds and words, while still maintaining many nonverbal ways to communicate.

(4) Use Self-Talk and Parallel Talk

Self-talk is talk that adults use to describe what they are doing while with the infant or toddler. For example, a teacher who is diapering a baby might say, "I'm getting your diaper. Now I'm lifting your feet. I'm putting the diaper on. All done." **Parallel talk** occurs when an adult talks about what a child is doing. For example, while the child is playing or eating, the adult might say, "Mmm, you're eating your toast" while pointing to the toast. These strategies tie language to an act or object manipulation, making words come alive and have meaning for the child.

(5) Talk Often with the Child, Using a Rich and Varied Vocabulary

How you talk and how much you talk, sing, and look at picture books together with an infant or toddler matters. Research shows that the number and quality of the conversations that adults have with infants and toddlers directly affects how they learn to talk (51, 52). Researchers Hart and Risley found astounding differences in how much parents talk with their children. Some infants and toddlers hear an average of 600 words an hour, whereas others hear as many as 2,100 words an hour. Some children hear 100 different words an hour, whereas others hear 500 different words an hour. These differences in the amount of language that children heard made a difference in their language development. By age 3, the children with talkative parents were talking more and with a richer vocabulary. They were averaging three times as many statements per hour and twice as many words per hour than the children of quieter parents: "The more time that parents spent talking with their child from day to day, the more rapidly the child's vocabulary was likely to be growing and the higher the child's score on an IQ test was likely to be at age 3" (53, p. 3). The number of total words and different words that the parent uses with the child daily, the number of conversations, and the positive affirmations from the parent are all related to infants' and toddlers' language development (54).

Use language-rich routines and many interactions with infants and toddlers to build their vocabulary. Diapering, for example, is a perfect time for a parent or teacher to talk about "first" we get a clean diaper, "second" we take off your diaper, and so forth. Talking about hands, nose, ears, and toes enlightens the baby about body parts and makes diapering an easier job for you.

(6) Use Joint Attention Strategies

Adults in Western cultures often look at or point to the people or objects under discussion when talking with their young children, thereby directing their children's attention. Joint attention occurs when both the adult and the child are focusing on the same thing at the same time. Adults who look at or point at the object of discussion or wait until the infant or toddler is looking at an object to talk about it ensure that the child will attach the language label to the correct object. This type of shared attention enhances language development (55).

(7) Use the Four Es Approach

Adults can *encourage, expand, elaborate* and *extend* children's language. *Encourage* children to communicate by listening, responding, and not correcting their language. *Expand* on both the meaning and the grammar of a child's words and conversational turns. For example, if a toddler exclaims, "A dog, a dog" as she looks out her window. The adult could say, "Yes, that's a brown dog. The dog is running." *Elaborate* on (make more complex) and *extend* (lengthen) the sounds, words, and sentence—for example, by adding a different sound, a new word, or a slightly longer sentence. Imitating and then expanding on the language of the child models the next step in development. The child hears your expansion and is likely to begin to use the newly modeled language forms. An added benefit of using the four Es is that infants and toddlers feel *effective* and a language *equal*, promoting further use of language to communicate.

(8) Use Semantically Responsive Talk

When adults took language turns with toddlers and stayed on the same topic, children were significantly more likely to reply than if the adult responded but changed the topic (56). Although a conversation made up of cooing sounds may seem as if it would be boring to an adult, the delight in an infant's eyes, the emotional connection, and the continuous development of the infant's language is reward enough to the caring adult. The adult's **semantic elaboration** supports the child's tendency to stay on the topic, as well. If a toddler is talking about the "airplane" and the listening adult responds semantically with information about the shape or color of the airplane, then the toddler is likely to stay on the topic and say something more about the airplane.

(9) Use Infant-Directed Speech

> *Janna, 13 months old, played quietly with a ball, rolling it and scrambling after it, only to roll it again across the carpet. When she tired of rolling the ball, she looked at her grandfather. Her grandfather sat on the floor beside her and said, "Ball, let's roll the ball." Janna smiled as she rolled the ball in Grandpa's direction. "Ball," she said quietly, imitating her grandpa's word.*

We've all heard that we shouldn't talk baby talk to an infant, but parents and teachers *do* use a special language when they interact with their infants because young children are more attentive when adults use it. This special language is often called, *infant directed speech, parentese, child-directed talk* because all parents and most adults use it with infants. Adults in most cultures use these practices, and in so doing, they are communication partners and language models for infants and toddlers. Parents who use infant-directed speech are modeling bite-size pieces of language that infants and toddlers can digest and practice.

As parents and teachers generally try to simplify language in order to maintain the infants' attention and teach them to use language, they use speech with a child that is significantly different from speech with an adult. For example, parents might stress a key word such as "jumping" in the phrase, "You are *jumping*." Adults using infant-directed speech also point or direct the child's attention to the focus of the conversation—for example, pointing to a cup while saying "cup." Adults repeat words—for example, they might say to an infant or young toddler, "Look, a *bird*. The *bird* is flying." Examples would include the following strategies:

- Use responsive talk.
- Use shorter sentences and decreased vocabulary.
- Exaggerate the pitch and intonation of your voice.
- Direct your communication at the infant or toddler.
- Use longer pauses between words and utterances.
- Frequently repeat words.
- Don't be afraid to be redundant—for example, say, "A *bird*—a blue *bird*," repeating the word *bird*.
- Elongate the vowels in words ("Oooh, whaaaat is that?").

- Use diminutive words ("blanky," "piggy," "doggy").
- Use frequent paraphrasing or recasting of previous utterances (toddler says "We go" and parent recasts by saying "Yes, we're going").
- Talk about what is immediately present.
- Use frequent phrases and parts of sentences in isolation ("in the car").
- Use questions and attempts to elicit speech.
- Label words—nouns and actions—in context.

Many adults use fewer functions when speaking directly to an infant or toddler. For example, we use language for a variety of social goals: to inform, question, promise, request, refuse, play, and direct others (functions of language). Parents use fewer functions when infants are young and gradually increase the number and types of functions as the infant grows to become a preschooler and can better understand the intentions of language.

By 13 months, young toddlers may need more than infant-directed speech. They will need adults who responsively talk about past events, future events, feelings, and reasons for actions as well as adults who use sentences that are slightly above the child's level of language (57).

Infant-directed strategies, however, also build the affectionate relationship between parent and child. Although most adults stop using these strategies as infants become toddlers and preschoolers, some words are like emotional glue that binds an adult and child together across time and space. Some special words a parent and child will use forever when they are together. A mother of a 30-year-old might ask her grown child if she would like some "pasgetti" (spaghetti). This reminds both of them of the early years when the child could not say "spaghetti" and the close attachment between them. A grandmother's name may become "Ta-ta" forever, because those were the first sounds that the infant made when laying peacefully in the grandmother's lap.

(10) Use Questions and Control Carefully

Adults often use questions to start a conversation with a child, to take a conversational turn, or to gain information. Some questions are **true questions** that are asked because the teacher doesn't know the answer. Other questions are asked to test children—for example, "What is that?" as they point to a toy on the floor. These questions are often referred to as **closed questions** because they usually have only one correct answer. There are thoughtful **open-ended questions** that have more than one acceptable answer, such as, "What song do you want to sing next?" **Choice questions** —for example, "Do you want juice or milk?"—are perfect questions for toddlers who are exerting their independence from adults.

Infants and toddlers enjoy and benefit from interactions with teachers who use a conversation-eliciting style. Conversation-eliciting adults take more language turns with children. This style is in contrast to a directive style. An adult who uses a directive style uses negative instructions ("I told you to clean your plate") and speeches (58).

Use *behavior control* carefully. Behavior control refers to statements that are used by teachers to elicit group participation around a common activity or to manage safety concerns. Frequent prohibitions from adults (e.g., "stop that," "don't") result in less favorable child outcomes than when adults use more active listening strategies of repeating, paraphrasing, and extending infants' and toddlers' statements (59).

(11) Listen with Your Eyes

> *A 3-year-old child's mother picked her up from her infant-toddler program and took her home immediately, so that the mother could prepare dinner. As the mother was pulling food out of the refrigerator, the little girl tried to tell her mommy about something that had happened during the day. The mother, focused on her task, commented, "Hmm, oh, that's nice." The little girl, obviously very frustrated with her mother's lack of response, said, "Mom, listen to me with your eyes."*

Toddlers enjoy listening to stories, singing songs, and doing finger-plays in informal groups.

Pearson Education

Infants and toddlers—in fact, all human beings—love to be listened to with another person's full engagement and focus. The little girl described in the previous example wanted her mom to look at her and "listen with her eyes." Infants and toddlers thrive, learn to listen, and take language turns, when adults in their lives do the same with them. They learn that holding a conversation means taking turns with listening and talking, so they will look at you intently, waiting as patiently as they can for you to finish what you want to say. If a child or family member from a particular culture believes that it is disrespectful to "look into your eyes" while talking, he may prefer for you to listen carefully with your ears and voice, acknowledging that you've heard.

(12) Read, Sing, Use Finger-Plays and Social Games Like Peek-a-Boo Often

Playful activities are crucial to enjoyable language learning. Chapter 13 discusses these topics, including literacy development and experiences, in great detail.

Culture and Language

Culture and language are intertwined. Language communicates a culture's values, beliefs, style, and purpose for speaking. "**Communicative-linguistic parameters** such as the language used in the home, the communication patterns, and the values underlying those patterns affect every aspect of how we learn about ourselves and the world around us" (60). Language is a powerful medium, then, for infants and toddlers to learn about their own value within their culture and what is of value to learn.

> *Language is a major medium for transmitting culture across generations. Through language socialization, adults convey to children, from infancy onward, culturally valued beliefs, behaviors, and processes. (Lee, Davis, & MacNeilage)*

> *In all cultures, language is one of the most powerful symbolic systems through which children learn to understand and interpret human behavior. (Harwood, Miller, & Irizarry)*

OBSERVATION INVITATION **9.3**

Click the play button to watch this video of Kai and his grandfather again from earlier in this chapter. Which of the 12 strategies listed in this chapter (e.g. use infant directed speech, using the four Es) is the grandfather using to encourage the toddler's language development? Answer questions about the video in your Pearson eText.

Differences in When and How Language Is Used

When we observe children's language development through a cultural lens we can see that culture is revealed in the content of talk and in how language is used in social contexts. See Figure 9.2 for a list of the aspects of language that may differ based on family and cultural values.

Ritual and System Constraints

The following scenario describes how Jamie, Cara, Mary, Tamika, and Carmen communicate their hunger differently to their teacher:

> *Jamie looks directly at her infant-toddler teacher as she demands "Eat," to tell her teacher very clearly that she is hungry and expects to be fed. Cara looks at the teacher with a longing look to tell her she is hungry. Mary moves in closely to the teacher, takes the teacher's face gently in her hands, and asks for milk by saying "milk" in a quiet voice, waiting up to 30 seconds for her favorite teacher to respond. Tamika waits until the teacher approaches her and asks her if she is hungry. Carmen starts to wail when she gets a hungry feeling in her tummy.*

These five children's way of getting their needs met differ because of system constraints and ritual constraints (61). **System constraints** refer to how the child opens and closes a conversation and takes language turns. In the previous example, Mary opens a "conversation" with her caring teacher by moving close to her

FIGURE 9.2   **Features of language that may differ based on family and cultural values.**

- When talk is appropriate.
- Who a child can speak to, and what are the appropriate ways of addressing people of different status or age.
- What is the acceptable volume or tone of voice for speech and when talk should be brief, discreet, or dispassionate.
- When the use of language can be unguarded or emotional, and how this varies by situation.
- Where you can talk and where is it important to be quiet.
- How much time you wait for someone to talk after you have stopped talking.
- How much eye contact you should give when you are talking to someone and the person is talking to you.
- How much personal space you allow between yourself and the listener when you are talking.
- What constitutes a "good" story and who can tell it.

and holding the teacher's face in her hands. She waits quietly for the teacher to respond before she takes her turn in the conversation. Jamie, on the other hand, opens the conversation about her rumbling tummy by approaching the teacher and telling her, in no uncertain terms, that she wants to eat. **Ritual constraints** refer to how the child controls her communication with others and how she protects her feelings. Tamika may be regulating her communication and feelings by waiting until the teacher approaches her. Carmen uses a different style. She loudly, and with a great deal of feeling, expresses her hunger to her understanding teacher. Ritual and system constraints are windows into different cultural and individual language styles rather than language limitations.

Children as Conversational Partners in Different Cultures

How children converse with you may depend on their culture. Are children treated as partners and participants in conversations in their culture or are they expected to listen and learn language by overhearing? When you listen to children and talk about what they want to talk about, then you are treating them as conversational equals. This practice is used by many families in the United States and Western Europe. (62). Adults adapt their talk with children to a developmental level that is slightly above the child's level of talk. The adult treats the child as a person who is capable of taking a conversational turn, including waiting while the adult speaks.

In some cultures, however, infants and toddlers learn language mostly by listening to adults talk. Children learn how to communicate by listening to stories and adults converse with each other. Adults in these cultures think that children can participate in conversations more when they are older. In the Mayan culture, for example, researchers found that whereas infants do not hear much child-directed speech, children between the ages of 13 and 35 months do hear more adult speech directed toward them. These adults may believe that the child is learning language by being a conversational partner in a social situation, but at an older age than in Western societies (63).

As you work with children and families, it will be important for you to observe the particular patterns of communication of children and families. You will then appreciate how, why, when, and where a child communicates to peers and adults.

Language Content and Culture

The content of adults' language with children may also differ by families and cultures. For example, families can differ in how they talk about past events with their children. Some parents may engage their young children in lengthy conversations. They also describe, elaborate, reminisce, and extend information about the past event. Other parents do not elaborate, but rather tell the more practical aspects of the past experience, prompting their child to remember, and asking many questions. Both of these styles may have their cultural value and purpose and prepare a child for styles of language use that succeed in their particular culture (64).

Dual Language Learners

Children may be learning two or more languages. Most infants and toddlers do have the brain capacity to hear the differences in the sounds and sequence of different languages. Young children are also able to learn the vocabulary of both languages and to speak two languages simultaneously (65). In fact, certain parts of the brain are dedicated to detect the different patterns in the languages that they hear. This allows the infant or toddler to learn multiple languages at the same time.

Newborns are prepared to learn two languages simultaneously. Those newborns who heard their mothers speak one language (e.g., English) while they were still in the womb preferred to hear that language over another language (e.g., Tagalog—a language spoken in the Philippines). However, newborns whose mothers spoke both English and Tagalog while pregnant showed equal preference for the two languages they heard prenatally (66). This demonstrates the remarkable ability of humans to learn languages.

Parents and teachers ask for information on dual language learning. One reason is that the population of the United States is quickly becoming more culturally and ethnically diverse. More than ever, many families have the opportunity to raise their children to be bilingual, but should they?

Let's first define what we mean by dual language learners, bilingual, monolingual, trilingual, and bidialectical.

- "Dual language learners are children learning two (or more) languages at the same time, as well as those learning a second language while continuing to develop their first (or home) language." (67)
- Bilingual children and adults speak more than one language.
- *Monolingual* children and adults speak one language only.
- *Trilingual* children and adults are learning three languages.
- *Bidialectical* children are learning two or more dialects. (A *dialect* is a particular version of a language, and although children who are bidialectical are learning basically the same language, such as English, they are learning two forms of that language.)

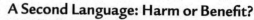

CULTURE CLOSE UP

A director of a program was surprised to hear that children who are learning two languages have a cognitive advantage over other children and that learning two languages is not harmful to their language development. He had been telling families that they should speak only one language, English, to their children so as to not confuse them. However, that was difficult for immigrant families that could not speak English well. He was concerned that he had actually caused harm to families because of his advice. He wanted to know all of the latest research and struggled with how to help the teachers and families in his program understand his profound change in how to think about dual language learning. He now wanted them to know all of the benefits of bilingualism and how to support children's learning of two or more languages starting at birth. Yet, he didn't want families who speak only one language to their children to begin to pressure young children to learn two languages. How would you present the research you have just read to families and teachers?

A Second Language: Harm or Benefit?

The answer is that learning two languages is quite beneficial for infants' and toddlers' brain development and ability to process language.

The ability to attend, shut out distracting information, and multitask (executive functioning) also improves with dual language learning children. Dual-language learning infants at 6 months of age were better than monolingual children at processing information and memory tasks (68). Twenty-four-month-olds' who were bilingual were better able to perform tasks without being distracted (69). Bilingualism was also found to improve abstract reasoning, working memory, and selective attention among low-income minority children in Portugal (70). If dual language learning children speak one language better than another, it is probably because they hear and interact with people more in that language (71, 72).

Now that we know that learning two or more languages at the same time actually benefits children, what are some strategies that adults can use to support infants and toddlers while they learn two languages?

Strategies for Adults with Infants and Toddlers Learning a Second Language

From an infant's or toddler's perspective, it may be easier to learn two languages if one adult, such as the father, primarily speaks one language with the child and a second adult, such as the teacher, speaks a second language with the child. This allows the child to consistently hear the differences in the sounds and words of the two languages. Although children may first confuse sounds and words in the two languages, they soon begin to keep the specific sounds, words, and sentence structure of each language separate and use the appropriate language with the right person who speaks that language with them. DeHouwer (73) recommends that parents of children learning two or more languages can support their children's language development if they use the strategies identified in Figure 9.3.

Honoring the Home Language

Many educators believe that infants and toddlers who attend programs need at least one teacher who speaks the child's native language in order to provide the child and family someone with whom they can communicate well. With so many languages spoken in the United States, however, administrators of programs may find it difficult to find teachers to speak the languages of the young children in their programs. But, even if a teacher can't speak a child's home language, she can learn words and songs in that language to use frequently. Words of endearment that help the infant or toddler feel safe and loved are especially important to learn and use. Both the children and the families will benefit if the teacher makes an attempt to honor the child's home language.

The parent should be encouraged to continue speaking the home language to the infant or toddler. Infants and toddlers deserve **linguistic continuity** (74).

FIGURE 9.3   **Strategies for supporting children who are learning two languages.**

- Make sure that children hear both languages frequently and in a variety of circumstances.
- Create opportunities for your children to use the languages that they hear.
- Read books to and with your children in each of the languages that are important to their lives.
- If you feel strongly about your children using one particular language with you, encourage them to use it in all of their communication with you.
- However, do not punish or criticize your children for using or not using a particular language. Instead, encourage them or offer them the appropriate words in the language you want them to speak.
- If a child is not learning either language well, ask a doctor for a hearing test in order to rule out medical problems.

Source: Based on DeHouwer, A. (1999, July). Two or more languages in early childhood: Some general points and practical recommendations. *ERIC Digest* (ED433697). District of Columbia: ERIC clearinghouse on Languages and Linguistics.

Programs that try to impose "English-only" rules on families may be doing harm. "In fact, the abrupt end of the use of the home language by a child's parents may lead to great emotional and psychological difficulties both for the parents and for the child. After all, language is strongly linked to emotion, affect, and identity" (75, p. 2). Also, if the parent doesn't have a great command of a language other than the home language, the language models as well as the emotional interactions may be limited for the child. Another language that is gaining in importance as a form of communication for all young children is sign language (76, 77).

Using Sign Language

Just as with a second verbal language, young children are capable of learning a sign symbol system to communicate. There are many books and Websites available that help parents and teachers learn how to teach their infants signs before they can talk. Infants can sign before they can speak because the fine motor development in their hands matures before the body parts needed to speak words, giving them a way to communicate prior to using words.

Dawson, at 1 year of age, could sign "more" and "down" because his parents modeled the sign "more" when he wanted more juice and the sign "down" when he wanted down from his high chair. Now Dawson, an 18-month-old, signs "more" and says the word as well. Learning sign language when he was younger helped him communicate with his parents and did not interfere with learning verbal language and won't as long as his parents use words with him as well as sign language.

 Watch this video which demonstrates the signs that a barely one-year-old infant knows. While we usually do not recommend quizzing children as this mother does, we understand that she is demonstrating how many signs the child knows, which is remarkable. Note how the mother emphasizes that she always says the word with the sign.

https://www.youtube.com/watch?v=7gSZfW4gVhI

When infants are taught to use sign language, they do not learn and say words more quickly. Learning sign language does not interfere with infants learning to say words, either (78). However, parents and teachers are discovering that when 11-month-olds sign words like "more" and "drink," the adults can use this powerful tool to help them be responsive to the infants' needs. A baby who learns signs may be less frustrated, as he can communicate his needs. The mothers of 20 infants who were taught how to teach their infants from 8 to 20 months sign language were more responsive to their infants' nonverbal cues and encouraged more independent behavior. "With infant signs, infants reveal their thoughts, feelings, interests, and personalities in their own contexts through everyday interactions. Babies open our minds to their minds" (79, p. 115). When infants learn sign language we have another window into their thinking before they can talk. This helps us respect how capable they are at communicating.

Summary of Dual Language Learning

The following statement provides an excellent summary to this section concerning children learning two languages:

> (1) A bilingual environment is most often a necessity, not a choice; (2) hearing two or more languages in childhood is not a cause of language disorder or language delay; (3) children's use of two languages within one sentence is not a sign of confusion; and (4) children do not just "pick up" a language; they need a strongly supportive and rich environment (80).

STRATEGIES TO SUPPORT LANGUAGE DEVELOPMENT AND LEARNING

1. Recognize the capacities of infants and toddlers to understand language and communicate using gestures, facial expressions, sounds, and words.

2. Identify language delay early in a child's life so that the child and family receive support in developing language skills.

3. Follow recommendations for parents of children learning two or more languages during the infant and toddler years.

4. Honor a child's home language by encouraging parents to continue using the language, employing native language speakers in the program, and using words and phrases from the child's home language during routines and interactions with the child.

5. Use the dozen strategies identified in this chapter to support children's language learning.

6. Understand that adults' use of responsive and sensitive language strategies is related to children's language development.

7. Use intervention strategies that help parents use language during routines such as eating.

 Check Your Understanding 9.3
Click here to check your understanding of the concepts in this section.

Program Practices that Enhance Language Learning and Development

As many infants and toddlers venture outside the home environment to participate in child care and learning programs, family child care homes, or early intervention programs such as Early Head Start or programs for children with disabilities, they develop relationships that can enhance or discourage language development.

Child Care and Learning Programs: Relationships and Responsive Interactions

The results of the NICHD Early Child Care Research Network, (81) study, following 500 to 800 infants and toddlers in 10 sites in the United States including a variety of types of child care programs as well as those at home with a parent most of the time, found that the overall quality of child care and language stimulation in particular was related to children's language development at 15, 24, and 36 months. Also, the quality of the environment is correlated with the language outcomes for infants and toddlers, both receptive language and expressive communication skills.

Early Prevention and Intervention Programs

When parents are stressed, their children's language may be harmed. However, Early Head Start supports young children's early language development. Even though the parents who are low-income experience stress, girls' language is "boosted." Boys' language development is "protected." Although boys and girls are affected differently, their language development is supported in Early Head Start (82, p. 695). This may be because teachers are taught to engage in descriptive language discussions with children. Teachers also work closely with family members in Early Head Start.

Early intervention programs include programs for infants and toddlers at risk for learning challenges because of their socioeconomic status and programs for young children identified by assessment teams as having disabilities. The parents of a child at risk or with a disability may receive home visits from a family support program or attend a family-centered child care center or intervention play group.

The communication enhancement strategies in Figure 9.4 acknowledge the strengths of each child, ensure the child's success, emphasize adult-child interactions as crucial for the language achievements of the child, and promote language development in the environments where the children use language.

FIGURE 9.4 **Effective strategies for improving language development in young children with disabilities.**

1. Facilitate language interactions with parents and teachers during routines, such as bath time, feeding and eating, and trips to the grocery store
2. Accept the child's communication bids by showing affection, attention, and verbal feedback
3. Use a facilitative (encouraging) versus a directive style (demanding)
4. Contingently respond through expansion of the child's sounds, words, and sentences
5. Using augmentative communication devices for children who cannot speak (picture symbols that the child uses or computer-like devices that speak for the child)

Source: From Prizant, B., Wetherby, A., & Roberts, J. (1993). Communication disorders in infants and toddlers. In J. Charles & H. Zeanah (Eds.), *Handbook of infant mental health.* New York: Guilford Press.

DEVELOPMENTAL TRENDS AND RESPONSIVE INTERACTIONS

LANGUAGE LEARNING AND DEVELOPMENT

Infants and toddlers develop the capacity to understand, express, and use language.

Development	Example

0–4 months (infant)

Development	Example
• Infants may startle if they hear a loud sound. • Infants hear the differences in all of the sounds spoken. • Infants may stop crying when they hear a familiar adult's voice. • Infants prefer to hear "parentese," a simpler version of language with many repetitions, directed toward infants. • Infants listen when an adult talks or sings to them while looking at them. • Infants cry when they are in pain, are hungry, or are distressed. • By 1 months of age, babies have different cries for hunger and pain. • Infants smile by 6 weeks and laugh toward the end of this age period. • Infants coo (make soft vowel sounds). • Infants will stare at interesting pictures in books.	Terrell's arms flew out as if to grasp on to his parent when he heard a big bang. Matt looked at his infant and with an excited voice and a big smile said, "Look at you. You are smiling. Yes, you are smiling." Erica gave her father a big smile when he picked her up out of her crib. Brenda held Jordon so they could gaze into each other's eyes. Jordon cooed softly and Brenda cooed back. Then she waited for Jordon to take another turn.

4–8 months (infant)

Development	Example
• Infants turn their head toward a noise or someone speaking their name. • Infants enjoy adults talking, singing, and laughing with them. • Infants vocalize with intention to get a response from the adult. • Infants make high-pitched squeals. • Infants practice their sounds when exploring and with favorite adults. • Infants begin to babble—at first with one consonant and then by combining two consonants. • Infants engage in turn-taking conversations with adults. • Babies will look at different pictures in a book and get excited at a favorite one or at the enthusiastic tone of an adult who is reading to them. • At the end of this age period, infants tune into the sounds of the language(s) they are hearing and begin to lose the ability to hear the difference in sounds spoken in other languages.	As Danielle, the infant teacher, was holding Donovan on her lap, she pointed to the pictures in the sturdy board book. "Look," she said, pointing to the picture, "a ball. There's your ball," as she pointed to a ball on the floor. Donovan looked at the picture, then at the ball on the floor, and back to the picture. "Tt" said Afi as he lay in his teacher's arms looking up at her. "Tada" exclaimed his teacher back to him. "Tt, ta" repeated Afi as he took his turn in the conversation.

8–12 months (infant)

Development	Example
• Infants are beginning to play social games such as peek-a-boo or "so big." • Infants enjoy listening to sound play (rhymes), songs, and finger-plays. • Babbling continues to develop with combined syllables such as "dada," "mama," "nana," and "tutu," but now the infant may be using these sounds specifically for mom or dad. • Infants will use sounds consistently for an object or person or animal. • If they hear another language *with* an adult through interactive conversational strategies, then infants can "keep the brain open to the sounds of a second language." • Infants may begin to use single words. • At the end of the age period, infants may begin to point to engage an adult. • They are using facial expressions and gestures such as shaking head or arms out to be picked up to communicate to adults or peers.	Deanna raised her hands and smiled when her mother said, "So big!" One of Trishanna's first words was "dada," which she excitedly said over and over again when she saw her father. Thomas used the sounds, "ba ba" to indicate he wanted his bottle of milk.

Teacher or Parent-Child Interaction	Environment
0–4 months (infant)	

Teacher or Parent-Child Interaction	Environment
• Use infant-directed speech. • Hold and talk to babies. Engage in long eye gazes while taking conversational turns. • Respect the baby if he needs a break and turns his head away, closes his eyes, or arches his back. • Repeat the sounds that infants make and wait for the infant to make the sound again (turn taking). • Be an empathic language partner—comment on the baby's feelings. • Use words and sounds to comfort babies. • Interpret babies' burps, cries, yawns, stretching, and sounds as forms of communication. Say, "Oh, you're telling me you're sleepy." • Sing lullabies and other songs. • Read books with rhythmic phrases and books with one picture on a page with 2- to 4-month-olds.	• The best environment is in the arms of a caring adult who holds the baby and talks softly. • Provide toys that make pleasant sounds. Gently hold the toy and share the sounds with the baby. • Provide interesting materials to touch while you comment on the textures. • Add mirrors low along a wall. Babies will look and possibly make sounds.

4–8 months (infant)	

Teacher or Parent-Child Interaction	Environment
• Use infant-directed speech. • Talk with babies often. Show them new objects and people and name them. • Repeat the sounds that infants make and wait for the infant to make the sound again (turn taking). • Use sign language for several familiar items such as "milk," "dog," or "more." • Sing songs and say finger-plays. • Use words to describe children's feelings expressed through gestures, body postures, and sounds. • Read simple books with one to two pictures on a page. Point to the pictures as you say the name of the picture. • Read the same books over and over. • Use joint attention strategies—point at a toy or picture in a book when you say the name or talk about it.	• Provide interesting toys and materials for babies to handle and explore. • Provide cardboard books with handles so that babies can crawl to them and pick them up. • Books with handles encourage babies to hang on to them. • Make a peek-a-boo picture book by gluing a piece of cloth over each picture. • Create a cozy book corner where teachers can be comfortable and read to babies. • Provide sound boxes (safely sealed) with different objects in them that make different sounds when shaken. • Add puppets to the environment. Use them at times to "talk" to the child. Put the puppet on the child's hand and wait to see what the child says or does.

8–12 months (infant)	

Teacher or Parent-Child Interaction	Environment
• Play familiar games such as peek-a-boo, pat-a-cake, or "how big are you?" • Respond to infants' nonverbal communication with words. • Sometimes look at and wait for infants to initiate sounds or words. • Imitate the sounds and then expand, elaborate, and extend the infants' language. • Model the next step in language development. • Use self-talk and parallel talk. • Talk often in a responsive way using a varied vocabulary. Don't bombard the child. • Read books with enthusiasm—changing the tone of your voice with different characters. • Talk about the pictures and the story as you read it. Engage babies in the story with your voice and gestures. • Wait while looking at a picture for babies to initiate with sounds, pointing, or facial expressions.	• Create a cozy book corner where babies can easily reach and handle books. • Create an "All About Me" book—small photo albums for each child with pictures of themselves, their family, their favorite toys, peers, teachers, and the family pets. Make them available to the children. Change the pictures as the child grows. • Musical push toys encourage infants to handle them and make sounds.

DEVELOPMENTAL TRENDS AND RESPONSIVE INTERACTIONS (Continued)

Development	Example

12–18 months (young toddler)

- Young toddlers can follow simple directions such as "Come here" or "Go get your shoes" without you gesturing.
- Young toddlers can play a social game without you demonstrating the action–for example, when you say "Wave bye-bye," they wave even though you don't show them how.
- Young toddlers will point to engage adults and peers.
- Rapid word learning—a language explosion—may occur with the children learning many new words.
- Young toddlers will combine words toward the end of this age period.
- Young toddlers will jabber (stringing many sounds together) using the intonation that adults use.
- Young toddlers will use gestures and language to reject, request, comment, refuse, demand, and name objects and people.
- Young toddlers use gestures and language to maintain an interaction or conversation with an adult or peer.

Janeika's teacher said, "Let's play pat-a-cake," and Janeika started clapping her hands together.

Ross looked up expectantly at his teacher, jabbering many sounds together as if asking her a question.

18–24 months (toddler)

- Toddlers can go get familiar toys from another room in the house when an adult asks them to and can follow directions such as "close the door."
- Toddlers combine words to name things ("that cat"), to deny ("no bite"), and to reject ("no more").
- Toddlers are combining two to three words with meaning.
- Toddlers use language for a variety of purposes, including asking "What that?"
- Toddlers point to an increasing number of pictures in books when an adult talks about the picture.

"Hi, Kitty," "open door," and "hat on" were just a few of the two-word combinations Cheral used at 20 months of age.

Tyra moved quickly over to the bookshelf, picked up a book with a bright cover, and rushed back to his teacher. After sitting comfortably in her lap, he opened the book and enthusiastically started pointing to the pictures as his teacher named them.

24–36 months (toddler)

- Toddlers understand more complex directions and remember words to short songs and finger-plays.
- Toddlers are using many two- to four-word sentences.
- Toddlers can point to and name many body parts.
- Toddlers add "ing" to words.
- Toddlers begin using prepositions such as "on" and "in."
- Toddlers add an "s" to words to indicate plurals.
- Toddlers may begin to ask "Why?"
- Toddlers will begin to tell you stories about what they did or what they saw.
- Toward the end of this period, a toddler can use the pictures to tell you what is happening in a story.

"I love you, you love me" sang DeLila.

Darien yelled, "I want go outside"

Mindy started to add "ing" to words she had been saying for several months. She said, "I running" and "I eating" rather than "I run" and "I eat."

"Why I kick wall?" "Why rain?" asked Hiawanda.

"Look, he's playing," exclaimed Treat as he pointed to a picture in his favorite book.

Teacher or Parent-Child Interaction	Environment

12–18 months (young toddler)

- Stay on topic in a conversation with a young toddler. See how many turns the child will take.
- Respond to the intonation of the child's jabbering. For example, if it seems as if the child is asking a question, answer what you think the child might be asking.
- Respond to young toddlers' pointing and other nonverbal communication with language.
- Use words that describe and compare sizes, shapes, and sounds.
- When a young toddler uses words such as "I jump," model the next step in language development by saying "You're jumping," adding the "ing" to the word. Do this with both the content of the words and the structure of the words or sentences.

- Introduce art materials such as play dough, clay, and paint.
- Add paper towel rolls for young toddlers to make sounds.
- Musical pull toys entice young toddlers to walk and pull objects behind them or push them.
- Sturdy music boxes encourage young toddlers to push buttons to "make music."
- Drums and other musical instruments can be made available.
- Add a sturdy CD player with a story from a parent taped on it.
- Use a tape recorder to tape young toddlers' voices and play it back to them.
- Provide bubble-making materials.
- Provide spaces for two or three children to encourage peer conversation.

18–24 months (toddler)

- Read books with longer stories, pausing as you go through the book to encourage toddlers to talk about the pictures and the story. Ask open-ended questions such as "How does the bear feel?"
- Wonder often with the child: "I wonder what will happen to the bear."
- Engage toddlers in conversation, trying to stay on the same topic as the child.
- Introduce new conversations about interesting objects and events.

- Set up an elaborate obstacle course and use words such as "in," "out," "over," "through," "around," "up," and "down" as the toddler goes through the course.
- Provide new books each week but keep children's favorites available.
- Provide a wider variety of art materials.
- Provide sensory materials.

24–36 months (toddler)

- Answer their "why" questions with patience and enthusiasm. This is how children learn and engage in social interactions.
- Listen with your eyes to the "stories" toddlers tell.
- Model saying words that are plurals, such as "dogs," "elephants," and so on.
- Use descriptive words such as "mozzarella cheese" rather than just "cheese," or "blue jay" rather than just "bird." Then say, "A blue jay is a bird."
- Have long conversations with toddlers, following their lead.
- Read books to small informal groups or to individual children.

- Provide pictures for children to match.
- Puzzles of animals, people, vehicles, and food are important.
- Books with many pictures and short stories can be added to the environment.
- Dramatic play materials encourage conversation.

> **Check Your Understanding 9.4**
> Click here to check your understanding of the concepts in this section.

Summary

Infants and toddlers have the capacity to become proficient language learners in the first 3 years of life.

- Language is used for communication with others and is affected by the quality of the child's relationships, the social context, and the environment. Throughout the first 3 years, infants and toddlers learn to make the sounds of the language spoken to them; combine sounds into words and combine words into sentences; learn the syntax, pragmatics, and prosody of language; learn the meaning of an astonishing number of words; and communicate in a variety of ways—the furrowing of a brow, a loud screech, whining, pointing, talking, and shouting. Girls do seem to talk earlier and speak more than boys in the first 20 months of life. However, differences in language development between boys and girls do not seem to last, and after age 20 months, fewer differences are found in the vocabularies of boys and girls.

- Infants and toddlers progress in receptive and expressive language, pragmatics, and prosody. Hearing loss and prematurity are two factors that affect language development in young children.

- Young children do have the capacity to learn two languages simultaneously, and there are strategies to support infants and toddlers as they are learning. Adults can use 12 major strategies to support language development. When infant-toddler teachers are more responsive and sensitive, then the language development of the children increases. Cultural differences exist in how children are viewed as conversational partners.

- Program practices that enhance children's language development include overall quality of the program, quality of the environment, and the quality of language stimulation. Children who attend Early Head Start improve in language development. There are specific strategies to use with children with language disabilities that enhance their language learning.

Key Terms

choice questions
closed questions
communication
communicative-linguistic
  parameters
contingent interactions
conversational dance

fast mapping
language
language delay
language explosion
linguistic continuity
multimodal input
open-ended questions

parallel talk
phonological
ritual constraints
self-talk
semantic elaboration
system constraints
true questions

Reflections and Resources for the Reader

REFLECTIONS

1. What are the key strategies that adults can use to support children as they learn two languages?
2. Identify the important features of a child care and learning setting that support infants' and toddlers' language learning and development.

OBSERVATION AND APPLICATION OPPORTUNITIES

1. Jeff is 2-months-old and his parents want him to learn to speak both English and Spanish. His dad speaks Spanish and English quite well and his mom speaks English. What advice would you give them?
2. Choose one capacity (e.g., receptive language) and discuss how children progress from prenatally to age 3. What are the implications of the information for parents and teachers?
3. Choose one of the strategies listed under the heading Development and Learning in Adult-Child Relationships for promoting language development and give examples of a conversation between an adult and a child, with the adult using the strategy.
4. Observe infants or toddlers in a child development and learning setting. Identify the skills that two children of different ages have in receptive and expressive language.

SUPPLEMENTARY ARTICLES AND BOOKS TO READ

Honig, A. S. (n.d.). Infants & toddlers: How to read to very young children. *Scholastic.* Retrieved from *www.scholastic.com/teachers/article/infants-toddlers-how-read-very-young-children*

Hulit, L. M., Fahey, K. R., & Howard, M. R. (2014). *Born to talk: An introduction to speech and language development, Video-Enhanced Pearson eText—Access Card/Edition 6.* NJ: Pearson.

Owens Jr., R. E. (2015). *Language development: An introduction, Enhanced Pearson eText —Access Card.* NJ: Pearson.

Zangl, R. (2014). *Raising a talker. Easy activities for birth to age 3.* Lewisville, NC: Gryphon House.

INTERESTING LINKS

Search for the American Speech-Language-Hearing Association (ASHA) for information on the causes of hearing loss in young children.

Search for the *Head Start Early Childhood Learning & Knowledge Center (ECLKC).* This site provides numerous excellent resources for infant/toddler educators.

Search for The Program for Infant/Toddler Care (*PITC*). This site provides many materials on language development.

Search for *ZERO TO THREE*: *Early Language & Literacy* This site offers articles, podcasts, handouts, and instructional materials.

10

Motor Learning and Development

Pearson Education

Joella flapped her arms and ran around the yard with glee. Every inch of her body spoke to her energy and excitement.

Michael froze in place, a serious, uncertain look on his face. His body was slightly hunched as he listened intently to the distant sound of a barking dog.

Raj squatted to study a bug moving across the play yard, a picture of concentration.

Helen, their infant-toddler teacher, watched them and thought, "I know so much about what they feel and think by watching their little bodies."

The motor system is how infants and toddlers move their bodies, gesture with their hands and arms, and show expressions on their faces. It is not just how they move. It is how they communicate. In many ways we think of infants and toddlers in terms of their motor development. We even name an entire stage of development after the toddling, balancing gait of the beginning walker. Our first thoughts of milestones, aside from smiling and sleeping through the night, tend to be motor milestones—rolling over, crawling, standing, and walking. It's not just the adults who think about motor development, either. Motor development occupies much of an infant's or toddler's time and effort: moving her body to get where she wants to be, and reaching and holding to bring objects to look at and taste.

Each Child is Capable and Unique

Each child is constantly adjusting his or her movements in response to a changing body, abilities, and the environment. Each child finds solutions to motor tasks in the moment. Temperament and gender contribute to each child's motor learning.

Temperament

Temperament affects motor development directly. The motivation of an active child to move, or the inhibition of a more fearful child, certainly affect the competence a child achieves in motor skills. Some children are *motor driven*, wanting to try everything and highly motivated to learn and practice motor skills. Others are *motor cautious*, needing time to watch others before trying new activities (1).

Teachers should consider temperament in planning motor activities for infants and toddlers. The motor driven child may be surprisingly competent. Or reckless. In these early years, the infant-toddler teacher uses her observation skills to determine how much freedom to move is safe for each child. The very skilled child may run, climb,

Terry is demonstrating how interrelated the areas of development can be. She is resisting gravity and balancing to stand. She has isolated a finger to strike the key. She is using language and imitation to sing a song and she is socially engaged with her audience.

Pearson Education

and jump off of sofas with an accurate sense of his own safety. For this child, the teacher tries to provide space and opportunity to move. Another motor driven child might need constant, close supervision because she lacks any sense of danger.

A motor cautious toddler may need support and encouragement to practice motor skills. Infant-toddler teachers can playfully offer a toy to the side to lure a young infant into rolling over. Sofa pillows on the floor become an obstacle course for crawlers. Crouching a few feet away from a new walker with your arms outstretched in welcome is a good motivator to keep a toddler moving.

Amazingly, competence in motor skills and exploration at 5 months has been associated with academic competence at the age of 14 (2). A process called a **developmental cascade** begins with motor maturity and active exploration at 5 months. A developmental cascade is a process of changes over time in which skills emerge and build on one another within a person. For example, an infant who can sit unsupported is able to use her hands to hold and handle objects. She coordinates her vision with her hands to learn about objects. Her ability to maintain balance while moving her hands and head help her to actively explore her environment. This core body strength will soon support crawling. Experience with objects is building mental concepts and curiosity that, in turn, inspire more exploration in the young crawler and walker. The rich experiences of infancy cascade throughout childhood producing a focused, competent learner at age 14.

OBSERVATION INVITATION **10.1**

What do you see in this picture that suggests Rosie is an active explorer? Click on the icon to answer a question about the photo.

Gender

The bodies of men and women certainly differ. Men tend to be bigger and stronger, with bodies evolved to be hunters. Women are smaller, with bodies evolved to reproduce. But are these differences present in infants and toddlers? Infant and toddler boys and girls are pretty similar in motor learning and development. In fact, there are no real differences in motor ability by gender in infancy (3). Where there are differences, we don't always know whether it is because of their bodies, their experiences, or simply, stereotypes.

As with all other areas of development, we look increasingly at the effect of genes and hormones. Genes and hormones may influence gender related behavior. At the same time, experiences can cause genes to activate or stop them from expressing. Looking for the biological explanation is one approach to understanding gender related behavior. Early animal studies introduced male hormones to the womb of a pregnant guinea pig and produced female pups with male sexualized behavior. Clearly, this is not an option with humans. However, studies have looked at situations in which female human fetuses are exposed to an unusually high level of testosterone in the womb. There is a genetic disorder that causes the female fetus to produce testosterone. The young girl then develops more traditionally male physical and play behavior. Toddler boys and girls with high levels of testosterone prefer toys that move in space such as balls. Both also have more physical aggression, and more dominance in play. The same is true for young girls whose mothers took male hormones during their pregnancies (4).

Adult attitudes and expectations may contain **gender bias**. Gender bias means a person has different expectations for performance based on sex. If an adult has stereotypical ideas about boys being more active than girls, she may arrange play spaces differently. An infant-toddler teacher may offer boys more opportunities to play in open spaces and steer little girls toward books and dolls. In one study, mothers of 11-month-old infants were asked to predict how their child would perform on a task of crawling up or down a slanted ramp. Mothers tended to underestimate how well their daughters would do and overestimate how well their sons would do. The babies' performances did not differ by gender (5). In general, the typical boy and girl have very similar activity levels. Still, the most active child in a group is likely to be a boy and the least active, a girl (6).

Reflexes

Reflexes determine the earliest movements. Infants are moving long before they are born. Using ultrasound, doctors have seen movements of the upper spine as early as 5 to 6 weeks of gestation, and movements of arms and legs by 8 to 9 weeks (7). The body and brain develop and store information about movement patterns when the fetus is active. Movement helps the fetus develop muscles and move through the birth canal.

Newborns are also physically active. Reflexes drive much of their activity. Traditionally reflexes have been understood to occur at the brainstem level, automatically keeping the infant alive. Now we understand adults help to regulate reflexes and even that reflexes are influenced by culture (8). Of the nearly 75 reflexes present in the newborn, the most well-known support feeding, gazing, and grasping—as you can see in Figure 10.1.

The first reflexes used by an infant are referred to as **primitive reflexes**. The **rooting reflex** and **sucking reflex** help the newborn find the nipple and begin to eat.

FIGURE 10.1   Primitive reflexes.

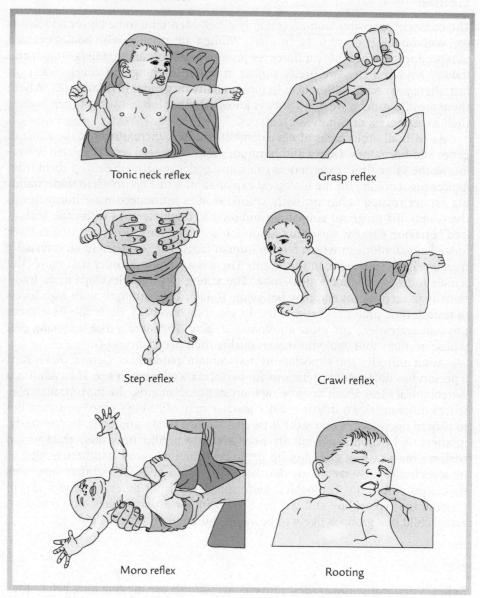

Tonic neck reflex

Grasp reflex

Step reflex

Crawl reflex

Moro reflex

Rooting

Babies also root and suck on their own hands to comfort themselves. When the baby feels a slight pressure against his cheek, he turns his head toward the pressure, "rooting" around for the nipple. When his lips come in contact with a surface, he begins sucking. Newborns are already practiced at sucking; it is reflexive and does not need to be learned. Newborns also have a reflex that protects them from swallowing anything other than liquids. They have a tongue thrust reflex that pushes everything out of the mouth. It's a good idea to wait to begin spoon feeding until this reflex disappears.

 Watch this video to see infant reflexes. How do these reflexes help survival?

https://www.youtube.com/watch?v=hDiqATUYjX4

The **Moro reflex**, or startle reflex, is a physical response to a loud sound or the sense of falling. The infant throws back her head, extends her arms and legs, and then pulls them back in. The posture also seems to act as communication to parents and teachers that the baby is stressed and needs to be picked up and comforted. The **tonic neck reflex** moves the arms in response to the infant's head turning in supine (lying on his back) position. When the baby's head is turned to the right, his right arm will thrust out, his left will be raised straight up. If he turns his head to the left, the arms will adjust. This may help the infant keep one hand in front of his eyes. This reflex begins to disappear as the baby begins to bring his hands together in the midline, where he can see them easily. The **palmar grasp reflex** causes the baby to close her fingers around something placed in the palm. She will grasp an adult's finger or hair, or a toy. Her feet will also curl when lightly brushed. When a baby is held upright, with her feet touching a solid surface, the **step reflex** makes the baby appear to be walking.

These primitive reflexes are very effective for the first few months and then begin to fade. As the primitive reflexes fade, another set of reflexes begins to emerge. **Postural reflexes** help the infant resist gravity and provide the basis for developing balance, posture, and voluntary movement. The postural reflexes become part of the central nervous system and function throughout life. These reflexes help a person turn his head or shift his weight to regain balance. They also help modulate the muscle tone so that a person may, for example, move his head without throwing his entire body into a reaction.

Check Your Understanding 10.1
Click here to check your understanding of the concepts in this section.

Knowing the Child

Changes in motor skills over the first three years do not come simply from growing bigger and older. Current theories of motor development propose that it is a complex, ongoing process of learning (9). Infants and toddlers are always responding to changes in their own height, weight, proportion, and posture. They are motivated by the opportunities and constraints in the environment. Adults encourage or discourage movement.

With a healthy brain and muscles, babies make remarkable progress in their ability to use their bodies to perceive sensory information and move toward or manipulate the source of the information. Within the first 3 years, babies make the journey from little controlled movement to running and jumping, and they advance from sucking on a hand to calm themselves to using buttons and zippers to get dressed. For the infant-toddler teacher, understanding how motor learning and development happens will help you in supporting this area of learning and development.

Dynamic Systems Theory

Dynamic systems theory, developed by Esther Thelen (10), says motor skills develop as the young child finds the best solution to using his body to make something happen in his environment. All of the changing parts of his body come into the solution (height, weight, proportions, center of gravity, abilities). The opportunity for action in the environment is called an **affordance**. For example, if an infant-toddler teacher holds a small doll in front of a 3-month-old, the child will flail her arms in an unsuccessful attempt to reach for it. A month later, she will make a successful, although ragged, reach. At 7 months, she will make a smooth and accurate reach. The affordance is the doll within reach. The solutions are the result of the body's systems working together. In the 3-month-old, there is not enough muscle control for success. The 4-month-old has gained strength and control, brings her attention to the task, and coordinates her eyes and her hands. She uses her trunk strength to hold her body still, her limb muscles for reaching and her finger muscles for grasping. By 7 months, the action has become automatic.

In the first 3 years, the child's body is constantly changing. The infant's and toddler's body is growing and changing height, weight, and proportions. Experiences build muscle strength and motor skills. These changes require dynamic solutions. For example, if a 4-week-old child wants to suck his thumb, he bends his short arm at the shoulder. At 6 months, he will bend his longer arm at the elbow. Each new posture brings the infant into contact with new aspects of the world, new perceptual information. Being able to see and touch the bottom bookshelf presents the goal of emptying the shelf of its books. Being able to see and touch the cupboard door presents the goal of opening and closing it. Each new posture requires practice in reestablishing balance and control in pursuit of other interests (11).

The environment is also changing. Different materials and experiences may be available. As the seasons change, the child may have more or less opportunity to play outdoors. A toy that was too heavy for the 1-year-old new walker may be easy for the 18-month-old walking pro to carry. Adults, siblings, and peers are also part of the environment. When others take delight in the infant's or toddler's new motor skills, the child is likely to repeat her efforts. As a teacher, the physical opportunities you provide and your enjoyment and encouragement are important parts of each child's motor learning.

 Watch this video to see Esther Thelen's studies of movement. Do you see how every motor skill is refined with learning?

https://www.youtube.com/watch?v=RI3t_hsFzX0

An affordance is the way the environment is perceived as having possibilities for action. In order for infants and toddlers to engage in new small or large motor actions, the environment must offer opportunities or invitations. Using a popular evaluation tool, the *Affordances in the Home Environment for Motor Development* (12), researchers look at outside space, inside space, daily activities, fine and large motor toys, and child and family characteristics. Studies find that these affordances in infancy can predict motor and cognitive success later in life (13). This same group, not surprisingly, found that families in higher socioeconomic brackets provided more affordances. Infant-toddler teachers and families need to understand the impact of these opportunities and provide them during the first year of life. Thinking in terms of possibilities is an effective intervention.

Respect, Reflect, Relate

<u>Respect</u>: Joey, a very competent crawler at 11 months, is beginning to walk. Two steps and down. Two steps and down. Picking up a toy throws off his balance. The steps up to the slide are suddenly impossible. Yet, he keeps going.

<u>Reflect</u>: Every new posture and form of locomotion requires new learning. Joey is refining his movements with each attempt.

<u>Relate</u>: Appreciate Joey's energy and motivation. Encourage him to keep moving but keep a close eye on him. He will not have much judgment to bring to his new skills.

Principles of Motor Development

Some parts of motor development seem to be fairly constant across cultures or relationships. The main principles are that development is

- **cephalocaudal**, muscle control moves from the head (cephalo) to the tail (caudal) or top down. The infant achieves head control long before he can control his legs and feet.
- **proximal-distal**, beginning with the midline (proximal or near) and progressing outward and downward (distal or distance). The infant gains control of the trunk months before he controls his hands.
- beginning with the large muscle groups and proceeding to the small muscle groups. The infant controls his arms before he controls his fingers.

Two other important principles of motor skills are **balance** and **resisting gravity**. Balance is the ability to move or stay in one position without falling by shifting weight. In every **posture** and form of **locomotion**, the child is constantly making tiny corrections to maintain balance. This is easy to observe in watching a 7-month-old working to master sitting without support. He will use his hands to touch the ground or spread his arms outwards for balance. He shifts his shoulders and turns his head if he feels himself slipping to one side. New walkers stretch both arms out to the side like tightrope walkers. Movement in early infancy is an ongoing attempt to resist gravity. The young infant's large, heavy head needs a strong trunk and neck to lift it when the baby is on her tummy (prone). Strong leg muscles make resisting gravity by kicking much easier when the infant is supine. The effects of gravity come front and center again as the new walker takes two steps and falls to her bottom.

Carrying objects while crawling or walking is an important activity in the second year of life. Experienced crawlers may carry a toy in their mouths or in a hand that is also being used to support weight and propel the child forward. One may carry a toy under the arm while scooching on the bottom. Experienced walkers may carry one or more toys in their hands while walking. New crawlers and walkers are much less likely to bring their hands into the action (14).

 Watch this video to see pre-locomotor skills in infants. How do the principles of motor development appear in the sequence of motor skills shown in the video?

https://www.youtube.com/watch?v=WpxR_KUSC8o

Locomotion

For infants and toddlers, motor skills are a way to achieve their goals in relationships (staying close to the to the familiar adult) and in learning (figuring out how rings fit a stick). Most importantly, achieving new motor skills is a goal in itself. Infants and toddlers work tirelessly, attempting a new skill and practicing it over and over until they are proficient. However, they may go about their motor tasks in unique ways.

Locomotion, or movement, follows the principles of proximal-distal and cephalocaudal development. Trunk and neck strength allow head control. Together with arm movements, these body parts work to create rolling. Kicking and reaching build muscle strength and control that contribute to crawling. Crawling appears in many forms, combat crawls, scooching on the bottom while sitting up, and the traditional hands and knees. Some children never crawl. Standing without holding on to something and cruising, walking while holding on the edge of a sofa or a coffee table, usually come before those first steps.

As Lois Barclay Murphy (15) describes so beautifully, the first steps are not the end of the locomotive adventure for the toddler or two:

> As I sat on a bench at the side of the road in the zoo, watching the children brought by their mothers or fathers, I rarely saw a little boy walking quietly beside his parent. One was hopping, another was jumping. Others were leaping, or skipping, or loping, raising each foot higher than it needed to be lifted for ordinary walking. Some children waved their arms. Each one seemed to savor the feeling of the moment, wanting to discover the possibilities of locomotion (p. 1).

OBSERVATION INVITATION 10.2

Click the play button to watch this video and answer questions about infants finding their own answers on how to move forward. How do these examples illustrate the dynamic systems theory?

Changes in locomotor skills require new learning and new solutions to the familiar problems of a developing body, balance, and resisting gravity. It seems that new forms of movement require new information about things like slopes and edges. A new crawler may try to go headfirst down a steep slope or off the edge of a step. An experienced crawler will judge the slope or the drop-off and stop if it is too steep. That same excellent judge of drop-offs, as a new walker, will try to walk down the steep slope or off of a step. It seems that they can't bring their hard won knowledge about the world into the new posture and movement (16).

In fact, experienced crawlers give up a lot to become walkers. They are shaky and uneven in their steps. They fall down often. After studying new walkers, researchers found that there are many benefits to being upright that help the toddler want to keep trying. These benefits include covering more space in less time. They see more. They can experience richer visual input, access and play more with distant objects. They also interact in qualitatively new and different ways with caregivers (17). Adults also respond with so much enthusiasm and excitement to a toddler's first steps that a child feels the effort is worthwhile.

 Watch this video to see toddler locomotion. What locomotive affordances are available for these new walkers?

https://www.youtube.com/watch?v=Y0j4K8DEER8&spfreload=10

Manipulation

Typical milestone charts are organized in ways that separate large and small muscle skills, but development is more holistic than that. For example, as a 3-month-old is gaining head and neck control, she will enjoy being on her tummy and looking around. As the control strengthens, she will be able to use a hand to hold something while she holds her head up and rests on one arm. At 4 months, she will be able to reach for hanging objects if her trunk is supported on the floor or in a seat. When she is able to sit with stability, not using her hands to balance, both hands are suddenly free to handle and play with objects. It is only after she has mastered stable sitting that she will develop the ability to pick things up, move them from hand to hand, put them into containers, and throw them. Toward the end of the first year, infants are using their hands to fill a bucket with blocks, place rings on a stick, stack cups, and manage simple shape boxes. In the second year, toddlers use their hands with simple puzzles, take off and later put on their shoes, and use tools such as forks and spoons for eating. They coordinate using their hands with walking by carrying toys, and pushing and pulling wheeled toys. In the third year, twos may undress and partially dress themselves. They use markers and thick paint brushes to create marks on paper. They can put large pegs in pegboards and thread wooden beads. The Developmental Trends and Responsive Interactions chart at the end of this chapter lists the motor milestones.

The Senses and Motor Skills

We have more than the common five senses of sight, hearing, taste, touch, and smell. Two senses speak directly to our motor system. We get our sense of balance or equilibrium from the **vestibular system**. As you walk along, the vestibular system in your inner ear is constantly monitoring your balance and your movements. Information about your muscles, tendons, and joints comes from

OBSERVATION INVITATION **10.3**

Click the play button to watch the video of a young toddler playing with a stacking toy and answer questions related to the video. How is he using his fingers to explore and manipulate the materials?

the **proprioceptive system**. It detects the motion or position of the body or a limb. Your proprioceptive system is telling your brain about your physical position, right now. This sensory information is part of the motor system.

Eleanor Gibson (18), proposed that all action and all learning begin with perception. The senses perceive meaningful information from the environment. The brain immediately processes the information and guides the body to take action adaptively. The quality of the actions continually improves with experience. This theory complements Thelen's dynamic systems theory. Both propose that motor skills are constantly being learned and that learning happens through perceptual-motor activity.

Several studies have attempted to determine exactly what sensory information infants use to plan the motor act of reaching. In one study, 6-month-old infants were presented with objects that gave off sounds under three conditions of light: in full vision, in the dark with the object glowing and making a sound, and in the dark with the object identified by sound alone. The babies used the same reaching motions with the same frequencies for objects in the light and for glowing objects in the dark. The reaches for the objects emitting sounds in the dark were faster, of shorter duration, and had more errors compared to the other conditions. These findings indicate that vision of their hand did not appear to affect infants' reaching in this situation, whereas vision of the target did (19).

A second study set up a more complex problem. Infants had to predict an object's trajectory and anticipate how and where to reach to capture the object. Infants were tested twice, at 5 and 7½ months of age. They were presented with a moving object under two lighting conditions to investigate the role of vision in early reaching. In one trial, light shone on the moving object. In the other trial, the same object was painted with glow-in-the-dark paint and shown to the baby in the dark. Infants successfully contacted the glowing object on about half of their attempts at both ages, although 7½-month-olds reached more often. Infants took into account the motion of the target object by aiming their reaches ahead of the object. These results suggest that proprioceptive feedback of their own arm and the sight of the target allow for successful reaching even with limited visual information. The infants' success also demonstrates their ability to adapt their movements and reaching strategy to the speed and trajectory of the target object (20).

When infants and toddlers cannot use sensory information, they may need supports. Some children are overly sensitive to sensory information. For example, an infant who cannot stand to be touched because she is hypersensitive may find it difficult to bond with a parent or teacher. She may be hungry but unable to tolerate a nipple in her mouth. The proprioceptive experience of being lifted and put down again can be overwhelming. All of the caregiving activities that are meant to soothe and comfort may feel like assaults. Adults caring for hypersensitive babies need to develop a firm and gentle touch. They need to use gentle pressure around the mouth to make feeding more comfortable. And they need to stay calm and limit the variations in position and handling used with the baby.

This young child's proprioceptive system is at work as he reaches into the basket and responds to the texture of the soft material.

Bodily Self-Awareness

Awareness of self is usually thought of in the emotional domain. That is the invisible, internal self. Researchers are now exploring how the very young child learns about his own body. In a series of fascinating studies, researchers are finding ways to "ask" children in what ways they are aware of their bodies: first, in relation to the sizes of openings and objects; second, as a group of parts that work together in many ways to make a whole (21). One series of experiments looked at bodily self-awareness, or topography, with toddlers between 18 and 30 months. The tasks are:

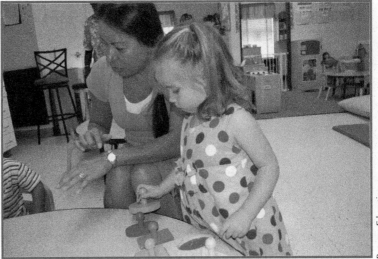

Aimee has mastered standing and can concentrate on the cognitive and fine motor tasks of doing this puzzle.

Sticker task: The toddler and parent, an examiner (E) and the examiner's assistant (A) are together. The E says, "Look, I'm going to put a sticker on A there. See, I put a sticker there (touching or pointing). E gives child a sticker and says, "Now you put this sticker on you right there (no pointing) so it's just like A." The child's doing so demonstrates an ability to experience oneself internally but also as others see you.

Body size tasks:

- *Too small clothes.* E dresses a 12-inch doll in a dress, coat, and hat. Then E hands the child an identical item and says, "Here's your coat. Put it on." Actually trying to put the tiny clothing demonstrates a lack of awareness of body size.
- *Door size.* With the parent on the other side of a Styrofoam board, the toddler needed to choose between two doors to reach her. One was 12 inches by 12 inches and easy to crawl through. The other was about 3 inches wide and 3 feet tall—impossible for the toddler to pass. The choice of door size reflected the child's body size awareness.
- *Replica toys.* First, the toddlers were in a room with several toys their size (table and chairs, slide, and car to drive). The children then went to another room with toy-sized replicas of the first toys. If the child tried to sit on the tiny chair or put his foot in the car, it reflected a lack of awareness of body size.

Body Mapping in the Brain

Another way we are coming to understand what young infants know about their bodies is through body mapping. Body mapping uses functional magnetic resonance imaging (fMRI) to watch which part of the brain is active at a certain time. Scientists lightly brushed the skin of an infant's hand or leg. Certain areas of the brain would be active giving the researchers the impression that specific neural networks are used to create a map of the parts of the body in the brain. The child is aware, on some level, of his body and its parts (22).

Perception-Action in the Brain

In chapter 8, we described how when an infant perceives someone else doing something like waving their hand, two parts of the infant's brain become active. The part that sees, or perceives, the action and the part of the brain that would make that action happen in the child both become active. So the child understands the action as though she was performing it herself (23). This also helps us understand how babies learn about their bodies and movement. They learn by watching and use imitation. This happens through a network of mirror neurons, brain cells that work together to perceive and experience action almost in the same moment.

Children with Special Needs

Infants and toddlers spend much of their time practicing existing motor skills and trying new ones. Healthy motor development needs the brain, the central nervous system, the muscles, the bones, and the opportunities infants have for practice. Motor development, often taken for granted, can have setbacks.

Cerebral Palsy

Injury, prenatal substance exposure, poor nutrition, and disease can all affect motor development. Motor disorders may have a variety of symptoms, as described in Figure 10.2.

The most common motor disorder in infancy is **cerebral palsy (CP)**. CP is a disorder caused by damage to the motor (muscle) control area of the brain: "The diagnosis is dependent upon two findings: Evidence of non-progressive damage to the developing brain and the presence of a resulting impairment of the motor (neuromuscular) control system of the body; the latter usually accompanied by a physiological impairment and functional disability" (24). Next to cognitive disorders, CP is the most common disorder of the developing brain. 70 percent of cerebral palsy occurs prenatally, 20 percent in the birthing process, and 10 percent in the first 2 years of life.

CP is a somewhat general term for a variety of conditions. Infants and toddlers with CP may keep their primitive reflexes. They have reflexive reactions rather than developing voluntary movement. There are three types of CP. **Spastic cerebral palsy** causes muscles to be so tight that the child cannot make voluntary movements. This could affect the legs, one side of the body, or the whole body, depending on the location and severity of the injury to the brain. **Athetoid cerebral palsy** affects the entire body with changing muscle tone that may result in uncontrolled movements and difficulty speaking or eating. **Ataxic cerebral palsy** affects balance and coordination, creating an unsteady walk or difficulty with fine motor tasks (25). Physical therapy can help children achieve the maximum possible control of their bodies within these conditions.

 Watch this video to see a toddler with cerebral palsy working playfully with dad on stretching and control. How does his father combine therapy with play?

https://www.youtube.com/watch?v=u0kTAPDCo7A

Effects of Motor Disorders

Motor disorders may affect more than movement. When a child is unable to participate in his part of the attachment relationship, the parent-child relationship

FIGURE 10.2   Warning signs of motor disorders.

Infants do not
- Bring hands together at midline
- Open fists to grasp, use individual fingers to point
- Lift and hold head up steadily
- Have normal muscle tone, muscles are tight or floppy
- Reach with two hands or reach at all
- Use both sides of their bodies equally
- Roll over (by 5 months)
- Sit independently (by 7 months)

Toddlers do not
- Crawl (by 1 year)
- Stand independently (by 14 months)
- Walk (by 18 months)
- Push a wheeled toy (by 18 months)

may suffer. If the child is unable to smile at parents, to follow their movements visually, to reach out to be lifted, or to cuddle when held, the adults may be confused as to the child's feelings. Infant-toddler teachers and early interventionists are often most helpful by pointing out the ways the child signals his pleasure and comfort in being with familiar, well-loved people.

Emotional and cognitive development may not be affected by a motor disorder. Sometimes adults need to learn to read the unique cues of the child. At other times changes or adaptations need to be made to materials in the environment. Many child assessment tools use motor skills to look at cognition. For example, we expect an infant to pull a cloth off a hidden object to demonstrate object permanence or to stack several blocks to demonstrate the ability to imitate. Children who do not have the motor ability to perform these actions will look like they do not understand the concepts. Unfortunately, because of the limits of the testing situation, these children may have no way to demonstrate their knowledge.

Check Your Understanding 10.2
Click here to check your understanding of the concepts in this section.

Learning Through the Adult-Child Relationship

The infant's and toddler's interest in her parents and in the play opportunities they provide, are important factors in early motor development. Being supported in various positions (tummy, back, snuggly, on the hip or shoulder) provides many opportunities to practice head and trunk control, using arms for support, and legs for kicking. If simply the position and amount of time we carry our babies affect their motor development, then imagine the impact of the opportunities we provide for movement or the handling of objects, of our comfort with movement, and our attitudes toward safety and risk taking. Although infant-toddler teachers do not make a genetic contribution to a child's motor abilities, they are certainly having an influence at the environmental level.

Adults have different comfort levels with activity. Very active adults are more comfortable with active infants and toddlers. Some adults are more comfortable with young children taking risks in climbing or using balance bikes. Sometimes, infants in group care are kept in swings, bouncers, or baby seats for hours at a time. Teachers caring for many infants may want to keep them quiet and so, keep them contained. It is heartbreaking to enter a room and see a group of infants looking dazed and limp, not allowed to move and explore.

 Watch this video to see a toddler being active with the support of his father. How does this toddler's joy illustrate his understanding of hula hoops?

https://www.youtube.com/watch?v=uBmUiouilQY

Adults support activity directly through interactions and indirectly through affordances. During tummy time, an adult may also lay on her tummy and be on eye level, playing with an infant. We might dangle a toy for an infant on his back. We offer toys to encourage reaching and rolling. We put toys a few inches ahead of a new crawler. We help beginning walkers by holding their hands as they walk back and forth, over and over.

Not all adults believe in helping infants and toddlers with motor skills. The organization, Resources for Infant Educarers (RIE®) is a popular approach to parenting. It was founded by Magda Gerber, based on her training in Hungary. The approach is characterized by a deep respect for the infant as a competent human being. One part of the approach is stated in these basic principles:

> We have basic trust in the infant to be an initiator, to be an explorer eager to learn what he is ready for.
>
> Because of this trust, we provide the infant with only enough help necessary to allow the child to enjoy mastery of her own actions (26).

RIE® teaches that infants and toddlers move when and in the ways for which they are ready. They would not approve of pulling a young infant to sitting or helping a new walker cross a room. They would never contain a baby or prevent movement, either. Most children will roll, crawl, and walk when they are ready. However, some children are helped when a caring adult supports motor learning.

Opportunities for Locomotion

Affordances, or opportunities, for movement are another way adults support motor learning and development. Adults protect young infants enjoying tummy time or time on their back on the floor. Crawling infants have clear spaces with no obstacles or choking dangers. Walkers have a nice variety of surfaces to offer just the right amount of challenge. These include platforms, ramps, and steps. Here are some suggestions for materials and experiences adults may make available in the environment to encourage locomotion.

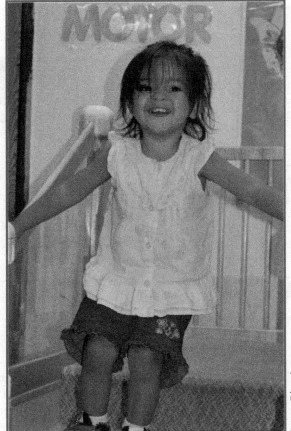

Aida is smiling with the challenge of walking down a ramp.

Pearson Education

Open spaces to encourage locomotion.

Clean and safe setting because health and safety are always our first concerns with young children. This includes no obstacles in the floor, shelving bolted to the wall, no choking hazards and everything kept clean.

Firm, washable mats for tummy and back time to strengthen trunk, arm and leg muscles.

Sitting supports (such as Boppy pillows) to help young infants close to sitting alone have opportunities to use their hands together.

Balls of various sizes and textures for holding, throwing, rolling and kicking.

Climbing structures to build strength and balance. These include structures like ladder rungs attached to an interior wall.

Riding toys for leg and trunk strength and balance. These include toys that move when a toddler squats and pushes off the floor with her feet, balance bikes, and pedal tricycles that are close to the ground.

Wagons and other pull toys encourage walking.

Music, musical instruments, and scarves seem to naturally motivate movement and develop rhythm.

OBSERVATION INVITATION **10.4**

Pearson Education

Pearson Education

 Look at how the children are using the art materials. How are these art experiences also fine motor experiences? Click on the icon to answer a question about how the children are using the art materials.

Large foam blocks for building, carrying and creating paths.
Child-sized tables and chairs so toddlers use tables independently (27).

There is one piece of equipment we must caution you about. Read about walkers in Box 10.1.

BOX 10.1

Baby walkers are dangerous!

Even when babies are supervised, they can be injured while using baby walkers. Documented injuries include the following:

- *Rolling down stairs:* Most common accident causing broken bones and head injuries
- *Burns:* Higher reach and mobility lead to burns from coffee cups, pots on stoves, radiators, fireplaces, and space heaters
- *Drowning:* Falls into pools, bathtubs, or toilets
- *Poisoning:* Higher reach for access to household chemicals
- *Pinched fingers and toes:* Caught between walker and furniture

Source: Based on AAP (American Academy of Pediatrics). (2004). *U.S. government should ban baby walkers.*

Baby Walkers

We have described many pieces of equipment as not good for development because they prevent movement. The mobile walker promotes movement but it is dangerous. It should not be in any program. A mobile baby walker holds a baby, who is too young to stand and walk, in a standing position. When the baby's feet touch the ground, small pressures of weight cause the walker to roll. The American Academy of Pediatrics (28) and the National Association for Children's Hospitals and Related Institutions have urged the Consumer Product Safety Commission to ban their manufacture and sale in the United States. The Canadian government has already banned the sale, advertisement, and importation of baby walkers.

Even following years of recalls and new standards, 3,600 children under age 5 were injured by baby walkers between 2004 and 2006. Five deaths resulted (29). Most of these injuries happened when adults were watching but were unable to respond quickly enough—a mobile walker can move more than 3 feet in 1 second! The American Academy of

Pediatrics further urges parents not to leave their child in care anywhere that mobile baby walkers are used (see Box 10.1).

It seems as though the early experience of walking would be beneficial and enriching. A study of the effect of early experiences with walkers (30) finds the opposite is true. The authors describe the use of walkers as problems because the infant or young toddler cannot see her own moving legs and feet. Walker babies sat, crawled, and walked later than babies who did not use walkers. The walker babies also scored lower on the Bayley Scales of Mental and Motor Development, a widely used assessment of cognitive, language, and motor development. The authors concluded that the risks far outweigh the benefits of walker use.

Opportunities for Manipulation

As infants and toddlers strengthen the large muscles of their neck, trunk, arms and legs, they are building a foundation for use of the small muscles in their fingers. Eventually, this will lead to the ability to sit and write in school. A very young infant holding his head and chest up from his tummy will soon also reach for and hold a small toy in one hand. The big benefit in sitting is being able to handle objects with two hands. Manipulative activities involve eye-hand coordination and the creation of new concepts such as size, spatial relationships, gravity, balance, and orientation. Here are some affordances adults may provide for manipulation learning and development:

Rattles are small and light enough for babies to hold, shake and examine.
Dangling toys refine the arm, hand and fingers in reaching.
Small, washable objects such as figures of people, animals, and vehicles for handling, banging together, tossing, mouthing, and moving hand to hand.
Stacking cups are used as individual objects before they are used more carefully for stacking by size.
Rings on a stick, a lid to fit into a slot in a plastic container, and shape boxes challenge a child to refine manipulation skills.
Puzzles also require hand and eye coordination. Toddlers may range from one to several piece puzzles by the time they are age 3.
Bristle blocks and magnetic blocks stick to each other during play and need pressure to pull apart.
Wooden blocks are great for building a sense of balance using the hands.

Culture and Motor Development

Cultural beliefs and practices differ in approaches to motor development. Cultures offer different opportunities for early movement. The timing and the quality of mastering motor movements are different because of this. This has led to questions about motor development. Are certain early experiences necessary for motor development? Do genes run the timeline of motor development? On the other hand, do children develop the motor skills needed for living in their own culture?

Adults provide different motor experiences for infants and toddlers around the world. They vary from carrying the baby at all times to encouraging sitting, crawling, and walking. The developmental milestone timelines used in the United States may be relevant only for babies in our own culture.

Some cultures emphasize keeping infants in vertical postures and others in horizontal postures. Much of the cross-cultural research was done in the 1960s

STRATEGIES TO SUPPORT MOTOR DEVELOPMENT AND LEARNING

Infants and toddlers are highly motivated to use their bodies to move and to use tools. These skills do not develop automatically, though. Some strategies you can use to support motor development follow:

1. Provide supervised opportunities for young babies to play on their tummies. Tummy time helps babies strengthen their trunk and neck control.

2. Limit the use of swings, infant seats, bouncers, or other furniture that restrains infants. When caring for several children at once, offer toys on the floor for tummy time, space for crawlers, or hanging toys for reaching from supine. Restraining babies makes them passive and discourages active exploration. Think of using their bodies as active, learning opportunities.

3. When young babies are playing on the floor on their backs, offering toys a little off to the side and above the head encourages reaching and turning, which develops into rolling over.

4. Create an environment that encourages movement at every stage of motor development. Think about how you can help infants and toddlers develop an active lifestyle from the beginning, countering the possibility of childhood obesity.

5. Firm, washable cubes, pads, and inclines can be arranged to create interesting and challenging surfaces for crawling, creeping, walking, and climbing.

6. As young toddlers begin cruising, they need long, low, stable surfaces to hold. In homes, they use sofas and coffee tables. In centers, if they are using shelving units, be sure they are bolted to the wall.

7. Small stairs with platforms, climbing bars bolted to walls, and sturdy structures encourage toddlers to climb. If the stairs and platform provide access to a window or the climbing bars face a mirror allowing the toddlers to see themselves, there is even more motivation for climbing.

8. Use music for movement, not just as background sound. Infants love being held while you dance with them, swooping and spinning to the rhythm. Toddlers love singing and playing instruments while dancing or marching.

9. Spend as much time outdoors as the climate allows.

10. Be aware of the child's changing abilities to handle objects and offer materials that match these abilities. Young infants need lightweight rattles, older infants need small objects they can pick up with a raking grasp but large enough to prevent choking when they mouth them.

11. New walkers enjoy carrying objects in each hand. Older infants and also toddlers enjoy the precision of fitting rings on sticks, stacking cups, or fitting pegs in pegboards.

12. Use small chairs and tables for meals, allowing toddlers to sit and rise by themselves.

and 1970s. The Zinecanteco Indians of southeastern Mexico carry their babies in a *rebozo*, a sling across the mother's belly. The infants are quiet and alert but not very exploratory. They develop motor skills in the same order as children in the United States, even though their environment has been so different. The timeline of acquiring these skills is about a month later than children in the United States (31).

The Ache mothers of eastern Paraguay carry their infants all of the time. An Ache baby is in a sling on his mother's body 93 percent of the daylight hours and on her lap all night. Even at 1 year, their mothers will hold them 40 percent of the day. At 18 months, toddlers are taught to ride in baskets or piggyback on their father's back (32). Ache children begin walking about 9 months later than children in the United States.

The !Kung San, known as the Bushmen of the Kalahari Desert, have infants and toddlers with advanced motor skills compared to babies in Western countries. San mothers carry young infants positioned vertically in a sling. They massage their infant's legs. They invest time in promoting motor skills such as standing and walking and encourage babies to explore by 7 months. San children achieve motor skills earlier and better and concentrate harder than American toddlers (33).

Some cultural practices may seem at odds with promoting motor development (34). Adults who dress and feed older toddlers and even preschool-age children serve the cultural values of the Latino and Asian traditions. The Hopi and Navajo practice of keeping babies in cradleboards serves their traditional mother-infant relationships. When your cultural background differs from that of the families in your child care setting, it is important to remember that children from all cultural practices do achieve the same motor milestones eventually. Cultural practices and beliefs affect motor development, and cultural values need to be considered in the child care and learning program's curriculum for motor development.

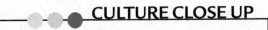

CULTURE CLOSE UP

A very friendly, enthusiastic Kenyan woman became a teacher in an infant room. Her English was competent and children and families loved her. Every day she found time to massage and exercise the legs of the young infants. She would hold them up as they "walked." The children seemed to enjoy the active play and many began walking at about 9 months. Parents were sort of pleased but not altogether. In some ways, the parents felt the teacher was pushing the children. In addition, the parents were not expecting their children to walk that early. Rather, the parents were expecting much longer periods of children's relative immobility when the parent could better control when and where the child moved. The director knew he was looking at a clash of cultures, wasn't sure that one was more "right" than the other, and was not at all sure what was best for the children. How might you think it through? What might you do?

Check Your Understanding 10.3
Click here to check your understanding of the concepts in this section.

Program Practices That Enhance Motor Learning and Development

Many of those reading this text and entering the early childhood field are young. Your memories of outdoor play may consist of organized sports more than playing in your yard or wandering through parks. Today's young children have even less access to outdoors than you did. Time outdoors might be the most important program practice for young children's health and motor skills.

Benefits of Outdoor Play

Humans may need to be outdoors and in nature. Safety, family work hours, and our wired-in culture all contribute to a generation of children who rarely spend time outdoors. One author describes them as suffering from "nature deficit disorder" (35). Not being outdoors may contribute to obesity, depression, diabetes, and attention deficit disorder. Benefits of being outdoors include helping the body and the mind. In fact, there is a bacterium, sometimes found in dirt, which improves cognition in mice who ingest it through dust (36). It is possible that it has the same positive effects on children.

Health Benefits

Toddlers playing outdoors will be more active, playing in ways that promote fitness and strengthen the heart, lungs and muscles. Active play sets habits that help prevent childhood obesity. Outdoor play strengthens infants' and toddlers' immune systems. It exposes them to fresh air with fewer germs. Today's infants and toddlers are increasingly deficient in Vitamin D. The easiest way to get Vitamin D is being in sunshine. This vitamin prevents future bone problems, diabetes, and even heart disease. Some experts suggest putting sunscreen on after children are exposed to sunlight for a few minutes. Sunscreen blocks Vitamin D along with harmful rays. Being outdoors may also prevent nearsightedness. Exposure to bright, natural light appears to help the lens and retina maintain the right distance (37).

Mental Benefits

Being outdoors also helps the mind. Children who faced significant life stresses had less anxiety if they lived in high-nature settings rather than low-nature settings (38). In fact, being outdoors gives children a sense of peace and well-being. Children with attention deficit hyperactivity disorder have better attention if they play in a space that has grass and trees than indoors or on a built structure (39). Even brief exposure to green spaces can help children and adults with attention and impulse control. When early childhood staff are able to be outdoors, they report better job satisfaction.

Learning in the Outdoors

Everything that happens indoors can happen outdoors—and so much more! Every area of the curriculum can be brought outdoors. Some skills such as developing friendships and problem-solving may be better outdoors. Each outdoor space holds the potential for many kinds of learning. Every interaction with an adult has lessons in emotional experience and self-regulation. Adults bring meaningful language to each experience. Play has endless social possibilities. Discoveries of how one's body can move abound in the outdoors. Curiosity about the natural world builds the approaches to learning as well as a store of information.

There are learning benefits to the many elements of an outdoor play space. Look at Table 10.1, Elements of an Outdoor Play Space.

Safe Outdoor Play Areas

Of course, safety is always our first concern in a setting for infants and toddlers. The most important source of safety are the adults paying attention to and interacting with the children. There are many things to consider and policies should be set with advice from health professionals or sources such as *Caring for Our Children: National Health and Safety Performance Standards; Guidelines for Early Care and Education Learning* (41).

Weather

Children should spend at least an hour a day outdoors except in extreme weather. The National Weather Service at weather.gov provides a color-coded warning system for extreme weather throughout the country and a local

TABLE 10.1   Elements of an Outdoor Play Space

Places to Play	Benefits	Example
Open Spaces	Open spaces provide room for toddlers to walk, run, squat, roll, and jump. The popular toddler game of "Copy me!" has room for movement. Movement becomes the means for social connection. Sharing space promotes problem-solving.	Grass is the best surface for crawling, toddling, walking, and running.
Stationary Pieces	This equipment offers some challenge but because it cannot change, it has limited learning value.	Slides, climbing structures, and riding toys anchored on springs
Nature	Outdoor play should lead to learning about nature. Children learn about wind, rain, snow, sun, clouds, and temperatures. Natural elements include variations in ground surfaces such as mounds or slopes. Even a small mound presents a sense of risk to a new crawler or walker. Non-toxic plants and flowers help create beauty and a sense of welcome. Stepping stones are both a physical and cognitive challenge as toddlers plan their steps and jumps. A log can be a seat for chatting or a challenging, but safe, balance beam.	Trees, stumps, boulders, long grass, water, pebbles, flowers, vegetables, bushes.
Push, Pull, and Riding Toys	Infants and toddlers learn to cooperate with others on paths and develop large-muscle groups. Offering a variety of wheeled toys challenges children with different ability levels. Include helmets to promote safety at an early age.	Low-riding tricycles, wagons, pull and push toys
Sand	Sand has so many different properties when it is wet or dry. It can build or hide. It is fun alone or with friends. It is always changing. Mud is harder to clean up but offers additional opportunities. Worms and bugs can be found in rich soil.	Sand, mud.
Water	Toddlers can learn how water moves and changes. Science information comes through playing with sinking and floating, water carrying leaves or sticks, and watching water flow	Fountains, waterfalls, hoses, spray bottles, and sprinklers
Movable Pieces	Movable pieces are parts that children can move to create new play and movement spaces. Slices of logs can create seats, stepping stones, or define a space. Think of loose parts as the building blocks of the outdoors.	Pinecones, milk crates, building blocks, and small stumps, logs, or branches.

weather report for your zip code. Do not take children outdoors in lightning and thunder storms, blizzards, or very hot or cold temperatures. Temperatures that are dangerous are at or over 90′ F or at or below a wind chill factor of minus 15. Toddlers can be outdoors for a short period of time in moderate rain and snow with proper clothing and protection. How cozy to read stories on a covered porch in a gentle rain! What fun to lift your head and stick out your tongue to catch drifting snowflakes!

DEVELOPMENTAL TRENDS AND RESPONSIVE INTERACTIONS

MOTOR LEARNING AND DEVELOPMENT

Infants and toddlers develop motor skills for locomotion, for using tools, and for coordinating perceptual information and motor actions.

Development	Example
0–4 months (infant)	
• Infants lift head when held at shoulder—hold head steady and erect.	Rosie held her head up and looked around at the other children as Sharon held her against her shoulder.
• On tummy, infants lift their head and shoulders off the ground and can hold a toy in hand.	Robert, on his tummy on a blanket, lifted his head to see himself in the mirror mounted at floor level on the wall.
• Infants turn head toward a familiar voice.	
• Infants hold body still to pay attention; wiggle and move to encourage continued interaction.	
• On back, infants thrust arms and legs in play.	Jen held a rattle placed in her hand but seemed unaware it was there.
• Infants turn from side to back.	
• Infants hold finger, light toy with reflexive grasp.	Filipe brought his fingers to his mouth and sucked on them, while looking intently at the toddlers.
• Infants suck on own fingers and hands, objects.	
• Infants move arms and legs.	
4–8 months (infant)	
• Infants turn from back to side, later roll from back to front.	Micky rolls from his back to his tummy to reach a toy, then rolls back over to play with it.
• Infants sit—first with support but steady alone by the end of this period.	
• Infants reach with one arm.	Erin, sitting steadily alone, loves using both hands to pick up objects and study them.
• Infants use raking grasp.	
• Infants crawl.	
• Infants shake, bang, hold, let go of objects.	Freddy loves being held while he has his bottle, but he insists on holding it himself.
• Infants move objects from hand to hand.	
• Infants can hold their own bottle.	
• Infants can bring objects to their mouth.	
8–12 months (infant)	
• Infants pull to stand.	Hershel crawls to his teacher's side, then holds her leg as he pulls up to stand.
• Infants cruise.	
• Infants stand alone.	
• Infants walk with help and then alone.	
• Infants sit in a chair.	
• Infants finger feed.	Jem sits at the lunch table, alternating between using her spoon and her fingers to enjoy her meal.
• Infants use spoon and tippy cup.	
• Infants use pincer grasp.	
12–18 months (young toddler)	
• Toddlers stack and line up blocks.	Gary stood at the table, carefully using both hands to build a tower with colored blocks.
• Toddlers can dress and undress self, arm into sleeve and foot into shoe.	
• Toddlers can walk.	
• Toddlers walk while carrying objects in each hand.	Michelle toddled across the room, with her teddy bear in one hand and her blanket in the other.
• Toddlers climb stairs.	

Teacher or Parent-Child Interaction	Environment
0–4 months (infant)	
• Change the infant's position; sometimes on his back, sometimes on his tummy. Even when holding the baby, sometimes cradle him in your arms, sometimes hold him upright against your shoulder. • When an infant is on the floor, lie down face-to-face with him. • When an infant is on her back, reaching for toy a little beyond her head, support her trunk as she rolls over.	• A stiff blanket (to prevent the danger of suffocation) on the floor provides space for early movements. • Small, interesting toys, pictures, and books to look at will encourage infants to lift their heads. A mirror bolted to the wall at floor level always provides something interesting to look at. • As infants begin to reach, they enjoy stable bars that dangle toys for them to bat at or reach and grasp.
4–8 months (infant)	
• Stay near the infant who is just beginning to sit alone. • Know the progression of motor development; emotionally encourage and physically support new attempts. • Believe in the lifelong health benefits of an active lifestyle.	• Provide safe places for rolling, sitting, and crawling. Protect infants from anything that might fall on them. • Provide small, washable lightweight objects (too large for choking) for handling and tossing, and provide containers for objects.
8–12 months (infant)	
• Stay alert to when practicing walkers need a little help—and when to let them keep trying. • Allow time for older infants to practice feeding themselves.	• Safe places to pull up to stand. • Push and pull toys to help support practicing walkers. • Busy boxes. • Board books for turning pages, lifting flaps, and poking fingers through holes.
12–18 months (young toddler)	
• Imitate a toddler's growing variety of movements. • Introduce songs with little dances and movements. • Provide time and patience while a toddler practices putting on his own jacket.	• Stable, low-to-the-ground riding toys. • Stable, low-to-the-ground rocking toys. • Skill-based manipulatives such as stacking cups and rings on a stick.

DEVELOPMENTAL TRENDS AND RESPONSIVE INTERACTIONS (Continued)

Development	Example
18–24 months (toddler)	
• Toddlers point to objects to communicate. • Toddlers make marks on paper. • Toddlers pound, shape clay. • Toddlers run. • Toddlers sit on and get up from small chairs alone. • Toddlers are developing spatial confidence—exploring their body in space.	Mindy rolled the dough with her hands, then used tools to make designs. Joseph sat down at the table to eat, then took his dirty dishes to the tub.
24–36 months (toddler)	
• Toddlers thread beads, use scissors, paint with fingers or brushes, and do simple puzzles. • Toddlers throw and kick a ball. • Toddlers stand on one foot. • Toddlers stand and walk on tiptoes. • Toddlers walk upstairs with one foot on each step. • Toddlers climb, slide, and jump. • Toddlers eat with spoon and fork. • Toddlers can dress self. • Toddlers can pour milk from small pitcher.	Robert doesn't even have to think about his body as he runs to greet his dad at the end of the day. Peggy and Misha make a game out of imitating each other's tiptoe steps, postures, and gestures. Lawrence and Evelyn use the dress-up clothes for their game, struggling a little to pull on the pieces.

The Centers for Disease Control and Prevention suggest keeping children safe in warm weather by doing these things:

- Dress infants and children in loose, lightweight, light-colored clothing.
- Schedule outdoor activities carefully, for morning and evening hours.
- Cover up. Clothing that covers your and your child's skin helps protect against UV rays.
- Use sunscreen with at least SPF (sun protection factor) 15 and UVA (ultraviolet A) and UVB (ultraviolet B) protection every time you and your child go outside.
- Keep children well-hydrated and frequently offer water to drink.

In cold weather, children should wear:

- A hat
- A scarf or nit mask to cover the face and neck
- Sleeves that are snug at the wrist
- Water-resistant coat and boots
- Several layers of loose-fitting clothing.

Teacher or Parent-Child Interaction	Environment
18–24 months (toddler)	
• Provide materials that challenge toddlers' growing use of their fingers. • Stay present with toddlers as they try new skills and support them. • Provide opportunities for climbing, walking, and running.	• Art materials with thick paintbrushes and markers, large surfaces for painting. • Smaller, skill-based manipulatives such as threading beads and pegboards. • Lots of space for movement—dancing, balls, riding toys, climbing, and slides.
24–36 months (toddler)	
• Be aware of the balance of time between active and quiet activities. • Watch for increasing accuracy in fine motor skills, as subtle issues may begin to be apparent. • Be available with encouragement and patience as toddlers increasingly feed, dress, and toilet themselves.	• Provide a variety of materials to practice fine motor skills: simple puzzles, shape boxes, threading beads, table blocks, clay, and art materials. • Space, opportunity, and structures to encourage movement—outdoor time, obstacle courses, dancing, and riding toys.

Protective Substances and Medications

Sunscreen and bug repellents should be used with the advice of a health professional. As mentioned earlier, some experts suggest a few minutes of exposure to the sun before applying sunscreen for the skin to soak in Vitamin D from the sun.

You need an outdoor first aid kit for your local area. This includes materials for treating bug bites and stings. Any medications that children need close by such as EpiPens or inhalers must be kept at proper temperatures (42).

Maintenance

Outdoor spaces need extra safety checks. Check equipment daily for loose bolts, broken pieces, or slivers. Hazardous materials found outdoors include poisonous, sharp, or choking hazards; buried objects; animal feces; and rodents. Check drainage of surfaces following rain or melting snow. Standing water can breed mosquitos. Sand boxes need to be covered when not in use. Icy paths or very hot equipment also present dangers (43).

Climbing equipment needs to be on resilient surfaces. Equipment needs to be safe and developmentally appropriate.

Check Your Understanding 10.4
Click here to check your understanding of the concepts in this section.

Summary

- Unique characteristics within each child influence their motor learning and skills. Temperament affects motor skills. Motor driven children take more opportunities to move and refine skills but they may be reckless. Motor cautious children move less and have fewer opportunities to refine skills. There are no gender differences in motor performance in infancy. There are differences in adult's expectations by the child's gender. Mothers overestimate their young son's performance and underestimate their young daughter's performance on a motor task.

  □ Motor learning and development include a constant interplay of physical changes and finding motor solutions. Primitive reflexes are present in the womb and for the first several months of life. Primitive reflexes drive most movement at first. Many early reflexes support breathing, eating, and attachment. Postural reflexes emerge and stay with us for life, helping us maintain balance in movement. Dynamic systems theory says motor skills develop as the young child finds the best solution to using his body to make something happen in his environment. All of the changing parts of his body come into the solution (height, weight, proportions, center of gravity, abilities). The opportunity for action in the environment is called an affordance.

- Development is proximal-distal, cephalocaudal, and proceeds from large muscles to small muscles. Locomotion describes movement skills. Manipulation describes object handling. Bodily awareness describes the ways infants and toddlers are aware of the parts of their bodies and how the parts relate as a whole. The senses, or perception, are an ongoing element of motor activity. The most common motor disorder in infancy is cerebral palsy (CP). CP is a disorder caused by damage to the motor (muscle) control area of the brain. Voluntary movement is inhibited. Cognition, social-emotional, and language may or may not be impaired.

- Adults and culture influence motor learning and development. Adults support motor activity with their encouragement and attitudes. Adults provide affordances for movement by not using containing equipment, providing surfaces and materials that invite movement and offer appropriate challenge. Adults provide affordances for manipulation by encouraging exploration of materials that roll, stack, fit into one another, and offer appropriate challenge. Culture affects how families handle their infants and support early movement.

- Infant-toddler care and learning programs affect children's motor development through policies and practices. Benefits of daily outdoor time include preventing obesity, reducing nearsightedness, countering depression and anxiety, and increasing Vitamin D. Learning in all domains occurs outdoors. The unique materials and space available outdoors offer special opportunities for learning about wind, sun, rain, snow, clouds, water, mud, bugs, birds, and the life cycle. Safety is important in every aspect of infant and toddler care. Outdoor safety requires good policies for weather conditions, procedures for keeping the outdoors clean and hazard free, and vigilant adult supervision.

Key Terms

affordance
ataxic cerebral palsy
athetoid cerebral palsy
balance

cerebral palsy (CP)
cephalocaudal
developmental cascade
dynamic systems theory

gender bias
locomotion
Moro reflex
palmar grasp reflex

posture
postural reflexes
primitive reflexes
proprioceptive system

proximal-distal
resisting gravity
rooting reflex
spastic cerebral palsy

step reflex
sucking reflex
tonic neck reflex
vestibular system

Reflections and Resources for the Reader

REFLECTIONS

1. Does your image of an ideal infant or toddler include a child who is always active and on the move? Our inactive lifestyles are contributing to childhood obesity, but many of our child care and learning programs are designed to keep children sitting quietly. How does your image of a healthy child affect how you would set up your space?

2. Are you naturally active? Would your personal preferences for activity or inactivity contribute to the kinds of motor activities you make available to the infants and toddlers in your care?

OBSERVATION AND APPLICATION OPPORTUNITIES

1. Observe an infant or toddler. How does she use her body to achieve some personal goal?

2. Notice how an infant or toddler handles objects. What sort of grasp does he use? Does he manage the objects well? Can he move them from hand to hand? Can he throw or release at will? Can he carry objects while moving around? Do different children use different ways of handling objects?

3. What materials would you offer infants and toddlers at different stages to support their increasingly effective grasps? Make a poster of the grasp and the materials that would support it. Share it in class.

SUPPLEMENTARY ARTICLES AND BOOKS TO READ

Adams, E. (2013). Nature-based learning. Taking infants and toddlers outside. *Young Children, 68*(3), 94–96.

Early Head Start National Resource Center. (2012) *News you can use: Outdoor spaces*. Author: Washington, D.C. Retrieved from the Early Childhood Learning and Knowledge Center.

Honig, A. (2015). *Experiencing nature with young children: Awakening delight, curiosity, and a sense of stewardship*. Washington, DC: The National Association for the Education of Young Children.

Petersen, S. H., & Wittmer, D. S. (2013). *Endless opportunities for infant and toddler curriculum: A relationship-based approach* (2nd ed.). Upper Saddle River, NJ: Pearson.

Spencer, K. H., & Wright, P. M. (2014). Toddlers and preschool quality outdoor play spaces for young children. *Young Children, 69*(5), 28–34.

INTERESTING LINKS

On the Move: The Power of Movement in Your Child's First Three Years

ZERO TO THREE Search online for the ZERO TO THREE Web site and once on the home page, search for "On the Move: The Power of Movement in Your Child's First Three Years." This article discusses how movement activities are critical not just for children's physical development, but for their overall development.

Physical Development.

*Virtual Lab School_* Five interactive, Web-based lessons on aspects of physical development and learning.

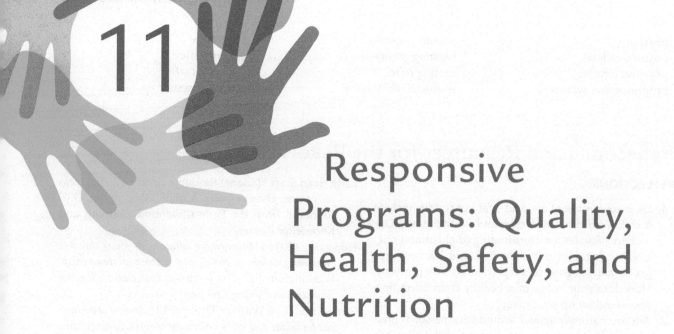

11

Responsive Programs: Quality, Health, Safety, and Nutrition

LEARNING OUTCOMES

After reading this chapter, you will be able to:

- Identify the elements of quality in infant/toddler care and learning programs.
- Describe the basic policies and procedures necessary to keep infants and toddlers in group care safe and healthy.
- Demonstrate familiarity with tools used to evaluate quality and identify the policies, laws, and systems that support quality in infant/toddler care and learning programs.

Pearson Education

Sheila wanted to be responsive to each child. But she could barely get through feeding and diapering. She was alone with five infants—and there was no way to do anything but run from one crying infant to another. She understood the importance of quality, but quality depended on more than her good intentions.

Almost 2 million children younger than age 1 are in nonmaternal care at least part of the week (1). The quality of care that young children receive is directly related to their well-being, skill development, and subsequent adjustment (2). We know the effects of early relationships and experiences on the development of the brain. Therefore, we should ensure that the hours infants and toddlers spend in group care are filled with safe, loving, responsive, and enriching experiences.

Unfortunately, quality care is expensive to provide. More than half the parents of infants and toddlers in America have to use child care and learning programs that are of mediocre or poor quality. Studies of infant/toddler care and learning programs have helped clarify which elements are most important to ensuring quality. Low ratios, small group sizes, and well-trained infant/toddler teachers are necessary for the focused, warm, enriched relationships infants and toddlers need for good development (3). These factors, of course, make for an expensive service.

What Is Quality and Why Does It Matter?

Every description of quality includes these four items:

- The safety of the child.
- Communication between the family and the teacher about the child.
- A warm, responsive relationship between the infant/toddler teacher and the child.
- An engaging, developmentally appropriate learning environment.

The definition of quality, however, is not that simple. Each of these items—safety, families, a warm relationship, and an engaging environment—has its own defining elements. Safety includes more than keeping the environment clean and free of **hazards**. It includes preventing the spread of **infection** and promoting healthy practices and good **nutrition**. Communication between families and infant/toddler teachers begins with supporting the parent-child relationship. It includes having clear **policies** that families are able to understand. Program staff respect differing cultural beliefs and child-rearing practices. They have ways to resolve conflicts that may arise. The quality of the relationship between the infant/toddler teacher and the child are affected by the teacher's own relationship history, training, knowledge, and skills. Relationships and environments are affected by the program's curriculum, ratios and group sizes.

All of these elements need to be considered in creating a high-quality program. In some ways it seems like a mix of apples and friendships. Some are concrete and easily observable. Others are subtle, subjective, and relationship based. Every element is influenced by the societal attitudes and policies toward care and learning programs. So, we will separate them into **structural variables** (concrete) and **process variables** (affecting the interactions) (4). Structural variables can affect process variables but process variables cannot change structural variables.

Benefits of low ratios include secure attachment relationships and more complex play with peers.

Pearson Education

Structural Variables of Quality

The structural variables of quality provide the foundation for quality. The variables include low **child-to-teacher ratios**, small **group size**, **primary caregiving**, **continuity of care**, and a well-educated, well-compensated, stable workforce. Safe and healthy environments are important structural variables. Management structures are also part of the underlying structure. In looking at this set of variables, it is clear that providing the foundation for a high-quality infant/toddler program is an expensive endeavor. Therefore, adequate financing is also a structural variable. Let's explore some of these variables more deeply.

Ratios and Group Sizes

Caring well for only one child can be a full-time job. It takes time for teachers to provide responsive care that promotes healthy development, one teacher cannot be responsible for more than a few infants and toddlers. Very young children, in turn, are easily overwhelmed by the noise and activity of large groups of people. In order for them to focus and learn, they need to be in groups of limited size.

Benefits of low ratios include secure attachment relationships, more complex play with peers and objects, more proficient adaptive language, and fewer behavior problems, such as aggression and anxiety. Better ratios were also related to better communication skills in 12-month-olds and higher scores on the Bayley Mental Development Index.

The funding challenges of infant/toddler care and learning programs make it difficult to keep group sizes small and ratios low, although the benefits have been known for a long time. Ratio and group size tend to be determined by licensing regulations–and states vary in their legal requirements for infant/toddler programs, requiring from 3 to 12 infants per teacher in regulated centers.

Early Head Start defines the ratios and group size requirements in the Program Standards. Several national organizations have also weighed in with recommendations for best practices. Table 11.1 illustrates these recommendations with the ratio of infant/toddler teacher to children given followed by the recommended group size.

Primary Caregiving

Primary caregiving is the practice of one infant/toddler teacher being most responsible for each child. The teacher and child develop a predictable and deepening relationship. The family has one person to depend on for sharing of information. At its best, the primary caregiver is with the child for as long as the child is in the program. Primary caregiving does not mean exclusive caregiving. Generally, more than one teacher is in a room with a group of infants or toddlers, and all teachers strive to have warm, affectionate relationships with all of the infants and toddlers.

The emphasis on primary caregiving comes from the importance of early relationships for healthy development. Infants and toddlers take time to trust new

TABLE 11.1   Recommended ratios (teachers: children)/Group sizes

Children's Age	Early Head Start (required)	American Academy of Pediatrics	NAEYC	ZERO TO THREE
Birth to 12 months	1:4/8	1:2/6	1:3/6 or 1:4/8	1:3/6
13 to 24 months	1:4/8	1:2-3/8	1:3/6 to 1:4/12	1:3/6
24 to 35 months	1:4/8	1:5/10	1:4/8 to 1:6/12	1:4/12

people. They don't know if they will be understood and cared for. They come to count on an adult who has shown she understands them (5). Emotionally available, attentive teachers help infants and toddlers understand relationships. Children learn about turn taking and cooperation (6). Consistent relationships can promote interest in exploration, pleasure in play, and abilities to manage stressful and challenging situations (7, 8).

For the infant/toddler teacher, observing, documenting, and thinking about the same three or four infants or toddlers, deepens her understanding. Her responses will be more individual and accurate. She will plan experiences that match each child's abilities and interests. The result should be better child development outcomes. Extended time together supports a child's sense of history of herself with the teacher. It helps a child believe that people remain in her life in caring, meaningful ways–that she can rely on and safely love other people.

When continuity of care is provided by a primary teacher, there are also many opportunities for the infant/toddler teacher and parents to develop a caring relationship. When a child and teacher spend at least a year together, they have higher levels of interactive involvement in caregiving (9). Infant/toddler teachers may learn from parents how the infant or toddler expects to be handled and any cultural or personal care practices the family utilizes. The teacher, in turn, may inform the family on the thinking behind some of the care practices in the program. Open, genuine communication between parents and teachers increases the continuity of the child's experiences between home and the infant/toddler program. For families experiencing multiple challenges (e.g., unstable housing leading to multiple moves, unstable employment, or numerous adults or other individuals rotating in and out of the home), continuity in the caregiving environment is especially beneficial for the young child.

Continuity of Care

Continuity of care extends the assignment of the primary teacher over a long period of time, preferably from the time of enrollment until the child is at least 3 years of age. By allowing the caregiving relationship to exist over years, the child is able to experience the time and intimacy needed to learn about himself and form meaningful relationships. When infant/toddler teachers change frequently, the child may experience both the grief of losing a valued friend and the stress of having to learn a new person's expectations (10). When relationships are repeatedly disrupted early in life, an infant or toddler may stop investing the effort needed to build new relationships, and life can become very distressing for the child. A poignant case study of two toddlers transitioning into a preschool classroom in the same program demonstrates the depth of feeling in the established child-teacher relationship.

> *Scott and Robbie transitioned into a preschool room from their infant-toddler room at about 2½ years. They were supported by visits with their toddler teachers and everyone thought they would do well. Scott had entered the infant room at 2 months and had spent his whole life with his primary teacher and the environment of the infant room. Robbie had spent only 10 months in the program, his third in 2 years. Robbie seemed to make the transition easily, although remaining watchful and distant. He remained watchful until leaving this program a few months later. Scott resisted the new rules and structure, cried, and took a long time developing a relationship with his new teachers. However, over time, drawing on his good history of relationships, he became comfortable and thrived in the new classroom.*

Continuity of care had provided time for Scott to develop a deep attachment relationship that provided a sense of safety in the infant room. He mourned and resisted the loss of this attachment relationship. Nonetheless, continuity of care built a foundation for him to create secure relationships with his new teachers over time. Robbie appeared to have an easier time of transition. However, he never developed a secure attachment with his new teacher. His history of disrupted relationships taught him not to trust these teachers who come and go.

Structure of continuity of care.   Continuity of care between a infant/toddler teacher and a child may be achieved in several ways. The two most important elements of continuity of care approaches are

1. The day-to-day interactions between the primary teacher and the child that give the child a sense of predictability in her daily experiences.
2. The deepening relationship and shared memories created through the enduring, year-after-year relationship between the primary teacher and the child.

Different structures for continuity of care include **mixed age groups** of infants and toddlers nurtured by primary teachers throughout their first 3 years, similar to the design of family child care. Another model is remaining with the same children in a close age group, and as the children grow older moving to a new, age-appropriate space with the same teacher, thus providing the infant/toddler teacher and child with the opportunity to maintain long-lasting bonds. As time progresses, teachers in this arrangement work with various age groups over several years. A third method is to maintain a close age group with the same teacher but modify the environment as the children's abilities and interests change.

Although some infant/toddler teachers may feel more competent with specific age groups and prefer to work, for example, only with young infants or only with 2-year-olds, the teacher and child will reap mutual benefits from a more long-term relationship spanning the duration of the child's enrollment. Infant/toddler teachers can feel confident of their ability to really know a child, to be able to read each cue, and to know how to individually comfort and challenge each child. The teacher avoids the stress of constantly *learning* new infants and toddlers.

Benefits of continuity of care.   Extended time together supports a child's sense of history of herself with the infant/toddler teacher. It helps a child believe that people remain in her life in caring, meaningful ways—that she can rely on and safely love other people.

When primary caregiving is responsive and continuous over at least a year, children have fewer difficult behaviors at home and are more cooperative in both the home and child care and learning environments. Their play with other children is more positive and there are fewer problem behaviors in toddlers. When a child and infant/toddler teacher spend at least a year together, they are more interactive during caregiving (11). On the other hand, children who experienced changes in caregivers before 24 months were more aggressive as toddlers.

Other benefits for children who experience primary caregiving and continuity of care are described in a lovely article titled "It's Good to See You Again!" (12) include:

- Children experience less stress.
- Children are supported through difficult and challenging parts of life.
- Children are supported in developing relationships with other children.
- Children are more successful communicating nonverbally and verbally.
- Children are more comfortable engaging in play, taking risks, and trying new things.
- Parents feel more welcome and at ease about leaving their child in group care.
- Parents and caregivers have stronger relationships and more open communication.
- Caregivers are better able to track development and plan meaningful activities for children.
- It's fun for children to be with someone they know and feel connected to.

Infant/toddler Teacher Characteristics

Personal characteristics—such as warmth, comfort with intimacy, a sense of humor, and enjoying children—are important for infant/toddler teachers. However, other factors such as general education level and specific training in child development (13), compensation and stability in the workplace, and the structure for ongoing supervision by the director consistently correlate to better child outcomes in studies of early care. Unfortunately, teachers of infants and toddlers have the lowest educational requirements, the lowest salaries, and the highest turnover in the field (14).

For those working with children age 3 to 5 years, 45 percent have a bachelor's degree, compared to 19 percent of those working with infants and toddlers. Conversely, 28 percent of those working with infants and toddlers have a high school diploma or less, compared to just 13 percent of those working with 3- to 5-year-olds (15).

Infant/toddler teachers with either a bachelor's degree or specialized training at the college level are more sensitive and less harsh with children, are warmer, more enthusiastic, and more developmentally appropriate in their communication (16). Teachers who are sensitive, use more stimulating materials, have more academic training and smaller group sizes have children with stronger academic skills. In child care homes, caregivers who were better educated and had higher and more recent levels of training demonstrated more positive caregiving (17). Infant/toddler teachers with as little as two courses at the community college level are less authoritarian than those with no training at all (18).

Infant/toddler teachers with more education maintain cleaner, healthier environments and reduce the number of accidental injuries in their classrooms. Their classrooms are likely to receive higher scores on global quality rating scales, such as the Infant/Toddler Environment Rating Scale (ITERS). (ITERS and other rating scales are discussed later in this chapter.) However, most health and safety practices are best maintained when a program has established ongoing monitoring of its own practices.

Watch the video to learn more about characteristics of early childhood teachers. Upon reflection, are you a good match for the field?

https://www.youtube.com/watch?v=a6m3ZQBY31E

The stability of teachers in their positions is also related to their education. Early childhood teachers with more education are more likely to remain in the field. Family home providers participating in initial training tend to seek out additional training and increase their commitment to their jobs.

Of course, whereas education tends to improve both the performance and stability of the teacher, the low wages and lack of benefits in most infant/toddler program jobs make it difficult to recruit and retain people who have invested in their own education. In a review of the 2011 wage by occupation figures, no occupations earned less than child care workers. Gas station attendants, ushers, and laundry workers all earned slightly more than the average $22,000 per year of child care workers (19). Family child care providers earn about $30,000 with a 55-hour workweek (20). Benefits such as health insurance are rare, and wages are so low that workers often cannot afford to pay their share even when employers pay a portion of the cost. The low wages result in a poorly trained workforce with a turnover rate of nearly 40 percent.

The most important predictor of the quality of care . . . is staff wages. (Joan Lombardi)

These structural variables—low ratios, small group sizes, primary caregiving, continuity of care, and well-trained and supported infant/toddler teachers—provide an environment that makes possible the kind of caring, responsive interactions by which we can ultimately judge the quality of a child's experience in an infant/toddler program. Without the foundation of these structural variables, process variables, discussed next, cannot possibly contribute to quality.

Process Variables of Quality

The moment-by-moment experiences of children in an infant/toddler program must be observed to really understand quality from the child's perspective. These process variables include the interactions between children and infant/toddler teachers and among children, and the play, learning, and health activities in which the children participate (21).

The process variables of greatest importance to infants and toddlers are responsive caregiving and planning, cultural and linguistic continuity, meeting the needs of the individual within the group context, and the physical environment. These topics

Nothing is more important than the ongoing relationship between the teacher and the children.

Pearson Education

are covered in depth in other chapters. A brief summary of the definition of these items as related to the broader concept of quality follows.

Responsive Teaching

Responsive teaching, of course, describes the process of understanding the child's experience and knowing how to respond appropriately. Lally (22) writes of seven gifts that good infant/toddler care and learning programs offer. The gifts of nurturance, support, security, and predictability help children believe that they will be loved and cared for in the program setting. The gifts of predictability, focus, encouragement, and expansion support the child's intellectual engagement and understanding of the world. These gifts provide a clear description of responsive teaching.

Cultural and Linguistic Continuity

Infants and toddlers develop expectations of how they will be cared for in their first days of life. They become familiar with the sound of their family's language, even in the womb. Infant/toddler teachers, ideally, would be of the same culture and home language as the family. In today's diverse communities, it is unlikely that all children will have a teacher from their native culture. Infant/toddler teachers can, however, learn the words of affection from families and try to match the family's practices. They can include pictures, toys, or artifacts of a specific culture in their environment, and they must always speak of the child's culture with respect. In Chapter 12, we discuss specific strategies for developing relationships with families from diverse cultures.

CULTURE CLOSE UP

A group of highly educated and influential infant-toddler program directors and college faculty had the opportunity to visit Reggio Emilia infant programs in Italy. In the atelier, a specialized art room shared by all the children, were beautiful displays of recycled objects. These included well-worn sea stones, nuts and bolts, thumbtacks, corks, sharp scissors—all displayed in glass containers within the children's reach. Some teachers were outraged at the lack of safety: "This would never be allowed in the United States. These things are far too dangerous for 1-year-olds." The Italian teachers responded, "We believe in children's strengths. We have never had children swallow something dangerous or otherwise harm themselves. They learn how to use all kinds of materials." On the bus afterward, the U.S. teachers had a lively discussion about what they would want to do if licensing were not an issue.

Meeting the Needs of the Individual Within the Context of the Group

Infant/toddler teachers need to find ways to respect the individual temperament, moods, preferences, and routines of each child in their care. This includes feeding on demand, being helped to fall asleep, and diapering or toileting as needed. Low ratios and small group sizes are critical factors in whether an infant/toddler teacher will be able to attend sensitively to the individual and the group.

This is a good time to reflect on **temperament**. In a toddler room, for example, feisty Syrita is alternating between climbing the wall ladder and rocking on the rocking horse. Jem is watching everyone from a cozy corner. William and Keisha are playing with dolls in the kitchen. Marty, one of their infant/toddler teachers, is welcoming children as they arrive. Pip, their other teacher, is trying in turn to keep Syrita from getting too wound up, helping Jem to enter the play, and expanding on William and Keisha's play. Each of the children is doing exactly what he or she needs to do. Their needs from their teachers, however, are very diverse.

Physical Environment

The environment must be kept particularly clean, given the immature immune systems of infants and toddlers, and especially safe for young children who may mouth and swallow anything and are constantly developing new abilities in movement. The play spaces must offer interesting opportunities for exploration without being overwhelming with too many choices. Above all else, the environment must be set up and monitored to ensure the health and safety of the children in care.

Check Your Understanding 11.1
Click here to check your understanding of the concepts in this section.

An Emphasis on Health and Safety

Two resources are rich with up-to-the-moment information for infant and toddler health and safety. *Caring for Our Children: National Health and Safety Performance Standards; Guidelines for Early Care and Learning Programs* (23) is the most thorough, well-researched, and reviewed material available. The practices in this section come from that source and we highly recommend that every infant/toddler teacher use the original document available on the internet. The second is the Health section on the Early Childhood Learning and Knowledge Center (ECLKC), a Web site run by the Office of Head Start.

Keeping children safe and healthy in infant/toddler care and learning programs is a foundation of quality, but it is not enough. Health and safety practices in infant/toddler care and learning programs include a range of activities for the purpose of avoiding injury and infection and promoting health, including the following:

* Sanitizing and preventing the spread of disease,
* Promoting safety and preventing injuries, and
* Adopting policies that promote and protect health.

 Watch the video to learn the strengths and concerns found in a study of health and safety in centers. Are these concerns familiar to you from programs you know?

https://www.youtube.com/watch?v=vmpUCGivuYg&index=7&list=PL84B845702CB6C26A

Sanitizing and Preventing the Spread of Disease

Infants are vulnerable. In the first weeks of life, they cannot even support their own heads when being held. They cannot take action to keep themselves dry, warm, fed, or safe—and they cannot, at the end of a day of care, tell us whether they were treated kindly. As parents, we are so aware of this vulnerability that we watch their breathing as they sleep, to reassure ourselves. And the most basic demand we make of non-parental care is that our infants will be healthy and safe.

This vulnerability is not simply our perception of infants. In the last 2 months of gestation, the mother's immune system creates enormous amounts of immunoglobulin, the protective agent against most infections, and sends it to the child across the placenta. At birth, the newborn has a higher immunoglobulin count than his mother. However, also at birth, the child stops receiving the

BOX 11.1

Caring for Our Children: National Health and Safety Performance Standards: Guidelines for Early Childhood Care and Learning Programs: Third Edition

Caring for Our Children was created by the American Academy of Pediatrics and the National Resource Center for Health and Safety in Child Care to provide the most current, evidence-based information on health and safety practices for group care. Standards describing best practices, scientific rationales, and comments address these areas:

- Staffing
- Program: Activities for healthy development
- Health promotion and protection in child care
- Nutrition and food service
- Facilities, supplies, equipment, and transportation
- Infectious diseases
- Children who are eligible for services under IDEA

- Administration
- Licensing and community action

Specific procedures for hand washing, diapering, cleaning and sanitizing, food handling, and every aspect of maintaining a safe and healthy environment are included.

The entire document is available online (http://nrckids.org), and updates are regularly posted as the current science provides new information for our decision making.

Source: Based on Caring for Our Children: National Health and Safety Performance Standards; Guidelines for Early Care and Learning Programs, Third Edition, *American Academy of Pediatrics, American Public Health Association,* Published by American Academy of Pediatrics, 2011.

immunoglobulin from his mother and the protection slowly decreases. Breastfed infants continue to receive antibodies from the mother through her milk (25). Newborns have a unique and developing immune system, but infants are considerably more prone to infection, and less resilient in recovering from infection, than people at any other stage of human development.

First, we understand the vulnerability to infection in the infant and toddler. Then we add the risks of repeated exposures to infection that are inherent in group care compared to being at home with one's family. It is clear that infant/toddler teachers have a responsibility to maintain a sanitary environment. See Box 11.1 for ways to find more information on health and safety practices for group care. For teachers of infants and toddlers, preventing the spread of disease depends on scrupulous attention to hand washing, diapering, sanitizing (toys, furniture, and bedding), and excluding children who are ill.

Hand Washing

Hand washing is the primary defense against illness in infant/toddler care and learning programs. It is such a basic step in hygiene that it is amazing how often it is either not done when it should be or is done improperly and ineffectively. Unwashed or improperly washed hands spread infection and may be the cause of diarrhea outbreaks among both children and staff. Centers that have implemented hand-washing training programs have decreased the incidence of diarrhea by 50 percent. Hand washing also reduces the spread of colds and respiratory infections and protects the children, as well as the infant/toddler teacher, from illness.

For these children, hand washing is a routine part of the day.

Keeping hands clean through improved hand hygiene is one of the most important steps we can take to avoid getting sick and spreading germs to others. Teachers, volunteers, and children should wash their hands before and after preparing food and before eating food. Adults should wash their hands and the child's hands after diapering a child. Everyone should wash hands after the using the toilet. Adults should wash their hands after blowing their nose or wiping a child's nose. Everyone should also wash their hands after handling animals, garbage, or playing in sand. (26, Standard 3.2.2).

Infant/toddler teachers should receive training in proper hand-washing procedures and be monitored for the accuracy of their use of the procedure and whether they are hand washing in every required situation. Infant/toddler care and learning programs should post proper hand-washing procedures above sinks. Specific procedures need to be in place describing how teachers will wash the hands of infants too young to do it themselves, or assist toddlers in washing their own hands.

Diapering

A second important area of hygiene in group care is diapering. Diapers must fit snuggly to hold solids and be able to absorb and hold liquids. Teachers should have a routine of regularly checking diapers every couple of hours but should also respond quickly when they feel or smell that a diaper needs changing.

Stool carries germs that cause gastrointestinal illnesses. The germs in stool spread widely among children in diapers and those learning toileting. Adults who diaper and assist children with toileting can also spread germs. The keys to infection control in diapering/toileting are:

- Diaper children on an elevated surface used only for diapering, away from food preparation, and within reach of hand washing.
- After diapering and toileting, both child and adult must wash their hands.
- Clean and disinfect the diapering surface after each use.
- Clean and disinfect toileting areas daily and when soiled.
- Discard dirty diapers in a covered step can.

Avoid having staff who change diapers prepare food. (27, Standard 3.2.1)

The changing table that is used must also be diligently sanitized using a solution, such as the one described in Box 11.2. Changing tables must be made of a nonporous material, cleaned and sanitized after each use to remove visible soil, and followed by wetting with a sanitizing solution such as the diluted bleach solution. The sanitizer must be left on for the required contact time. Some sanitizers need to be wiped off afterward with water, but bleach does not as the chlorine evaporates, leaving only water on the surface (28, Standard 3.3).

Sanitizing Toys, Furniture, and Bedding

The Standards also provide directions to clean and **sanitize** all aspects of the child care area. Infants and toddlers are likely to touch any surface they can reach. They are both spreading infectious agents and coming in contact with contaminated surfaces anywhere in the environment. One precaution in the standards that is only for infant rooms is the requirement that people either cover their street shoes or replace them with slippers before walking on the infant room floor (29, Standard 5.2.9.14). Infants and toddlers spend so much time with their hands and faces on or near the floor. Floor cleanliness is a special issue for those rooms.

Infants and toddlers sneeze and cough without covering their noses or mouths. They mouth any toy or object and they drool when they are teething. The potential for spreading disease is impressive. A routine for cleaning and sanitizing all surfaces should be established, implemented, and monitored by all programs.

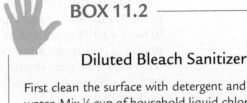

BOX 11.2

Diluted Bleach Sanitizer

First clean the surface with detergent and rinse with water. Mix ¼ cup of household liquid chlorine bleach in 1 gallon of water (or 1 tablespoon of bleach to 1 quart of water). Sprayed onto a cleaned surface, the sanitizer requires 2 minutes of surface contact to kill the usual infectious agents found in feces.

Excluding Children Who Are Ill

The Standards suggest that children who are ill be excluded from child care for a short period of time. Each state's licensing standards may have specific regulations regarding when children should be excluded from care. **Health consultants** or health advisory committees should also be consulted. However, the basic guidelines from the National Health and Safety Performance Standards include specific conditions for **exclusion** from the program. For instance, a child should be excluded if the illness prevents her from participating in the activities or the illness requires infant/toddler teachers to provide less care to the other children. A child with any of the following conditions should be excluded from group care: fever; symptoms and signs of severe illness (e.g., lethargy, uncontrolled coughing, persistent irritability or crying, difficulty breathing, wheezing, or other unusual signs); diarrhea; blood in stools; vomiting; persistent abdominal pain; mouth sores with drooling; rash with fever; purulent conjunctivitis (pink eye); pediculosis (head lice); scabies; tuberculosis; impetigo; strep throat; chickenpox; pertussis; mumps; hepatitis A virus; measles; rubella; respiratory tract illness; shingles; or herpes simplex.

Excluding children with mild infections has only a small effect on limiting the spread of infection because many viruses are spread before the child actually exhibits any symptoms of the disease. Infant/toddler care and learning programs should also consider the child's comfort and the needs of the staff when they create policies for excluding children who are ill (30, Standard 3.6.1.1).

Administering Medication

When children with mild illnesses or chronic conditions require medication, the child care program may be involved in **medication administration**. The

National Health and Safety Performance Standards, the Head Start program performance standards, and most state licensing regulations require programs to have a written policy and procedures for medication administration. The best option is that medication be prescribed in ways that allow parents to administer it before or after the hours the child is in care. However, young children are prone to illnesses, and it is sometimes necessary for programs to take on the responsibility.

When programs must administer medications, the National Health and Safety Performance Standards have several standards concerning this issue, including Permissible Administration of Medication, Labeling and Storage of Medications, and Training of Teachers to Administer Medication. These standards limit the administration of medications to prescribed medications ordered by a health care provider with written permission of the parent or legal guardian. Nonprescription (over-the-counter) medications must also be recommended by a health care provider for a specific child or for a specific circumstance for all children, with written permission from the parent or legal guardian. So, a health care provider could write a standing order for the use of sunscreen or acetaminophen for use in specific circumstances (exposure to sun or fever higher than 101°F). Parents must be notified of each application of any medication and each application should be logged.

Prescribed medications brought into the child care and learning facility should be in their original containers, dated, labeled with the child's first and last names, the date the prescription was filled, the name of the health care provider who wrote the prescription, the expiration date, the instructions for administration, and the name and strength of the medication. Over-the-counter medications should be brought in their original container and labeled by the parent with the child's name and instructions from the health care provider. All medications should have child-resistant caps, be stored away from food, and be kept inaccessible to children.

Promoting Safety and Preventing Injuries

In addition to the vulnerability of very young children to disease, infants and toddlers are quite susceptible to injuries through accidents. They are just developing the ability to move around and do not automatically understand how to keep their balance. They may fall over steep edges. They get stuck in tight places they have somehow managed to squeeze into. Infants and toddlers who are so interested in the ideas of *in* and *out* apply those ideas to tiny objects that can choke them or to interesting openings in walls where adults plug in lamps and CD players. The world can be a dangerous place for the curious explorer who brings limited experience to his movements or the consequences of his actions. It can be challenging to find a balance between keeping the child care area safe and still providing an environment that invites children to play, learn, and explore.

Accident Prevention

Teachers who care for infants and toddlers are constantly scanning the environment for anything that may cause injury to their charges. A key to keeping the environment safe for infants and toddlers is to see the area through their eyes.

Getting down on the floor and taking a child's eye view can alert the teacher to dangers she might not see from an adult height. Are tall shelves bolted to the wall so they can't fall down on a climbing child? Are outlets covered? Are more remote parts of the carpet vacuumed as frequently as the open spaces? Are all sharp or breakable items out of children's reach? Are cleaning products, medications, and other poisons in a locked closet or cabinet? Are small toys that could cause choking out of the reach of all children under 3? Are there doors, gates, or other barriers to prevent children from falling down stairs? Are sharp edges and corners of furniture covered to protect children (32)?

A child's-eye view can alert teachers to dangers and hazards in the environment.

Accident prevention requires an awareness of potential hazards, eliminating known hazards, knowing what to do in an emergency, and teaching children about safety

With infants and toddlers, the teacher's vigilant observation of the children and the space is the most important factor in preventing accidents and injuries. Teachers arrange furniture to allow visual access to children at all times. Furniture is checked for stability. Door edges are protected to prevent pinched fingers. Electrical cords are not dangling or within reach of children. Outlets are covered. Infants and toddlers are never left unattended in high chairs, infant seats, or swings. Choking hazards, such as small objects, broken parts of toys, curtain cords, balloons, popcorn, peanuts, hot dogs, grapes, gum, and hard candies are kept out of the environment. Infant and toddler toys should be greater than 1¼ inches in diameter to avoid choking. Toys are chosen for their age-appropriateness, checking the labels for age recommendations. Toys should be **nontoxic**, wooden toys kept free of splinters, and cloth toys must be flame retardant.

All cleaning supplies and medications should be kept locked and out of the children's reach. Other potentially **toxic substances** include poisonous plants, small batteries, salves used in diapering, and even art materials. Colored inks used in magazines may contain lead.

Outdoor play must also be well supervised. Children should be dressed appropriately for whatever weather is present. Children must be kept well hydrated and safe from the sun. Playgrounds should be designed for infants and toddlers and provide surfaces that provide protection from the inevitable falls.

Despite all precautions, accidents may still occur. Teachers need to have current first aid and infant-toddler CPR training, fully stocked first aid kits kept handy, and written plans for reacting to emergencies. Infant/toddler care and learning programs should practice evacuation drills for fires, hurricanes, and tornados. Infant programs should have evacuation cribs to provide for quick transport of a group of infants.

Adopting Policies That Promote and Protect Health

All programs serving young children need health and safety policies that are written out, approved by a health consultant or health advisory committee, and understood by staff. Infant/toddler teachers should receive training on the policies and procedures and be monitored for their adherence to them. Hand washing, cleaning, sanitizing, diapering, and accident prevention are all areas that should be covered by those policies. Schedules that promote a balance between active and quiet play and rest times, good nutrition, and the constant presence of a responsive, caring adult all promote health.

Two additional areas are important to emphasize in a discussion of infant/toddler care and learning programs: safe sleep positioning and child abuse reporting.

Back to Sleep

In 1992, the American Academy of Pediatrics (AAP) Task Force on Infant Positioning and SIDS (sudden infant death syndrome) made the strong recommendation that young infants be placed to sleep supine (on their backs) to reduce the risk of SIDS. Their public awareness effort became known as the *Back to Sleep* campaign. Between 1992 and 2001, the SIDS rate had been reduced by 53 percent. All infant/toddler care and learning programs should ensure safe sleeping positions as a policy. The most recent AAP (33) policy statement on SIDS makes these recommendations:

1. Place infants on their backs to sleep.
2. Use a firm sleep surface.
3. Keep soft objects and loose bedding out of the crib.
4. Do not smoke during pregnancy.
5. Provide a separate nearby sleeping environment (recommended).
6. Offer a pacifier at naptime and bedtime.
7. Avoid overheating.

Child Abuse and Prevention

Child abuse and neglect are sensitive, emotionally charged issues for everyone. Parents fear for their child's safety when left in group care, with abuse sometimes being one of those worries. Infant/toddler teachers are often the first to recognize and identify signs of parental abuse and then have the difficult task of reporting the abuse or neglect to authorities. There is a Federal law that defines child abuse as

> Any recent act or failure to act on the part of a parent or caretaker, which results in death, serious physical or emotional harm, sexual abuse, or exploitation, or an act or failure to act which presents an imminent risk of serious harm (34).

Abuse may include

- Non-accidental injury
- Neglect
- Sexual molestation
- Emotional abuse

Infant/toddler teachers are required to report all suspected cases of abuse and neglect. It is important to have training in recognizing signs of possible abuse and characteristics of child abusers. It is also important to understand the **legal mandate for reporting** in your state, as well as the procedures for reporting suspected abuse or neglect. Infant/toddler care and learning programs should have policies in place to ensure that abuse never occurs within the program. They should have a method for investigating any accusations of abuse. Although this topic requires greater depth of training than can be given here, a short description of each of these issues will be helpful. A teacher's recognition of an indicator of abuse or neglect should be considered within the context of explanations given by the family, the medical history, and the ability of the child to participate in the activities said to cause the accident. It is not your responsibility to determine abuse or neglect. It is your responsibility to report any reasonable suspicions.

The indicators of abuse or neglect are as follows:

- *Indicators of physical abuse:* Any injury on an infant such as burns, fractures, bruises, bites, welts, cuts, scrapes, head injuries, fear of adults, appearance of pain
- *Indicators of emotional abuse:* General unhappiness, reacting without emotion to unpleasant statements or actions, delayed emotional development, or for infants an appearance of freezing as though withdrawing completely from the present moment
- *Indicators of sexual abuse:* Difficulty in walking or sitting; torn, stained, or bloody underclothing; pain when urinating; bruises or bleeding in vaginal or anal areas, mouth, or throat, or vaginal infections; unwillingness to have clothing changed; being fearful of a particular person; or unusual interest in or knowledge of sexual matters
- *Indicators of physical and emotional neglect:* Infants or toddlers left in the care of other children, dressed inadequately for the weather, poor hygiene, not getting regular well-child care, no weight gain, or always hungry (35).

Characteristics of child abusers include these traits:

- Isolated, under stress, mental health issues
- **Substance abuse**
- Unmet emotional needs for nurturance and support
- Immaturity
  - impulsive behavior
  - using the child to meet the adult's own emotional or physical needs
  - a constant craving for change and excitement
- Lack of interpersonal skills
- Lack of parenting knowledge
- Likely to feel that violence is an acceptable way of dealing with problems (36).

Reporting suspected child abuse is one of the most difficult things infant/ toddler teachers may have to do, but it is not a choice. If you suspect abuse or neglect, you are legally required to report your suspicions to authorities. Each state has its own definition of what constitutes abuse or neglect. You are never required to have proof before reporting and must report an incident as soon as it is noticed. Part of your program's policy should include knowing which agency to call in your community. Many states will take an anonymous report over the phone, but it is useful to provide your contact information.

Infant/toddler teachers may also need to consider how their program's discipline policy may be seen in light of issues of abuse and neglect. Corporal punishment may never be used in child care. Discipline must never interfere with a child's schedule of eating, sleeping, or toileting. However, a responsive teacher will not use discipline with infants and toddlers. Her own good skills, an engaging but serene environment, and positive interactions with children will provide the guidance very young children need as they learn to control their own behavior. Chapter 14 presents specific strategies in regard to guidance for infants and toddlers.

The Importance of Good Nutrition

The nutrition infants and toddlers receive directly affects the ability of the brain to form and develop and may have a lifelong effect on the child's ability to learn, to cope with difficult circumstances, and to grow and have strong bones. Mothers who are severely malnourished in pregnancy produce infants with smaller head circumferences and smaller brain weight. The enormous spurts of growth in the last months of gestation and the first years of life require sufficient amounts of food and sufficient quantities of particular nutrients.

Infant/toddler care and learning programs may play an important role in ensuring that infants and toddlers in care have adequate nutrition. We help to establish healthy eating habits and get used to a variety of healthy choices. We need to use proper food-handling techniques. Programs can influence the patterns children set early in life. Infant/toddler teachers must establish healthy eating habits, good sleep routines, a balance between active and quiet play, and some time outdoors every day to lay the foundation for good growth and development.

Nutritional Needs of Infants and Toddlers

Human breast milk is the best food for young human infants. The composition of the mother's milk changes as the child grows, giving the child exactly what she needs at the time. The protein is easily digested and the vitamins and minerals are almost entirely absorbed, compared to only 10 percent of iron and vitamins from formula. Certain fats found in breast milk, but not in formula, are used by the developing central nervous system and the photoreceptor rods in the retina (37, 38). The American Academy of Pediatrics strongly endorses breast-feeding, in part because of the significant immunological benefits. More than 50 immune agents are transferred through breast milk, giving infants protection from otitis media (middle ear infections), fewer respiratory infections, and fewer gastric infections causing diarrhea (39). Breast-fed infants may have a lower incidence of SIDS, allergies, childhood lymphoma, childhood-onset diabetes, and obesity (40). Infant/toddler care and learning programs can support mothers in their breast-feeding by encouraging them to visit their child during the day to breast-feed or to express milk to use in bottles. Infants weaned before 12 months of age should be fed iron-fortified formula.

Bottles of breast milk, formula, milk, or juice should never be propped for a child to use without being held. The nurturing, social aspect of feeding is nearly as important as the nutrition for infants. Bottles should never be used as a way to help a child fall asleep because the prolonged contact with the natural sugars in the liquids can cause tooth decay. Even very young infants should have their gums wiped with a moist cloth after feeding to remove any remaining liquid that could turn to plaque and cause tooth decay (41, Standard 4.3.1).

Certain micronutrients (vitamins and minerals) are essential for healthy growth and development. Iron, iodine, and zinc are all necessary for proper cell development. Infants are born with enough iron for the first 4 to 6 months; infants get iron from breast milk, iron-fortified formula, iron-fortified cereal, beans, vegetables, and meats. Iron is used by the body in the development of red blood cells and in brain tissue, including the network of neurotransmitters used for information processing (42). Toddlers with **iron deficiency anemia** have lower scores on both the mental and psychomotor indices of the *Bayley Scales of Infant Development* and are more wary, hesitant, easily tired, and less attentive, involved, and playful than children with adequate iron (43). Iron deficiency is often associated with poverty, but iron-fortified formulas or iron supplements can prevent anemia.

Between 4 and 6 months, infants begin to supplement breast milk or formula with foods such as rice cereal or unsweetened applesauce—foods that are unlikely to trigger allergic reactions. Solid foods should be introduced one at a time, with a few days passing before introducing the next new food so that any reactions to the food can be easily identified. The introduction of these soft solid foods coincides with the child's developing abilities to move the food in his mouth and swallow it.

From 6 months to the first birthday, infants continue to rely on breast milk or formula for most of their nutrition, but they are increasing the amount and variety of solid foods they are eating. At this time, infants eat pureed cereals, fruits, vegetables, and meats. They learn to eat a wide variety of healthy foods, incorporating more solid foods as they have teeth for chewing. Foods that are likely to cause allergies or choking should not be introduced. Water is offered to quench thirst. Infants begin to finger-feed themselves toward the end of the first year and enjoy holding their own spoon while they are being fed. Important habits are being developed during this time. Infants should be fed when they express their hunger through crying, sucking on their fist, fussiness, or pointing to places where food is kept. They eat quickly when hungry and will begin to slow down and explore or socialize as the hunger abates. When the child signals through a closed mouth or turning away that she is full, the infant/toddler teacher should end the feeding. One of the lessons the child is learning is to understand her own body's signals of hunger and fullness.

Infants cannot eat a great deal at a time, and they need food that is packed in healthy calories to ensure their growth and development. Infants need fat in their diet but they do not need salt or sugar to flavor their foods, and both salt and sugar should be kept to a minimum in their diets. High salt intake can lead to hypertension in adults, and it is not necessary to teach a child to develop a desire for it. Sugar is linked to hyperactivity, diabetes, tooth decay, and other chronic diseases later in life (44).

Breast-fed infants may continue nursing after their first birthday if it is working well for the mother and the child. However, formula-fed infants usually switch to cow's milk at about 1 year of age. Between 1 and 2 years, a toddler's daily nutritional needs include about 16 ounces of milk; 1 cup each of fresh fruits and vegetables; 2 one-ounce servings of meat, poultry, fish, eggs or beans; about 200 to 500 calories of other good foods such as fortified cereal, breads, and legumes; and water for thirst. Between 2 and 3 years, toddlers need 16 ounces of milk; 1-½ cups each of fresh fruits and vegetables; 3 to 4 ounces of meats, poultry, fish, or eggs; about 400 to 800 calories of foods, such as fortified cereal, breads, and legumes; and water for thirst (45). Infant/toddler teachers must be sure to avoid serving foods that cause choking, such as hot dogs (whole or cut into rounds), raw carrot rounds or sticks, whole grapes, hard candy, or nuts. Other foods that present choking dangers include seeds, raw peas, popcorn, chunks of peanut butter, and chunks of meat (46).

As toddlers are becoming skillful eaters with increasing appetites, teachers and parents can be teaching and encouraging healthy choices. Toddlers enjoy feeding themselves, having some choice in what they eat, eating when they are hungry, and being allowed to determine when they are through. Infant/toddler care and learning programs should not even have unhealthy salty or sugary foods available as possible choices. Children should see child care as a place where only healthy foods are available. As toddlers naturally use their mouths to explore during the second year of life, give them opportunities to explore a wide variety of foods. By age 2, children can have a repertoire of as many as 200 foods that they enjoy. Toddlers

Pearson Education

Serving themselves lunch can become an important part of the day. It takes a lot of skill and concentration.

may want to eat the same food day after day for every meal and then suddenly get bored and refuse to touch those very foods at all. As long as children are getting a well-rounded diet that meets their nutritional needs, with ongoing opportunities to broaden their tastes, it is all right to allow them to make choices about what they eat at any one meal.

Infant/toddler Care and Learning Programs Supporting Safe and Healthy Nutrition

When providing foods for infants and toddlers in programs, the changing nutritional needs are only part of what teachers need to know. The emotional and social environment of snacks and meals are important. You need to know about the safe handling of foods and the utensils used in meal preparation and eating. Your program needs policies that ensure each infant or toddler has an individualized diet plan including how to respond to family preferences or allergic reactions to food.

The Social Environment of Feeding

It is almost impossible to separate the importance of nutrition from the importance of being held, touched, and talked to while being fed. In child care, as well as with parents, infants should always be held during bottle-feeding. Bottles should never be propped in a crib or carried around by the child. Teachers should also feed infants on demand, and a consistent adult, preferably the primary teacher, being the one to feed the child as often as possible. The primary teacher develops the ongoing relationship with the child that allows them to understand each other's cues and develop expectations about the rhythm and pattern of the feeding. The consistent adult partner will recognize signs of hunger before the child is so distressed that he is crying (47, Standard 4.5). As older infants begin to eat solid foods, they may at first be spoon-fed in the teacher's arms as part of the meal, which is still primarily bottle-feeding. However, as the child is able to sit, and the amount of solid food is increasing, the child should be in a supported chair. The infant/toddler teacher should be talking with the child and creating a pleasant tone for the feeding and always communicating a positive attitude toward the food, with words such as, "Oh yummy. These peas are soooo good. Green beans are so good for you! You really enjoy this, don't you?" Older toddlers will begin to have meals and snacks in small groups, the adult sitting with them, promoting the social aspects of mealtime, such as passing foods to one another and having conversations.

Infant/toddler teachers should never force children to eat or prevent them eating. Food may not be used as a punishment and should not be used as a reward (48, Standard 4.5.0.11).

Safe Handling of Food and Utensils

As in all areas of health and safety, the recommendations for the safe handling of food, eating areas, and utensils are thoroughly described in the National Health and Safety Performance Standards. Some of the most important points include having seating arrangements for infants and toddlers during meals in which they can sit comfortably, with tables coming between stomach and mid-chest levels, on seats that allow their feet to rest on a firm surface while eating. This provides the most comfort and increases the developing independence of the child. Seats that attach to the side of a table leaving little feet hanging in midair would not meet this recommendation (49, Standard 4.5).

Utensils and eating surfaces must, of course, be kept clean and sanitized to prevent the spread of disease. Eating utensils should enable children to eat at their developmental level and should never have sharp edges that could cut the tissue inside a child's mouth; plates and utensils must be free from chips; single-use materials, such as paper plates or napkins must be discarded after one use. Washable bibs, placemats, napkins, or tablecloths must be washed and sanitized after each use. Imported dishware must be certified to be free from lead or other heavy metals. All surfaces in contact with foods must be lead free. Table surfaces and even high chair trays appear to be much more likely to be contaminated by microorganisms than single-use or washed and sanitized dishes (50, Standard 4.5).

The food preparation areas must be kept separate from areas of the program used for eating, play, laundry, toileting, bathrooms, and any area where animals are permitted. Sinks used for food preparation may not be used for hand washing or any other purpose. Sinks used for hand washing and diapering may not be used for food preparation. Refrigeration must be able to keep foods at 40°F or lower, and freezers must maintain 0°F or lower at all times. No staff with symptoms of illness should handle food. Food that was unfinished on individual plates or family-style serving bowls should be discarded. The storage of foods, washing of dishes, and transporting of meals purchased from off-site food services should follow the regulations of the National Health and Safety Performance Standards and the Child and Adult Care Food Program of the U.S. Department of Agriculture (51).

Policies Supporting Safe and Healthy Food Services

In a role similar to that of a health consultant to a program, each child care and learning program should have a **nutrition consultant**. This nutritionist can help determine how to meet individual requests from families (e.g., vegetarian, kosher), how to train and plan for food-related emergencies (e.g., allergic reactions or choking), and how to be sure that feeding plans for individual children are meeting their nutritional needs. A program might develop policies regarding the consistent feeding by one adult for bottle-fed infants or limit the number of children per adult during a small group meal. Program policies can articulate the training and monitoring of staff for safe food-handling practices.

An additional role for a nutrition consultant may be to provide nutrition education for families or help teachers plan nutritional learning activities for toddlers. The consultant may help educate staff and parents about programs that can support their ability to provide healthy foods such as the Child and Adult Care Food Program (CACFP) described in Box 11.3.

  Check Your Understanding 11.2
Click here to check your understanding of the concepts in this section.

BOX 11.3

The Child and Adult Care Food Program (CACFP)

CACFP is a federal program that provides healthy meals and snacks to children and adults receiving day care. It plays a vital role in improving the quality of child care and making it more affordable for many low-income families. CACFP reimburses participating centers and child care homes for their meal costs. It is administered at the federal level by the Food and Nutrition Service (FNS), an agency of the U.S. Department of Agriculture. The state education or health department administers CACFP in most states. Independent centers and homes and sponsoring organizations enter into agreements with their state agencies to operate the program.

In order to participate in CACFP, homes and centers must agree to meet the nutritional meal and snack requirements of the program. In turn, the program receives reimbursements for each snack and meal served.

Child Care Centers. Public or private nonprofit child care centers, Head Start programs, and some for-profit centers that are licensed or approved to provide day care may serve meals and snacks to infants and children through CACFP.

Family Day Care Homes. CACFP provides reimbursement for meals and snacks served to small groups of children receiving nonresidential day care in licensed or approved private homes. A family or group day care home must sign an agreement with a sponsoring organization to participate in CACFP. The sponsoring organization organizes training, conducts monitoring, and helps with planning menus and filling out reimbursement forms.

To learn more about CACFP, contact your state agency. If you have questions about any of USDA's nutrition assistance programs, check the information on the other pages of the USDA FNS Web site.

Source: Child and Adult Care Food Program. (2015) *Child and adult care food program.* Retrieved from: www.fns.usda.gov/cacfp/child-and-adult-care-food-program. U.S. Department of Agriculture.

Systems, Laws, and Policies That Support Quality Programs

If you recall the bioecological theory described earlier in this text, you know that quality in programs would require systems, laws, and policies to support them. Determining whether programs have high quality depends on a strong system of evaluation. We describe some tools that are currently in use to evaluate infant/toddler care and learning programs. Next we look at the Child Care Development Fund (CCDF), program licensing, quality rating and improvement systems, and program accreditation. Together, these initiatives are working toward improving quality in infant and toddler programs.

Program Evaluation

Given the aspects that contribute to quality already described in this chapter, it should be evident by now that assessing quality is anything but clear. When we walk into a program and find infants and toddlers quietly and intently engaged in their play and learning and looking to teachers for a moment of emotional connection, the teachers calm and interested in the children, we know we are looking at high quality. Understanding each child's experience is, of course, the most important way to assess quality, but it is very subjective. The evaluation tools available for infant/toddler care and learning programs use both structural and process variables as researchers develop increasingly sophisticated measures of quality.

There are several reasons to assess the quality of care. Researchers are continuously trying to determine which elements of quality have most impact on the developmental outcomes of young children. Policy makers use that information to determine where to invest resources. Parents use quality indicators to help them choose the best care possible for their own child. Large public programs such as Early Head Start use program evaluation as a measure of accountability for the use of public funds. Programs can use measurement tools to assess their own quality and develop their own plans for improvement. Following are descriptions of some of the most frequently used measures.

Infant/Toddler Environment Rating Scale

The ITERS–Revised (52) is one of the most widely used measures of quality in the United States. It is part of a series of measures used for specific age groups or settings, including preschool, family child care, and school-age care. In its new revision, the ITERS–Revised consists of 39 items organized into seven subscales: space and furnishings, personal care routines, listening and talking, activities, interaction, program structure, and parents and staff. The observer has to notice materials or interactions taking place. Each item is measured on a 7-point scale ranging from inadequate to minimal to good to excellent. Each subset is scored and a global score is given. The information available from the measure can be helpful for a program working on improving quality.

The ITERS–Revised is often used in research as a reliable, valid measure. Many states have adopted its use as one factor to provide higher child care reimbursement rates to programs that offer higher quality. The ITERS–Revised and its related scales are sometimes criticized as overemphasizing the structural variables and not being sensitive to the subtleties of responsive caregiving.

Classroom Assessment Scoring System

The Classroom Assessment Scoring System (CLASS) for preschool has been established as part of the official monitoring of Head Start programs. Now there is also a CLASS for infants and one for toddlers. These tools concentrate on the interactions between infant/toddler teachers and children in center-based programs. For infants, the CLASS looks at these dimensions of responsive caregiving: the relational climate, teacher sensitivity, facilitated exploration, and early language support. For toddlers, the CLASS evaluates emotional and behavioral support: positive climate, negative climate, teacher sensitivity, regard for child perspectives, and behavior guidance. They also rate engaged support for learning: facilitation of learning and development, quality of feedback, and language modeling.

Quality of Caregiver-Child Interaction for Infants and Toddlers

The Quality of Caregiver-Child Interaction for Infants and Toddlers (QCCIIT) has been developed by Mathematica Policy Research under the Office of Program Research and Evaluation in the Administration for Children and Families (ACF). The Head Start Act of 2007 required programs to use scientifically based measures to support instruction and program evaluation. At that time, ACF felt that there was not a good selection of tools available to infant/toddler care and learning programs. They funded and guided the development of this new tool. Like the CLASS, the QCCIIT focuses on infant/toddler teacher-child interactions in center-based or family child care home. The tool looks at: sensitivity/responsiveness, support for language/literacy, support for cognitive development, support for social-emotional development, positive regard/warmth, behavior guidance, and support for peer interaction.

At the time of writing this text, the QCCIIT was still being field tested.

Laws and Policies

The Head Start Program Performance Standards (53) (HSPPS) are a good example of how government uses regulations to influence quality. The HSPPS provide detailed descriptions of what is required of every aspect of the program; a system of technical assistance is available to help programs achieve the standards, and the programs are reviewed every 3 years against the full set of standards. Whenever public funds are used for programs, some set of regulations provides the limits within which those funds may be used. The Office of Head Start, the Office of Child Care, state and city governments—all have policies and regulations ranging from minimum standards of safety to standards of quality. Public money and private institutions also provide a wide network of programs to support and encourage quality. Although this is not a comprehensive list, it will give students of child development an idea of the wider system in which they will be working.

Child Care Development Fund

The federal government provides funding for child care through the Office of Child Care in the ACF within the U.S. Department of Health and Human Services (DHHS). The CCDF provides each state with funds to subsidize the cost of child care for families that are in work or education programs as they transition from welfare assistance. A portion of each state's CCDF funds is to be used for increasing quality, and a specific portion has been earmarked for infants and toddlers. States use their infant-toddler earmarked funds to make infant-toddler—specific improvements in facilities, such as appropriate playgrounds or bathrooms. They support infant-toddler—specific training for teachers and infant-toddler specialists in the resource and referral networks. Some states use these funds to raise public awareness of the importance of the early years and the impact of good- or poor-quality child care on later development. CCDF is used to promote quality in child care, but there is not sufficient funding or authority to ensure quality care from the federal government. The overall quality of a child care system depends on the licensing regulations and initiatives of the individual state.

Licensing

Every state requires programs providing child care to be licensed. The actual licensing requirements and the range of settings that are exempt from licensing vary widely from state to state. At minimum, a state has basic safety requirements for a setting and age requirements for teachers. Many states have detailed regulations determining group sizes, ratios, training requirements for staff, health and safety practices, and even plans for learning activities. Most states have specific licensing requirements for programs serving infants and toddlers. However, even the most minimal requirements are not always enforced because of the many programs that may be exempt from licensing or may be operating illegally without a license.

Each state has an office administrating the CCDF and child care licensing. These may not be the same offices, or even the same departments of state government. Nonetheless, each of these groups would like to be able to ensure safe and high-quality child care for every infant and toddler who requires out-of-home care. If it were possible, each state would set licensing requirements that ensure low ratios, small group sizes, highly trained staff, and strong health and safety policies at every program.

Unfortunately, high-quality child care is expensive, and states fear that by requiring high-quality child care and highly trained workers, they would reduce the availability of care—as private owners and nonprofit organizations would be unable to meet the cost of providing quality child care on the basis of the tuition they can collect. The states themselves are struggling with large deficits and are unable, or unwilling, to commit precious funds to supporting infant-toddler care and learning when their public schools and colleges are struggling for survival.

Unable to ensure high-quality child care by legislation, states and national organizations are trying a number of other strategies to promote and inspire quality. States are developing quality rating systems wherein they rate the quality of particular programs, either as a way of informing consumers or as the basis of providing differential subsidy reimbursements. National child care organizations offer accreditation to programs as a statement of recognized quality. We examine these two strategies next.

Quality Rating Improvement Systems and Tiered Reimbursement

Tiered quality systems are one way for states to inspire, recognize, and reward quality. A compendium of quality rating improvement systems (QRIS) was completed in 2010, assessing the QRIS from 26 states (54). In tiered reimbursements, states give higher subsidy payments to child care centers and homes that demonstrate quality beyond the requirements of licensing. These may include having a national accreditation or a variety of factors such as group size, ratios, teacher training, compensation, family involvement, and ratings on standardized tools. Some states have only two tiers, licensed and above. Other states have more complex systems, often symbolized by a rating of 1 to 4 stars. Quality rating systems, sometimes called star rating systems, may be tied to higher reimbursement rates, or they may be aimed primarily at getting consumers to demand higher quality. These systems are a sort of report card for programs. When they are most effectively used, programs are able to receive increased funds for better quality but are also able to receive technical assistance and support to help them make improvements.

 Watch the video to learn about Michigan's QRIS. What are benefits to programs for participating?

https://www.youtube.com/watch?v=wz9ZR9c22qk

Accreditation

Many national early childhood organizations offer program accreditation as a way of promoting and recognizing high quality in child care. The two major national accreditation programs are from the National Association for the Education of Young Children (55) for centers, and the National Association for Family Child Care (56) for home and family programs. The NAEYC has more than 8,000 accredited child care programs around the country serving more than 700,000 children and families. Both NAEYC and NAFCC require an in-depth self-study by the program. The self-study report is validated by a team of trained visitors to the program (or individual to a home). The validated self-study is then submitted to a national commission; if the program is judged to be in compliance, it is granted accreditation for a limited number of years. In order to maintain accreditation, the program must submit yearly reports on progress and its responses to suggestions from the national organization. Accreditation carries considerable respect within the field of child development.

 Check Your Understanding 11.3
Click here to check your understanding of the concepts in this section.

Summary

The potential of infant/toddler care and learning programs to have either positive or negative effects on infants and toddlers depends entirely on the quality of the program involved.

- Many elements contribute to high quality in infant/toddler care and learning programs. For infants and toddlers to experience warm, nurturing, ongoing relationships, programs need low child-to-teacher ratios and small group sizes. They need continuity of care, children staying with the same teacher over the course of years. Infant/toddler teachers should be warm, comfortable with intimacy, and enjoy children, as well as being well educated (specifically in infant and toddler development), well compensated, and well supported in their work. Infant/toddler care and learning programs must have cultural and linguistic continuity with the home. The environment should be comfortable and homelike with daily exposure to family-like routines, as well as engaging learning experiences.

- For infants and toddlers to be safe and healthy in a program, teachers must maintain good procedures for
  □ Sanitizing and preventing the spread of disease
  □ Hand washing
  □ Excluding children who are ill
  □ Administering medication
  □ Promoting safety and preventing injuries and accidents
  □ Meeting the nutritional needs of infants and toddlers
  □ Providing safe handling of food

- Quality in infant/toddler care and learning programs may be assessed with a variety of tools that examine the environment and the interactions. These include the ITERS, the Infant and Toddler CLASS, and the Q-CCIIT. Quality is supported by structures at the federal government and the state government and through national professional organizations offering accreditation.

Key Terms

child-to-teacher ratios
continuity of care
exclusion
group size
hazards
health consultants
infection
iron deficiency anemia

legal mandate for reporting
medication administration
mixed age groups
nontoxic
nutrition
nutrition consultants
policy
primary caregiving

process variables
sanitize
structural variables
substance abuse
temperament
tiered quality systems
toxic substances

Reflections and Resources for the Reader

REFLECTIONS

1. If our greatest concern for quality, after the basics of health and safety, is the responsiveness of the teacher, why do we measure quality by the structural variables of group size and ratios?
2. Infant/toddler care and learning programs can be very busy places. What can a program do to ensure that care is always being taken with health, safety, and nutrition?

OBSERVATION AND APPLICATION OPPORTUNITIES

1. Visit an infant-toddler program and ask to review its health, safety, diapering, and food-handling policies. Do you see the policies as thorough enough to provide guidance to the staff? Is there a system for monitoring how the policies are implemented? Would you make any changes?
2. Contact a program in your community that has been accredited by the National Association for Family Child Care or the National Association for the Education of Young Children. Interview a staff member about the process of accreditation.
3. Contact a child care licensing agent in your community and interview him or her about the role of licensing in supporting quality.

SUPPLEMENTARY ARTICLES AND BOOKS TO READ

American Academy of Pediatrics. (2015). *Back to sleep, tummy to play.* Retrieved from: healthychildren.org

Lally, R. (2001) The art and science of child care. Program for Infant Toddler Care. Retrieved from: *pitc.org/cs/pitclib/query/q/2915?author=Lally&search_year=2001&name=Art%20and%20Science%20of%20Child%20Care&x-template=pitclib.search.form*

Snyder, C. (2011, Spring). It's good to see you again! Continuity of care in infant and toddler program. *ReSource,* 11–15. Retrieved from highscope.org

INTERESTING LINKS

National Resource Center for Health and Safety in Child Care

This Web site includes the full text of *Caring for Our Children: National Health and Safety Performance Standards for Out-of-Home Child Care* (3rd ed.). It also has links to each state's licensing standards.

Healthy Child Care America The Web site for Healthy Child Care America, a joint project of the Child Care Bureau and the Maternal and Child Health Bureau, is a great source of information on healthy practices in child care.

HealthyChildren.org

This Web site, supported by the American Academy of Pediatrics, includes up-to-date health and safety information and many brochures such as, *A parents' guide to safe sleep* and *A child care provider's guide to safe sleep.*

12

Creating a Relationship-Based Curriculum

LEARNING OUTCOMES

After reading this chapter, you should be able to:

- Describe the foundational elements of a responsive, relationship-based program.
- Explain and evaluate the teachers' roles in a relationship-based program.
- Explain how to create a family and culturally sensitive program.
- Describe how to plan in a responsive, relationship-based format.

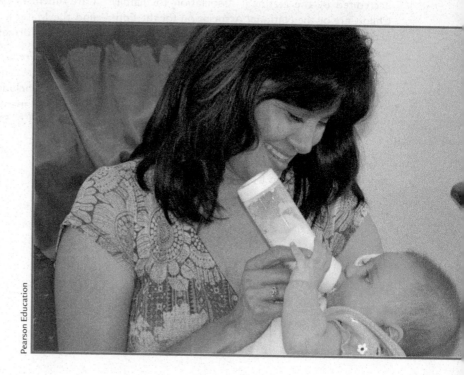

Pearson Education

Hours in infancy have more power to shape us than months in middle age. The relative impact of time—time lost or time invested—is greatest early in life. Indeed, humanity was created in childhood. (Perry)

What do you do with infants and toddlers? They really can't do much, can they? These are questions you may have heard before. In this chapter we are going to answer those questions. We will talk about how to design an interesting, responsive curriculum for infants and toddlers. We will think about what curriculum means to children, teachers, and families in an infant-toddler program or a family child care home. The major elements of a child-centered, responsive, relationship-based curriculum for infants and toddlers are described.

A curriculum for infants and toddlers is everything that happens to and with a child from the moment they are carried, walk, or run into the program until the time they leave. This approach to infant and toddler curriculum focuses on the importance of relationships to infants, toddlers, families, and teachers. Thus, even after a family leaves with the child for the day, the family carries with them the essence of the curriculum—the importance of their relationship with their child. The planning strategies and interactions are responsive to individual children's needs, interests, and strengths (in collaboration with families). The curriculum roots are in Developmentally Appropriate Practice. This means that it is age, individually, and culturally appropriate (1). The relationship-based approach discussed in this book adds a planning process of *respect, reflect,* and *relate;* child-centered planning guides; and further detailed illumination of a relationship-based approach.

This video describes key aspects of a developmentally appropriate program. Are there other aspects to consider and add for a quality, responsive infant/toddler program?

A responsive, relationship-based curriculum focuses on the mental health of infants and toddlers. The curriculum is based on the perspectives and needs of the very young children. The adults are attentive to the responsive, caring, moment-to-moment and day-to-day experiences that lead to valuable, enduring, and nourishing relationships in each child's life.

Relationships are created over time, and they require a teacher's emotional commitment to each child's well-being. In a program using a caring, responsive curriculum, the more enduring relationships—between the children and their families, the teachers and the children, and the teachers and families—provide the foundation for children to love and learn and experience joy. The curriculum is truly *day to day, the relationship way!*

The teacher is empathic with children's joy and pleasure and responds to children's unhappiness and distress with tender care (2). Teachers are kind, caring, considerate, and compassionate with young children's and their families' feelings, needs, and learning goals and know how to develop an enriched environment that supports important relationships in children's lives. The teachers use a

Pearson Education

A relationship-based curriculum requires teachers' emotional commitment to the well-being of each child.

philosophy of mind-mindedness (3,4), which means that teachers consider infants and toddlers to have a mind that can readily process information and express thoughts, feelings, and needs. Thus teachers are constantly trying to consider the perspectives and feelings of the children and families. This teacher behavior is related to a child's secure attachment (5).

Table 12.1 describes the eight components of curriculum planning that are considered in Chapters 12, 13, and 14. Components 1 through 4 are discussed in this chapter and components 5 through 7 will be highlighted in Chapter 13. Component 8 is covered in Chapter 14.

TABLE 12.1   Important components of a curriculum

1. A way of thinking about infants and toddlers

What are your beliefs and assumptions about the nature of infants and toddlers?

What are the needs of infants and toddlers?

What is important for infants and toddlers to learn?

How do infants and toddlers develop and learn?

2. The teachers' roles in a relationship-based program

What is the program's view of

the roles teachers play in the creation of a relationship-based program community?

the nature of teacher-child interactions?

the importance of teachers' emotional connections with the children?

3. Relationships with families and culturally sensitive care

How does the program create partnerships with families?

How do program teachers respond sensitively to a child's and family's culture?

4. Responsive, relationship-based planning

What is the planning process of respect, reflect, and relate?

How do teachers individualize the curriculum for each child?

How do teachers plan for groups?

5. Transitions and routines—A time for relationships

What is the value placed on transitions, routines, rituals, and schedules?

6. Responsive and relationship-based environments for "day to day, the relationship way"

How is the environment developed, created, and adapted to individual children and groups?

7. Responsive experiences and opportunities

How are interactions, materials and experiences chosen and provided?

8. A relationship-based approach to guidance

What is the philosophy and what are the strategies used to guide infants and toddlers?

A Way of Thinking About Infants and Toddlers

A way of thinking about infants and toddlers includes teachers' beliefs and assumptions about

- the nature of children,
- children's emotional and social needs,
- *what* is important for children to learn, and
- *how* children develop and learn.

Let's begin with the beliefs and assumptions about the nature of children.

What Are Your Beliefs and Assumptions About the Nature of Infants and Toddlers?

A framework for an infant-toddler program is based on certain principles and beliefs regarding the nature of infants and toddlers. Here are two questions you might consider regarding the nature of young children: Do infants and toddlers have human rights and responsibilities? Are they capable learners?

Most adults think that young children have rights—the rights to be protected, to learn, to be loved and to love, and to be treated with respect. They have the right to belong and participate in their family, culture, and social life. The United Nations developed the Convention on the Rights of the Child in 1989 (6). The following video highlights the human rights of children everywhere.

 After watching this video on the 20th anniversary of the UN Convention on the Rights of the Child, answer this question: What are the basic rights of children?

https://www.youtube.com/watch?v=A-icxE5qrNg

In addition to believing that children have rights, many adults also know that infants and toddlers are capable learners—that they enter this world as active learners, discoverers, and problem solvers. When they are offered responsive, empathic care and an enriched environment, they quickly construct their knowledge in interaction with caring adults, family members, and peers. Jerome Bruner (7) emphasizes this point: "The child is *not* merely ignorant or an empty vessel, but somebody able to reason, to make sense, both on her own and through discourse with others" (p. 57).

 Watch the video on a hundred languages of children. What does Malaguzzi mean when he talks about a hundred languages of children?

https://www.youtube.com/watch?v=5ayT-x3Htv4

Adults' beliefs about the nature of children influence the attitudes that they have about their role in children's lives. If children are viewed as having rights and as being capable learners, then they are treated with respect for their "personhood" (8). In a relationship-based, responsive program, adults trust that very young children need and want to belong to a social group, that they strive to develop well and to be healthy, and that they would like to and can master their environment if given the opportunity and responsive care. Adults trust that meeting infants' and toddlers' basic needs for protection and nurturance will result in children who are more likely to be competent, caring, and courageous.

When an infant leans in and puts her head on the shoulder of the teacher, we know she feels safe.

Pearson Education

What Are the Needs of Infants and Toddlers?

As discussed in previous chapters, infants and toddlers need strong, positive, emotional connections with their families, teachers, and peers in order to thrive. Children have a neurobiological expectation for affection and nurturance (9). This means that children are biologically programmed to expect to be protected and cared for in loving ways—and if they are, then they are more likely to develop optimally. As highlighted in Chapter 5, brain development occurs best when children receive tender and compassionate care, when adults take the perspective of what it is like to be an infant or toddler and respond sensitively and perceptively to the children's needs. Young children need protection. They need to feel safe; they need adults whom they can count on to be emotionally and physically available to them. Ideally, there is one person who is "just crazy about him" (10), thinks he is precious, and knows him well.

How can parents and teachers meet the basic needs of babies? As Gonzalez-Mena and Eyer (11) have said, "infants and toddlers need attention to their physical and psychological needs" (p. 6). They state that one of the most important needs of an infant is the pacing of care—a thoughtful, unhurried, finely **attuned** dialog between the infant and teacher. Lally, Torres, and Phelps (12) stress that settings for infants should offer "security, protection, and intimacy" to meet infants' and toddlers' needs.

Some teachers may become concerned about becoming *too attached* to an infant or toddler in their care. Yet, as we read in Chapter 6, children who are securely attached to the important, special people in their lives at home are more resilient, more trusting, and more likely to develop positive relationships with others. As we might expect, infants and toddlers in infant-toddler programs who are securely attached to their teachers are also more likely to be socially and emotionally competent (13) than children who experience insecure attachment with their teachers.

> Securely attached children have a more balanced self-concept; more advanced memory processes; a more sophisticated grasp of emotion; a more positive understanding of friendship; and greater conscience development (14, pp. 236–237).

We can see that infants and toddlers feel securely attached if the following happen:

- They can generally be comforted by the teacher and relax in the teacher's arms.
- They can engage in long, mutually satisfying gazes and conversations of sounds and words with the teacher.
- They show that they feel valued and loved by the teacher.
- They are generally happy to see the teacher.
- They can experience joy with the teacher.
- They (toddlers) move away from the teacher and explore the environment but hurry back if they sense danger or need a hug.

- They can focus and engage with toys, materials, and the environment.
- They seek the teacher for food, safety, assistance, nurturing, scaffolding, and guidance.

Teachers need to understand that even when young children spend a significant amount of time in infant-toddler programs, the parents are the most influential adults in their lives (15), and teachers should do everything possible to support children's primary relationships with their families. It is critical that infants and toddlers have a secure relationship with their parents or primary caregivers. At the same time, teachers should not underestimate the importance of their own relationship with the child. Children cannot thrive in the absence of secure relationships with both parents and teachers. Each child who experiences healthy relationships carries within him hope and optimism for his current and future relationships.

What Is Important for Infants and Toddlers to Learn?

Children's motivation toward mastery, self-regulation and social commerce and their reliance on relationships with trusted teachers for support and guidance [are] seen as central to program planning. (Gandini & Edwards)

The knowledge, skills, and dispositions important for infants and toddlers to learn have been described extensively in Chapters 6–10 in this book. The Head Start Early Learning Outcomes Framework and the states' Early Learning Guidelines are good sources for guidance in what children should know and be able to do. Gandini and Edwards (16) also emphasize that teachers should consider what children learn about themselves and what they learn about how to relate to others when creating the curriculum.

How is the child viewed—what needs, competencies, desires, are determined by the adult to need nurturing or to be squashed? (Szanton)

Lally (17) discusses how teachers must focus on helping infants and toddlers develop a sense of identity as a person of worth—what he calls a **working sense of self**. In addition to learning about themselves and others, infants and toddlers are learning about how the world works. What is grass, how does applesauce taste, where do caterpillars go when they crawl away, how many blocks can fit in a basket, what are the properties of water, and what is a friend are among the important things that young children learn about the world. There is so much for infants and toddlers to learn in the first 3 years of life,

This child is developing a working sense of self as curious, calm, and engaged.

Pearson Education

and there are so many exciting opportunities for nurturing adults to help these children enjoy being in and learning about the world.

How Do Children Develop and Learn?

In addition to the question of *what* is important for infants and toddlers to learn, there is the question of *how* they develop and learn. We know that only when a child is secure in his relationship with the important adults in his life is there freedom to be independent in play with toys and peers (18,19). The way infants and toddlers develop and learn can be summarized as follows:

1. Learning is integrated.
2. Learning is developmental.
3. Children learn through play.

Let's start with integrated learning.

Learning Is Integrated

> *Marilee crawled across the carpet with great speed, making babbling noises to the cat. Her mother commented to her, "You are so fast!" Marilee picked up a colorful soft toy and turned it upside down, studying it carefully. She looked at her mother to see if she was still there sitting on the floor. Marilee smiled and crawled toward her mom.*

As all children do in almost any experience, Marilee is developing in emotional, social, cognitive, language, and motor domains in one sequence of behavior. She develops emotionally and socially as she learns to trust her mother. She learns language as she practices babbling and hears her mother match words to her actions. As she studies the toy, her cognitive development is enhanced as she learns about how an object looks from another viewpoint. Her crawling is an important aspect of motor development. As she crawls toward her mother, she is establishing an emotional bond as well as improving her motor skills. Marilee is growing in all domains, not just sequentially, but simultaneously. Her learning is integrated with all developmental domains in use and affecting one another: "In infants and toddlers, all domains of development are interrelated. Each is a thread in the same cloth; pull one, and the others follow" (20, p. 4).

Adults divide children's development into the different domains to help themselves observe and learn about children, but children are including and applying all of their skills together to accomplish their goals. Development in one domain also affects development in another domain.

 Watch this video to observe two boys playing. What are these children learning in the emotional, social, cognitive, language, and motor development domains as they play? Is their learning integrated?

Learning Is Developmental

An infant-toddler care and learning program looks different for infants (0 to 12 months of age) than it does for young toddlers (12 to 18 months) or for older toddlers (18 to 36 months). Children of these different ages have distinct needs and learning goals (21), although we also know that they exhibit a broad range of individual differences. If we listen and watch, infants and toddlers tell us what they are experiencing and how we can respond to these changing needs. Teachers learn how to **dance up and down the developmental ladder** (22). They observe children and figure out where each child is functioning in the different domains (emotional, social, language, motor, and cognitive) of development. Teachers then provide materials and interactions that are developmentally appropriate for each child.

We can easily see how infants and toddlers change physically over time. It is more difficult, however, to detect the emotional, social, learning, and language changes in a child as he grows from a dependent baby to a more independent person. Only caring, observant adults can provide a responsive program for both the group and the unique individuals within the group that meets their emotional and social needs. Following is a quick summary of the emotional, social, learning and language needs of the different age groups.

Infancy: 0 to 12 months.   Infants rely completely on parents and teachers to meet their emotional and social needs; to provide nurturing, sensitive care, and calm and interesting environments; and to present opportunities for the infants to move and explore objects. Ideally, during the first 12 months of life, infants will become emotionally attached to their parent(s) as well as to primary teacher(s). Infants want to be with these special persons in their lives, receive comfort from them, and learn from them. The baby will turn to the sound of this person's voice, brighten when spoken to, and give a special smile just for the person(s) she is growing to love. The infant learns what to expect, how that person will treat her, and the tone of that person's voice. As early as several weeks of age, infants feel more comfortable when they are with their special person(s) and can become distressed when they are not. The most important thing that babies this age are learning is that they can trust adults to take care of them rather than having to defend and protect themselves most of the time. They need adults who can hold, rock, sing, and talk quietly to them, and who can play "follow the leader" by imitating the baby's eye-blinks, sounds, and facial movements and then waiting for the baby to take a turn.

The environment must be tailored for infants. Infants need safe places to be on the floor to practice their "tummy" moves, sitting, and crawling. They need quiet, calm places to sleep and places to sit (without being knocked over), to bang objects on the floor or together in their hands. As they approach 8 months of age, many of the infants are ready to pull themselves up to a standing position. This requires that there be space for an adult on the floor. The infant can then inch himself up the trustworthy adult's body to look her in the eye or collapse safely in her arms.

Younger toddlers: 12 to 18 months.   Young toddlers are on the move. They are often crawling, walking, and fitting their bodies into a variety of spaces. Infants who are on the move need nurturing adults who provide the emotional and social base from which they explore their world. Toddlers are often dashing back or fussing when an emotional connection to a caring teacher is needed. The most important thing that young toddlers learn in your care is that they can "make things happen" with both people and objects. This is **Velcro time** with language, a term (23) used to describe how older infants and toddlers stick like Velcro to the teachers' responsive words, finger-plays, and book reading as their language bursts forth. The environment also changes as children develop.

The environment requires open spaces and cozy corners to encourage both *interaction time* with teachers and peers and *alone time* to gather energy for the next adventure. For young toddlers, life is truly an adventure as they make exciting discoveries with toys and peers. Open-ended toys (with no correct product) encourage stacking, pulling, pushing, throwing, and filling.

As young toddlers reach 18 months, they are ready for fat crayons, art materials, large beads and string, and more challenging motor activities. Children thrive in a room or family child care home that has space to explore, interesting materials to investigate, and peers to imitate. They especially need caring adults who admire their blossoming skills.

Older toddlers: 18 to 36 months.   Toddlers need loving, understanding people in their lives who think of them as very special with all of their new skills and antics. As stated by Lerner and Dombro (24), "For babies, the world is a banquet to be gobbled up with eyes, ears, nose, mouth, and fingers" (p. 20). The light in a toddler's eyes when he discovers a bug, listens with his ears to the bathtub drain to hear where the water goes, or sees a kitten for the first time recharges an adult's sense of wonder and delight in learning about the world. This in turn provides emotional energy for the child to continue learning.

Experienced teachers even love when toddlers say "No," because they understand the emotional struggles of very young children who are so brave to stand up to a person more than twice their size. Living with toddlers requires that parents and teachers be ready for anything, as toddlers experiment with what happens when they poke a friend or when they pull all of the tissues out of a tissue box. It helps parents and teachers to remember that toddlers are learning with all of their senses. Their experimentation is their enthusiastic way of learning about their world.

Toddlers are little scientists who are inventing, taking apart, creating, and exploring on their way to figuring out the ways of the world. They have to touch to learn. They look at an object and they have to investigate it. They watch and they have to manipulate objects. They are problem solvers and it is the teachers' and parents' role to give them a physically and emotionally safe environment in which to explore and learn. It is also easier to be a teacher of toddlers when you understand that they are not purposely trying to frustrate you, but rather that they are experiencing important internal struggles on their way to becoming good decision makers and problem solvers.

For all of these ages—infancy, young toddlers, and older toddlers—play is the way to learn.

Children Learn Through Play

Many theorists and researchers strongly believe, based on their observations and the results of research, that children learn through play and active exploration of their environment (25,26,27). Bettelheim (28) defines play as a child's activities characterized by freedom from all but personally imposed rules (which are changed at will). Play is an opportunity for pure enjoyment and is also important for many other reasons.

Play is vital for the developing child: "We learn best when we are having fun" (29 p. 24). Play enhances "verbalization, vocabulary, language, comprehension, attention span, imaginativeness, concentration, impulse control, curiosity, more problem-solving strategies, cooperation, empathy, and group participation"

Why is play so important for young children?

(30, p. 220). "It is only through acting on the world using developmentally appropriate skills during exploratory play that infants build a meaningful understanding of the environment" (31, pp. 67–68). Complex play as a toddler predicts a child's prosocial behavior as a preschooler and less aggressive and less withdrawn behavior as a 9-year-old. It seems that as young children play, they learn many cognitive and social skills that result in social competence later in their childhood (32).

What will infants and toddlers do when they are playing? This will vary according to a child's developmental level. Generally, they are trying to figure out how the world works. Infants will mouth, bang, shake, and pound on toys to learn about them. They will watch other children with great interest. They vocalize and responsive caregivers respond. Older infants and toddlers will imitate each other during play, turn objects around, put objects in and take them out of containers, and pull and push objects to see out how they work. They engage in games such as peek-a-boo with their favorite caregivers, who they trust will not really disappear. Toddlers will try many strategies to learn—change strategies, adapt strategies, try another strategy, go away from the problem, come back eons later (2 minutes or 2 days) and try again with toys, materials, and people. Older toddlers will begin to pretend as their understanding of symbols progresses (for example, using a toy telephone as if it were a real telephone), and, as we learned in Chapter 7 on social development, play becomes more reciprocal with peers. We can begin to appreciate how children work hard while playing when we see them move a large toy, position a block on top of a tower, or gain the attention of special adults and peers, not because they have to, but because they want to learn.

How to Encourage Play

Once we understand that toddlers learn by active involvement with people and by manipulating objects, it becomes clear that such activities as coloring books, worksheets, and models made of clay or other materials that children are expected to imitate are inappropriate. (Lally, Provence, Szanton, & Weissbourd)

Box 12.1 is a "letter" from a toddler that reminds us how important play is for young children.

Infants and toddlers learn by active involvement. To support infants' and toddlers' active involvement and play, provide long play times where they can make

BOX 12.1

Letter from a Toddler

For young children, play with others and by themselves is a way to learn. If toddlers could, they might describe what goes on in a good infant-toddler care and learning setting that encourages play in the following way:

Dear Teacher of Mine,

You looked a little tired and discouraged when the parents were coming to pick all of us up today. Then, when that one dad said, "Did they learn anything today or did they just play?" I thought you'd just about had it. I'm writing to cheer you up and tell you that I'm learning lots because you help us play.

Tonight at supper my big sister said that she learned "the nines table" in school today. I'm not sure what the "nines table" is but everyone seemed pleased and excited that she'd learned it.

I learned a lot today too. Unfortunately, I can't talk enough to describe what I learned about how the world works. I know that dumping out bins of toys, climbing, knocking over blocks, and squashing bananas on my feeding tray doesn't sound as mysterious as "the nines table," but I'm sure grateful that you know how important it all was.

Thank goodness you know I have to play to learn. For example, remember today how every time you'd kneel down and open up your arms, I'd run to you for a big hug? We were playing a game, of course, and we'd both laugh—but just the act of running was learning for me. Babies and toddlers learn through their big muscles, you know. When I ran into your arms, it not only made me feel loved and happy, it gave me a chance to practice the movements of using my arms and legs together. I'm brand new at that. Running strengthens those muscles too. It was fun. I wanted to do it over and over. I'm glad you had time to play so that I could learn. Thank you.

And I'm glad you noticed today how much fun I had tapping with the xylophone hammer, remember? I tapped the xylophone for a while, then the wall, then the floor and lots of other objects. I discovered so many different sounds—metallic, strong, soft. Oh, by the way, sorry about Robby's head. It sure scared me when he cried so loud. Thanks for finding all those boxes and pans for me to tap. I am beginning to understand so much more about the world now because you realized I was learning, not "just playing."

I heard you say, "Tappers need things to tap!" You must believe that "dumpers need things to dump" too, because you filled up that coffee can with clothespins over and over and let me dump it out as much as I wanted to. You must have realized that I wasn't trying to make a mess when I dumped out all the tubs of toys yesterday. I need to dump things out. I'm so curious about how something can be full one minute and empty the next—and that I can make it happen.

Dumping things out makes me feel big. After lots of play at dumping, I'll want to try filling. It's really the very first step toward being able to put things away neatly—when I'm older.

Thanks to your helping me play, I'm learning that it's good to be curious, it's good to explore and learn and understand. I get the feeling you think my play is pretty valuable. My play is all my own idea, you know. You must think that my ideas are pretty valuable, too. Hey, that must mean you value me, too. I'm important, and what I learn is important—even if it isn't "the nines table."

Please don't be discouraged. You helped me play today. You gave me gifts of learning and self-worth that nobody can ever take away. See you tomorrow!

A Toddler in Child Care (author unknown)

Source: Louisiana's Early Learning Guidelines and Program Standards: Birth through Three, 2005 , pg 137. http://www.dss.state.la.us/assets/docs/searchable/OFS/LAEarlyLearningGuide.pdf.

choices with comforting and challenging materials, persist at activities, explore, and even have conflicts with peers that provide a foundation for future social relationships. This builds a child's confidence, sense of competence, and motivation to learn. When infants are kept in car seats, swings, walkers, and other containers and not allowed to move freely, they can feel trapped and become inactive and passive. Rather than all toddlers doing the same thing at the same time—such as everyone going first to the puzzle table, then a circle time, then an art activity, then back to a large group story time—they need time to explore alone, with peers, and with their favorite adults. When young children are not allowed to make choices during play we have seen them become passive and sad. From the outside looking in, it may seem that these toddlers are quiet and "well behaved," but a closer look at their faces tells us that they are not engaged in the activities. When toddlers (or adults) aren't engaged and interested, they are not learning.

Infants and toddlers need to move their bodies, explore sensory materials, manipulate toys, and experience the consequences of their decisions in order to learn. The program in which children are provided a rich array of materials in a well-organized environment can, in fact, be noisy at times with the sounds of children learning through choice and initiation. Provide opportunities for children to explore materials on their own in their own way, with a favorite teacher close by for emotional support.

CULTURE CLOSE UP

Different family cultures have different beliefs about how children develop and learn and what is important to learn. Saliah wanted to create a toddler classroom that had many opportunities for children to explore by themselves, with peers, or with teachers, as she believed that children wanted to learn and could learn through experimentation with materials. She had seen a toddler spend a great deal of time at a low water table, closely supervised, but given time to pour water out of containers, watch water pour out of a sieve, and try to hold water in his hands. Saliah believed that because this child was closely attached to her, he could move away from her and feel safe exploring the environment. She believed that what the child chose to explore, play with, and investigate were the most important topics for the child to learn.

However, some parents wanted her to teach the toddlers their alphabet letters so that they would be ready for preschool. They had heard that there was testing in the preschools that asked children to name the letters, and they were nervous that their children weren't learning what they needed to learn in the toddler room so that they could be successful in the preschool room. Some parents also thought that there was too much play and not enough group lesson time.

What would you do to be culturally sensitive to the parents' needs and wishes while also providing a developmentally appropriate curriculum?

Check Your Understanding 12.1
Click here to check your understanding of the concepts in this section.

The Infant-Toddler Professional's Role—
Creating a Relationship-Based Program

Developing a relationship-based program requires professionals who are special people who value emotional connections. Responsive, relationship-based teachers think about

- the roles teachers play in the creation of a relationship-based program community,
- the nature of teacher-child interactions, and
- the importance of teachers' emotional connections with children.

BOX 12.2

The Top Eight Responsibilities of an Infant-Toddler Teacher

Whether in an infant-toddler care and learning center or family child care home, the responsibilities of an infant-toddler teacher include the following eight components:

1. Develop the foundation for a relationship-based program.
2. Structure the program to emphasize the importance of relationships—provide primary care and continuity of care to the children. Take care of children's physical needs—keep children safe and healthy. Provide responsive and reciprocal interactions—give/take, engage/break, negotiate, and cooperate. Care for the spirit of the child—meet the emotional and social needs of children.
3. Build caring, responsive relationships with families, diverse cultures, and the community.
4. Use a responsive planning process—day to day the relationship way. Facilitate individual child development.
5. Create a flexible schedule with responsive routines.
6. Set up the environment for routines, nurturing, playing, learning, and relationships.
7. Provide toys, materials, and opportunities that are individually, culturally, and age appropriate.
8. Use a relationship-based approach to guidance that involves family members and other staff.

The Roles Teachers Play in the Creation of a Relationship-Based Program Community

Communities are places where a group of people work and play together. Programs are communities where infants and toddlers and their teachers often spend many hours together. Programs for young children and the staff, who spend many hours at work, should resemble a home more than an institution to reduce staff's and children's stress and to develop a physical environment and structure to the day that "connects and nurtures people" (33, p. 71). There are many creative ways to make a program more home-like. Teachers may include interesting colors, a variety of textures and natural elements such as plants and rocks, cozy lighting, and framed pictures of children and families. The term **homebases** can be used rather than *classrooms* in center-based programs. Classrooms are considered homes and there are common areas such as playgrounds where children and teachers from the different homes gather at times (34). Children can be organized into **attachment groups**—small groups that emphasize continuity of care for children with their special teachers throughout their years in a center program (35). Whatever arrangement is chosen, infants and toddlers need to feel safe and nurtured and have a sense of belonging.

Creating programs that are homelike with homebases and attachment groups are just several ways that teachers create a relationship-based program community. Box 12.2 summarizes the roles the infant and toddler teachers play in developing a relationship-based program.

 Watch the video on what quality looks like in care and learning of children under 2 years old. Think about the different roles listed in Box 12.2 that the professional plays.

https://www.youtube.com/watch?v=xs9bd1RV_Fw

The first role of the teacher is to create a strong foundation for the program (highlighted in the first part of this chapter). Providing positive emotional connections and healthy relationships with children is also a primary responsibility of teachers and programs.

The Importance of Teachers' Emotional Connections and Healthy Relationships with Infants and Toddlers

Because children's emotional development is the foundation for children to love and learn, teachers think about the well-being of the child from the child's perspective and ask, "What's it like to be an infant or toddler in this program?" and "What can I, as the adult, do to support this child emotionally?" Teachers' interactions must care for the spirit—the emotional health and vitality—of the child by demonstrating a profound respect for each child's emotional experiences. When you are a teacher in a center program or family child care home for infants and toddlers, always ask the question, "How would it feel to be an infant or toddler in this setting?" and then respond to help infants and toddlers feel loved, safe, and competent.

Table 12.2 includes examples of teaching practices that focus on supporting the emotional capacities of infants and toddlers through recognizing cues of communication and responding in ways that are satisfying to the infant or child. Teachers are not only responding to infants and toddlers, but also watching and learning from the children about what those children like and how those children think. Many of these concepts were introduced in earlier chapters in this book, but we discuss them now as they apply to teacher-child interactions and relationships in a program setting. Let's examine how these responsive teacher and parent strategies support emotional development, the foundation for learning.

TABLE 12.2   **How adults can meet infants' and toddlers' emotional needs**

- Develop strong, positive, secure relationships with children.
- Be attuned emotionally and physically to children's cues and communication attempts, reflect on their meaning, and relate as needed by child.
- Interact by taking balanced turns (reciprocal interactions) and matching the pace of interactions with the child.
- Be approachable, accessible, and available to children, both emotionally and physically.
- Maintain a pleasant and positive emotional tone throughout the day.
- Respond to children's distress and intense emotional outbursts and other displays of displeasure calmly and in a way that comforts them and helps them regulate themselves physically and emotionally.
- Notice, identify, encourage, and show admiration for strengths, interests, and new skills in each and every child in the group.
- Appreciate development and differences—help children feel appreciated for their uniqueness.

Develop strong, positive relationships with children.

The responsive teacher is kind, affectionate, warm, empathic, caring, and compassionate with children. The teacher helps each child feel safe, secure, lovable, loving, worthy of love, and cherished.

Infants and toddlers need affection and kindness, to learn how to be affectionate and kind themselves. They need touch–people hugging, holding, and sitting near them—for healthy mental and social development. Infants and toddlers need adults who will hold them when they need to be held, are positive with them when they choose or need to be close, and are always kind to them. Teachers' frequent smiles result in young children's affectionate responses (36). Without affection, children learn to be on the defensive, to protect themselves, to be on guard, and to generally distrust people. With affection, they learn that they are worthy of being loved.

Teachers show affection and warmth to children through smiles, gentle touches, and mutual gazes. Honig (37) emphasizes that teachers need to be intimate with infants and toddlers. Being intimate with infants and toddlers means that there are warm, friendly relationships that include emotional connections of caring between adults and children and a commitment to the children's well-being. While each adult in group care may not cherish all of the children, each child needs to be cherished by at least one adult in the group and all adults need to be warm and affectionate with all children.

A teacher can ask herself whether she does any of the following in a day:

- Uses frequent responsive, caring touch
- Uses kind words with children
- Shows affection for children
- Empathizes and shows compassion with children's feelings ("Ooh, that must hurt," or "I can tell you are feeling sad")

Be attuned to children's cues.

The responsive teacher is consistently attuned emotionally and physically to children's cues and communication attempts, reflects on their meaning, relates as needed by the child, and interprets children's cues and communication attempts.

Infants and toddlers need teachers who are attuned to their obvious and subtle communication signaling and who notice and understand the intentions and feelings of the child. Being attuned means that a teacher is sensitive to and understands what very young children are trying to communicate with facial expressions, sounds, gestures, or words. For example, the teacher might say "You want up" in response to a child's upraised arms, or say "It seems like you are feeling sad" to a child with a sad expression on her face. When a caregiver is well attuned to a child, she will mirror the infant or toddler's experiences in observable ways. A teacher might reflect on whether she does any of the following during the day:

- Shares a child's delight
- Asks children what they want or how they are feeling and helps them express feelings
- Focuses on what the infant or toddler is trying to communicate
- Actively listens with eyes and ears to the infant's or toddler's facial expressions, gestures, body movements, sounds, and words

Magda Gerber, an early infancy expert, would say to a baby, "I don't know what you are trying to tell me, but I want to figure it out" (38). She believed that when an adult responds to an infant or toddler's communication attempts, the baby gains a positive concept of self and others as communication partners. The children will learn to use words to express their thoughts and emotions rather than crying, yelling, or whining much of the time.

When adults cannot respond physically to a child, they can respond verbally. For example, while the teacher is changing one baby's diaper, he might respond in a reassuring voice to an infant who is crying, "I'm changing Jareem's diaper.

I'll be there soon." A teacher can reflect on whether he uses any of the following strategies during the day:

- Looks for and reads both clear and subtle communication cues
- Uses words to identify feelings
- Responds quickly and positively to children's questions and other bids for attention

Encourage reciprocal interactions.

A reciprocal interaction is one in which there is a sense of give and take, of shared moments, of balanced turns, and of joint attention. The teacher matches the pace of interactions with the child. This important teacher skill not only promotes communication skills in young children but also meets their emotional need for "making things happen." If the infant coos, the teacher coos back. If the infant rolls the ball to the teacher, she rolls the ball back. The teacher may initiate the interaction by picking up a book and offering it to the toddler. The toddler then takes the book, sits down beside the teacher, and holds up the book to be read.

These are examples of balanced, reciprocal turn taking. Although not all interactions may be quite this even, taking balanced turns promotes a child's sense of confidence and skills as an interactive partner. Reciprocity helps a child feel some control over what happens to him or her—which is important if the child is to have motivation to learn. This sense of control and efficacy helps infants and toddlers become more engaged in an activity and tolerate small frustrations.

A teacher might watch for moments like these to reflect on her abilities to follow the infant or toddler's lead and promote reciprocity:

- Being sensitive to an infant's or toddler's cues in interaction
- Taking balanced turns in play, eating, and communicating
- Waiting to approach a young child without interrupting or disrupting his activity (noticing that Henry is concentrating on stacking blocks, so waiting a few minutes to change the toddler's diaper)
- Approaching children from within their visual range, rather than swooping them up from behind (leaning down or getting on the floor with the child and telling him what is happening next: "After you finish playing with your toy, I'm going to change your diaper.")
- Asking the child what he wants, how he is feeling, and/or what he would like to do next, either with gestures or verbally (rather than assuming that the child wants to be picked up, asking the child and then waiting for the child to respond with a look, a gesture, or words)

Be available, both emotionally and physically.

The responsive teacher is consistently approachable, accessible, and available both emotionally and physically to children. Infants and toddlers develop a sense of security when an adult is emotionally and physically available to them. Reciprocal interactions are more likely to occur when a teacher is physically on the child's level; infants and toddlers learn to maintain focus and attention when emotionally available adults engage them in longer turn-taking exchanges through games such as peek-a-boo or through conversational interactions. If infants and toddlers approach an adult and are rejected (often because teachers mistakenly don't want the children to become too dependent on them or attached to them), infants and toddlers may actually become more dependent and clingy because they are not feeling safe and secure (39).

A teacher might use these strategies to ensure her emotional and physical availability to children:

- Spend time with children by sitting on the floor with them—allow them to come close, to move away, and then come back to sit in or near her lap at their discretion
- Spend one-on-one time with each child each day
- Limit talking time with other adults so that infants and toddlers feel her emotional presence
- Sit on the infant or toddler's physical level to encourage eye contact and touch

Maintain a pleasant emotional tone.

The responsive teacher consistently maintains a pleasant and positive emotional tone throughout the day: "When adult voice tones are hurried, sharp, critical, or upset, babies pick up the emotional tone of any adult worry. They may cry, become distracted from play, and show tension in body and facial muscles. The calmer your voice tones, the more peaceful your classroom will be" (40, p. 28). Infants and toddlers pay considerable attention to the moods and emotions of the adults who care for them. Teachers have an impact on each child in their program all of the time, not only when they are in direct interactions. The teachers need to provide a sense of calm, comfort, and joy as they encourage the children to approach life with a sense of hope and optimism.

The teacher creates a positive atmosphere in the room or family child care home when she or he uses these strategies:

- Finds ways to reduce her own stress
- Creates a peaceful environment by playing soft music and making the room beautiful
- Remains calm and reassuring throughout the routines of the day

Respond to children's distress in a calm, comforting way.

The responsive teacher consistently responds to children's distress and intense emotional outbursts and other displays of displeasure calmly and in a way that comforts children. The teacher tries a variety of strategies to comfort children and helps infants and toddlers regulate and express a range of emotions in socially and culturally acceptable ways. The teacher reduces stress and distress in the room or child care home.

Maintaining a sense of calm in an infant-toddler program may be a challenge when children express their feelings intensely. Teachers can encourage children to express feelings in appropriate ways. Even infants need to hear comments such as "You seem tired" or "You don't like it when I have to change your diaper. I'll hurry so I can rock you and make you feel better." When parents and teachers encourage infants and toddlers to express feelings, there are fewer tantrums because they feel heard and acknowledged, and over time they learn to use their words. Honig acknowledged the feelings of a friend's toddler, Dana, when her mother was gone by saying, "You are so sad, and you are so mad." When Dana's mother returned, Dana, with her hands on her hips, stated emphatically, "Me so mad and me so sad" (41).

Teachers might try these strategies for supporting self-regulation in moments of distress:

- Being willing to comfort a child to help her regulate her behavior

- Trying different strategies with individual children to calm and be calming
- Responding to initiations from a child for comfort (an infant may crawl over to you and want you to hold him for a minute; a toddler may want you to put a Band-Aid on a boo-boo)
- Responding to emotional outbursts and other displays of displeasure calmly and with a kind, understanding voice; trying to soothe the child, staying close rather than abandoning the child emotionally; saying things like (choose words appropriate to the age and experience of the child) "You seem angry," "You feel like stomping your feet," "You wanted the toy," "You can tell me what's wrong—I'd like to help you," or "Do you need a hug?"

Encourage the developing skills in every child.

The responsive teacher consistently notices, identifies, encourages, and admires the strength, interests, and new skills in each child in the group.

Young children gain a sense of self-worth when they are noticed in positive and caring ways. Young children thrive when adults share "joy and true delight" (42) in their efforts and accomplishments. Say things like "You jumped up" or "You picked up the blue toy" rather than just giving praise, such as "Good" or "That's nice." Specific encouragement gives children more information than vague, general praise and encourages their sense of intentionality.

Teachers might use these strategies to encourage and show admiration for the infants and toddlers in their care:

- Affirming the worth of each child by noticing and identifying the strengths of each child; saying things like "You are such a helpful person" or "You can make people smile"
- Being specific and avoiding phrases such as "good," "nice," "wonderful," and "cute" that have a different meaning to each person
- Showing admiration for new skills such as climbing, walking, jumping, talking, and helping
- Identifying at least five strengths of each child and talking about them often

Appreciate development and differences.

The responsive teacher consistently appreciates children's developmental stages and differences and helps each child feel appreciated for his or her uniqueness.

Just as adults appreciate when others accept them for who they are, infants and toddlers develop a sense of identity as a unique person with special skills and attributes. A sound background in child development helps the teacher accept children's behavior that is developmentally appropriate—including thumb sucking, spilling food (because the wrist movement isn't fully developed), falling into another toddler, or saying "No" as often as possible when they start to develop autonomy and want to do things by themselves.

Teachers can demonstrate their understanding of child development and individual development by using these strategies:

- Showing approval for children attempting and mastering new skills without being critical or scolding
- Helping children enter play if they need the support
- Staying with children in new situations until they feel comfortable
- Checking in frequently with quiet children and providing active children with opportunities to use their energy

- Helping children negotiate challenges when they need help
- Accepting developmental stages (sucking thumb, needing blanket, trying to use spoon but spilling)

 As you watch this video clip, think about which strategies identified in Table 12.2 the infant/toddler teacher uses to meet the child's emotional needs.

Helping Infants and Toddlers Learn

While children's emotional needs are met there are also ways that infant and toddler teachers support children's learning. We now know how important these ways of being with infants and toddlers are for both the well-being and learning of the young child (see Table 12.3).

Let's look at each of these strategies in detail.

TABLE 12.3   Helping Infants and Toddlers Learn

Teachers protect children and help them feel safe and healthy.
Teachers help children feel a sense of belonging.
Teachers are intentional.
Teachers follow children's lead for what they need.
Teachers imitate and encourage the child in an interaction.
Teachers scaffold learning in all domains of development.

Teachers Protect Children and Help Them Feel Safe and Healthy

Infants and toddlers must feel protected and safe in order to love and learn. Sometimes we say the adult **holds and enfolds** the child. Holding infants and toddlers is, of course, a familiar idea. The concept of enfolding means to surround each child with a caring and supportive personal and physical environment. A teacher can reflect on whether she uses any of the following strategies during the day:

- Holds a crying infant
- Uses a calm voice and respectful words
- Interacts with children in a gentle way
- Protects children from other children hurting them
- Puts her arm around a toddler who is sitting near to her
- Let a child lean on you or crawl in your lap when you are sitting on the floor
- Responds helpfully to an infant or toddler who becomes upset when another parent comes into the room

Teachers Help Infants and Toddlers Gain a Sense of Belonging

A sense of belonging is one of the primary needs of infants and toddlers. It is a sense of being comfortable with an adult, a group, or a peer. It is a sense that this is where I'm meant to be at this moment. It may be one of the most important feelings that we can help infants and toddlers attain. Teachers help young children feel a sense of belonging by greeting them warmly each morning and saying, "Good-bye, I'll see you tomorrow," when they leave. They belong when their name and other children's names in the group are used frequently. They feel they belong when their strengths are appreciated and their challenges are accepted.

Teachers Are Intentional

Infant and toddler teachers are deliberate in how they support children's development. Sometimes when a person who doesn't understand a responsive curriculum peeks into an infant-toddler care and learning program or family child care home and sees infants and toddlers playing or sitting on teachers' laps for a snuggle, the person may think that not much teacher planning occurs. Indeed, we know that teachers of young children carefully plan a responsive environment that meets the developmental needs of each child in the room. They also know how to *use the moment* to support children's development in emotional, social, language, cognitive, and motor development. They are purposeful in how they develop strong and positive relationships with families.

Teachers Follow Children's Lead for What They Need

Adults follow children's leads for what they need in both moment-to-moment adult-child interactions and in weekly planning for changes in adult-child interactions and the environment. In the moment-to-moment responsive interactions, the professional or parent observes the child, reads the child's cues, tries to determine what the child is thinking, and then responds by continuing to observe or by responding to the child in a way that encourages further action on the part of the child. A 1-year-old, for example, may cover an adult's foot with a blanket, the adult wiggles his foot under the blanket, and then the infant laughs and pulls the blanket off the foot. The adult shares the delight of finding his own foot under the blanket. The infant covers the foot again as if to ask "Will the foot wiggle again?" It does! Again, the infant is delighted. This 1-year-old is not only sharing an emotionally gratifying moment with the adult, but he also is exploring cause-and-effect principles. He is learning how to learn and will likely explore different ways to make that foot move. At times, following children's lead may mean that the adult observes that the child is ready for the adult to initiate an opportunity for the child to use strategies to learn.

For example, after the adult offers a toy, rolls a ball to the child, or sits on the floor with a book, the adult then watches to see if the child is interested in these opportunities. Does the infant or toddler begin to use strategies to pursue his own goal—starting to play with the toy, rolling the ball back to the adult, or showing delight in listening to the book? When the infant-toddler professional or parent sometimes leads and sometimes follows, the interactions feel like a satisfying dance to both the adult and the child:

> Learning and growing together is like dancing. Step by step, day by day, you and your child learn about each other and how your relationship works. Sometimes you lead, and sometimes you follow your child in the dance you create together (43, p. 1).

Teachers Imitate and Encourage the Child in an Interaction

When an adult imitates a child, the child, in turn, is stimulated to imitate the adult by increasing his output in the task at hand. (Forman & Kuschner)

Remember from Chapter 8 that children's ability to imitate is an important way that children learn. Providing a model for the children to imitate is another effective teacher strategy. Teachers can imitate children, too. Imitating children not only helps the adult tune into their developmental level, but also stimulates children to continue their play and discoveries. An infant will bat at a musical toy and it will make a jingly sound. The adult bats at the toy and looks at the infant. The infant is likely to bat the toy again and may bat it in a different way. She will be discovering that the different ways to bat the toy result in different sounds. She is exploring cause and effect and is more motivated to continue because of a partner in the exploration.

Teachers Scaffold Learning in All Domains of Development

Teachers and other adults, as well as peers, can support children's learning through scaffolding (as discussed in Chapter 3). Just as a scaffold holds a painter to keep the painter from falling, a teacher figuratively holds the infant or toddler while the child learns. Rather than painting for the painter, the scaffold helps make it possible for the *painter* to paint—to figure out *how* best to paint. Scaffolding a young child's learning in all developmental domains is similar. For example, if a toddler is challenged while trying to put together a three-piece puzzle, the teacher could do one of several things to scaffold the child's goal of mastering the puzzle. Toddlers often have a theory that pushing hard on the pieces will make them "work" in the puzzle. Rather than tell the toddler that pushing doesn't work, it is important to provide teacher support while the toddler experiments. The teacher could hold the frame of the puzzle so the toddler could "push" the pieces in to see how they fit. The teacher could suggest that they take out one piece of puzzle at a time and look carefully at each piece. This helps the toddler see the colors or pictures on the puzzle pieces and then the toddler can more easily put the pieces back in the puzzle frame in the right places. If the toddler is getting frustrated, a teacher might suggest that the toddler turn the piece slightly so that it will fit, thus helping the child *learn a strategy* for how to put puzzles together.

Or, to scaffold for the future, a teacher might add several two-piece puzzles to the environment or three-piece puzzles with handles on each piece to support the toddler when he experiments with strategies for putting a puzzle together. The teacher is providing a supportive personal and physical environment to help the child experiment and learn different strategies to achieve his goals. Although completion of a task provides satisfaction to the child, the most important goal is not that the toddler completes the puzzle, but rather that the toddler learns different strategies for how to put a puzzle together.

The secret to scaffolding is to support children's thinking about *how* to use a tool for learning—initiating to a peer, learning how to express emotions, building, dumping, filling, or asking—and to take the next step in development. Another aspect of scaffolding is to provide the materials to support children's learning. When a teacher observes that a toddler is trying to learn how to jump off a short platform, she can provide a mat on the floor. An environmental prop often is just the thing to encourage a tentative child to try something new.

One of the most important ways to scaffold young children is to develop an emotional climate for exploration. Show an interest in what a child is trying to learn. Your smiles and attention will encourage him to continue his "work." Listening demonstrates that you value what the child has to say. Holding the hand of a child learning to jump or a toddler learning to climb (when they want you to) scaffolds a next step in development. Do not worry that you will make the child dependent on you—a child who is motivated to learn won't always want your hand. For now, your hand provides the emotional and physical support the child needs to have the courage to try.

Check Your Understanding 12.2
Click here to check your understanding of the concepts in this section.

Relationships with Families and Culturally Sensitive Care

Considerations for families and culture were covered in Chapter 2. Here we highlight strategies that teachers can use to create relationships with families in the context of an early care and learning program.

Strategies for Developing Partnerships with Families

Teachers' relationships with families and the community weave a network of support for infants and toddlers that provides for their well-being. Positive relationships and interactions with families begin at the first telephone call or visit of the family to the infant-toddler program. An intake form is usually completed with a program director or family child care provider and parent together. Not only is crucial information collected from the family that supports the child's development, but budding relationships are formed that provide a firm foundation for all future interactions with the family. Information is exchanged—teachers provide information about the program and parents provide information on how to best meet the child's needs. Table 12.4 highlights some strategies for developing a family-centered program: one that recognizes and respects the child's need for a strong, positive relationship with his family and that provides as much consistency as possible for the child across the two settings.

Strategies for Responding Sensitively to a Child's and Family's Culture

Each family has a culture. As *culture* pertains to child-rearing practices, it is a set of beliefs about how children should be viewed and the role that parents and teachers should play in a child's life (44). Teachers will have their own cultures as well. Infant-toddler program teachers, Early Head Start teachers, or family child care home providers may agree or disagree with parents about how to care for a child. Areas of agreement or difference may include when

One way that teachers and administrators build strong, positive relationships with families is to support the child's transition to the parent at the end of the day.

TABLE 12.4 **Characteristics of a family-centered program**

Support the relationship between each child and his family.

- Display photographs of each child's family around the room and place them where children can easily see them. They may be laminated and held to the wall with Velcro, so that an infant or toddler can take the picture of his family and carry it around. Or, the children's family photos could be displayed on a large poster board with a piece of fabric over each picture, so that toddlers can play peek-a-boo with their own and others' family pictures.
- Be sure books or photograph albums with pictures of the children and their families are available to the children.
- Ask family members to make tape recordings, telling a story or singing a song.

Make family members feel welcome in the program through your own welcoming attitude and through a friendly classroom environment.

- Institute an open-door policy for families. They can be with their children at all times of the day and for as long as they like, visiting and interacting with the children.
- Have a family-friendly bulletin board that describes opportunities for families to visit and volunteer and that includes notices and announcements.
- Provide a private area for family members who want to give their child a bottle or breast-feed their babies or spend some moments alone with their children.
- Have a "family information" space (filing box or cabinet, for example) with information on resources, discipline, reading to children, and so on that parents can add to it or help themselves to articles, pamphlets, and brochures that build family-child relationships.

Involve families in the program. Whereas certain strategies will fit one type of program more than another, as well as one type of family more than another, the important factor is creating a feeling of partnership between the program and the child's family.

- Survey families concerning the different ways that they would like to be involved.
- Include families in policy decisions by inviting families to serve on a board of directors or policy council for the program.
- Plan social events, with family input, that include the whole family.
- Invite parents into the program to take pictures of children or record language samples that can then, for example, be made into a display of children's interests and learning.
- Develop a sense of community by including parents in the planning and writing of a monthly newsletter that includes interesting information about the program, monthly events, children, and families.
- Involve parents in fund-raising activities.
- Provide opportunities for family members to help at home by making homemade toys (sock puppets, "feely boxes," beanbags, lotto games) for the program.
- Provide opportunities and information about resources for family support—for example, learning a second language, divorce support groups, teenage parenting, and learning about Medicaid and Medicare.

Develop a system for daily exchange of information between families and staff.

- Create a friendly place inside the room or family child care home where information concerning a child's needs for the day can be written by a family member and shared with the teacher.
- Create a friendly place inside the room or family child care home where information about each child's day is kept so that families can easily pick up the information and talk to teachers about how the day went.
- Create a friendly "Conversation Corner" somewhere in the center or family child care home so that teachers and families can have a private place to talk.

Be sure families have ample opportunity to continually express preferences, beliefs, values, and concerns regarding the practices of the center or family child care home.

- Develop a process for communicating with parents who speak a different language from the teachers. If necessary, obtain a translator to assist in communication with children and/or families.
- On a regular basis, ask parents to share information indicating their own and their child's needs, interests, developmental history, and any other relevant information that will help make the program more responsive to the child's individual needs.

children should start feeding themselves, when and how children should learn to use the toilet, what types of food children should eat and when, to what degree children should be kept clean, or whether a baby should be placed on the floor (or on a blanket or mat). These varying convictions about children's behavior are supported by conscious or unconscious beliefs about the meaning of what happens, for example, when infants and toddlers start feeding themselves (45,46). For many families, the child's ability to feed himself means that he is no longer as dependent on the parent. For some families, this is a good thing and means that the child is on the road to independence, a valued trait in those families. Other families might believe that children need to be dependent longer in order to develop strong family bonds, so it is not a positive thing if a child is feeding himself with his hands or a spoon at 1 year of age. For some families, food should not be wasted, so the parents feel strongly that they must spoon-feed their 1-year-olds rather than let them pick up food from a high chair tray and, more than likely, drop some precious food on the floor as well as smear it all over their faces. How can infant-toddler teachers be responsive to parents' wishes and cultures?

With healthy dialog, teachers and families can negotiate an agreed-upon practice in the infant-toddler program. And, as always, a relationship of mutual respect—of asking and listening–can be developed between parents and teachers in regard to the most important issues about child rearing. Gonzalez-Mena (47) states wisely "no matter what culture a person comes from, a goal should be to develop a person-to-person relationship. Treating people with respect solves many cross-cultural problems" (p. 16).

Whereas the items in Table 12.4 are important, it is the relationships between teachers and families that are most important. Developing healthy relationships with families involves listening to them and dialoging with them on key issues of potential conflict. Gonzalez-Mena (48) recommends that teachers dialog with families rather than trying to convince them that the teacher is right. Arguing involves trying to win somebody over to your side through persuasion, she says, whereas in dialoging everyone tries to understand the other's perspective. She summarizes the difference between arguments versus dialoging as follows:

- The object of an argument is to win; the object of a dialog is to gather information.
- The arguer tells; the dialoger asks.
- The arguer tries to persuade; the dialoger tries to learn.
- The arguer tries to convince; the dialoger tries to discover.
- The arguer sees two opposing views and considers the valid or better one; the dialoger is willing to understand multiple viewpoints (p. 4).

When teachers and parents take time to dialog, then issues about feeding, schedules, whether the child should wear pull-ups or pants while learning to use the toilet, and what the infant or toddler could be learning become opportunities to build relationships. These relationships are built on trust that the other will listen, try to understand, and problem solve to find the best solution at that moment in time.

Teachers must be able to self-reflect about their own cultural values and how those are represented in their behavior. Something as simple as whether a teacher sits on the floor with a child illustrates that teacher's cultural values regarding the role of children. Table 12.5 lists ways that teachers can provide culturally responsive care.

TABLE 12.5 **Providing culturally responsive care**

Families
- Always take time to talk to families about their beliefs about child rearing.
- Include questions about routines (separation, feeding, diapering, sleeping) and time for the teacher and family to dialog about routines when the child enters the program and again frequently throughout the year.
- Invite families to share a day in play at your care and learning center or family child care home.
- Invite families to help redecorate the room; discuss the important aspects of a diversity-rich and stereotype-free environment.

Language
- Use important words from the infants' and toddlers' home languages whenever possible.
- Ask the families for words of endearment in the home language and use them with children.

Eating and feeding
- Encourage families to let you know what their children like to eat.
- Encourage families to let you know how and when their children like to eat.

Toys
- Ask families what the child's favorite toy is and try to provide it.
- Select toys and dolls that represent different cultures (and not just the cultures represented in the classroom).

Books
- Select books that demonstrate a variety of cultures in positive roles.
- Select books that show women and men in a variety of roles.

Songs
- Ask families to share their favorite cultural songs, CDs, and other music.
- Ask a family member to come in and sing with the infants and toddlers as they play.
- Play and sing a variety of music from a variety of cultures including your own.

Posters, pictures, and wall hangings
- Display pictures of children's families (including pets), laminated and adhered to the wall at the child's level. Allow a child to pull off a picture and carry it around.
- Provide small pillows with a picture of the family tucked inside a pocket. Let infants and toddlers carry them around.
- Display posters of a variety of cultures.
- Display quilts, cloths, paintings, and wall hangings from a variety of cultures (always ask your licensure person what is safe).

Dramatic play
- Include clothing, shoes, and accessories from a variety of cultures.
- For toddlers, include clothing, hats, shoes, tools, and other items from different types of jobs and roles in the community.

To become more culturally self-aware teachers can

1. Engage in conversations with other teachers and families about cultural issues
2. Read books such as *Skilled Dialogs* by Barrera, Kramer, & Macpherson (49) and Leading Anti-Bias Early Childhood Programs-A Guide for Change (50).
3. Engage in discussions with professionals and parents from diverse cultures to learn their points of view on early care and learning issues
4. Attend conferences or sessions at conferences about diversity
5. Keep a private journal of thoughts about cultural issues and reflect on beliefs and bias

Providing culturally responsive care is a skill that teachers can learn.

Check Your Understanding 12.3
Click here to check your understanding of the concepts in this section.

Responsive, Relationship-Based Planning

Curriculum planning is a continuous circle of energy that flows from the children through perceptive infant-toddler teachers and returns to the children with the power to motivate, recharge, and inspire them. (Wittmer)

In a responsive, relationship-based curriculum, the moment-to-moment, day-to-day, and weekly needs and interests of the children and their families guide teachers' planning process. The infant-toddler teacher does not start planning the curriculum with a list of activities, but rather starts planning for the day or week by observing what the children are doing and learning in all developmental domains. (See the Developmental Trends and Responsive Interactions charts at the end of Chapters 6 through 10.)

The Planning Process: Respect, Reflect, and Relate

The infant-toddler teacher observes, documents her observations, and uses the information to plan interactions and changes in the environment and experiences provided for the child that support the child's learning and relationships. For example, the teacher observes and documents that Hiawanda is starting to walk. She also considers that starting to walk influences Hiawanda's development in the social, emotional, and cognitive domains because he will be seeing and experiencing the world in new ways. Based on her *respect* for Hiawanda's internal motivation to walk, her *reflections* on how his efforts influence his development in all domains, the teacher *relates* (communicates, shares feelings, observes with interest) to the child. She responds by frequently sitting on the floor to provide a secure base for Hiawanda's walking adventures. She also responds by examining

BOX 12.3

What teachers can do to plan responsively

Respect: Value what the child is trying to do and how the child feels. Admire the child's feelings, goals, and how the child is learning.

Reflect: Observe, think, and feel. How is the child showing you how he or she feels? What are the child's goals? What is the child learning? How is the child trying to learn it? What does the child need?

Relate: Be responsive by observing with interest, interacting, communicating, sharing feelings, or changing the physical environment.

the environment to ensure that he has space to take his first steps. The teacher has thought about changes in the environment and her responsive interactions based on her observations of Hiawanda's goals that he is setting for himself. She has used the 3 R approach to curriculum planning—respect, reflect, and relate. Box 12.3 defines these terms.

The process begins with *respect.* At the beginning of the chapter, we discussed the concept of respect for the personhood of infants and toddlers. As Emde (51) puts it: "Each child is valued as a child, not just for what adults want the child to become" (p. viii). Children will pursue their goals in an emotionally supportive and physically interesting environment. A child who is figuring out how to stack blocks will often work on it for a long period of time. A child who is learning to walk will practice until she "gets it right" (p. xi). No one has to say, "Now it is time to practice your walking—start walking." A teacher who respects the internal motivation of young children to work at goals that they set for themselves and their ability to "figure things out" will then be intentional about reflecting on the children's goals and feelings and what the child is learning, how the child is learning it, and what the child is "telling" you he needs.

Reflecting includes both observing and thinking about what you are observing. It also is a self-reflective process because you consider how you (the adult) are feeling and what you are thinking. Often, reflection takes place in a split second when you have to respond to a screaming child, but it may also take place over time as you ponder the meaning of observations and interactions with the child.

Relating includes the actions that you take after you respect and reflect. Relating includes being responsive by continuing to observe with interest, interacting, communicating, sharing feelings, or changing the physical environment for and with the child with a focus on healthy relationships—again, both in the moment and over time.

How to Plan for Each Child

We have provided individual and group planning forms that infant-toddler teachers can use to plan a curriculum that is responsive to children's individual and group needs and interests. See Appendix D for full-page ready-to-use planning forms. The individual planning forms are completed by the teacher(s) responsible for planning for a few specific children. If the primary care system is used, then each teacher is responsible for completing guides on a small number of children each week. Infant and toddler professionals conduct home visits complete these forms with the family. Teachers should try to complete two individual guides a week to document the child's feelings, discoveries, and explorations.

There are two versions of individual planning forms. Version 1 (Box 12.4) and Version 2 (Box 12.5) allow for documenting children's interests with photos or anecdotal records. Both guides ask you to think about what the child is doing as well as what the child may be feeling (inference) and also what the child is learning (concepts and developmental milestones). Under the Respect

BOX 12.4

Individual Child Planning Guide: Version 1

Child's name: <u>Sophie Age: 26 months</u>
Plans for week of (date): <u>March 9–13, 2016</u>
Person(s) completing the guide: <u>Matt and Carla</u>
Respect: Child's emotions, effort, goals, learning, and relationships
Write an observation or use a photograph(s) or other documentation here—date all notes: 3/9/16

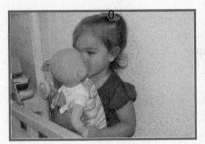  

Respect and Reflect	Relate

Respect and Reflect

What am I doing?
- I am kissing my favorite doll, wrapping her in a blanket, and tucking her in the doll bed.

How am I feeling?
- I am feeling safe to focus on taking care of the doll.

What am I learning?
Emotional
- I am gaining self-confidence in my ability to make things happen. I am learning how to focus (self-regulation) and express and manage my feelings (emotional regulation). I am learning how to nurture others.

Social
Cognitive
- I am learning about spatial concepts.
- I am learning about cause and effect (I can do something that will have an effect).
- I am pretending and engaging in symbolic play.

Language
- I am learning how to communicate that I like something or someone (with a kiss).

Motor
- I am learning to control my body so that I can wrap the doll in the blanket and place her carefully in the doll bed. I am gaining both fine-motor and large-motor skills as I play.

Relate

What will you do to support my development and learning?
(These are examples. A team of teachers would choose which ones to focus on during the week.)
Responsive interactions
- We will use language to describe what you are doing.
- We will continue to model how to be gentle, caring, and prosocial.

Environment, toys, materials, and experiences
- We will bring in toys that provide opportunities for you to explore cause/effect and spatial concepts.
- We will place different dolls, different sizes of blankets, baby bottles, and other baby toys in the dramatic play area to support your ability to nurture.
- We will talk with your family to learn more about how you nurture others at home and how you engage in symbolic play.
- We will think about providing more experiences for the children to participate in dramatic/symbolic play, document children's experience, and then plan additional opportunities.

BOX 12.5

Individual Child Planning Guide: Version 2

Child's name: <u>Sheila</u> Age: <u>9 months</u>
Plans for week of (date): <u>March 9–13, 2016</u>
Person(s) completing the guide: <u>Chloe</u>

Respect: Child's emotions, effort, goals, learning, and relationships
Write an observation or use a photograph or other documentation here—date all notes:
3/9/16: Sheila is on the floor lying on a blanket on the carpet. She is lying on her back shaking a ring toy up and down. She has a smile on her face. She is making sounds such as "ba," "ma." She then rolled over onto her tummy and crawled crablike across the floor.
3/10/16: When Dad came to pick her up today she was sitting in Chloe's lap. She squealed loudly and smiled when she saw her dad.

Reflect
What am I doing?
- I have started to crawl. I put my hands forward, bunch up, and crawl crablike across the floor. I can express my emotions by squealing with a big smile on my face when I see my dad at the end of the day. I hold the plastic ring toys when I am on my back and make them jingle loudly—shaking them quickly up and down while looking at them. I am starting to make sounds like "ba," "ma."
How am I feeling?
- I seem to feel very happy when my dad comes. I enjoy making noise with the ring toys.
What am I learning?
- I am learning that Dad will respond happily when I squeal in delight when I see him and that I can make things happen (jingly ring toy). I'm also learning that I can make the jingly noise (cause and effect) when I shake the ring toy and that toys can make noises. My language is growing. I'm learning to communicate by babbling. I'm learning to move in different ways.

Relate
What will you do to support my development and learning?
Responsive interactions
- I will ask your father what you like to do at home.
- We will babble back to you and then wait for you to take a turn. We will use one and two word sentences with you as well.
- Martha will be your primary care teacher. She will try to be the one to feed you and rock you to sleep.

Environment, toys, materials, and experiences
- I will bring in some different ring toys for you to shake.
- We'll add other cause-and-effect toys to several of the cozy corners.
- We'll make sure that there is a clear space to crawl.

and Reflect sections, Version 1 asks teachers to write what the child is learning in each developmental domain, whereas Version 2 asks teachers to write a response that integrates learning. For a brief list of possible concepts that the child might be exploring, see Table 12.6. Teachers and parents can add more to the list as they observe children. They could also use an observation system such as the Ounce Scale (52) to describe behaviors, knowledge, and developmental steps (such as beginning to use two words together or beginning to crawl). Teachers in center programs or family child care homes can ask the family members to share information about what they have observed at home.

On the individual planning guides, the teachers and/or parents use the observation to plan for the changes that could be made in regard to responsive interactions (teacher-child, parent-child, peer-peer, and teacher-family), including routines and a responsive environment (environmental arrangement, equipment, materials, and experiences offered to children) to support the child's learning in all domains of development. We have discussed responsive interactions, but routines, environment, and experiences will be described in Chapter 13. After reading Chapter 13 and seeing several models of individual planning guides, you will be ready to complete the Relate section of the individual planning guide.

Many of these changes are implemented immediately, in the moment-to-moment interactions with the infant or toddler, and some may be implemented over time.

How Do You Plan for Groups?

There are two forms for group planning as well. The form shown in Box 12.6 is to be used at the end of a week to plan special opportunities for the following week. When teachers develop the group plan together, they bring the individual planning guides and share information so that all of the teachers can contribute to the recommended changes in interactions and the environment. As you plan, you build on the concepts and developmental steps, interests, and strengths of the children in the group.

The second group planning form in Box 12.7 provides space for teachers in center or home programs to reflect on routines of the day and develop a community of caring and should be completed at least once a month. The group planning guides could also be used by home visitors to plan with families to make routines, such as bath time, more successful for everyone involved.

Planning is a process of respect, reflect, and relate. Teachers plan responsively for individuals in the group and, using that information, then plan thoughtfully for the group.

TABLE 12.6   "I'm exploring and learning . . . "

Emotional/ Attachment	Social/Peers	Cognitive	Language/ Literacy	Motor
My own self-worth: Whether I am worthy of love	What peers do	How to solve problems	How to communicate my needs including what I don't want	How to move my large muscles: roll over, sit, crawl, pull to stand, walk, run, jump, climb stairs . . .
Who will protect me and keep me safe	How to play beside and/or with peers— e.g., parallel aware, simple social play, complementary and reciprocal social play	What will happen when I'm curious	Expressive language: How to communicate with sounds, facial expressions, sign language, gestures, coos, babbles, words, and sentences	How to navigate new environments: Walk in snow, walk down a ramp, use indoor play equipment, and outdoor playground equipment
How to get my needs met	Who will play with me and how peers differ in how they play	How I can use tools to accomplish a goal: pull a toy with a string, use my fingers to make music on a toy piano	Receptive language: How to listen and understand what another is saying, how to follow directions	How to maintain balance and how to control my body
Who I can trust to take good care of me	Who will treat me kindly and who will hurt me	About concepts such as light/dark, up/down, in/out, high/low, how shadows are created, how gravity works.	How to use language in different pragmatic ways: telling, requesting, questioning, demanding . . .	How to use my body: move and/or carry objects around, to get my needs met or accomplish goals
How others feel about me	How to engage peers: join play; make a peer smile, laugh, and/or follow me	The properties of objects and materials: hard/soft, weak/strong	How to take language turns with another person	How to use fine motor skills: touching, reaching, holding, letting go, picking up, waving, clapping hands together.
How to get adults to pay attention to me and be with me	Prosocial: How I can comfort, help, and/or nurture a peer	Cause and effect: How I can make things happen and what causes what	Who will respond to my sounds, words, and language	How to use my hands and eyes together to accomplish a goal: complete a puzzle, put pegs in pegboard, eat food

TABLE 12.6   "I'm exploring and learning . . . " (Continued)

Emotional/ Attachment	Social/Peers	Cognitive	Language/ Literacy	Motor
How to express my feelings: sadness, discomfort, happiness, joy, anger, affection, frustration, and disappointment	How to protect myself or my things in socially acceptable ways	Symbols: How to understand symbols and participate in symbolic play	Who I can enjoy communicating with	How to use different types of grasps: raking, scissors, and pincer
How to interpret and respond to others' emotional expressions	How to handle conflict. How to negotiate and cooperate.	Spatial relationships: How to fit objects or myself into a space and/ or how objects fit together	How words fit together to make a sentence (syntax)	How to cooperate with and enjoy when someone is feeding or dressing me
How to self-regulate: express emotions without falling apart, wait, comfort myself	How to make a friend and be a friend	Object permanence: Where objects/people go when they disappear. How to make objects/people disappear/appear	How to add endings to words to express meaning (semantics)	How to communicate what I want and don't want to eat or if I'm uncomfortable
My self-esteem and sense of self-worth: What I am capable of doing or not doing	How to make a peer go away	How to use different strategies to accomplish my goals	How to enjoy books: hold books, listen to a story, look at the pictures	How to control my body in different situations
How to persist at a task	How to negotiate with gestures, actions, or words	Time	How to interact with adults or peers with books	How to use my fingers, hands, and/ or eating utensils to feed myself
How to separate from my loved ones	How to share space, materials, or toys and other objects	How to seriate: put objects in sequence based on height, width, length, gradations of color	How to interpret pictures in books including how pictures relate to real objects, people, or animals	How to self-care: brushing teeth, pulling a shirt off, pulling off, putting shoes in a special place
How I should react to strangers	How to share the special adults in my life	How to classify/ sort objects: by one dimension (color or shape) or two dimensions	How to open and close books, turn pages, and/or take good care of books	How to use the toilet including how to communicate the need to use the toilet

BOX 12.6

Individually Responsive Group Planning Guide

Name of children in group: <u>Silvia, Sophie, Sheila, and Juan</u>
Week of: <u>March 16–20, 2016</u>
Person(s) completing this guide: <u>Matt, Carla, Chloe</u>

Respect and reflect
(Use information from the individual planning guides.) The children in my group are . . .
Exploring cause and effect
Gaining self-confidence as they learn new things and make things happen
Trusting adults to respond to them and have fun with them
Learning to express themselves through squealing and words

Relate: Plans for the week to meet children's interests and needs
Songs/Finger-plays
Continue singing songs with children in a responsive way.
Sit on the floor and start singing several children's favorite songs.
Bring in pictures or real objects to accompany the songs.
Sing the bubble song while playing with bubbles.

Stories/Books
Build on Sophie's interest in cause and effect.
Sit on the floor and invite children to listen to a story several times a day.
Respond when a child wants a story read.

Responsive interactions
Be sure to follow children's lead in interactions.
Be sure to comment on children's feelings.
Respond to children's language:
    Respond to Sheila's babbling by babbling back and saying words to her.
Use new words with Sophie and other children.

Environment, toys, materials, and opportunities
To build on Sophie's interest in cause and effect add flashlights to the cozy corner to provide opportunities for children to explore turning them on.
In the middle of the week add colored cellophane.
Make sure there is room for Sheila to crawl.
Add a cause-and-effect toy (a waterwheel) to the water table. Add "tubs for two" with water to encourage social interactions. During the middle of the week add bubbles to the water table and "tubs for two" for opportunities for them to learn more about bubbles.
Develop an obstacle course outside.
Add different sizes of balls to the active area with baskets of various sizes.
Add more ring toys to provide opportunities for cause-and-effect play.

Experiences with families
Exchange information with families about how their children explore cause and effect and make things happen at home and in the program.
Ask families for ideas about what toys, materials, experiences their children might like during the day in the program.

Special experiences
Silvio's dad will visit on Tuesday and will play his flute.

BOX 12.7

Group Planning for Routines

Group Planning for Routines

Name of children in group: <u>Silvia, Sophie, Sheila, and Juan</u>

Week of: <u>March 16–20, 2016</u>

Persons completing this form: <u>Matt, Carla, Chloe</u>

Developing a caring community: Think about what is happening and what could happen to develop a relationship-based program for children, families, and teachers.

Routine	What is going well for the children and teachers	What could we do to improve the experience for children, families, and the teachers
Greeting time or good-bye time	A teacher is greeting each parent and getting information on how the child's night was.	Place the forms for parents to write on about their child's night or any special information closer to the door. Provide a comfortable adult chair by the door.
Feeding infants and toddler eating times	The toddlers are enjoying the songs that we are singing when they are seated and are waiting for the food.	To make the atmosphere more pleasant we could provide placemats and some flowers on the table for the toddlers.
Infant sleep and toddler nap time	The toddlers are falling asleep easily after we read stories to those who want a story read to them.	To make the transition from lunch to nap time easier, we will give each toddler a special hug before going to sleep.
Diapering	We are talking to them and they are talking to us.	No change.
Toileting	The older toddlers are beginning to use the toilet. There is no pressure, but when one starts to sit on the toilet several others do as well.	Remember to encourage them but not to ever force them. We want to emphasize that they are learning how rather than that we are training them how.
Play times	Most of the toddlers are engaged in play most of the morning.	Continue to plan based on what we are observing are their interests and needs.
Outdoor times	We created some shade so that the toddlers can sit in the shade while outside.	Ask families to help build a sandbox with a lid.
Transitions	Singing the "cleanup" song has helped establish a routine for cleanup.	Put pictures of several items on the shelf so that they can match the object to the picture
Other routines		

Check Your Understanding 12.4
Click here to check your understanding of the concepts in this section.

Summary

- The emotional development of infants and toddlers creates a foundation for the child to learn and love. Teachers' responsive strategies promote children's sense of well-being; meet infants' and toddlers' emotional needs for affection, love, and encouragement; and help them learn. Scaffolding is an adult strategy that can be used to promote emotional, social, language, cognitive, and motor development. Teachers observe and document children's learning and use the information for planning to develop a responsive curriculum.

  □ A curriculum for infants and toddlers is responsive to individual children's needs, interests, and strengths (in collaboration with families) and focuses on the development of children's healthy relationships. A curriculum is everything that children experience from the beginning to the end of the day—they are constantly learning. There are eight components to a curriculum, with components 1 through 4 discussed in this chapter.

  □ The teachers' beliefs about the nature and needs of infants and toddlers, what is important for them to learn, and how they best learn form the philosophical foundation for a curriculum. Play is an important way that infants and toddlers learn.

- One of the most important roles of the teacher is to create a relationship-based community to ensure that infants and toddlers feel safe, nurtured, and experience a sense of belonging. Teachers are intentional in how they scaffold children's emotional, social, language, cognitive, and motor development and follow children's lead for what they need. Nine dimensions of adult-child interactions promote children's emotional development, the foundation for all learning.

- Explain how to create a family and culturally sensitive program. When teachers develop strong, positive relationships with families from a variety of cultures, they weave a network of support for the well-being of infants and toddlers. To create respectful relationships, teachers and parents must take time to dialog.

- In a responsive, relationship-based curriculum the moment-to-moment, day-to-day, and weekly needs and interests of the children and their families guide the planning process. A responsive planning process that includes *respect, reflect,* and *relate* will ensure that the curriculum is truly "day to day, the relationship way!"

Key Terms

attachment groups
attuned

dance up and down the
    developmental ladder
holds and enfolds

homebases
Velcro time
working sense of self

Reflections and Resources for the Reader

REFLECTIONS

1. What are the key components to planning a curriculum for infants and toddlers? Which are most important?
2. What do you think are the most important goals for infants and toddlers? Compare your answers with another person in your group.
3. What does it mean to respect an infant or toddler?
4. What are the nine responsive strategies that teachers use to promote infants' and toddlers' emotional development—a foundation for learning? Why are these strategies important for children, families, and teachers?

OBSERVATION AND APPLICATION OPPORTUNITIES

1. Use the items in Tables 12.4 and Table 12.5 to observe an infant and toddler program and to interview the teachers to determine how they develop responsive relationships with families in general and also families from diverse cultures. Write a summary of your observations and interviews and make recommendations for improvement.
2. Analyze the following: Abria is 28-months-old. Abria's parents want the teachers to feed her with a spoon and do not want her to play with her food at lunchtime. In the program that Abria attends, the toddlers sit together at a table and feed themselves with a spoon, even though it is often messy.

Sometimes they get tired and pick up food with their fingers. The teachers in the program think that it is important for children to learn to feed themselves. How would you dialog to discuss this issue with the family?

SUPPLEMENTARY ARTICLES AND BOOKS TO READ

Follari, L. (2014). *Valuing diversity in early childhood education*. New York: Pearson.

Lally, R. (2013). *For our babies*. New York: Teachers College Press.

ZERO TO THREE. (2008). *Caring for infants and toddlers in groups: Developmentally Appropriate Practice* (2nd ed.). Washington, DC: Zero to Three Press.

INTERESTING LINKS

PITC.org. The Program for Infant/Toddler Care.
This site includes video clips from PITC's video—*The next step: Including the infant in the curriculum.* A new video, titled, *"The social womb"* was written and narrated by J. Ronal Lally.

UNICEF
This Web site includes a link to the Convention on the Rights of the Child. Available on this link is the full text of this international human rights treaty, which articulates a new world vision committed to protecting children's rights.

Routines, Environments, and Opportunities: Day to Day, the Relationship Way

LEARNING OUTCOMES

After reading this chapter, you will be able to:

- Explain how to provide responsive transitions and routines.
- Create a responsive, relationship-based environment including quality learning spaces, equipment, toys, and materials.
- Explain how to provide a variety of learning opportunities.
- Describe various curriculum approaches.

Pearson Education

In this chapter, you will learn how to establish respectful routines and create an enriched environment in a responsive curriculum. You will also learn how to provide opportunities for very young children to develop within the context of relationships, and you will see examples of the *respect, reflect,* and *relate* (3 R) planning process. At the end of the chapter, we describe other infant and toddler curriculum approaches to use in group settings. But first, see Box 13.1, where you can peek into an infant and toddler classroom that focuses on responsive interactions and relationships. The infants and toddlers in the program described

BOX 13.1

A Responsive Classroom

Every infant in Angie Hicks's classroom shares the attention of a teacher with just two or three other children. Designated teachers have primary responsibility for three or four children. These teachers spend the bulk of their day with their children and monitor their basic needs. On the day of our visit, this arrangement is evident in the children's behavior. When one of the teachers goes to get a bottle, Samantha's eyes trail after her, then start to tear up. The other teacher, seeing Samantha's concern, says comfortingly, "Are you getting sad because Jeannie is leaving?"

The large infant rooms are very calm. Soft music plays at times for the children who are awake. Two additional rooms contain cribs as well as a quiet area where mothers can breast-feed. Teachers rock children to sleep in their arms and often sing lullabies before placing the babies in a crib.

The room is well organized and well labeled so teachers do not have to spend time searching for supplies. Personal belongings, including diapers and pacifiers, are all kept in labeled locations. Food allergies and sunscreen requirements are posted in large letters on the wall. The providers are fastidious about health precautions, maintaining clean facilities, washing their hands between feedings and diaper changes, and using plastic gloves while wiping children's noses. Parents frequently call to check on their children.

Most important, the infant teachers have worked consistently with babies for many years. As Director Burroughs says, "The teachers in this room prefer to work with very young children and have not experienced the burnout" so common in the infant care profession. Their devotion to the children is apparent. One teacher lovingly hugs a child who had just awakened, then rubs his back, allowing him to transition slowly into the activities of the day. Conversations are filled with encouraging and caring comments. "Keep crawling—you are almost there!" "Thank you for handing that to me!" Teachers convey their excitement to parents, proudly reporting on the children's activities.

The teachers follow the children's lead. When one child carries a book to one of the teachers, the gift prompts a group reading session. When an infant pushes back on the firm pillows supporting him and begins to cry, a teacher takes the cue to move him onto his back, where he becomes immediately content. Another teacher asks a toddler, "What are you trying to tell me, Jenny? Do you want to blow the bubbles?" Jenny gives an enthusiastic "Bubba ba ba." The teacher helps Jenny blow the bubbles herself, then encourages other children to come join the activity.

Because toddlers learn to communicate verbally, most of the conversation in the toddler room develops out of the children's ideas. Astar holds out a plastic ice cream cone and says, "Daddy." The teacher responds, "Does Daddy buy ice cream?" When Astar then picks up a milkshake cup, she asks, "Is that a milkshake you are making? Let's all go and get some ice cream." In the house area, the toddlers play ice cream scenarios. After a while, a boy excitedly announces that he has made a cake. The teacher and the children start to sing "Happy Birthday."

Source: Kinch, A. F., & Schweinhart, L. J. (2004) *Achieving high-quality child care: How ten programs deliver excellence parents can afford,* pp. 16–17. Copyright © NAEYC®. Reprinted with permission.

Watch the video on what quality looks like in care and learning of children under 2 years old in New Zealand. What are the quality aspects of an infant/toddler program?

https://www.youtube.com/watch?v=xs9bd1RV_Fw

here are having profound experiences that will influence how they view themselves, relationships, and the world. Considered alone, each experience may not seem important, but when they are combined, they are transformed into who a child is and will become.

How do we give young children the experiences they deserve—day to day, the relationship way? One of the most important experiences for infants and toddlers is how they transition into a program and the routines that they experience each day.

Transitions and Routines—A Time for Relationships

Transitions and **routines** are important opportunities for strengthening a child's relationships and learning with teachers, families, and peers. *Transitions* are times of change that occur in a child's life, such as when an infant or toddler enters a care and learning center or family child care home or when an infant changes rooms in a center as he grows and has new needs (hopefully with a familiar teacher moving "up" with him). Daily transitions occur when a child or group moves from one experience to another—for example, from indoor play to outdoor play. *Routines* are regularly occurring events that the child experiences during a day, such as diapering time, feeding time, or moving from play into nap time.

Transition of Entering a New Infant-Toddler Program

One of the more difficult times for babies may be when they enter a center program or child care home for the first time. Teachers and parents can work closely to support the child during this time of separation and adjustment to a new environment, new adults, and new experiences. Notice how difficult it is for Tim in the following example reported by Pawl and St. John (1):

> Tim stood just inside the entrance to the big playroom. He was sturdy for two and a half years, but short. The noise was jarring, and he looked around for the woman his mother talked to when they came in. She had said to his mother, "He'll be fine—I'll get him started," and she had taken his hand. But now, just as fast, she was gone. It scared him as much as the other time. This was not a good place to be. He wanted his mother, and he wanted to go home. A boy running past bumped him hard and Tim nearly fell, but he caught himself and made his way to the corner of the room. He still couldn't see that big person or the other one—just lots and lots of small kids. He sat down and fingered some colored blocks on the floor. A big boy came and grabbed one and stepped on Tim's hand. Tim yelped and cried and looked around. He held his hurt hand in the other, and the tears ran down his cheeks. No one saw. (p. 12).

What could have made it easier for Tim, his mother, and the teacher? Remembering how hard it is for us to separate from a loved one helps us take the perspective of the child and parent. The parent may feel anxious and/or guilty, as if she were giving up a part of herself. T. Berry Brazelton, pediatrician and child development expert, noted that some parents may express their feelings openly, others seem distant as they prepare themselves to separate from their baby, and others seem angry as they attempt to maintain control but really feel out of control (2). Babies like Tim can be confused and sad.

Transitions To and From the Program Each Day

At the beginning of the day, parents and teachers could use *ciao* time—a word that means both "hello" and "good-bye" in Italian—instead of *dropping off*.

Ciao time is an emotional exchange of the child from the parent to the teacher at the beginning of the day and from the teacher back to the family at the end of the child's day in the program.

The morning is "good-bye" time from the infants' and toddlers' perspectives, as the babies say good-bye to their parents. However, it is also "hello" time, as the infant or toddler and the parents say hello to the child's teacher. Thus, it is both good-bye and hello if we think about this transition time from the child's perspective.

An infant's or toddler's good-bye to the parent and hello to the teacher time must be handled with care, as it is an emotional exchange of the child between the parent and teacher. Although a baby is held emotionally through time and space by the physically absent parent, an infant or toddler will not be able to think about how the parent still loves her after the parent disappears (according to the child's perspective). The child has to transition her trust from the parent to the teacher—not an easy task unless the relationships with both are positive.

A routine provides child, parent, and the teacher predictability—a sense of expectancy—about ciao time, leading to smoother transitions for all.

> As an infant, Kia's mom made sure she was comfortable in the child care home and sang her one song before saying good-bye. The teacher always greeted Mom and Kia and asked how the baby's night had been and if there were any special needs for the day. As a young toddler, the teacher did the same thing, only now she greeted Kia with a special hug. Kia's mom sang one song and read one story and then said good-bye with hugs and kisses, telling Kia that she would be back after Kia's nap in the afternoon. The teacher made sure she was near and ready to pick up Kia, hold her, or read a story to help Kia settle in for the day. In the toddler room, the teacher sat at a table near the door with interesting things like play dough, books, or new toys. When Kia came in the door with her parent, the teacher could be right there asking the parent about special needs and greeting Kia with a smile. Kia took off her shoes and put on her special slippers for the day. This routine helped her make the transition into the center and she was able to say good-bye to her mother with a big hug and a kiss.

These transition times at the beginning of the day are repeated at the end of the day in a similar way to smooth the child's transition from program to home.

Watch the video and think about how the teacher(s) help the children and parents feel safe and comfort. Which supports were given to help the child and family members with transitions?

Transitions During the Day

Transitions during the day are important times for building teacher-child relationships. Inform children before individual and group transitions occur and give them time. For example, to an infant who needs to have a diaper change, says things like, "It is time to change your diaper . . ." *before* you pick up the child. Help them finish a task before toddling toward the diaper table. Snatching infants and toddlers from their play for diaper changes can result in child sadness and anger. Remember, when you transition to another part of the room or out of the room, it is also a change for the children. To help children feel more secure, you can tell infants and toddlers when you are leaving to change another child's diaper or fix food, and when you will be back. Transitions from one room to another in a center as children age are difficult for infants and toddlers unless there is continuity of care where at least one teacher moves to a new room with a *group* of children.

Responsive Routines

Caregiving routines in a program are patterned interactions that occur with predictable regularity during the day. These routines include diapering and toileting, feeding and eating, and sleeping times. There are many benefits of responsive routines. Routines strengthen teacher-child relationships and child learning. A responsive routine meets young children's physical and *emotional* needs. Infants and toddlers gain a sense of self-worth and learn about the kindness of others. They learn that their needs will be met. They learn that they can communicate their needs and someone will respond. Infants and toddlers develop relationships with those who meet their needs in responsive, caring ways. They learn whether adults are trustworthy. Infants and toddlers learn language and cognitive skills when teachers use words with them during routines, such as "up," "down," "over." With responsive routines, infants and toddlers become self-regulated and gain a sense of inner control. Their brains become organized as they experience the patterns of routines (3).

Group time / Child's choice
11 – 11:45 A.M.

Hand washing/Lunch
11:45 - 12:30 P.M.

Nap/Diapers
12:30 P.M. - 3 P.M.

Pearson Education

Schedules and routines are negotiated with parents to ensure that they are responsive to children's needs.

As you watch the video, think about how responsive care is demonstrated. Notice how individual children are feeling. What do teachers do to help toddlers feel safe as they transition to nap and as they nap? What more could the teachers do to create a calm and relaxing personal and physical environment?

For infants, routines are individualized and responsive to their needs. Babies feel they are hungry or overwhelmed and usually let you know. The teacher reads the cues of the child concerning an empty or full tummy, a need for interactions, or a diaper change. These interactions form the core of relationship building between the infant and teacher. They also begin the formation of the infant's identity as someone who can trust others and who feels lovable. For toddlers, routines are times for shared relationships as they participate in conversations (cooing, babbling, first words, and sentences) with teachers during diapering, eating, and time for sleep.

Infants and toddlers are included in the diaper-changing process. When a teacher says, "It is time to take your diaper off. I'm putting on a clean diaper" the routine is completed *with* the child, not *to* the child. Toddlers share routine times with teachers and peers as, over time, diapering time turns into toilet time, feeding turns into eating with peers at small tables, and helping infants fall asleep becomes supporting toddlers as they transition to nap time. Teachers can use Table 13.1 to determine how responsive their routines are for the infants and toddlers in their program.

Routines happen continuously in a program and there is a danger that they will become routinized (monotonous). Teachers may wonder why they are wiping noses, cleaning bottoms, and feeding toddlers. They may wonder what routines have to do with teaching. When we recognize that these times represent opportunities for learning and emotional connections, then we will treat them for what they are—perhaps the most important part of the day.

CULTURE CLOSE UP

Mia, the coach who visited rooms in infant-toddler programs to support teachers, was clearly upset. She called her mentor when she observed that an almost 3-year-old was being treated like a young infant by being lifted up on a changing table (rather than climb up a set of safety stairs), fed with a spoon and not allowed to touch his food, and talked to in "baby talk." Mia was encouraged by her mentor to ask the teacher, Shaleen, respectful questions about her practices. Mia found that Shaleen was being responsive to the child's parents' wishes, although questioning whether it was the right thing to do for the child. However, Shaleen had learned and was trying to understand that in the child's family, interdependence rather than independence was encouraged. Shaleen was being responsive to the parents so as not to confuse the child with different practices at home and at the center because the family had just recently arrived in the United States. What are your thoughts on Mia's, Shaleen's, the child's, and the family's experiences?

TABLE 13.1   Responsive routines

Responsive daily routines
- Provide a daily routine that follows each infant's need for feeding and sleep.
- Implement a flexible routine (eating, sleeping, play time, inside-outside) that the toddlers learn to predict.
- Use routines as opportunities for emotional interaction and learning.
- Provide primary caregiving.

(continued)

TABLE 13.1   Responsive routines (continued)

Responsive routines for infant feeding and toddler eating
- Provide a private place for parents to feed an infant, if parent desires.
- Respect the mother's wish to breast-feed or not.
- Ask families about their cultural and family preferences for the child's eating habits, needs, and food preferences.
- Sit with toddlers for eating rather than hovering above.
- Respond to young children's requests and comments while feeding and eating with the children—name foods; use words that describe the color, shape, size, texture, and taste of foods; and talk about pleasant events while feeding and eating with the children.
- Hold infants gently for bottle-feeding. Babies need to be held for feeding to ensure safety and to meet babies' emotional needs. Talk softly, hum, sing, or remain quiet according to the infant's needs.
- Speak in a soft, kind, friendly, gentle, encouraging, and positive way to the children during feeding and eating activities.
- Respond when infants or toddlers indicate that they are hungry or want more food, and respect children when they indicate that they are satisfied or want to stop eating.
- Use plates and place mats instead of napkins or paper plates to serve toddlers.
- Provide opportunities for toddlers to begin to serve themselves, pour milk out of a small pitcher, and clean the table with a sponge.
- Provide a system for giving daily information to families concerning how, when, what, and with whom the child ate.
- Provide a system for documenting families' wishes on issues related to weaning from the breast or bottle.

Responsive routines for diapering and toilet learning
- Provide pictures of family members or other interesting pictures on the wall at the infant's or toddler's eye level in the diapering area.
- Make diapering a special time for adults to talk and sing. Use encouraging and positive words and self-talk, such as "first," "next," and comforting words.
- Coordinate toilet learning with the parents to provide continuity from home to program.
- Help toddlers and talk gently to them when they use the toilet.
- Never force toddlers to use or stay on the toilet.

Responsive routines for sleeping
- Provide long, luxurious holding times for infants and toddlers.
- Gently rock or pat infants who need help to get to sleep, respond positively and quickly when they signal that they want out of crib.
- Provide each toddler with a cot that is labeled, both with her or his first name and a special symbol or picture. Label sheets, pillows, and blankets in the same way.
- Plan and implement a transition time from play to sleep with a predictable sequence for toddlers. To build positive relationships, read stories, talk gently, and/or pat a child gently to sleep according to the child's needs. Toddlers may pick a special book or have their own stuffed toy or blanket if needed.
- Allow toddlers to sleep as long as they need. Plan a quiet activity for toddlers who wake up.
- Help toddlers transition from nap to wake time.
- Prepare the nap area for toddlers before lunch, so that if a toddler is tired or falls asleep during lunch the teacher can help the child transition to nap time.

Responsive greeting and good-bye times
- Greet each infant, toddler, and parent warmly in the morning. Help children transition from home to the program at the beginning of the day. Give family members a chance to communicate needs, priorities, and concerns.
- Greet each family member warmly when the family picks up their child. Help children transition from the program to parent at the end of the child's day. Talk about the daily record with the family. Give each infant and toddler a special good-bye.

Check Your Understanding 13.1
Click here to check your understanding of the concepts in this section.

Creating Responsive, Relationship-Based Environments

The infant-toddler professional creates a relationship-based, responsive environment with equipment, materials, and opportunities that support children's development. There are many elements of a quality environment that infants, toddlers, and their teachers would enjoy:

1. It supports children's individual and social development.
2. It encourages explorations, focused play, and cooperation.
3. It provides choices for children and supports **self-directed learning**.
4. The walls and learning areas are uncluttered and provide opportunities for learning.
5. The environment meets "our need to gather, be comforted, rest, and explore" (4, p. 75).
6. It supports the teacher-child relationship.
7. It minimizes management and custodial activities, allowing teachers more time for interactions, observation, and facilitation of children's development.

A Quality Environment for Centers and Child Care Homes

A learning environment begins with recognizing what infants and toddlers need to *do* and determining how to maximize their opportunities to have the appropriate experiences. Greenman asks, "What do babies do for a living?" He answers, "Most simply, it is to make sense of the world of people and things and to develop their capacities to the fullest. Babies are explorers and scientists; they test and discover their own properties, the properties of objects and people, and the relationships between the elements of the world." (5, p. 99)

And, of course, we can't forget infants' and toddlers' needs for environments that promote relationships—both adult-child and peer relationships. With all of these purposes in mind, teachers can set up an environment that is a home away from home. See Figures 13.1 and 13.2 for examples of floor plans for an infant room and a toddler room. For babies to feel both safe and motivated to learn, a quality environment needs the elements found in Table 13.2. Environments need learning spaces and special places for infants and toddlers to delight in their surroundings.

 Watch this video about an infant and toddler center. Use Table 13.2 to evaluate this infant room.

https://www.youtube.com/watch?v=nzYcAjc5mtk&list=PLBrTAvoznpga86R8glEo3NL6QK0BxuJDU&index=60

Learning Spaces and Special Places

Learning spaces are well-defined places with materials that support relationships and learning. Integrated learning in all domains (emotional, social, language, cognitive, and motor) occurs in all areas of the room. As teachers set up these

FIGURE 13.1 Floor plan for an infant and young toddler room (2 months to 18 months)

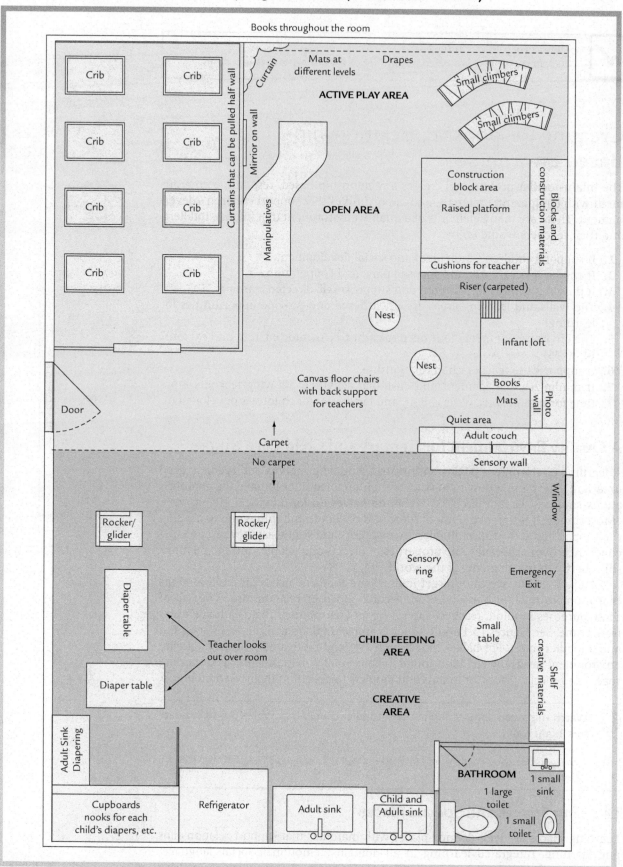

FIGURE 13.2   Floor plan for a toddler room (18 months to 3 years)

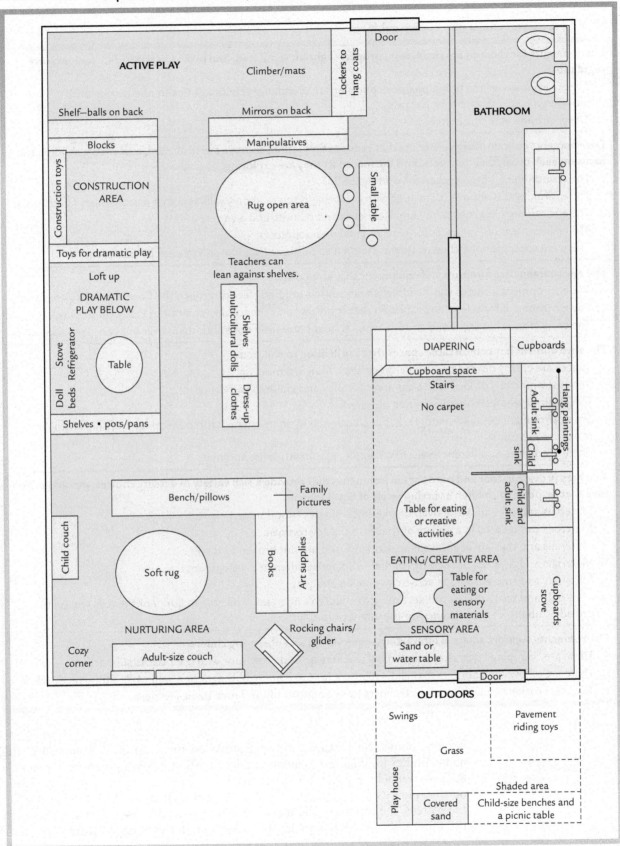

TABLE 13.2   Environment observation guide

Environments for children are clean, safe, properly lighted, ventilated, and provide appropriate temperature regulation.
- The environment is free of materials or conditions that endanger children's health and is constantly monitored by the teachers for hazards.
- The environment is clutter free.

Environments contain design elements that reduce stimulation, create a sense of calm, and enable children to focus on each other, their teachers, and the materials they are exploring.
- The environment is bright, cheerful, and beautiful.
- The environment is not overstimulating with paint that is too bright or wallpaper that has too many figures on it.
- The environment has soft items—small couches and pillows, and a variety of textures.
- The environment offers spaces for teacher-child interactions.
- There are spaces for one child or several children to be alone (but can still be seen by the teacher).

The environment has furniture and equipment that is child size.
- The environment includes short toddler chairs so that toddlers' feet can touch the floor when they are sitting.
- The environment includes short tables so that toddlers can sit in toddler chairs and easily eat or play.
- The environment has short and sturdy shelves so that babies will not knock them over but can reach toys easily.

The environment has comfortable spaces that are inviting to children.
- Spaces are clearly divided by low shelves or cloth hung from ceiling.
- The environment is divided into clear areas for play and children can delineate.
- The environment feels organized—not cluttered.
- The environment contains features that encourage children to interact and develop relationships with each other.
- There are spaces at different levels, for example, platforms, lofts, and mats.

Teachers provide indoor and outdoor environments that provide a rich variety of activity choices, materials, and toys that respond to children's varying levels of development.
- Materials and toys are attractively displayed on shelves (not dumped into a toy box).
- Materials can be used in a variety of spaces in the environment.
- Materials and toys are in good shape, working, and are not broken or dirty.
- Materials and toys can be used by children who are at different developmental levels.
- Materials and toys encourage active exploration and play.
- Materials and toys are changed according to children's interests, while the majority of the toys remain to provide stability and consistency for the infant or toddler.

Environments support adults in interacting, supervising, and observing children.
- There are "camping" type chairs that allow teachers to sit on the floor with their backs supported.
- There are pillows and bolsters that allow teachers to lean comfortably against a wall while sitting on the floor.
- There are rocking chairs that allow teachers to sit comfortably and rock babies to sleep.

corners, nooks, cozy spaces, and special places, they can think about all of the opportunities for children to laugh and learn. All of the equipment and materials are not available at one time, but instead the teachers alternate materials based on the interests and developmental levels of the children. As a teacher sets up these areas, she can think about each child in her group and how that child might use these materials. Remember, play is the way for children to learn—and they will play, explore, experiment, eat, and rest if enticing spaces are created. The teacher is physically and emotionally available to promote children's emotional well-being, their feelings of safety, enduring relationships with adults and peers, and learning in all of the developmental domains.

Spaces invite, entice, and engage children. Table 13.3 describes a variety of spaces that could be created in an infant and toddler room in a center and adapted for a family child care home. Provide the equipment, toys, and opportunities based on children's individual interests and developmental level.

TABLE 13.3   Creating responsive spaces

A quiet space

- A quiet space away from active play (a cozy corner)
- A space with
  - a mat or layers of mats with a low mirror on the wall beside it
  - family photograph books, dolls and blankets, soft toys, quiet toys, puppets, and books
  - a nest
  - boxes large enough for child to crawl in and out

A nest provides a special place to nurture infants and toddlers.

Special places for nurturing children

- A comfortable space away from active play for teachers to sit on the floor (with back support) and hold a child
- A loft
- An adult-size couch
- A mat on the floor against the wall with firm pillows with washable covers
- A glider to rock and feed infants and toddlers

Spaces for delighting the senses

- Short tables for toddlers for play dough and other creative materials
- A space with
  - small tubs, other containers, or water tables with water for infants and toddlers (always monitor children very carefully with water—children have drowned in an inch of water in a container)
  - containers or tables for sand and other natural materials
  - a light table (see Reggio materials)
  - wading pools filled with different textured balls or other safe materials
  - a space to use feeling and sound boxes and bubbles with various sizes of wands
  - a sticky wall

Sand delights children of all ages.

(continued)

TABLE 13.3 Creating responsive spaces (Continued)

A space to use materials to create

- A space without carpet for painting on paper on the floor
- A space to use nontoxic paint; thick crayons; clay; play dough; large pieces of paper to tear, draw, and paint on; brushes; short easels
- A table for toddlers to use materials to create

A small table invites toddlers to draw.

A space for peek-a-boo and other social games

- A space made with a cloth hanging from ceiling with a mirror on the wall
- Boxes of various sizes with holes cut out of the sides—add cloth over the holes for variation and "peek-a-boo" games
- Lofts with a Plexiglas panel in the floor so children that are up can look down and children that are down can look up and enjoy one another

Create spaces for social opportunities.

A space for active play

- Floor space so that children can move freely with
  - balls of all sizes
  - couches to walk around and climb up on
  - ramps and short climbers to climb
  - rocking boats
  - tunnels to crawl through
  - mats at different levels for climbing
  - objects that can be moved such as child-size shopping carts, doll strollers, and riding toys
  - a bar fastened to the wall on various levels so that children can pull to stand
  - large empty appliance boxes with windows cut out of them and/or the end off of them so that children can crawl through the box

Mats at different levels provide a place for older infants and toddlers to climb.

A space for toys and other manipulatives

- Short shelves and space in front of shelves to play on the floor with
  - a child-size table and chairs for toddlers
  - toys that move, make noise, and change shape
  - toddler nesting blocks, ring towers, large beads, cause-and-effect and "take apart" toys, blocks, shape sorters
  - wooden animals, little houses, multiethnic play people, trucks and cars
  - small balls, blocks of various sizes, large pegs, large beads for stringing, puppets, puzzles, dolls, toy telephones
  - tubes of varying lengths and sizes

A puzzle with a handle on each piece is perfect for infants and toddlers.

TABLE 13.3   **Creating responsive spaces (Continued)**

A space to build and construct

- A platform for building
- Blocks of all sizes, shapes, and textures
- Wooden animals, little houses, play people, trucks and cars

A space for dramatic play with

- Mirrors, low pegs to hang clothing, scarves, purses, safe kitchen utensils, hats, pots and pans, containers of various sizes, dress-up clothes
- Multiethnic dolls, doll blankets, baby bottles, baby bed
- Puppets of varying sizes and shapes
- Child-size tables, stoves, sinks, refrigerators, pots and pans, dishes (for older toddlers)

Toddlers pretend with a child-size stove and sink.

A space for reading to children

- A special place that is designed for older infants and toddlers to choose books from an attractive, easily reached display and "read" or be read to in comfort
- Also place books around the room (any space is a great space for reading to a child)

This attractive book holder shows the covers of the books.

Feeding and eating spaces with

- Comfortable floor chairs for adults to feed infants sitting in their arms
- Gliders for feeding bottles to infants and younger toddlers
- Child-size chairs and tables for toddlers to eat
- A refrigerator
- A sink at children's level for toddlers
- An adult-size sink

Sleeping, diapering, and toileting spaces

- Sleeping
  - cribs for infants
  - cots or mats for toddlers
- Diapering
  - a diaper table with storage space
  - sturdy stairs with sides for toddlers to climb to diaper table
  - an adult-size sink
- Toileting
  - child-size toilets for toddlers who are learning to use the toilet
  - a child-size sink

Outdoor spaces with

- Open areas for large motor development
- An area for fine-motor play
- A shaded area to protect children from the sun and heat
- A comfortable area where children can look at books or teachers can read to children
- Areas with equipment that children can move around to create and problem-solve
- Areas that encourage social interaction such as a small climber

No space is marginal, no corner is unimportant, and each space needs to be alive, flexible, and open to change. (Malaguzzi)

How the space is organized, the equipment, and the materials all provide opportunities for relating and learning. As Greenman (5) states, "Teachers are sure to think about how to creatively use each corner in the room to entice and tempt babies to explore." Teachers also provide special opportunities for learning in each of the learning spaces.

 Watch this video of a toddler room, which shows different learning areas. Use Table 13.3 to evaluate the learning areas in this toddler room.

https://www.youtube.com/watch?v=isSgq1k4AhU

 Check Your Understanding 13.2
Click here to check your understanding of the concepts in this section.

Responsive Opportunities

Don't think in terms of activities; think in terms of each child's and the group's interests and levels of development. Think of providing opportunities for learning from which children choose—and then *respecting, reflecting,* and *relating* to children as they experience these opportunities.

It is not the quality of the object that holds a child's interest, but the opportunity it affords the child for action. (Torrence & Chattin-McNichols)

Teachers can buy many books full of activities and experiences for children. Some have experiences that are responsive and that provide a rich array of opportunities to entice infants and toddlers to explore, problem solve, and discover. Some, however, are much too structured for infants and toddlers and require enforced group time and products that are not appropriate for children so young. The questions in Figure 13.3 will guide you as you think about whether the opportunity is appropriate for the children in your group.

FIGURE 13.3   Choosing materials and opportunities

1. Does it meet one or more children's needs and strengths?
2. Does it provide for a variety of developmental levels (infants, younger and older toddlers)?
3. Is it safe? Durable? Washable? Nontoxic?
4. Does it support learning in a variety of developmental domains (motor, communication, thinking, social, emotional, and cultural)?
5. Does it spark the interest of a child or a number of children?
6. Does it support a child doing a number of different things with the toy or material (for example, with a ball a child may chew on it, bounce it, roll it, put it in a container, etc.)? A toy may lend itself to one response (such as a puzzle); however, a child could explore the toy in a variety of ways.
7. Does it support non-gender-biased, multicultural thinking, and nonviolent-prosocial behavior?
8. Can I use the materials or the activities by offering them as opportunities for children rather than a forced activity?
9. Can the material or experience be adapted for children with special needs?
10. Are vocabulary-rich, expansive interactions suggested?

Following is an example of how a teacher used the guidelines to decide whether an experience was appropriate for the children in her group:

> *Mara, a teacher in a room for children 18 months to 3-years-old, had several children in her room who loved to play with balls. She read about an experience that she might provide in her room in a book, Infant and Toddler Experiences, by Hast and Hollyfield (1999, p. 133). The experience entailed bringing balls of different textures, sizes, and qualities into the room as well as baskets or containers to put the balls in. The activity recommended that she fill the room with all of the balls and let the toddlers discover them. After thinking about the questions in Figure 13.3 she thought that she would try it. She decided, however, that instead of filling the room, she would place the balls and containers in the active area so that the children would not be overstimulated. For Tommy, who couldn't walk yet, she would place a small basket and small balls near him to explore with other children.*

Let's explore some wonderful opportunities (see Figure 13.4) for children that could be provided in the learning spaces. Not all of these experiences are available at one time and the environment, materials, and opportunities change in response to children's needs and interests. Teachers may *plan* for opportunities to occur in specific places, such as the ball experiences described previously in the active area or literacy experiences in the corner where books are available. Opportunities for creative activities with crayons or paints will likely take place in the creative arts learning area. However, we want to emphasize that most of the following opportunities can take place in *all* of the learning spaces described in Table 13.3—for example, opportunities for nurturing; social, prosocial, language, cognitive, and motor learning and development; delighting the senses, music, and learning about literacy and numeracy happen in *all* of the learning spaces. If teachers are *reflective* of the possibilities for learning in all of the areas, they will *respect* infants' and toddlers' choice of equipment, toys, and materials and will *relate* to children based on the opportunities for learning inherent in all of children's experiences (Petersen & Wittmer, 2013).

FIGURE 13.4   Opportunities for infants and toddlers

Quiet and calm opportunities
Nurturing opportunities
Social and prosocial opportunities, and opportunities for social experiences for and with
   children with disabilities
Language opportunities
Cognitive opportunities
Delighting-the-senses opportunities
Creative opportunities
Writing and drawing opportunities
Music, song, and creative movement opportunities
Numeracy, space, and shape opportunities
Opportunities for active play and motor development
Outdoor opportunities

Quiet and Calm Opportunities

Quiet spaces create opportunities for children to calm themselves; suck their thumbs; gather their energies; and rest alone, with another peer, or the teacher or a parent. These spaces have softness in them—quiet, visually pleasing toys, and firm pillows for older infants and toddlers. A large inner tube with a stiff blanket that covers the inner tube creates a nest inside which an infant or two can be placed or where a toddler can relax. Boxes on a side with firm, washable pillows in them for older infants and toddlers provide a place to hide away from the group, slow down, and unwind.

Nurturing Opportunities

Opportunities for children to experience nurturing can happen in many spaces and at many times throughout the day. Nurturing children is one of the most important roles of the infant or toddler teacher—for example, when a toddler falls and cries and an adult finds a Band-Aid (the magic cure). Examine a room. Are there places for teachers or parents to nurture their children? Quiet spaces may double as nurturing places, but rooms will also need gliders (that can't pinch little fingers), a stuffed chair, or a comfortable corner for two or three.

- Create areas where the adult and children can be cozy together and the teacher can hold and comfort children.
- Create comfortable areas where the adult can sit with his back supported— then infants and toddlers can sit close, lean on the adult, or plop on a lap.
- Create spaces where the teacher can see eye-to-eye with children.
- Provide a firm mat on the floor in front of a safety mirror hung low on the wall, so that infants, toddlers, and teachers can enjoy looking in the mirror, patting the images they see, singing songs to their reflections, and making faces at the faces looking back at them.
- Provide pictures of families that teachers laminate so that the children can carry them around.
- Provide peek-a-boo pictures of children and family members on a board with a piece of cloth over each one so children can lift up the cloth and see the picture.

Social and Prosocial Opportunities

As discussed in Chapter 7, infants and toddlers show great interest in peers very early in their lives. Teachers can support children's early interactions and developing friendships by

- Supporting infants' interest in each other by placing or sitting children near each other. For example, place infants close enough so they can touch each other.
- Providing long periods of play during which infants and toddlers can imitate, approach, follow, and try to engage other children.
- Sharing the strategies that infants and toddlers use to engage others. Continually document through pictures or video how young children enjoy each other. Share the information with parents. Encourage parents to share their pictures and examples of their child's interest in other children. See Box 13.2 for an

example of how a teacher might plan for a child based on a photograph of a social interaction.

- Setting up learning areas for several children—for example, a box for one or two or more, a small couch, and a nook under the loft.
- Providing two or more of each favorite toy or similar toys so that children can enjoy them together. Sometimes the best "friendships" develop for toddlers when each has her own materials and can easily see and interact with one other child.
- Using large motor equipment that promotes social play, such as a climber or a rocking boat. Conflict between peers occurs less often with large pieces of equipment than with small toys (although those are necessary as well).
- Providing places for infants and toddlers to have alone time to promote emotional and social development. Private spaces, such as a box on its side that one toddler can fit into, allow for **emotional refueling**. Too much togetherness, and no opportunity for alone time, *for some infants and toddlers* can contribute to their feelings of stress.

Language Opportunities

Teachers of infants and toddlers play a significant role in facilitating their language development. Each interaction and experience that the child has with teachers and peers provides opportunities for children's language to blossom. Review the 12 strategies for language learning in Chapter 9 and use them often throughout the day. As a child climbs on the climber, you can use parallel talk and say, "You are climbing up. Now you are climbing down." When you are responding to an infant's or toddler's sounds or words, you can elaborate and expand the child's language. When a child climbs into your lap, you can ask him how he is feeling today. An astute teacher doesn't bombard children with comments and questions but rather uses responsive talk and turn-taking strategies at all times so that infants and toddlers experience the joy of communicating.

Miller (6) describes materials that teachers can add to the environment to encourage language development and communication between children. Large, empty gift-wrap tubes provide opportunities for children to experiment with how their voices sound different when they talk through the tube. Toddlers will use pretend phones to "talk" to Mommy, Daddy, or Grandma. Picture cards of favorite people, animals, toys, and babies that teachers laminate and place in a box provide opportunities for children to name the pictures. Miller suggests putting a different object in a hinged box each day to provide an opportunity for naming and conversing about the "surprise" object.

Cognitive Opportunities

Cognitive activities occur every day at all times. With cognitive development, the environment, toys, and materials facilitate children's development of the learning sparkle. The materials in the environment and the adult-child interactions will facilitate each child's sense of wonder, joy, interest, and discovery in all areas of

BOX 13.2

Day to Day, the Relationship Way

Individual Child Planning Guide

Child's name: <u>Brogan</u>

Plans for week of (date): <u>Sept. 7–11, 2016</u>

Person(s) completing the guide: <u>Denmon</u>

Respect: Child's emotions, effort, goals, learning, and relationships

Write an observation or use a picture or other documentation here—date all notes:

Pearson Education

Respect and Reflect

9/7/16

What am I doing?
I was crawling through the tunnel and now I am peering out . . . seeing what the world looks like on this side of the tunnel.

How am I feeling?
I am enjoying playing and moving my muscles.

What am I learning?
Emotional
- I am learning how to focus (self-regulation).
Social
- I'm learning how to lead a friend through the tunnel.
Cognitive
- I am learning about spatial concepts like "in" and "out" and "through."
- I am learning about cause and effect (I can do something that will have an effect).
Language
- My teacher said to me: "Look, you crawled through the tunnel."
Motor
- I am learning to use my large muscles and maintaining balance.

Relate

What will you do to support my development and learning?
Responsive interactions
- We will continue to provide a long play time during the day to provide an opportunity for peer play and self-mastery.
Environment, toys, materials, and experiences
- We will bring in more challenging cause-and-effect toys to enjoy with friends.
- We will continue to provide more objects and play equipment for you and your friends to explore spatial concepts such as "through," "over," and "under."
- We will document the children's understanding and exploration of spatial concepts.

the room. It is this sense of wonder that leads to learning and the love of learning.

Provide toys that adapt to changes in the child's development. For example, a stacking toy can usually be chewed and examined and passed from hand to hand by an infant. It can also be stacked, at first incorrectly and then correctly (after much experimentation) by a toddler. The toy hasn't changed, but the way that the child plays with the toy has changed. This toy is adaptable and can be used by children who are at different developmental stages in their ability to play with this toy and

Pearson Education

by the same child as he develops. Adults also provide opportunities for children to develop the foundations for learning discussed in Chapter 8 through the materials that they provide and their responsive interactions.

Infants and toddlers gain confidence in their ability to initiate, be intentional, persist at tasks, and problem solve when they are given opportunities to discover what they can do with toys and materials. This may include tasting, sucking, banging together, tapping, moving, dumping, building, and tasting again. To help them gain confidence and the desire to problem solve give them many opportunities to succeed by providing materials that interest them and that are at or slightly above their developmental level.

Long periods of exploration time are important for infants and toddlers to investigate toys and materials and have time to be intentional and problem solve.

Toddlers often gravitate toward different and interesting materials, such as using crayons with corrugated cardboard—two materials that often aren't used together. The cardboard provides a challenge that sparks the child's problem solving and initiation. Toddlers like surprises. Provide a container with a hole in the bottom or a slotted spoon in the water table, a solid block in with the stacking rings, or a toy that doesn't make music with a small basket of musical toys. Toddlers enjoy and are surprised by contact paper with the sticky side up. Tape it to a wall or the floor. Place toys, feathers, and other material nearby so that toddlers can experiment with placing and removing items on the paper. These materials create a sense of wonder in young children.

Also, create and share the "wow" moments with infants and toddlers. Create and look for the moments when an infant seems puzzled by a wobbly toy or when a toddler has the look of surprise when she discovers how balls sound different from blocks as they are dumped from a basket. Share those wow moments with your own surprised looks to build an emotional feeling of excitement about learning. When teachers support children's curiosity they support children's desire and confidence to learn. They also build positive relationships with the children.

Delighting-the-Senses Experiences

Infants and toddlers are using all of their senses—hearing, seeing, feeling, tasting, and smelling—in all areas of the room. When children delight their senses, they are learning about object permanence, cause and effect, and attributes of objects and materials. With a responsive teacher and peers, infants' and toddlers' language development grows by leaps and bounds. As they play with sand and water, they are also developing their small motor skills.

Sand provides a delightful sensory experience. Sand in a short sand/water table indoors and outdoors encourages toddlers to feel the texture, pour sand through their fingers, and experiment with filling and emptying cups and other containers. Waterwheels, funnels, sifters, containers of different sizes, and plastic animals encourage toddlers to experiment. Create a sandbox beach inside for toddlers, with a small swimming pool full of sand, safe low beach chairs, large plastic sunglasses, beach towels, and magazines.

Provide water in a variety of containers for toddlers (always watch carefully to prevent drowning). (In Box 13.3, Vernon [7] provides a wonderful example of how toddlers enjoyed water in her program.) Provide small basins of water or short water tables for toddlers. Add different materials each day or week to encourage exploration. Refill the containers of water often to reduce the spread of infection. Water tables have drains on the bottom for ease of emptying. Squeeze bottles and paintbrushes encourage toddlers to use water outdoors to "paint" a fence.

Provide infants with materials of different textures to touch. Feely bags (cloth or paper bags) with different objects in them delight older infants and toddlers as they cautiously put their hands in the bags.

BOX 13.3

Sink Play

When it is too cold for water play outside, we invite the children to immerse themselves in water at the sinks [standing, with only diapers on, in front of low sinks filled partially with water and toys]. I always find it interesting to observe the different ways children play even while standing right next to each other. Kevin and Trent stood side by side, each engrossed in his own task. Trent concentrated intently on filling the large bucket and carefully pouring it out again into the sink. He poured water on a single washcloth and then would hold it up and watch the water drip steadily down into the sink.

Kevin was interested in filling many small containers with water and then pouring them into each other. He also used a bottle with a squeeze-lid to spray the water into the containers. He used the bottle to "feed" his baby doll and also to wash the baby's hair. He experimented by filling a container to the top, pushing his hands and arms into the container, and watching the water pour out.

The children were using many words to describe what they were doing: "pour," "top," "wash baby," "water," "my baby," "mine." Not only do the children enjoy playing in the water, it also seems to soothe them, and they learn many things about their world. They also learn about such concepts as cause and effect, size, shape, and quantity. And, they get to share a pleasurable experience with their classmates and learn from each other.

Source: Vernon, F. (2003, Spring). Sink play. *Focus on Infants and Toddlers, 15*(1), 5. © 2003 ACEI

Provide materials of different textures for infants and toddlers to explore.

Think about how to offer opportunities for children to explore with their other senses in addition to touch. Make listening boxes by placing different items in each box (be sure to tape them up well). Stop and have the children listen when there is a new noise. Use "loud," "soft," "noisy," and "quiet" and other descriptive words to enhance language development while exploring sound. Provide visually pleasing materials such as bottles (again, taped closed very carefully) with oil and food coloring combined in them.

Pearson Education

> Serena was excited. She hurried over to the paints and large pieces of paper that the teacher had placed carefully on the low table. Serena's teacher helped her put her smock over her head and then adjust it, Serena grasped a wide-handled paintbrush in a hammer grip, dipped the brush part into the short-side containers of paint, lifted the brush, and watched as the beautiful yellow paint dripped off the end. As she started to move the pretty paintbrush toward her mouth to taste it, the teacher said, "Here, put the paint on this paper," and helped guide Serena's hand toward the paper on the table. Serena was fascinated by the yellow mark that appeared.

Creative Opportunities

Infants and toddlers love to create—make messes, invent new sounds, make a toy move in a surprising way, or put two or more items together in an innovative manner. When watching young children, adults can see the joy and wonder expressed when toddlers make marks on paper with crayons or when they glue two pieces of wood together. When young children are making messes, dumping, mushing, exploring, discovering, inventing, collecting, imagining, observing, and playing with materials, they are creating.

Being a creative person begins in infancy. An infant reaches out to touch his parent's face, the parent's eyes open wide in delight, and the infant has created an emotional connection. The infant squeezes a toy and creates a funny, squeaky noise. She plays with her mouth and creates new sounds. He bats at a musical toy and creates a beautiful tune. A young toddler, who is just beginning to walk, creates a stir as adults marvel at this new development. Toddlers throw toys into a box and create crashing noises. They place one block beside another and begin to create a row. One day they stack a block on top of another and create a tower. A toddler will accidently stick his finger into the neck of an empty water bottle and create a new toy that waves around when he moves his finger. Turning the pages of a cardboard book creates a new scene to enjoy.

Display children's open-ended art on the wall.

Pearson Education

Colorful marks made with crayons and nontoxic paints are masterpieces to a toddler budding artist. Groups of toddlers with colorful scarves create a kaleidoscope of colors. As infants and toddlers create in this way they learn that they can produce, build, generate new ideas, and construct—all aspects of being a creative person. They also develop a healthy sense of mastery; a positive self-concept; and a feeling of being effective, capable, and competent.

Honig (8) notes "working with art materials gives sensory joy to toddlers as they knead play dough or watch in awe as cornstarch goop stretches in their fingers" (p. 22). Creative, sensory, open-ended materials engage children and often reduce stress. Open-ended materials are those that allow the child to use them in a variety of ways. Teachers make the materials available and young children experiment rather than try to make a product. The process of feeling, pouring, dumping, lifting, examining, turning over, and testing is what is important for very young children—not the end product.

Offer play dough and clay, then stay close and watch the wonderful exploration and investigation that occurs. As they delight their senses, children are learning about the composition of materials and how to shape and reshape them, number, quantity, and mass. All of these activities provide perfect opportunities for teachers to support the language development of infants and toddlers. Toddlers are also learning social skills as they negotiate space and share the materials.

Create a corner where children play with play dough on the floor or on a short table. Place separate piles of play dough on the table or provide one large ball of play dough in the middle of the table. If the materials are available for lengthy periods of time and almost every day, infants and toddlers will relax as they trust that the materials will be available and have time to test their theories about how the material works.

Young children enjoy painting. Nontoxic paint that is especially made for young children and purchased through catalogs or in a teacher supply store can be offered to toddlers with large pieces of paper on a table or on the floor. Toddlers can use their hands or large paintbrushes with the paint to test their theories on how to make a mark on a page. Short easels for toddlers spark their creativity with crayons and paint. Smocks (aprons) can be purchased to cover toddlers' clothing if parents or the children are concerned about getting paint on their clothes. Toddlers can learn to go get their smocks before they begin to paint but often need help from a teachers or peer to get them on correctly.

Ditto sheets to color or requiring toddlers to create products such as egg carton caterpillars are not appropriate tasks for toddlers because they stifle creativity. Toddlers are *making something happen* rather than *making something*. Be open to all of the possibilities for what children do with the materials. Materials should always be offered as a choice, and children should not ever be forced to touch or play with them. Let them wash their hands as soon as they would like, to build enjoyment in the experience of being creative.

Writing and Drawing Opportunities

Infants and toddlers make their mark on the world through drawing with nontoxic crayons, magnetic boards with an attached large pen, and markers (without the lids, which are a choking hazard). Toddlers like Dawson (as shown in Box 13.4) grasp the big pen with an overhand grasp, using the large muscles in his arm to make big circles on the paper. Infants will bang or jab their crayon on the paper, but soon they will make lines. Vertical lines usually appear before horizontal lines. Dawson has had quite a bit of experience using crayons and other writing materials, so he is already making circles with his pen on his magnetic board.

Provide comfortable small chairs, such as Dawson is using, or create a learning area with a small table where toddlers can use nontoxic crayons and large pieces of blank paper. Opportunities to use crayons on sandpaper and other unusual materials, chalk outside, and finger painting spark a toddler's interest in writing and drawing. Infants and toddlers who have experience with writing tools have better school readiness skills in handwriting in kindergarten.

Opportunities with Blocks

Blocks may be small or large, plastic or wooden, of various sizes and shapes. Hirsch (1996) has identified six stages of block development: carrying, stacking and placing in rows, bridging, building enclosures, creating patterns, and representational play (9). An infant will mouth the blocks, a younger toddler will carry them around and begin to explore their properties, and many toddlers will begin to stack them one on top of the other. Soon rows of blocks will appear, and then varying forms of bridges. You may see a toddler creating an enclosure with blocks on all sides to contain a zoo full of wooden animals. Patterns may appear—for example, a toddler may use four blocks of the same size to support a large unit block. Toward the end of the toddler period, children may begin to use the blocks as **symbols** for another object, such as a firefighter's hose, and may begin to pretend—for example, to be a firefighter.

Blocks provide opportunities for learning at all ages and provide opportunities to support development in all domains. As infants and toddlers manipulate the blocks and then play with them in a purposeful way, they are developing self-regulation. Playing with blocks is often a social experience and provides opportunities for children to learn to play together and resolve conflicts. Creativity blossoms as toddlers build with blocks. Toddlers will also knock down a block tower that they have built to create a noise and to create a mess. Knocking down blocks, as well as building with them, is about learning about the properties of materials. They are also using many problem-solving strategies, as described in the following example:

Sam, 2, discovered that another child had built a bridge out of three blocks and had placed it on the floor in the block area. He found a toy car and pushed it under the bridge. The bridge came tumbling down because the car was too big. Sam looked around and found a smaller car. He picked up the blocks and stacked them one on top of the other but soon realized that his blocks did not have a space under them. He experimented with making bridges until his little toy car fit under the bridge. Sam had figured it out.

BOX 13.4

Day to Day, the Relationship Way

Individual Child Planning Guide

Child's name: <u>Dawson</u>

Plans for week of (date): <u>Sept. 7–11, 2016</u>

Person(s) completing the guide: <u>Torren and Nicole</u>

Respect: Child's Emotions, Effort, Goals, Learning, and Relationships

Write an observation or use a picture or other documentation here—date all notes:

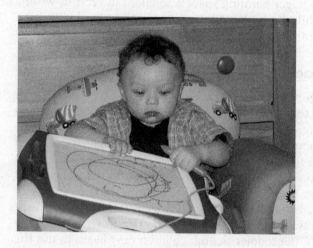

Respect and Reflect

9/7/16

What am I doing?
I am making large circles on a magnetic board. I am holding the large attached pen with my left hand and holding the board with my right. This is called holding and operating. I am using an overhand grasp, which is typical for my age and allows me to use the large muscles in my arm to draw.

How am I feeling?
I am feeling very focused. I am intent on what I am doing.

What am I learning?
I am learning how to use the large muscles in my arms and the small muscles in my hands to write and to create. I am learning to focus and attend when I want to accomplish something. I am learning, "I can do it," and I am learning about cause and effect.

Relate

What will you do to support my development and learning?

Responsive interactions
We will talk with your parents about how much you enjoyed this experience and we will ask them what you like to do at home. We will use words to describe what you are doing (parallel talk).

Environment, toys, materials, and experiences
We will provide other creative experiences such as play dough, finger paints, and crayons as well as other "cause and effect" toys.

When an older toddler pretends to build a house, a fence around a pretend playground, or a birthday cake, he is building a foundation for literacy development. Stroud (10) identifies ways that block play supports success in literacy development:

Block areas invite young children to have fun as they learn many spatial concepts.

Pearson Education

1. Children learn about **representation** and symbols as they pretend with blocks and block structures. When children begin to reproduce and name their buildings, for example, block building becomes representational and serves as an introduction to symbolization: "The blocks themselves become symbols for other objects, just as printed letters and words are symbols for objects and ideas" (p. 9).

2. **Visual discrimination**—a skill necessary for distinguishing similar letter and word formations during the reading process—is enhanced by block play. Children are continually looking at, comparing, and matching blocks of varying shapes and sizes. Cleanup provides another opportunity to sort and return blocks to a labeled position on storage shelves.

3. Fine-motor strength and coordination used for writing are developed with blocks. Writing skills needed to manipulate crayons and pencils are developed through grasping, carrying, and stacking blocks.

4. Oral language develops as young children label the toys as "blocks," describe them, and talk about them with others.

Stroud also recommends adding books and writing materials to the block area to encourage literacy experiences.

Children's receptive and expressive language develops as adults and peers name the blocks, describe their attributes, and talk about spatial concepts. An adult says, "You put the red block on the blue block" and then waits for the infant or toddler to respond with a sound, a gesture, an action, or words. The adult listens for these language expressions and responds by observing, imitating, expanding, elaborating, or extending the child's language.

Motor capacities develop as toddlers handle the blocks with their hands (small motor), pick up blocks and carry them around (large motor), and explore how they feel and listen to how they sound when they fall (sensory development).

When infants and toddlers play with blocks of all sizes and shapes, create a learning area where blocks and materials are displayed and easy for children to reach. Children need room for floor play with the blocks. Place blocks on a low shelf with each shelf clearly labeled. As almost 3-year-olds "clean up" after playtime, they learn to classify as they replace the blocks on the shelves in their designated places. Add responsive teachers and the possibilities for learning in all of the developmental domains is endless.

Music, Song, and Creative Movement Opportunities

> *Sarah, just a year old, laughed as her teacher played pat-a-cake with her. As her teacher began singing the song, Sarah clapped her hands together repeatedly with delight. After the song ended, Sarah's teacher pointed to Sarah's hands with delight and said, "You clapped your hands." Sarah looked joyfully at the teacher as if to say, "Do it again."*

While playing with Jamika, her teacher sings, "You have ten little *fingers*, and ten little *toes*, two little *arms*, and one little *nose*." As her teacher touches her fingers, her toes, her arms, and her nose, Jamika wriggles in delight at hearing this familiar tune. Soon Jamika will start chiming in with her teacher as she sings this song.

Teachers can sing songs throughout the day. A good-morning song helps infants and toddlers transition from home to a caring program. A good-bye song signals that a parent is here to pick up his child. Songs sung throughout the day comfort children or help them transition from one activity to another, such as from indoor play to outdoor play. As Jamika waits for her mom and dad at the end of the day, one teacher sings to Jamika, modeling how to clap and tap: "Two little hands go clap, clap, clap. Two little feet go tap, tap, tap." Soon, several toddlers are sitting with the teacher. Jamika watches her friends intently as they clap and tap in all different and unique ways. These familiar activities are opportunities for young children to enjoy music and learn concepts in fun, responsive, sensitive ways. Teachers don't have to have the best singing voices in the world to sing to infants and toddlers. Infants and toddlers love to hear songs and it doesn't matter to them how a teacher sings them—children love the warm feelings that are conveyed. There are many benefits to children of singing, listening to music, making rhythms, and moving their bodies. These experiences

- Provide opportunities for pure joy
- Provide opportunities to move, practice crawling, pull to stand, jump, run, experience rhythms, and feel comfortable with their bodies in space
- Increase self-awareness and worth
- Provide opportunities for children to learn concepts such as "up" and "down"
- Provide opportunities for children to interact and learn prosocial behavior
- Help children make transitions and make routines and learning times fun
- Provide opportunities for children to learn words and longer sentences in their own and other languages
- Encourage children to listen and follow directions
- Encourage creativity and problem solving
- Provide opportunities for representational and symbolic play—for example, when toddlers sing "Twinkle, Twinkle, Little Star" they use their hands to represent stars
- Comfort and soothe children and help them fall asleep

Literacy Opportunities

Literacy experiences are among the most important that a teacher can provide to young children. What is literacy? How does it develop? What is the relationship between talking, social experiences, and learning to read and write? Literacy is learning that writing and reading are ways of making, understanding, and communicating meaning.

Becoming literate is about learning to read and write—and *becoming* begins in infancy when an infant hears the sounds of language and begins to make sounds herself.

Many people believe that children learn to read and write in kindergarten or first grade; however, the foundation for literacy skills is laid years before children enter school. Emergent literacy, much like any other cognitive skill, begins at birth. During the early years, children develop competency in language and literacy not through a set curriculum, but through interactions and experiences with the adults around them (11, p. 9).

Language is a strong bridge that connects to later reading and writing because infants and toddlers learn how to communicate—the ultimate purpose of reading and writing. Play is a necessary bridge—playing with sounds and words, and making marks on a page. Learning about symbols is also a connecting bridge to literacy as toddlers learn that a picture or an object (a plastic apple) can represent something real that is seen and touched. This leads to a later understanding that squiggly lines called letters have meaning. Experiences with water, sand, toys, animals, and people are essential bridges to literacy. With these types of experiences children can understand what is read, and when they are older, they can write stories based on their many rich understandings. And certainly, one of the most important bridges to becoming literate is the love of books. This is a foundational bridge that provides a link to later reading and writing. Positive relationships with special adults and peers are the supports that strengthen the bridges to literacy.

Learning to Love Books

> Ezra, 26 months old, snuggles against his teacher's arm as she reads a book to him and two other toddlers who are sitting together on the floor. He likes turning the brightly colored pages with the pictures of familiar toys. He especially likes to hear his teacher's animated voice as she reads the story aloud. Ezra loves books and often finds books in the room and runs to his teacher holding out the book for her to read.

Most young infants adore looking at visually interesting images found in books. They tune into the reader's voice and learn about the rhythms, tones, and sounds of language. Nursery rhymes and poetry can soothe a baby with their reassuringly rhythmic sounds. Books with one word and picture on a page spark an infant's interest as the adult "reads" the pictures. Cloth and soft vinyl books allow infants to grasp, chew, suck, and crinkle books as they learn through all their senses. Sitting in a teacher's lap is the perfect way for an infant to see the pictures and enjoy a fun, colorful book.

Toddlers love to look at books as they sit, walk, and toddle around. For both younger and older toddlers, books are playthings that can be touched and turned, and they reveal a world of surprises with every flip of the page. Because toddlers are absorbing language and learning new words every day, they're beginning to relate the pictures in books to objects in real life. A book about toys or animals is a great choice for this age group. Choose short books with simple stories. Books made of heavy cardboard allow toddlers to use newly developed motor skills to turn pages.

Toddlers love stories about familiar animals, objects, and people. Pictures with a few printed words on every page can keep a busy toddler's attention as she points to the pictures and asks, "What's that?" Interactive pop-up books, with their hidden surprises, trigger grins of delight from curious toddlers.

Allow toddlers to choose from books displayed on shelves with the cover showing—rather than thrown in a box, where they're hard to identify. Even toddlers are beginning to learn how books work: that you start at the front and read from top to bottom, that the story is usually about the picture, and that some of those strange squiggles sound the same each time an adult reads it.

Here are some ways you can help infants and toddlers have fun with and learn to love books:

- *Create "reading" corners.* Equip these corners and nooks with a small, soft-covered mattress, with a cover you can easily clean, and for toddlers a short couch just their size. Make sure that the corner is comfortable for teachers to lie on their backs while holding up a book with a baby by their side, who is looking up as well. Or, create a place where teachers can sit with their backs supported by the wall or camping chair. Toddlers will enjoy looking at books together.
- *Place books around the room.* That way, they greet and tempt a child at every turn. Be creative. Putting a book about bears right next to a stuffed bear makes that book hard to resist!
- *Read throughout the day.* Infants can look and listen when teachers hold them in their comfortable laps. Toddlers like one-on-one time with a teacher as well, but also enjoy clustering together around a favorite teacher on a couch, in a cozy corner, or wherever books are in the room. Take your cues from the children and read whenever they ask you. Instead of having a structured reading time for toddlers, teachers can entice them to listen to a story by sitting down where toddlers can join together. Don't be surprised if other toddlers come running to hear the story as well. Let them come and go—they will soon learn to sit for a whole story. When toddlers are forced to sit in groups to listen to a story, they often become disinterested quickly and their love of books can be jeopardized. Toddlers learn to love books when they are shared with an adult who makes them feel safe, loved, excited, soothed, or important, depending on the child's need at the time.
- *Choose books carefully.* Cloth and heavy cardboard books (sometimes called board books) are sturdy and can be transported, carted, stashed, put in containers, and "read" by curious infants and energetic toddlers. Choose books with rhythmical language, touch-and-smell books, and books with clear pictures. Select books with pictures of children and families from a variety of cultures and books that show both boys and girls in a variety of activities.
- *Read responsively.* Notice which pictures children seem to enjoy, point to them, name them, and when possible, point out the real objects they represent. Interact with children as you read the story and encourage their engagement. Encourage infants to make sounds and toddlers to discuss their experiences as you read a story. Answer their questions. Avoid pestering children with too many one-right-answer questions such as "What's this?" and "Who's that?" Have fun reading, use lots of feeling, exaggerate sounds, and wait for infants and toddlers to respond with their own sounds, words, and gestures.
- *Exchange information with families through home visits, book bags to borrow, and information about the importance of reading as well as how to read to infants and toddlers.* The ZERO TO THREE Web site (zerotothree.org) and the National Center for Family Literacy (NCFL) Web site (famlit.org) provide tip sheets, activities, and research related to supporting families. Ask families what books their infants

and toddlers like at home and what secrets they have for sparking their children's interest in books.

- *Provide a literacy-rich environment.* Books and printed words should be found in all parts of an infant or toddler room. Make photograph albums of family members, friends, and pets available with the name of the pet, for example, written at the bottom of the page. Add their names and photos to their cubbies. Rather than quiz children, comment with excitement when a child is looking at a word.

Math, Space, and Shape Opportunities

All of the materials in an infant-toddler room or home offer opportunities for learning about numerals (the symbols that represent numbers, such as the numeral 2) and numbers (the concept of amount—there are two blocks) as well as other math concepts. As an infant holds one block in one hand and another block in another and looks back and forth from one to the other, he is learning about numbers. He is learning that he now has more blocks than he did before when he was holding one block. "More" becomes evident as the infant feels what two are like compared to one.

Teachers and parents can nurture infants' and toddlers' understanding of mathematical concepts (12). An adult's role is to set up a rich menu of math opportunities for young children. Teachers then support children's interest and exploration through math interactions. Teachers and parents can promote children's ability to process information—how to think.

To support mathematical understanding, toddlers are not given worksheets and they are not drilled in their numbers and shapes by adults. Rather, possibilities for learning about math concepts in a play environment are found everywhere that children go and in many interactions that occur daily with teachers. Adults who are knowledgeable about mathematical concepts see the possibilities for supporting mathematical understanding every day in relaxed and informal ways. Teachers take advantage of playful moments and the environment to help young children learn. Here each concept is defined and a list of materials and interactions that promote mathematical understanding are described. Understand though, that most materials and interactions have the possibility of promoting many concepts—for example, a finger-play with a toddler (such as "Round and round the garden, like a teddy bear, one step, two steps, tickle you under there") uses concepts of shape (round and round the garden) and counting (one step, two steps), as well as builds relationships. (Use your finger to trace a circle around and around the palm of a young child's hand. Walk your fingers up the baby's arm as you say "one step, two steps" and then if the baby is enjoying the finger-play, gently tickle the baby under the arm. Wait at least 5 seconds to see if the baby puts out her hand for another turn. If so, repeat the finger-play. If not, try again another time.)

Opportunities for Learning About Counting

Infants and toddlers learn to count in myriad ways if the adults in their lives are aware of the many daily opportunities for counting. *Model* counting during play as you point to and count children, toys, and books. For toddlers, start counting "1" and then point to the next item and wait to see if the toddler counts the next item. If not, continue modeling in a warm tone of voice. Routines provide opportunities as adults count children's fingers and toes in playful and responsive ways.

Snack time provides many opportunities for counting pieces of food, cups, plates, and silverware. Once adults are aware that it is important that they model counting for children, then they will see many opportunities during the day to count. As always, count when the infant or toddler seems receptive and the counting doesn't interfere with a goal that the child is attempting to achieve, such as carefully stacking blocks.

Opportunities for Learning About One-to-One Correspondence

One-to-one correspondence occurs as babies begin to understand that there is a number for each item that is counted. Provide an environment that contains a variety of objects that work together in a one-to-one relationship: cars and garages, containers with lids, and dolls with beds. Provide opportunities for toddlers to put the plates on the table for a snack or meal—one for each child in the group or one for each member of the family. You can say, "One plate for Daddy, one plate for Mommy, and one plate for you," as you point to the plates.

Opportunities for Learning How to Classify

Infants and toddlers are also learning concepts about classifying people and objects. Classification is a concept that describes a child's actions of comparing similarities and differences, sorting by various attributes, putting objects into different categories, and arranging objects by various characteristics. Infants, for example, begin to categorize which adults are friendly and which aren't. Older infants and toddlers try to figure out which items make a noise when shaken or which items roll. Use responsive planning to provide the child with objects that make noise and objects that don't to encourage further discoveries. Table 13.4 includes a number of opportunities that teachers can provide to encourage infants' and toddlers' exploration of classification, spatial relationships and shapes, quantity, patterning, and seriation.

Opportunities for Active Play and Motor Development

Opportunities for active play and motor development include large motor and fine motor/ manipulatives.

Large Motor

Provide spaces for infants and toddlers where they can use their large muscles to crawl, pull to stand, stand, walk, climb, toddle, and run. They will need space away from the quiet, nurturing, and creative areas. The equipment in this indoor area usually includes mats stacked to create different levels, a rocking boat, a short climber, a large tube to climb through, or a few steps to a loft area. These large pieces of equipment promote social as well as motor development. For small spaces, these pieces of equipment can be shared with other homebases in centers and teachers can alternate these exciting opportunities.

At various times, depending on the interests and needs of the children, balls of various sizes and shapes, large containers and boxes, push and pull toys, small "grocery" carts, riding toys, wagons, and blankets with toys on them for pulling can be introduced. Miller (13) describes large-muscle motor opportunities; for example, place large boxes with the ends cut out end to end and cover them with blankets to create box tunnels. Punch a hole in the ends of shoeboxes and tie them together, end to end, to make a little train. Leave a string about 10 inches long on one end so that the child can pull the train. Children

TABLE 13.4   Learning opportunities: Sorting, numeracy, space, and shape

Opportunities to learn about classification (sorting)
- Compare objects—point out similarities and differences in color, shape, and size.
- Provide an environment that includes a variety of manipulatives (parquetry blocks, unit cubes), collections (rocks too big to swallow, plastic animals), dramatic play props (variety of clothing, dishes, dolls), and art materials (fabric samples) in different colors, shapes, and sizes to offer classifying and sorting experiences throughout the day.
- Provide opportunities for children to assemble collections (walk to the park to collect pinecones or fallen leaves) and talk about why the children sort, classify, and order objects in a certain way.
- Use language and point out similarities and differences in, for example, toys and blocks, as toddlers put them on the shelf during cleanup time.
- Compare collections one-to-one to determine "more," "less," and "same as."
- Provide opportunities for toddlers to sort objects according to two characteristics at the same time (big red, small red, big yellow, small yellow). Understand, though that this is challenging for toddlers.

Opportunities to learn about spatial relationships and shapes
- Provide opportunities for infants and toddlers to explore spatial relations (next to, above, below, inside, outside) during the day. You can say as you point, "Sarah is sitting *next to* Amanda." "Oh, you're putting the block *in* the basket." "Put the puzzles on the shelf *above* the blocks."
- Provide opportunities for children to build complex 2-dimensional and 3-dimensional shapes by putting simple shapes together (pattern blocks, tangrams, unit blocks).

Opportunities to learn about quantity
- Provide different sizes of containers during water and sand play.
- Provide opportunities for infants and toddlers to experiment with full and empty.

Opportunities to learn about patterning
- Provide opportunities for children to notice patterns (visual pattern in bricks in the sidewalk, auditory pattern in the melodies of music, repetitive language of predictable stories, physical patterns in exercise).

Opportunities to learn about seriation (ordering by one or more dimensions)
- Provide materials for toddlers to explore seriating (various sized cups in water table to sort by size, paint-chip samples to seriate by color hue, fabric squares to sort by texture from softest to least soft).
- Use terms such as *short*, *tall*, *high*, *low*, *wide*, *thin* to compare objects.

will place various toys from around the room into the boxes to give them a little ride. These open-ended materials (no one correct way to use them) provide numerous opportunities for infants and toddlers to problem solve and explore their multiple uses.

Fine Motor and Manipulative Opportunities

Provide spaces for infants and toddlers where they can use their large muscles to crawl, pull to stand, stand alone, walk, climb, toddle, and run. They will need space away from the quiet, nurturing, and creative areas. The equipment in this indoor area usually includes mats stacked to create different levels, a rocking boat, a short climber, a large tube to climb through, or a few steps to a loft area. These large pieces of equipment promote social as well as motor development. For small spaces, these pieces of equipment can be shared with other homerooms in centers and teachers can alternate these exciting opportunities.

Outdoor Opportunities

> Joshua looked with anticipation at his teacher when she announced, "Time to go outside."
> This was the time of day that Joshua seemed to like best. When the door to the outside
> opened, Joshua was the first to toddle outside. He put his face to the sun and then scurried to
> the sandbox to bury his hands deep into the cool sand. It was all his teacher could do to keep
> up with him as she carried a big box of sand toys to the area.

Outdoor time brings opportunities for infants and toddlers to poke and dig in the
sand and dirt, push and pull wagons, touch everything in sight, and feel the soft
breezes on their faces. They savor the scent of flowering trees, learn new outside
vocabulary, and gain a sparkle in their eyes from invigorating and challenging
physical experiences such as walking in sand and climbing over safe obstacles.

Outdoor time also brings challenges for teachers as they strive to provide
interesting and exciting experiences for infants and toddlers, allow them to
explore with all of their senses, and yet provide a sense of security and safety that
infants and toddlers need so much, indoors or outdoors (see Table 13.5).

TABLE 13.5 Security and safety issues for outdoor time

Age	Activities (Delighting the Senses)	Security and Safety Issues
Birth–12 months (infants)		
During this age period infants will begin to turn over, then roll, and crawl.	Place infants on a soft blanket to allow them to practice their physical skills.	Young infants need to know that their special teacher is near and nurturing.
Fine motor skills improve and soon everything in sight, including grass and bugs, may go to the mouth.	Bring each infant's manipulatives outside. Small plastic swimming pools in the shade (without water in them) provide a separate and safe place for young infants.	Infants need particular care when outdoors to protect them from the sun and extreme temperatures.
	Continue activities like "reading" picture books, repeating sounds, and providing responsive toys.	
12–18 months (young toddlers)		
Crawling, toddling, and running are skills that may emerge during this period. Walking backward and climbing up and down a low set of stairs are challenging tasks for this age.	Provide equipment that is safe for cruising infants to pull themselves up on and walk around. Gather push-and-pull toys such as small trikes and wagons for the walking crowd. Balls and stacking toys are great outdoors as well as inside.	Children tire easily and need a lap to sink into to regroup and gain energy for the next physical tasks. "Watching them like a hawk" has special meaning at this age to prevent unwanted and unknown objects from finding their way to the mouth.
Small motor skills improve greatly during this period. Many very small and large items go straight to the mouth.	Fill small plastic pools with balls or safe manipulatives.	

TABLE 13.5   **Security and safety issues for outdoor time (Continued)**

Age	Activities (Delighting the Senses)	Security and Safety Issues
Young toddlers like being near each other, exchanging looks, touches, and sometimes even toys.	Large boxes with doors and windows cut out are the perfect places for young toddlers to play peek-a-boo and crawl-in-and-out.	Provide shady spots for all sun-sensitive young toddlers. Watch water play, even in very small containers, because infants and toddlers have drowned in pails or small pools of water.
Older infants in this stage may learn to say "Mine" and clutch items closely.	Small individual tubs of water are perfect for this age, but need one-on-one attention for safety reasons. Language develops as teachers comment on walking, jumping, climbing, in, out, up, down, over, and around.	Provide nutritious safe snacks and plenty of fluids.
18–36 months (toddlers)		
This age delights in practicing all of their physical skills. They will challenge themselves to climb and jump higher and farther. Imitating an adult or a peer occurs frequently. Toddlers may become frustrated easily because they want to do more than their physical skills allow. Some toddlers may begin to "pretend" to be firefighters or other characters that they have experienced live or on TV. They want to be with peers and will play beside or with others. Toddlers alternate between wanting to "do it myself" and wanting adults to help them. They need special teachers who understand how they struggle between wanting to be grown up, but still need loving, nurturing, and holding (on their terms, of course).	Sand and water are favorites. Provide sand areas large enough for several toddlers and expect them to sit right in the middle of the area. Bring *many* sand toys for pouring, digging, and poking safely. Pulling or pushing a "friend" in a wagon will result in squeals of delight from both. Expect conflicts over toys, just as indoors. Paintbrushes and water go together for an outdoor art experience. Set up other art materials such as crayons, paints, and a variety of paper on the ground or a low table. Dolls, trucks, cars, and other play materials encourage interactions among peers. Blankets on the ground or over a card table for puzzles, stories, and manipulatives provide a spot for a quiet break. Provide a nurturing place with blankets and pillows for a toddler to "refuel" emotionally with a special teacher.	Remember, toddlers need time to experiment, problem solve, and explore materials alone and with peers. When they tire they will need to be near an adult whom they trust and like. Try to accumulate many outdoor toys for toddlers Otherwise, they will become bored with the few toys available. Provide nutritious, safe snacks and plenty of fluids. Survey the playground for sharp objects and broken equipment before allowing children outside each day.

Infant and toddler professionals can challenge themselves to think about the potential for children's learning in all of the equipment, materials, and experiences available in a center, a family child care home, or a family's home environment. Children choose from these opportunities and learn from each experience that they have in a carefully planned environment and in teacher and peer interactions that happen moment to moment and day to day the relationship way.

We have described the experiences that can be offered as opportunities for learning. Teachers are very intentional about setting up an environment that engages infants and toddlers and they choose from the opportunities. Almost any opportunity that they choose offers possibilities for children to learn in all domains of development.

Check Your Understanding 13.3
Click here to check your understanding of the concepts in this section.

Curriculum Approaches

We have shared information on seven components of planning a responsive, relationship-based curriculum. Many curricula and programs available to purchase share these components. Some, however, emphasize the importance of relationships more than others. With any of the following that we describe here, however, a teacher's emphasis on the importance of relationships and responsive interactions and planning can complement the materials available. Let's start by discussing a program that has led the way in promoting a relationship-based approach to curriculum planning.

The Program for Infant/Toddler Care

We begin by describing the Program for Infant/Toddler Care (PITC), a comprehensive training program for infant-toddler teachers, because this program has greatly informed the authors of this book. The goal of PITC is to help teachers recognize the crucial importance of giving tender, loving care and assisting in the infants' intellectual development through an attentive reading of each child's cues. The PITC videos, DVDs, guides, and manuals are designed to help administrators and teachers become sensitive to infants' cues, connect with the children's families and cultures, and develop responsive, relationship-based care. The training materials provide the foundation for teachers to study the children in their care, reflect on and record information about the children's interests and skills, and search for ways to set the stage for the child's next learning encounters.

As a relationship-based approach, PITC particularly emphasizes the importance of primary caregiving, continuity of caregiving, small group sizes, low ratios, and responsiveness as foundations of settings in which infants and toddlers are able to learn and thrive. PITC holds an image of the child as an active learner who will make important discoveries about the world through her own exploration, if supported by a responsive adult in an engaging environment. Videos and training materials for PITC are available from www.pitc.org.

The Creative Curriculum® for Infants, Toddlers, & Twos

Creative Curriculum for Infants, Toddlers, and Twos, (14), provides extensive information for planning a responsive curriculum. Table 13.6 describes the main components of this well-known curriculum. Also see teachingstrategies.com for information on the philosophy, goals, strategies, assessment tools, and resources available.

TABLE 13.6   Five components of the *Creative Curriculum for Infants, Toddlers & Twos* curriculum

1. **Knowing infants, toddlers, and twos**

   Describes development and the unique characteristics of children

2. **Creating a responsive environment**

   Describes how to set up an environment that is responsive to individual children

3. **What children are learning**

   Describes relationships, interactions, materials, and experiences that are building blocks of learning

4. **Caring and teaching**

   Describes the diverse roles of teachers including how to use ongoing assessment

5. **Partnering with families**

   Describes how to partner with families in a respectful and responsive way

Sources: Berke, Rudick, & Dodge (2007); Dodge, Rudick, Berke, & Dombro (2006).

Reggio Emilia

According to researchers, "For the last three decades, certain Italian regions and localities have been sites of extraordinary efforts by educators and public officials, working together with parents and other citizens, to build high-quality public systems of care and learning to serve families with young children" (15, p. 1).

One of the fundamental points of the Reggio philosophy is an image of a child who experiences the world, who feels a part of the world right from birth; who is full of curiosities, full of desire to live; a child who is full of desire and ability to communicate from the start of his or her life; a child who is fully able to create maps for his or her personal, social, cognitive, affective, and symbolic orientation. Because of all this, a young child reacts with a competent system of abilities, learning strategies, and ways of organizing relationships (16, pp. 50–51).

Bambini: The Italian Approach to Infant/Toddler Care by Gandini and Edwards (2001) describes the Reggio Emilia approach in detail. The Italian approach to early childhood education grows from a well-articulated image of the child. The image of the infant and toddler as highly capable of making discoveries and constructing knowledge is, of course, congruent with research findings on early learning. This image drives the organization of the infant-toddler centers in Reggio Emilia.

Respect for very young children's ability to construct knowledge from their relationships and their environment is central to the organization of the early childhood programs and the environments, relationships, and experiences they offer in supporting learning. The key tool used by teachers is purposeful observation and documentation of the children's activities. This documentation process is not simply recording activities or accomplishments—it is a method of coming to thoughtful, reflective understanding of the children's activities and thinking, and it is the basis of the teacher's planning for introducing new activities or materials into the center. The documentation process consists of forming a question or hypothesis; observing, recording, and collecting artifacts; organizing observations and artifacts; analyzing and interpreting the observations and artifacts, which leads to building theories; possibly reframing the original questions; and then planning and responding from one's understandings of the children's knowledge and interests (17).

> **Check Your Understanding 13.4**
> Click here to check your understanding of the concepts in this section.

Summary

- Responsive routines that provide stability, consistency, and opportunities for learning for infants and toddlers are a key component of a relationship-based program.

- An environment set up with learning spaces and places and the opportunities provided within this environment entice children to choose, play, develop, relate to others, be nurtured, and learn.

- Every experience offers an opportunity for children to develop their capacities in the emotional, social, cognitive, language, and motor domains.

- A variety of infant and toddler curricula are available to purchase and each offers unique possibilities for child development.

Key Terms

emotional refueling
one-to-one correspondence
representation

routines
self-directed learning
symbols

visual discrimination

Reflections and Resources for the Reader

REFLECTIONS

1. How do responsive environments support infants' and toddlers' relationships with adults and peers?
2. How would you interact with a toddler during diaper time to help him or her feel safe and enjoy the time with you?

OBSERVATION AND APPLICATION OPPORTUNITIES

1. Use the environment guide (Table 13.2) at the beginning of this chapter to observe an infant or toddler environment. What components does the environment include? What do you think needs to be added or changed in the environment?
2. Observe an infant or toddler program. What literacy and math opportunities do you see provided for children (interactions, environment, materials, and experiences)? Are children able to choose among these literacy and math opportunities?
3. Choose one curriculum described at the end of this chapter and report to other students on the eight components of a curriculum described at the beginning of Chapter 12.

SUPPLEMENTARY ARTICLES AND BOOKS TO READ

Curtis, D., & Carter, M. (2014). *Designs for living and learning, transforming early childhood environments* (2nd ed.). Minneapolis, MN: Redleaf Press.

Kuh, L. (2014). *Thinking critically about environments for children: Bridging theory and practice (Early Childhood Education)*. New York: Teachers College Press.

Luckenbill, J., & Schallock, L. (2015). Infants and toddlers. Designing and using a developmentally appropriate block area for infants and toddlers. *Young Children, 70*(1), 8-17.

ZERO TO THREE. (2014). New Parenting App - *Let's Play!* is a free parenting app from ZERO TO THREE with fun activities, organized by age and routine, for parents to use to support their young child's early learning - Download from iTunes or Google Play Store.

ZERO TO THREE (2014). *Play*. ZERO TO THREE. Retrieved from http://www.zerotothree.org/child-development/play/

INTERESTING LINKS

Better Brains for Babies: Search for the Better Brain for Babies Web site. This site provides research-based information about brain development and numerous resources to support young children's development.

National Child Care Information Exchange: The NCCIC has several Web pages of helpful information about literacy development.

PITC Demonstration Programs: Virtual Tours: To get ideas for an infant and toddler environment, take a virtual tour through five California community college children's centers that are implementing the PITC approach to infant-toddler care.

ZERO TO THREE: Go to zerotothree.org and search for the following slideshows and resources.

- *Help Your Child Learn Through Play*—View this slideshow to learn more about how and what babies and toddlers learn through play.
- *Birth to 12 Months: Becoming Aware*—View this slideshow to see what types of play captures babies' interest across the first twelve months of life.
- *12 to 24 Months: Becoming Active Explorers*—View this slideshow to learn how young toddlers develop new skills through play and exploration.
- *24 to 36 Months: Becoming Complex Thinkers*—View this slideshow to see how older toddlers use play to develop critical thinking skills and master other important milestones.
- *Playtime True & False*—This slideshow highlights little-known truths and common myths about play in the early years.
- *How Caregivers Can Nurture Play Skills*—Download this resource on how to support early play skills for your child's caregiver.

14

Respect, Reflect, and Relate: The 3 R Approach to Guidance

LEARNING OUTCOMES

After reading this chapter, you will be able to:

- Explain the difference between the terms *discipline* and *guidance*.

- Describe the meaning of *respect*, *reflect*, and *relate* in a relationship-based approach to guidance and explain in detail 10 strategies to use in a relationship-based approach.

- Describe why relationship realignments are a necessary part of the teacher/child relationships.

- Describe strategies and programs that are effective with children who exhibit challenging behavior and experience mental health issues.

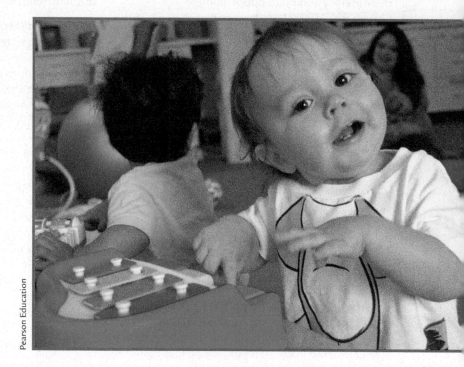

Pearson Education

This chapter is the eighth component of planning a curriculum: a relationship-based approach to guiding infants' and toddlers' behavior while meeting their emotional needs. We use the 3 R approach (respect, reflect, and relate). The 3 R approach helps us focus on children's development and the reasons for their behavior. This approach also emphasizes the importance of adults responding in ways that build children's social and emotional skills. The 3 R approach helps us think about the importance of children's relationships with family, teachers and peers.

This approach to guidance builds on the relationship-based model presented in Chapter 1. This model reminds us to think about the uniqueness of each child and how this affects the child's behavior and our response to the child. The model also helps us focus on how the child's family, culture, and ecology affect the quality of the child's relationships, which then influence a child's development and behavior.

The 3 R approach gives us a framework for helping children with developmental issues—for example, separation anxiety, biting, tantrums, and toilet learning. These are everyday challenges that teachers and family members experience with children at home and in programs. Adults who have increased knowledge of what the child is experiencing during these times of emotional change, and sometimes turbulence, are more likely to use empathic responses that promote children's capacities.

Unfortunately, sometimes children who are experiencing problems in their lives engage in challenging behaviors to get their needs met. In the last part of the chapter, we discuss ideas for understanding and helping children who are angry, aggressive, sad, or anxious or who have experienced **traumatic events**. Let's begin with a discussion of the difference between guidance and discipline and why we use the word *guidance* in this chapter.

The Difference Between Guidance and Discipline

Jose takes off his diaper during playtime. William starts playing with his food. Lynn bites peers who get too near to her when she is tired. Laura grabs toys from other children when she wants them. Before the teacher can stop them, Deanna and John quickly jump up on a chair in order to see better, but the chair topples over and they tumble to the floor.

What do these examples have in common? They are opportunities for adults to socialize children to the ways of a culture, to guide them to try different strategies of relating and getting their needs met, and to teach them in order for them to be successful in a world that requires social and emotional competence.

The term **discipline** has traditionally been used to mean adult control, restraint, and authority as well as child obedience—but another meaning of the term discipline is *to teach*—to teach infants and toddlers new behavior. Because of the confusion between the two meanings of the term discipline, we will use the term **guidance** to indicate a developmental, relationship-based, problem-solving approach to supporting young children's social and emotional competence.

A guide shows the way and supports those she guides on the journey. A guide encourages, models, and structures a journey so that everyone can be successful. Guiding means that infants and toddlers are supported as they learn an enormous amount of information in such a short period of time—how to use a spoon or why they shouldn't take off their own diaper in the middle of the room in the middle of the day. They learn the important guidelines for their culture, such as when it is acceptable to laugh and how to help another person in distress. They can also learn how to get what they need without using aggression. Guidance implies the use of a positive philosophy and strategies for supporting children as they become **socialized** in the cultures in which they live.

Guidance includes assistance, facilitation, and setting limits. It goes on throughout the day and doesn't occur just when children "misbehave." In fact, it describes a way for teachers and parents to help children become capable and caring human beings who can guide their own behavior.

 Check Your Understanding 14.1
Click here to check your understanding of the concepts in this section.

BOX 14.1

A Relationship-Based Approach to Guidance

Respect:
- Respect for children's emotional needs and their goals
- Respect for individual differences in children
- Respect for the power of development
- Respect for self

Reflect:
- What is the child experiencing? What is the child communicating that he wants or needs? What is the purpose of the child's behavior?
- What, when, where, how, and with whom does the behavior occur?
- What do we want the child to do now? What characteristics do we want the child to develop? What are our long-term goals for the child?

Relate:
- Support children's healthy relationships with all of the important people in their lives
- Focus on adult-child responsive interaction strategies that promote children's capacities
- Create and change the environment

A Relationship-Based Approach to Guidance

The 3 R Approach to guidance starts with respect, then asks teachers to reflect, and then relate to children. See Box 14.1 for a summary of the 3 R strategies.

Respect

Respect for infants and toddlers includes respect for their emotional needs, respect for individual differences and strengths, and respect for the power of development.

Respect for Children's Emotional Needs and Their Goals

Respect begins with an understanding of infants' and toddlers' needs.

Protection.   Infants and toddlers need to feel safe with you. They need to know that you care enough to stop them if they are hurting themselves or others. They need to feel that they can run into your arms when they are feeling frightened or hurt.

Secure and caring relationships.   Infants and toddlers need to feel that you really care about them. If they are securely attached and feel a positive emotional connection to you, they are more likely to be cooperative with you. They feel as if you are there for and with them. They can count on you.

Responsive interactions.   Infants and toddlers need adults who respond to their gestures, cries, words, and interests. They need to feel that you are listening to and understanding them. They trust that they can bury their head in your shoulder when they are sad. They know that you will comfort them when they are hurt. They know that you are emotionally present when they are struggling to learn to walk or climb or talk, empathizing with them. With your words, expressions, and gestures you are saying: "I see you are unhappy." "You make me laugh when you are so funny." "I'll keep you safe." "I won't let you hurt Matty." "I feel so good holding you."

A sense of self-worth through mastery and learning.   Infants and toddlers need your affirmation and encouragement. Rather than saying, "That's good!" we need to be more specific in our affirmation. We can say, "You worked so hard," or "You did it. You climbed up on the mat." They trust that you will respond with affection so that they can see their own self-worth in your eyes and voice. They need opportunities to learn and master new skills.

It is important to think about each one of these needs. They are the foundation for how we think about guidance.

Respect for Individual Differences in Children

Respect for infants and toddlers also entails appreciation for what children bring to a relationship in terms of their unique styles of interacting and learning. When we recognize that each child is different, we will reflect on how their temperament, personality, needs, and strengths influence how we are guiding them. We will individualize our guidance strategies for each child.

Tune into children's temperament, strengths, culture, **sensory challenges** and their effects on you.

Temperament.   An infant's or toddler's temperament influences how that child will react to the differences in quality of care. Among 66 toddlers between 24 and 35 months observed in an infant-toddler program, children with reactive temperaments were more socially integrated when the quality of the environment and teacher-child interactions was higher (1). Reactive toddlers were quite responsive to the sensitivity, intrusiveness, and detachment of the teacher and the quality of the environment. Other researchers (2) found that among 70 children age 15 months, "children with a relatively difficult temperament were less involved in contacts initiated by peers although only in cases of lower quality childcare" (p. 709). Although infants or toddlers with reactive and more negative temperaments may be challenging for teachers, their knowledge and awareness of a child's temperament will help them meet the children's needs for responsive sensitivity and social involvement.

The following example demonstrates how a teacher is accepting of Tim sucking his thumb, knowing that he uses it to self-regulate before he courageously crawls into the midst of play:

> *Tim sat on the floor sucking his thumb contently while watching all of the action in his child care home. Martha, his teacher, watched Tim and reflected on how Tim liked to observe before crawling into the midst of the other infants playing on the floor. She admired his ability to regulate and calm himself by sucking his thumb. Martha smiled at Tim, Tim smiled back, and he began to crawl toward another baby.*

Tim has found a unique way to ready himself for peer play by jumping into the fray only after he is ready. Sucking his thumb helps him self-regulate and gain strength and confidence. Martha's respect for Tim's style of playing and temperament allows him to develop at his pace and in his own way.

Strengths.   Perceptive adults also focus on children's strengths and what they can do rather than what they can't do. Build on what the child can do and think of each child in terms of his or her competencies. Avoid labeling a child as, for example, an "aggressive child," which seems to define the very essence of who this child is. For example, Sal is a helper, builder, or a climber rather than a biter. He happens to be biting right now, but biting doesn't define his character. When teachers think of the strengths of each child, they are building the identity and spirit of the child. Thinking about strengths also provides a road map for strategies that will help the child focus on what he can do rather than what he can't do.

Culture.   Gonzalez-Mena (3, 4) emphasizes that we need to show respect for cultural differences in children's families. Recognizing these differences will influence the strategies we use. Some children require more personal space around them whereas others require less. Some children smile to be friendly whereas others smile only when they are happy. Some children may have learned that they convey respect by looking downward rather than into an adult's eyes. If we recognize these differences in ourselves and others, we can value them rather than misinterpret them.

Children's effect on you.   Have you experienced an infant or toddler who doesn't respond to your attention? Vallotton (5) observed student teachers interacting individually with infants between 4 and 19 months who were being taught "baby signing." The teachers interacted more with babies who responded to the adults' initiations and attempts at communication with gestures or signs. It is paramount that adults who interact with children are aware of how an infant's responsiveness, language, temperament, and behavior influence them. We need to be more responsive to infants and toddlers who are not engaging others.

Sensory challenges.   Some children experience sensory processing challenges. They may react differently than other children to the texture of foods. They may not like sensory experiences such as water, sand, or finger paints. These children may react when there is too much visual or auditory stimulation by withdrawing or losing control. They may have difficulty with light touch that would be pleasant to other children. These children are at risk of being considered uncooperative, disruptive, or anxious. You will want to tune in to children's differing abilities to process sensory experiences.

Children's temperament, strengths, culture, sensory challenges, and their effects on you are a just a few examples of how children will demonstrate their individual personalities. We can embrace each child's uniqueness and adapt experiences and the environment to individual needs, strengths, and interests.

Respect for the Power of Development

We understand that children are developing their emotional and social skills. It takes time to learn new skills and ways of being. During some periods of their life, for example, when they are first separating from their parents or when they are using to learn the toilet, life is even more challenging for them. Each stage of development may require different adult strategies. What do we need to understand about child development in relation to guidance strategies?

An infant cries when he sees someone new, and a young toddler sucks her thumb when she gets tired. A young child just learning to use a spoon will get tired and start picking up food with his hands. A toddler suddenly starts saying "No" to everything and has to have his bib tied just the right way to be happy.

As we can see in these examples, when infants and toddlers mature in emotional, social, cognitive, language, and motor domains—they go through different stages. These stages of achievement can also be times of disquiet and disequilibrium for both infants or toddlers and their parents and teachers (e.g., when an infant begins to experience stranger anxiety). If teachers don't understand the forces of development, they may have unrealistic expectations that contribute to demanding too much of children (such as expecting a toddler to eat without spilling food). When this happens, infants and toddlers become very frustrated or feel increasingly incompetent.

On the other hand, if a teacher does not notice a certain behavior, such as a 9-month-old patting his hands together, the teacher may not provide interesting, developmentally appropriate interactions such as playing pat-a-cake. Teachers can use the Developmental Trends and Responsive Interactions charts at the end of Chapters 6 through 10 and in the appendices in this book to observe the development of the child, gain realistic expectations, and provide experiences that are responsive to child development.

If an infant or toddler has a developmental delay or disability in one area of development, a second area of development may be affected as well. You will remember from previous chapters that a developmental delay is a lag or difference in development that is caused by a variety of genetic or environmental factors. Several researchers have discovered that when young children, especially toddlers, are experiencing language delay, they are more likely to also be experiencing social and emotional delays (6). Teachers and parents must give infants and toddlers with language delay extra support to help them learn to communicate their needs in socially appropriate ways. Watch for these types of connections between delays in other domains of development.

When teachers understand the power of development, they will observe children carefully and wisely study child development.

Respect for Self

Know yourself. What has your culture taught you about how children should behave? How does this influence the way you guide young children? Think about what makes you angry, sad, frustrated, and anxious when you are with children. The more you know yourself and why you respond as you do, the more you will use reflective practice.

Reflect

Reflection includes thinking about what an experience is like for a child, observing what children are communicating through their behavior, and deciding what you would like the child to do instead. The following reflection strategies pave the way for relating in a way that meets children's emotional needs and teaches them a new behavior.

Reflecting includes taking time to figure out what emotions children are experiencing.

Pearson Education

Reflect on Child's Experience

Tasha cries every morning when her mother says good-bye and Richard has a hard time transitioning from lunch to nap time. What is each child experiencing? It may be difficult to think about what they are experiencing rather than what we, as adults, are experiencing with them. When we understand what the experience is like from the child's perspective, then we are much more likely to empathize and offer support in ways that are helpful to the child. Tasha may really miss her father. Richard may be afraid to be alone on his cot when he can't see his favorite teacher.

What is the purpose of the child's behavior? Take the example of Serena, discussed by Van De Zande and the Santa Cruz Toddler Care Center Staff (7). Although this child's thought processes are not this sophisticated, she is experimenting with what happens when she spits in various places and at different times with different people:

> "How interesting," Serena seems to think. "Mommy gets mad if I spit on the table! . . . Was that just at breakfast or also at lunch? . . . What about dinner? . . . Just yesterday, or also today? . . . It seems okay to spit in the bathtub. . . . She made me spit out a bug . . . what if I spit on these papers on her desk?" (p. 15)

After thinking with Serena and taking her perspective, an understanding adult will give Serena more information about where and when it is okay to spit rather than punish her without explanation.

What is the child communicating? Young children communicate their needs in a variety of ways. Infants yawn or turn away when they need a break from an interaction. When they are extremely upset, they may arch their back or kick their feet. Older infants and young toddlers may crawl away or cling to you to tell you they are upset or afraid. They may throw a toy down on the floor to tell you that they are frustrated. Toddlers fall into a heap crying when they are trying to tell you that they intensely want something or are trying to assert their independence and separateness from you. Some children may try to distract you with cute faces and antics to avoid having to do something they don't want to do. Some children may hit other children to either get what they want or to tell you, "I'm not feeling safe and I have to protect myself." Some children may even want you to leave them alone—they have learned that adults aren't to be trusted. Children can't usually tell us with words, but they tell us with their behavior what it is they need or want. We can often decide what they need or the purpose of their behavior by using the observation system depicted in Table 14.1.

TABLE 14.1   **Observation of Julie to determine the purpose of her behavior**

Date	What Happens Before	The Child's Behavior	What Happens After	Possible Purposes of the Behavior
12/1	Tasha took Julie's crayon out of Julie's hand.	Julie hit Tasha with an open hand on Tasha's side.	Tasha cried and dropped the crayon. Julie picked it up and started using it.	To get her crayon back
12/5	Dale stepped on Julie's block structure.	Julie hit at Dale's leg when Dale went by her.	Dale left the area and Julie continued playing.	To get Dale to leave her alone

Reflect With Whom and When the Behavior Occurs

Observe frequently to try to understand when, where, and with whom a child may be behaving in a certain way. For example, after observing that Peter, a toddler, seemed upset on Mondays, the teacher realized that when he came into the toddler room on those days, he needed several hours to readjust to the room, his peers, and his teachers. He possibly needed time to adjust after a weekend with his mom, who was experiencing stress in her life. Tara, the teacher, tried to make him feel welcome by having him stay by her side as she checked the classroom pets. Soon, Peter was off playing and checking back with her occasionally when he needed a hug. The information that the teacher gathered was a guide to the strategies she chose.

Reflect on New Behaviors

What do the family and teachers and peers want the child to do now instead of the behavior the child is using to communicate her needs? Will the new behavior help the child meet her needs? Once you have determined what it is that you want the child to do, then you can begin to support the child to learn new ways to meet her needs. In the example in Table 14.1, the parents and teachers decided that they wanted Julie to learn to say "Stop" to other children when they try to take something away from her or interfere with her play.

"What characteristics do we want the child to develop?" and "What are our long-term goals for the child?" are more difficult questions. These questions require conversations with families. For example, as you are trying to help a child stop biting his peers, it is important to think about what kind of child his or her family has said that they want the child to be. Has the family said that they want the child to be a kind child? Has the family emphasized that they want their child to learn to help others? The goals that we have for children become important as we consider the strategies to use with the child.

    Watch Bruce Perry talk about the six core strengths for healthy child development. Are these characteristics that you want children to develop? How can we guide children to help them gain these strengths?

https://www.youtube.com/watch?v=skaYWKC6iD4

Relate

Respecting and reflecting may give adults insight that needs no further response on their part to support the child. However, they will often relate (use strategies) to help children learn and express their individual personalities and develop positive and healthy relationships. Box 14.2 summarizes the relate strategies that are described in detail in this section.

These strategies create children who have internal guides to behavior and who can uniquely contribute to the well-being of themselves and others through engaging in positive relationships. Let's start with building relationships.

Relate: Support Children's Healthy Relationships with All of the Important People in Their Lives

In other chapters, we have emphasized the importance of teachers supporting the family-child relationships as the key ongoing foundation in a child's life. We

BOX 14.2

A Summary of Relate Strategies

Support children's healthy *relationships* with all of the important people in their lives

- Support the child's relationship with his or her family.
- Continuously communicate with families and other staff to learn about their culture, wishes, and guidance practices.
- Use a problem-solving approach with families.
- Build a strong, positive relationship with each child—a truly caring relationship.
- Use primary care and continuity of care systems to promote ongoing, secure teacher-child, teacher-family, and peer relationships.

Focus on adult-child responsive interaction strategies that promote children's capacities

- Empathize with the child's goals, struggles, and feelings.
- Build emotional vocabulary—acknowledge and help children express strong feelings.
- Patiently guide children toward controlling their own impulses and behavior.
- Recognize behavior as communication, and teach children to communicate.
- Explain and teach the child what to do. Make clear, positive statements to children.
- Provide limits that keep the child safe, others safe, and materials safe.
- Help children take the perspective of others through other-oriented guidance.
- Help children learn how to problem solve and handle conflicts.
- Give children choices that you can live with.
- Create routines to provide security for infants and toddlers.
- Gradually build toddlers' ability to wait or to handle disappointment.
- Use time-in rather than time-out.

Create and change the environment

- Create an environment that contributes to children's engagement and relationships—cozy corners, private spaces, spaces for two, and interesting things to do.
- Change the environment as needed to ensure positive behavior and help children be successful.

also know that the quality of other relationships that the child might observe or experience affects the relationships that the child has, for example, with teachers or peers. In studies of aggression in toddlers, Brook (8) researchers found that there were associations with parenting style and marital relations. When the relationship between the mother and father was strained, toddlers were more likely to exhibit aggressive behavior with their peers. This is a good example of how important it is to consider the ecological and relationship factors that influence a very young child's behavior. Let's think about how a teacher might support the parent-child relationship.

Support the child's relationship with his or her family.

> *Karin seemed happy all day at the infant-toddler care and learning center, but when her father came to the door each evening, she fell apart.*

In this example, how can teachers use a relationship-based approach as a framework to think about solutions to this challenge for Karin? The teacher wonders how to handle it so that her relationship with Karin and Karin's relationship with her father are both strengthened. It is tempting to think that Karin likes her teacher better than her father, but this could be a mistake. Brazelton (9) talks about how children can "hold it together" emotionally during the day, but that they can literally "fall apart" as the day ends and transitions occur. The teacher can acknowledge how hard the end of a day is for both Dad and Karin and do what she can to support them both. She decides to ask Dad if he could call ahead when he left work and then the teacher could prepare Karin that Dad was coming and help her get ready to go. This strategy of respecting the importance of all the relationships in Karin's life influenced how the teacher promoted and supported parent-child relationships as well as the teacher's relationship with Karin. The teacher can also partner with everyone who has a relationship with the child—including parents, siblings, grandparents, and other teachers.

Continuously communicate with families and other staff to learn about their culture, wishes, and guidance practices.   Daily conversations and periodic conferences with family members will ensure that you are involving them in all aspects of their children's care and learning. It is very important to share the strengths, interests, likes, and dislikes of the children in an ongoing way rather than just sharing children's challenges. Encourage family members to share both the positive experiences of the children with you and to share their own and their children's challenges related to the care and learning of their children. Ongoing conversations will prevents problems from escalating.

Use a problem-solving approach with families.   Bromwich (10) recommends a six-step problem-solving approach that teachers, home visitors, and other infant-toddler professionals can use when talking with families about guidance issues (See Box 14.3)

Build a strong, positive relationship with each child—a truly caring relationship.   In a truly caring relationship the child feels mutual affection. There is a sense of felt security.

Use primary care and continuity of care systems to promote ongoing, secure teacher-child and peer relationships.   These strategies ensure that

BOX 14.3

Bromwich's Problem-Solving Approach with Parents

Listen empathetically to the parent.

Try to see things from the parent's perspective, and try to understand his/her perceptions of the child and of himself/herself in the context of the family. Listen carefully and convey that what the parent says, does, and feels is important to you. Comment on the parent's feelings—for example, to a parent who is concerned about the child screaming, say, "It must have felt pretty frustrating to have him continue screaming after you picked him up and tried to cuddle him." However, be careful about not encouraging the parent to talk about issues and feelings before she indicates that she wants to talk about them. Try not to become involved in highly personal matters for which you do not have the knowledge and skills to help the parent. Discuss with other staff when to refer the family to a therapist or human services agency.

Observe.

Help the parent become a sensitive observer in order to read his infant's or toddler's cues and respond to them. Observe with the parent to call the parent's attention to the details of behavior that reveal important developmental changes in the child, no matter how small. Observing *with* the parent means that parent and staff share with each other what they have observed.

Ask.

Ask the parent to share what she knows about her child that you do not know, recognizing that the parent knows the child best. Build on the parent's strengths by asking him/her to describe his/her successful handling of the child in one situation. For example, ask a mother how she calms her child so successfully when he is fussy on weekends. These ideas can be applied to other times when the parent is having difficulty with her baby when she fusses and also when you are trying to calm the baby. Ask parents specific questions as a first step in the cooperative problem-solving process, such as, "What situations seem to happen right before the child has a tantrum?" or "When did the behavior start?"

Comment positively.

Comment positively on what you see the parent is doing that seems to work with her child. Be specific—for example, "Your baby really lights up when she sees you smiling at her."

Discuss.

Discussion usually includes sharing information on typical development. For example, you might say to a parent who is concerned because her child drops things off her high chair, "Many children in this age range drop things from the high chair to experiment with what happens to them and to play." Focus on the observations of the child's current behavior and relate the discussion to those observations. The developmental information may help the parent respond more effectively or anticipate the next stage in development.

Experiment.

Problem solve with the parent to determine a variety of ways to interact with the child. With the baby who was fussy, the parent may notice that the baby is calmer when wrapped snugly in a blanket. You may have noticed that the baby is calmer when the room is quieter. One solution will not work forever and some may not work at all. If you talk with the parent about experimenting, then you don't set up the parent for failure. This encourages both you and the parent to try new things and share information about how the solutions worked. If they don't work, then you can begin the six-step process over again–all in the spirit of collaboration.

Source: Bromwich, R. (1997). *Working with families and their infants at risk.* Austin, TX: Pro-Ed.

infants' and toddlers' need for enduring, secure relationships with teachers is met. Continuity of care also ensures that infants' and toddlers' peer relationships are protected and valued as peers move together to a new room with a beloved teacher.

Relate: Focus on Adult-Child Responsive Interaction Strategies That Promote Children's Capacities

All of the strategies discussed in Chapter 12 on how to support infants' and toddlers' emotional and social development—such as "noticing and encouraging strengths and positive behavior," "showing affection," and "being responsive" provide the foundation upon which guidance interaction strategies are based. Now would be a good time to review those strategies, as they are critical to remember as the underpinnings to building children's capacities. Approaches that you can use to guide children are discussed here, but they are not likely to be effective if you are not using the basic strategies. Following are the 12 additional strategies that teachers and parents can use to guide adult-child interactions with infants and toddlers.

Empathize with the child's goals, struggles, and feelings.

> *Eight-month-old Marku seemed tired and crabby all day. He cried easily and wouldn't sit by himself on the floor. He wanted to be in the teacher's lap and sobbed whenever she had to put him down to help another child.*

What is Marku feeling? We don't know for sure, but we can tell that he is not happy. The teacher said to Marku, "I can tell you are unhappy today. What can I do to make you feel better?" Although Marku couldn't understand all of the teacher's words, he could feel that she really cared and empathized with him. She didn't think he was spoiled or "just trying to get attention." Instead, she trusted that Marku had special emotional needs today and that there was a reason, which she didn't understand yet, for why he was clingy. She knew that today was a "care for the spirit of Marku" day, that her special care would help him learn to trust her, and that their positive relationship would provide a foundation for Marku to feel safe to feel, express, and regulate his emotions.

Always start by trying to state what you think the child may be feeling, trying to communicate to you, or trying to achieve. This will help you "tune in" to the child and take the child's perspective in the situation. Then ask, "What can I do to help?"

Honig (11) recommends saying, "You wish...." to the child to help yourself tune into the child's feelings and acknowledge that you are listening to the messages that the child is communicating to you. For example, you could say, "I know you wish you could have that toy. Tina Marie has it now."

Build emotional vocabulary—acknowledge and help children express strong feelings.

- This strategy is similar to the first one, but focuses on helping children describe their own emotions. For infants, teachers describe the emotions that they think the child *might* be feeling. Teachers are making their best guess as they read the child's facial expressions and body movements. For young toddlers, teachers frequently use emotion words to describe the child's feelings and encourage the child to say a word—for example, "You can tell me you feel sad." Teachers continue describing a broader range of feelings for toddlers–for example, "You look disappointed"—and continue encouraging the child to express his feelings in a variety of situations.

Patiently guide children toward controlling their own impulses and behavior.

> *Nate stood at the sand table, gleefully throwing sand on the floor and then listening to the sounds he could make with his shoes. Cara, the teacher, got down on his level and said, "Sand stays in the sand table. Let's see if we can make noises with the shovel in the table," recognizing his interest in cause and effect and making different sounds.*

Because of the teacher's patience, Nate is learning that he can control his own behavior as he starts making noises with his shovel in the table.

Recognize behavior as communication, and teach children to communicate.
The toddler who runs over and kicks another toddler's blocks is possibly communicating that he wants to play but doesn't know how to do so. He needs help learning new strategies of communication for entering play with another child, because his present strategy certainly isn't working very well!

In Chapter 9, sign language was discussed as a useful means of communicating with infants and toddlers. Parents and teachers are reporting that when they use a few signs, such as those for milk or more, then infants and toddlers learn these signs from the modeling of the adult, begin to use them around 9 months of age, and are less frustrated because they can communicate their needs.

"Use your words" is a phrase that is often repeated by teachers of toddlers as they try to teach children to use words rather than aggression to obtain a prized toy from another child or protect themselves or a toy that another toddler covets (12). Saying "Use your words" is helpful only if the toddler knows the words to use. It is more helpful in the beginning to tell the toddlers the specific words that can be used, such as "Please" (often said as "peas") when they want a toy, or "No" or "Later" when they don't want someone to take a toy from them. When adults model words, then toddlers soon begin to use them—a step toward becoming a communicator in social situations.

Building children's emotion vocabulary and vocabulary in general is important for the development of their ability to control and express emotions. Researchers (13) collected data on toddlers who were 13, 24, and 36 months and found that children's language skills, particularly

What are these children's gestures communicating? What could you say that would help these children express their feelings with words?

Pearson Education

their vocabulary, influenced girls' self-regulation and the rate of change in boys' self-regulation.

Explain and teach the child what to do. Make clear, positive statements to children.   Give short reasons and explanations to help young children begin to internalize the rules and their reasons. To help infants and toddlers begin to understand why they should touch a breakable item very gently, give simple explanations such as "Touch gently, it is fragile."

To Verina who just bit Sarah, say, "No biting; that hurt Sarah. Look, she's crying. Tell her what you wanted."

Make positive statements about what to do—for example, instead of saying "Don't run," say "Please walk." When a teacher says "Don't run," a young child may just hear the word "run."

When Mario, 28-months-old, picked up an interesting piece of dirt and started putting it in his mouth for a taste, he said aloud to himself, "I put it in my mouth. I no do it. It dirty."

The words that he heard from his teachers and parents now became an internal guide to behavior. At the moment and more likely in the future, he will not need someone telling him to keep strange things out of his mouth. When infants and toddlers hear the reason for doing or not doing a certain behavior, then that reason becomes a part of them. They will then have self-control rather than always needing external control from adults.

Provide limits that keep the child safe, others safe, and materials safe.

Dina climbed up on the chair and looked at the teacher to see what she would do. The teacher helped Dina down, held her in her arms, and said, "I will keep you safe. I don't want you to climb on the chair. You could get hurt." After several days of this, Dina seemed more relaxed and could concentrate on playing in a more focused way.

Follow through when a child hurts himself, another child, or materials.

Andrew, 18-months-old, pushed Julie hard on his way to get the box of blocks. The teacher took him gently in her arms and said firmly, "You pushed Julie. That hurt Julie. I want to keep everyone in the room safe. You can go around her like this" taking his hand and showing him the way.

Help children take the perspective of others through other-oriented guidance.

Joshua stepped over Jerry as he toddled fast to the new blocks. The teacher walked over to Joshua, bent down to Joshua's level, and helped him look back at Jerry, who was crying. "Look, he's crying. You stepped on him. That hurt his hand. Let's go help Jerry," as the teacher gently took Joshua's hand and led him over to Jerry.

When teachers use **other-oriented guidance**, they steer children to begin to think about how others feel. Guiding toddlers to look at the face of another child, interpreting the feeling of the other child, and then thinking aloud about how to help a child who is hurt, for example, starts a child on the challenging and often bumpy road of taking other people's perspective.

Help children learn how to problem solve and handle conflicts.   Thirty-month-old children of mothers who used **justification** (use of reason), **resolution** (trying to bring the conflict to a solution agreeable to all), and **mitigation** (trying to lessen the conflict) during conflict with their children had higher levels of social and emotional development at 36 months of age (14). Conflict is inevitable; for example, a toddler might decide that he doesn't want to get dressed or put on a coat. When teachers and parents talk with toddlers and negotiate solutions, toddlers learn important lessons about the give and take of making decisions.

Infants and toddlers benefit from participating in conflicts with peers (15, 16, 17) if teachers and other adults help them learn how to negotiate, develop emotion regulation and self-regulation, learn problem-solving skills, and most importantly learn that others have perspectives that are different than their view of the world (theory of mind). Instead of using directions, distractions, warnings, and threats, teachers can ask open-ended questions, invite children to participate in dialogue, offer choices, and help them make decisions. Toddlers and twos can learn to problem solve (16). When a teacher asks, "What could we do to help Amy?" or "What could you do if you want the toy?" then toddlers begin to understand the nature of problem solving. They will need continuous help to think of possible answers, but if teachers keep asking and modeling answers, then toddlers become great problem solvers as they grow.

Give children choices that you can live with.   Give more choices to toddlers with each passing month. Carmen, the toddler teacher knows that Lulu's diaper needs to be changed, but Lulu is very busy putting blocks in and out of a can. The teacher approaches Lulu, bends down to her level, and asks, "I see you need to have your diaper changed." Lulu loudly says, "No!" "I can see that you are enjoying your blocks," replies Carmen, "I'll be back in a few minutes to change your diaper." After a few minutes, Carmen approaches Lulu again. "It is time to have your diaper changed; would you like to walk or would you like me to carry you?" Lulu holds her hands up to be carried.

Create routines to provide security for infants and toddlers.   A routine becomes a habit and provides emotional security to the child. Children can predict what will happen when routines are consistent. Details of how to proceed do not have to be explained each day. Use a cleanup song when it is time to put away toys: "It's cleanup time. It's cleanup time. It's time to put our toys away." Use routines for saying good-bye and a routine for going outside. Sing songs if you have to wait for lunch to arrive. Use a routine for moving from lunch to nap time, so toddlers know that when they are done eating, they can get their "blankie" or "lovie" and a teacher will read to them on their mats.

Gradually build toddlers' ability to wait or to handle disappointment.

> Toddlers who don't learn gradually about disappointment lose their resilience through lack of practice in give-and-take with other people's needs. They can become self-centered, demanding, and difficult to like or to be with (Lieberman).

As infants become toddlers, they can gradually learn about waiting for the food to be warm enough to eat or to go outside, for example. Children are more likely to learn patience and to take the perspective of others if adults talk in a soothing voice to children while they are waiting. Disappointment may occur when children can't go outside because of the weather or because a favorite teacher is absent for a day. Thinking about how you feel when you are disappointed will remind you of how important it is for adults to explain what is happening, acknowledge toddlers' disappointed feelings, and demonstrate coping strategies for how to handle frustration and sadness.

Use time-in rather than time-out.   **Time-out** is a strategy that has often been used by parents and teachers to punish children by placing them in a time-out chair, a cubby, or a place alone away from everyone else after the child has "misbehaved." When teachers use time-out, it is often in a punitive way; the teacher angrily places the child in a separate place and tells the child to stay there until he can "learn not to bite." The child usually focuses on protecting himself in a time-out situation rather than focusing on what happened, why it happened, how he and the other child feel, and what else he could have done instead. **Time-in** is a strategy that involves a parent or teacher spending time with a child who, for example, bit another child. The teacher calms the child and teaches the child what to do instead of biting. If a cozy area of the room with soft toys and pillows is always available as a "cozy corner," toddlers, when upset, may go there by themselves to calm themselves. Or, they may ask or pull a teacher to come with them to the cozy corner.

Relate: Create and Change the Environment

> *The young toddlers in the child care home began to crawl up the stairs, so Melissa put a baby gate across the bottom of the stairs. The toddlers were continually running at full speed through the room until the teachers placed a small climber in the center. Instead of blaming the children for the challenges, the teacher examined what she could do to change the environment to be more developmentally appropriate.*

Create an environment that contributes to children's engagement, self-regulation, and relationships—cozy corners, spaces for two, and interesting things to do. If the environment includes caring people and interesting equipment, toys, and materials with which the child can be successful, then children are more likely to be engaged. If an environment is attractive and calm, then children are more likely to be able to self-regulate.

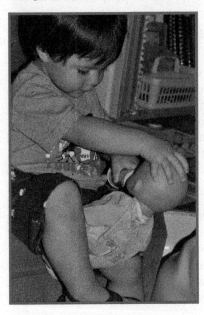

Pearson Education

What about this environment helps this child self-regulate, engage with the materials, and practice nurturing another?

Change the environment as needed to ensure positive behavior and help children be successful. Always ask, "How can I change the environment to help this child be successful?" If a toddler seems to have difficulty falling asleep, try creating a more private space in the room so that you can sing the toddler to sleep without distractions. A small change in the environment can make a big difference for a child.

Check Your Understanding 14.2
Click here to check your understanding of the concepts in this section.

Relationship Realignments

When infants and toddlers experience separation anxiety, resisting behavior, tantrums, biting others, and learning to use the toilet, then their relationships with caring adults are often challenged. At these times, relationships require a readjustment or change. The child is feeling fear, anger, a loss of control, or a need for independence. The child needs support and guidance. The adults need to change how they are relating to the children because the children are in a new phase of development. Adults will need to try new strategies that meet children's needs in hopes of regaining relationship rapport.

Separation Anxiety

> *For months, Karin's dad had been dropping off his 10-month-old daughter at the same care and learning program without seeing so much as a tear from her. But lately, after the usual good-bye hugs and kisses, Karin has started wailing, clinging fast to Dad's leg. Martha, Karin's special teacher, was surprised by this sudden change in behavior and tried to distract the baby with a favorite toy. As the crying continued, however, she and Karin's dad wondered, "What are we doing wrong?"*

With new knowledge comes the fear of being abandoned, unloved, or physically damaged. (Lieberman)

A young baby may cry when a parent leaves, but at about 7 months of age infants may actively show **separation anxiety**. They search for their loved one, scowl, cry, push away others who offer comfort, and have difficulty saying good-bye. New cognitive understandings contribute to the infant's growing awareness of "out of sight, but not out of mind." Often infants don't want their favorite teacher to disappear, even behind the bathroom door. Separation anxiety can occur for several months, but the length of this stage varies in children. There are children who by 18 months feel very comfortable saying good-bye to parents, but there are also children who have difficulty with separation all of their life. Teachers can hold an infant, allow her to stay as close as she wants, talk to her in nurturing tones, and appreciate the emotional struggle that the infant is experiencing.

When children enter an infant-toddler care and learning program between 1 and 2 years of age, they may take several weeks to several months to adjust to the new situation. The first several days may go smoothly, but as the toddler begins to realize that the new setting is where he is going to be each day, he may begin to protest more. Other children are frightened from the beginning of this new separation from parents and protest vehemently. Yet, they don't have the language skills to express themselves clearly. Children of this age have a difficult time cognitively understanding where the parent is going and when he or she will return. Many children this age seem very sad after their parents leave and in the midst of their play, they may turn to the door with a hopeful "Mommy?" when they hear someone enter. They then feel sad all over again when it isn't their loved one returning. When adults understand that cognitive development affects social and emotional development, and vice versa, they can help young children during this scary time by being emotionally and physically available and commenting on the child's (even a young baby's) feelings. For example, a teacher could say, "I know you thought that was Mommy. Mommy will be here after your nap."

A child can also experience separation anxiety as she leaves the program at the end of the day. She may cry and fuss at having to make another transition. Teachers support children and parents in as many ways as possible to ease the transition from program to home with the parent. Teachers can make sure the child is ready to transition with a clean diaper and a full tummy. Or, if the parent wants to feed the child, the teacher supports the parent-child relationship by timing the feedings (while still being responsive to the child) so that the parent can experience bonding time with the child. If a child fusses at leaving his favorite teacher it is important that teachers help build the parent-child relationship through interpreting the feelings of the child. Teachers can say to the parent, "She is happy to see you. She wasn't quite ready to have her coat put on" or "She just seems tired today—I think she needs some cuddle time with her dad."

Toddler Resistance

Teachers and parents of toddlers often feel as if they are on an emotional roller coaster with their children. Toddlers are sometimes pushing for independence and at other times want to be taken care of as if they were still infants. Toddlers are learning how to be autonomous, or self-directing. They often attempt to gain control but become frustrated at their lack of control. A toddler can feel mixed up, sometimes wanting to be a grownup and the next minute feeling scared, lonely, or just out of energy and wanting to sit in your lap. Toddler teachers often experience the full range of emotions that toddlers feel in the course of a day—from pure delight and contagious giggles to overwhelming frustration.

Toddlers can get frightened when they are resisting. If a parent or teacher doesn't stop them from doing something dangerous; they can feel that there is no one there to hold, help, restrain, or contain them (18). They say "No" to tell you that they are people who can express feelings and to test the safe limits and boundaries of the world, but they still want to feel safe. It helps teachers and parents if they appreciate that developmental change can occur rapidly between 18 months and 3 years of age. It is the teacher of this age group who masterfully gives toddlers opportunities to be self-directing while providing the boundaries for behavior that keep children feeling safe and emotionally secure.

Tantrums

Both young and older toddlers may have what adults call **tantrums**—times of distress when they literally seem to fall apart. Some children cry loudly, scream, whine, flail, fall to the floor, stomp their feet, or become stiff or floppy. A teacher may not have put a bib on a child in quite the right way or the teacher may have denied a child a second banana. It is difficult to predict when a young child might have a tantrum. They are very taxing and challenging to both the child and the teachers. Let's now take a look at Keri, who has started having tantrums, to see how many of the guidance strategies discussed in this chapter can be applied to a real-life situation, one that teachers often face in their work with children ages 15 months to 3 years:

> Keri, 2-years-old, is in a family child care home for 3 days a week. She eats her banana with great delight. After swallowing the last delicious crumb, [and with banana still dribbling out of her mouth], she gestures to her care provider that she would like another one, only to hear, "I'm sorry, Keri, just one banana today. It sometimes gives you a tummy-ache if you eat two bananas." Keri scowls, jumps up from her chair, stomps her feet, and puts her hands on her hips. As her teacher approaches, Keri suddenly falls to the floor in a heap, crying as loudly as she can.

As toddlers begin to assert themselves, strong emotions and resistance—**negativism**—can occur out of the blue. As Lieberman (18) explains,

> When toddlers are unable to speak about urgent matters, they must resort to crying or screaming. This happens even with adults. The voice is the carrier of emotion, and when speech fails us, we need to cry out in whatever form we can to convey our meaning. Often, what passes for negativism is really the toddler's desperate effort to make herself understood (p. 38).

What is Keri feeling, and what is she trying to say? Is she more likely to have a tantrum on certain days or times of the day? What are Keri's language skills? Very young children are starting to use words and voice intonation to express strong feelings—but their language skills are still developing, so they often fall back on using tears and tantrums. Recording the observations of Keri can result in strategies that meet her needs. The strategies that adults use in these situations can either set up negative communication patterns between adults and children or support children emotionally as they learn new ways of expressing strong feelings.

Strategies to use include: accentuating Keri's strengths, using responsive interactions in the moment, using responsive interactions beyond the moment, and changing the environment.

A Child Who Tantrums: Accentuate the Child's Strengths

Instead of thinking of Keri as the little girl who has tantrums, think of Keri's strengths and what she loves to do. She is enthusiastic about everything that she does and she loves it when she can make a choice. Keri's teachers decided to build on this enthusiasm and Keri's desire to make choices by offering her more choices throughout the day. For example, they ask her if she would like a blue bib or a white bib as they move toward the table, or if she wants to have her diaper changed before or after a favorite puzzle.

A Child Who Tantrums: Use Responsive Interactions in the Moment

Will responding to children's tantrums encourage their negative behavior and spoil them? Or, can we, as adults, respond to tantrums in a way that helps children learn to use words to communicate their feelings? When deciding how to react, think of outbursts as part of a developmental stage most toddlers go through.

Your job is to teach children new ways to express strong emotions, not to discourage these feelings by ignoring them. Your support through this difficult stage will help children learn to communicate more maturely. Following are some ways in which you can encourage this process when a child is having a tantrum:

- *Validate children's feelings.* Even though you won't give Keri another banana, you can let her know you understand why she's upset. By saying in a soothing voice, "Keri, you seem very frustrated. I realize you want another banana," you're sending the message that she's been heard and that it's okay to have strong feelings.
- *Build children's emotional vocabulary.* Children can learn, from you, the words to express how they feel. So, when you comment on a child's emotions, model words she can use. You might say, with feeling, "Keri, you seem sad. You're crying. You can tell me, 'I'm sad.'"
- *Observe facial expressions, gestures, and body movements.* Learn when a toddler might be getting ready to tantrum. Catching the toddler before she tantrums is one of the keys to preventing tantrums and helping her learn new ways to express disappointment, frustration, and anger.
- *Encourage problem solving by offering choices.* Providing options helps toddlers discover new solutions to old problems. For example, giving Keri a choice of more juice or more milk (instead of another banana) will help her feel as if she has some power in the situation. It will give her a sense of control over herself and her environment, while letting her know that a loving adult is watching out for her well-being.
- *Model ways to express strong feelings.* To let Keri know she isn't the only person who has feelings, share how you feel with her. You might say, with the appropriate expression, "Keri, I wish you could have another banana!"

Discussing feelings is neither giving in to children nor giving them everything they want (common adult fears). Rather, when you show children how to communicate through words and gestures, you're helping them take the next developmental step toward becoming good communicators and problem solvers. You are also providing them safe and healthy boundaries in which to build relationships and learn.

A Child Who Tantrums: Build Relationships Beyond the Moment

Whereas many toddlers tantrum because they are overwhelmed in the moment, events that happened at home or in the infant-toddler care and learning program may have affected Keri. Teachers and parents should aim to have a strong, positive relationship so that there can be an open discussion about whether there has been any change in Keri's life that may be affecting her emotionally, such as sudden changes in who is taking care of her at home.

 Watch this video on handling children's tantrums by meeting their emotional need for empathy. Which techniques are recommended?

https://www.youtube.com/watch?v=UwuIvk0Hg9U

A Child Who Tantrums: Create and Change the Environment in Responsive Ways

If adults find themselves saying "No," "Stop that," "You can't do that," or constantly removing children from dangerous situations, then the environment definitely needs to be improved so that children, peers, and adults are safe and engaged in many fulfilling and interesting activities together. When there is a "No" environment, toddlers will feel quite frustrated and confused concerning what they can and cannot do. The environment can be changed to be more interesting, less stimulating, and more supportive of the child's emotional and social development.

Children Who Bite

One of the biggest challenges for group programs is children biting each other and the teacher. So let's explore the topic of why children bite and the strategies that adults can use to deal with the problem.

> Jaheed's mother is coming to the door of the infant-toddler center to pick up Jaheed and take him home. About an hour ago, Jaheed bit Aaron. Jaheed didn't break the skin, but Aaron cried for a long time after Jaheed bit him. What are you going to say to Jaheed's mother? What are you going to say to Aaron's mother?

Before babies have teeth, they gum, mouth, and suck on any object they can get into their mouths. Babies are encouraged to "bite" their food and try new oral delights. It is no wonder that as they become more physically active and enter the stage of "true experimentations" between 12 and 18 months, people become one of the new objects that must be tested and tried to see how they taste.

Biting, then, provides babies with comfort (as they suck their fists, fingers, and food) and opportunities to learn (as they discover what is soft, hard, chewy, tasty, or yucky). Yet, biting, which is so enjoyable and so necessary, can get the toddler into trouble when it extends into the world of adults, children, themselves, and animals.

Children may bite other people for various reasons. It will help you handle a child who bites if you think about the many possible reasons toddlers bite others. You can then try the solutions based on the particular reason a particular child is biting people. Table 14.2 presents the reasons children bite, as well as possible solutions.

When an infant or toddler bites another person, show the child who bites with your voice and facial expression that you are very concerned. Speak in a serious voice with the child. Look directly into the child's eyes. Hold the child gently by the shoulders if necessary. For example, you might say, "You bit Candace" (state the behavior). "She doesn't like it. She's crying" (pointing out how the bite's behavior affected the other child). "You can bite this cloth" (food, biting toy, etc.), or "You can tell Candace how you feel" (what the child can do instead). Use words appropriate to the child's developmental level and try to restore the relationship between the two children. With toddlers and twos, an adult can ask the victim to tell the biter what would make him feel better.

Help the victim of the biter. If the skin is not broken or broken, wash it well with soap and water. If possible, bring the biter along to assist the victim (however, the victim may appropriately want the biter to stay far away). Call the parent of the child who received the bite. If the skin is broken, then the parent must take the child to a doctor.

Often the biter is as frightened about what happened as the victim. If punishment for the biter is too harsh, the young child who bites nurses her own hurt rather than concentrating on and helping the victim of the bite. If you punish or yell at the child or put her in time-out, she will try to protect herself, think only of herself, and will not be open to learning about alternatives to biting others.

TABLE 14.2   Why Children Bite: Relationship-Based Solutions

Reason for Biting: Holding On and Letting Go

As children's muscles mature, toddlers experiment with two simultaneous ways of handing experiences: *holding on* and *letting go*. Toddlers are learning to both hold on and let go of (1) parents and other adults, (2) toys, (3) bowel movements, etc. Thus, they are also learning to hang on/let go with their mouths.

Program Solution: Help ease infant or toddler separations (letting go) from their parents. If the baby cries when the parent leaves, then say to the baby, "You're feeling very sad that Mommy/Daddy has to leave. It's hard to say good-bye. Mommy/Daddy will come back after lunch/nap" (some concrete event). Give toys to baby for hanging on/letting go, such as blocks to put into containers. Don't pressure toilet learning. Wait until the child shows that he or she can "let go" in other areas of life.

Reason for Biting: Autonomy

Toddlers are developing autonomy: doing things for themselves, making choices, needing to control, making demands of adults and the environment, wanting power, moving out and away from adults. Biting can be an expression of a toddler's separation from the adult; infants and toddlers are no longer one with adults if they can bite the adult. Infants and toddlers are showing control of the other person and the situation when they bite. Biting gives children power over others. Toddlers may be allowed to get "out of control" by loving adults who are hesitant to set limits for them.

Program Solution: Toddlers need help to achieve a balance between their need for control and their need for loving, firm limits to be placed on their often-uncontrollable urges. Because there are so many situations in which adults must control toddlers, allow and provide as many situations as possible when they can choose and have power. For example, you can say, "Do you want the red marker or the blue marker?" "The apple or the pear?" Set up the environment so that infants and toddlers can have long stretches of time to make choices and have control over how long they play with a toy.

Reason for Biting: Sensory Exploration

Biting is a part of sensorimotor exploration. Toys, food, and people must be touched, smelled, and, of course, tasted if the toddler is to learn. Infants and toddlers are sensuous creatures who learn through their all of their senses and their motor actions.

Program Solution: Provide a variety of sensorimotor experiences. Infants and toddlers should experience closely supervised play with water, paints, play dough, and sand. Infants and toddlers can crawl and tumble over a variety of hard, soft, rough, and smooth surfaces. A colorful array of toys that can be mouthed and easily washed should be available.

Reason for Biting: Teething

Teething can cause an infant's or toddler's mouth to hurt. Babies often need something or someone to gnaw on to comfort them.

Program Solution: Provide infants and toddlers with teething toys, frozen bagels, and chewy foods that disintegrate in the mouth and will not cause choking. Older toddlers can be encouraged to bite on firm teething toys. Clean frozen cloths provide cooling relief for teething toddlers (and for the child who has been bitten).

Reason for Biting: Desire for Peer Interaction

Infants and toddlers are just beginning to learn how to engage peers in positive ways. Infants usually do not understand they are hurting others when they bite them (older toddlers may). Infants and toddlers do not know how to approach their peers in acceptable ways. They often express their interest by biting, pulling hair, pushing, etc.

Program Solution: Children need lots of social experiences in order to learn how to interact with others. Take their hand as they reach out to others roughly and say, "Touch gently—that makes her feel happy." Acknowledge their interest in other children by saying, "I know you like Darin—you can give him a toy." Provide enough age-appropriate materials and equipment so children can play beside and with each other. Notice positive peer interaction such as one child hugging another, giving a toy to another, and smiling to another.

TABLE 14.2 Why Children Bite: Relationship-Based Solutions (Continued)

Reason for Biting: Cause and Effect

Infants and toddlers truly investigate cause-and-effect relationships. It is as if they are saying, "What will happen if I bite Susie? What reaction will I get?" Biting gets a reaction—usually a very strong one! The infant often receives a loud scream from the other baby, and a yell of protest from an adult.

Program Solution: Provide extensive time for play. Provide toys that "do something" when the child acts on the toy (cause and effect). For example, when a button is pushed, a figure pops up, or when a knob is turned, music plays. Sand, dirt, water, paints, blocks, and crayons allow for creative, open-ended experiences that offer many opportunities for the child to make something happen. Help them notice the positive reaction they get when they pat, hug, or give a toy to another child.

Reason for Biting: Imitation

Infants and toddlers learn by imitating others, and biting is one behavior that is often learned from other young persons. After 15 months, infants can observe a behavior (such as biting), store it in their memory, and perform the act later when conditions are right. This skill is called *deferred imitation*. Research has shown that children who are physically punished are much more likely than their peers to be aggressive with both adults and peers—especially younger, smaller peers. Children learn that hitting and biting others is an acceptable way of handling their anger if they see adults responding in that way.

Program Solution: Model loving, nurturing, sharing, polite, positive behavior for young children to imitate. Develop a repertoire of responses for handling children's negative behavior. Redirect them to a positive activity or acknowledge their feelings (e.g., "You are feeling angry at Sarah—she took your toy and that made you feel angry"). Teach the child alternative positive behavior. Positive techniques do work! Children comply more readily and they learn positive ways of interacting with others.

Reason for Biting: Attention

The young child may bite to get attention from others. It is true that negative attention seems to be better to many toddlers than no attention at all. Everyone hates to be ignored, and children younger than age 3 are no exception. Some children may actually be receiving more negative attention from teachers and peers than positive attention, thus continuing the cycle of negative behavior.

Program Solution: Saturate the child who bites with positive, warm, nurturing attention. This can be difficult, especially when adults are feeling extremely frustrated. Remember, however, that when children's positive, busy, curious, helpful, productive behaviors are noticed and encouraged, the children are much more likely to continue those behaviors. Comment on young children's efforts rather than saying, "Good boy." Say, "You are working so hard." Children learn the positive behaviors and behave that way more often. Break into that negative cycle of child behavior with adult positive comments and hugs.

Reason for Biting: Frustration

Young children may bite others due to feelings of anger and frustration because of lack of language skills, or needs that are not met. A child who cries or whose more positive bids for attention go unheard may feel that they need to bite to get attention. A child who is hit, slapped, yelled at, or bitten by adults may become a frustrated, angry, biting child. Too many children, too high adult-to-child ratios, or not enough space can lead to biting.

Program Solution: Help young children develop their own repertoire of behaviors for gaining attention from adults and peers. Help children handle frustrations and angry feelings. Help children learn to say "Not now!" or sign "No" to another child who grabs a toy. Teach children to say, "I feel frustrated" to adults and peers. If infant-toddler professionals or parents are using punitive techniques, they need opportunities to learn about the effects of positive versus hostile discipline techniques. Children who have been severely punished will need time to develop trust in adults who use positive strategies.

TABLE 14.2   **Why Children Bite: Relationship-Based Solutions**

> **Reason for Biting: Anxiety**
>
> Young children may be experiencing generalized anxiety about events happening to them or around them (such as parents' divorcing or fighting, the loss of or separation from loved ones, etc.). Anxiety may lead to biting others to relieve tension (just as adults smoke cigarettes, chew gum, or bat a ball around).
>
> **Program Solution**: Work with parents to determine the source of anxiety. Provide calming activities such as water or sand play. Allow children to suck a thumb and/or hold transitional objects (such as blankets or stuffed animals). Provide time for one-on-one with a special adult. Pat backs and sing songs at nap time to quiet toddlers into sleep. Use infant massage strategies to calm a child. Play soothing lullabies. Stay close to nurture children and help them through transition times.

If one child's biting continues after several days of repeating these techniques, meet with the family and other teachers to determine what might be causing the child to bite and plan together to provide consistency across home and the infant-toddler care and learning program. The infant or toddler deserves our best planning, caring, and teaching. Implement a more intense program of time-in and emotional connection with an adult. An adult stays near the child, meets the child's emotional needs, shows the child affection and encouragement, catches her before she bites, teaches her alternative behaviors, and teaches her how to be gentle or use sign language or words to express her needs.

Keep in mind the following points:

- When adults hit or bite children for biting others, the child learns that biting is OK if you are bigger and stronger than the other person. The child will be more likely to bite peers (especially smaller ones).
- Observe when the biting and attempts to bite occur. Keep records. The biting may occur before lunch or when others crowd the child.
- Explore with the parents what the reasons for biting may be. Try a solution based on the possible reasons. Work with the parents of the biter so that the guidance techniques used at home and at the center are consistent.
- Have a staff meeting. Review all the reasons that toddlers bite and all the techniques that can be used. Individualize strategies for each child and then work together to provide consistency for that child. Staff can help one another be consistent in the use of the techniques.
- Before parents and family members become upset about a biting problem, hold a parent meeting or send a newsletter home to let parents know what techniques they and the staff can use. Parents need to know why toddlers bite, that it is a common problem whenever toddlers are brought together in a group, and that the name of the biter will not be revealed. Tell parents that the staff will do everything possible to ensure the safety of the children.

If a solution works, give yourself a big pat on the back. If a solution does not work, provide the time-in approach. If the child continues biting, bites viciously, or bites and then smiles, seek professional help. Too many parents are asked to take their child out of a center for biting. This solves the problem for the program but not for the child or the family. In collaboration with the parent, you can seek support for the child from professionals in the local early intervention team in your school district (see Chapter 15). These professionals will provide an assessment and ongoing support if needed to parents and teachers. Children can learn that infant-toddler teachers are there to help them learn new positive ways of interacting with peers and adults.

BOX 14.4

Readiness for Toilet Learning

Parents

- Are willing to collaborate with teachers to provide consistency for the child.
- Are willing to be encouraging and not punitive with the child.
- Respect the child's timetable (e.g., a child may start the process and then stop for a period of time).
- Agree that the child is ready to learn.

Teachers

- Have an adult-to-child ratio that is conducive to a teacher being available to the child learning to use the toilet.
- Have a trusting relationship with the child.

The child

- Has an interest in imitating adults when they use the toilet.
- Can communicate his or her needs with sign language, gestures, or words to adults.
- Is not in a resistant stage of development.
- Is willing to sit on the toilet with and without diapers.
- Can pull pants off and on fairly easily.
- Has sphincter (anal) muscles that are sufficiently developed to hold on and let go of a bowel movement.
- Has a dry diaper for longer periods of time indicating that the child's bladder is maturing.

Toilet Learning

Here's what children do in order to use a toilet. Children must (1) feel the urge to eliminate; (2) understand the urge is a signal to eliminate—"Hey, I gotta go, NOW!"; (3) suppress the immediate urge; (4) get to the toilet (quickly!); (5) pull clothing out of the way; (6) situate and balance on the potty; and (7) relax urinary or sphincter muscles to eliminate. (19, p. 78)

And, those are just the physical skills necessary for toddlers to be successful using a toilet. There are also emotional issues. As mentioned in our discussion of toddler resistance, toddlers do want to be grown up—but they often want to grow up on their own timetable.

Most child development specialists who have written about toilet learning recommend waiting until the child shows signs of readiness (see Box 14.4). They use the term *toilet learning* rather than *toilet training* to indicate that children are learning on their own terms, rather than adults training them on the adult's timetable. Learning to use the toilet is a "step up to independence" (20). It is an opportunity for the toddler to express his autonomy. If forced, he will express his autonomy by resisting the adult. We want the child to feel as if it is his idea, not ours, for him to use the toilet and it is his accomplishment, not ours, when he does.

Brazelton and Sparrow (21) have written a book outlining Brazelton's method for helping toddlers learn to use the toilet. They recommend a relaxed method of taking the child to the toilet and letting him sit on it with his clothes on. If there is no resistance, then take the child to the toilet without a diaper on. Always let the child get up and leave if he wants to. At some point you will "catch" the child's urine or stool, and the child will begin to get the idea of how to use the toilet. If the child resists or the process does not seem to be working, wait at least a month before trying again. Be encouraging but be careful not to praise too loudly or too much. The child is doing this for himself, not just for you. To provide consistency for the child at home and in a program, it is best if the parents and teachers meet to discuss the toilet learning process.

Toddlers may touch their own genitals while they are learning to use the toilet, and infants may during diapering. This is typical behavior and should not be punished. If you ignore this normal behavior, their curiosity will be satisfied.

When they share their observations of the child, parents and teachers can usually agree on methods and a cooperative plan of action—especially if a relationship of mutual trust has been established.

The goal is that toddlers end up with a sense of pride in using the toilet—a very grown-up thing to do—rather than a sense of shame due to failure or anger because he is being forced against his will. And finally, "Anticipate accidents by asking parents to provide at least three pairs of extra LABELED underwear, pants/shorts, and an extra pair of shoes. When accidents occur, don't spank, threaten, ridicule, tease, or otherwise punish a child. Reassure them that every boy and girl has accidents when learning to use the toilet" (22, p. 80).

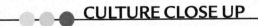

CULTURE CLOSE UP

Toilet learning can be a frustrating time for parents if they would like to complete the process quickly to eliminate the costly expense of diapers and not have to clean up the sometimes "big messes" that toddlers can make in their diaper. In some cultures, parents may "train" children early (in the first 2 years of life) by learning to read the signs that a child gives when he is going to urinate or defecate and then placing the child on the toilet or a potty chair. The parent may ask you to do the same in the program. This can be challenging in a program where a teacher often has at least three infants to take care of, and even more if the teacher works with toddlers. How would you use the dialog methods recommended in Chapter 12 for listening to parents and negotiating strategies with them?

Check Your Understanding 14.3
Click here to check your understanding of the concepts in this section.

Challenging Behavior and Mental Health Issues

Managing challenging behaviors in infants and toddlers are just that—a challenge! Infant and toddler teachers and parents have listed children's behaviors that are challenging to them: sadness; flat affect; distress or crying frequently; continuously hurting others (biting, pushing, grabbing, hitting); hurting self; frequently having tantrums and falling apart; not sleeping; excess clinginess; noncompliance; defensive, angry, anxious, or fearful behavior; and a general lack of response to guidance strategies. Note that these behaviors more seriously affect and disrupt infants' and toddlers' sense of well-being, long-term behavior, and sense of self-worth. They represent a more serious challenge for the child, family members, teachers, and peers and are beyond typical development issues that respond to socialization and guidance strategies. These expressions of a child's need engender intense feelings on the part of everyone involved and are often difficult to understand. Challenging behaviors can leave adults feeling powerless as they try to problem solve to help the child toward well-being and away from distress.

In this section, we again emphasize that behavior is a way for young children to communicate their joys, needs, and frustrations. If we can "read" the behavior, then we have a key for unlocking the meaning of the behavior for the child. The child is clearly telling us that he or she needs help.

When adults talk about challenging behavior, they usually mean that the child is challenging them. They may mean that their typical guidance strategies just aren't working. However, the child is feeling challenged, too. Infant mental health specialists have helped teachers and parents understand that infants and toddlers can and do have strong feelings in response to their experiences in life and that it is important to intervene early if the child is feeling challenged.

What do children with behavioral challenges have in common? Often they are communicating their distress through their behavior rather than using language. They may be ill, tired, or overwhelmed by stimulation. A child who "doesn't listen" may not be hearing well. A child who falls apart frequently and with intensity when there is too much stimulation may be sensitive to noise. A child may be delayed in language development, which then affects how well she can communicate her needs. Children may not be able to tell you with their words, but they are telling you with their behavior that something doesn't feel right.

A child who is feeling challenged may feel overprotected or underprotected. If adults are watching every move and constantly warning the child of dangers, then the child may feel as if the world is a scary place. The child then feels afraid to venture out and explore the environment. This child may feel overprotected. Alternatively, if an adult is not setting limits for the toddler—such as "hitting hurts" or "jumping off high furniture is not safe"—a toddler may feel as if he has too much power and thus will not feel safe. This toddler may do "daring" things as if to say "Doesn't someone care enough to stop me?" In these cases, children may feel underprotected. Let's examine some emotions that infants and toddlers may express, what they mean, and what teachers can do to support the child and family.

Anxious, Fearful, Vigilant

A child who is anxious, fearful, or vigilant (on guard) may have multiple or specific fears; become agitated easily; or display uncontrollable crying or screaming, facial tics, and tension. The child may be easily upset, not explore, cling to an adult, or run and hide when something fearful happens. Children who are anxious may seem to be constantly watchful of others and the environment. Anxiety is increased by helplessness and lack of knowledge, which makes infants and toddlers very prone to it (23).

The child may have had overwhelming, frightening experiences or be experiencing sensory overload. There may be too much stimulation for this particular child's temperament and ability to process information through several senses at once.

You can help these children by doing the following:

- Offer challenges gradually.
- Speak in a calm voice.
- Keep your promises to read a book or to help the child.
- Do not send the child over to a new situation. Go with her and draw her in. Stay with her until her mood has changed.
- Say often, "This is a safe place. I will keep you safe."
- Provide a primary caregiver model where at least one caregiver "moves up" to the next classroom with the child.

Work closely with families. Families' marital relationships influence infant behavior (24). They found that aggressive marital conflicts predicted infant withdrawal at 6 months. The results of this study demonstrate how important it is for early educators to think about children's behavior within the context of the family from a bioecological perspective and provide as many family-friendly policies and opportunities as possible. When talking directly with families, use the 6-step problem-solving approach discussed earlier and the 10-point problem-solving guide at the end of this chapter.

Angry and Defiant

Infants and toddlers can feel angry. Infants may cry loudly. Their faces may scrunch up and turn red as they express their rage. An angry toddler may throw things such as toys or scratch another child who gets too near. An angry toddler may even throw chairs. A very upset toddler screams many angry words—words that you didn't think a young child could say. A defiant toddler might destroy materials or toys, throw things, and threaten others.

What might contribute to this behavior? Perhaps this child is easily over-stimulated and has difficulty with self-regulation. Perhaps an adult in the child's life doesn't understand development, and so scolds or punishes typical behavior. This child may have difficulty trusting others because she hasn't experienced pre-dictable, kind, understanding, or responsive relationships. A child who is angry may have experienced a traumatic event or events. If you look closely, you may actually see a fearful child who is lashing out to protect himself—before someone hurts him.

An angry child can make the adults around her angry, too. It is hard to stay calm in the face of so much feeling from a child so young. Your anger, though, is not helpful to the child. The child may be trying hard to trigger your anger, because that is what the child expects from adults. When we understand the intention of the child, we then can respond with the message (through words or actions) that "I'm not going to respond to you the way you have come to expect." Instead, value the feelings of the child. Help identify the child's feelings by saying, "You are very angry!" in a tone that tells the child you understand. You may need to repeat this several times. Tell the child what he can do instead of hurting others or destroying property. Say, "You can stomp when you are angry" and then show him how. Figure out what the child is trying to communicate and what the child needs; help the child learn appropriate ways to get those needs met. Adapt your solutions to the needs of the individual child. Some possible responses may include the following:

- Take time to be emotionally available—be a respite in the storm. Sit on the floor near the child. Hold and comfort the child as often as possible. Give the child one-on-one time each day.
- Be firm about toddlers using aggression to express anger. Say (depending on what the child can understand), "Hitting hurts and we need to keep everyone safe. You can tell me, 'I'm angry.'"
- Help the child feel safe.
- Be responsive so the child feels he can "make something happen" in socially acceptable ways.
- Give choices—for example, say, "Do you want juice or milk?"
- Provide a quiet area (cozy corner) in the room where the child can go when he is angry. Do not force him to stay in that area, but rather encourage him to use it when he is angry.
- Provide places for boisterous play such as climbing and running.
- Provide a calm environment with places for cuddling, comforting, and caring.

Meet together with children's families in a supportive way. Parents and teachers must know that "toddlerhood represents a critical period when behavioral and emotional problems of potentially clinical significance emerge" (25, p. 12). The children's families and teachers must be involved in problem-solving solutions (26). The children who exhibit extreme oppositional and defiant behavior should receive extensive support from infant mental health professionals.

Children Who Behave Aggressively

Aggression is defined as behavior that harms others either directly through physical damage or indirectly through manipulation of peer relationships. An adult in an infant or toddler room may experience children who bite, scratch, hit, kick, spit, or pull hair. A toddler may call another child names or purposely ignore another child. Children may be initiating aggression or reacting to another's aggression (27).

Always look for physical reasons first. Children who have delayed receptive language development may not be able to process language and communicate their needs, so they resort to physical aggression (28). A child with delayed receptive language may have **neurocognitive challenges**.

Observe these children so that you can understand what they are communicating to you through their behavior. They may be communicating that they don't want other children to be near them or that they need to feel powerful. A toddler may have learned that she gets her needs met (attention, noticed, out of an activity) when she is aggressive. Or, she may be experimenting with new behaviors that she observed other toddlers use. The infant or toddler may be angry.

Children who are aggressive may feel "out of control" and frightened because there are no clear or consistent rules or boundaries and they are not learning to regulate their behavior. Your observation and discussions with family members will help you determine what the child is trying to communicate.

We must recognize that children's problematic aggressive behavior can begin in infancy. Many toddlers use aggressive behaviors as they are learning how to interact with others. However, most toddlers, with adult support, learn alternative ways of expressing their needs (29). There are some toddlers who do not learn alternative ways. In a longitudinal study of 10,658 Canadian children, one-sixth of the children demonstrated a consistent pattern of high levels of aggression from toddlerhood to preadolescence. These children were primarily boys from low-income families whose parents used **"hostile/ineffective parenting strategies"** (30, 31. p. 71). Other studies support the Canada research. When toddlers experience mutually angry and hostile mother-toddler interactions at 24 to 42 months, these young children are more likely to have behavior problems at 5 to 6 years of age (32). On the other hand, parental sensitivity is related to a *decrease* in angry, acting out behavior (33). Also, when mothers use more reasoning with their older toddlers the children are more socially competent with more developed self-concepts at age 3 (34).

Spanking children can lead to aggression (35). In one study 3-year-olds who were spanked more than twice in the prior month by both parents had increased aggression at 5 years of age. Another study found that the more children were spanked at age 1, the more likely they were to have behavioral challenges at age 3. Those with behavioral challenges at age 3 were more likely to have social challenges at age 5 (36).

We can ask, "Does spanking work to stop undesired behavior?" In one study 73 percent of the time children received corporal punishment, they misbehaved again within 10 minutes (37). Spanking didn't seem to stop undesired child behavior. Intervention with families can work to decrease spanking. Parents, who had positive attitudes toward corporal punishment were provided very brief summaries of the negative effects of corporal punishment. Parents who read the brief summaries demonstrated significant decreases in their positive attitudes about corporal punishment (38).

This research supports the importance of listening to and supporting families when their children are infants and toddlers. If parents are using hostile/ineffective parenting strategies in these early years, provide them opportunities for home visits, parent-to-parent stress reduction classes, and guidance classes. Innovative prevention programs are being developed. One innovative program developed to help parents in a child maltreatment prevention program used iPhones to connect parents with home visitors (39).

You can help these children by doing the following:

- Refer the child to the local child find team affiliated with the local school district for a full evaluation of emotional, social, cognitive, language, and motor development.
- Work hard to develop the child's trust in you and a positive relationship. Greet the child warmly each day and provide one-on-one teacher-child cozy, comforting time. Help the child get his needs met in more positive ways.
- Make 10 times more positive remarks than negative ones: Notice, notice, notice positive behavior.
- Keep teaching prosocial behavior.
- Talk to the child about his character in a positive way. Say, "You are the kind of child who helps others."
- Give the toddler a toy or stuffed animal and say, "This is your toy, and you can hold it all day if you'd like—you don't have to share it. The other toys are for all of the children to share and use."
- If the toddler hits you, hold the toddler's hand and say, "I don't like to be hit. It hurts. You can tell me, 'I'm mad.'"
- Help the child take the perspective of the other child. Say, "No biting, that hurt him—look, he's crying."
- Say, "I know you are angry, but I do not want you to kick him. Kicking hurts."
- Reduce stimuli, create a calm and safe environment, provide cozy corners and a private place for the child (can be an open box), so the child can be alone when needed (this is not a time-out spot).
- Create an interesting environment with cause-and-effect toys so the child can feel more powerful.
- Reduce spaces for running in a classroom, but provide places for large motor activities.

The toddler years are critical for supporting children's use of prosocial rather than aggressive behaviors (40).

Posttraumatic Stress Disorder

Unfortunately, some infants and toddlers experience extremely unpleasant events such as a car accident, hospitalization, abuse, or witnessing domestic abuse or even murder. **Posttraumatic stress disorder** can occur after an infant or toddler experiences a traumatic event. Gaensbauer (41), a professor of psychiatry who helps children who experience trauma in their lives, reports that young children usually relive the trauma through their actions rather than verbally. He reports that a child placed in foster care at 4 months of age had been severely traumatized by a mother with mental illness. She would undress him and wrap him in cold towels. At 9 months of age, when he was reunited with his mother for a supervised visit, she started to undress him. At that moment the infant started to scream and the visit was stopped. He seemed to have a memory of the trauma from when he was 4 months old.

 Watch this video on how *you* can make a difference in the lives of children who are experiencing trauma. How does one secure relationship make a difference in a child's life? What did one narrator mean when she said, "You have permission to meet children's needs?"

https://www.youtube.com/watch?v=RYj7YYHmbQs

A person, object, or event may trigger memories of the painful, disturbing, or upsetting experience. These memories of the experience may cause fear, anxiety, withdrawal, aggression, crying, or shock. The infant or toddler may become still with vacant eyes or hyperactive with frantic looks. A toddler who experienced cockroaches in his diaper while suffering neglect in his home became frenzied when he felt a prickly or crawling sensation on his skin (42). It may seem as if the toddler is having a tantrum, but he is expressing fear. A child may cling to a blanket or piece of clothing that reminds her of her deceased mother. A child may begin to panic when she sees a pair of scissors because this is what her mother used to protect herself during a domestic violence incident. An open hand raised to help a toddler may cause a child to "freeze" or panic because of parental abuse with an open hand. These children may want to over control their environment and people or may withdraw in order to keep themselves safe. The overwhelming feeling that a child (or an adult) seems to experience during the traumatic event is one of helplessness, inability to control the situation, and feelings of not being safe or protected. Adapt your strategies to the individual child's temperament and experience. The purpose of your strategies is to assure the child that you will keep him safe. You can do the following:

- Talk with a mental health specialist for support and strategies that meet this particular child's need.
- Observe and document the child's behavior.
- Help the child learn strategies when lost in a flood of anxiety—for instance, go to the teacher or a safe place at home or in classroom.
- Always tell when you are going out of the room—and say "I'm back" when you return.
- Help the child feel competent with toys and materials at her developmental level.
- Acknowledge the child's feelings—say, "It looks as if you are feeling afraid. I'm here, I'll keep you safe." Say, "This is a safe place."
- Use contingently responsive strategies—for instance, when a child pops up out of a box, say, "Oh, there you are" in a surprised voice. The child may replay the scene over and over to feel as if he is "making something happen." The child

may also be playing out the theme of separation by separating from you and then returning to see if you are still there.

- Provide a primary caregiver, continuity of care, and a consistent routine.
- Provide a cozy corner or "safe place" with boundaries and comforting toys (could be a box).
- Simplify things for the child—provide her own bin of water for water-play instead of a bin for two, so the child doesn't have to share for a while.
- Provide water play—it *may* be soothing to a child.
- Take obnoxiously loud toys out of the environment.

Work with a mental health specialist as you support the family. If the child has been removed from his home, you may be working with the foster parent(s). Help families understand, and learn from families how the child is expressing his or her reaction to trauma. Problem solve with the family on how to comfort the child. And, of course, if you suspect abuse, you must report it.

What Philosophy Will You Use?

A responsive care, relationship-based model that includes a family- and culture-centered approach works very well for helping us think about how to help a child who is challenged and challenges parents, teachers, and peers. Ask: "What strategies promote healthy relationships and are responsive to the child's needs? What strategies make the child feel safe, secure, and able to express emotions in a healthy way? What helps him regulate his own behavior, problem solve, and want to be prosocial? How can you win the heart of a child with challenging behavior?"

Are the important adults in the child's life working together to improve all of the child's relationships? If the child is to be helped, it isn't enough to improve only the relationship between the teacher and the child, although that can certainly help the child emotionally. The child's relationship with his or her parents, siblings, or grandparents must also be improved for long-term results. There is no place for blaming the child (as in "He's mean")—but rather, it is the responsibility of adults to positively support the child and work toward the child's mental health and well-being.

Following is a 10-point process for helping children with challenging behavior. The key people in the child's life work together to answer the following questions that then lead to a relationship-based approach with the child. Only after all of the key people reflect on the questions can appropriate strategies be developed that truly meet the child's needs.

1. *Who is this child?* Who has positive relationships with this child? What are his strengths? Who likes what about this child?

   It is important to see the "whole" child with strengths, interests, and needs rather than defining the child only by the challenging behavior.

2. *Clearly define the behavior that is challenging the child, the teacher, or family members.*

   Before deciding on strategies, the behavior must be clearly defined. Write down the behavior (he bites other children), not an attribute of the child (the child is aggressive). What is the challenge for the child? For example, "The child bites peers." How often does it occur? How long has it occurred? Who does it happen with? Where does it happen? Is it developmentally appropriate?

3. *Why is the behavior a challenge?*

   Why is the behavior a challenge for the child, the parent, the teacher, and peers? How are the parents and teachers feeling about it? (Angry, sad, rejected, proud, frustrated?) How is it affecting the child and others? Who is it a problem for? What's the meaning for the family and teachers? What are the cultural issues?

4. *Why do the family and teacher think the child does the behavior?*

   Brainstorm several possibilities. Always rule out any medical problems first. Then observe the child. Observe for temperament, developmental level, delay, disability, coping style, sensory needs, imitation, anxiety, fear, anger, stress, hypersensitivity, sleep deprivation, grief, depression, need for positive attention, recent loss or transitions, trauma, or abuse. Think about how the child is keeping himself safe. Has he learned to avoid adults to protect himself or has he learned to "make himself heard" and use more intense ways of getting the attention of the adult in order to be protected?

5. *What's the purpose of the behavior? What is the child trying to communicate?*

   The behavior is working for the child and helping her cope. What does the child gain from the behavior? (If the child hits, the child gets a toy away from a peer.) After observing, complete the following chart:

Date	What Happens Before	The Challenging Behavior	What Happens After	Possible Purposes of the Behavior

6. *What is the child feeling and experiencing?* What's the emotional need being expressed by the child? How is the child feeling challenged? Look at behavior from the child's perspective.

7. *What are the child's short-term and long-range social and emotional needs?*

8. *What do the family, teachers, and peers want the child to be able to feel and do instead of the challenging behavior?* Is it developmentally appropriate? Will it help the child meet his needs? Does the child possess the skills to meet the need in a more appropriate way?"

9. *Think about the strategies you've tried.* What's worked, what hasn't? How did they work? How did these make the child feel? How did they make the adult feel? Were the strategies consistent with achieving the goal(s) for the child? Were they consistent with your beliefs about what infants and toddlers need and how they learn?

10. *What support do the adults and peers need to help this child?* Who can help the child, the family, peers, and the teachers? What are some strategies that meet children's needs; help children achieve their goals; guide children to

use more positive behavior; and are developmentally, individually, and culturally appropriate?

Whoever has a strong, positive relationship with the child should be the key persons to help.

Check Your Understanding 14.4
Click here to check your understanding of the concepts in this section.

Summary

This chapter completed our discussion of the components of a curriculum by examining component 8 (a relationship-based approach to guidance).

- The term *discipline* has traditionally been used to mean adult control, restraint, and authority as well as child obedience—but another meaning of the term discipline is to teach infants and toddlers new behavior. Because of the confusion between the two meanings of the term discipline, we will use the term *guidance* to indicate a developmental, relationship-based, problem-solving approach to supporting young children's social and emotional competence. When adults guide young children, they are teaching them in order for them to be successful in a world that requires social and emotional competence.

- A relationship-based approach to guidance is important. There are respect, reflect, and relate strategies to use in a relationship-based approach.

  □ Respect for infants and toddlers includes valuing their emotional needs, individual differences and strengths, and the power of development. Teachers must also respect themselves and know how their culture and past experiences affect their beliefs about how children should behave and become socialized.

  □ When adults reflect, they think about what an experience is like for a child, observe what the children are communicating through their behavior,

and decide what they would like the child to learn to do instead.

  □ When adults relate with infants and toddlers, they support children's healthy relationships with all of the important people in their lives, focus on adult-child responsive interactions that promote children's capacities and development, and create a supportive environment.

- Relationship realignments are a necessary part of the teacher/child relationships.

  □ Separation anxiety, toddler resistance, challenges with learning to use the toilet, tantrums, and biting peers and adults are behaviors that are sure to happen with infants and toddlers.

  □ When adults understand that young children experience times of emotional turmoil as they develop and learn new behaviors, they can be more understanding and supportive.

- There are specific strategies and programs that are effective with children who exhibit challenging behavior and experience mental health issues.

  □ Some infants and toddlers may feel anxious, fearful, and vigilant; angry and defiant; aggressive; or may experience posttraumatic stress disorder.

  □ Use a relationship-based philosophy to collaborate with all of the adults in a child's life to support the child's emotional and social development when the child is feeling challenged.

Key Terms

discipline
guidance
justification
hostile/ineffective
   parenting strategies
mitigation

negativism
neurocognitive challenges
other-oriented guidance
posttraumatic stress disorder
resolution
sensory challenges

separation anxiety
socialized
tantrums
time-in
time-out
traumatic events

Reflections and Resources for the Reader

REFLECTIONS

1. Elaborate on the 3 R approach (respect, reflect, and relate) for thinking about guidance. What would you add to each step of the process?
2. What is the child experiencing when he or she is having a tantrum? How do you or other adults you know usually handle toddler tantrums? What would you do to support a child who is having a tantrum and help the child learn new ways to express emotions?
3. Trishanna is 20-months-old, in a family child care setting, and feels very angry much of the time. She bites her peers, kicks furniture, and resists any efforts on the part of the teacher to comfort her when she is distressed. What would you do if you were the provider?

OBSERVATION AND APPLICATION OPPORTUNITIES

1. Observe an infant-toddler program. How do the adults guide young children's behavior? Are the strategies supporting the infants' and toddlers' social and emotional development and helping them learn new appropriate behaviors?
2. Choose one of the challenging behaviors discussed in this chapter and read more about children who

may be experiencing anxiety, fear, anger, or posttraumatic stress disorder.
3. Choose one of the developmental issues discussed in this chapter. Develop a guidebook for parents on strategies that they can use when their children are experiencing separation anxiety, biting, tantrums, or learning to use the toilet. Help them understand the issue from the child's perspective.

SUPPLEMENTARY ARTICLES, BOOKS, AND DVDS

Kaiser, B., & Rasminsky, J. S. (2016). *Challenging behavior in young children* (4th ed.). Pearson.

Lieberman, A. F., & Soler, E. (2013). Child exposure to violence as a public health emergency. *ZERO TO THREE Journal, 34*(2), 4–10.

NAEYC. *Daily dilemmas: Coping with challenges (DVD)*. Washington, DC: NAEYC

Osofsky, J. D., & Reuther, E. T. (2013). Young children and disasters: Lessons learned about resilience and recovery. *ZERO TO THREE Journal, 34*(2), 46–54.

Yeary, J. (2013). Promoting mindfulness. Helping young children cope with separation. *Young Children, 68*(5), 110–112.

Stone, J. (2014). *A guide to discipline* (Revised Edition). Washington, DC: NAEYC.

INTERESTING LINKS

Center on the Social and Emotional Foundations for Early Learning: This national center focuses on strengthening the capacity of child care and Head Start programs to improve the social and emotional outcomes of young children.

https://www.youtube.com/watch?v=jYyEEMlMMb0 Search for "Trauma" and "Healing" to find this video that sensitively explains the effects of trauma and what you can do to help children heal.

Child Trauma Academy *childtrauma.org/* This site offers educational materials and articles concerning child trauma, including sections for caregivers and interdisciplinary teams.

Technical Assistance Center on Social Emotional Intervention challengingbehavior.org The center promotes the use of evidence-based practice to meet the needs of young children who have, or are at risk for, challenging behavior.

The Clearinghouse on Early Education and Parenting ceep.crc.uiuc.edu/poptopics/biting.html CEEP provides an article on biting and other resources on biting for parents and teachers.

15

Including Infants and Toddlers with Disabilities in Child Care and Learning Programs

LEARNING OUTCOMES

After reading this chapter, you will be able to:

- Describe the major infant and toddler disabling conditions, the challenges they bring, and ways teachers can support these children.
- Explain the elements of Part C of the early intervention system.
- Discuss how early care and learning programs can be effective natural environments.
- Describe the Americans with Disabilities Act (ADA) and the professional policy statements regarding inclusion.

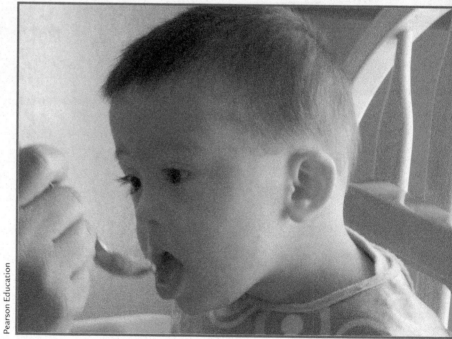

Pearson Education

Diane stopped in the doorway of the toddler room in the child care and learning center as she entered to pick up her daughter Lucy at the end of the day. She couldn't stop the tears that were welling up. Pat, Lucy's teacher, rushed over to her, concerned. "I'm OK," Diane said. "It's just that for a moment, when I looked around the room, I didn't know which one was Lucy. They're all busy and playing. I've never seen her just blend in before."

Moments like this are possible for Diane because community-based child care and learning programs are increasingly likely to include children with special needs. According a report on the settings where infants and toddlers are receiving **early intervention (EI)** services, the huge majority are in the child's home with the parents present. Up to about 20 percent of children from birth through 2 years are served in community settings. Out of almost 35,000 children served outside the home, only several hundred were enrolled in settings only for children with disabilities (1). At this point, many teachers have served many infants and toddlers with disabilities—and served them well.

Throughout this book, we have included information on infants and toddlers with disabilities. Most of their needs will be met through the same knowledge and strategies used with typically developing children. We included this information to illustrate our own commitment to the full inclusion of children with disabilities in programs.

However, there is further, specific information teachers need about children with disabilities.

This chapter provides a description of more common types of disabilities and challenges to development found in infants and toddlers. We describe the EI process. Finally, we discuss some specific strategies teachers can use to help these children participate in experiences and develop friendships with other children.

What Disabilities Do We See in Infants and Toddlers?

Before naming a list of disabling conditions, it is worth pointing out that terms such as *disability* or *special needs* are so general they are almost meaningless. Yet, for any individual, these words can be fraught with meaning. In addition, the diagnosis of a disability does not fully describe a particular child. The disability is only one aspect of the child. There is no meaningful way, for example, to describe infants with Down syndrome. Any one infant with Down syndrome is born into a particular family with its unique resources and stressors, as well as its own understanding and meaning of the disability. The child may be born relatively healthy or with complicating health issues. The child has his own personality and temperament and quickly establishes his own history, a sense of who he is, and his own expectations of the world. He may be an only child, a new child among siblings, or live within an extended family. The surrounding culture

CULTURE CLOSE UP

In 1982, an immigrant Hmong family gave birth to a little girl in California. Early on, she developed a seizure disorder. When she was 4, she suffered a grand mal seizure that left her without language or the ability to move. In her culture a seizure meant, *the spirit captures you and you fall down*, describing the belief that a powerful spirit was now living inside her. Was this child being gifted as a shaman or was her brain being destroyed by seizures? Anne Faddiman reported their story in a book subtitled *A Hmong Child, Her American Doctors and A Collision of Two Cultures* (2). This was a fascinating story of the American medical culture and the Hmong spiritual culture both trying to help this child—and tragically getting in each other's way. Is illness or disability physical or spiritual? What happens when an early childhood care and learning program and a family have very different beliefs? Ms. Lee died in 2012 at the age of 30, in her mother's home, surrounded by family.

may contribute particular beliefs about Down syndrome, a wealth or lack of supporting resources, and a welcoming or rejecting attitude.

Thus, because no child can be described fully by the name of his disability, we use **person-first language**: We say *a person with a disability* or *a child with a disability* or *a child with Down syndrome*, not *a disabled child* or *a Down's child*. The child is a person *first* with all of the differing individual characteristics, strengths, needs, interests, and desires that all children have. The disability is a part of who that child is, but only a part.

Groups of Disabilities

Nonetheless, we do classify disabling conditions. The disabilities most often identified in infancy tend to be relatively significant. These include genetic syndromes, sensory disorders, and central nervous system disorders. These conditions tend to have serious impacts on a child's ability to take information from the world, to process and understand that information, and to control the movement of his own body. Causes may include circumstances around the gestation and birth such as substance exposure, prematurity, low birth weight, or toxic stress. They may be conditions such as Down syndrome, cerebral palsy, or seizures that are known to cause delays. Language and communication impairments are often secondary disabilities caused by the primary condition. Producing speech requires considerable muscle control, and learning language requires both sensory and processing abilities.

It is impossible to name each potential disability and explain its effects. There are thousands of genetic syndromes alone. Nonetheless, young teachers frequently request some overview that would help them understand the kinds of disabling conditions that may present themselves. In this section, we describe some disabling conditions that would fit under the category *established biological risk*, some of their potential effects on development, and some interventions that support development for children with these conditions. Remember, children with each of these conditions have been successfully included in child care and learning programs.

Chromosomal Abnormalities and Genetic Syndromes

As described in Chapter 5, the gene is the basic component of inherited information, carrying traits from parent to child. The gene reproduces at each cell division and produces exact copies of its DNA and proteins. Normally, each cell in the body, except the egg and sperm, has 23 matching pairs, or 46 chromosomes. Each gene is located on a specific spot of the DNA of a particular chromosome.

Genetic syndromes occur when the genes are damaged in cell division or when sets of genes from the mother and/or father carry defective information that prevents the gene from expressing itself. **Chromosomal abnormalities** occur when there are too many or too few chromosomes, or when a chromosome has missing pieces, extra pieces, or pieces attached to another chromosome (3).

Chromosomal abnormalities and genetic syndromes are often identified prenatally, at birth, or soon after birth. Some common chromosomal and genetic abnormalities include the following:

Down Syndrome

Caused by an extra, or third, 21st chromosome. Because of the cause of the syndrome, it is also known as *trisomy 21*. This occurs most often when the 21st chromosome duplicates in either the egg or the sperm as a pair, rather than as a single chromosome. Down syndrome has a number of visible characteristics such as an upward slant to the eyes, a small mouth and facial features, small stature, a flattened back of the head, and small hands with a single crease across the palm. Children with Down syndrome may have congenital heart defects, poor muscle tone that can delay motor development, and varying degrees of cognitive challenges. Although children with Down syndrome eventually develop speech, they often begin communication successfully by using sign language (4).

Supporting development.   Given low muscle tone, infants and toddlers with Down syndrome may need support in sitting and in being engaged to stay near the other children. Physical therapists may recommend experiences to develop muscle tone. During the first year of life, they will benefit from using sign language or other communication systems as they have much to communicate but are likely to be delayed in language. Teachers use responsive interactions as a way to help these infants and toddlers focus and maintain their attention and learning. Responsive interactions include:

- *Contingency*—respond immediately to little behaviors
- *Reciprocity*—take one turn and wait
- *Affect*—interact for fun
- *Match*—do what the child can do
- *Nondirective*—following the child's lead (5).

 Watch this video to hear a young mother describe her first 2 years with her daughter who has Down syndrome. Would you have hope for Maddox's future?

https://www.youtube.com/watch?v=uPy2WsHAls8

Fragile X Syndrome

Caused by a partially broken area (fragile) on the X chromosome. Because girls have two X chromosomes and boys have only one, the damage usually has more impact on boys. Children with fragile X syndrome are likely to have mild to severe intellectual disabilities, although they may also have normal intelligence. They may have a large head with noticeably large forehead, nose, jaws, and ears. Some children with fragile X syndrome have attention problems and some have autistic-like tendencies (6).

Supporting development.   Children with fragile X syndrome have traditionally been identified at or later than the age 3, but amniocentesis and newborn screening are providing early identification (7). Infant-toddler teachers may need to help overcome feeding difficulties and promote social interest and language and motor imitation.

Cystic fibrosis

A disorder in which genes lack the enzymes to break down and absorb fats, causing malnutrition. Thick secretions cause chronic lung damage. Teachers may be involved in performing exercises to help the infant or toddler clear his lungs (8). Cystic fibrosis is the most common, inherited, deadly disease of Caucasians in the United States.

Supporting development.   Teachers may learn to position the infant or toddler with cystic fibrosis and tap the chest and back in ways that help loosen the mucus so that it may be coughed out.

Many syndromes show no symptoms in the first months of life.

Pearson Education

Sickle cell anemia

An abnormality in which some red blood cells are crescent or sickle shaped. The red blood cells carry hemoglobin to the cells throughout the body delivering oxygen. The sickle cells live for half the time of a healthy cell and greatly reduce the total number of red cells in the body. Sickle cell occurs primarily in African Americans, causes fevers and great pain in joints and the abdomen, and is incurable (9).

Supporting development. Infants and toddlers with sickle cell anemia must have an individualized health care plan that informs teachers what symptoms are of concern and steps to be taken from notifying parents to initiating transport to an emergency medical facility.

Sensory Impairments

Hearing, Visual, Tactile, and Processing

Sensory impairments describe the categories of problems that can occur with receiving or processing information through the senses. Sensory impairments can occur prenatally or as a result of illness or injury, ranging in severity from mild to total. Hearing impairment, for example, may range from a mild loss of ability to hear to complete deafness. Visual impairment also includes a range from easily correctable issues to complete blindness. Tactile defensiveness, or hypersensitivity to touch, is a less well-known disorder. It involves a child's difficulty in receiving information from his body and results in poor motor planning and poor body awareness (10). Sensory processing disorders may make it difficult for a young child to manage loud noises, certain textures, eating, and changes in routine. Social interactions, so vital to learning and development, may be physically uncomfortable.

Supporting development.   Teachers will work with EI teams and families to meet the needs of infants and toddlers with sensory impairments. Teachers may change the environment, adding a darkened space with light-oriented activities for infants and toddlers with visual impairments. Teachers will carefully provide tactile-rich and language-rich experiences. They may learn and use sign language with all of the children, if there is a child with a hearing impairment. Teachers may learn to do exercises with tactile defensive children to help them become more comfortable with touch.

Metabolic Disorders

Metabolic disorders result from inherited deficiencies of particular enzymes. The enzymes are not available to break down materials such as amino acids, which then build up and cause damage to the brain. Some metabolic disorders can be diagnosed and treated, such as phenylketonuria (PKU). Others, such as Tay-Sachs, cannot be treated and are fatal.

PKU and Tay-Sachs

PKU is a condition in which children cannot break down the enzyme phenylalanine, which is present in almost all foods. Without treatment, phenylalanine builds up in the bloodstream and causes brain damage and mental retardation. PKU is a genetic disease. Newborns are now tested at all U.S. hospitals, and it is recommended that babies tested within the first 24 hours be retested at 2 weeks (11).

Tay-Sachs is also an inherited metabolic disorder, caused by the absence of a vital enzyme called hexosaminidase A (Hex-A). Without Hex-A, a fatty substance (or lipid) called GM2 ganglioside accumulates abnormally in cells, especially in the nerve cells of the brain. There is progressive damage to the cells and children do not live past early childhood. People of European Jewish descent are most likely to be carriers of the defective gene (12).

Supporting development. Because Tay-Sachs is a severe medical condition usually resulting in death in the first 4 years of life, program staff must carefully consider how they will provide emotional support to the teachers, parents, the child, and the child's peers.

Central Nervous System Disorders

The brain and the spinal cord make up the central nervous system. They receive information from the body through a network of nerves. The brain and spinal cord can be malformed in the womb because of exposure to toxic substances, poor nutrition, maternal infections, or poor migration of cells. Neural cells may also be damaged during the birth process if the baby is deprived of oxygen. The nervous system may not develop well after birth if the child is in a chaotic or barren environment, if nutrition is poor, or if the child is exposed to environmental toxins such as lead. The central nervous system may also be damaged by high fevers, disease, and injury.

Some commonly seen **central nervous system disorders** include the following:

Cerebral Palsy

A disorder of motor and postural control from non-progressive damage to the brain. The type and severity of the disorder depend on the area of the brain that is affected and the degree of damage. Cerebral palsy ranges from a mild motor impairment to almost no voluntary control of movement. Intelligence is not necessarily affected by the damage, but seizures often occur with cerebral palsy (13). This condition was described in Chapter 10.

Supporting development. Children with cerebral palsy are included in group care very successfully, with the support of the family and the early intervention team. Teachers will have to learn the individual child's strengths and needs for support. Supports may include physical positioning, feeding, individual learning capacities, and alternate communication systems.

 Watch this video to learn about cerebral palsy from a 2-year-old's point of view. What does Cohen think is the most important thing for you to know?

https://www.youtube.com/watch?v=Kzb1XYGO0IQ

Spina Bifida

A birth defect that occurs because the neural tube did not close entirely while forming prenatally. The effect of spina bifida depends on which vertebra are exposed and can range from almost no effect to complete paralysis below the spinal opening and severe mental retardation. Some 70 percent of the cases of spina bifida could be prevented with adequate intake of folic acid during pregnancy (14).

Supporting development.   Most children with spina bifida have normal intelligence and should be responsive learners and relationship partners. They are likely to have significant problems with mobility and bladder and bowel problems. Special services concentrate on these issues.

Shaken Baby Syndrome

A set of symptoms found when an infant or toddler has been violently shaken. Symptoms include brain swelling and bleeding in the brain and the retinas of the eyes. It can result in cognitive and motor damage and often results in death (15). If the child survives the shaking, he may develop these symptoms over time: lethargy, vomiting, poor sucking or swallowing, lack of smiling, unequal pupil size, and an inability to focus visually or to lift his head.

In recent developments, some question has arisen as to whether the symptoms described above are enough to diagnose shaken baby syndrome or abusive head trauma. The presence of bruises and bone fractures may be needed to prove abuse (16).

Supporting development.   The teacher may be the one to recognize the symptoms of this head trauma. Every program must have a plan in place for how to report suspected child abuse.

Congenital Infections

Congenital infections are diseases that affect the baby prenatally. As briefly described in Chapter 5, maternal infections do cross the placenta and can cause harm to the fetus. The most commonly seen infections, grouped under the acronym STORCH or TORCH-S, are syphilis, toxoplasmosis, other infections (such as HIV or hepatitis B), rubella, cytomegalovirus, and herpes. These infections, when transmitted in the womb or at birth, can cause mental retardation, growth retardation, sensory impairments, and even death (17).

Disorders Secondary to Exposure to Toxic Substances

Toxins that the mother actively inhales or ingests, such as tobacco, illegal drugs, and alcohol, as well as toxins to which the mother is passively exposed, such as cleaning solvents, lead, pollutants and pesticides, are all able to cross the placenta and harm the developing nervous system of the fetus. Damage to the nervous system can cause cognitive impairments and diminished growth. The range of effects depends to some extent on the timing and dosage of exposure. These conditions are described more fully in Chapter 5.

Chronic Illness

Chronic illnesses requiring some use of medication or medical technology are increasingly common in child care and learning settings. Asthma and allergies are very common chronic conditions. Hemophilia is less common but is often reported by caregivers in workshops on disabilities.

Asthma, Allergies, and Hemophilia

Asthma is a chronic respiratory disorder causing wheezing, coughing, and difficulty breathing. Ten to twelve percent of American children have asthma and the numbers are rising, although no one is sure why. It is usually attrib-

Conditions such as asthma are on the rise, probably because of pollution.

uted to the increase of pollution and allergens in the air, particularly because the greatest increase is in African American boys living in poverty (18). Teachers sometimes administer medication for asthma with a machine called a nebulizer.

Allergies are a sensitivity to normally harmless substances. Allergic reactions may include rashes, irritability, vomiting, swelling, difficulty in breathing, or even shock. Individualized health care plans include instructions for how to respond to known allergic reactions.

Hemophilia is an X-linked disorder caused by a lack of proteins needed for blood clotting. Children may have dangerous internal bleeding from falls or bumps or be unable to stop bleeding from minor cuts.

Supporting development.   Teachers must have plans in place describing how to recognize and respond to symptoms. These conditions are episodic and may be emergencies; nonetheless, on a day-to-day basis teachers should be using their well-developed skills of responsive caregiving, individualized planning, and relationship building.

Pervasive Developmental Disorders

Pervasive developmental disorders (PDD) comprise another group of developmental disorders, including autism spectrum disorders (ASD), Rett syndrome, childhood disintegrative disorder, and PDD, that are characterized by impairment in social interaction and communication skills, extreme reactions to change, and obsessive and repetitive behaviors. PDD can have moderate to severe effects on a child's ability to function. You read about autism in Chapter 6. The other disorders are quite rare.

 Watch this video to learn the early signs of autism. Which signs help identify autism by two years?

https://www.youtube.com/watch?v=9Ithxd5KWhw

A Reminder

Although there are thousands of potentially disabling conditions, no condition or diagnosis defines a child. Early childhood educators need to learn about each child, her likes and dislikes, her personality, her routines and expectations, and the effects of the disabling condition. No one needs to know about all disabilities and their effects; a teacher simply needs to know how to understand one child at a time, how to read her cues, and how to develop a relationship with that one child.

Above all, it is important to remember that with children with special needs, there is a little person with whom the teacher has all the necessary skills and compassion to develop a meaningful and loving relationship. This child is part of a family that is quickly learning a great deal of new information. They may be dealing with a shock. Perhaps they are first-time new parents. They are very possibly worrying about how they will be welcomed anywhere. Early childhood programs can serve infants and toddlers with disabilities well. A program can provide wonderful opportunities for learning and relationships and can be welcoming and reassuring to the family. If the infant-toddler program conveys a message that "We are a program, a community, and a society that has room for all children," it will always be deeply appreciated by families.

 Check Your Understanding 15.1
Click here to check your understanding of the concepts in this section.

Early Intervention: Part C of IDEA

Early childhood programs play an important role in the lives of families. However, they do not have the responsibility for providing therapeutic services. The federal Individuals with Disabilities Education Act (IDEA) provides special education services to children between 3 and 21 years of age. Part C of IDEA is a grant program from the federal government to the states to help them provide EI services for infants and toddlers through age 2 and their families. The Program for Infants and Toddlers with Disabilities (Part C of IDEA) was designed to

- Enhance the development of infants and toddlers with disabilities
- Reduce the need for later special education through EI
- Minimize the likelihood of institutionalization and maximize independent living
- Enhance the capacity of families to meet their child's needs (19).

The state has to meet a set of components, as shown in Box 15.1 and must ensure that it will meet the needs of every eligible child and family.

Public Awareness

The purpose of Part C is to identify children with delays early so they can receive services. Many of these children will not need further services after the infant-toddler years. EI can promote optimal development and help children overcome early challenges.

Each state has an ongoing effort that keeps the families, health professionals and the general public informed about the EI program. Your state should have materials available to help you know what makes a child eligible for services and

BOX 15.1

Required Components of a State's Part C (IDEA) System

1. Public awareness program
   a. Central directory of services, resources, and research and demonstration projects
   b. Information for parents
2. Comprehensive Child Find and referral system
   a. A rigorous definition of developmental delay and procedures for determining eligibility
   b. Timely and comprehensive multidisciplinary evaluation of needs of children and assessment of each child and family
   c. Referral procedures following Child Find
   d. Post referral timeline
3. Individualized family service plan development, review and evaluation and service coordination
   a. Appropriate early intervention services based on scientifically based research, to the extent practical, available to all infants and toddlers with disabilities and their families, including Indian and homeless infants and toddlers
   b. Policies and procedures to ensure that to the maximum extent appropriate, early intervention services are provided in natural environments except when early intervention cannot be achieved satisfactorily in a natural environment
4. Administrative

   a. Comprehensive system of personnel development
   b. Policies and procedures for personnel standards
   c. Single line of authority in a lead agency designated by the governor
   d. Procedural safeguards
   e. System for compiling data on the early intervention system
   f. State interagency coordinating council

Source: Individuals with Disabilities Education Act, 20 U.S.C. § 1400 (2004). *U.S. Department of Education.*

how to make a referral to Part C services. Some child care and learning programs are required because of federal funding to have a written agreement with the EI provider. The lead agency in the state should have brochures and other resources to help you and families know how to get services for a child.

The lead agency also compiles and maintains a directory of all the services and other resources for children and families receiving Part C services. The federal government also funds research and special projects for improving services. These projects have included special training and supports for inclusion, using video to integrate intervention into daily routines, and developing processes for cross-disciplinary teams. If your state has any of these funded projects, they are also in the directory.

Comprehensive Child Find and Referral System

Each state must create a process for finding the infants and toddlers who are eligible for Part C services. The state determines criteria for **eligibility**. It develops a process for finding children who are eligible for services. The state develops a

BOX 15.2

Conditions of Established Risk

- Chromosomal abnormalities
- Genetic or congenital disorders
- Severe sensory impairments, including hearing and vision
- Inborn errors of metabolism
- Disorders reflecting disturbance of the nervous system
- Congenital infections
- Disorders secondary to exposure of toxic substances, including fetal alcohol syndrome
- Severe attachment disorders

Source: Individuals with Disabilities Education Act, 20 U.S.C. § 1400 (2004). *U.S. Department of Education.*

process for evaluating children and assessing the family's strengths and needs. Then, there is a plan and a timeline for making referrals for services if the child is eligible for Part C.

Eligibility

Part C requires each state to determine its own criteria for eligibility. All states are required to provide services to children who have conditions of **established risk**, a diagnosed physical or mental condition that has a high probability of resulting in developmental delay (see Box 15.2).

In addition to these conditions, many states add biological conditions that increase the likelihood of, but do not necessarily result in, developmental delays. These would include low birth weight, intraventricular hemorrhage at birth, chronic lung disease, and failure to thrive. Some states also choose to provide services to children who are considered to be at environmental risk for development because of factors such as parental substance abuse, parental mental illness, and child abuse or neglect.

 Watch this video to learn the definition of an infant or toddler with a disability. Why did Congress want the definition of a disability to be broad in Part C?

https://www.youtube.com/watch?v=iETUyOs1irA

Child Find

The Child Find mandate in Part C describes the state's responsibility to identify, locate and evaluate every child with a disability. The responsibility for Child Find rests with the school districts. However, for Part C, it may be managed by the EI providers. Child Find staff may hold developmental screenings at community events. They may be available to train infant/toddler teachers on how to recognize delays and make a referral.

The Child Find staff take referrals from families, health professionals, and early childhood teachers. They have 45 days from the date of the referral to perform a multidisciplinary evaluation of the child.

Multidisciplinary Evaluation

When a family expresses concern over their child's development, the EI team conducts an evaluation of the child's

Pearson Education

Certain disorders make a child automatically eligible for Part C because we know they can delay development.

abilities and developmental delays. People from two or more professional disciplines must take part in the evaluation. They may use several sources of information including standardized tests, observation, family reports, and their own **informed, clinical opinion**. This evaluation determines whether the child is eligible for services under the state's definition of a disability.

At the same time, the family is assessed "to identify the resources, priorities, concerns and the supports, and services necessary to enhance the family's capacity to meet the needs of their child" (20). The Child Find process should be directed by the family. Together, the family and the Child Find team decide on the child's and family's needs, the child's goals, and the needed services. The final step is making referrals to the appropriate service providers.

Family Assessment

A family-directed assessment must be conducted by qualified personnel in order to identify the family's resources, priorities, and concerns and the supports and services necessary to enhance the family's capacity to meet the developmental needs of the family's infant or toddler with a disability. The family-directed assessment must: (1) be voluntary on the part of each family member participating in the assessment, (2) be based on information obtained through an assessment tool and also through an interview with those family members who elect to participate in the assessment, and (3) include the family's description of its resources, priorities, and concerns related to enhancing the child's development.

Individualized Family Service Plan Development, Review and Evaluation and Service Coordination

Once a child is found to be eligible for services, the family and the EI team develop an **Individualized Family Service Plan (IFSP)**. The plan is a blueprint for the interventions over the next six months. It includes a timeline for being reviewed and a plan for evaluating how progress will be measured. A **service coordinator** is identified and works on the development of the IFSP.

IFSP

The IFSP documents the intended outcomes for the child, and the services and supports needed to achieve them. The IFSP includes:

- The child's present levels of functioning and needs in the areas of his or her physical, cognitive, communication, social/emotional, and adaptive development.
- Family information (with their agreement), including the resources, priorities, and their concerns, as parents, and other family members closely involved with the child.
- The major results or outcomes expected to be achieved for the child and family.
- The specific EI services the child will be receiving.
- Where in the **natural environment** (e.g., home, community) the services will be provided (if the services will not be provided in the natural environment, the IFSP must include a statement justifying why not).
- When and where the child will receive services.
- The number of days or sessions the child will receive each service and how long each session will last.
- Who will pay for the services.
- The name of the service coordinator overseeing the implementation of the IFSP.

• The steps to be taken to support your child's transition out of early intervention and into another program when the time comes.

The IFSP may also identify services the family may be interested in, such as financial information or information about raising a child with a disability (21).

Ideally, each IFSP looks quite different from any other and takes into consideration the priorities, strengths, and needs of each family and child. If a program is providing child care and learning services, the director or teacher should be included as a member of the intervention team. She can provide valuable information about how the child manages his interactions with other children and can offer her own expertise on typical development.

EI Services

Under Part C, infants and toddlers with disabilities may receive services from early childhood special educators, speech-language therapists, physical therapists, occupational therapists, or psychologists. A service coordinator manages the variety of services and often coordinates many sources of funding. Part C requires states "to have policies and procedures in place to ensure that to the maximum extent appropriate, early intervention services are provided in natural environments" (22).

Early childhood special educators help infants and toddlers to explore and learn. They may make adaptations to materials and the environment. They support learning by structuring some experiences to break skills into smaller steps. Speech-language therapists help infants and toddlers with disabilities with speaking or other forms of communication. They might teach sign language or provide picture boards or digital devices.

In many states, the EI services are offered within the child care and learning program. At the very least, EI teams provide ongoing consultation to the staff. Early interventionists may provide advice on how to physically position a child to maximize his ability to control and use his body. They may offer strategies for adapting toys and materials. They help teachers make the most of learning opportunities. They may have tips to make feeding more efficient and satisfying. They may also offer a variety of communication alternatives to help adults understand the cues and signals of the infant or toddler with disabilities. Physical therapists (PT) work with normalizing muscle tone and mobility. For children with cerebral palsy, the PT works with the child to reduce the tight muscles. She may provide adapted materials such as toys that run on **switches**. For a child with Down syndrome, the PT is trying to strengthen low muscle tone. An occupational therapist will also work on muscle tone; especially in service of the child's being able to manage her environment.

States have different rules limiting the medical procedures that can be performed by anyone other than a nurse. These rules are outlined in each state's Nurse Practice Act. The program's health consultant should be

Most children with disabilities fit in well in family child care and infant and toddler classrooms.

Pearson Education

involved in planning care for a child who requires a feeding tube, nebulizer treatments, or any other actions that might be construed as practicing medicine.

The requirement for offering services in natural settings was designed to take full advantage of the benefits to the child with disabilities that are inherent in an inclusive environment. Every infant and toddler has a natural interest in her peers. This motivates children with disabilities to actively work to join their friends in their very compelling activities. The play and exploration of typically developing children can be highly engaging for the child with disabilities and can provide models of a variety of ways to play. All children benefit when they learn to create friendships with children with differing skills.

BOX 15.3

The Intervention Process

The steps in the intervention process are as follows:

1. Family contacts Part C provider with concerns.
2. Multidisciplinary assessment of child's development is made.
3. Eligibility is established.
4. Service coordinator is assigned.
5. IFSP is developed.
6. Services are delivered.
7. Evaluation and plan are reviewed at 6-month intervals.

Service Coordination

Service coordination is provided by one person who assists and enables the child and family to receive EI services and rights under Part C. The service coordinator also assists the family in gaining any other services identified in the IFSP.

Service coordination may include any of these activities:

- Helping infants and families access necessary treatment and supports from qualified providers
- Making appropriate referrals and scheduling appointments for assessments and services
- Coordinating early intervention and other services (e.g., educational, social, and medical that are not provided for diagnostic or evaluative purposes)
- Coordinating evaluations and assessments
- Being involved in the development, review, and evaluation of the IFSP
- Conducting referral and other activities to assist families in identifying available providers
- Coordinating, facilitating and monitoring the delivery of services in a timely manner
- Conducting follow-up activities
- Advising families of their rights and procedural safeguards
- Coordinating funding sources for required services
- Facilitating the development of transition plans (23)

Check Your Understanding 15.2
Click here to check your understanding of the concepts in this section.

A Natural Environment

Part C requires that EI services be provided in the most natural setting: places where the child would be if he did not have a disability. For a large majority of infants and toddlers, these services are provided in the child's home with the parents. However, for several hundred children, EI occurs in early care and learning programs. This section offers some effective strategies for inclusion. It provides guidance for when the program raises concerns about a child's development and wants to make a referral to EI. In closing the chapter, we introduce you to the position statements of your profession that direct professionals to embrace inclusion.

Strategies for Inclusion

Even now, in the 21st century, despite laws such as the ADA designed to prevent discrimination, some teachers, directors, and home family providers routinely turn away any child identified as having a disability. In studies and workshops on this topic, teachers frequently voice concerns about not having the knowledge to care for children with disabilities, about children with disabilities requiring one-on-one care, and about the discomfort other children and families may feel (24). Family care providers are concerned that the child with disabilities will require so much attention that they will have to serve fewer children and thus reduce their income (25). Although that may be true for an infant with multiple disabilities—for example, on a respirator and gastrostomy tube, with visual and hearing impairment—that description would match only a very few of the thousands of infants and toddlers identified each year with disabilities.

Teachers and families who have experienced inclusive services describe them as having many benefits. Teachers with positive experiences in serving infants and toddlers with disabilities enjoy their jobs more and have more positive attitudes toward serving other children with disabilities. When they were given opportunities to prepare themselves, learn additional strategies, and establish the supports they felt they needed, teachers were positive about supporting a child's membership in their community. Those teachers who approached the challenge with confidence believed that inclusion promotes gains in socialization among all children (26). Here are some strategies for successful inclusion.

Maintain a Positive Attitude

The attitudes of the adults involved are the biggest factor in the success or failure of inclusion. Teachers should reflect on their own feelings about disabilities and discuss any concerns they might have about serving a child with disabilities. Concerns might include possibly harming the child through lack of knowledge or skills or being unable to manage the regular ratios when the group has a child perceived to have high needs. Program directors or EI team members may be helpful in participating in this conversation.

Ask for Information Sharing

Teachers need adequate information in order to serve every child. Teachers should have the opportunity to form their questions and have them answered by the family, health professionals, or EI providers. Families should also feel free to ask questions regarding the program's ability to provide any specific services or adaptations needed by their child. If Part C is serving the child, the service coordinator can be helpful in facilitating the conversation. Inclusion is most successful when teachers and parents have frequent opportunities to exchange information, when they are open to each other's suggestions and ideas, and when they value each other's contributions to the children and the success of the experience (27).

TABLE 15.1   **Sarah's favorite things to do!**

Toys	Meals	Outdoors
Sarah loves hugging and carrying her doll, being just like her own mommy. Sarah can put the rings on the stick and the shapes in the box—and she likes to practice that a lot!	Sarah is a good friend at the table. She drinks from a cup and feeds herself finger food snacks. She smiles and laughs and is interested in her friends. Sarah signs to Miss Rose to tell her what she wants at mealtimes.	Sarah stays close to Miss Rose outdoors. She likes pulling the "horsie" riding toy around the playground as much as riding it. Sarah loves playing in sand and water.
Friends	**Grown-ups**	**Nap Time**
Sarah looks for Ona and Peter when she gets to school. She likes to be near friends and to give hugs.	Sarah loves her mommy, daddy, and grandmas. She especially likes to be with Miss Rose during the day. Sometimes Sarah likes grown-ups to help her when she gets frustrated with a toy or a puzzle.	Sarah gets tired at school and sleeps heavily at nap time. She likes to listen to stories, quiet music, and have her back rubbed as she falls asleep. Cuddling in the glider is a big treat!

Document Children's Competence

Documentation can be useful in helping teachers maintain positive attitudes toward children with disabilities. Documentation of infants and toddlers with disabilities can reflect images of active, productive, and social experiences back to the child, as well as help keep positive images of the child in the teacher's mind. Although it is easy to see how this sort of chart (see Table 15.1) would be appropriate for any child, it can be particularly helpful in keeping the child's strengths, rather than needs and disabilities, in the teacher's mind. The chart shown in Table 15.1 describes the interests and abilities of an 18-month-old girl with Down syndrome.

Adapt Materials and Activities

The large list of disabling conditions described at the beginning of this chapter demonstrated that disabilities might have all sorts of functional effects. Some children have normal or high intelligence but are unable to control their bodies. Some move well but have difficulty processing and understanding information. Some have difficulty focusing attention. Some have difficulty in social relationships. Some have poor sensory abilities. Obviously, different strategies serve different children.

Without question, there is no easier age group for full inclusion than infants and toddlers. Infant and

Pearson Education

This child is feeling the sponge used for painting, tentatively but with interest. She explores new tactile experiences very slowly.

toddler services are already highly individualized. In fact, early childhood educators are constantly making unconscious little adjustments to particular needs: Riley needs protected space to play, Freddie won't eat foods of a certain texture, Rachel needs lots of warning before a transition, and Li needs moments of quiet connection and cuddling throughout the day. Teachers make these adjustments without thinking about them. High-quality programs have low ratios and small groups. The typically developing infants and toddlers haven't lived long enough to greet their peers with disabilities with any preconceived biases. Still, a number of considerations and strategies ensure that inclusion results in a successful, meaningful experience for everyone involved:

> One of the roles of teachers in inclusive child care settings is to serve as *inclusion facilitators*. Facilitating inclusion simply means making sure that children with special needs are incorporated into all of the ongoing activities of the classroom, including daily living activities as well as play activities. An emphasis on facilitating inclusion ensures that children who have disabilities are not set apart from the other children, such as by eating separately because they need individual care, being kept indoors when the other children are on the playground, or being entertained by one teacher while other children are involved in group activities (28, p. 35).

As shown in Table 15.2, adapting toys and materials for infants and toddlers with special needs is a three-step process: (1) understand what the children are learning and how they learn, (2) provide materials that contain the information in a relevant form, and (3) ensure that the materials are stable. One of the first considerations in planning learning activities for infants or toddlers with disabilities is to understand which concepts and skills are currently emerging for them and which kinds of toys and materials they find interesting. For example, infants who are just beginning to learn that they can hold on to an object and move it enjoy rattles that are light, fist size, and make noise. Infants who are beginning to explore spatial relationships enjoy putting objects into containers and dumping them out again. Infants and toddlers with disabilities are making the same cognitive discoveries as typically developing infants, although possibly not on the same timeline or through the same sources of information. Provide materials that are

TABLE 15.2   Principles of adapting toys and materials

Stability	Usefulness of Information	Achieving Goals Through Play
Increases child's control of objects, ability to explore and learn • Use Velcro or tape to hold items to table. • Large handles make an item easier to pick up or move. • A weighted bottom makes the item less likely to tip over. • Use thicker materials (e.g., board books rather than paper).	Provides information through senses and use of body most effective for the child • Simplify materials by offering fewer pieces. • Use sharp contrasts for child with visual impairment. • Remove sound-makers for children who are sensitive to too much stimulation. • If working on matching, for example, begin with two pieces that match exactly and one very different distractor (2 spoons and a ball). Work toward 2 spoons and fork and ultimately, 2 spoons that are not exactly the same.	Naturally engages child to attempt goals such as bringing hands together at midline, isolating fingers, or making sounds • Offer toys that require both hands to hold them. • Blow bubbles to pop when hands are clapped together. • Poke at bubbles with one finger. • Offer toys that require an isolated finger such as a little piano or telephone.

responsive to the actions they are capable of producing. Infants and toddlers with disabilities do well when the materials they use are stable enough to stay in one place and not be easily knocked over or roll away. The information must be available to them in ways that make sense—for example, simplify the information in stacking cups by offering fewer at a time or use a light table as the playing surface for a child with visual impairment.

Arrange the Environment

As older infants become mobile, it might become necessary for the teacher to move the young child with physical impairments to be able to stay close to her friends. Supportive seating that allows the toddler to sit at the snack table with everyone else is more conducive to participation than a seat with its own tray. Children with visual impairments, in particular, need the furniture and pathways in the environment to remain unchanged so that they are able to learn how to get from one area to another on their own.

 Watch the video for a demonstration of learning opportunities in a natural environment. How does the adult enrich the experience?

https://www.youtube.com/watch?v=BOJ-zKV6HOI

Use Group Affection Activities

In so many ways, we encourage infants and toddlers to be kind to each other. We remind them to be gentle in their touch and give them the general advice to "Be nice." We can be specific in our directions to children as to how they can be most helpful to a child with a disability. It might be "Take her hand," or it might be "Just wait—he'll get it." Teachers can reinforce the toddler with special needs, using positive descriptive words, when he stays close to the other children and observes or imitates their social play: "You really like watching Andre with those trucks. Andre has a good time playing cars and trucks." A further step would be to help the typically developing child invite the child with special needs into the activity: "Andre, would you please give this truck to Jack?" (29, p. 22).

Meet Therapeutic Goals

Infants and toddlers with disabilities should have an EI team working with them and an IFSP defining the child's therapeutic goals. Teachers can promote the mastery of these goals through well-chosen play activities, wherein the toys and materials inherently suggest the desired actions. Children with nervous system and motor disorders are often working on goals such as using both hands at midline, loosening their fists to use their fingers, using fingers in isolation, and using increasingly sophisticated grasps. Play activities that promote these goals would include offering toys large enough to require both hands be used together, toy pianos, cd players, and other single-button-activated toys. Small toys—but not so small as to be a choking hazard—and foods such as bits of bananas or cereal pieces all encourage grasps. One of the best materials for promoting these actions is bubbles. Smashing bubbles with both hands clapping is a great way to bring the hands to midline. Poking bubbles promotes the use of isolated fingers.

Teachers may use a variety of positioning techniques to support children with motor issues to maximize their use of their bodies. Therapists may show teachers how to use simple material such as rolled-up towels to support positions or may provide standing boards or special chairs. Children with severe motor issues may be introduced to toys that run on switches, devices that direct battery-operated toys through the use of whatever part of the body has most control. Switches may be operated through touch, sound, head position, sucking, or blowing. The EI team should provide these materials to child care and learning programs.

Many therapeutic goals for infants and toddlers require only the same materials and teacher interactions as those for typically developing children. Teachers create environments that encourage focus, attention, and exploration. They expand play and language. They provide an emotional tone of calm interest to support learning and joyful celebration to support accomplishment. They respond to vocalizations from infants as though they were words spoken with meaning. They promote kindness and empathy toward other children. These actions all support the achievement of therapeutic goals by infants and toddlers with disabilities.

Making Referrals

Some children may come to your program already identified by Part C and receiving services. Or your program may have some concerns about a child you are serving. It is important for every infant and toddler program to understand how to access the Part C program in its community and how to talk to families about making a **referral**. If the family is concerned about the child's development, Part C must provide an evaluation to determine whether the child is eligible for services.

There are many ways to gauge child development. Many programs routinely review development with a brief assessment called a **screening**. Screening tools (see Box 15.4) are usually a list of a few items describing typical development in each domain. Sometimes teachers may set up situations in which to observe whether a child is performing the task. They may also answer the items from ongoing observations. Some screening tools ask families to use their experience to report on development. Screening tools do not determine delays but can help identify areas of possible concern. All programs could use screening tools periodically as part of their system of observing and recording development. Concerns can be addressed quickly and with mutual understanding when each child's development is part of the ongoing conversation between families and the program.

If a program and family are sufficiently concerned about a child's development in one or more areas, the family may request an evaluation from the Child Find program in the community. The results from regular screening in the child care and learning program can provide useful information to the early intervention team. Besides the tools

BOX 15.4

Screening Tools

The Ages & Stages Questionnaire is filled out by parents every several months. Teachers then code the results to track children's development. The pamphlets utilize parent observations while helping inform parents of the predicted course of development. They can be used with children from 2 months to $5\frac{1}{2}$ years (search for Brookes Publishing online for more information and samples).

Ages & Stages Questionnaires®: Social-Emotional, Second Edition (ASQ:SE-2™) is filled out by parents every several months to identify young children at risk for social and emotional concerns. The tool screens for self-regulation, compliance, communication, adaptive behaviors, autonomy, affect, and interaction with people.

The Denver Developmental Screen II is used by professionals or trained paraprofessionals to track development. A few items in each developmental domain are scored at each observation to see if the child's development is within the normal range. It can be used from birth to 6 years and is known as the Denver II.

presented in Box 15.3, ongoing assessments such as the Ounce (30) may also be used to document children's development. An example of the Ounce Scale and how it is used was presented in Chapter 12.

Remember that your role as an infant/toddler teacher qualifies you to make judgements about whether development is on track. It does not qualify you to diagnose a child with a particular disability. When you bring your concerns to a family, please be aware that it can be upsetting and frightening for a family to learn that their child may be struggling. Be respectful and careful as you enlist the family's attention to the child's development.

Check Your Understanding 15.3
Click here to check your understanding of the concepts in this section.

Professional Positions

We have tried to explain the benefits of inclusion and provide strategies for successful inclusion. There are additional reasons to think about inclusion. One is that unless you have a very sound reason for excluding a child with a disability, you are required by law to be inclusive. On a more positive note, though, several entities in early childhood have issued position statements in favor of inclusion.

The ADA

The ADA was passed in by Congress in 1990 as a civil rights bill for people with disabilities. Among other things, the ADA prohibits discrimination by child care centers and family child care providers against individuals with disabilities. Child care centers may not discriminate against a child because the child has a disability. Each child and family are evaluated on a case-by-case basis. There are three kinds of **accommodations** that may be required of programs:

- Changes in policies, practices, or procedures,
- Provision of auxiliary aids and services to ensure effective communication, and
- Removal of physical barriers in existing program facilities.

The program does not need to serve the child if doing so would

- In cases of changes in policies, practices or procedures, the accommodation would fundamentally alter the nature of the program or services offered.
- In the case of auxiliary aids and services, the accommodation would fundamentally alter the nature of the program or pose an undue burden (i.e., pose a significant difficulty or expense).
- In the case of the removal of physical or structural communication barriers, the accommodation is not readily achievable (31).

In the first case, for example, an accommodation that fundamentally alters the nature of the program or services offered might be a child who is on a respirator. This child needs full-time nursing care and cannot fully participate in the program's experiences. The child's needs would fundamentally alter the services being offered. The program does not generally offer nursing care. In the second case, using the same example, that full-time nurse may cost $85,000 each year. Paying that salary would pose an undue financial burden on a program. The

BOX 15.5

Child Care and the ADA

1. The ADA applies to privately run and publicly run child care centers and the program's interactions with children, parents, guardians, and potential customers as well as in their employment practices. Child care centers run by religious organizations may be exempt.

2. The ADA has these specific requirements for child care centers:

   • Centers cannot exclude children with disabilities from their programs unless their presence would pose a *direct threat* to the health or safety of others or require a *fundamental alteration* of the program.

   • Centers have to make *reasonable modifications* to their policies and practices to integrate children, parents, and guardians with disabilities into their programs unless doing so would constitute a *fundamental alteration*.

   • Centers must provide appropriate auxiliary aids and services needed for *effective communication* with children or adults with disabilities, when doing so would not constitute an *undue burden*.

   • Centers must generally make their facilities accessible to persons with disabilities. Existing facilities are subject to the *readily achievable* standard for barrier removal, whereas newly constructed facilities and any altered portions of existing facilities must be *fully accessible*.

Source: U.S. Department of Justice. (1997). *Commonly asked questions about child care centers and the Americans with Disabilities Act.* Retrieved from *www.ada.gov/childq%26a.htm*

third is a little harder to illustrate because infants and toddlers are unlikely to be in wheelchairs, yet. Physical accommodations to a building are unlikely to be required. (See Box 15.5 for highlights of the ADA).

Federal Agency Policy Statement on Inclusion

The U.S. Department of Health and Human Services and the U.S. Department of Education issued a policy statement on inclusion in early childhood programs (32). These two agencies affect a huge proportion of programs through direct funding, meals or child care subsidies to families.

> It is the Departments' position that all young children with disabilities should have access to inclusive high-quality early childhood programs, where they are provided with individualized and appropriate support in meeting high expectations (32, p. 1).

This policy statement does not have requirements for programs. It describes the importance of high quality programs for all children. It lays out the science that supports the benefits of inclusion for everyone involved. It also highlights the legal requirements for inclusion. Programs such as Head Start, which are fully federally funded, have specific requirements for including children with disabilities.

The policy statement also describes the major challenges to inclusion. The first and largest is the attitude of people involved. Related to that are lack of staffing, training, and expertise of the early childhood workforce. It is true that the infant toddler workforce has fewer training requirements and is the most poorly compensated. However, the staff at a program with high quality should have the skills and knowledge to serve most children. It can be helpful to remember that we are only talking about one infant or toddler at a time.

Joint Position Statement on Inclusion

The Division for Early Childhood (DEC) and the National Association for the Education of Young Children (NAEYC) have a Joint Position Statement on Early Childhood Inclusion (33). DEC is the professional organization for early childhood special education and related services. NAEYC is the professional organization for the wider earlier childhood field.

The position statement defines inclusion in this way:

Early childhood inclusion embodies the values, policies, and practices that support the right of every infant and young child and his or her family, regardless of ability, to participate in a broad range of activities and contexts as full members of families, communities, and society. The desired results of inclusive experiences for children with and without disabilities and their families include a sense of belonging and membership, positive social relationships and friendships, and development and learning to reach their full potential. The defining features of inclusion that can be used to identify high quality early childhood programs and services are access, participation, and supports (p. 32).

This statement says the defining features of high quality are access, participation, and supports. Access means the opportunity to be present in the early childhood program. It is the first step in meaningful inclusion. Participation involves the intentional efforts of the teachers to support each child during play and learning activities. A teacher might provide additional structure ("Here, Angie, hold the strainer in this hand"). She might join in the play with the child ("Sam and I are going to play with you!"). Or, she might prompt a peer ("Rami, can you hand the other ball to Sari?"). Supports refers to the adaptations, accommodations, equipment, knowledge, consultation, and services needed for the child to be successful in the group setting. For most children with disabilities, some information and an ongoing, working relationship with the family and EI team will be enough. For other children, special equipment for sitting, standing, or walking may be needed. In the first three years of life, it would be highly unusual to need extra staff.

Belonging is the true goal of all inclusion efforts. Every child learns and grows better when they feel accepted, well-liked, and enjoyed. Each child with the capacity to like and accept others has valuable qualities for his future relationships.

Check Your Understanding 15.4
Click here to check your understanding of the concepts in this section.

Summary

- Infant and toddler teachers today routinely serve children with disabilities in their community settings. High-quality practices serve children with disabilities well, but it is helpful for teachers to know some additional things:

  - The major infant and toddler disabling conditions include:

    1. Chromosomal abnormalities and genetic syndromes
    2. Sensory disorders
    3. Metabolic disorders
    4. Central nervous system disorders
    5. Congenital infections
    6. Exposure to toxic substances
    7. Chronic illness
    8. Pervasive developmental disorders

  - Each type of disorder brings its own challenges. Teachers best support these children with their own observation skills and knowledge of child development. Additional supports may be suggested and provided by the family or the EI team.

- The Program for Infants and Toddlers with Disabilities (Part C of the IDEA) provides EI services for eligible children and their families. Elements include evaluation, eligibility, service coordination, an IFSP, and services such as physical therapy, occupational therapy, speech therapy, and special education. All services should be provided in the most natural environment.

- EI teams serving infants and toddlers with disabilities should be able to support the child in child care and learning. Teachers may have a copy of the IFSP, which describes the developmental goals and strategies to help the child achieve the goals. The early interventionists may provide special equipment needed to support the child. EI services may actually be provided within the child care and learning setting.

  □ Teachers use many strategies to adapt materials and activities for their successful use by the infants and toddlers with disabilities. Toys need to be stable, match the child's current interests, and provide contingent responses to the child's actions. Teachers need to promote the close physical proximity of infants and toddlers with disabilities to typically developing children as well as the social and emotional connections among children.

  □ Well-trained infant-toddler educators have the ability to serve all children well because the elements of quality are the same for all children. It is the willingness of the teacher to include a child with disabilities that is the greatest indicator for success emotional connections among children.

- The ADA requires that child care programs serve children with disabilities. A policy statement and position statement from early childhood's leading agencies and organizations strongly support inclusion as a cornerstone of the profession.

Key Terms

accommodations
central nervous system disorders
chromosomal abnormalities
early intervention (EI)
eligibility
established risk

genetic syndromes
Individualized Family Service Plan (IFSP)
informed, clinical opinion
natural environments
person-first language

referral
screening
sensory impairments
service coordinator
switches

Reflections and Resources for the Reader

REFLECTIONS

1. Our own life experiences, or lack of experiences, around people with disabilities may influence our comfort with inclusive services. Reflect on your experiences and how they influence your feelings about serving infants and toddlers with disabilities in a child care and learning program.
2. If you were designing an inclusive infant-toddler environment, would you do anything differently from what you would do only for children without disabilities?

3. If you were preparing a parent handbook for an infant-toddler program, what would you include to let families know that you serve all children? Have a parent review the handbook and give you feedback on the relevance and completeness of the document.

their use of a child development and education program, and their EI experiences.
2. Observe an inclusive infant-toddler program. What works well? What would you change?

OBSERVATION AND APPLICATION OPPORTUNITIES

1. Contact the Part C coordinator in your community and see if you could talk to parents of an infant or toddler with a disability about their child's disability,

SUPPLEMENTARY ARTICLES AND BOOKS TO READ

Brekken, L. (2011). Early Head Start and early intervention. Partnerships that make a difference for young children with disabilities and their families. *ZERO TO THREE JOURNAL, 31*(4), 32–38.

Cook, R., Klein, M., Chen, D., & Tessier, A. (2012). *Adapting early childhood curricula for children with special needs* (8th ed.). Columbus, OH: Pearson.

Gebhard, B., & Oser, C. (2012). Putting the pieces together for infants and toddlers. Comprehensive, coordinated systems. *ZERO TO THREE.* Retrieved from *www.zerotothree.org/public-policy/policy-toolkit/systemssinglesmarch5.pdf*

Parlakian, R. (2013) Inclusion in infant/toddler child development settings: More than just including. Retrieved from: *https://prezi.com/ttpn2uo1u2ao/inclusion/*

Raver, S.A., & Childress, D.C. (2013). *Family-centered early intervention. Supporting infants and toddlers in natural environments.* Baltimore, MD: Brookes Publishing Co.

INTERESTING LINKS

Early Childhood Technical Assistance Center (ECTA) The Early Childhood Technical Assistance Center is funded by the Office of Special Education Programs to improve state EI and early childhood special education service systems, increase the implementation of effective practices, and enhance the outcomes of these programs for young children and their families.

YouTube Use the key words "infants" "disabilities" or a specific disabling condition when searching for videos on YouTube.

16

The Infant-Toddler Professional

LEARNING OUTCOMES

After reading this chapter, you will be able to:

- Describe the infant and toddler profession including standards and competencies, the code of ethics, professional development, and professional organizations.

- Explain key aspects of being an infant-toddler teacher including the nature of the relationships with children, families, colleagues, and yourself.

- Describe elements of a relationship-based, reflective program including the 3R approach (respect, reflect, and relate), reflective supervision, and mentoring and being mentored.

Pearson Education

This chapter focuses on you—in a profession, as a professional, and your experience in a relationship-based, reflective program. We examine whether early childhood is a profession. It has several of the elements of a profession but not the preparation or compensation. We discuss the aspects of working in the infant and toddler field that make it unique, particularly the intense and intimate nature of the relationships. Finally, we describe some parts of how a relationship-based, reflective program works.

The Infant and Toddler Profession

Teaching and nurturing infants and toddlers is critically important work. In these early years, the child's brain is being built. The moment-to-moment interactions and experiences of the infant or toddler create the brain. Today policy-makers recognize that the people who care for infants and toddlers need age-specific knowledge and skills and compensation equal to the importance of their work. The infant-toddler field is becoming a **profession**.

Elements of a Profession

You may think that professions are medicine, law, and education of older children and adults. However, the field of early childhood meets the requirements of a profession. Look at these elements.

- The well-being of a society is served.
- Enough emotional distance is maintained from those served that the professional can exercise clear judgment.
- There are agreed-upon principles and ethics.
- A specialized knowledge base is present and maintained.
- Prolonged and specialized training is required.
- There are clear standards of practice.
- Work is performed with some autonomy on the part of the client (i.e., professionals are not supervised every moment of the day).
- There is an altruistic mission or vision (1).

Infant-toddler professionals nurture and teach a new generation of citizens. When you do your work well, the well-being of society is being served. You are taking classes now and hopefully you will be a life-long learner, building your professional skills and knowledge. You will care for children making hundreds of decisions on your own. You will be altruistic because when you care for young children, you must put their well-being ahead of your own. Their needs are urgent and their dependence is great.

There are ways in which we fall short of being a profession (2). First, emotional distance may not be a good thing for working with young children. On the contrary, we need to use our knowledge to guide the closeness we experience with children and families. That is different from professional distance. The requirement for prolonged training does not apply to most of our field. In many states, a person can care for young children with almost no training. Throughout the field, compensation does not begin to look like a professional salary.

We may be considered an emerging profession. We are building the components of a profession. Our profession has **standards**, a **code of ethics**, descriptions of **core competencies** and **best practices**. **Professional development** opportunities are offered by **professional organizations**. Professional development describes the continued training infant-toddler teachers receive while they are working.

Professional organizations are established groups dedicated to furthering the professionalism of the early childhood field. In our emerging profession research expands our knowledge. Accreditation systems describe quality. Standards of practice or core competencies define the knowledge, skills, and characteristics that all professionals should possess. Some standards for early childhood professionals are for professionals who work with children from birth to 8 years of age. Others provide specific standards for an infant-toddler teacher. We do not have one, overarching list of competencies but we have great agreement on the important knowledge, skills and dispositions for our field.

Standards for Teachers of Children from Birth to 8 Years Old

There is not one, universally accepted set of practices for early childhood teachers, family child care providers and home visitors working with children from birth to 8 years old. The most influential standards are the NAEYC standards for early childhood professional preparation programs, the DEC recommended practices, and the NAFCC standards.

National Association for the Education of Young Children Standards for Early Childhood Professional Preparation Programs

The National Association for the Education of Young Children (NAEYC) has standards for early childhood professionals (3). These standards include the values of the profession as well as a vision for the preparation of early childhood teachers. These standards (see Table 16.1) identify the knowledge, skills, and **dispositions** (attitudes and values) early childhood teachers (including infant-toddler teachers) need. These standards are taught in an approved college or university that is recognized by NAEYC as an accredited institution.

Division for Early Childhood Recommended Practices

The Division for Early Childhood (DEC) of the Council for Exceptional Children (CEC) developed standards for professionals working with young children with disabilities (4). These standards are for **early childhood special education** (ECSE) teachers. These standards state that ECSE teachers should have knowledge and skills related to the following:

- The development and characteristics of learners,
- Individual learning differences,
- Instructional strategies,
- Learning environments and social interactions,
- Language,
- Instructional planning,
- Assessment, and
- Professional and ethical practice.

The CEC Web site (www.cec.sped.org) contains detailed information concerning the standards. NAEYC and CEC collaborated in writing both sets of standards. There are also specific

This family child care provider knows how to develop a relationship-based program.

Pearson Education

TABLE 16.1   NAEYC standards summary

Standard 1: Promoting child development and learning
   1a: Knowing and understanding young children's characteristics and needs
   1b: Knowing and understanding the multiple influences on early development and learning
   1c: Using developmental knowledge to create healthy, respectful, supportive, and challenging learning environments

Standard 2: Building family and community relationships
   2a: Knowing about and understanding diverse family and community characteristics
   2b: Supporting and engaging families and communities through respectful, reciprocal relationships
   2c: Involving families and communities in young children's development and learning

Standard 3: Observing, documenting, and assessing to support young children and families
   3a: Understanding the goals, benefits, and uses of assessment
   3b: Knowing about and using observation, documentation, and other appropriate assessment tools and approaches
   3c: Understanding and practicing responsible assessment to promote positive outcomes for each child
   3d: Knowing about assessment partnerships with families and with professional colleagues

Standard 4: Using developmentally effective approaches
   4a: Understanding positive relationships and supportive interactions as the foundation of their work with children
   4b: Knowing and understanding effective strategies and tools for early education
   4c: Using a broad repertoire of developmentally appropriate teaching/learning approaches
   4d: Reflecting on own practice to promote positive outcomes for each child

Standard 5: Using content knowledge to build meaningful curriculum
   5a: Understanding content knowledge and resources in academic disciplines.
   5b: Knowing and using the central concepts, inquiry tools, and structures of content areas or academic disciplines
   5c: Using own knowledge, appropriate early learning standards, and other resources to design, implement, and evaluate developmentally meaningful and challenging curriculum for each child

Standard 6: Becoming a professional
   6a: Identifying and involving oneself with the early childhood field
   6b: Knowing about and upholding ethical standards and other early childhood professional guidelines
   6c: Engaging in continuous, collaborative learning to inform practice
   6d: Integrating knowledgeable, reflective, and critical perspectives on early education
   6e: Engaging in informed advocacy for young children and the early childhood profession

Source: National Association for the Education of Young Children (NAEYC). (2009). *NAEYC standards for early childhood professional preparation.* Washington, DC: NAEYC. Retrieved from *www.naeyc.org/files/naeyc/files/2009%20Professional%20Prep%20stdsRevised%204_12.pdf.* Copyright © NAEYC®. Reprinted with permission.

established standards for infant-toddler teachers that are described in the next section.

National Association for Family Child Care Standards

National Association for Family Child Care Standards (NAFCC) established standards for family child care providers who provide care and learning opportunities to children from birth to 8 years of age (5). A provider may earn accreditation through meeting standards in these categories:

- Relationships
- The environment

- Developmental learning activities
- Safety and health
- Professional and business practices

NAFCC sponsors the only nationally recognized accreditation system designed specifically for family child care providers. Accreditation is awarded to family child care providers who meet the eligibility requirements and the quality standards for NAFCC accreditation. Family child care providers achieve this high level of quality through a process that examines all aspects of the family child care program, that is relationships, the environment, developmental learning activities, safety, health, and professional and business practices.

Standards and Competencies for Infant-Toddler Teachers

There are a number of standards or competencies for infant-toddler teachers. The Child Development Associate (CDA) for teachers, family child care providers, and home visitors is most established. ZERO TO THREE has developed competencies specifically for infant and toddler educators. New York, like other states, has a credential for their infant and toddler group leaders. The field of early childhood mental health has several competency-based endorsements.

The CDA Credential

The CDA credential is awarded to people who demonstrate skills related to nurturing children's physical, social, emotional, and intellectual growth. Only the Council for Professional Recognition in Washington, DC, can award a CDA credential. There are four types of CDA credentials:

- Center-based preschool
- Center-based infant-toddler
- Family child care
- Home visitor

The CDA competency standards are the core of the CDA program. The *goals* and *functional areas* are statements of the skills needed to be a competent teacher. The competency goals establish the framework for caregiver behavior. The 13 functional areas describe the major tasks or functions teachers must complete in order to carry out the competency goals. The goal areas and functional areas are the same for each type of credential, but the content varies with each credential. The competency goals are as follows:

Goal I: To establish and maintain a safe, healthy learning environment
Goal II: To advance physical and intellectual competence
Goal III: To support social and emotional development and to provide positive guidance
Goal IV: To establish positive and productive relationships with families
Goal V: To ensure a well-run purposeful program responsive to participant needs
Goal VI: To maintain a commitment to professionalism

If an infant/toddler teacher does not have a degree in early childhood education or early intervention, then earning a CDA credential is important. See Web site www.cdacouncil.org for more information on the requirements of earning the CDA credential, including why it is important to do so.

Critical Competencies for Infant Toddler Educators™

ZERO TO THREE (ZTT) has developed *Critical Competencies for Infant Toddler Educators™* (6). ZTT developed these competencies to support educators who work in group settings. It identifies important, observable skills that educators use to support infants' and toddlers' learning and development. It was prepared, in part, in response to the national report on the workforce (7) that called for specific and specialized competencies for working with infants and toddlers.

The first part of this document identifies eight domains of knowledge and that cut across all early childhood programs (see Box 16.1). As you can see, these domains have each been addressed in this text, as part of your professional development.

The critical competencies focus on social-emotional, cognitive, and language and literacy learning and development. For each of these there is a set of competencies in the sub-areas you see in Box 16.2.

The New York State Infant Toddler Care and Education Credential

A state may require a specific infant and toddler credential as well. New York, for example, provides the New York State Infant Toddler Care and Education credential to formally recognize a professional's specialized knowledge of infant and toddler care and development. This credential is one of the options required of infant-toddler teachers to be head of a group in a center program.

A Code of Ethics

Ethics is how we treat children, families, colleagues, and community members—the people we work with, work for, and come to work to serve. (Israel)

NAEYC and CEC have developed codes of ethical conduct for early childhood professionals. A code of ethics states the values of the profession and the guidelines for responsible behavior. See Box 16.3 for definitions of *code of ethics*, *values*, and *core values*.

BOX 16.1

The Eight Cross-Sector Core Competency Domains

Domain #1: Early childhood development
Domain #2: Family-centered practice
Domain #3: Relationship-based practice
Domain #4: Health and developmental protective and risk factors
Domain #5: Cultural and linguistic responsiveness
Domain #6: Leadership to meet family needs and improve services and systems
Domain #7: Professional and ethical practices
Domain #8: Service planning, coordination, and collaboration

Source: Dean, A., LeMoine, S., & Mayoral, M. (2015).*Critical competencies for infant toddler educators™*. Washington, D.C.: ZERO TO THREE

BOX 16.2

Critical Competencies Sub-Areas

Supporting social-emotional development

- Building warm, positive, and nurturing relationships
- Providing consistent and responsive caregiving
- Supporting emotional expression and regulation
- Promoting socialization
- Guiding behavior
- Promoting children's sense of identity and belonging

Supporting cognitive development

- Facilitating exploration and concept development
- Building meaningful curriculum
- Promoting imitation, symbolic representation, and play
- Supporting reasoning and problem solving

Supporting language and literacy development

- Promoting language and literacy development
- Expanding expressive and receptive language and vocabulary
- Promoting early literacy

Source: Dean, A., LeMoine, S., & Mayoral, M. (2015).*Critical competencies for infant toddler educators™*. Washington, D.C.: ZERO TO THREE

BOX 16.3

Ethics Terminology

code of ethics: document may outline the mission and values of the business or organization, how professionals are supposed to approach problems, the ethical principles based on the organization's core values and the standards to which the professional is held.

values: principles or standards of behavior; one's judgment of what is important in life.

core values: guiding principles that dictate behavior and action.

Source: Copyright © NAEYC. Reprinted with permission.

NAEYC's *Code of Ethical Conduct and Statement of Commitment* (8) is divided into sections:

Section I identifies the ethical responsibilities to children.

Section II identifies the ethical responsibilities to families.

Section III identifies the ethical responsibilities to colleagues.

Section IV identifies the ethical responsibilities to community and society.

Infant/toddler teachers are encouraged to become familiar with this code of ethics and apply it to their work with children, families, colleagues, and the community and society.

The DEC of the CEC has developed a *Code of Ethics* for professionals working with children with disabilities (9). The code provides principles and guidelines for practice including professional practice, professional development and preparation, responsive family practices, and ethical and evidence-based practices. For example, the principle professional practice states that "We shall demonstrate in our behavior and language respect and appreciation for the unique value and human potential of each child."

 Watch this video of Sue Bredekamp talking about changes in the field of early childhood. As you listen, think about how the field is becoming more of a profession.

Professional Organizations

Professions have professional organizations. These associations are usually nonprofits that seek to further a particular profession, the interests of individuals engaged in that profession and the public interest. They may participate in disseminating research. They may lobby the government for the betterment of the profession.

NAEYC is the largest professional organization in our field. It promotes high-quality early learning for all young children, birth through age 8, by connecting early childhood practice, policy, and research. NAFCC plays a similar role for family child care. The DEC in the CEC is the professional organization for early intervention and early childhood special education. ZERO TO THREE offers membership to people working with infants and toddlers.

 Check Your Understanding 16.1
Click here to check your understanding of the concepts in this section.

The Infant-Toddler Professional

The infant/toddler teacher's work is different from those who work with older children. The adult's relationship with infants and toddlers is more intimate and intense. Infants and toddlers are highly vulnerable and evoke strong feelings in adults. Self-knowledge is important for managing those feelings. The field is young and needs advocates to work for appropriate standards and funding. Finally, the knowledge requirements for entering the field are minimal and the knowledge base keeps increasing. Ongoing learning experiences are important to keep growing as a professional.

Intense and Intimate Relationships

The infant and toddler field is built on relationships. Relationships with children, families, colleagues, and employers. The primary difference between infant/toddler teachers and professionals who work with older children centers on the intensity and intimacy of relationships.

The Relationship with the Infant or Toddler

There is a physical and emotional intensity about working with infants and toddlers (10). In this work professionals provide more intimate contact and physical support with infants and toddlers than they do when working with older children.

The infant/toddler teacher performs the most intimate routines with the child—holding, diapering, toileting, feeding, wiping noses, and drying tears. The emotional nature of the work requires that children develop an attachment to an adult—an emotional connection. It is professional for adults to have an emotional connection with each child. Infants and toddlers need that to thrive. Young children use relationships to develop their sense of self-worth. They develop their basic ability to trust others. They form ideas of how adults and people in general will treat them. They learn how effective they can be in relationships and in mastering their environment.

Infant/toddler teachers create an environment in which everyone can live together, not just learn together. Infant and toddler care and learning programs should have a homelike environment. Children and adults live together, often for many hours during the day, so care and learning settings should be great places to live.

The Relationship with Families

The primary work of the infant/toddler teacher is to support the parent-child relationship. Infant/toddler teachers provide information and emotional support to families. Your ideas may conflict with some parents about what is best for the children. It can be challenging for families to share the care with teachers without becoming jealous or resentful, especially if the teacher develops that important, close relationship with the infant or toddler. It can be challenging for the teacher not to become competitive with the family over who knows what is best for the child. More so than teachers who work with older children, infant/toddler teachers must have very close

An infant/toddler teacher knows how important it is to spend time with children individually or in very small informal groups.

Pearson Education

relationships with families—constantly sharing information, delicately negotiating conflicts, and enthusiastically supporting the parent-child relationship.

The Relationship with Other Staff

The adults work as a team in infant and toddler care and learning programs. When an infant or toddler needs to have a diaper changed in a center program, the teacher who is diapering trusts that the other teachers are close to the other children. Much of the communication is nonverbal. Teachers work closely together, often in a small space. They need to respect each other's style of interacting with the children. Goals for the children must be made explicit. Tasks must be divided fairly. A good colleague is pleasant, appreciative of the work others do, and does her fair share of the work. A good employee is able to listen to constructive feedback, learn from it and improve her performance (11).

Self-knowledge

Infant/toddler teachers must have self-awareness. This means that teachers try to be aware of their feelings and reactions to be sure that they are being realistic. Sometimes, adults impose their personal needs onto their relationships with children. Or they project intentions onto an infant or toddler, such as thinking that an infant is crying just to aggravate them or that a toddler is saying "No" just to annoy them. Teachers can do some internal personal history searching to make them more responsive teachers:

> One interesting way for caregivers to feel more comfortable about floor games and creative games with babies is to do some internal personal history searching. Inside each of us are old record players. Some records play positive praises and comforting comments from our past. Some of our old personal records carry warning, shaming, prohibitions about being a silly child, a naughty child, a bad baby. A caregiver needs to leave on the nurturant positive record players that can support and encourage safe explorations and expressions of curiosity and delight. She or he may have to work hard to turn off punitive and disapproving records playing from the past. Such hard work will pay off as the caregiver becomes a person who is freer to enjoy toddlers with their "messiness" and with their delightful whimsies (12, p. 209).

Adults working with infants and toddlers need to be comfortable with closeness and intimacy. They also need to handle separation and grieving. Teachers may have their hearts broken when they say good-bye to a child who has been with them since he was an infant as he transitions to a preschool. But they are willing to have their hearts broken because they have invested in a strong, positive relationship with a child for 3 years. They know that the emotional connections developed because of continuity of care and primary care are absolutely vital for young children's development.

> Knowing ourselves involves exploring our strengths and vulnerabilities. We need to wonder about, and try to understand the meaning of, our reactions ("I got angry so quickly. Why is that?"), our frustrations ("I really get aggravated with judgmental staff members."), and the parts of our job that bring us joy ("I love it when families graduate from the program."). This exploration can sometimes be difficult or uncomfortable (13, p. 6).

When infant/toddler teachers are self-reflective, we can better manage our emotional responses, better recognize our limitations, and better leverage our skills and strengths.

Becoming an Advocate

Never doubt that a small group of committed citizens can change the world. Indeed, it is the only thing that ever has. (Margaret Mead)

The role of being an advocate for children, families, programs, communities, and yourself is the last characteristic of an infant-toddler teacher that we will discuss. An **advocate** is an enthusiastic supporter of a cause. We hope that you will become an advocate for the importance of the early years and relationship-based practice. As Margaret Mead stated, a small group of committed citizens can change the world. You have learned information in this book that will guide your advocacy efforts.

Early learning begets later learning and early success breeds later success. (Heckerman)

Much of our profession is controlled by laws, regulations, and funding. These all come from government groups. Advocates stay informed about possible changes to any of these through their professional organizations. Advocates may write letters or call legislators when they are reviewing laws to increase funding or change regulations. In a presentation at a conference, officials from Seattle explained how they came to support funding for young children. They explained that Patricia Kuhl, a leading infancy researcher spoke to the city council and explained the research on brain development. When they understood the importance of high-quality programs, they provided funding. And one person added, "And when support begins to drop, we just have her come back!"

 Watch this video to see and hear teachers advocating for early childhood. What did these teachers say to lawmakers on their advocacy day?

https://www.youtube.com/watch?v=OM-kPodg6os

Sometimes early childhood advocates take their children to visit the city council or state legislature during the Week of the Young Child. Programs invite elected officials and agency representatives to visit. Your first steps could be attending to what candidates for office have to say about early childhood issues—and vote!

Professional Development

As authors, we hope you have established a strong foundation of knowledge about infants and toddlers, their families, and how to provide group care. This is just the beginning of your learning as a professional. We hope that you stay in this field and keep growing as a teacher. Another aspect of a profession is an established array of opportunities for continued learning and development. There are many ways you might continue your learning. You may take more classes, work with a coach, attend professional conferences, and read journals. Some additional approaches will be described later in the chapter.

Classes

If you are reading this text, it is likely that you are taking classes now. There are not many communities in the United States that offer coursework focused on infant and toddler learning and development. The report *Transforming the Workplace for Children Birth Through Age 8: A Unifying Foundation* (14) promotes the requirement of a bachelor's degree for people working with infants and toddlers. However, they recognize that compensation will have to significantly increase to make the coursework worthwhile for the workforce.

> *A majority of voters think that early childhood teachers should have college degrees and matching compensation to improve quality. Teachers working in the field agree (15).*

Coaching

Coaching is an ongoing relationship between a coach and a coachee of observation, reflection, and conversation aimed at improving practices with children and families. Coaching has gained in popularity as a strategy for changing practice in early childhood over the last decade. It is clear that teaching someone a skill does not translate into their being able to perform that skill. A coach will join the teacher in the classroom, or the home visitor or family child care provider in the home. In most coaching models, the coach watches the coachee work on an already agreed upon goal or skill. Afterward, they will discuss and reflect upon what happened, the good practices observed and areas for improvement.

Sometimes coaching is offered as part of a course of study to support translating training into practice. Sometimes it is centered on a set of practices such as the items in the *Classroom Assessment Scoring System (CLASS)* (16) which articulates sets of teacher skills. Coaching may focus on competencies or standards.

Meetings

NAEYC and its state and local affiliates regularly hold conferences, presentations and meetings to provide specialized training. To find your state's NAEYC office, go to the NAEYC Web site and search for your state by name. Nationally, NAEYC holds a huge national conference in November and a smaller Professional Development Institute in June. ZERO TO THREE holds a national conference in December.

> *When Jeffrey, an infant teacher at Wee Care Child Care, walked out into the sunshine on the first day of the National Early Childhood Conference, he felt like a professional for the first time. After attending several sessions, he realized that he really did have some specialized knowledge about how to work with infants and their families. He felt good about his chosen profession.*

Smaller meetings may be held by a state, a local community, or a program. The best way to be notified of these events is to be a member of your state's NAEYC affiliate.

Journals

Professions share information through journals. Some journals share more strategies for the classroom or home visits. Some report research. *Young Children* is NAEYC's journal. It has articles on working with children from birth to 8 years. It comes with a membership in the organization. *Exchange Magazine* supports center administrators with workable strategies, practical advice, and down-to-earth ideas for dealing with the serious responsibilities and demands they face each day. ZERO TO THREE has a journal especially for people working with infants and toddlers. It is oriented more toward issues, research, and program models. It is aimed at the wider field including child care, infant mental health, health, and early intervention.

The National Center for Early Childhood Development, Teaching, and Learning is offering a service called *Text4Teachers* that sends research-based information to teachers on their smart phones.

Your Vision

If we are going to have infant care, then why not create places where babies love to go and we love to have them go? Instead of setting our sights so low, why not create places where our children will be amazed, enlivened, and overjoyed each day? Why stop at "Do no harm?" (17).

What is your vision for the type of community you want for infants and toddlers?

Part of being a reflective, theory-based professional is to reflect on your vision for children and families. How do you hope to affect the lives of children and families by becoming an infant-toddler teacher?

Your values and vision will guide you to make important difficult decisions regarding your practice. What if teachers in a center are being bounced around from classroom to classroom each day with no regard for the relationship that you know is critical for infants' development? Teachers have knowledge of and a value for the importance of relationships, including primary caregiving and continuity of care. They problem solve with others to try to make the situation better for infants and toddlers. Your values and vision are a guide to your behavior in this situation and others.

Imagine the child care of our dreams, not just child care that's good enough. (Whitebook)

To develop your vision, ask, "What kind of life and experiences do I want for children and families?"

- What is the primary purpose of my work?
- What do I wish for infants and toddlers?
- What do I wish for families of infants and toddlers?
- What do I wish for programs for infants and toddlers?
- What do I wish for my community, nation, and world to support infants' and toddlers' optimal development?

 Check Your Understanding 16.2
Click here to check your understanding of the concepts in this section.

Relationship-Based, Reflective Practice

Your personal and professional relationships with colleagues affect your feelings about your work and your career. A relationship-based community sets a positive tone for the workday—and the work. Other supports for the intense and intimate work of our field includes reflective supervision and mentoring.

Developing a Professional Relationship-Based Community

The skills needed to create a supportive and inspiring workplace include *respect, reflect,* and *relate*. We can apply these concepts to professionals' relationships with each other as well as their relationships with children. Professionals need to discover who they can be together: "To build a group culture and a sense of community, we need to know who we are and why we are here, and to begin to discover who we can be together" (18, p. 85). This process starts with respect.

Respect with Relationships in Mind

Respect for your colleagues includes recognizing their humanity. Each person needs to feel as if she is a contributing and valued member of the team. The need for emotional connections is just as strong for adults as it is for children. And, each person has strengths and can contribute in different ways.

The following questions capture part of what it means to respect others on your team (19):

- At meetings, do you listen well to others?
- When you disagree with others, how often do you differ with the idea, not the person, encouraging members to share even unusual ideas or minority opinions?
- How often do you recognize special talents of your colleagues by asking them for input on particular projects?
- If other members miss a meeting, how often do you let them know that they were missed, perhaps expressing disappointment because you would have liked their input on something?
- How often do you personally compliment team members when they offer ideas, facilitate decision making, or put aside personal interests for the good of the group?

Besides respecting the strengths of others, you can also reflect on your own emotional and recognition needs as a team member and how you are contributing to the program.

Reflect with Relationships in Mind

To become a relationship-based team member, you can ask yourself: "What are my communication skills? How do I handle conflict?" When you are communicating with others, do you express yourself clearly? Do you listen with your eyes by looking at the speaker? Do you let others finish their sentences before you respond? What are your **responding habits**?

Here are some questions that can help you reflect on your responding habits. We have added the examples after each question that are relevant to the infant and toddler profession.

- Do you demonstrate that you are listening by reflecting the feeling of the speaker? *("So, you are feeling upset with the parent who yelled at you.")*
- Do you check your understanding of what others say by paraphrasing the content? *("Your main concern is finding time to talk with Visha's parent?")*

- Do you try to expand your understanding of what was said by asking related questions? (*"Are you saying that Visha's mom was upset with you because she thought you didn't talk with her enough?"*)
- Do you begin your response with agreement first and objections second? (*"I agree with you about the importance of having a special conference with each parent each month. I'm concerned about how we will find time to do that."*)
- When disagreeing, do you state under what conditions you agree? (*"I could go along with that idea if we can do it within the workday and not have to come out again at night."*)
- When disagreeing, do you show respect for the individual's thinking, sharing, and taking a risk? (*"That's a creative idea; let's talk to the coordinator about discussing it at the next staff meeting."*) (20).

Despite reflecting on and using great communication skills, conflicts happen! Infant and toddler teachers work closely together. Sometimes, decisions with teammates have to be made quickly. You live together every day for long periods of time. There are going to be differences of opinion, disagreements about practice, and diversity in how people relate to each other. How you and your teammates resolve conflicts will make or break your experience in the workplace. **Conflict resolution skills** are among the most important that you can learn. Here are steps to a win-win conflict management strategy:

1. Prepare powerfully.
   - Identify your position/interest. Ask, "What do I want? Why do I want it?"
   - Speculate on the other party's stated position and underlying interests. Ask, "What do they want? Why do they want it?"

2. Approach positively.
   - Acknowledge that you have thought about the other party's needs: "I've thought about what's important to you. You'd like _____. Is that pretty close?"
   - State your win-win intent: "I really want to find a solution that will satisfy both of us."
   - Seek commitment to a win-win (collaborative) process.

3. Clarify both points of view.
   - Check any areas of agreement: "Let's review where we agree. We both want _____. Right?"
   - Clarify areas of disagreement: "Let's review where we differ. You would like _____, and I would like _____. Right?"

4. Create alternatives.
   - Agree not to evaluate solutions, but to generate possibilities.
   - Brainstorm alternatives together.

5. Select a solution and agree on implementation. (21).

Some conflicts need to be resolved through finding information, not resolving opinions. Conflicts about the health, safety, or emotional well-being of infants and toddlers, for example whether or not to pick up crying toddlers, require information. You need a discussion of why you think as you do. Draw upon research and what you know about a child learning to trust others and develop self-regulation. Being an ethical professional entails supporting your point of view with scientific evidence and standing by your principles of "do no harm" and "meet the emotional and social needs of children." You may need to ask a third person to help you and the other staff member sort out the reasons why a certain practice is critical to the health and well-being of children and families. Having an attitude of "let's find out" what information is available can lead to collaborative learning as a way to solve conflict.

Relate with Relationships in Mind

Relate to others by developing and committing to agreements. Agreements that are created in a collaborative way make explicit basic values for how professionals will treat each other. Here are some areas for staff agreements, and approaches to criticism when those agreements are broken:

1. We will each have an attitude of flexibility and cooperation in our work here, thinking of the needs of others and the group as a whole, along with our own needs.
2. We will each carry a full share of the workload, which includes some extra hours outside our work schedule (i.e., parent-teacher conferences, meetings, planning and preparation of activities, record keeping, progress reports).
3. We will each communicate directly and honestly with each other. We will be respectful and honorable in our interactions.
4. When problems or difficulties related to our work arise, we will address them rather than ignore or avoid them.
5. We will all be informed of significant problems that affect the center. These will be communicated in person as soon as possible and in writing as necessary.
6. We understand that it is appropriate to seek help from the director on sensitive or difficult issues.
7. When necessary, we will use a criticism/self-criticism discussion process to identify attitudes and behaviors that are negatively affecting our agreements (22, p 78–79).

Agreements are necessary for those times when the core values for how professionals treat each other are violated. However, responding to others in a caring and compassionate way that supports positive relationships can usually prevent troubles and lead to mutually satisfying solutions to problems.

The terms *respect, reflect,* and *relate* can remind professionals of the important steps in developing a community of caring. By making a commitment to your own and others' sense of well-being in the workplace, you are modeling your focus on the importance of healthy relationships for families and children.

Reflective Supervision

Carly was looking forward to her weekly meeting with her reflective supervisor. Mia actually listened to her and empowered her to think through problems. Carly couldn't wait to tell Mia about her problem with Sheila, a new toddler in her class who was biting Cal, the smallest child in her group.

"Reflective supervision is a collaborative relationship for professional growth that improves program quality and practice by cherishing strengths and partnering around vulnerabilities" (23, p. 8). A collaborative relationship is a partnership where individuals bring their best thinking to identify strengths or address concerns around the families and children they serve. No one is expected to know all the answers. Reflective supervision entails regular meetings during which the two parties discuss what they are feeling and thinking with a supportive and thoughtful partner (24, 25).

There are three necessary ingredients for reflective supervision to work—regularity, collaboration, and reflection (26). Each member of the relationship shares power. There are mutual expectations for the relationship. There is open communication. Reflective supervision requires trust in one another, confidentiality, and trust in the ability of the supervisee to solve her own problems. The reflective supervisor provides the time and space for thoughtful reflection. The reflective supervisor engages in active listening (rephrasing the meaning of what the other says and does) and thoughtful questioning.

Reflective supervision has been particularly useful in the infant and toddler field. The intensity and intimacy of the relationships can bring out strong feelings in teachers and home visitors. Infants and toddlers are so vulnerable. Or sometimes so frustrating. Sometimes parents act in ways that are disturbing to the teacher. Sometimes, it is a part of our own history that triggered an outburst. A teacher may want to talk with her supervisor about how her skills with comforting crying babies just doesn't work with Jamie—and it makes her angry. Perhaps that feeling of helplessness is coming from something much older than Jamie. Quiet time to reflect with an interested partner may lead to insight about the teacher's own crying as a child— crying that received no comfort from the adults in her life. She may remind herself that it was long ago. She is no longer helpless. Maybe the next day, Jamie's tears will not be so overwhelming.

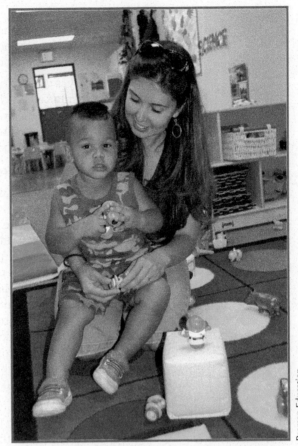

This teacher benefits from reflective supervision and mentoring to help her improve her practice. She knows that sensitive responding to infants' and toddlers' needs is part of being a professional.

 Watch this video to observe a reflective supervision session. How does reflection support this supervisor to gain deeper understanding of her work?

https://www.youtube.com/watch?v=f-pvfocphaQ

Mentoring and Being Mentored

Mentors are guides and role models who help whomever they are mentoring—their **protégés**—to develop their own professional goals. They are capable of developing a supportive relationship with their protégés that is based on trust and confidentiality (27).

Responsibilities of the Mentor

The responsibilities of the mentor include:

- Share information
- Link their protégés to appropriate resources
- Share teaching strategies and information
- Guide and give ideas

- Assist the protégé—for example, in setting up the classroom
- Observe and discuss what was observed
- Promote self-observation and analysis
- Encourage reflection and model professionalism (28).

Technology is enhancing the ability of mentors to provide opportunities for both new and experienced teachers to improve their practice. Protégés may videotape themselves teaching and watch with their mentors. They may use a smartphone to capture a moment they find particularly challenging or rewarding. If agreeable to both parties, the protégé may even text a question to a mentor, in the moment.

Responsibilities of the Protégé

Protégés also have responsibilities as they participate in the relationship for learning. Protégés think about what they want to learn, are willing to examine their own practices, and engage in problem solving for change and improvement (29).

The mentoring relationship is built on trust, confidentiality, and commitment (30). Mentors do not evaluate the protégé's job performance. That is the responsibility of a **supervisor**. The protégé and the mentor must be able to discuss difficult issues and the challenges that the protégé is experiencing without fear of reprisal or judgment. The only exception, of course, is if the mentor suspects that the protégé is neglecting or abusing children. It must be made clear at the beginning of the relationship that the mentor is ethically and legally required to report suspected child abuse.

The following questions can be used to create a more positive reflective supervision and mentoring relationship. If you are the one being supervised, then you could suggest that you would like to complete the questionnaire to help your mentor get to know you.

1. How did you become interested in infant-family issues?
2. When did you join the program? What positions have you held with this program?
3. Where did you work before?
4. What is your educational background?
5. How long have you been in your current position?
6. What are the best things about your job? What are the things you like the least about your job?
7. What do you find really motivating about working here?
8. What would you change about your job if you could? The organization?
9. What are your long-term goals? What would you like to be doing 5 years from now?
10. What do you think you are learning on the job right now? What are you struggling with at the moment?
11. What skills or abilities would you like to develop? (31, p. 19)

In the first chapter we said our goal is that you gain an appreciation for how vitally important the prenatal period and the first 3 years of life are for children and the future adults they will become. Our hope is that you will become knowledgeable about and gain a passion for promoting the well-being, competence, and quality of life for infants and toddlers and their families.

We hope that we have accomplished our goal.

Check Your Understanding 16.3
Click here to check your understanding of the concepts in this section.

Summary

We end the book by coming full circle in our quest for quality experiences for infants and toddlers. The infant-toddler teachers are the ones who ensure that quality will be created and will continue. The following points are covered in this chapter:

- The infant and toddler profession meets most of the criteria determined to be necessary in order to be a profession. Professionals commit to a standard of performance that earns the respect of others. Early childhood professional standards include the values of the profession as well as a vision for the preparation of early childhood professionals. It is important for professionals to know the code of ethics of their profession. Ongoing professional development includes classes, coaching, meetings, journals, and membership in professional organizations.

- The primary difference between infant/toddler teachers and professionals who work with older children centers on the intensity and intimacy of relationships. Infant/toddler teachers develop close emotional bonds with the children and the families. Teachers work in teams and need respectful, pleasant working relationships. Infant/toddler teachers need self-knowledge to manage the strong feelings infants can evoke. Finally, teachers should be advocates in this severely underfunded, vitally important field.

- The 3R approach (respect, reflect, relate) supports relationship-based programs. A **reflective practice model** includes reflective supervision and mentoring, two systems that build on the strength of relationship to improve practices.

Our goal in this book was for you to recognize the importance of relationships and responsive adult-child interactions for the optimal development of infants' and toddlers' capacities in emotional, social, cognitive, language, and motor domains. Our hope is that you will become knowledgeable about and gain a passion for promoting the well-being, competence, and quality of life for infants and toddlers and their families.

Key Terms

advocate
best practices
code of ethics
conflict resolution skills
core competencies
dispositions

early childhood special education
mentor
profession
professional development
professional organizations
protégé

reflective practice model
responding habits
standards
supervisor

Reflections and Resources for the Reader

REFLECTIONS

1. For you, what are the benefits and drawbacks of the increasing professionalism of the field of early childhood?
2. As you look at the standards of practice and competencies expected of you in this field, does it affect your sense of being a professional?
3. What are the unique challenges of the infant-toddler teacher?
4. For you, what are the benefits and drawbacks of relationship-based coaching, mentoring, or reflective supervision?

OBSERVATION AND APPLICATION OPPORTUNITIES

1. Design a vision statement for an infant/toddler care and learning program.
2. A teammate is using practices that you think are harmful to the children (such as not comforting an infant who is crying). What are your ethical responsibilities to the children, families, colleagues, and the community and society? How would you communicate your concerns to your teammate?
3. Write a letter to a legislator on the importance of the infant and toddler years.

SUPPLEMENTARY ARTICLES AND BOOKS TO READ

ZERO TO THREE. (2016). *Professional development for the infant-toddler early care and education workforce.* Retrieved from: zerotothree.org/resources/467-professional-development-for-the-infant-toddler-early-care-and-education-workforce

Early Head Start National Resource Center. (2015). *Tips on becoming a reflective supervisor and a reflective supervisee.* Retrieved from: *https://eclkc.ohs.acf.hhs.gov/hslc/tta-system/ehsnrc/comp/program-design/tips-reflective-supervisor-supervisee.html*

Feeney, S. & Freeman, N. K. (2015, March). Smartphones and social media: Ethical implications for educators. *Young Children.* Retrieved from: http://www.naeyc.org/yc/columns/focusonethics/smartphones_and_social_media

INTERESTING LINKS

Child Care Information Exchange. This site promotes the exchange of ideas among leaders in early childhood programs worldwide through its magazine, books, training products and seminars, and international conference.

Early Educator Central. This site has information on education and career pathways for the infant-toddler workforce and for those who support the workforce.

Families and Work Institute. The institute is a nonprofit center providing data on the changing workforce, family, and community. It offers some of the most comprehensive research on the U.S. workforce available.

The National Center for Research on Early Childhood Education. This Web site supports research, disseminates research findings, and provides leadership to improve the quality of early childhood education.

Appendices

Appendix A

Portraits of Development

Portraits of Infants and Toddlers

Acknowledgments to Florida State University Center for Prevention & Early Intervention Policy, *http://www.cpeip.fus.edu*, for their formatting suggestions for this material.

	Development	Example
	0–4 months	
Emotions/ Attachment	• Infants are taking in a lot of information about the world. • Infants can get overwhelmed and begin to yawn, look away, or fuss. • Infants begin to calm themselves by sucking on their hands or listening to an adult talk quietly to them. • Infants gaze into their teacher's eyes as she feeds them. • Infants turn their heads toward a familiar voice. • Infants relax and allow themselves to be comforted by familiar people. • Infants cry when they are hungry, tired, or uncomfortable.	Carlos followed Karen with his eyes wherever she went in the room. When she came close to him, he looked at her as though he wanted her to join him. Accepting his invitation to play, she sat with him on the floor. As he began to tire and fuss, she swaddled him in a blanket, held him close, and spoke softly to him.
Learning with peers	• Infants like to look at each other (visual regard). • Infants prefer to look at faces, especially the edges and the eyes. • Infants may cry when they hear other babies cry (contagion).	After the teacher put Tamika near Sam on a blanket on the floor, Tamika stared intently at Sam.
Cognitive	• Infants follow a moving object visually. • Infants cry to bring an adult to comfort or feed them. • Infants will look around the room with interest. • Infants begin to reach for a toy. • Infants notice that their arms or legs made something happen and will repeat the movement. • Infants recognize familiar people and objects. • Infants begin to bring objects to mouth.	• Megan lifted her head, resting on her arms as she lay on the blanket. With a serious expression on her face, she watched the teachers and children around her. • Willie kicked the mobile hanging over him and made it wiggle. He stopped, looked at it, and then kicked some more, watching the mobile to see if anything might happen.
Language	• Infants may startle if they hear a loud sound. • Infants hear the differences in all of the language sounds spoken. • Infants may stop crying when they hear a familiar adult's voice. • Infants prefer to hear "parentese," a simpler version of language with many repetitions, directed toward them. • Infants listen when an adult talks or sings to them while looking at them. • Infants cry when they are in pain, are hungry, or are distressed. • By 2 months of age, babies have different cries for hunger and pain. • Infants may smile by the end of this age period. • Infants "coo" (make soft vowel sounds). • Infants will stare at interesting pictures in books.	• Terrell's arms flew out as if to grasp on to his parent when he heard a big bang. • Erica gave her father a big smile when he picked her up out of her crib. • Brenda held Jordon so they could gaze into each other's eyes. Jordon cooed softly and Brenda cooed back. Then she waited for Jordon to take another turn.

Teacher-Child or Parent-Child Interaction	Environment
0–4 months	

Teacher-Child or Parent-Child Interaction	Environment
• Keep young babies close to you, in your arms, in a snuggly, or on a blanket nearby. • Recognize the signals that indicate a baby wants to be with you—intent gazing, reaching, a happy look—and respond with quiet, verbal and nonverbal turn taking. • Recognize the signals that indicate a baby needs a break—yawning, drooling, looking away—and sit back quietly and wait while the baby regroups. • Comfort babies whenever they cry.	• Being close to a familiar teacher is best. • A serene, quiet space with gentle lighting limits the information an infant needs to take in. • Avoid playing background music all day. • Limit the number of objects, sounds, color, and movements around a young infant. • The teacher is the most interesting thing for a baby to watch, but other babies, mirrors, and toys within the baby's visual range of focus are also interesting.
• Hold two babies so they can look at each other. • Place a few babies on a blanket on the floor so that they can look at and touch each other.	• The arms of teachers provide the best environment. • Blankets on the floor—put two babies beside each other so their toes are touching.
• Slowly move a small toy from one side to another while the infant follows it with his gaze. • Respond quickly to the baby's cries. • Provide quiet time for babies to look at what is happening around them. Talk about what they see. • React to infants' expressions with clear, even exaggerated facial expressions and language.	• Arrange the space so that infants can see some activity but still be protected. • Provide a few interesting things to look at—small toys on the floor during tummy time, dangling toys when infants are on their backs. • Provide nonbreakable mirrors.
• Use infant-directed speech. • Hold and talk to babies. Engage in long eye gazes while taking conversational turns. • Respect the baby if he needs a break and turns his head away, closes his eyes, or arches his back. • Repeat the sounds that infants make and wait for the infant to make the sound again (turn taking). • Be an empathic language partner—comment on the baby's feelings. • Use words and sounds to comfort babies. • Interpret babies' burps, cries, yawns, stretching, and sounds as forms of communication. Say, "Oh, you're telling me you're sleepy." • Sing lullabies and other songs • Read books with rhythmic phrases and books with one picture on a page with 2- to 4-month-olds.	• The best environment is in the arms of a caring adult who holds the baby and talks softly. • Provide toys that make pleasant sounds. Gently hold the toy and share the sounds with the baby. • Provide interesting materials to touch while you comment on the textures. • Add mirrors low along a wall. Babies will look and possibly make sounds.

Development	Example
0–4 months	

Motor
- Infants lift head when held at shoulder—hold head steady and erect.
- On tummy, infants lift their head and shoulders off the ground and can hold a toy in hand.
- Infants turn head toward a familiar voice.
- Infants hold body still to pay attention, wiggle and move to encourage continued interaction.
- On back, infants thrust arms and legs in play.
- Infants turn from side to back.
- Infants hold finger, light toy with reflexive grasp.
- Infants suck on own fingers and hands and on objects.
- Infants move arms and legs in what seem like random motions but are called "body babbling", akin to language babbling.

Example:
- Rosie held her head up and looked around at the other children as Sharon held her against her shoulder.
- Robert, on his tummy on a blanket, lifted his head to see himself in the mirror mounted at floor level on the wall.
- Jen held a rattle placed in her hand but seemed unaware it was there.
- Filipe brought his fingers to his mouth and sucked on them, while looking intently at the toddlers.

4–8 months

Emotions/Attachment
- Infants like to look at their hands and feet.
- Infants wave their arms and kick in excitement when they see a familiar person.
- Infants will smile at a teacher expecting her to smile back.
- Infants use their faces and bodies to express many feelings: everything from frowning and crying to laughing out loud.
- Infants express their feelings more clearly to familiar people and are more reserved with strangers.

Example:
Deborah loves being carried in her teacher's arms as they move around the room "talking" about the things they see. Her eyes are wide and bright, she smiles, and she makes cooing sounds as though taking her turn in the conversation. When a visitor enters the room, Deborah gets very quiet and serious and holds tightly to her teacher's shoulder as she looks at the visitor.

Learning with peers
- Infants touch a peer, vocalize to each other, get excited, approach other babies, smile and laugh at each other.
- Babies may treat other babies like objects–crawling over them, licking or sucking on them, or sitting on them. They are just learning the difference between people and objects. Infants may poke, push, or pat another baby to see what that other infant will do. They often look very surprised at the reaction they get.

Example:
Anna crawled over to Nadia who was lying on the floor. Touching Nadia's hair, Anna laughed out loud.

Cognitive
- Infants like to examine toys.
- Infants like to make toys do something—make a sound, put one inside another.
- Infants imitate adult expressions and gestures.
- Infants turn toward a sound to see where it came from.
- Infants look for toys they dropped.

Example:
- Angela is interested in everything. She watches her friends and then looks at the teacher and smiles.
- Roger reaches out to touch a dangling toy. When it swings, making a sound, he reaches out to do it again.

Teacher-Child or Parent-Child Interaction	Environment

0–4 months

• Change the baby's position: sometimes on his back, sometimes on his tummy. Even when holding the baby, sometimes cradle him in your arms, sometimes hold him upright against your shoulder. • When baby is on the floor, lie down face-to-face with him. • When baby is on her back, reaching for a toy a little beyond her head, support her trunk as she rolls over.	• A stiff blanket (to prevent the danger of suffocation) on the floor provides space for early movements. • Small, interesting toys, pictures, and books to look at will encourage babies to lift their heads. A mirror bolted to the wall at floor level always provides something interesting to look at. • As babies begin to reach, they enjoy stable bars that dangle toys for them to bat at or reach and grasp.

4–8 months

• Provide opportunities for babies to look in mirrors as they play. • Mirror the emotional expressions of the infant and add appropriate words: "I'm so excited to see you today!" • Respond to babies in a way that helps them be calm and active; if babies are crying, soothe them.	• Mount unbreakable mirrors on walls. • Provide floor time where babies play with their feet while on their backs and move around on the ground. • Books and posters of photographs of real faces with different emotional expressions are very interesting to infants.
• Move to music with a baby in each arm. • While holding one baby in your lap, point out and talk about what another baby is doing. • Place two babies on their tummies facing a mirror. • Instead of saying "Don't" or "Stop that" to exploring babies, say "Touch gently." Tell children what you want them to do—model it for them.	• Hang a safety mirror horizontally on the wall, so the bottom is touching the floor. • Cover an inner tube with soft cloth. Sit two babies in the inner tube so that their feet are touching.
• Hold the infant in your arms as you walk around, looking at things and talking about them. • Sit nearby and talk to the baby about the toys she is looking at. • Call the baby by name from a short distance to reassure her you are nearby.	• Provide a variety of small toys to handle and examine. • Provide toys that make sounds when a baby moves them, fit inside each other, or dangle and move when touched. • Offer board books.

	Development	Example
	4–8 months	
Language	• Infants turn their head toward a noise or someone speaking their name. • Infants enjoy adults talking, singing, and laughing with them. • Infants vocalize with intention to get a response from the adult. • Infants make high-pitched squeals. • Infants practice their sounds when exploring and with favorite adults. • Infants begin to babble—at first with one consonant and then by combining two consonants. • Infants engage in turn-taking conversations with adults. • Babies will look at different pictures in a book and get excited at a favorite one or at the enthusiastic tone of an adult who is reading to them. • At the end of this age period, infants tune into the sounds of the language(s) they are hearing and begin to lose the ability to hear the difference in sounds spoken in other languages.	• As Danielle, the infant teacher, was holding Donovan on her lap, she pointed to the pictures in the sturdy board book. • "Look," she said, pointing to the picture, "a ball. There's your ball," as she pointed to a ball on the floor. Donovan looked at the picture, then at the ball on the floor, and back to the picture. • "Tt" said Afi as he lay in his teacher's arms looking up at her. "Tada" exclaimed his teacher back to him. "Tt" repeated Afi as he took his turn in the conversation.
Motor	• Infants turn from back to side, later roll from back to front. • Infants sit—first with support but steady alone by the end of this period. • Infants reach with one arm. • Infants use raking grasp. • Infants crawl. • Infants shake, bang, hold, and let go of objects. • Infants move objects from hand to hand. • Infants can hold their own bottle. • Infants can bring objects to their mouth.	• Micky rolls from his back to his tummy to reach a toy, then rolls back over to play with it. • Erin, sitting steadily alone, loves using both hands to pick up objects and study them. • Freddy loves being held while he has his bottle, but he insists on holding it himself.
	8–12 months	
Emotions/ Attachment	• Infants may be fearful with strangers. • Infants will call upon familiar adults to help them when they are upset. • Infants will look at a familiar adult to determine whether a situation is safe or dangerous. • Infants will cling to a familiar adult when they are in a strange situation. • Infants will find humor in silly games and adults making big facial expressions.	Jamie is enjoying his new ability to quickly crawl anywhere he wants to go. He loves the little climber that lets him look out the window. But when the ramp feels a little shaky, he likes to look back at his teacher, Fred—just making sure he's still safe.

Teacher-Child or Parent-Child Interaction	Environment

4–8 months

- Use infant-directed speech.
- Talk with babies often. Show them new objects and people and name them.
- Repeat the sounds that infants make and wait for the infant to make the sound again (turn taking).
- Use sign language for several familiar items such as "milk" or "dog."
- Sing songs and say finger-plays.
- Use words to describe children's feelings expressed through gestures, body postures, and sounds.
- Read simple books with one to two pictures on a page. Point to the pictures as you say the name of the picture.
- Read the same books over and over.
- Use joint attention strategies—point at a toy or picture in a book when you say the name or talk about it.
- Stay near the baby who is just beginning to sit alone.
- Know the progression of motor development; emotionally encourage and physically support new attempts.
- Believe in the lifelong health benefits of an active lifestyle.

- Provide interesting toys and materials for babies to handle and explore.
- Provide cardboard books with handles so that babies pick them up.
- Make a peek-a-boo picture book by gluing a piece of cloth over each picture.
- Create a cozy book corner where teachers can be comfortable and read to babies.
- Provide sound boxes (safely sealed) with different objects in them that make different sounds when shaken.
- Add puppets to the environment. Use them at times to "talk" to the child. Put the puppet on the child's hand and wait to see what the child says or does.
- Provide safe places for rolling, sitting, and crawling. Protect babies from anything that might fall on them.
- Provide small, washable lightweight objects (too large for choking) for handling and tossing, and provide containers for objects.

8–12 months

- Encourage Infants to move off and explore by reassuring them that you are watching and keeping them safe.
- Understand that Infants may become afraid of new situations that wouldn't have been frightening a few months ago. Be comforting and reassuring.

- Play peek-a-boo.
- Read stories about mothers and fathers who go away and come back.
- Read books with flaps to lift to find things.
- Keep room arrangements and routines predictable.

	Development	Example
	8–12 months	
Learning with peers	• Infants may show a peer an object, sit by each other, crawl after and around each other, play chase-and-retrieve games. • Babies smile and laugh at each other. • Babies make sounds to and with each other—may say first words with peers. • Peek-a-boo is a favorite game as babies explore separation: coming and going, in sight and out of sight. • Infants can learn to touch each other gently. • Because infants become more goal oriented at this age, they may push another baby's hand away from a toy or crawl over another baby to get a toy.	Shamaine peeked around the low toy shelf and saw Carla crawling toward her. Shamaine quickly turned around and crawled away with Carla close behind. Kai crawled over Bridger's legs to get a toy on the other side of Bridger.
Cognitive	• Infants like to take the pieces of a toy apart and put them back together. • Infants like toys that do something when you touch them, pull them, bang them. • Infants begin very simple pretend play, such as lifting a cup to their mouth. • Infants like to find small toys hidden under a cloth or cup. • Infants like to pick up and examine a tiny item like a Cheerio. • Infants point to objects, knowing you can also see them.	• Charlie loves to take each plastic animal out of the bucket and look at it. When the bucket is empty, he tosses it aside. • Aliya likes the push button and the swinging doors on the busy box but can't work all the mechanisms yet. Her teacher expresses surprise with Aliya when the doors pop open, and everyone once in a while shows her how to work another of the knobs.
Language	• Infants are beginning to play social games such as peek-a-boo or "So big." • Infants enjoy listening to sound play (rhymes), songs, and finger-plays. • Babbling continues to develop with combined syllables such as "dada," "mama," and "tutu," but now the infant may be using these sounds specifically for mom or dad. • Infants will use sounds consistently for an object or person or animal. • If they hear another language with an adult through interactive conversational strategies, then infants can "keep the brain open to the sounds of a second language." • Infants may begin to use single words. • At the end of the age period, infants may begin to point to engage an adult. • They are using facial expressions and gestures such as shaking head or stretching arms out to be picked up to communicate to adults.	• Deanna raised her hands and smiled when her mother said, "So big!" • One of Trishanna's first words was "dada," which she excitedly said over and over again when she saw her father. • Thomas used the sounds, "baba" to indicate he wanted his bottle of milk.

Teacher-Child or Parent-Child Interaction	Environment

8–12 months

- Name parts of infants' bodies as two infants sit close to each other:
    - *Here is baby's eyes*
    - *Here is baby's nose*
    - *Touch the part that sees*
    - *Touch the part that blows*
- Place a baby with one other baby (pairs), because more frequent, complex, and intense peer interaction occurs than when a child is with many peers.
- Understand that infants are not being "naughty" when they push another child's hand away. Say "Jenny was holding that toy. Let's find you a different toy."

- While feeding, place high chairs so children can see each other.
- Set up cozy corners in the room where babies can "disappear" (but adults can still see them).
- Hang a long wide cloth (so babies won't get tangled in it) from the ceiling. Babies love to crawl around it.
- Place containers with different sizes of blocks in them between two babies. Sit beside them as they begin to explore the materials. Talk about what each one is doing.

- Help the baby focus on what is interesting to him, using your presence, your interest, and your enthusiasm to support his attention and exploration.
- Use your emotional expressions and words to show the mobile infant that you delight in his discoveries.
- Use words to describe the child's activity: "Look, you found a Cheerio. You're picking it up with your fingers."

- Provide toys like stacking cups, rings on a post, pop-beads, and tubs full of small, interesting objects such as toy animals.
- Provide child-size replicas of dishes or household tools.
- Provide toys that respond to children's actions—busy boxes, water-filled pads.
- Provide sensory materials such as water and sand with a variety of tools.
- Provide board books with photos.

- Play familiar games such as peek-a-boo, pat-a-cake, or "How big are you?"
- Respond to infants' nonverbal communication with words.
- Sometimes look at and wait for infants to initiate sounds or words.
- Imitate the sounds and then expand, elaborate, and extend the baby's language.
- Model the next step in language development.
- Use self-talk and parallel talk.
- Talk often in a responsive way using a varied vocabulary. Don't bombard the child.
- Read books with enthusiasm, changing the tone of your voice with different characters.
- Talk about the pictures and the story as you read it. Engage babies in the story with your voice and gestures.
- Wait while looking at a picture for babies to communicate sounds, point, or use facial expressions.

- Create a cozy book corner where babies can easily reach and handle books.
- Create an "All About Me" book—small photo albums for each child with pictures of themselves, their family, their favorite toys, peers, teachers, and the family pets. Make them available to the children. Change the pictures as the child grows.
- Musical push toys encourage infants to handle them and make sounds.

Development	Example
8–12 months	
Motor • Infants pull to stand. • Infants cruise. • Infants stand alone. • Infants walk with help and then alone. • Infants sit in a chair. • Infants finger-feed. • Infants use spoon, tippy cup. • Infants use pincer grasp.	• Hershel crawls to his teacher's side, then holds her leg as he pulls up to stand. • Jem sits at the lunch table, alternating between using her spoon and her fingers to enjoy her meal.
12–18 months	
Emotions/ Attachment • Young toddlers will imitate the actions of familiar adults, such as using the phone or caring for a baby doll. • Young toddlers will seek adult attention by pulling on their leg or taking their hand. • Young toddlers will use a favorite blanket or stuffed animal to help calm themselves. • Young toddlers will protest loudly when their parents leave them. • Young toddlers will relax and be comforted by cuddling with a familiar adult. • Young toddlers will let their likes and dislikes be clearly known.	Amelia carries her teddy bear around all morning. Sometimes she copies her teacher Sophia's actions, patting its back or "feeding it a bottle." When she gets tired, she rubs teddy against her ear and sucks her thumb.
Learning with peers • Imitation (motor) and interactive turns begin. Toddlers may copy each other—if one gives a toy to another child, the other may imitate. • Young toddlers begin to talk to each other. • Infants may show concern when other babies are distressed. • Young toddlers may take a toy away from another child, say "No," push away another child, clutch toy to self and say "Mine." • Toddlers are little scientists at this age, experimenting to see how things work. This affects how they get along with peers. They are constantly doing things to other children to see what response they will get. • Biting may appear as toddlers bite others "to see what happens," to get the toy they want, or to express frustration. Toddlers are on the cusp of communicating well; they may communicate through their mouths in the form of a bite.	• Rashinda banged her spoon on the table; soon two others tried it. They seemed to be physically following each other's lead (as in a conversation). • First, Carmen tried pushing Toby away from her rocking horse. When that didn't work, she leaned over and took a bite out of his arm.

Teacher-Child or Parent-Child Interaction	Environment

8–12 Months

- Stay alert when practicing walkers need a little help—and know when to let them keep trying.
- Allow time for older infants to practice feeding themselves using their fingers.

- Safe places to pull up to stand.
- Push and pull toys to help support practicing walkers.
- Busy boxes.
- Board books for turning pages, lifting flaps, and poking fingers through holes.

12–18 months

- Demonstrate your interest in toddlers' activities.
- Show your pride in toddlers' accomplishments.
- Let toddlers use you as a secure base from which to explore the world.
- Let toddlers know you understand their feelings and respond with respect.
- These are still very young children who needs lots of cuddling and holding.

- Provide child-size copies of tools adults use, such as telephones, dishes, keys, and so on.
- Post photographs of the toddlers with their family on the wall.
- Laminate photos of the toddlers with their family for carrying around.
- Make photo albums of the children at your program and talk about the pictures.
- Have adult chairs and quiet, comfortable spaces for holding children.

- Show young toddlers how to roll down a small hill together.
- Help toddlers learn each other's names by singing greeting and good-bye songs with the children's names in them: "Here is Tanya, how are you?" and "Here is Henry, how are you?" as you point to or touch each child who comes by you or is sitting in your lap.
- Comment on prosocial behavior. Say "You gave him the doll. He likes that!" Young toddlers may not understand your words, but they will be able to tell by your tone of voice that you are pleased with them.
- They will enjoy looking at books together by forming an informal group (this means they move in and out of the group) around the legs, lap, and arms of a favorite parent or teacher.

- Provide a large cardboard box, open on each end. Encourage babies to crawl in and out of the box with each other. Windows on the side encourage babies to peek at each other through the windows.
- Dolls, trucks, cars, and other play materials encourage interactions among peers.
- They love sand and water and playing with different sizes of safe bottles and balls. When each has his own bin or tub of water or sand, play goes more smoothly.
- Outside, large sandboxes or push toys encourage interactive play.

Development	Example
12–18 months	

<ul><li>Young toddlers like to use their mobility to explore—crawling, walking, climbing, and running.</li><li>Young toddlers enjoy playing with sand, water, and play dough with different kinds of tools.</li><li>Young toddlers are interested in spatial relationships in puzzles and pegboards.</li><li>Young toddlers use tools such as keys or telephones in their pretend play.</li><li>Young toddlers enjoy looking at books and naming objects, animals, or body parts.</li></ul>	<ul><li>Alexis and Dan are gleeful about being on two feet. They follow each other around, one daringly balancing his way up the sloping surface with the other right behind. Sometimes they both try to squeeze into the area under the slide.</li><li>Meredith loves to cuddle on her teacher's lap, pointing at pictures in books while her teacher names the animals, or asks her to find a certain animal.</li></ul>
Language <ul><li>Young toddlers can follow simple directions such as "Come here" or "Go get your shoes" without you gesturing.</li><li>Young toddlers play a social game without you demonstrating the action—for example, when you say, "Wave bye-bye."</li><li>Young toddlers will point to engage adults and peers.</li><li>Rapid word learning—a language explosion—may occur with the children learning many new words.</li><li>Young toddlers will combine words toward the end of this age period.</li><li>Young toddlers will jabber (stringing many sounds together) using adultlike intonation.</li><li>Young toddlers will use gestures and language to reject, request, comment, refuse, demand, and name objects and people.</li><li>Young toddlers use language to maintain an interaction or conversation with an adult or peer.</li></ul>	<ul><li>Janeika's teacher said, "Let's play pat-a-cake," and Janeika started clapping her hands together.</li><li>Ross looked up expectantly at his teacher, jabbering many sounds together as if asking her a question.</li></ul>
Motor <ul><li>Young toddlers stack and line up blocks.</li><li>Young toddlers can dress and undress self, arm into sleeve, foot into shoe.</li><li>Young toddlers can walk.</li><li>Young toddlers walk while carrying objects in each hand.</li><li>Young toddlers climb stairs.</li></ul>	<ul><li>Gary stood at the table, carefully using both hands to build a tower with colored blocks.</li><li>Michelle toddled across the room, with her teddy bear in one hand and her blanket in the other.</li></ul>
18–24 months	
Emotions/ Attachment <ul><li>Toddlers begin to control some impulses, saying, "No, no, no" as they begin to throw blocks.</li><li>Toddlers may stop their actions when told to by a teacher.</li><li>Toddlers may not want to stop playing when their parent comes to pick them up.</li><li>Toddlers may cry when they are unable to master what they are trying to do.</li><li>Toddlers know their own names and may use "me" and "mine."</li></ul>	Frankie climbs up onto the table, looking his disapproving teacher right in the eye and says "No, no, no."

Teacher-Child or Parent-Child Interaction	Environment

12–18 months

• Allow young toddlers protected time and space to explore. • Stay nearby to express interest, provide words, and make the activity more elaborate and complex. • Help young toddlers express their interest in each other gently. • Express enthusiasm for the things that interest young toddlers. • Stay on topic in a conversation with a young toddler. See how many turns the child will take. • Respond to the intonation of the child's jabbering. For example, if it seems as if the child is asking a question, answer what you think the child might be asking. • Respond to young toddlers' pointing and other nonverbal communication with language. • Use words that describe and compare sizes, shapes, and sounds. • When a young toddler uses words such as "I jump," model the next step in language development by saying "You're jumping," adding the "ing" to the word. • Read longer stories, pausing to encourage young toddlers to talk about pictures and story.	• Provide simple puzzles, pegboards, shape forms, wooden beads with thick strings. • Provide small climbers, tunnels, interesting pathways. • Provide toys that respond to winding, turning on and off. • Provide simple props for pretend play. • Introduce art materials such as play dough, clay, and paint. • Add paper towel rolls for young toddlers to walk and pull objects behind them or push them. • Musical pull and push toys entice young toddlers to walk and pull objects behind them or push them. • Sturdy music boxes encourage young toddlers to push buttons to "make music." • Drums and other musical instruments can be made available. • Add a sturdy CD player with a story from a parent recorded to play on it. • Record young toddlers' voices and play it back to them. • Provide bubble making materials. • Provide spaces for two or three children to encourage peer conversation.
• Imitate toddlers' growing variety of movements. • Introduce songs with little dances and movements. • Provide time and patience while a toddler practices putting on his own jacket.	• Stable, low-to-the-ground riding toys. • Stable, low-to-the-ground rocking toys. • Skill-based manipulatives such as stacking cups, rings on a stick.

18–24 months

• Keep your sense of humor. Understand that sometimes toddlers can stop themselves from doing things, but sometimes they cannot. • Respect the strong feelings of toddlers. Taking turns and sharing come later—now "me" and "mine" are an important part of developing a strong sense of self.	• Provide spaces that allow children to explore without ever being out of sight. • Have enough copies of the same toy for several children to each have one without sharing or taking turns. • Let children bring comfort items like blankets or stuffed animals to your program. Provide a quiet place where they can comfort themselves.

	Development	Example
	18–24 months	
Learning with peers	• Friendships can develop early. Friends are more likely to touch, lean on one another, and smile at each other than are children who are not friends. • Toddlers imitate each other's sounds and words and talk to each other and begin to communicate with others across more space. • Toddlers give or offer a toy or food to another toddler. • Toddlers may get an adult or pull an adult to help another child or for example, will help another child by getting a tissue. • Toddlers can show kindness to other babies who are feeling distressed. A mobile infant or toddler, however, may assume that what will comfort him will also comfort the distressed child. • Children take turns (e.g., with a ball, or jumping up). They may have toddler kinesthetic conversations as they follow a leader in moving around the room—moving in and out of the group, taking turns as leader and follower—as if in a conversation of listening and talking, learning valuable turn-taking skills. • Pushing, shoving, grabbing, and hitting may occur as children struggle over "mine for as long as I want it" and "yours, but I want it, too." Toddlers may fight over small toys more than large, unmovable objects.	• Paulie looked as if he was waiting by the door for Jamie to appear at the beginning of the day. When Jamie and his mom came in the door, Paulie toddled over and took Jamie's hand, a big smile on his face. • Tanya jumped (half fell) off a board several inches off the ground. Soon three young toddlers were standing on the board and half jumping, half stepping off and on the board, enjoying the activity immensely.
Cognitive	• Toddlers enjoy the ease of their movement and like to use their hands to carry things around. • Toddlers understand they can cause things to happen. • Toddlers understand and remember the details of routines. • Toddlers use objects as substitutes for other objects in their pretend play. • Toddlers enjoy increasingly challenging materials that suggest activities such as building, sorting, matching shapes.	• Before breakfast, Chris puts out his hands for the little song. When a child arrives and joins the table late, he reaches out for everyone to sing again. • Lynn and Matt build little towers of blocks and then drive play trucks into them and knock them down. • Fran takes out the box of 2-inch blocks and makes one pile of red blocks, one pile of blue blocks.
Language	• Toddlers can go get familiar toys from another room in the house when an adult asks them to and can follow directions such as "Close the door." • Toddlers combine words to name things ("That cat"), to deny ("No bite"), and to reject ("No more"). • Toddlers are combining two to three words together with meaning. • Toddlers use language for a variety of purposes, including asking, "What that?" • Toddlers point to an increasing number of pictures in books when an adult talks about the picture.	• "Hi, Kitty," "Open door," and "Hat on" were just a few of the two-word combinations Cheral used at 20 months of age. • Tyra moved quickly over to the bookshelf, picked up a book with a bright cover, and rushed back to his teacher. After sitting comfortably in her lap, he opened the book and enthusiastically started pointing to the pictures as his teacher named them.

Teacher-Child or Parent-Child Interaction	Environment
18–24 months	

- When inside or outside, nurture toddlers as they come and go to "refuel" emotionally with a special teacher, encouraging several toddlers to sit together beside you or in your lap. Allow toddlers to touch each other gently.
- Encourage several toddlers to make animal sounds together and imitate each other as you show them the pictures in a book.
- Ask one child to help another child by getting a tissue, turning the faucet on, opening a door, etc.
- Encourage kindness with one another. If one toddler cries, ask another what "we" could do to help.
- Encourage two peers to set a table together or sponge it off together after eating. Watch them imitate each other.
- Sing songs, encouraging toddlers to take turns with the actions.

- Inside and outside: Provide sand areas large enough for several toddlers and expect them to sit right in the middle of the area.
- Blankets on the floor or ground or over a table provide a spot for peers to play.
- Provide wagons: Pulling or pushing a friend in a wagon will result in squeals of delight.
- Provide balls and pull-toys that encourage interactive play.
- Places to jump safely encourage social exchanges.
- Provide musical toys, several of each kind, so children can make beautiful music together. Sometimes one will lead and another will follow, or vice versa.

- Maintain predictable routines, reminding children of the order with questions like, "It's time to eat. What do we do?"
- Keep materials in orderly and predictable places.
- Provide scaffolding as toddlers think about their activities, with questions such as "What will you do next?" or "What will you buy at the store?"

- Have toys and materials arranged so that toddlers can make choices, reach them, and put them away (with reminders).
- Frequently review the materials you have available to ensure that you are keeping a balance between what is familiar and what is a little challenging.

- Read books with longer stories, pausing as you go through the book to encourage toddlers to talk about the pictures and the story. Ask open-ended questions such as "How does the bear feel?"
- Wonder often with the child: "I wonder what will happen to the bear."
- Engage toddlers in conversation, trying to stay on the same topic as the child.
- Introduce new conversations about interesting objects and events.

- Set up an elaborate obstacle course and use words such as "in," "out," "over," "through," "around," "up," and "down" as the toddler goes through the course.
- Provide new books each week but keep children's favorites available.
- Provide a wider variety of art materials.
- Provide sensory materials.

	Development	Example
	18–24 months	
Motor	• Toddlers point to objects to communicate. • Toddlers make marks on paper. • Toddlers pound, shape clay. • Toddlers run. • Toddlers sit on and get up from small chairs alone. • Toddlers are developing spatial confidence—explore their body in space.	• Mindy rolled the dough with her hands, then used tools to make designs. • Joseph sat down at the table to eat, then took his dirty dishes to the tub.
	24–36 months	
Emotions/ Attachment	• Toddlers can sometimes be independent, but they like to know the teacher is close by. • Toddlers like to study pictures of themselves, their friends, and their families. • Toddlers listen to your words and the tone of your voice when you talk about them. They want you to be interested and proud of them. • Toddlers need clear and consistent limits. They will forget rules, or test rules, but feel secure when you remind them and help them to follow the rules. • Toddlers may use words to express their feelings, or they may hit or bite. • Toddlers care about the feelings of others and will comfort someone who is sad or hurt.	Kiki carried her baby doll over to the photos of her own family on the wall. She crooned to her baby while looking at her own mother's face.
Learning with peers	• Toddler friendship is "proximity seeking," wanting to be close and to show affection, such as smiling, laughing, and hugging. Friendships continue to develop and deepen. • They exchange information and can imitate past action of others. • Toddlers may congregate and cluster together. When a teacher begins an interesting activity with one child, children often come running from the corners of the room. • Some toddlers are capable of inventing a variety of ways to help others who are hurt or sad. • Peers work together toward a common goal, with one the leader and one the follower. • Object, personal space, and verbal struggles can occur. Toddlers also engage in playful exchanges—rough and tumble, run and chase, and verbal games. • Some children may gain a reputation with peers for aggressive or kind behavior. • Dominance of one child over another can occur.	• Maria and Sally played on opposite sides of the small shelf of toys for 30 minutes, peeking over at each other every few minutes, and telling each other, "boat" "my boat," "hi," "want juice," "look at me," and saying each other's names over and over. • When a fire truck went by outside, several toddlers rushed to the window to look. • Josh and Mike pushed, pulled, rolled, and grunted as they worked hard to roll the huge pumpkin from inside to the playground where the toddlers and their teachers were going to cut it open and scoop out all of the seeds.

Teacher-Child or Parent-Child Interaction	Environment

18–24 months

- Provide materials that challenge toddlers' growing use of their fingers.
- Stay present with toddlers as they try new skills and support them.
- Provide opportunities for climbing, walking, and running.

- Art materials with thick paint brushes and markers, large surfaces for painting.
- Smaller, skill-based manipulates such as connecting beads and pegboards.
- Lots of space for movement—dancing, riding toys, climbing, and slides.

24–36 months

- Establish clear and consistent rules. Be prepared to remind the toddlers frequently of how to follow the rules: "We don't bite. Biting hurts." "We are kind to our friends."
- Give toddlers enough of your time and attention so that they feel understood.
- Echo the enthusiasm toddlers can bring to their play.
- Notice and comment on the interactions that toddlers are watching and thinking about.

- Provide many photographs of the children with their family: on the walls, in little books, and laminated to carry around.
- Provide protected spaces for quiet play.
- Maintain predictable routines and room arrangement.
- Provide books that tell simple stories of coming and going, of families, and of friendship.
- Sing songs about feelings such as "When you're happy and you know it" and "When you're sad, angry . . . "

- Create situations in which two toddlers need to work together—for example, to roll a pumpkin from one place to another or carry a bucket of "heavy" blocks from inside to outside.
- Put a Band-Aid on a doll's arm or leg and encourage toddlers to take care of the baby.
- Ask the toddlers, "How can we help Joey? He's sad. He's crying."
- Try to change the image of a child who is gaining a reputation for aggression. Keep the child close, show her how to touch gently, and comment on her helpful behavior. Give her an interesting toy that might interest other children to engage with her. Stay close and teach her how to play.

- Place hats and easy-to-put-on dress-up clothes in a cozy corner with a big mirror.
- Toddlers will enjoy each other as their friends change appearances under a floppy hat or wearing big shoes.
- Spaces on or under a short loft encourage peer interaction.
- Provide several types of dolls as well as safe feeding utensils, blankets, and small beds. Sit close and watch as toddlers pretend to care for their babies.
- Provide open-ended materials such as blocks, and activities that require cooperation such as painting with big brushes and water on outside walls or filling a big bucket with water from smaller containers.
- Large motor equipment such as climbers or rocking boats encourage toddlers to work together toward a common goal: everyone moving to the top of the climber or rocking the boat with everyone in it.

	Development	Example
	24–36 months	

	Development	Example
Cognitive	• Toddlers begin to understand concepts such as color, size, shape, time, and weight. • Toddlers are interested in the story and pictures in storybooks. • Toddlers create new stories in pretend play or new structures in block building, becoming more imaginative and creative. • Assign roles to toys and other children in pretend play; use chairs, blankets, and bookcases as substitutes for items in pretend play.	• Erick is feeling a little sad and carries a picture of his mommy around with him, saying, "After nap." • Sara takes charge of the dramatic play corner, handing out dolls and stuffed animals. She puts on a hat and says, "Mommy going shopping."
Language	• Toddlers understand more complex directions and remember words to short songs and finger-plays. • Toddlers use many 2- to 4-word sentences. • Toddlers can point to and name body parts. • Toddlers add "ing" to words. • Toddlers begin using prepositions such as "on" and "in." • Toddlers add an "s" to words to indicate plurals. • Toddlers may begin to ask "Why?" • Toddlers will begin to tell you stories about what they did or what they saw. • Toward the end of this period, a toddler can use the pictures to tell you what is happening in a story.	• "I love you, you love me" sang DeLila • Darien yelled, "I want go outside." • Mindy started to add "ing" to words she had been saying for several months. She said, "I running" and "I eating" rather than " I run" and "I eat." • "Why I kick wall?" "Why rain?" asked Hiawanda.
Motor	• Toddlers thread beads, use scissors, paint with fingers or brushes, and do simple puzzles. • Toddlers throw and kick a ball. • Toddlers stand on one foot. • Toddlers stand and walk on tiptoes. • Toddlers climb stairs with one foot on each step. • Toddlers climb, slide, and jump. • Toddlers eat with spoon and fork. • Toddlers can dress self. • Toddlers can pour milk from small pitcher.	• Robert doesn't even have to think about his body as he runs to greet his dad at the end of the day. • Peggy and Misha make a game out of imitating each other's tiptoe steps, postures, and gestures. • Lawrence and Evelyn use the dress-up clothes for their game, struggling a little to pull on the pieces.

Teacher-Child or Parent-Child Interaction	Environment

24–36 months

• Ask children how they might solve problems that occur and let them figure out answers. • Support children working together with materials to share ideas. • Use language that describes time (now, later, before nap, after lunch), weight (heavy, light), size (bigger, smaller). • Count things during the day.	• Provide play opportunities that promote comparison of sizes, weights, colors, shapes, and quantities. • Have books available in all areas of the program. Have several copies of old favorites and bring in new books. • Allow children to combine materials from different areas in creative ways. • Present new material or new combinations of materials.
• Answer their "why" questions with patience and enthusiasm. • Listen with your eyes to the "stories" toddlers tell. • Model saying words that are plurals, such as "dogs," "elephants," and so on. • Use descriptive words such as "mozzarella cheese" rather than just "cheese," or "Blue jay" rather than just the word "bird." • Have long conversations with toddlers, following their lead. • Read books to small informal groups or to individual children.	• Provide pictures for children to match. • Puzzles of animals, people, vehicles, and food are important. • Books with many pictures and short stories can be added to the environment. • Dramatic play materials encourage conversation.
• Be aware of the balance of time between active and quiet activities. • Watch for increasing accuracy in fine motor skills, as subtle issues may begin to be apparent. • Be available with encouragement and patience as toddlers increasingly feed, dress, and toilet themselves.	• Provide a variety of materials to practice fine motor skills—simple puzzles, shape boxes, threading beads, table blocks, clay, and art materials. • Space, opportunity, and structures to encourage movement—outdoor time, obstacle courses, dancing, and riding toys.

Appendix B

Portraits of Development–Spanish

Retratos de Bebés y Niños Pequenos

Desarrollo		Ejemplo
0 a 4 meses (bebé)		
Los sentimientos/ Las ataduras	• Los bebés absorben una gran cantidad de información acerca del mundo. • Los bebés pueden sentirse abrumados y comenzar a bostezar, mirar hacia otro lado o molestarse. • Los bebés comienzan a calmarse chupándose las manos o escuchando a un adulto que les hable suavemente. • Los bebés miran fijamente a los ojos de su maestra mientras les da de comer. • Los bebés voltean la cabeza hacia voces conocidas. • Los bebés se calman y se consuelan con personas conocidas. • Los bebés lloran cuando tienen hambre o están cansados o incómodos.	Carlos seguía a Karen con los ojos por donde quiera que fuera por el salón. Cuando ella se le acercó, la miró como si quisiera que ella se quedara con él. Karen aceptó la invitación a jugar y se sentó con él en el piso. En cuanto comenzó a cansarse y a ponerse molesto, Karen lo envolvió en una manta, lo abrazó estrechamente y le habló con voz suave.
El aprender entre los pares	• A los bebés les gusta mirarse mutuamente (mirada visual). • Los bebés prefieren mirar caras, especialmente los bordes y los ojos. • Puede que los bebés lloren cuando oyen llorar a otros bebés (contagio).	Después de que la profesora puso a Tamika y a Sam sobre una manta en el piso, Tamika se quedó mirando fijamente a Sam.
La Cognición	• Los bebés siguen visualmente un objeto en movimiento. • Los bebés lloran para atraer la atención del adulto a fin de que los consuele o les dé de comer. • Los bebés miran a su alrededor por el salón con interés. • Los bebés comienzan a intentar alcanzar juguetes. • Los bebés notan que sus brazos y piernas han causado algo y repiten el movimiento. • Los bebés reconocen personas y objetos. • Los bebés comienzan a llevarse objetos a la boca.	Megan levantó la cabeza, apoyándose en los brazos mientras estaba recostada sobre la manta. Con una expresión seria miró a la maestra y a los niños a su alrededor. Willy comenzó a patear el móvil que colgaba encima y logró que se meneara. Luego paró, lo miró y volvió a patearlo mirándolo para ver si pasaba algo.

Interacciones entre Maestro o Padre/Madre–Niño	Ambiente
0 a 4 meses (bebé)	
• Mantenga a los bebés pequeños cerca, en brazos, en un saco de bebé, o sobre una manta. • Reconozca las señales de por qué el bebé quiere estar con usted—mirada fija, tenderle los brazos, mirada feliz—y respóndale hablándole suavemente, alternando la comunicación verbal y no verbal. • Reconozca las señales que indican que el bebé necesita un descanso—bostezar, babear, mirar hacia otro lado—y apártese en silencio esperando a que el bebé se recupere. • Consuele a los bebés cuando lloren.	• Estar cerca de una maestra conocida es lo mejor. • Un espacio sereno y tranquilo con luces bajas, limita la información que el bebé necesita absorber. • Evite tener música de fondo todo el día. • Limite el número de objetos, sonidos, colores y movimientos alrededor de un bebé pequeño. • La maestra es lo más interesante que el bebé tiene para mirar, pero para otros bebés, los espejos y juguetes que se encuentran en su campo visual, también son interesantes.
• Sostenga a dos bebés para que puedan mirarse mutuamente. • Ponga varios bebés sobre una manta en el piso para que puedan mirarse y tocarse entre sí.	• Los brazos de la maestras ofrecen el mejor ambiente. • Ponga a dos bebés sobre unas mantas en el piso—uno junto a otro, de manera que los dos se estén tocando con los dedos de los pies.
• Mueva lentamente un juguete pequeño de lado a lado mientras el bebé lo sigue con la mirada. • Responda rápidamente al llanto del niño. • Déles tiempo a los bebés para que estén tranquilos mirando lo que pasa a su alrededor. Hable acerca de lo que ven. • Reaccione ante las expresiones de los bebés con expresiones y lenguaje claro y hasta exagerado.	• Organice el espacio de manera que los bebés puedan ver actividad sin dejar de estar protegidos. • Suministre unos cuantos objetos interesantes para mirar—juguetes pequeños en el piso, cuando están boca abajo; juguetes colgantes cuando los bebés están boca arriba • Ponga espejos irrompibles a disposición de los bebés.

	Desarrollo	Ejemplo
	0 a 4 meses (bebé)	
El Lenguaje	• Los bebés se pueden asustar si oyen un ruido fuerte. • Los bebés captan las diferencias entre los sonidos. • Los bebés pueden dejar de llorar cuando oyen la voz de un adulto conocido. • Los bebés prefieren oír hablar cuando se les habla a ellos de forma directa. • Los bebés escuchan cuando un adulto les habla o les canta mientras los mira. • Los bebés lloran cuando sienten dolor, tienen hambre o están afligidos. • A los 2 meses de edad, los bebés tienen llantos específicos de hambre y dolor. • Los bebés "arrullan" (producen sonidos vocálicos suaves). • Hacia el final de este período, los bebés sonríen y se ríen. • Los bebés miran fijamente imágenes interesantes en libros.	Brenda sostenía a Jordán de manera que pudieran mirarse a los ojos. Jordán arrulló suavemente y Brenda le arrulló también. Luego, ella esperó a que Jordán lo volviera a hacer. Érica le sonrió de oreja a oreja a su padre cuando él la levantó de la cuna.
El desarrollo musculoso	• Los bebés levantan la cabeza cuando los llevan en brazos contra el hombro; sostienen la cabeza firme y erguida. • Boca abajo, los bebés levantan la cabeza y los hombros y pueden sostener un juguete en la mano. • Los bebés giran la cabeza hacia una voz conocida. • Los bebés se quedan quietos para prestar atención; se contonean y se mueven para inducir la continuación de la interacción. • De espaldas, los bebés estiran los brazos y las piernas a manera de juego. • Estando de lado, los bebés se dan vuelta para quedar de espaldas. • Los bebés sujetan un dedo o un juguete liviano con agarre reflejo. • Los bebés se chupan los dedos, las manos y otros objetos. • Los bebés mueven los brazos y las piernas.	Rosie mantuvo la cabeza erguida y miró a su alrededor a los otros niños mientras Sharon la llevaba contra el hombro. Robert, boca abajo sobre una manta, levantó la cabeza para mirarse al espejo montado a nivel del suelo en la pared. Jen tenía un sonajero en la mano, pero no parecía darse cuenta de que lo tenía. Filipe se llevó los dedos a la boca y se los chupó mientras miraba atentamente a los niños pequeños.

Interacciones entre Maestro o Padre/Madre–Niño	Ambiente
0 a 4 meses (bebé)	

0 a 4 meses (bebé)

- Use lenguaje dirigido al bebé.
- Tenga a los bebés en brazos y hábleles suavemente. Mírelos largamente a los ojos mientras baila conversando. Respete al bebé si necesita un descanso y aparta la cabeza.
- Lea libros con frases rítmicas y con una sola imagen en una página, con 2 imágenes a los de 4 meses de edad.
- Interprete los eructos, llantos, bostezos, estiramientos y sonidos de los bebés como formas de comunicación. Diga "Ah, me estás diciendo que tienes sueño".
- Cante canciones de cuna y otras canciones.
- Sea un compañero de lenguaje que se identifique y comente los sentimientos del bebé.
- Diga palabras y produzca sonidos para consolar a los bebés.

- El mejor ambiente son los brazos de un adulto afectuoso que tenga al bebé en brazos y le hable suavemente.
- Suministre juguetes que produzcan sonidos agradables. Sostenga con cuidado el juguete e intercambie sonidos con el bebé.
- Suministre materiales interesantes para tocar mientras comenta las texturas.
- Coloque espejos bajos a lo largo de una pared. Los bebés se miran y es posible que produzcan sonidos.

- Cambie la posición del bebé; a veces de espaldas, otras boca abajo. Cuando lleve en brazos al bebé, acúnelo en sus brazos o sosténgalo erguido contra el hombro.
- Cuando el bebé está en el piso, acuéstese cara a cara junto a él.
- Cuando la bebé está de espaldas y trata de alcanzar un juguete un poco más allá de su cabeza, sosténgale el tronco mientras rueda.

- Una manta rígida (contra el riesgo de asfixia) en el suelo da espacio para los primeros movimientos.
- Los juguetes pequeños e interesantes, las imágenes, y los libros para mirar cuando quieran animan a los bebés a levantar la cabeza. Un espejo atornillado a la pared a nivel del suelo siempre ofrece algo interesante que mirar.
- A medida que comienzan a estirarse para alcanzar, a los bebés les gustan las barras estables con juguetes colgantes que puedan batear, alcanzar y agarrar.

Desarrollo		Ejemplo
	4 a 8 meses (bebé)	
Los sentimientos/ Las ataduras	• A los bebés les gusta mirarse las manos y los pies. • Los bebés agitan los brazos y patalean emocionados cuando ven a una persona conocida. • Los bebés le sonríen a la maestra esperando que ella les sonría también. • Con la cara y el cuerpo, los bebés expresan muchos sentimientos: desde fruncir el ceño y llorar hasta reírse a carcajadas. • Los bebés expresan sus sentimientos claramente ante personas conocidas, y son más reservados con los desconocidos	A Deborah le encanta que la maestra la lleve en brazos mientras va por el salón "hablándole" de lo que ven. Tiene los ojos bien abiertos y brillantes, sonríe y hace ruiditos de arrullo cuando le corresponde hablar en la conversación. Cuando un visitante entra en el salón, Deborah se queda muy callada y seria, y se sujeta firmemente al hombro de la maestra mirando al visitante.
El aprender entre los pares	• Los bebés tocan a otros bebés, se dirigen vocalizaciones, se entusiasman, se acercan a otros bebés, sonríen y se ríen unos de otros. • Los bebés pueden tratar a otros bebés como si fueran objetos - pasándoles por encima al gatear, lamiéndolos, chupándolos, sentándose encima. Están simplemente aprendiendo la diferencia entre personas y objetos. Los bebés pueden pinchar con el dedo, empujar, dar palmaditas a otros bebés, para ver lo que el otro bebé va a hacer. A menudo se sorprenden con la reacción que logran.reacción que logran.	Ana le pasó por encima gateando a Nadia que estaba acostada en el piso. Tocándole el pelo a Nadia. Ana se rió a carcajadas.
La Cognición	• A los bebés les gusta examinar los juguetes. • A los bebés les gusta hacer que los juguetes hagan algo—sonar, encajarse uno dentro de otro. • Los bebés imitan las expresiones y los gestos de los adultos. • Los bebés se vuelven hacia los sonidos para ver de dónde vienen. • Los bebés buscan juguetes que han dejado caer.	Ángela se interesa en todo. Mira a sus amigos y luego mira a la maestra y sonríe. Roger se estira para tocar un juguete colgante. Cuando se balancea y suena, Roger se estira para hacerlo de nuevo.
El Lenguaje	• Los bebés giran la cabeza hacia un ruido, o una persona que dice su nombre. • A los bebés les gusta que los adultos hablen, canten y se rían con ellos. • Los bebés vocalizan con la intención de obtener una respuesta del adulto. • Los bebés dan chillidos agudos. • Los bebés practican sus sonidos cuando exploran y cuando están con adultos conocidos. • Los bebés comienzan a balbucear; al principio una consonante y luego combinaciones de dos consonantes. • Los bebés participan en conversaciones turnándose con los adultos. • Los bebés miran distintas imágenes de un libro y se emocionan cuando ven una que les gusta o cuando les gusta el tono entusiasta del adulto que lee.	Mientras sostenía a Donovan en su regazo, Daniela, la maestra del bebé, señalaba con el dedo las imágenes del libro de tapas de cartón. "Mira," dijo señalando la imagen, "una pelota." Luego dijo "Ahí está tu pelota" y señaló hacia una pelota en el piso. Donovan miró la imagen, luego la pelota en el piso y finalmente volvió a mirar la imagen. "Tt" dijo Afi cuando estaba en brazos de su maestra mirándola. "Tada" le dijo la maestra. "Tt" repitió Afi cuando le tocó hablar en la conversación.

Interacciones entre Maestro o Padre/Madre–Niño	Ambiente
4 a 8 meses (bebé)	

• Déles a los bebés oportunidades para que se miren al espejo mientras juegan. • Refleje las expresiones emocionales del bebé y agregue palabras apropiadas: "Estoy tan contenta de verte hoy." • Responda a los bebés de una manera que les ayude a calmarse y mantenerse activos. Si el bebé llora, cálmelo.	• Monte espejos irrompibles en las paredes. • Deje que los bebés pasen un rato en el piso mientras están boca arriba, jugando con sus pies y moviéndose por el piso. • Los libros y los álbumes de fotografías con caras reales mostrando diferentes expresiones emocionales son muy interesantes para los bebés.
• Muévase al ritmo de la música con un bebé en cada brazo. • Con un bebé sobre el regazo, apunte y hable sobre lo que el otro bebé está haciendo. • Ponga a dos bebés boca bajo frente a un espejo. • En vez de decirles "No" y "Deja de hacer eso" a los bebés que están explorando, dígales, "Tócalo con cuidado." Dígales a los niños lo que usted quiere que hagan$ . . . $muéstreselo.	• Cuelgue un espejo seguro en la pared de manera horizontal, para que la parte de abajo esté tocando el piso. • Cubra la cámara de aire de la rueda de un auto con un paño suave. Siente a dos bebés en la cámara para que se toquen con los pies.
• Lleve en brazos al bebé, mientras camina por el salón mirando cosas y hablando acerca de ellas. • Siéntese cerca y háblele al bebé sobre los juguetes que está mirando. • Llame al bebé por su nombre a poca distancia para asegurarle que está cerca.	• Suministre una variedad de juguetes pequeños para que los manipule y los examine. • Suministre juguetes que suenan cuando se mueven, se encajan unos dentro de otros o se cuelgan y mueven cuando se tocan. • Ofrezca libros de tapas de cartón.
• Use lenguaje dirigido al bebé. • Hable a menudo con los bebés. Muéstreles objetos y personas nuevos y nómbrelos. • Repita los sonidos que los bebés producen y espere a que repitan el sonido (turnarse). • Refiérase a varios artículos conocidos, tales como "leche" o "perro," con lenguaje de señas. • Cante canciones y haga juegos de dedos. • Describa con palabras los sentimientos de los niños expresados a través de gestos, posturas corporales y sonidos. • Léale libros sencillos con una o dos imágenes por página. Señale con el dedo las imágenes mientras dice el nombre de la imagen. • Léale los mismos libros una y otra vez. • Aplique estrategias de atención conjunta—señale con el dedo un juguete o una imagen de un libro diciendo el nombre o hablando al respecto.	• Suministre juguetes y materiales interesantes para que los bebés los manipulen y examinen. • Suministre libros de cartón con asas para que puedan gatear hasta ellos y tomarlos. • Los libros con asas animan a los bebés a llevarlos. • Haga un libro de imágenes *de te veo, no te veo* pegando un pedazo de tela sobre cada imagen. • Forme un rincón de lectura acogedor donde las maestras puedan estar cómodas y leer a los bebés. • Suministre cajas de sonido (bien selladas) con distintos objetos adentro que produzcan distintos sonidos al sacudirlas. • Incorpore títeres al ambiente. Úselos a veces para "hablar" con el niño. Coloque los títeres en la mano del niño y espere a ver lo que el niño dice o hace.

Desarrollo		Ejemplo
	4 a 8 meses (bebé)	
El desarrollo musculoso	• Los bebés de espaldas se ponen de lado y luego se vuelven a poner de espaldas. • Al final de este período, los bebés se sientan; primero con apoyo pero luego estables y solos. • Los bebés se estiran para alcanzar objetos con el brazo. • Los bebés agarran rastrillando. • Los bebés gatean. • Los bebés sacuden, golpean, sujetan y sueltan objetos. • Los bebés se pasan objetos de una mano a otra. • Los bebés pueden sostener su biberón. • Los bebés se pueden llevar objetos a la boca.	Estando de espaldas, Micky rueda para quedar boca abajo y alcanzar un juguete, luego vuelve a rodar para jugar con el juguete. A Erin, sentada sola establemente, le gusta recoger objetos con las dos manos y examinarlos. A Freddy le gusta que lo tomen en brazos mientras toma su biberón, aunque insiste en sujetarlo solo.
	8 a 12 meses (bebé móvil)	
Los sentimientos/Las ataduras	• Los bebés móviles pueden tenerle miedo a los desconocidos. • Los bebés móviles pueden llamar a los adultos conocidos para que los ayuden cuando están enojados. • Los bebés móviles miran al adulto conocido para determinar si una situación es peligrosa o no. • Los bebés móviles se aferran al adulto cuando están en una situación desconocida. • A los bebés móviles les parecen divertidos los juegos tontos y las expresiones faciales exageradas que ponen los adultos.	Jaime está disfrutando de su nueva habilidad, que es ir gateando rápidamente a donde quiera ir. Le encanta el pequeño trepador que le permite mirar por la ventana. Pero cuando siente que la rampa es un poco inestable, se vuelve a mirar a Federico, su maestro, para asegurarse de que no hay peligro.
El aprender entre los pares	• Los bebés pueden mostrar a otros bebés un objeto, sentarse juntos, perseguirse gateando y jugar a perseguir y recoger objetos. • Los bebés se sonríen y se ríen entre sí. • Los bebés se dirigen sonidos—y es posible que sus primeras palabras se las digan entre sí. • Uno de los juegos preferidos de los bebés es el *te veo, no te veo* mientras exploran la separación: irse y volver, aparecer y desaparecer. • Los bebés pueden aprender a tocarse uno al otro con cuidado. • Como a esta edad los bebés actúan en gran medida en función de sus objetivos, pueden apartar la mano de un bebé que esté tocando un juguete, o gatearle por encima para alcanzar un juguete.	Shamaine miró la estantería baja de juguetes y vio que Carla venía gateando hacia ella. Shamaine se dio la vuelta rápidamente y se alejó gateando con Carla siguiéndola de cerca. Kai pasó gateando por encima de las piernas de Bridger para alcanzar un juguete que estaba al otro lado de Bridger.

Interacciones entre Maestro o Padre/Madre–Niño	Ambiente
4 a 8 meses (bebé)	

• Quédese cerca del bebé que recién comienza a sentarse solo. • Conozca el avance del desarrollo motor; anime emocionalmente y apoye físicamente al bebé en sus nuevos intentos. • Crea en los beneficios a largo plazo para la salud de un estilo de vida activo.	• Deles lugares seguros para rodar, sentarse y gatear. Proteja a los bebés de cualquier cosa que pueda caerles encima. • Deles objetos livianos pequeños y lavables (grandes para evitar que se asfixien) para que los manipulen y los lancen, y deles recipientes para los objetos.
• Anime a los bebés móviles a moverse y explorar asegurándoles que usted los está mirando y cuidando. • Entienda que los bebés móviles pueden asustarse ante situaciones nuevas que quizás no los habrían asustado hace unos meses. Consuélelos y tranquilícelos.	• Juegue al *te veo, no te veo*. • Léales cuentos sobre madres y padres que se van y vuelven. • Léales libros con solapas que se pueden levantar para encontrar cosas. • Mantenga una previsibilidad de hábitos y rutinas del salón.
• Nombre partes del cuerpo del bebé mientras dos bebés están sentados juntos: • Estos son los ojos del bebé Esta es la nariz del bebé Toca la parte con que ves Tócate la parte que te suenas • Ponga un bebé con otro (en parejas) porque las interacciones más frecuentes, complejas e intensas entre niños se producen cuando un niño está con varios compañeros. • Comprenda que los bebés no son "malos" cuando le apartan la mano al otro. Diga "Jenny tenía ese juguete. Vamos a buscarte otro."	• Mientras están comiendo, coloque las sillas altas de manera que los niños se puedan ver unos a los otros. • Disponga de rincones agradables en el salón donde los bebés puedan "desaparecer" (pero pudiendo aún ser vistos por adultos). • Cuelgue del techo un paño largo y ancho (para que los bebés no se enreden en él). A los bebés les encanta gatear alrededor. • Ponga contenedores con bloques de diferentes tamaños entre dos bebés. Quédese sentada junto a ellos mientras comienzan a explorar los materiales. Hable acerca de lo que está haciendo cada uno.

Desarrollo	Ejemplo
8 a 12 meses (bebé móvil)	

	Desarrollo	Ejemplo
La Cognición	• A los bebés móviles les gusta desarmar los juguetes y luego volver a armarlos. • A los bebés móviles les gustan los juguetes que hacen algo cuando se tocan, se jalan o se golpean. • Los bebés móviles comienzan juegos imaginarios muy simples, tales como llevarse un vaso a la boca. • A los bebés móviles les gusta encontrar juguetes pequeños debajo de un paño o de un vaso. • A los bebés móviles les gusta levantar y examinar objetos pequeños tales como un Cheerio. • Los bebés móviles muestran objetos con el dedo sabiendo que usted también puede verlos.	A Carlos le encanta sacar cada uno de los animales de plástico del balde y mirarlo. Cuando el balde queda vacío, lo lanza a un lado. A Aliya le gusta el botón que se aprieta y las puertas oscilantes de la caja mecánica, pero todavía no puede hacer funcionar todos los mecanismos. Su maestra expresa sorpresa a Aliya cuando las puertas se abren y, de vez en cuando, le enseña cómo funciona otra de las perillas.
El Lenguaje	• Los bebés móviles comienzan a participar en juegos sociales tales como el *te veo, no te veo* o el *"así de grande."* • A los bebés les gusta escuchar juegos de sonidos (rimas), canciones y juegos de dedos. • El balbuceo continúa desarrollándose con sílabas com-binadas tales como "dada," "mama," "nana" y "tutu" y a esta altura el bebé puede usar estos sonidos específicamente para referirse a su mamá o su papá. • Los bebés repiten sonidos consistentemente para referirse a un objeto, una persona o un animal. • Si oyen otro lenguaje *con* un adulto a través de estrategias conversacionales interactivas, los bebés pueden "tener una actitud abierta hacia los sonidos de un lenguaje extranjero." • Los bebés pueden comenzar a decir palabras aisladas. • Al final de este período, los bebés pueden comenzar a señalar con el dedo para atraer la atención de un adulto. • Los bebés emplean expresiones faciales y gestos tales como agitar la cabeza o los brazos para que los tomen en brazos, y así comunicarse con los adultos o con sus compañeros.	Una de las primeras palabras de Dana fue "mamá," y la repetía una y otra vez cuando veía a su madre. Una de las primera palabras de Trishanna fue "mamá," y la repetía con entusiasmo una y otra vez cuando veía a su madre.
El desarrollo musculoso	• Los bebés móviles jalan de algo para ponerse de pie. • Los bebés móviles se pasean. • Los bebés móviles se quedan de pie solos. • Los bebés móviles caminan con ayuda al principio y después solos. • Los bebés móviles se sientan en una silla. • Los bebés móviles comen con los dedos. • Los bebés móviles pueden usar una cuchara y un vaso hermético. • Los bebés móviles agarran atenazando.	Hershel gatea hasta su maestra, luego se agarra de su pierna y jala para ponerse de pie. Jem se sienta a la mesa del almuerzo, y alterna la cuchara y los dedos para disfrutar de la comida.

Interacciones entre Maestro o Padre/Madre–Niño	Ambiente

8 a 12 meses (bebé móvil)

• Con su presencia, su interés y su entusiasmo, ayude al bebé a concentrarse en lo que le interesa para apoyarlo en su atención y exploración. • Con sus expresiones y palabras afectivas, demuéstrele al bebé móvil que usted disfruta de sus descubrimientos. • Con palabras, describa la actividad del niño: "Mira, encontraste un Cheerio. Lo estás recogiendo con los dedos."	• Suministre juguetes tales como vasos para apilar, anillos en poste, piezas que se interconectan y cubos llenos de objetos pequeños interesantes, tales como animales de juguete. • Suministre réplicas tamaño infantil de platos o herramientas domésticas. • Suministre juguetes que reaccionen—cajas mecánicas, almohadillas llenas de agua. • Suministre materiales sensoriales, como agua y arena con una variedad de herramientas. • Suministre libros de tapas de cartón con fotos.
• Organice juegos conocidos tales como te veo—no te veo, palmitas—palmitas o *"¿cómo eres de grande?"* • Responda con palabras a la comunicación no verbal de los bebés. • Observe y espere a que los bebés inicien sonidos o palabras. • Imite los sonidos y luego expanda, detalle y amplíe el lenguaje del bebé. • Modele el siguiente paso en el desarrollo del lenguaje. • Emplee hablarse a sí mismo y hablar en paralelo. • Hable a menudo de manera receptiva con un vocabulario variado. No bombardee al niño con palabras. • Lea los libros con entusiasmo—cambiando el tono de su voz con los distintos personajes. • Hable sobre las imágenes y el cuento a medida que lee. Involucre a los bebés con la voz y los gestos. • Mientras miran una imagen, espere a que el bebé produzca sonidos, señale con el dedo o haga expresiones faciales.	• Cree un rincón de lectura acogedor en que los bebés puedan alcanzar fácilmente los libros y manipularlos. • Haga un libro "Todo sobre mí"—álbumes pequeños de fotos para cada niño con imágenes de ellos, su familia, sus juguetes preferidos, sus compañeros, sus maestras y los animales domésticos de la familia. Déjelos al alcance de los niños. Cambie las imágenes a medida que el niño crece. • Los juguetes musicales para empujar animan a los bebés a manipularlos y producir sonidos.
• Esté atenta para saber cuándo ayudar al bebé que comienza a caminar y cuándo dejar que lo siga intentando. • Dé tiempo para que los bebés mayores practiquen comer solos.	• Lugares seguros para ponerse de pie apoyándose en algo. • Juguetes para empujar y jalar para que los que comienzan a caminar puedan jalar y empujar. • Cajas mecánicas. • Libros de cartón para pasar las páginas, levantar las solapas y meter los dedos a través de los agujeros.

Desarrollo	Ejemplo
8 a 18 meses (bebé móvil)	

Los sentimientos/ Las ataduras

- Los bebés móviles imitan las acciones de los adultos conocidos, tales como hablar por teléfono o llevar en brazos a una muñeca bebé.
- Los bebés móviles intentan atraer la atención del adulto jalándole la pierna o tomándole la mano.
- Los bebés móviles se calman con su manta o su animal de peluche favorito.
- Los bebés móviles protestan ruidosamente cuando sus padres los dejan.
- Los bebés móviles se relajan y se consuelan acurrucándose con un adulto conocido.
- Los bebés móviles hacen saber claramente lo que les gusta y lo que no les gusta.

Amelia carga toda la mañana su osito de peluche por todos los lados. A veces copia las acciones de Sofía, su maestra, dándole al osito palmaditas en la espalda o alimentándole con biberón. Cuando se cansa, se frota el osito contra la oreja y se chupa el pulgar.

El aprender entre los pares

- Comienzan los turnos imitativos (motores) e interactivos. Los niños pequeños pueden imitarse unos a otros—si un bebé le da un juguete a otro, el otro puede imitarlo.
- Los bebés móviles comienzan a hablarse unos a otros.
- Los bebés pueden demostrar preocupación cuando otros bebés están afligidos.
- Los bebés móviles pueden quitarle el juguete a otro bebé, decirle "no," empujarlo, agarrar firmemente el juguete y decir "mío."
- A esta edad, los bebés son pequeños científicos que experimentan para ver cómo funcionan las cosas. Esto afecta la relación que tienen con sus compañeros, pues están constantemente haciéndoles cosas para ver cómo reaccionan.
- Morder puede aparecer cuando los bebés muerden a otros "para ver lo que pasa," para obtener el juguete que quieren, para expresar su frustración. Los bebés están al borde de comunicarse bien; pueden comunicarse por la boca en forma de mordedura.

Rashida golpeó la mesa con la cuchara; poco después, otros dos comenzaron a hacerlo. Parecían estar siguiendo el ejemplo físicamente (como si estuvieran conversando).

Primero, Carmen intentó alejar a Toby del caballito de balancín. Cuando eso no dio resultado, se inclinó hacia él y lo mordió en el brazo.

La Cognición

- A los bebés móviles les gusta poner en práctica su movilidad para explorar gateando, caminando, trepando, corriendo, etc.
- Los bebés móviles disfrutan jugando en la arena, el agua, con plastilina y varios tipos de herramientas.
- A los bebés móviles les interesan las relaciones espaciales de rompecabezas y tableros con agujeros.
- Los bebés móviles utilizan herramientas tales como llaves o teléfonos en sus juegos imaginarios.
- Los bebés móviles disfrutan al mirar libros y nombrar objetos, animales o partes del cuerpo.

Alexis y Dan están contentísimos de estar de pie. Se siguen mutuamente por todas partes, uno subiendo atrevidamente por un plano inclinado, con el otro inmediatamente detrás. A veces los dos intentan meterse debajo del tobogán.

A Meredith le encanta acurrucarse en el regazo de su maestra y mostrar con el dedo imágenes en libros mientras la maestra nombra los animales o le pide que encuentre uno en particular.

Interacciones entre Maestro o Padre/Madre–Niño	Ambiente

12 a 18 meses (bebé móvil)

- Muestre interés en las actividades del bebé.
- Muestre su orgullo por los logros del bebé.
- Deje que los bebés la utilicen como una base firme, para explorar el mundo.
- Deje que los bebés sepan que usted entiende lo que sienten y responda respetuosamente.
- Estos niños son todavía muy pequeños, y necesitan que se les acurruque y abrace mucho.

- Disponga de objetos de mayores en tamaño infantil: teléfonos, platos, llaves, etc.
- Ponga fotografías de bebés con su familia en la pared.
- Lamine las fotos del bebé con su familia para que las lleve consigo.
- Haga álbumes de fotos de los niños del programa y hable acerca de las fotos.
- Disponga de sillas de adulto y espacios tranquilos y cómodos para tener a los niños en brazos.

- Muéstreles a los niños pequeños móviles cómo rodar juntos por una pequeña pendiente.
- Ayude a los niños pequeños móviles a que aprendan los nombres de los demás, cantando canciones de saludo y despedida incluyendo los nombres de los niños: "Esta es Tania, ¿cómo estás?" y "Este es Enrique, ¿cómo estás?" y apuntando o tocando a cada niño que pasa junto a usted o al que está sentado en su regazo.
- Comente el comportamiento social activo. Diga "Le diste la muñeca. Eso le gusta." Puede que los bebés no entiendan sus palabras, pero son capaces de darse cuenta por el tono de voz que usted está contenta con ellos.
- A los bebés les gusta mirar libros juntos, creando grupos informales (esto significa que entrar y salir del grupo) alrededor de las piernas, el regazo y los brazos del padre, la madre o la maestra que más les gusta.

- Suministre una caja de cartón grande abierta por los dos lados. Anímelos a entrar y salir de la caja gateando juntos. Ventanas a los lados de la caja estimulan a los bebés para que se miren entre ellos por la ventana.
- Muñecas, camiones, autos y otros materiales de juego, promueven las interacciones entre compañeros.
- A los bebés les encanta la arena y el agua y jugar con botellas y pelotas seguras de diferentes tamaños. Cuando cada uno tiene su propio contenedor o cubo con agua o arena, el juego se desarrolla sin altibajos.
- Al aire libre, grandes cajas de arena o juguetes para empujar, estimulan el juego interactivo. Tendencias de Desarrollo e Interacciones Receptivas.

- Déle a los bebés móviles tiempo y espacio protegido para explorar.
- Quédese cerca para expresar interés, sugerir palabras y hacer que la actividad sea más elaborada y compleja.
- Ayude a los bebés móviles a que expresen su interés en otros bebés cuidadosamente.
- Exprese entusiasmo por lo que les interesa a los bebés móviles.

- Suministre rompecabezas simples, tableros con agujeros, formas, cuentas de madera con cordones gruesos.
- Suministre trepadores pequeños, túneles y trayectos interesantes.
- Suministre juguetes que funcionen al darle cuerda, o que se enciendan y apaguen.
- Suministre artículos simples para el juego imaginario.

Desarrollo	Ejemplo
18 a 24 meses (niños pequeños)	

	Desarrollo	Ejemplo
El Lenguaje	• Los bebés móviles pueden seguir instrucciones sencillas tales como "Ven aquí" o "Trae tus zapatos" sin que haya que hacer gestos. • Los bebés móviles pueden jugar socialmente sin que haya que demostrar la acción. Por ejemplo, cuando usted dice "Dile adiós" ellos mueven las manos aunque usted no les muestre cómo hacerlo. • Los bebés móviles señalan con el dedo para llamar la atención de los adultos y de sus compañeros. • Se puede producir un aprendizaje rápido de palabras—una explosión de lenguaje—en los niños que están aprendiendo muchas palabras nuevas. • Hacia el final de este período, los bebés móviles combinan palabras. • Los bebés móviles farfullan (hilando muchos sonidos) con la misma entonación que los adultos. • Los bebés móviles hacen gestos y se valen de palabras para rechazar, pedir, comentar, negarse, exigir y nombrar objetos y personas. • Los bebés móviles se valen del lenguaje para mantener una interacción o conversación con un adulto o uno de sus compañeros.	La maestra de Janina le dijo "Juguemos a dar palmitas, palmitas," y Janina comenzó a aplaudir. Ross miró a su maestra con expectación, farfullando muchos sonidos juntos como si le hiciera una pregunta.
El desarrollo musculoso	• Los bebés móviles apilan y alinean bloques. • Los bebés móviles pueden vestirse y desvestirse solos, meter el brazo en una manga y el pie dentro de un zapato. • Los bebés móviles pueden caminar. • Los bebés móviles caminan con objetos en las manos. • Los bebés móviles suben escaleras.	Gary se paró frente a la mesa y construyó cuidadosamente con las dos manos una torre con bloques de colores. Michelle caminó por la habitación con su osito de peluche en una mano y su manta en la otra.
18 a 24 meses (niños pequeños)		
Los sentimientos / Las ataduras	• Los niños pequeños comienzan a controlar ciertos impulsos diciendo "no, no, no" a medida que comienzan a lanzar bloques. • Los niños pequeños pueden dejar lo que están haciendo cuando la maestra se lo dice. • Los niños pequeños pueden no querer dejar de jugar cuando su padre o su madre viene a buscarlos. • Los niños pequeños pueden llorar cuando no consiguen hacer algo que están intentando. • Los niños pequeños saben su propio nombre y puede que usen el "mi" y "mío."	Francisco se sube a la mesa mientras mira directamente a los ojos de la maestra que desaprueba lo que él hace, y dice "no, no, no."

Interacciones entre Maestro o Padre/Madre–Niño	Ambiente

12 a 18 meses (bebé móvil)

- Mantenga el tema en una conversación con un bebé móvil. Vea cuántas veces hablará el niño.
- Responda a la entonación del parloteo del niño. Por ejemplo, si parece que el niño hace una pregunta, responda a lo que usted cree que el niño puede estar preguntando.
- Responda con palabras a las señales hechas con los dedos y otros medios de comunicación no verbal de los bebés móviles.
- Describa y compare con palabras tamaños, formas y sonidos.
- Cuando un bebé móvil dice palabras tales como "Yo salto," modele el próximo paso en el desarrollo del lenguaje diciendo "Tú estás saltando," añadiendo "ando o iendo" a la palabra. Haga esto tanto con el contenido de las palabras como con la estructura de las palabras u oraciones.
- Léale libros con cuentos más largos, haga pausas a medida que avanza por el libro para animar a los bebés móviles a hablar sobre las imágenes y el cuento.

- Introduzca materiales de arte tales como plastilina, arcilla y pintura.
- Déle rollos de toallas de papel a los bebés móviles para que produzcan sonidos.
- Los juguetes musicales para jalar animan a los bebés móviles a caminar y jalarlos o empujarlos.
- Las cajas de música resistentes animan a los bebés móviles a apretar botones para "hacer música."
- Se pueden poner a disposición tambores y otros instrumentos musicales.
- Incorpore un reproductor de CD resistente con un cuento que haya grabado el padre o la madre.
- Grabe las voces de los bebés móviles con una grabadora y haga que las escuchen.
- Suministre materiales para hacer burbujas.
- Facilite espacios para animar a dos o tres niños a conversar con sus compañeros.

- Imite la cada vez mayor variedad de movimientos del bebé.
- Introduzca canciones con pequeños bailes y movimientos.
- Dé tiempo y tenga paciencia mientras el niño pequeño practica ponerse solo la chaqueta.

- Juguetes para montar estables y no muy altos.
- Juguetes mecedores estables y no muy altos.
- Juegos de manipulación basados en habilidades, tales como apilar vasos o ensartar aros en un palo.

- Mantenga su sentido del humor. Entienda que los niños pequeños pueden dejar de hacer ciertas cosas a veces, pero no siempre.
- Respete los sentimientos fuertes de los niños pequeños. El turnarse y compartir viene después; ahora "mí" y "mío" son una etapa importante del desarrollo de un sólido sentido de identidad.

- Disponga espacios que permita que los niños exploren, pero siempre sin perderlos de vista.
- Tenga suficientes juguetes iguales para que varios niños puedan tener el suyo, sin tener que compartir o turnarse.
- Deje que los niños traigan al programa artículos que los calmen, tales como mantas o animales de peluche. Asígneles un lugar tranquilo donde puedan consolarse solos.

	Desarrollo	Ejemplo
	12 a 24 meses (bebé móvil)	

| El aprender entre los pares | • Las amistades pueden desarrollarse a muy temprana edad. Los amigos son más propensos a tocarse, apoyarse y sonreírse entre sí, que otros niños que no son amigos.
• Los niños pequeños imitan mutuamente los sonidos y las palabras que dicen y se hablan y comienzan a comunicarse con los demás a mayores distancias.
• Los niños pequeños dan u ofrecen un juguete o comida a otros niños pequeños
• Los niños pequeños pueden llamar a un adulto y jalar al adulto para que ayude a otro niño, o pueden ayudar a otro niño llevándole un pañuelito de papel, por ejemplo.
• Los niños pequeños demuestran bondad hacia otros bebés que se sienten afligidos. Sin embargo, el bebé o niño pequeño móvil puede suponer que lo que lo consuela a él, también consuela al afligido
• Los niños pueden turnarse, por ejemplo, con una pelota o para saltar. Pueden tener conversaciones cinéticas de niño pequeño mientras siguen a un líder por el salón—entrando y saliendo del grupo, turnándose para ser líder y seguidor— como si estuvieran en una conversación, en la cual escuchan y hablan, aprendiendo la importante habilidad de cómo turnarse.
• Empujar, dar empujones, agarrar y golpear pueden ocurrir a medida que los niños luchan con la idea de "mío durante todo el tiempo que yo quiera" y "tuyo, pero yo también lo quiero." Los niños pequeños puede que se peleen más por juguetes pequeños, que por objetos grandes que no se mueven. | Paulie parecía estar esperando en la puerta a que apareciera Jamie al principio de la jornada. Cuando Jaime y su mamá llegaron, Paulie se dirigió hacia ellos y le tomó la mano a Jaime con una gran sonrisa en la cara.
Tania saltó (medio se cayó) de una tabla situada a varias pulgadas del suelo. Pronto tres niños pequeños estaban parados sobre la tabla, y casi saltando, casi bajando de la tabla y disfrutando inmensamente de la actividad. |
| La Cognición | • Los niños pequeños de corta edad disfrutan de su facilidad de movimiento y les gusta llevar cosas en las manos.
• Los niños pequeños entienden que pueden hacer que ocurran cosas.
• Los niños pequeños entienden y recuerdan los detalles de las rutinas.
• Los niños pequeños sustituyen unos objetos por otros en su juego imaginario.
• Los niños pequeños disfrutan cada vez más de los materiales problemáticos que sugieren actividades tales como construir y hacer corresponder formas. | • Mantenga rutinas predecibles recordándole a los niños el orden de las etapas con preguntas tales como "Es hora de comer. ¿Qué hacemos?"
• Tenga los materiales en lugares predecibles y ordenados.
• Con preguntas tales como "¿Qué vas a hacer ahora? ¿Qué vas a comprar en la tienda? Apoye a los niños pequeños cuando piensen en sus actividades. |

Interacciones entre Maestro o Padre/Madre–Niño	Ambiente
18 a 24 meses (niños pequeños)	

- Ya esté adentro o afuera, atienda a los niños pequeños cuando entran a "reponerse" emocionalmente con su maestra especial animando a varios niños pequeños a sentarse junto a usted o en su regazo. Permita que los niños pequeños se toquen mutuamente con cuidado.
- Anime a que varios niños pequeños hagan sonidos de animales y se imiten entre sí mientras les muestra las imágenes de un libro.
- Pídale a un niño que ayude a otro, trayendo un pañuelito de papel, abriendo la llave del agua, abriendo la puerta, etc.
- Estimule la bondad mutua. Si un niño pequeño llora, pregúntele a otro lo que "podríamos" hacer para ayudarlo.
- Anime a dos niños pequeños a que pongan la mesa o la limpien después de comer. Mire como se imitan.
- Cante canciones, animando a los niños pequeños a que se turnen con las acciones.

- Adentro y afuera: Ponga a su disposición áreas con arena que sean suficientemente grandes para varios niños pequeños, es de esperar que se sienten justo en el medio del área.
- Las mantas sobre el piso, el suelo o una mesa son un centro para que los niños pequeños jueguen.
- Suministre vagones: Empujar o jalar a un amigo en un vagón dará como resultado chillidos de deleite.
- Suministre pelotas y juguetes para jalar que estimulen el juego interactivo.
- Lugares para saltar sin peligro estimulan los intercambios sociales.
- Suministre juguetes musicales, varios de cada clase, para que los niños puedan tocar juntos una música bella. A veces uno dirigirá y el otro le seguirá, o viceversa.

- Mantenga rutinas predecibles recordándole a los niños el orden de las etapas con preguntas tales como "Es hora de comer. ¿Qué hacemos?"
- Tenga los materiales en lugares predecibles y ordenados.
- Con preguntas tales como "¿Qué vas a hacer ahora? ¿Qué vas a comprar en la tienda? Apoye a los niños pequeños cuando piensen en sus actividades.

- Tenga los juguetes y los materiales organizados de manera que los niños pequeños puedan escogerlos, alcanzarlos y guardarlos (con recordatorios).
- Revise frecuentemente los materiales a su disposición para asegurarse de que mantiene un equilibrio entre lo que es conocido y lo que es un poco difícil.

	Desarrollo	Ejemplo
El Lenguaje	Los niños pequeños pueden ir a buscar juguetes conocidos en otra habitación de la casa cuando un adulto se los pide, y pueden seguir instrucciones tales como "cierra la puerta." Los niños pequeños combinan palabras para nombrar cosas ("ese gato"), para negar ("no muerde") y para rechazar ("no más"). Los niños pequeños combinan dos o tres palabras con significado. Los niños pequeños se valen del lenguaje para varios propósitos, tales como preguntar "¿Qué eso?" Los niños pequeños señalan una cantidad de imágenes cada vez mayor en los libros cuando un adulto les habla sobre la imagen.	"Hola Kitty," "puerta abierta" y "sombrero puesto" fueron sólo algunas de las combinaciones de dos palabras que Cheral dijo a los 20 meses de edad. Tyra corrió rápidamente hasta el librero, tomó un libro con tapa brillante y regresó de prisa hasta su maestra. Después de sentarse cómodamente en su regazo, abrió el libro y comenzó a señalar con entusiasmo las imágenes mientras su maestra las nombraba.
El desarrollo musculoso	Los niños pequeños señalan objetos con el dedo para comunicarse. Los niños pequeños hacen marcas en un papel. Los niños pequeños trabajan y dan forma a la plastilina. Los niños pequeños corren. Los niños pequeños se sientan y se levantan solos de sillas pequeñas. Los niños pequeños están desarrollando su confianza espacial; explorando su cuerpo en el espacio.	Mindy estiró la plastilina con las manos y luego hizo figuras con las herramientas. Joseph se sentó a la mesa para comer, luego llevó los platos sucios al fregadero.
	24 a 36 meses (niños pequeños)	
Los sentimientos / Las ataduras	Los niños pequeños a veces pueden ser independientes, pero les gusta saber que la maestra está cerca. A los niños pequeños les gusta mirar fotos de sí mismos, sus amigos y su familia. Los niños pequeños oyen sus palabras y el tono de su voz cuando usted habla acerca de ellos. Quieren que usted se interese en ellos y se enorgullezca de sus logros. Los niños pequeños necesitan límites claros y consistentes. Olvidarán o pondrán a prueba las reglas, pero se sentirán a gusto cuando usted les recuerda las reglas y les ayuda a obedecerlas. Los niños pequeños pueden utilizar palabras para expresar sus sentimientos, o pueden dar golpes o morder. Los niños pequeños se ocupan de los sentimientos de los demás, y consuelan a quien esté triste o le llevan una curita a quien se haya lastimado.	Kiki llevó su bebé a ver las fotos de su propia familia en la pared, y la arrullaba mientras miraba la cara de su propia madre.

Interacciones entre Maestro o Padre/Madre–Niño	Ambiente

18 a 24 meses (niños pequeños)

• Léale libros con cuentos más largos, haga pausas a medida que avanza por el libro para animar a los niños pequeños a hablar sobre las imágenes y la historia. Haga preguntas abiertas tales como "¿Cómo se siente el oso?" • Pregúntese a menudo con el niño: "Me pregunto qué va a pasar con el oso." • Haga que los niños pequeños conversen intentando mantenerse en el mismo tema que el niño. • Introduzca nuevas conversaciones sobre objetos y eventos.	• Disponga una pista de obstáculos complicada y use palabras tales como "adentro," "afuera," "por arriba," "a través," "alrededor," "arriba" y "abajo" mientras el niño pequeño recorre la pista. • Suministre libros nuevos todas las semanas, pero mantenga cerca los libros preferidos de los niños. • Suministre una mayor variedad de materiales de arte. • Déle materiales que estimulen los sentidos.
• Ponga a disposición de los niños materiales pequeños que los induzcan a poner en práctica su creciente capacidad de manipulación de objetos con los dedos. • Quédese con los niños pequeños y apóyelos mientras intentan poner en práctica capacidades recientemente desarrolladas. • Deles oportunidades de trepar, caminar y correr.	• Materiales de arte tales como brochas gordas, marcadores y superficies grandes para pintar. • Artículos pequeños, tales como cuentas que se interconectan y tableros para clavijas, para practicar actividades de manipulación. • Mucho espacio para el movimiento: bailes, juguetes para montar, estructuras para trepar, toboganes.

18 a 36 meses (niños pequeños)

• Establezca reglas claras y consistentes. Esté preparada para recordar a los niños pequeños con frecuencia, la manera de obedecer las reglas: "No se muerde; morder duele." • Dedique a los niños pequeños suficiente tiempo y atención para que se sientan comprendidos. • Haga eco al entusiasmo que los niños pequeños pueden darle a su propio juego. • Note y comente las interacciones que los niños pequeños están mirando y en las que están pensando.	• Tenga muchas fotografías de niños con sus familias en las paredes, en libros pequeños, y laminadas para que las lleven consigo. • Disponga espacios protegidos para el juego tranquilo. • Mantenga rutinas y disposiciones de salón previsibles. • Tenga libros con cuentos simples sobre ir y venir, familias y amistad. • Canten canciones sobre sentimientos tales como "Cuando estás contento y lo sabes" y "Cuando estás triste y enojado$ . . . $"

	Desarrollo	Ejemplo
	24 a 36 meses (niños pequeños)	

	Desarrollo	Ejemplo
El aprender entre los pares	• La amistad de los niños pequeños es "búsqueda de proximidad," deseo de estar cerca y mostrar cariño como sonreír, reírse y abrazarse. Los amigos se prefieren mutuamente como compañeros de interacción. Las amistades continúan desarrollándose y se profundizan. • Los niños pequeños intercambian información y pueden imitar las acciones pasadas de los demás. • Los niños pequeños pueden congregarse y amontonarse. Cuando una maestra comienza a hacer una actividad interesante con un niño, por lo general los otros llegan corriendo de todas partes del salón. • Algunos niños pequeños son capaces de idear maneras diferentes de ayudar a otros cuando se han lastimado o están tristes. Algunos pueden tener un impresionante repertorio de comportamientos altruistas, y si algo no funciona, intentan hacer otra cosa. • Los compañeros colaboran hacia metas comunes, haciendo uno de líder y otro de seguidor. • Pueden producirse peleas por objetos, espacio personal y palabras. Los niños pequeños también se dedican a intercambios juguetones, tal como empujar y caerse bruscamente, correr y perseguirse, y realizar juegos verbales. • Algunos niños pueden ganarse cierta reputación entre sus compañeros por comportamiento agresivo o bondadoso. • Los niños se vuelven más positivos y menos negativos en su juego social entre los 24 y los 36 meses de edad. • Puede haber dominación de un niño sobre otro.	María y Sally jugaron durante 30 minutos en extremos opuestos de la pequeña estantería de juguetes, mirándose mutuamente cada varios minutos y diciéndose "barco," "mi barco," "hola," "quiero jugo," "mírame" y llamándose por su nombre una y otra vez. Cuando pasó un camión de bomberos afuera, varios niños pequeños se acercaron corriendo para mirar por la ventana. José y Miguel empujaron, jalaron, rodaron y resoplaron haciendo rodar una gran calabaza desde dentro hasta el patio de juegos, donde los niños pequeños y sus maestras iban a abrirla y sacarle las semillas.
La Cognición	• Los niños pequeños de más edad comienzan a entender conceptos tales como el color, el tamaño, la forma, el tiempo y el peso. • Los niños pequeños de más edad se interesan en las historias y en las imágenes de libros de cuentos. • Los niños pequeños mayores crean nuevos cuentos en el juego imaginario o nuevas estructuras en la construcción de bloques y se vuelven más imaginativos y creativos. • Asigne papeles a los juguetes y a otros niños en el juego imaginario; utilice sillas, mantas y estanterías como sustitutos en el juego imaginario.	Eric se siente un poco triste y lleva una foto de su mamá diciendo, "después de siesta." Sara se encarga de la esquina de juego dramático entregando muñecas y animales de peluche. Se pone un sombrero y dice "la mamá va a comprar."

Interacciones entre Maestro o Padre/Madre-Niño	Ambiente
24 a 36 meses (niños pequeños)	

- Organice situaciones en que dos niños pequeños deban trabajar juntos—como por ejemplo, hacer rodar una calabaza de un lugar a otro, o traer de afuera un balde con bloques "pesados."
- Póngale una curita a una muñeca en el brazo o en la pierna y anime a los niños pequeños a que cuiden al bebé.
- Pregunte a los niños pequeños "¿cómo podemos ayudar a José? Está triste, está llorando."
- Intente cambiar la imagen de la niña que se está ganando una reputación de agresividad. Téngala cerca, muéstrele cómo tocar con cuidado y comente su comportamiento servicial. Déle un juguete interesante que pueda inducir a otros niños a jugar con ella. Manténgase cerca y enséñele a jugar.

- Coloque sombreros y ropa que sea fácil de poner, en un rincón acogedor y con un espejo grande.
- Los niños pequeños disfrutarán de una mutua compañía cuando los amigos cambian de aspecto poniéndose un sombrero de ala ancha o unos zapatos grandes.
- Los espacios que quedan encima o debajo de un ático bajo estimulan la interacción entre los niños pequeños.
- Suministre varios tipos de muñecas, así como cubiertos de mesa no peligrosos, mantas y camas pequeñas. Siéntese cerca y mire como los niños pequeños juegan a cuidar a sus bebés.
- Suministre materiales sin propósito específico, como bloques, y actividades que requieran cooperación, tales como pintar con agua un muro exterior utilizando una brocha gorda, o llenar de agua un balde grande con envases pequeños.
- Un equipo de motor grande, como los trepadores o los barcos de balancín, animan a los niños pequeños a colaborar para alcanzar una meta común: todos se van a la parte de arriba del trepador, o balancean el barco con todos dentro.

- Pregúntele a los niños cómo podrían resolver problemas que se presentan y luego deje que los resuelvan solos.
- Apoye a los niños que trabajan juntos con materiales para que compartan ideas.
- Hable con un lenguaje que describa el tiempo ("ahora," "más tarde," "antes de la siesta," "después de almuerzo"), peso ("pesado," "ligero"), tamaño ("grande," "pequeño").
- Cuente cosas durante el día.

- Facilite oportunidades de juego que promuevan la comparación de tamaños, pesos, colores, formas y cantidades.
- Ponga por todas partes libros para los niños. Tenga varias copias de libros favoritos antiguos, y traiga libros nuevos.
- Permita que los niños combinen materiales de diferentes áreas de maneras creativas.
- Presente nuevos materiales o nuevas combinaciones de materiales.

	Desarrollo	Ejemplo
	24 a 36 meses (niños pequeños)	

| El Lenguaje | • Los niños pequeños comprenden instrucciones complejas y recuerdan palabras de canciones cortas y juegos de dedos.
• Los niños pequeños se valen de muchas oraciones de dos a cuatro palabras.
• Los niños pequeños pueden señalar con el dedo y nombrar muchas partes del cuerpo.
• Los niños pequeños añaden "ando o iendo" a las palabras.
• Los niños pequeños comienzan a usar preposiciones tales como "sobre" y "dentro."
• Los niños pequeños añaden una "s" a las palabras para indicar plurales.
• Los niños pequeños podrían empezar a preguntar " ¿Por qué?"
• Los niños pequeños comienzan a contar historias sobre lo que hicieron o lo que vieron.
• Hacia el final de este período, el niño pequeño puede usar las imágenes para contar lo que ocurre en un cuento. | Mindy comenzó a añadir "ando o iendo" a las palabras que había estado diciendo durante meses. Dijo "Yo corriendo" y "Yo comiendo" en vez de "Yo corro" y "Yo como."
"Mira, está jugando," exclamó Treat mientras señalaba con el dedo una imagen en su libro preferido. |
| El desarrollo musculoso | • Los niños pequeños ensartan cuentas, usan las tijeras, pintan con los dedos o con pinceles, arman rompecabezas sencillos.
• Los niños pequeños lanzan y patean una pelota.
• Los niños pequeños se paran en un solo pie.
• Los niños pequeños se paran y caminan en puntillas.
• Los niños pequeños suben escaleras poniendo un pie en cada escalón.
• Los niños pequeños trepan, se deslizan y saltan.
• Los niños pequeños comen con cuchara y tenedor.
• Los niños pequeños se pueden vestir solos.
• Los niños pequeños pueden verter leche de una jarra pequeña. | Robert ni siquiera tiene que pensar en su cuerpo cuando corre para saludar a su papá al final del día.
Peggy y Misha inventan un juego imitándose mutuamente los pasos en puntillas, posturas y gestos. Forcejeando un poco, Lawrence y Evelyn juegan con la ropa para disfrazarse. |

Interacciones entre Maestro o Padre/Madre–Niño	Ambiente
24 a 36 meses (niños pequeños)	

Interacciones entre Maestro o Padre/Madre–Niño	Ambiente
• Responda sus preguntas de "por qué" con paciencia y entusiasmo. Así es como los niños aprenden y desarrollan interacciones sociales. • Escuche con sus ojos las "historias" que los niños pequeños cuentan. • Modele decir palabras plurales, tales como "perros," "elefantes," etc. • Use palabras descriptivas tales como "queso mozarella" en vez de sólo "queso" o "urraca de América" en vez de sólo "pájaro." • Tenga conversaciones largas con los niños pequeños, siguiendo lo que dicen. • Lea libros a grupos informales pequeños o a niños por separado.	• Déle imágenes para que los niños las hagan corresponder. • Los rompecabezas de animales, personas, vehículos y alimentos son importantes. • Se pueden agregar al ambiente libros con muchas imágenes y cuentos cortos. • Los materiales para el juego dramático estimulan la conversación.
• Esté consciente del equilibrio necesario entre el tiempo dedicado a actividades enérgicas y a actividades tranquilas. • Esté atento al aumento de precisión de las capacidades motrices ligeras, pues pueden comenzar a manifestarse sutiles problemas. • Esté a disposición de los niños pequeños animándolos y teniéndoles paciencia conforme comen, se visten y van al baño solos con más frecuencia.	• Ponga a su disposición una variedad de materiales para practicar capacidades motrices ligeras: rompecabezas simples, cajas de formas, cuentas para hacer collares, bloques de mesa, arcilla, materiales de arte. • Espacio, oportunidad y estructuras para fomentar el movimiento: períodos de tiempo al aire libre, carreras de obstáculos, bailes y juguetes para montar.

Appendix C

Developmental Trends and Responsive Interactions—Spanish

Tendencias de Desarrollo e Interacciones Receptivas (Capítulo 6)

Tanto los bebés como los niños pequeños desarrollan un sólido sentido de identidad a través del aumento de la autorregulación, el aprendizaje de la expresión emocional efectiva y el desarrollo de relaciones de cariño.

Desarrollo	Ejemplo
0 a 4 meses (bebé)	
• Los bebés absorben una gran cantidad de información acerca del mundo. • Los bebés pueden sentirse abrumados y comenzar a bostezar, mirar hacia otro lado o molestarse. • Los bebés comienzan a calmarse chupándose las manos o escuchando a un adulto que les hable suavemente. • Los bebés miran fijamente a los ojos de su maestra mientras les da de comer. • Los bebés voltean la cabeza hacia voces conocidas. • Los bebés se calman y se consuelan con personas conocidas. • Los bebés lloran cuando tienen hambre o están cansados o incómodos	Carlos seguía a Karen con los ojos por donde quiera que fuera por el salón. Cuando ella se le acercó, la miró como si quisiera que ella se quedara con él. Karen aceptó la invitación a jugar y se sentó con él en el piso. En cuanto comenzó a cansarse y a ponerse molesto, Karen lo envolvió en una manta, lo abrazó estrechamente y le habló con voz suave.
4 a 8 meses (bebé)	
• A los bebés les gusta mirarse las manos y los pies. • Los bebés agitan los brazos y patalean emocionados cuando ven a una persona conocida. • Los bebés le sonríen a la maestra esperando que ella les sonría también. • Con la cara y el cuerpo, los bebés expresan muchos sentimientos: desde fruncir el ceño y llorar hasta reírse a carcajadas. • Los bebés expresan sus sentimientos claramente ante personas conocidas, y son más reservados con los desconocidos.	A Deborah le encanta que la maestra la lleve en brazos mientras va por el salón "hablándole" de lo que ven. Tiene los ojos bien abiertos y brillantes, sonríe y hace ruiditos de arrullo cuando le corresponde hablar en la conversación. Cuando un visitante entra en el salón, Deborah se queda muy callada y seria, y se sujeta firmemente al hombro de la maestra mirando al visitante.
8 a 12 meses (bebé móvil)	
• Los bebés móviles pueden tenerle miedo a los desconocidos. • Los bebés móviles pueden llamar a los adultos conocidos para que los ayuden cuando están enojados. • Los bebés móviles miran al adulto conocido para determinar si una situación es peligrosa o no. • Los bebés móviles se aferran al adulto cuando están en una situación desconocida. • A los bebés m5óviles les parecen divertidos los juegos tontos y las expresiones faciales exageradas que ponen los adultos.	Jaime está disfrutando de su nueva habilidad, que es ir gateando rápidamente a donde quiera ir. Le encanta el pequeño trepador que le permite mirar por la ventana. Pero cuando siente que la rampa es un poco inestable, se vuelve a mirar a Federico, su maestro, para asegurarse de que no hay peligro.

Interacciones entre Maestro o Padre/Madre–Niño	Ambiente
0 a 4 meses (bebé)	

• Mantenga a los bebés pequeños cerca, en brazos, en un saco de bebé, o sobre una manta. • Reconozca las señales de por qué el bebé quiere estar con usted—mirada fija, tenderle los brazos, mirada feliz—y respóndale hablándole suavemente, alternando la comunicación verbal y no verbal. • Reconozca las señales que indican que el bebé necesita un descanso—bostezar, babear, mirar hacia otro lado—y apártese en silencio esperando a que el bebé se recupere. • Consuele a los bebés cuando lloren.	• Estar cerca de una maestra conocida es lo mejor. • Un espacio sereno y tranquilo con luces bajas, limita la información que el bebé necesita absorber. • Evite tener música de fondo todo el día. • Limite el número de objetos, sonidos, colores y movimientos alrededor de un bebé pequeño. • La maestra es lo más interesante que el bebé tiene para mirar, pero para otros bebés, los espejos y juguetes que se encuentran en su campo visual, también son interesantes.

4 a 8 meses (bebé)	
• Déles a los bebés oportunidades para que se miren al espejo mientras juegan. • Refleje las expresiones emocionales del bebé y agregue palabras apropiadas: "Estoy tan contenta de verte hoy." • Responda a los bebés de una manera que les ayude a calmarse y mantenerse activos. Si el bebé llora, cálmelo.	• Monte espejos irrompibles en las paredes. • Deje que los bebés pasen un rato en el piso mientras están boca arriba, jugando con sus pies y moviéndose por el piso. • Los libros y los álbumes de fotografías con caras reales mostrando diferentes expresiones emocionales son muy interesantes para los bebés.

8 a 12 meses (bebé móvil)	
• Anime a los bebés móviles a moverse y explorar asegurándoles que usted los está mirando y cuidando. • Entienda que los bebés móviles pueden asustarse ante situaciones nuevas que quizás no los habrían asustado hace unos meses. Consuélelos y tranquilícelos.	• Juegue al te veo, no te veo. • Léales cuentos sobre madres y padres que se van y vuelven. • Léales libros con solapas que se pueden levantar para encontrar cosas. • Mantenga una previsibilidad de hábitos y rutinas del salón.

Desarrollo	Ejemplo

12 a 18 meses (bebé móvil)

- Los bebés móviles imitan las acciones de los adultos conocidos, tales como hablar por teléfono o llevar en brazos a una muñeca bebé.
- Los bebés móviles intentan atraer la atención del adulto jalándole la pierna o tomándole la mano.
- Los bebés móviles se calman con su manta o su animal de peluche favorito.
- Los bebés móviles protestan ruidosamente cuando sus padres los dejan.
- Los bebés móviles se relajan y se consuelan acurrucándose con un adulto conocido.
- Los bebés móviles hacen saber claramente lo que les gusta y lo que no les gusta.

Amelia carga toda la mañana su osito de peluche por todos los lados. A veces copia las acciones de Sofía, su maestra, dándole al osito palmaditas en la espalda o alimentándole con biberón. Cuando se cansa, se frota el osito contra la oreja y se chupa el pulgar.

18 a 24 meses (niños pequeños)

- Los niños pequeños comienzan a controlar ciertos impulsos diciendo "no, no, no" a medida que comienzan a lanzar bloques.
- Los niños pequeños pueden dejar lo que están haciendo cuando la maestra se lo dice.
- Los niños pequeños pueden no querer dejar de jugar cuando su padre o su madre viene a buscarlos.
- Los niños pequeños pueden llorar cuando no consiguen hacer algo que están intentando.
- Los niños pequeños saben su propio nombre y puede que usen el "mi" y "mío."

Francisco se sube a la mesa mientras mira directamente a los ojos de la maestra que desaprueba lo que él hace, y dice "no, no, no."

24 a 36 meses (niños pequeños)

- Los niños pequeños a veces pueden ser independientes, pero les gusta saber que la maestra está cerca.
- A los niños pequeños les gusta mirar fotos de sí mismos, sus amigos y su familia.
- Los niños pequeños oyen sus palabras y el tono de su voz cuando usted habla acerca de ellos. Quieren que usted se interese en ellos y se enorgullezca de sus logros.
- Los niños pequeños necesitan límites claros y consistentes. Olvidarán o pondrán a prueba las reglas, pero se sentirán a gusto cuando usted les recuerda las reglas y les ayuda a obedecerlas.
- Los niños pequeños pueden utilizar palabras para expresar sus sentimientos, o pueden dar golpes o morder.
- Los niños pequeños se ocupan de los sentimientos de los demás, y consuelan a quien esté triste o le llevan una curita a quien se haya lastimado.

Kiki llevó su bebé a ver las fotos de su propia familia en la pared, y la arrullaba mientras miraba la cara de su propia madre.

Interacciones entre Maestro o Padre/Madre–Niño	Ambiente

12 a 18 meses (bebé móvil)

- Muestre interés en las actividades del bebé.
- Muestre su orgullo por los logros del bebé.
- Deje que los bebés la utilicen como una base firme, para explorar el mundo.
- Deje que los bebés sepan que usted entiende lo que sienten y responda respetuosamente.
- Estos niños son todavía muy pequeños, y necesitan que se les acurruque y abrace mucho.

- Disponga de objetos de mayores en tamaño infantil: teléfonos, platos, llaves, etc.
- Ponga fotografías de bebés con su familia en la pared.
- Lamine las fotos del bebé con su familia para que las lleve consigo.
- Haga álbumes de fotos de los niños del programa y hable acerca de las fotos.
- Disponga de sillas de adulto y espacios tranquilos y cómodos para tener a los niños en brazos.

18 a 24 meses (niños pequeños)

- Mantenga su sentido del humor. Entienda que los niños pequeños pueden dejar de hacer ciertas cosas a veces, pero no siempre.
- Respete los sentimientos fuertes de los niños pequeños. El turnarse y compartir viene después; ahora "mí" y "mío" son una etapa importante del desarrollo de un sólido sentido de identidad.

- Disponga espacios que permita que los niños exploren, pero siempre sin perderlos de vista.
- Tenga suficientes juguetes iguales para que varios niños puedan tener el suyo, sin tener que compartir o turnarse.
- Deje que los niños traigan al programa artículos que los calmen, tales como mantas o animales de peluche. Asígneles un lugar tranquilo donde puedan consolarse solos.

24 a 36 meses (niños pequeños)

- Establezca reglas claras y consistentes. Esté preparada para recordar a los niños pequeños con frecuencia, la manera de obedecer las reglas: "No se muerde; morder duele."
- Dedique a los niños pequeños suficiente tiempo y atención para que se sientan comprendidos.
- Haga eco al entusiasmo que los niños pequeños pueden darle a su propio juego.
- Note y comente las interacciones que los niños pequeños están mirando y en las que están pensando.

- Tenga muchas fotografías de niños con sus familias en las paredes, en libros pequeños, y laminadas para que las lleven consigo.
- Disponga espacios protegidos para el juego tranquilo.
- Mantenga rutinas y disposiciones de salón previsibles.
- Tenga libros con cuentos simples sobre ir y venir, familias y amistad.
- Canten canciones sobre sentimientos tales como "Cuando estás contento y lo sabes" y "Cuando estás triste y enojado . . ."

Tendencias de Desarrollo e Interacciones Receptivas (Capítulo 7)

Habilidades: Comunicarse con sus compañeros, ser socialmente activo, jugar con sus compañeros, y controlar emociones negativas y conflictos durante interacciones con los compañeros.

Desarrollo	Ejemplo
0 a 4 meses (bebé)	
• A los bebés les gusta mirarse mutuamente (mirada visual). • Los bebés prefieren mirar caras, especialmente los bordes y los ojos. • Puede que los bebés lloren cuando oyen llorar a otros bebés (contagio).	Después de que la profesora puso a Tamika y a Sam sobre una manta en el piso, Tamika se quedó mirando fijamente a Sam.
4 a 8 meses (bebé)	
• Los bebés tocan a otros bebés, se dirigen vocalizaciones, se entusiasman, se acercan a otros bebés, sonríen y se ríen unos de otros. • Los bebés pueden tratar a otros bebés como si fueran objetos—pasándoles por encima al gatear, lamiéndolos, chupándolos, sentándose encima. Están simplemente aprendiendo la diferencia entre personas y objetos. Los bebés pueden pinchar con el dedo, empujar, dar palmaditas a otros bebés, para ver lo que el otro bebé va a hacer. A menudo se sorprenden con la reacción que logran.	Amna le pasó por encima gateando a Nadia que estaba acostada en el piso. Tocándole el pelo a Nadia, Amna se rió a carcajadas.
8 a 12 meses (bebé móvil)	
• Los bebés pueden mostrar a otros bebés un objeto, sentarse juntos, perseguirse gateando y jugar a perseguir y recoger objetos. • Los bebés se sonríen y se ríen entre sí. • Los bebés se dirigen sonidos—y es posible que sus primeras palabras se las digan entre sí. • Uno de los juegos preferidos de los bebés es el *te veo, no te veo* mientras exploran la separación: irse y volver, aparecer y desaparecer. • Los bebés pueden aprender a tocarse uno al otro con cuidado. • Como a esta edad los bebés actúan en gran medida en función de sus objetivos, pueden apartar la mano de un bebé que esté tocando un juguete, o gatearle por encima para alcanzar un juguete.	Shamaine miró la estantería baja de juguetes y vio que Carla venía gateando hacia ella. Shamaine se dio la vuelta rápidamente y se alejó gateando con Carla siguiéndola de cerca. Kai pasó gateando por encima de las piernas de Bridger para alcanzar un juguete que estaba al otro lado de Bridger.

Interacciones entre Maestro o Padre/Madre–Niño	Ambiente

0 a 4 meses (bebé)

• Sostenga a dos bebés para que puedan mirarse mutuamente. • Ponga varios bebés sobre una manta en el piso para que puedan mirarse y tocarse entre sí.	• Los brazos de la maestras ofrecen el mejor ambiente. • Ponga a dos bebés sobre unas mantas en el piso—uno junto a otro, de manera que los dos se estén tocando con los dedos de los pies.

4 a 8 meses (bebé)

• Muévase al ritmo de la música con un bebé en cada brazo. • Con un bebé sobre el regazo, apunte y hable sobre lo que el otro bebé está haciendo. • Ponga a dos bebés boca bajo frente a un espejo. • En vez de decirles "No" y "Deja de hacer eso" a los bebés que están explorando, dígales, "Tócalo con cuidado." Dígales a los niños lo que usted quiere que hagan . . . muéstreselo.	• Cuelgue un espejo seguro en la pared de manera horizontal, para que la parte de abajo esté tocando el piso. • Cubra la cámara de aire de la rueda de un auto con un paño suave. Siente a dos bebés en la cámara para que se toquen con los pies.

8 a 12 meses (bebé móvil)

• Nombre partes del cuerpo del bebé mientras dos bebés están sentados juntos:
    Estos son los ojos del bebé
    Esta es la nariz del bebé
    Toca la parte con que ves
    Tócate la parte que te suenas
• Ponga un bebé con otro (en parejas) porque las interacciones más frecuentes, complejas e intensas entre niños se producen cuando un niño está con varios compañeros.
• Comprenda que los bebés no son "malos" cuando le apartan la mano al otro. Diga "Jenny tenía ese juguete. Vamos a buscarte otro."
	• Mientras están comiendo, coloque las sillas altas de manera que los niños se puedan ver unos a los otros.
	• Disponga de rincones agradables en el salón donde los bebés puedan "desaparecer" (pero pudiendo aún ser vistos por adultos).
	• Cuelgue del techo un paño largo y ancho (para que los bebés no se enreden en él). A los bebés les encanta gatear alrededor.
	• Ponga contenedores con bloques de diferentes tamaños entre dos bebés. Quédese sentada junto a ellos mientras comienzan a explorar los materiales. Hable acerca de lo que está haciendo cada uno.

Desarrollo	Ejemplo

12 a 18 meses (bebé móvil)

- Comienzan los turnos imitativos (motores) e interactivos. Los niños pequeños pueden imitarse unos a otros—si un bebé le da un juguete a otro, el otro puede imitarlo.
- Los bebés móviles comienzan a hablarse unos a otros.
- Los bebés pueden demostrar preocupación cuando otros bebés están afligidos.
- Los bebés móviles pueden quitarle el juguete a otro bebé, decirle "no," empujarlo, agarrar firmemente el juguete y decir "mío."
- A esta edad, los bebés son pequeños científicos que experimentan para ver cómo funcionan las cosas. Esto afecta la relación que tienen con sus compañeros, pues están constantemente haciéndoles cosas para ver cómo reaccionan.
- Morder puede aparecer cuando los bebés muerden a otros "para ver lo que pasa," para obtener el juguete que quieren, para expresar su frustración. Los bebés están al borde de comunicarse bien; pueden comunicarse por la boca en forma de mordedura.

Rashida golpeó la mesa con la cuchara; poco después, otros dos comenzaron a hacerlo. Parecían estar siguiendo el ejemplo físicamente (como si estuvieran conversando).

Primero, Carmen intentó alejar a Toby del caballito de balancín. Cuando eso no dio resultado, se inclinó hacia él y lo mordió en el brazo.

18 a 24 meses (niños pequeños)

- Las amistades pueden desarrollarse a muy temprana edad. Los amigos son más propensos a tocarse, apoyarse y sonreírse entre sí, que otros niños que no son amigos.
- Los niños pequeños imitan mutuamente los sonidos y las palabras que dicen y se hablan y comienzan a comunicarse con los demás a mayores distancias.
- Los niños pequeños dan u ofrecen un juguete o comida a otros niños pequeños.
- Los niños pequeños pueden llamar a un adulto y jalar al adulto para que ayude a otro niño, o pueden ayudar a otro niño llevándole un pañuelito de papel, por ejemplo.
- Los niños pequeños demuestran bondad hacia otros bebés que se sienten afligidos. Sin embargo, el bebé o niño pequeño móvil puede suponer que lo que lo consuela a él, también consuela al afligido.
- Los niños pueden turnarse, por ejemplo, con una pelota o para saltar. Pueden tener conversaciones cinéticas de niño pequeño mientras siguen a un líder por el salón—entrando y saliendo del grupo, turnándose para ser líder y seguidor—como si estuvieran en una conversación, en la cual escuchan y hablan, aprendiendo la importante habilidad de cómo turnarse.
- Empujar, dar empujones, agarrar y golpear pueden ocurrir a medida que los niños luchan con la idea de "mío durante todo el tiempo que yo quiera" y "tuyo, pero yo también lo quiero." Los niños pequeños puede que se peleen más por juguetes pequeños, que por objetos grandes que no se mueven.

Paulie parecía estar esperando en la puerta a que apareciera Jamie al principio de la jornada. Cuando Jaime y su mamá llegaron, Paulie se dirigió hacia ellos y le tomó la mano a Jaime con una gran sonrisa en la cara.

Tania saltó (medio se cayó) de una tabla situada a varias pulgadas del suelo. Pronto tres niños pequeños estaban parados sobre la tabla, y casi saltando, casi bajando de la tabla y disfrutando inmensamente de la actividad.

Interacción entre Maestra–Niño, o Padre/Madre–Niño	Ambiente

12 a 18 meses (bebé móvil)

- Muéstreles a los niños pequeños móviles cómo rodar juntos por una pequeña pendiente.
- Ayude a los niños pequeños móviles a que aprendan los nombres de los demás, cantando canciones de saludo y despedida incluyendo los nombres de los niños: "Esta es Tania, ¿cómo estás?" y "Este es Enrique, ¿cómo estás?" y apuntando o tocando a cada niño que pasa junto a usted o al que está sentado en su regazo.
- Comente el comportamiento social activo. Diga "Le diste la muñeca. Eso le gusta." Puede que los bebés no entiendan sus palabras, pero son capaces de darse cuenta por el tono de voz que usted está contenta con ellos.
- A los bebés les gusta mirar libros juntos, creando grupos informales (esto significa que entrar y salir del grupo) alrededor de las piernas, el regazo y los brazos del padre, la madre o la maestra que más les gusta.

- Suministre una caja de cartón grande abierta por los dos lados. Anímelos a entrar y salir de la caja gateando juntos. Ventanas a los lados de la caja estimulan a los bebés para que se miren entre ellos por la ventana.
- Muñecas, camiones, autos y otros materiales de juego, promueven las interacciones entre compañeros.
- A los bebés les encanta la arena y el agua y jugar con botellas y pelotas seguras de diferentes tamaños. Cuando cada uno tiene su propio contenedor o cubo con agua o arena, el juego se desarrolla sin altibajos.
- Al aire libre, grandes cajas de arena o juguetes para empujar, estimulan el juego interactivo.

18 a 24 meses (niños pequeños)

- Ya esté adentro o afuera, atienda a los niños pequeños cuando entran a "reponerse" emocionalmente con su maestra especial animando a varios niños pequeños a sentarse junto a usted o en su regazo. Permita que los niños pequeños se toquen mutuamente con cuidado.
- Anime a que varios niños pequeños hagan sonidos de animales y se imiten entre sí mientras les muestra las imágenes de un libro.
- Pídale a un niño que ayude a otro, trayendo un pañuelito de papel, abriendo la llave del agua, abriendo la puerta, etc.
- Estimule la bondad mutua. Si un niño pequeño llora, pregúntele a otro lo que "podríamos" hacer para ayudarlo.
- Anime a dos niños pequeños a que pongan la mesa o la limpien después de comer. Mire como se imitan.
- Cante canciones, animando a los niños pequeños a que se turnen con las acciones.

- Adentro y afuera: Ponga a su disposición áreas con arena que sean suficientemente grandes para varios niños pequeños, es de esperar que se sienten justo en el medio del área.
- Las mantas sobre el piso, el suelo o una mesa son un centro para que los niños pequeños jueguen.
- Suministre vagones: Empujar o jalar a un amigo en un vagón dará como resultado chillidos de deleite.
- Suministre pelotas y juguetes para jalar que estimulen el juego interactivo.
- Lugares para saltar sin peligro estimulan los intercambios sociales.
- Suministre juguetes musicales, varios de cada clase, para que los niños puedan tocar juntos una música bella. A veces uno dirigirá y el otro le seguirá, o viceversa.

Desarrollo	Ejemplo

24 a 36 meses (niños pequeños)

- La amistad de los niños pequeños es "búsqueda de proximidad," deseo de estar cerca y mostrar cariño como sonreír, reírse y abrazarse. Los amigos se prefieren mutuamente como compañeros de interacción. Las amistades continúan desarrollándose y se profundizan.
- Los niños pequeños intercambian información y pueden imitar las acciones pasadas de los demás.
- Los niños pequeños pueden congregarse y amontonarse. Cuando una maestra comienza a hacer una actividad interesante con un niño, por lo general los otros llegan corriendo de todas partes del salón.
- Algunos niños pequeños son capaces de idear maneras diferentes de ayudar a otros cuando se han lastimado o están tristes. Algunos pueden tener un impresionante repertorio de comportamientos altruistas, y si algo no funciona, intentan hacer otra cosa.
- Los compañeros colaboran hacia metas comunes, haciendo uno de líder y otro de seguidor.
- Pueden producirse peleas por objetos, espacio personal y palabras. Los niños pequeños también se dedican a intercambios juguetones, tal como empujar y caerse bruscamente, correr y perseguirse, y realizar juegos verbales.
- Algunos niños pueden ganarse cierta reputación entre sus compañeros por comportamiento agresivo o bondadoso.
- Los niños se vuelven más positivos y menos negativos en su juego social entre los 24 y los 36 meses de edad.
- Puede haber dominación de un niño sobre otro.

María y Sally jugaron durante 30 minutos en extremos opuestos de la pequeña estantería de juguetes, mirándose mutuamente cada varios minutos y diciéndose "barco," "mi barco," "hola," "quiero jugo," "mírame" y llamándose por su nombre una y otra vez. Cuando pasó un camión de bomberos afuera, varios niños pequeños se acercaron corriendo para mirar por la ventana. José y Miguel empujaron, jalaron, rodaron y resoplaron haciendo rodar una gran calabaza desde dentro hasta el patio de juegos, donde los niños pequeños y sus maestras iban a abrirla y sacarle las semillas.

Interacción entre Maestra-Niño, o Padre/Madre–Niño	Ambiente

24 a 36 meses (niños pequeños)

- Organice situaciones en que dos niños pequeños deban trabajar juntos—como por ejemplo, hacer rodar una calabaza de un lugar a otro, o traer de afuera un balde con bloques "pesados."
- Póngale una curita a una muñeca en el brazo o en la pierna y anime a los niños pequeños a que cuiden al bebé.
- Pregunte a los niños pequeños "¿cómo podemos ayudar a José? Está triste, está llorando."
- Intente cambiar la imagen de la niña que se está ganando una reputación de agresividad. Téngala cerca, muéstrele cómo tocar con cuidado y comente su comportamiento servicial. Déle un juguete interesante que pueda inducir a otros niños a jugar con ella. Manténgase cerca y enséñele a jugar.

- Coloque sombreros y ropa que sea fácil de poner, en un rincón acogedor y con un espejo grande.
- Los niños pequeños disfrutarán de una mutua compañía cuando los amigos cambian de aspecto poniéndose un sombrero de ala ancha o unos zapatos grandes.
- Los espacios que quedan encima o debajo de un ático bajo estimulan la interacción entre los niños pequeños.
- Suministre varios tipos de muñecas, así como cubiertos de mesa no peligrosos, mantas y camas pequeñas. Siéntese cerca y mire como los niños pequeños juegan a cuidar a sus bebés.
- Suministre materiales sin propósito específico, como bloques, y actividades que requieran cooperación, tales como pintar con agua un muro exterior utilizando una brocha gorda, o llenar de agua un balde grande con envases pequeños.
- Un equipo de motor grande, como los trepadores o los barcos de balancín, animan a los niños pequeños a colaborar para alcanzar una meta común: todos se van a la parte de arriba del trepador, o balancean el barco con todos dentro.

Tendencias de Desarrollo e Interacciones Receptivas (Capítulo 8)

Los bebés y los niños pequeños se conocen a sí mismos, a los demás y al mundo, a través de sus propias capacidades y atributos, utilizando instrumentos cognitivos de aprendizaje y conceptos básicos.

Desarrollo	Ejemplo
0 a 4 meses (bebé)	
• Los bebés siguen visualmente un objeto en movimiento.	Megan levantó la cabeza, apoyándose en los brazos mientras estaba recostada sobre la manta. Con una expresión seria miró a la maestra y a los niños a su alrededor.
• Los bebés lloran para atraer la atención del adulto a fin de que los consuele o les dé de comer.	Willy comenzó a patear el móvil que colgaba encima y logró que se meneara. Luego paró, lo miró y volvió a patearlo mirándolo para ver si pasaba algo.
• Los bebés miran a su alrededor por el salón con interés.	
• Los bebés comienzan a intentar alcanzar juguetes.	
• Los bebés notan que sus brazos y piernas han causado algo y repiten el movimiento.	
• Los bebés reconocen personas y objetos.	
• Los bebés comienzan a llevarse objetos a la boca.	
4 a 8 meses (bebé)	
• A los bebés les gusta examinar los juguetes.	Ángela se interesa en todo. Mira a sus amigos y luego mira a la maestra y sonríe.
• A los bebés les gusta hacer que los juguetes hagan algo—sonar, encajarse uno dentro de otro.	Roger se estira para tocar un juguete colgante. Cuando se balancea y suena, Roger se estira para hacerlo de nuevo.
• Los bebés imitan las expresiones y los gestos de los adultos.	
• Los bebés se vuelven hacia los sonidos para ver de dónde vienen.	
• Los bebés buscan juguetes que han dejado caer.	
8 a 12 meses (bebé móvil)	
• A los bebés móviles les gusta desarmar los juguetes y luego volver a armarlos.	A Carlos le encanta sacar cada uno de los animales de plástico del balde y mirarlo. Cuando el balde queda vacío, lo lanza a un lado.
• A los bebés móviles les gustan los juguetes que hacen algo cuando se tocan, se jalan o se golpean.	A Aliya le gusta el botón que se aprieta y las puertas oscilantes de la caja mecánica, pero todavía no puede hacer funcionar todos los mecanismos. Su maestra expresa sorpresa a Aliya cuando las puertas se abren y, de vez en cuando, le enseña cómo funciona otra de las perillas.
• Los bebés móviles comienzan juegos imaginarios muy simples, tales como llevarse un vaso a la boca.	
• A los bebés móviles les gusta encontrar juguetes pequeños debajo de un paño o de un vaso.	
• A los bebés móviles les gusta levantar y examinar objetos pequeños tales como un Cheerio.	
• Los bebés móviles muestran objetos con el dedo sabiendo que usted también puede verlos.	

Interacción entre Maestra-Niño, o Padre/Madre-Niño	Ambiente

0 a 4 meses (bebé)

• Mueva lentamente un juguete pequeño de lado a lado mientras el bebé lo sigue con la mirada. • Responda rápidamente al llanto del niño. • Déles tiempo a los bebés para que estén tranquilos mirando lo que pasa a su alrededor. Hable acerca de lo que ven. • Reaccione ante las expresiones de los bebés con expresiones y lenguaje claro y hasta exagerado.	• Organice el espacio de manera que los bebés puedan ver actividad sin dejar de estar protegidos. • Suministre unos cuantos objetos interesantes para mirar—juguetes pequeños en el piso, cuando están boca abajo; juguetes colgantes cuando los bebés están boca arriba. • Ponga espejos irrompibles a disposición de los bebés.

4 a 8 meses (bebé)

• Lleve en brazos al bebé, mientras camina por el salón mirando cosas y hablando acerca de ellas. • Siéntese cerca y háblele al bebé sobre los juguetes que está mirando. • Llame al bebé por su nombre a poca distancia para asegurarle que está cerca.	• Suministre una variedad de juguetes pequeños para que los manipule y los examine. • Suministre juguetes que suenan cuando se mueven, se encajan unos dentro de otros o se cuelgan y mueven cuando se tocan. • Ofrezca libros de tapas de cartón.

8 a 12 meses (bebé móvil)

• Con su presencia, su interés y su entusiasmo, ayude al bebé a concentrarse en lo que le interesa para apoyarlo en su atención y exploración. • Con sus expresiones y palabras afectivas, demuéstrele al bebé móvil que usted disfruta de sus descubrimientos. • Con palabras, describa la actividad del niño: "Mira, encontraste un Cheerio. Lo estás recogiendo con los dedos."	• Suministre juguetes tales como vasos para apilar, anillos en poste, piezas que se interconectan y cubos llenos de objetos pequeños interesantes, tales como animales de juguete. • Suministre réplicas tamaño infantil de platos o herramientas domésticas. • Suministre juguetes que reaccionen—cajas mecánicas, almohadillas llenas de agua. • Suministre materiales sensoriales, como agua y arena con una variedad de herramientas. • Suministre libros de tapas de cartón con fotos.

Desarrollo	Ejemplo

12 a 18 meses (bebé móvil)

- A los bebés móviles les gusta poner en práctica su movilidad para explorar gateando, caminando, trepando, corriendo, etc.
- Los bebés móviles disfrutan jugando en la arena, el agua, con plastilina y varios tipos de herramientas.
- A los bebés móviles les interesan las relaciones espaciales de rompecabezas y tableros con agujeros.
- Los bebés móviles utilizan herramientas tales como llaves o teléfonos en sus juegos imaginarios.
- Los bebés móviles disfrutan al mirar libros y nombrar objetos, animales o partes del cuerpo.

Alexis y Dan están contentísimos de estar de pie. Se siguen mutuamente por todas partes, uno subiendo atrevidamente por un plano inclinado, con el otro inmediatamente detrás. A veces los dos intentan meterse debajo del tobogán.

A Meredith le encanta acurrucarse en el regazo de su maestra y mostrar con el dedo imágenes en libros mientras la maestra nombra los animales o le pide que encuentre uno en particular.

18 a 24 meses (niños pequeños)

- Los niños pequeños de corta edad disfrutan de su facilidad de movimiento y les gusta llevar cosas en las manos.
- Los niños pequeños entienden que pueden hacer que ocurran cosas.
- Los niños pequeños entienden y recuerdan los detalles de las rutinas.
- Los niños pequeños sustituyen unos objetos por otros en su juego imaginario.
- Los niños pequeños disfrutan cada vez más de los materiales problemáticos que sugieren actividades tales como construir y hacer corresponder formas.

Antes del desayuno, Chris tiende las manos para la cancioncita de gracias. Cuando un niño llega más tarde y se sienta a la mesa, Chris tiende las manos para que todos canten nuevamente.

Lynn y Matt construyen pequeñas torres de bloques y luego las chocan con camiones de juguete para derribarlas.

Fran saca de la caja bloques de una pulgada y hace una pila de bloques rojos y una pila de bloques azules.

24 a 36 meses (niños pequeños)

- Los niños pequeños de más edad comienzan a entender conceptos tales como el color, el tamaño, la forma, el tiempo y el peso.
- Los niños pequeños de más edad se interesan en las historias y en las imágenes de libros de cuentos.
- Los niños pequeños mayores crean nuevos cuentos en el juego imaginario o nuevas estructuras en la construcción de bloques y se vuelven más imaginativos y creativos.
- Asigne papeles a los juguetes y a otros niños en el juego imaginario; utilice sillas, mantas y estanterías como sustitutos en el juego imaginario.

Eric se siente un poco triste y lleva una foto de su mamá diciendo, "después de siesta."

Sara se encarga de la esquina de juego dramático entregando muñecas y animales de peluche. Se pone un sombrero y dice "la mamá va a comprar."

Interacción entre Maestra-Niño, o Padre/Madre–Niño	Ambiente

12 a 18 meses (bebé móvil)

• Déle a los bebés móviles tiempo y espacio protegido para explorar.	• Suministre rompecabezas simples, tableros con agujeros, formas, cuentas de madera con cordones gruesos.
• Quédese cerca para expresar interés, sugerir palabras y hacer que la actividad sea más elaborada y compleja.	• Suministre trepadores pequeños, túneles y trayectos interesantes.
• Ayude a los bebés móviles a que expresen su interés en otros bebés cuidadosamente.	• Suministre juguetes que funcionen al darle cuerda, o que se enciendan y apaguen.
• Exprese entusiasmo por lo que les interesa a los bebés móviles.	• Suministre artículos simples para el juego imaginario.

18 a 24 meses (niños pequeños)

• Mantenga rutinas predecibles recordándole a los niños el orden de las etapas con preguntas tales como "Es hora de comer. ¿Qué hacemos?"	• Tenga los juguetes y los materiales organizados de manera que los niños pequeños puedan escogerlos, alcanzarlos y guardarlos (con recordatorios).
• Tenga los materiales en lugares predecibles y ordenados.	• Revise frecuentemente los materiales a su disposición para asegurarse de que mantiene un equilibrio entre lo que es conocido y lo que es un poco difícil.
• Con preguntas tales como "¿Qué vas a hacer ahora? ¿Qué vas a comprar en la tienda? apoye a los niños pequeños cuando piensen en sus actividades.	

24 a 36 meses (niños pequeños)

• Pregúntele a los niños cómo podrían resolver problemas que se presentan y luego deje que los resuelvan solos.	• Facilite oportunidades de juego que promuevan la comparación de tamaños, pesos, colores, formas y cantidades.
• Apoye a los niños que trabajan juntos con materiales para que compartan ideas.	• Ponga por todas partes libros para los niños. Tenga varias copias de libros favoritos antiguos, y traiga libros nuevos.
• Hable con un lenguaje que describa el tiempo ("ahora," "más tarde," "antes de la siesta," "después de almuerzo"), peso ("pesado," "ligero"), tamaño ("grande," "pequeño").	• Permita que los niños combinen materiales de diferentes áreas de maneras creativas.
• Cuente cosas durante el día.	• Presente nuevos materiales o nuevas combinaciones de materiales.

Tendencias de Desarrollo e Interacciones Receptivas (Capítulo 9)

Los bebés y los niños pequeños desarrollan la capacidad de entender, expresar y decir palabras.

Desarrollo	Ejemplo
0 a 4 meses (bebé)	
• Los bebés se pueden asustar si oyen un ruido fuerte. • Los bebés captan las diferencias entre los sonidos. • Los bebés pueden dejar de llorar cuando oyen la voz de un adulto conocido. • Los bebés prefieren oír hablar cuando se les habla a ellos de forma directa. • Los bebés escuchan cuando un adulto les habla o les canta mientras los mira. • Los bebés lloran cuando sienten dolor, tienen hambre o están afligidos. • A los 2 meses de edad, los bebés tienen llantos específicos de hambre y dolor. • Los bebés "arrullan" (producen sonidos vocálicos suaves). • Hacia el final de este período, los bebés sonríen y se ríen. • Los bebés miran fijamente imágenes interesantes en libros.	Brenda sostenía a Jordán de manera que pudieran mirarse a los ojos. Jordán arrulló suavemente y Brenda le arrulló también. Luego, ella esperó a que Jordán lo volviera a hacer. Érica le sonrió de oreja a oreja a su padre cuando él la levantó de la cuna.
4 a 8 meses (bebé)	
• Los bebés giran la cabeza hacia un ruido, o una persona que dice su nombre. • A los bebés les gusta que los adultos hablen, canten y se rían con ellos. • Los bebés vocalizan con la intención de obtener una respuesta del adulto. • Los bebés dan chillidos agudos. • Los bebés practican sus sonidos cuando exploran y cuando están con adultos conocidos. • Los bebés comienzan a balbucear; al principio una consonante y luego combinaciones de dos consonantes. • Los bebés participan en conversaciones turnándose con los adultos. • Los bebés miran distintas imágenes de un libro y se emocionan cuando ven una que les gusta o cuando les gusta el tono entusiasta del adulto que lee.	Mientras sostenía a Donovan en su regazo, Daniela, la maestra del bebé, señalaba con el dedo las imágenes del libro de tapas de cartón. "Mira," dijo señalando la imagen, "una pelota." Luego dijo "Ahí está tu pelota" y señaló hacia una pelota en el piso. Donovan miró la imagen, luego la pelota en el piso y finalmente volvió a mirar la imagen. "Tt" dijo Afi cuando estaba en brazos de su maestra mirándola. "Tada" le dijo la maestra. "Tt" repitió Afi cuando le tocó hablar en la conversación.

Interacción entre Maestra-Niño, o Padre/Madre-Niño	Ambiente

0 a 4 meses (bebé)

- Use lenguaje dirigido al bebé.
- Tenga a los bebés en brazos y hábleles suavemente. Mírelos largamente a los ojos mientras baila conversando. Respete al bebé si necesita un descanso y aparta la cabeza.
- Lea libros con frases rítmicas y con una sola imagen en una página, con 2 imágenes a los de 4 meses de edad.
- Interprete los eructos, llantos, bostezos, estiramientos y sonidos de los bebés como formas de comunicación. Diga "Ah, me estás diciendo que tienes sueño."
- Cante canciones de cuna y otras canciones.
- Sea un compañero de lenguaje que se identifique y comente los sentimientos del bebé.
- Diga palabras y produzca sonidos para consolar a los bebés.

- El mejor ambiente son los brazos de un adulto afectuoso que tenga al bebé en brazos y le hable suavemente.
- Suministre juguetes que produzcan sonidos agradables. Sostenga con cuidado el juguete e intercambie sonidos con el bebé.
- Suministre materiales interesantes para tocar mientras comenta las texturas.
- Coloque espejos bajos a lo largo de una pared. Los bebés se miran y es posible que produzcan sonidos.

4 a 8 meses (bebé)

- Use lenguaje dirigido al bebé.
- Hable a menudo con los bebés. Muéstreles objetos y personas nuevos y nómbrelos.
- Repita los sonidos que los bebés producen y espere a que repitan el sonido (turnarse).
- Refiérase a varios artículos conocidos, tales como "leche" o "perro," con lenguaje de señas.
- Cante canciones y haga juegos de dedos.
- Describa con palabras los sentimientos de los niños expresados a través de gestos, posturas corporales y sonidos.
- Léale libros sencillos con una o dos imágenes por página. Señale con el dedo las imágenes mientras dice el nombre de la imagen.
- Léale los mismos libros una y otra vez.
- Aplique estrategias de atención conjunta—señale con el dedo un juguete o una imagen de un libro diciendo el nombre o hablando al respecto.

- Suministre juguetes y materiales interesantes para que los bebés los manipulen y examinen.
- Suministre libros de cartón con asas para que pueden gatear hasta ellos y tomarlos.
- Los libros con asas animan a los bebés a llevarlos.
- Haga un libro de imágenes de te veo, no te veo pegando un pedazo de tela sobre cada imagen.
- Forme un rincón de lectura acogedor donde las maestras puedan estar cómodas y leer a los bebés.
- Suministre cajas de sonido (bien selladas) con distintos objetos adentro que produzcan distintos sonidos al sacudirlas.
- Incorpore títeres al ambiente. Úselos a veces para "hablar" con el niño. Coloque los títeres en la mano del niño y espere a ver lo que el niño dice o hace.

Desarrollo	Ejemplo

8 a 12 meses (bebé móvil)

- Los bebés móviles comienzan a participar en juegos sociales tales como el *te veo, no te veo* o el *"así de grande."*
- A los bebés les gusta escuchar juegos de sonidos (rimas), canciones y juegos de dedos.
- El balbuceo continúa desarrollándose con sílabas combinadas tales como "dada," "mama," "nana" y "tutu" y a esta altura el bebé puede usar estos sonidos específicamente para referirse a su mamá o su papá.
- Los bebés repiten sonidos consistentemente para referirse a un objeto, una persona o un animal.
- Si oyen otro lenguaje *con* un adulto a través de estrategias conversacionales interactivas, los bebés pueden "tener una actitud abierta hacia los sonidos de un lenguaje extranjero."
- Los bebés pueden comenzar a decir palabras aisladas.
- Al final de este período, los bebés pueden comenzar a señalar con el dedo para atraer la atención de un adulto.
- Los bebés emplean expresiones faciales y gestos tales como agitar la cabeza o los brazos para que los tomen en brazos, y así comunicarse con los adultos o con sus compañeros.

Ejemplo: Una de las primeras palabras de Dana fue "mamá," y la repetía una y otra vez cuando veía a su madre.

Una de las primera palabras de Trishanna fue "mamá," y la repetía con entusiasmo una y otra vez cuando veía a su madre.

12 a 18 meses (bebé móvil)

- Los bebés móviles pueden seguir instrucciones sencillas tales como "Ven aquí" o "Trae tus zapatos" sin que haya que hacer gestos.
- Los bebés móviles pueden jugar socialmente sin que haya que demostrar la acción. Por ejemplo, cuando usted dice "Dile adiós" ellos mueven las manos aunque usted no les muestre cómo hacerlo.
- Los bebés móviles señalan con el dedo para llamar la atención de los adultos y de sus compañeros.
- Se puede producir un aprendizaje rápido de palabras—una explosión de lenguaje—en los niños que están aprendiendo muchas palabras nuevas.
- Hacia el final de este período, los bebés móviles combinan palabras.
- Los bebés móviles farfullan (hilando muchos sonidos) con la misma entonación que los adultos.
- Los bebés móviles hacen gestos y se valen de palabras para rechazar, pedir, comentar, negarse, exigir y nombrar objetos y personas.
- Los bebés móviles se valen del lenguaje para mantener una interacción o conversación con un adulto o uno de sus compañeros.

Ejemplo: La maestra de Janina le dijo "Juguemos a dar palmitas, palmitas," y Janina comenzó a aplaudir.

Ross miró a su maestra con expectación, farfullando muchos sonidos juntos como si le hiciera una pregunta.

Interacción entre Maestra-Niño, o Padre/Madre–Niño	Ambiente

8 a 12 meses (bebé móvil)

- Organice juegos conocidos tales como te veo—no te veo, palmitas—palmitas o *"¿cómo eres de grande?"*
- Responda con palabras a la comunicación no verbal de los bebés.
- Observe y espere a que los bebés inicien sonidos o palabras.
- Imite los sonidos y luego expanda, detalle y amplíe el lenguaje del bebé.
- Modele el siguiente paso en el desarrollo del lenguaje.
- Emplee hablarse a sí mismo y hablar en paralelo.
- Hable a menudo de manera receptiva con un vocabulario variado. No bombardee al niño con palabras.
- Lea los libros con entusiasmo—cambiando el tono de su voz con los distintos personajes.
- Hable sobre las imágenes y el cuento a medida que lee. Involucre a los bebés con la voz y los gestos.
- Mientras miran una imagen, espere a que el bebé produzca sonidos, señale con el dedo o haga expresiones faciales.

- Cree un rincón de lectura acogedor en que los bebés puedan alcanzar fácilmente los libros y manipularlos.
- Haga un libro "Todo sobre mí"—álbumes pequeños de fotos para cada niño con imágenes de ellos, su familia, sus juguetes preferidos, sus compañeros, sus maestras y los animales domésticos de la familia. Déjelos al alcance de los niños. Cambie las imágenes a medida que el niño crece.
- Los juguetes musicales para empujar animan a los bebés a manipularlos y producir sonidos.

12 a 18 meses (bebé móvil)

- Mantenga el tema en una conversación con un bebé móvil. Vea cuántas veces hablará el niño.
- Responda a la entonación del parloteo del niño. Por ejemplo, si parece que el niño hace una pregunta, responda a lo que usted cree que el niño puede estar preguntando.
- Responda con palabras a las señales hechas con los dedos y otros medios de comunicación no verbal de los bebés móviles.
- Describa y compare con palabras tamaños, formas y sonidos.
- Cuando un bebé móvil dice palabras tales como "Yo salto," modele el próximo paso en el desarrollo del lenguaje diciendo "Tú estás saltando," añadiendo "ando o iendo" a la palabra. Haga esto tanto con el contenido de las palabras como con la estructura de las palabras u oraciones.
- Léale libros con cuentos más largos, haga pausas a medida que avanza por el libro para animar a los bebés móviles a hablar sobre las imágenes y el cuento.

- Introduzca materiales de arte tales como plastilina, arcilla y pintura.
- Déle rollos de toallas de papel a los bebés móviles para que produzcan sonidos.
- Los juguetes musicales para jalar animan a los bebés móviles a caminar y jalarlos o empujarlos.
- Las cajas de música resistentes animan a los bebés móviles a apretar botones para "hacer música."
- Se pueden poner a disposición tambores y otros instrumentos musicales.
- Incorpore un reproductor de CD resistente con un cuento que haya grabado el padre o la madre.
- Grabe las voces de los bebés móviles con una grabadora y haga que las escuchen.
- Suministre materiales para hacer burbujas.
- Facilite espacios para animar a dos o tres niños a conversar con sus compañeros.

Desarrollo	Ejemplo

18 a 24 meses (niño pequeño)

- Los niños pequeños pueden ir a buscar juguetes conocidos en otra habitación de la casa cuando un adulto se los pide, y pueden seguir instrucciones tales como "cierra la puerta."
- Los niños pequeños combinan palabras para nombrar cosas ("ese gato"), para negar ("no muerde") y para rechazar ("no más").
- Los niños pequeños combinan dos o tres palabras con significado.
- Los niños pequeños se valen del lenguaje para varios propósitos, tales como preguntar "¿Qué eso?"
- Los niños pequeños señalan una cantidad de imágenes cada vez mayor en los libros cuando un adulto les habla sobre la imagen.

"Hola Kitty," "puerta abierta" y "sombrero puesto" fueron sólo algunas de las combinaciones de dos palabras que Cheral dijo a los 20 meses de edad.

Tyra corrió rápidamente hasta el librero, tomó un libro con tapa brillante y regresó de prisa hasta su maestra. Después de sentarse cómodamente en su regazo, abrió el libro y comenzó a señalar con entusiasmo las imágenes mientras su maestra las nombraba.

24 a 36 meses (niño pequeño)

- Los niños pequeños comprenden instrucciones complejas y recuerdan palabras de canciones cortas y juegos de dedos.
- Los niños pequeños se valen de muchas oraciones de dos a cuatro palabras.
- Los niños pequeños pueden señalar con el dedo y nombrar muchas partes del cuerpo.
- Los niños pequeños añaden "ando o iendo" a las palabras.
- Los niños pequeños comienzan a usar preposiciones tales como "sobre" y "dentro."
- Los niños pequeños añaden una "s" a las palabras para indicar plurales.
- Los niños pequeños podrían empezar a preguntar "¿Por qué?"
- Los niños pequeños comienzan a contar historias sobre lo que hicieron o lo que vieron.
- Hacia el final de este período, el niño pequeño puede usar las imágenes para contar lo que ocurre en un cuento.

Mindy comenzó a añadir "ando o iendo" a las palabras que había estado diciendo durante meses. Dijo "Yo corriendo" y "Yo comiendo" en vez de "Yo corro" y "Yo como."

"Mira, está jugando," exclamó Treat mientras señalaba con el dedo una imagen en su libro preferido.

Interacción entre Maestra-Niño, o Padre/Madre-Niño	Ambiente

18 a 24 meses (niño pequeño)

• Léale libros con cuentos más largos, haga pausas a medida que avanza por el libro para animar a los niños pequeños a hablar sobre las imágenes y la historia. Haga preguntas abiertas tales como "¿Cómo se siente el oso?" • Pregúntese a menudo con el niño: "Me pregunto qué va a pasar con el oso." • Haga que los niños pequeños conversen intentando mantenerse en el mismo tema que el niño. • Introduzca nuevas conversaciones sobre objetos y acontecimientos interesantes.	• Disponga una pista de obstáculos complicada y use palabras tales como "adentro," "afuera," "por arriba," "a través," "alrededor," "arriba" y "abajo" mientras el niño pequeño recorre la pista. • Suministre libros nuevos todas las semanas, pero mantenga cerca los libros preferidos de los niños. • Suministre una mayor variedad de materiales de arte. • Déle materiales que estimulen los sentidos.

24 a 36 meses (niño pequeño)

• Responda sus preguntas de "por qué" con paciencia y entusiasmo. Así es como los niños aprenden y desarrollan interacciones sociales. • Escuche con sus ojos las "historias" que los niños pequeños cuentan. • Modele decir palabras plurales, tales como "perros," "elefantes," etc. • Use palabras descriptivas tales como "queso mozarella" en vez de sólo "queso" o "urraca de América" en vez de sólo "pájaro." • Tenga conversaciones largas con los niños pequeños, siguiendo lo que dicen. • Lea libros a grupos informales pequeños o a niños por separado.	• Déle imágenes para que los niños las hagan corresponder. • Los rompecabezas de animales, personas, vehículos y alimentos son importantes. • Se pueden agregar al ambiente libros con muchas imágenes y cuentos cortos. • Los materiales para el juego dramático estimulan la conversación.

Tendencias de desarrollo e interacciones receptivas (Capítulo 10)

Los bebés y los niños pequeños desarrollan capacidades motrices para la locomoción, el uso de herramientas y la coordinación de información perceptiva con acciones motrices.

Desarrollo	Ejemplo
0 a 4 meses (bebé)	
• Los bebés levantan la cabeza cuando los llevan en brazos contra el hombro; sostienen la cabeza firme y erguida.	Rosie mantuvo la cabeza erguida y miró a su alrededor a los otros niños mientras Sharon la llevaba contra el hombro.
• Boca abajo, los bebés levantan la cabeza y los hombros y pueden sostener un juguete en la mano.	Robert, boca abajo sobre una manta, levantó la cabeza para mirarse al espejo montado a nivel del suelo en la pared.
• Los bebés giran la cabeza hacia una voz conocida.	Jen tenía un sonajero en la mano, pero no parecía darse cuenta de que lo tenía.
• Los bebés se quedan quietos para prestar atención; se contonean y se mueven para inducir la continuación de la interacción.	Filipe se llevó los dedos a la boca y se los chupó mientras miraba atentamente a los niños pequeños.
• De espaldas, los bebés estiran los brazos y las piernas a manera de juego.	
• Estando de lado, los bebés se dan vuelta para quedar de espaldas.	
• Los bebés sujetan un dedo o un juguete liviano con agarre reflejo.	
• Los bebés se chupan los dedos, las manos y otros objetos.	
• Los bebés mueven los brazos y las piernas.	
4 a 8 meses (bebé)	
• Los bebés de espaldas se ponen de lado y luego se vuelven a poner de espaldas.	Estando de espaldas, Micky rueda para quedar boca abajo y alcanzar un juguete, luego vuelve a rodar para jugar con el juguete.
• Al final de este período, los bebés se sientan; primero con apoyo pero luego estables y solos.	A Erin, sentada sola establemente, le gusta recoger objetos con las dos manos y examinarlos.
• Los bebés se estiran para alcanzar objetos con el brazo.	A Freddy le gusta que lo tomen en brazos mientras toma su biberón, aunque insiste en sujetarlo solo.
• Los bebés agarran rastrillando.	
• Los bebés gatean.	
• Los bebés sacuden, golpean, sujetan y sueltan objetos.	
• Los bebés se pasan objetos de una mano a otra.	
• Los bebés pueden sostener su biberón.	
• Los bebés se pueden llevar objetos a la boca.	
8 a 12 meses (bebé móvil)	
• Los bebés móviles jalan de algo para ponerse de pie.	Hershel gatea hasta su maestra, luego se agarra de su pierna y jala para ponerse de pie.
• Los bebés móviles se pasean.	Jem se sienta a la mesa del almuerzo, y alterna la cuchara y los dedos para disfrutar de la comida.
• Los bebés móviles se quedan de pie solos.	
• Los bebés móviles caminan con ayuda al principio y después solos.	
• Los bebés móviles se sientan en una silla.	
• Los bebés móviles comen con los dedos.	
• Los bebés móviles pueden usar una cuchara y un vaso hermético.	
• Los bebés móviles agarran atenazando.	

Interacción entre Maestra-Niño, o Padre/Madre–Niño	Ambiente

0 a 4 meses (bebé)

- Cambie la posición del bebé; a veces de espaldas, otras boca abajo. Cuando lleve en brazos al bebé, acúnelo en sus brazos o sosténgalo erguido contra el hombro.
- Cuando el bebé está en el piso, acuéstese cara a cara junto a él.
- Cuando la bebé está de espaldas y trata de alcanzar un juguete un poco más allá de su cabeza, sosténgale el tronco mientras rueda.

- Una manta rígida (contra el riesgo de asfixia) en el suelo da espacio para los primeros movimientos.
- Los juguetes pequeños e interesantes, las imágenes, y los libros para mirar cuando quieran animan a los bebés a levantar la cabeza. Un espejo atornillado a la pared a nivel del suelo siempre ofrece algo interesante que mirar.
- A medida que comienzan a estirarse para alcanzar, a los bebés les gustan las barras estables con juguetes colgantes que puedan batear, alcanzar y agarrar.

4 a 8 meses (bebé)

- Quédese cerca del bebé que recién comienza a sentarse solo.
- Conozca el avance del desarrollo motor; anime emocionalmente y apoye físicamente al bebé en sus nuevos intentos.
- Crea en los beneficios a largo plazo para la salud de un estilo de vida activo.

- Deles lugares seguros para rodar, sentarse y gatear. Proteja a los bebés de cualquier cosa que pueda caerles encima.
- Deles objetos livianos pequeños y lavables (grandes para evitar que se asfixien) para que los manipulen y los lancen, y deles recipientes para los objetos.

8 a 12 meses (bebé móvil)

- Esté atenta para saber cuándo ayudar al bebé que comienza a caminar y cuándo dejar que lo siga intentando.
- Dé tiempo para que los bebés mayores practiquen comer solos.

- Lugares seguros para ponerse de pie apoyándose en algo.
- Juguetes para empujar y jalar para que los que comienzan a caminar puedan jalar y empujar.
- Cajas mecánicas.
- Libros de cartón para pasar las páginas, levantar las solapas y meter los dedos a través de los agujeros.

Desarrollo	Ejemplo

12 a 18 meses (bebé móvil)

- Los bebés móviles apilan y alinean bloques.
- Los bebés móviles pueden vestirse y desvestirse solos, meter el brazo en una manga y el pie dentro de un zapato.
- Los bebés móviles pueden caminar.
- Los bebés móviles caminan con objetos en las manos.
- Los bebés móviles suben escaleras.

Gary se paró frente a la mesa y construyó cuidadosamente con las dos manos una torre con bloques de colores.

Michelle caminó por la habitación con su osito de peluche en una mano y su manta en la otra.

18 a 24 meses (niño pequeño)

- Los niños pequeños señalan objetos con el dedo para comunicarse.
- Los niños pequeños hacen marcas en un papel.
- Los niños pequeños trabajan y dan forma a la plastilina.
- Los niños pequeños corren.
- Los niños pequeños se sientan y se levantan solos de sillas pequeñas.
- Los niños pequeños están desarrollando su confianza espacial; explorando su cuerpo en el espacio.

Mindy estiró la plastilina con las manos y luego hizo figuras con las herramientas.

Joseph se sentó a la mesa para comer, luego llevó los platos sucios al fregadero.

24 a 36 meses (niño pequeño)

- Los niños pequeños ensartan cuentas, usan las tijeras, pintan con los dedos o con pinceles, arman rompecabezas sencillos.
- Los niños pequeños lanzan y patean una pelota.
- Los niños pequeños se paran en un solo pie.
- Los niños pequeños se paran y caminan en puntillas.
- Los niños pequeños suben escaleras poniendo un pie en cada escalón.
- Los niños pequeños trepan, se deslizan y saltan.
- Los niños pequeños comen con cuchara y tenedor.
- Los niños pequeños se pueden vestir solos.
- Los niños pequeños pueden verter leche de una jarra pequeña.

Robert ni siquiera tiene que pensar en su cuerpo cuando corre para saludar a su papá al final del día.

Peggy y Misha inventan un juego imitándose mutuamente los pasos en puntillas, posturas y gestos.

Forcejeando un poco, Lawrence y Evelyn juegan con la ropa para disfrazarse.

Interacciones entre el niño y la maestra, el padre o la madre	Ambiente

12 a 18 meses (bebé móvil)

- Imite la cada vez mayor variedad de movimientos del bebé. - Introduzca canciones con pequeños bailes y movimientos. - Dé tiempo y tenga paciencia mientras el niño pequeño practica ponerse solo la chaqueta.	- Juguetes para montar estables y no muy altos. - Juguetes mecedores estables y no muy altos. - Juegos de manipulación basados en habilidades, tales como apilar vasos o ensartar aros en un palo.

18 a 24 meses (niño pequeño)

- Ponga a disposición de los niños materiales pequeños que los induzcan a poner en práctica su creciente capacidad de manipulación de objetos con los dedos. - Quédese con los niños pequeños y apóyelos mientras intentan poner en práctica capacidades recientemente desarrolladas. - Deles oportunidades de trepar, caminar y correr.	- Materi.ales de arte tales como brochas gordas, marcadores y superficies grandes para pintar. - Articulos pequeños, tales como cuentas que se interconectan y tableros para clavijas, para practicar actividades de manipulación. - Mucho espacio para el movimiento: bailes, juguetes para montar, estructuras para trepar, toboganes.

24 a 36 meses (niño pequeño)

- Esté consciente del equilibrio necesario entre el tiempo dedicado a actividades enérgicas y a actividades tranquilas. - Esté atento al aumento de precisión de las capacidades motrices ligeras, pues pueden comenzar a manifestarse sutiles problemas. - Esté a disposición de los niños pequeños animándolos y teniéndoles paciencia conforme comen, se visten y van al baño solos con más frecuencia.	- Ponga a su disposición una variedad de materiales para practicar capacidades motrices ligeras: rompecabezas simples, cajas de formas, cuentas para hacer collares, bloques de mesa, arcilla, materiales de arte. - Espacio, oportunidad y estructuras para fomentar el movimiento: períodos de tiempo al aire libre, carreras de obstáculos, bailes y juguetes para montar.

Appendix D

Planning Guides

Directions for Using the Planning Guides

Individual Child Planning Guides

1. **Choose which individual child planning guide you would like to use**. Version 1 divides the reflect section into developmental domains, whereas Version 2 provides a space under the reflect section for you to write a sentence or two about the child's development that integrates the domains.

2. **Choose the child or children to observe during the week**. In a center program, teachers decide which children each teacher will observe during the week. In a center using a primary caregiving system, each teacher will complete a guide on her primary group children. In a family child care home, the teacher can choose several children to observe during a particular week. For a home visiting program, the home visitor completes the guide with the family.

3. **Complete the respect section.** For both versions, each teacher writes an anecdotal record; uses a photograph (or series of photographs) of the child involved with the teacher, peers, equipment, toys, materials, and experiences; or uses other documentation (e.g., an example of the child's scribbling). You can attach these to the page.

4. **Complete the reflect section**. This section is completed by you, with other teachers, and/or with family members. When completing the section "What am I doing?", objectively describe the behavior represented under the respect section. You could use the chart of concepts and the Developmental Trends and Responsive Interaction charts found in Chapters 6 through 10 and the Concept table in Chapter 13 to help you complete "What am I learning?" For Version 1, describe what concepts the child is exploring and/or describe development. For Version 2, describe what concepts the child is exploring and what the child may be thinking.

5. **Complete the relate section**. This section is completed by you, with other teachers, and/or with family members. In both versions, decide what interactions and changes in the environment are responsive to the concepts the child is exploring and the development observed.

6. **Create a portfolio for each child and include the individual child planning guides**. Use them to reflect on changes in the child's interests and the child's developmental progress over time. Give the portfolios to the family of the child when the child changes rooms or when the child leaves the program.

Group Planning Guides

1. **Complete the individually responsive group planning guide with other teachers and/or with family members**. Each teacher in a center-based program brings her completed individual child planning guides to a team meeting. The team discusses the information from the individual guides and then completes the group guide by summarizing the concepts and developmental efforts of the individual children observed that week. You could use resource books that provide ideas about interactions, equipment, and experiences and then choose opportunities that are responsive to the individual children and the group. Provide the opportunities during the following week.

2. **Complete the group planning for routines guide each month.**

Individual Child Planning Guide: Version 1

Child's Name: _____   Plans for Week of (Date):_____

Person Completing the Guide: _____

Respect: Child's Emotions, Effort, Goals, Learning, and Relationships

Write an observation or use a picture or other documentation here—date all notes:

Respect and Reflect	Relate
	What will you do to support my development and learning?
What am I doing?	*Responsive Interactions*
How am I feeling?	
What am I learning? • *Emotional*	*Environment, Toys, Materials, and Experiences*
• *Social*	
• *Cognitive*	
• *Language*	
• *Motor*	

Individual Child Planning Guide: Version 2

Child's Name: _____   Plans for Week of (Date): _____

Person(s) Completing the Guide: _____

Respect: Child's Emotions, Effort, Goals, Learning, and Relationships

Write an observation or use a picture or other documentation here—date all notes:

Reflect

What am I doing?

How am I feeling?

What am I learning?

Relate

What will you do to support my development and learning?

Responsive Interactions

Environment, Toys, Materials, and Experiences

Individually Responsive Group Planning Guide

Name of Children in Group: _____

Week of: _____

Person(s) Completing This Guide: _____

_____

Respect and Reflect

(Use information from the individual planning guides.)

Relate: Plans for the Week to Meet Children's Interests and Needs

Songs/Finger-Plays

Stories/Books

Responsive Interactions

Environment, Toys, Materials, and Opportunities

Experiences with Families

Special Experiences

Group Planning for Routines

Name of Children in Group:_____

Week of: _____

Person(s) Completing This Form: _____

Developing a caring community: Think about what is happening and what could happen to develop a relationship-based program for children, families, and teachers.

Routine	What is going well for the children, families, and teachers?	What could we do to improve the experience for children, families, and teachers?
Greeting time or good-bye time		
Feeding infants and toddler eating times		
Infant sleep and toddler nap time		
Diapering		
Toileting		
Play times		
Outdoor times		
Transitions		
Summary		

References

Chapter 1

1. Erickson, M. F., & Kurz-Riemer, K. (1999). *Infants, toddlers and families: A framework for support and intervention.* New York: Guilford Press.

2. Johnston, M. V. (2009). Plasticity in the developing brain: Implications for rehabilitation. *Mental Disabilities Research Reviews, 15,* 94–101.

3. Center on the Developing Child. (2016). *Toxic stress.* Retrieved from *http://developingchild.harvard.edu*

4. ChildTrauma Academy. (2016). *Brain development and neuroscience.* Retrieved from *http://childtrauma.org/cta-library/brain-dev-neuroscience/*

5. Spelke, E. S. (2002). Developmental neuroimaging: A developmental psychologist looks ahead. *Developmental Science, 5*(3), 392–396.

6. Thompson, R. A. (2016). What more has been learned? The science of early childhood development 15 years after *Neurons to Neighborhoods. ZERO TO THREE Journal, 36*(3), 18–25.

7. National Scientific Council on the Developing Child. (2010). *Early experiences can alter gene expression and affect long-term development: Working paper 10.* Retrieved from *www.developingchild.harvard.edu*

8. National Scientific Council on the Developing Child. (2010). *Persistent fear and anxiety can affect young children's learning and development: Working paper 9.* Retrieved from *www.developingchild.harvard.edu*

9. Saffron, J. R. (2003). Statistical language learning: Mechanisms and constraints. *Current Directions in Psychological Science, 12*(4), 110–114.

10. Meltzoff, A. N., Kuhl, P. K., Movellan, J., & Sejnowski, T. J. (2009). Foundations for a new science of learning. *Science, 325,* 284–288. doi:10.1126/science.1175626

11. Meltzoff, A. N., & Kuhl, P. K. (2016). Exploring the infant social brain: What's going on in there? *ZERO TO THREE Journal, 36*(3), 2–9.

12. Moffitt, T. E., Arseneault, L., Belsky, D., Dickson, N., Hancox, R. J., Harrington, H., . . . Caspi, A. (2011). A gradient of childhood self-control predicts health, wealth, and public safety. *PNAS Proceedings of the National Academy of Sciences of the United States of America, 108*(7), 2693–2698. doi:10.1073/pnas.1010076108

13. Sektnan, M., McClelland, M. M., Acock, A., & Morrison, F. J. (2010). Relations between early family risk, children's behavioral regulation, and academic achievement. *Early Childhood Research Quarterly, 25*(4), 464–479.

14. Gonzalez-Mena, J. (2008). *Diversity in early care and education: Honoring differences* (5th ed.). Washington, DC: National Association for the Education of Young Children.

15. Small, M. F. (1998). *Our babies, ourselves: How biology and culture shape the way we parent.* New York: Anchor.

16. Waxman, S. R., Fu, X., Ferguson, B., Geraghty, K., Leddon, E., Liang, J., & Zhao, M. F. (2016). How early is infants' attention to objects and actions shaped by culture? New evidence from 24 month olds raised in the US and China. *Frontiers in Psychology, 7.*

17. Cassidy, J., & Shaver, P. R. (2008). *Handbook of attachment* (2nd ed.). Guilford Press.

18. Hinde, R., & Stevenson-Hinde, J. (1987). Interpersonal relationships and child development. *Developmental Review, 7,* 1–21.

19. Bronfenbrenner, U. (1979). *The ecology of human development.* Cambridge, MA: Harvard University Press.

20. Bronfenbrenner, U. (1986). Ecology of the family as a context for human development: Research perspectives. *Developmental Psychology, 22*(6), 723–741.

21. Bronfenbrenner, U. (1994). Who cares for the children. In H. Nuba, M. Searson, & D. L. Sheiman (Eds.), *Resources for early childhood: A handbook* (pp.113–129). New York: Garland.

22. Bronfenbrenner, U. (Ed). (2004). *Making human beings human: Bioecological perspectives on human development.* Thousand Oaks, CA: Sage.

23. Gonzalez-Mena, J. (2008). *Diversity in early care and education: Honoring differences* (5th ed.). Washington, DC: National Association for the Education of Young Children.

24. Barrera, I., & Corso, R. (2003). *Skilled dialogue: Strategies for responding to cultural diversity in early childhood.* Baltimore, MD: Brookes.

25. Sameroff, A. J., & Feise, B. H. (2000). Transactional regulation: The development ecology of early intervention. In J. P. Shonkoff & S. J. Meisels (Eds.), *Handbook of early childhood intervention* (2nd ed., pp. 135–159). New York: Cambridge University Press.

26. Child Welfare Information Gateway (2016). *Preventing child abuse & neglect.* Retrieved from *https://www.childwelfare.gov/topics/preventing/*

27. Gunnar, M., & Cheatham, C. L. (2003). Brain and behavior interface: Stress and the developing brain. *Infant Mental Health Journal, 24*(3), 195–211.

28. Drake, K., Fearon, R. M. P., & Belsky, J. (2014). From early attachment to engagement with learning in school:

The role of self-regulation and persistence. *Developmental Psychology, 50*(5), 1350–1361.

29. Gunnar, M. R., & Quevedo, K. (2007). The neurobiology of stress and development. *Annual Review of Psychology, 58*(1), 145.

30. Booth-Laforce, C., Oh, W., Kim, A. H., Rubin, K. H., Rose-Krasnor, L., & Burgess, K. (2006). Attachment, self-worth, and peer-group functioning in middle childhood. *Attachment & Human Development, 8*(4), 309–325. doi:10.1080/14616730601048209

31. Ibid.

32. Verissimo, M., Santos, A. J., Vaughn, B. E., Torres, N., Monteiro, L., & Santos, O. (2011). Quality of attachment to father and mother and number of reciprocal friends. *Early Child Development and Care, 181*(1), 27–38.

33. Mcquaid, N. E., Bibok, M. B., & Carpendale, J. I. M. (2009). Relation between maternal contingent responsiveness and infant social expectations. *Infancy, 14*(3), 390–401. doi:10.1080/15250000902839955

34. Kok, R., van IJzendoorn, M. H., Linting, M., Bakermans-Kranenburg, M., Tharner, A., Luijk, M. P. C. M., . . . Tiemeier, H. (2013). Attachment insecurity predicts child active resistance to parental requests in a compliance task. *Child: Care, Health & Development, 39*(2), 277–287. doi:10.1111/j.1365-2214.2012.01374.x

35. Kochanska, G., & Kim, S. (2012). Toward a new understanding of legacy of early attachments for future antisocial trajectories: Evidence from two longitudinal studies. *Development and Psychopathology, 24*(3), 783–806.

36. Tharner, A., Luijk, M. P. C. M., van IJzendoorn, M. H., Bakermans-Kranenburg, M., Jaddoe, V. W. V., Hofman, A., . . . Tiemeier, H. (2012). Infant attachment, parenting stress, and child emotional and behavioral problems at age 3 years. *Parenting: Science & Practice, 12*(4), 261–281.

37. Kochanska, G., Woodard, J., Kim, S., Koenig, J. L., Jeung, E. Y., & Barry, R. A. (2010). Positive socialization mechanisms in secure and insecure parent–child dyads: Two longitudinal studies. *Journal of Child Psychology & Psychiatry, 51*(9), 998–1009.

38. Abraham, M. M., & Kerns, K. A. (2013). Positive and negative emotions and coping as mediators of mother-child attachment and peer relationships. *Merrill-Palmer Quarterly, 59*(4), 399–425.

39. de Wolff, M. S., & van IJzendoorn, M. H. (1997). Sensitivity and attachment: A meta-analysis on parental antecedents of infant attachment. *Child Development, 68,* 571–591.

40. Beijersbergen, M. D., Juffer, F., Nakermans-Konenburg, M., & van IJzendoorn, M.H. (2012). Remaining or becoming secure: Parental sensitive support predicts attachment security from infancy to adolescence in a longitudinal adoption study. *Developmental Psychology, 48,* 1277–1283.

41. Finger, B., Hans, S. L., Bernstein, V. J., & Cox, S. M. (2009). Parent relationship quality and infant-mother attachment. *Attachment & Human Development, 11*(3), 285–306. doi:10.1080/14616730902814960

42. Ziv, Y., Aviezer, O., Gini, M., Sagi, A., & Koren-Karie, N. (2000). Emotional availability in the mother-infant dyad as related to the quality of infant-mother attachment relationship. *Attachment & Human Development, 2,* 149–169.

43. Biringen, Z. (2009). *The universal language of love: Assessing relationships through the science of emotional availability.* EA Press.

44. Philbrook, L. E., Hozella, A. C., Kim, B., Jian, N., Shimizu, M., & Teti, D. M. (2014). Maternal emotional availability at bedtime and infant cortisol at 1 and 3 months. *Early Human Development, 90*(10), 595–605. doi:10.1016/j.earlhumdev.2014.05.014

45. NICHD Early Child Care Research Network. (2004). Father's and mother's parenting behavior and beliefs as predictors of child social adjustment in the transition to school. *Journal of Family Psychology, 18*(4), 628–638.

46. Eshel, N., Daelman, B., de Mello, M., & Martines, J. (2006). Responsive parenting: interventions and outcomes. *Bulletin Of The World Health Organization, 84*(12), 991–998.

47. Mcquaid, N. E., Bibok, M. B., & Carpendale, J. I. M. (2009). Relationship between maternal contingent responsiveness and infant social expectations. *Infancy, 14*(3), 390–401.

48. Brophy-Herb, H., Schiffman, R. F., Bocknek, E. L., Dupuis, S. B., Fitzgerald, H.E., Horodynski, M., Onaga, E., Van Egeren, L., & Hillaker, B. (2011). Toddlers' social-emotional competence in the contexts of maternal emotion socialization and contingent responsiveness in a low-income sample. *Social Development, 20*(1), 73–92.

49. Howes, C., Phillips, D., & Whitebook, M. (1992). Thresholds of quality: Implications for the social development of children in center-based child care. *Child Development, 63,* 449–460.

50. Howes, C., & Smith, E. (1995). Relations among child care quality, teacher behavior, children's play activities, emotional security, and cognitive activity in child care. *Early Childhood Research Quarterly, 10,* 381–404.

51. Howes, C., & Hamilton, C. E. (1992). Children's relationships with caregivers: Mothers and childcare teachers. *Child Development, 63,* 859–866.

52. De Schipper, J. C., Tavecchio, L. W. C., & Van IJzendoorn, M. H. (2008). Children's attachment relationships with daycare caregivers: Associations with positive caregiving

and the child's temperament. *Social Development, 17*(3), 454–470. doi:10.1111/j.1467-9507.2007.00448.x

53. Werner, E. E. (1993). Risk, resilience, and recovery: Perspectives from the Kauai longitudinal study. *Development and Psychopathology, 9*(4), 503–515.

54. Werner, E. E. (2000). The power of protective factors in the early years. *ZERO TO THREE, 20*(3), 3–5.

55. Werner, E. E. (1993). Risk, resilience, and recovery: Perspectives from the Kauai longitudinal study. *Development and Psychopathology, 9*(4), 503–515.

56. Werner, E. E. (2000). The power of protective factors in the early years. *ZERO TO THREE, 20*(3), 3–5.

57. Garbarino, J., & Ganzel, B. (2000). The human ecology of early risk. In J. P. Shonkoff & S. J. Meisels (Eds.), *Handbook of early childhood intervention* (2nd ed., pp. 76–93). New York: Cambridge University Press.

58. Ibid.

59. Sameroff, A. J. (1998). Management of clinical problems and emotional care: Environmental risk factors in infancy. *Pediatrics, 102*(5), 1287–1292.

60. Belsky, J., Bakermans-Kranenburg, M., & van IJzendoorn, M. H. (2007). For better and for worse: Differential susceptibility to environmental influences. *Current Directions in Psychological Science (Wiley-Blackwell), 16*(6), 300–304. doi:10.1111/j.1467-8721.2007.00525.x

61. Jiang, Y., Ekono, M., & Skinner, C. (2013). *Basic facts about low-income children: Children under 3 years, 2013.* Retrieved from National Center for Children in Poverty (2016) *http://www.nccp.org/publications/pub_1096.html*

62. National Center for Children in Poverty. (2016). Retrieved from *http://www.nccp.org*

63. Penn, H. (2005). *Unequal childhoods: Young children's lives in poor countries.* London: Routledge.

64. Delamonica, E., & Minujin, A. (2007). Incidence, depth and severity of children in poverty. *Social Indicators Research, 82,* 361–374.

65. Ibid.

66. UNICEF. (2008). *The state of the world's children 2008.* Retrieved from *www.unicef.org/publications/files/SOWC_2008_Exec_Summary_EN_042908.pdf*

67. Rouse, K. (1998). Infant and toddler resilience. *Early Childhood Education Journal, 26*(1), 47–52.

68. Breslin, D. (2005). Children's capacity to develop resiliency: How to nurture it. *Young Children, 60*(1), 47–57.

69. Werner, E. E. (1993). Risk, resilience, and recovery: Perspectives from the Kauai longitudinal study. *Development and Psychopathology, 9*(4), 503–515.

70. Werner, E. E. (2000). The power of protective factors in the early years. *ZERO TO THREE, 20*(3), 3–5.

71. Masten, A. S., & Motti-Stefanidi, F. (2008). Understanding and promoting resilience in children: Promotive and protective processes in schools. In T. Gutkin & C. Reynolds (Eds.), *The handbook of school psychology* (4th ed., pp. 721–738). New York: Wiley.

72. Sapienza, J., & Masten, A. S. (2011). Understanding and promoting resilience in children and youth. *Current Opinion in Psychiatry, 24*(4), 267–273.

73. Bureau of Labor Statistics. (2012). *Table 6. Employment status of mothers with own children under 3 years old by single year of age of youngest child and marital status, 2010–2011 annual averages.* Retrieved from *http://www.bls.gov/news.release/famee.t06.html*

74. Mother's day: More than candy and flowers, working parent's need paid time-off. (2002). Retrieved from *www.childpolicyintl.org/issuebrief/issuebrief5.html*

75. Helburn, S. W. (Ed.). (1995). *Cost, quality, and child outcomes in child care centers* [Technical report]. Denver: Department of Economics, Center for Research in Economic and Social Policy, University of Colorado–Denver.

76. NICHD Early Child Care Research Network. (2000). Characteristics and quality of child care for toddlers and preschoolers. *Applied Developmental Science, 4*(3), 116–135.

77. NICHD Early Child Care Research Network. (2000). The relation of child care to cognitive and language development. *Child Development, 71*(4), 960–980.

78. Shalala calls for a new era of support to families with infants and toddlers. (1995). *Children Today, 23*(3), 4–5.

79. U.S. Department of Health and Human Services. (2001). Early Head Start shows significant results for low income children and parents. Retrieved from *http://www.hhs.gov/news/pres/20010112.html*

80. Early Head Start Research and Evaluation Project. (1996–Current). Retrieved from *www.acf.hhs.gov/programs/opre/ehs/ehs_resrch/index.html*

81. Love, J. M., Kisker, E. E., Ross, C., Raikes, H., Constantine, J., Boller, K., . . . Vogel, C. (2005). The effectiveness of Early Head Start for 3-year-old children and their parents: Lessons for policy and programs. *Developmental Psychology, 41*(6), 885–901.

82. Early Head Start Research and Evaluation Project. (1996–Current). Retrieved from *www.acf.hhs.gov/programs/opre/ehs/ehs_resrch/index.html*

83. Love, J. M., Kisker, E. E., Ross, C., Raikes, H., Constantine, J., Boller, K., . . . Vogel, C. (2005). The effectiveness of Early Head Start for 3-year-old children and their parents: Lessons for policy and programs. *Developmental Psychology, 41*(6), 885–901.

84. Early Head Start Research and Evaluation Project. (1996–Current). Retrieved from *www.acf.hhs.gov/programs/opre/ehs/ehs_resrch/index.html*

85. Schmit, S. (2012). *Early head start participants, programs, families and staff in 2011*. Retrieved from *http://www.clasp.org/admin/site/publications/files/EHS-PIR-2011-Fact-Sheet.pdf*

86. Blasco, P. M. (2001). *Early intervention services for infants, toddlers, and their families*. Boston: Allyn & Bacon.

87. NECTAC (National Early Childhood Technical Assistance Center). (2012). *Annual appropriations and number of children*. Retrieved from *http://ectacenter.org/partc/partcdata.asp*

88. Raikes, H. (1993). Relationship duration in infant care: Time with a high-ability teacher and infant-teacher attachment. *Early Childhood Research Quarterly, 8*, 309–325.

89. NICHD Early Child Care Research Network. (2001). Non-maternal care and family factors in early development: An overview of the NICHD study of early child care. *Journal of Applied Developmental Psychology, 22*, 457–492.

90. Howes, C., & Hamilton, C. E. (1993). The changing experience of childcare: Changes in teacher and in teacher-child relationships and children's social competence with peers. *Early Childhood Research Quarterly, 8*, 15–30.

91. Horm, D., Norris, D., Perry, D., Chazan-Cohen, R., & Halle, T. (2016). *Developmental foundations of school readiness for infants and toddlers, A research to practice report, OPRE Report # 2016-07*, Washington, DC: Office of Planning, Research and Evaluation, Administration for Children and Families, U.S. Department of Health and Human Services.

92. Brazelton, T. B., & Greenspan, S. I. (2000). *The irreducible needs of children: What every child must have to grow, learn, and flourish*. New York: Perseus.

Chapter 2

1. Goodnow, J. J., Cashmore, J., Cotton, S., & Knight, R. (1984). Mothers' developmental timetables in two cultural groups. *International Journal of Psychology, 19*, 193–205.

2. Gopnik, A., Meltzoff, A. N., & Kuhl, P. K. (1999). *The scientist in the crib: Minds, brains, and how children learn*. New York: Morrow.

3. Shonkoff, J. P. (2011). Protecting brains, not simply stimulating minds. *Science, 333*(6045), 982–983.

4. Small, M. F. (1998). *Our babies, ourselves: How biology and culture shape the way we parent*. New York: Anchor.

5. Keller, H. (2002). Culture and development: Developmental pathways to individualism and interrelatedness. In W. J. Lonner, D. L. Dinnel, S. A. Hayes, & D. N. Sattler (Eds.), *Online Readings in Psychology and Culture* (Unit 11, Chapter 1). Bellingham, WA: Center for Cross-Cultural Research, Western Washington University. Retrieved from *http://www.wwu.edu/culture/keller.html*

6. Keller, H., Lamm, B., Abels, M., Yovsi, R. D., Borke, J., Jensen, H., . . . Chaudhary, N. (2006). Cultural models, socialization goals, and parenting ethnotheories: A multicultural analysis. *Journal of Cross-Cultural Psychology, 37*, 155–172.

7. Keller, H., & Otto, H. (2009). The cultural socialization of emotion regulation during infancy. *Journal of Cross-Cultural Psychology, 40*(6), 996–1011.

8. Ibid.

9. Ibid.

10. Susman-Stillman, A., Appleyard, K., & Siebenbruner, J. (2003). For better or worse: An ecological perspective on parents' relationships and parent-infant interaction. *ZERO TO THREE, 23*(3), 4–12.

11. Hofferth, S., & Goldscheider, F. (2010). Family structure and the transition to early parenthood. *Demography, 47*, 415–437.

12. Bretherton, I. (1985). Attachment theory: Retrospect and prospect. *Monographs of the Society for Research in Child Development, 50*(1/2), 3–35.

13. Crowell, J. A., Treboux, D., & Brockmeyer, S. (2009). Parental divorce and adult children's attachment representations and marital status. *Attachment & Human Development, 11*(1), 87–101.

14. Volling, B., Notaro, P. C., & Larsen, J. J. (1998). Adult attachment styles: Relations with emotional well-being, marriage, and parenting. *Family Relations, 47*(4), 355–367.

15. Crowell, J. A., Treboux, D., & Brockmeyer, S. (2009). Parental divorce and adult children's attachment representations and marital status. Attachment & Human Development, 11(1), 87–101.

16. Bandy, T., Andrews, K. M., & Anderson, K. (2012). Disadvantaged families and child outcomes. The importance of emotional support. *Child Trends*. Retrieved from *http://www.childtrends.org*

17. Kesner, J. E., & McKenry, P. C. (2001). Single parenthood and social competence in children of color. *Families in Society: The Journal of Contemporary Human Services, 82*, 135–143.

18. Yeung, W. J., Sandberg, J. F., Davis-Kean, P. E., & Hofferth, S. L. (2001). Children's time with fathers in intact families. *Journal of Marriage and Family, 63*(1), 136–154.

19. Castillo, J. T., Welch, G. W., & Sarver, C. M. (2012). Walking a high beam: The balance between employment stability, workplace flexibility, and nonresident father involvement. *American Journal of Men's Health, 6*(2), 120–131. doi:10.1177/1557988311417612.

20. Edin, K. (2000). What do low-income single mothers say about marriage? *Social Problems, 47*, 112–133.

21. Stern, D. (2000). *The interpersonal world of the infant*. New York: Basic Books.

22. Sevón, E. (2012). "My life has changed, but his life hasn't": Making sense of the gendering of parenthood during the transition to motherhood. *Feminism & Psychology, 22*(1), 60–80. doi:10.1177/0959353511415076

23. Barnes, M. W. (2011). When couples become parents: The creation of gender in the transition to parenthood. *Journal of Marriage and Family, 73*, 310–312.

24. Dew, J., & Wilcox, W. B. (2011). If momma ain't happy: Explaining declines in marital satisfaction among new mothers. *Journal of Marriage and Family, 73*(1), 1–12. doi:10.1111/j.1741-3737.2010.00782.x

25. Milkie, M. A. (2011). Social and cultural resources for and constraints on new mothers' marriages. *Journal of Marriage and Family, 73*(1), 18–22. doi:10.1111/j.1741-3737.2010.00784.x

26. Redshaw, M., & Martin, C. (2011). Motherhood: A natural progression and a major transition. *Journal of Reproductive and Infant Psychology, 29*(4), 305–307.

27. Sevón, E. (2012). "My life has changed, but his life hasn't": Making sense of the gendering of parenthood during the transition to motherhood. *Feminism & Psychology, 22*(1), 60–80. doi:10.1177/0959353511415076

28. Howarth, A. M., Swain, N., & Treharne, G. (2011). Taking personal responsibility for well-being increases birth satisfaction of first-time mothers. *Journal of Health Psychology, 16*(8), 1221–1230.

29. Dew, J., & Wilcox, W. B. (2011). If momma ain't happy: Explaining declines in marital satisfaction among new mothers. *Journal of Marriage and Family, 73*(1), 1–12. doi:10.1111/j.1741-3737.2010.00782.x

30. Rizzo, K. M., Schiffrin, H. H., & Liss, M. (2012, June). Insight into the parenting paradox: Mental health outcomes of intensive mothering. *Journal of Child and Family Studies.* doi:10.1007/s10826-012-9615-z

31. National Fatherhood Initiative. (2012). The father factor: Data on the consequences of father absence. Retrieved from *www.fatherhood.org/media/consequences-of-father-absence-statistics*

32. Bronte-Tinkew, J., Carrano, J., & Guzman, L. (2006). Resident fathers' perceptions of their roles and links to involvement with infants. *Fathering: A Journal of Theory, Research, & Practice About Men as Fathers, 4*(3), 254–285.

33. Association of Maternal and Child Health Programs (AMCHP). (2009). Supporting evidence-based home visiting. Retrieved from *http://supportingebhv.org/home-visiting-models*

34. Cabrera, N. J., Hofferth, S. L., & Chae, S. (2011). Patterns and predictors of father-infant engagement across race/ethnic groups. *Early Child Research Quarterly, 26*(3), 365–375.

35. Brown, G. L., Mangelsdorf, S. C., & Neff, C. (2012). Father involvement, paternal sensitivity, and father-child attachment security in the first 3 years. *Journal of Family Psychology, 26*(3), 421–430.

36. Carlson, M., & McLanahan, S. (2002). *Characteristics and antecedents of involvement by young, unmarried fathers.* (Working Paper #02-09-FF). Princeton, NJ: Princeton University, Center for Research on Child Wellbeing.

37. Sano, Y., Smith, S., & Lanigan, J. (2011). Predicting presence and level of nonresident fathers' involvement in infants' lives: Mothers' perspective. *Journal of Divorce & Remarriage, 52*(5), 350–368. doi:10.1080/10502556.2011.586613

38. Coley, R. L., & Chase-Lansdale, P. L. (1999). Stability and change in paternal involvement among urban African-American fathers. *Journal of Family Psychology, 13*(3), 416–435.

39. Magill-Evans, J., Harrison, M. J., Benzies, K., Gierl, M., & Kimak, C. (2007). Effects of parenting education on first-time fathers' skills in interactions with their infants. *Fathering, 5*(1), 42–57.

40. Baumrind, D. (1991). The influence of parenting style on adolescent competence and substance use. *Journal of Early Adolescence, 11*(1), 56–95.

41. Maccoby, E. E., & Martin, J. A. (1983). Socialization in the context of the family: Parent-child interaction. In P. H. Mussen & E. M. Hetherington (Eds.), *Handbook of child psychology* (Vol. 4, pp. 1–102). New York: Wiley.

42. Baumrind, D. (1991). The influence of parenting style on adolescent competence and substance use. *Journal of Early Adolescence, 11*(1), 56–95.

43. Darling, N. (1999, March). Parenting style and its correlates. *ERIC Digest* (ED427896). Champaign, IL: ERIC Clearing-house on Elementary and Early Childhood Education.

44. Chao, R. K. (1994). Beyond parental control and authoritarian parenting style: Understanding Chinese parenting through the cultural notion of training. *Child Development, 65*(4), 1111–1119.

45. Dewar, G. (2011). Traditional Chinese parenting: What research says about Chinese kids and why they succeed. *Parenting Science.* Retrieved from *www.parentingscience.com/chinese-parenting.html*

46. Perrin, E. C. (2002). Technical report: Coparent or second-parent adoption by same-sex parents. *Pediatrics, 109*(2), 341–344.

47. Centers for Disease Control and Prevention. (2015). *Child Maltreatment: Risk and Protective Factors.* Retrieved from *http://www.cdc.gov/violenceprevention/childmaltreatment/risk-protectivefactors.html*

48. Weitzman, C., Edmonds, D., Davagnino, J., & Briggs-Gowan, M. (2014). *Young child Socioemotional/behavioral problems and cumulative psychosocial risk.* John Wiley & Sons, Inc. doi:10.1002/imhj.21421

49. Weitoft, G. R., Hjern, A., Haglund, B., & Rosén, M. (2003). Mortality, severe morbidity, and injury in children living with single parents in Sweden: A population-based study. *Lancet, 361*(9354), 289–294.

50. ChildStats. (2015). *Family structure and children's living arrangements: Percentage of children ages 0–17 by presence of parents in household and race and Hispanic origin, 1980–2014.*

Retrieved from http://www.childstats.gov/americaschildren/tables/fam1a.asp?popup=true

51. Pruett, M. K., McIntosh, J. E., & Kelly, J. B. (2014) Parental separation and overnight care of young children, Part I: Consensus through theoretical and empirical integration. *Family Court Review. 52*(2) 240–255

52. George, S., Solomon, J., & McIntosh, J. (2011). Divorce in the nursery: On infants and overnight care. *Family Court Review, 49.*

53. Altenhofen, S., Biringen, Z., & Mergler, R. (2010). Families experiencing divorce: Age at onset of overnight stays, conflict, and emotional availability as predictors of child attachment. *Journal of Divorce & Remarriage, 51*, 141–156.

54. Martinez, G., Daniels, K., & Chandra, A. (2012). Fertility of men and women aged 15–44 years in the United States: National survey of family growth, 2006–2010. *National Health Center Reports. Centers for Disease Control and Prevention.* Retrieved from *www.cdc.gov/nchs/data/nhsr/nhsr051.pdf*

55. ZERO TO THREE. (2012). *National baby facts: Infants, toddlers, and their families in the United States.* Retrieved from *http://www.zerotothree.org/public-policy/pdf/national-baby-facts.pdf*

56. Lick, D. J., Tornello, S. L., Riskind, R. G., Schmidt, K. M., & Patterson, C. J. (2012). Social climate for sexual minorities predicts well-being among heterosexual offspring of lesbian and gay parents. *Sexuality Research and Social Policy*, 1–14.

57. Patterson, C. (2006). Children of lesbian and gay parents. *Current Directions in Psychological Science, 15*(5), 241–244.

58. ChildStats. (2015). *Family structure and children's living arrangements: percentage of children ages 0–17 by presence of parents in household and race and Hispanic origin, 1980–2014.* Retrieved from *http://www.childstats.gov/americaschildren/tables/fam1a.asp?popup=true*

59. U.S. Census Bureau (2012). Profile American facts for features. Retrieved from *http://www.census.gov*

60. Minkler, M. (2002). *Grandparents and other relatives raising children: Characteristics, needs, best practices, & implications for the aging network.* Washington, DC: Administration on Aging, Department of Health and Human Services.

61. Smith, A. B., Dannison, L. L., & Vach-Hasse, T. (1998). When "Grandma" is "Mom": What today's teachers need to know. *Childhood Education, 75*(1), 12–16.

62. Children's Bureau. (2014). *Adoption and Foster Care Analysis and Reporting System (AFCARS) data for FY 2014.* Retrieved from *http://www.acf.hhs.gov/programs/cb/resource/afcars-report-22*

63. Stacks, A. M., & Partridge, T. (2011). Infants placed in foster care prior to their first birthday: Differences in kin and nonkin placements. *Infant Mental Health Journal, 32*(5), 489–508.

64. Ibid.

65. National Center for Parent, Family, and Community Engagement. (2011). *The Head Start parent, family, and community engagement framework.* Retrieved from *http://eclkc.ohs.acf.hhs.gov/hslc/standards/im/2011/pfce-framework.pdf*

66. Robertson, A. S. (1998). The parenting education spectrum: A look at the scope of parenting programs that should be available within a community. *Parent News: National Parent Information Network.*

67. MIECHV. (2015). *Maternal, infant, and early childhood home visiting.* Retrieved from *http://mchb.hrsa.gov/programs/homevisiting/*

68. Kearney, P., & Griffin, T. (2001). Between joy and sorrow: Being a parent of a child with developmental disability. *Journal of Advanced Nursing, 34*(5), 582–593.

69. Smith, P. M. (2003). *You are not alone: For parents when they learn that their child has a disability.* Kidsource Online. Retrieved from *www.kidsource.com/NICHCY/parenting.disab.all.4.2.html*

70. Müller, E. (2007). *Collaborative partnerships between SEAs and Parent Training and Information Centers (PTIs).* Retrieved from *http://nasdse.org/DesktopModules/DNNspot-Store/Product-Files/21_c9ec21a1-3101-4d8f-bc7e-de63e88225df.pdf*

71. Santelli, B. (2003). *Parent to parent support.* Retrieved from *www.nichcy.org/pubs/basicpar/bp2txt.html*

Chapter 3

1. Bowlby, J. (1969). *Attachment and loss: Vol. 1. Attachment.* New York: Basic Books.

2. Bowlby, J. (1982). *Attachment.* New York: Basic Books.

3. Bowlby, J. (1988). *A secure base: Parent-child attachment and healthy human development.* New York: Basic Books.

4. Ainsworth, M. D. S., Bell, S. M., & Stayton, D. J. (1971). Individual differences in the strange situation behavior of one-year-olds. In H. R. Schaffer (Ed.), *The Origins of Human Social Relations* (pp. 17–58). San Diego, CA: Academic Press.

5. Piaget, J. (2002). *The language and thought of the child.* New York: Routledge Classics.

6. Emde, R. N., & Robinson, J. L. (2000). Guiding principles for a theory of early intervention: A developmental-psychoanalytic perspective. J. P Shonkoff & S. J. Meisels (Eds). Handbook of Early Childhood (2nd Ed.), (pp. 160–178). New York: University Press.

7. Hinde, R. (1992). Ethological and relationship approaches. In R. Vasta (Ed.), *Six theories of child development: Revised formulations and current issues* (pp. 251–285). London: JKP Press.

8. Sameroff, A. J. (Ed.) (2009). The transactional model of development: How children and contexts shape each other. Washington, DC: American Psychological Association.

9. Sameroff, A. J., & Chandler, M. (1975). Reproductive risk and the continuum of caretaking casualty. In F. Horowitz,

M. Hetherington, & S. Scar-Salaperk (Eds.), *Review of child development research* (Vol. 4, pp. 187–244). Chicago: University of Chicago Press.

10. Sameroff, A. J. (2010). A unified theory of development: A dialectic integration of nature an and nurture. *Child Development, 81*, 6–22.

11. Bronfenbrenner, U. (Ed). (2004). *Making human beings human: Bioecological perspectives on human development.* Thousand Oaks, CA: Sage Publications.

12. Shonkoff J.P., & Garner, A.S. (2012).The lifelong effects of early childhood adversity and toxic stress. *Pediatrics, 129*(1), e232-246.

13. Barrera, I., Kramer, L., & Macpherson, T. (2012). *Skilled dialogue: Strategies for responding to cultural diversity* (2nd ed.). Baltimore, MD: Paul Brookes Publishing Co.

14. Hinde, R. (1992). Ethological and relationship approaches. In R. Vasta (Ed.), *Six theories of child development: Revised formulations and current issues* (pp. 251–285). London: JKP Press.

15. Pawl, J.J. (1995). The therapeutic relationship as human connectedness: Being held in another's mind. *Zero to Three, 15*(4), 2–5.

16. Hinde, R. (1992). Ethological and relationship approaches. In R. Vasta (Ed.), *Six theories of child development: Revised formulations and current issues* (pp. 251–285). London: JKP Press.

17. Ainsworth, M. D. S., Blehar, M. C., Waters, E., & Wall, S. (1978). *Patterns of attachment: A psychological study of the strange situation.* Hillsdale, NJ: Erlbaum.

18. Bowlby, J. (1969). *Attachment and loss: Vol. 1. Attachment.* New York: Basic Books.

19. Hinde, R. (1988). Introduction. In R. Hinde & J. Stevenson-Hinde (Eds.), *Relationships within families: Mutual influences* (pp. 1–4). Oxford, England: Clarendon.

20. Sameroff, A. J., & Chandler, M. (1975). Reproductive risk and the continuum of caretaking casualty. In F. Horowitz, M. Hetherington, & S. Scar-Salaperk (Eds.), *Review of child development research* (Vol. 4, pp. 187–244). Chicago: University of Chicago Press.

21. Ibid.

22. Sameroff, A. J., & MacKenzie, M. J. (2003). A quarter-century of the transactional model: How have things changed? *ZERO TO THREE, 24*(1), 14–22.

23. Sameroff, A.J., & Feise, B. H. (2000). Transactional regulation: The development ecology of early intervention. In J. P. Shonkoff & S. J. Meisels (Eds.), *Handbook of early childhood intervention* (2nd ed., pp. 135–159). New York: Cambridge University Press.

24. Sameroff, A. J. (2010). A unified theory of development: A dialectic integration of nature and nurture. *Child Development, 81*, 6–22.

25. Bronfenbrenner, U. (Ed). (2004). *Making human beings human: Bioecological perspectives on human development.* Thousand Oaks, CA: Sage Publications.

26. Ibid.

27. American Academy of Pediatrics (2012). Early childhood adversity, toxic stress, and the role of the pediatrician: Translating developmental science into lifelong health. Retrieved from *http://pediatrics.aappublications.org/content/129/1/e224*

28. Erikson, E. (1963). *Childhood and society* (2nd ed.). New York: Norton.

29. Erikson, E. (1994). *Identity and the life cycle.* New York: W.W. Norton. (Original work published 1959)

30. Maslow, A. H. (1968). *Toward a psychology of being.* New York: Van Nostrand Reinhold.

31. Bowlby, J. (1969). *Attachment and loss: Vol. 1. Attachment.* New York: Basic Books.

32. Stern, D. (2000). *The interpersonal world of the infant.* New York: Basic Books.

33. Erikson, E. (1963). *Childhood and society* (2nd ed.). New York: Norton.

34. Erikson, E. (1994). *Identity and the life cycle.* New York: W.W. Norton. (Original work published 1959)

35. Maslow, A. H. (1968). *Toward a psychology of being.* New York: Van Nostrand Reinhold.

36. Erikson, E. (1963). *Childhood and society* (2nd ed.). New York: Norton.

37. Erikson, E. (1994). *Identity and the life cycle.* New York: W.W. Norton. (Original work published 1959)

38. Ainsworth, M. D. S., Blehar, M. C., Waters, E., & Wall, S. (1978). *Patterns of attachment: A psychological study of the strange situation.* Hillsdale, NJ: Erlbaum.

39. Bowlby, J. (1982). *Attachment.* New York: Basic Books.

40. Stern, D. (2000). *The interpersonal world of the infant.* New York: Basic Books.

41. Ibid.

42. Vygotsky, L. S. (1962). *Thought and language.* Cambridge, MA: MIT Press.

43. Vygotsky, L. S. (1978). *Mind in society: The development of higher psychological processes.* Cambridge, MA: Harvard University Press.

44. Vygotsky, L. S. (1987). Thinking and speech. In N. Minick (Trans.), *The collected works of L. S. Vygotsky; Vol. 1.: Problems in general psychology.* New York: Plenum.

45. Vygotsky, L. S. (1962). *Thought and language.* Cambridge, MA: MIT Press.

46. Vygotsky, L. S. (1987). Thinking and speech. In N. Minick (Trans.), *The collected works of L. S. Vygotsky; Vol. 1.: Problems in general psychology.* New York: Plenum.

47. Piaget, J. (1952). *The origins of intelligence in children.* New York: Norton.

48. Piaget, J. (1954). *The construction of reality in the child*. New York: Basic Books.

49. Piaget, J. (1962). *Play, dreams and imitation in childhood*. New York: Norton. Routledge. (Original work published 1926)

50. Piaget, J., & Inhelder, B. (2000). *The psychology of the child*. New York: Basic Books. (Original work published 1969)

51. Flavell, J. H. (1977). *Cognitive development*. Upper Saddle River, NJ: Merrill/Prentice Hall.

52. Flavell, J. H. (1996). Piaget's legacy. *Psychological Science, 7*, 200–203.

53. Sutherland, P. (1992). *Cognitive development today: Piaget and his critics*. London: Chapman.

54. Bruner, J. (1966). *Toward a theory of instruction*. Cambridge, MA: Harvard University Press.

55. Bruner, J. (1996). What we have learned about early learning. *European Early Childhood Education Research Journal, 4*(1), 5–16.

56. Bandura, A. (1977). *Social learning theory*. Upper Saddle River, NJ: Merrill/Prentice Hall.

57. Bandura, A. (1989). Social cognitive theory. In R. Vasta (Ed.), *Annals of child development* (Vol. 6). Greenwich, CT: JAI.

58. Bandura, A. (2001). Social cognitive theory: An agentive perspective. *Review of Psychology, 52*, 1–26.

59. Bandura, A. (1997). *Self-efficacy: The exercise of control*. New York: Freeman.

60. Gergely, G., Bekkering, H., & Király, I. (2002). Rational imitation in preverbal infants. *Nature, 415(6873, 755)*

61. Bellagamba, F., Camaioni, L., & Colonnesi, C. (2006). Change in children's understanding of others' intentional actions. *Developmental Science, 9*(2), 182–188.

62. Meltzoff, A. N. (1995). Understanding the intentions of others: Reenactment of intended acts of others by 10-month-old children. *Developmental Psychology, 31*, 838–850.

63. Buttelmann, D., Zmyj, N., Daum, M., & Carpenter, M. (2013). Selective imitation of in-group over out-group members in 14-month-old infants. *Child Development, 84*(2), 422–428. doi:10.1111/j.1467-8624.2012.01860.x

64. Meltzoff, A. N., Kuhl, P. K., Movellan, J., & Sejnowski, T. J. (2009). Foundations for a new science of learning. *Science, 325*, 284–288.

65. Spelke, E., & Kinzler, K.D. (2007). Core knowledge. *Developmental Science, 10*(1), 89–96.

66. Ibid.

67. Schmuckler, M. A., Collimore, L. M., & Dannemiller, J. L. (2007). Infants' reactions to object collision on hit and miss trajectories. *Infancy, 12*(1), 105–118. doi:10.1111/j.1532-7078.2007.tb00236.x

68. Brooks, R., & Meltzoff, A. N. (2005). The development of gaze following and its relation to language. *Developmental Science, 8*(6), 535–543.

69. Wynn, K. (1992). Addition and subtraction by human infants. *Nature, 358*, 749–750.

70. Jordan, K. E., & Brannon, E. M. (2006). The multisensory representation of number in infancy. *Proceedings of the National Academy of Sciences, 103*, 3486–3489.

71. Vygotsky, L. S. (1962). *Thought and language*. Cambridge, MA: MIT Press.

72. Vygotsky, L. S. (1987). Thinking and speech. In N. Minick (Trans.), *The collected works of L. S. Vygotsky; Vol. 1.: Problems in general psychology*. New York: Plenum.

73. Johnson, M. (2005). *Developmental cognitive neuroscience* (2nd ed.). Oxford, England: Blackwell.

74. Kuhl, P. K. (2000). A new view of language acquisition. *PNAS, 97*(22), 11850–11857.

75. Kuhl, P. K. (2007). Is speech learning 'gated' by the social brain? *Developmental Science, 10*(1), 110–120.

76. Kuhl, P. K., Williams, K. A., Lacerda, F., Stevens, K. N., & Lindblom, B. (1992). Linguistic experience alters phonetic perception in infants by 6 months of age. *Science, 255*, 606–608.

77. Kuhl, P.K. (2000). A new view of language acquisition. *PNAS, 97*(22), 11850–11857.

78. Ibid.

79. Ramirez-Esparza, N., Garcia-Sierra, A., & Kuhl, P. (2014). Look who's talking: Speech style and social context in language input to infants are linked to concurrent and future speech development. *Developmental Science, 17*(6), 880–891.

80. Thiessen, E. D., Hill, E. A., & Saffran, J. R. (2005). Infant-directed speech facilitates word segmentation. *Infancy, 7*(1), 53–71.

81. Johnson, M. (2005). *Developmental cognitive neuroscience* (2nd ed.). Oxford, England: Blackwell.

82. Vygotsky, L. S. (1962). *Thought and language*. Cambridge, MA: MIT Press.

83. Vygotsky, L. S. (1978). *Mind in society: The development of higher psychological processes*. Cambridge, MA: Harvard University Press.

84. Vygotsky, L. S. (1987). Thinking and speech. In N. Minick (Trans.), *The collected works of L. S. Vygotsky; Vol. 1.: Problems in general psychology*. New York: Plenum.

85. Gesell, A. (1946). The ontogenesis of infant behavior. In L. Carmichael (Ed.), *Manual of Child Psychology* (pp. 295–331). New York: Wiley.

86. Adolph, K. E. (2008). Learning to move. *Current Directions in Psychological Science, 17*, 213–218.

87. Thelen, E. (2005). Dynamic systems theory and the complexity of change. *Psychoanalytic Dialogues, 15*, 255–283.

88. Adolph, K. E. (2008). Learning to move. *Current Directions in Psychological Science, 17*, 213–218.

89. Edwards, C., & Raikes, H. (2002). Extending the dance: Relationship-based approaches to infant/toddler care and education. *Young Children, 57*(4), 10–17.

90. Wittmer, D.S. (2008). *A focus on peers in the early years: The importance of relationships.* Washington, DC: ZERO TO THREE. (out of print)

Chapter 4

1. Jablon, J. R., Dombro, A., & Dichtelmiller, M. L. (2007). *The power of observation* (2nd Ed.). Washington, DC: Teaching Strategies.

2. National Association for the Education of Young Children (NAEYC). (2005). *Code of Ethical Conduct and Statement of Commitment.* Retrieved from http://www.naeyc.org/files/naeyc/file/positions/PSETH05.pdf

3. Division of Early Childhood (DEC). (2009). *Code of ethics.* Retrieved from http://dec.membershipsoftware.org/files/Position%20Statement%20and%20Papers/Member%20Code%20of%20Ethics.pdf

4. Jablon, J. R., Dombro, A., & Dichtelmiller, M. L. (2007). *The power of observation* (2nd Ed.). Washington, DC: Teaching Strategies.

5. Brownlee, J., & Bakeman, R. (1981). Hitting in toddler-peer interaction. *Child Development, 52*(3), 1076–1080.

6. Gandini, L., & Goldhaber, J. (2001). Two reflections about documentation. In L. Gandini & C. Edwards (Eds.), *Bambini: The Italian approach to infant/toddler care* (pp. 124–145). New York: Teacher's College Press.

7. Ibid.

8. Ibid.

9. Edwards, C., Gandini, L., & Forman, G. (Eds.). (1998). *The hundred languages of children: The Reggio Emilia approach—Advanced reflections.* Greenwich, CT: Ablex.

10. Marsden, D. B., Dombro, A. L., & Dichtelmiller, M. L. (2003). *The ounce scale user's guide.* New York: Pearson Early Learning.

11. Meisels, S. J., Dombro, A., Marsden, D. B., Weston, D. R., & Jewkes, A. M. (2003). *The ounce scale.* New York: Pearson Early Learning.

12. Ibid.

13. Marsden, D. B., Dombro, A. L., Dichtelmiller, M. L. (2003). *The Ounce Scale user's guide.* New York: Pearson Early Learning.

14. High/Scope. (2015). *Assessment.* Retrieved from http://www.highscope.org/Content.asp?ContentId=372

15. Bricker, D., & Squires, J. (2009). *Ages & Stages Questionnaires: A parent-completed child monitoring system* (3rd ed.). Baltimore, MD: Brookes.

16. Liu, J., Leung, P., Sun, R., Li, H., & Liu, J., (2012). Cross-Cultural application of Achenbach system of empirically based assessment (ASEBA): Process of instrument translation in Chinese, challenges, and future directions. *World Journal of Pediatrics, 8*(1), 5–10.

Chapter 5

1. Human Genome Project. (2008). *Human Genome Project information.* Retrieved from www.ornl.gov/sci/techresources/Human_Genome/home.shtml

2. National Scientific Council on the Developing Child. (2010). *Persistent fear and anxiety can affect young children's learning and development: Working paper 9.* Retrieved from www.developingchild.harvard.edu

3. National Women's Health Information Center. (2009). *Pregnancy and a healthy diet.* Retrieved from www.4woman.gov/

4. Ibid.

5. Kavle, J., Mehanna, S., Khan, G., Hassan, M., Saleh, G. & Galloway, R. (2014) *Cultural beliefs and perceptions of maternal diet and weight gain during pregnancy and postpartum family planning in Egypt.* Washington, D.C.: United States Agency for International Development.

6. Nag, M. (1994). Beliefs and practices about food during pregnancy. *Economic and Political Weekly,* 2427–2438.

7. Taylor, F., Ko, R., & Pan, M. (1999). Prenatal and reproductive health care. In E. Kramer, S. Ivey, & Y. W. Ying (Eds.), *Immigrant women's health: Problems and solutions* (pp. 121–135). San Francisco: Jossey-Bass.

8. Gottlieb, A. (2000). Luring your child into this life: A Beng path for infant care. In J. DeLoache & A. Gottlieb (Eds.), *A world of babies: Imagined child care guides for seven societies* (pp. 55–90). Cambridge, UK: Cambridge University Press.

9. Delaney, C. (2000). Making babies in a Turkish village. In J. DeLoache & A. Gottlieb (Eds.), *A world of babies: Imagined child care guides for seven societies* (pp. 117–144). Cambridge, UK: Cambridge University Press.

10. Pierroutsakos, S. L. (2000). Infants of the dreaming: A Warlpiri guide to child care. In J. DeLoache & A. Gottlieb (Eds.), *A world of babies: Imagined child care guides for seven societies.* Cambridge, UK: Cambridge University Press.

11. Arnold, C. M., Aragon, D., Shepherd, J., & Van Sell, S. L. (2011). The coming of the blessing: A successful cross-cultural collaborative effort for American Indian/Alaska Native families. *Family & Community Health, 34*(3), 196–201.

12. WomensHealth.gov. (2012). *Prenatal fact sheet.* Retrieved from http://womenshealth.gov/publications/our-publications/fact-sheet/prenatal-care.html#b)

13. Paintner, A., Williams, A. D., & Burd, L. (2012). Fetal alcohol spectrum disorders—Implications for child neurology, Part 2: Diagnosis and management. *Journal of Child Neurology, 27*(3), 355–362.

14. Szalavitz, M. (2010). *Missing out on mother's day.* Retrieved from www.thefix.com/content/mothers-day-addicted-pregnant-women-policy8710

15. Gouin, K., Murphy, K., Shah, P. S. & the Knowledge Synthesis Group on Determinants of Low Birth Weight and Preterm Births. (2011). Effects of cocaine use during pregnancy on low birthweight and preterm birth: Systematic review and meta-analyses. *American Journal of Obstetrics and Gynecology, 204*(4), 340–348.

16. Eiden, R. D., Schuetze, P., Colder, C. R., & Veira, Y. (2011). Maternal cocaine use and mother-toddler aggression. *Neurotoxicology Teratology, 33*(3), 360–369.

17. Hackshaw, A., Rodeck, C., & Boniface, S. (2011). Maternal smoking in pregnancy and birth defects: A systematic review based on 173,687 malformed cases and 11.7 million controls. *Oxford Journals, 17*(5), 589–604.

18. Ibid.

19. Centers for Disease Control and Prevention. (2016). *Effects of disasters on pregnant women: Environmental exposures.* Retrieved from *http://www.cdc.gov/ncbddd/disasters/environmental.html*

20. March of Dimes. (2013). *Sexually transmitted diseases.* Retrieved from *http://www.marchofdimes.org/complications/sexually-transmitted-diseases.aspx*

21. Tavernise, S. (2016). *Zika virus a global health emergency,* W.H.O. says. Feb. 1. Retrieved from *http://www.nytimes.com/2016/02/02/health/zika-virus-world-health-organization.html?_r=0*

22. National Scientific Council on the Developing Child (2014). *Excessive stress disrupts the architecture of the developing brain: Working paper 3.* Updated edition. Retrieved from *www.developingchild.harvard.edu.*

23. Davalos, D. B., Yadon, C., & Tregellas, H. (2012). Untreated prenatal maternal depression and the potential risks to offspring: A review. *Archives of Women's Mental Health, 15,* 1–14.

24. Epifanio, M. S., Genna, V., De Luca, C., Roccella, M., & La Grutta, S. (2015). Paternal and maternal transition to parenthood: The risk of postpartum depression and parenting stress. *Pediatric Reports, 7*(2), 5872. Retrieved from *http://www.ncbi.nlm.nih.gov/pmc/articles/PMC4508624/*

25. Hellmuth, J. C., Gordon, K. C., Stuart, G. L., & Moore, T. M. (2013). Risk factors for intimate partner violence during pregnancy and postpartum. *Archives of Women's Mental Health. 16*(1), 19–27. Retrieved from *http://www.ncbi.nlm.nih.gov/pmc/articles/PMC3547143/*

26. MedlinePlus. (2013). *Fetal development.* Retrieved from *https://www.nlm.nih.gov/medlineplus/ency/article/002398.html*

27. Medline Plus. (2011). *Fetal development. U.S. National Library of Medicine and the National Institute of Health.* Retrieved from *http://www.nlm.nih.gov/medlineplus/ency/article/002398.html*

28. Restak, R. (2001). *The secret life of the brain.* Washington, DC: Joseph Henry Press.

29. Chugani, H. T. (1998). A critical period of brain development: Studies of cerebral glucose utilization with PET. *Preventive Medicine, 27,* 487–497.

30. DeLoache, J. (2000). Cognitive development in infants. In D. Cryer & T. Harmes (Eds.), *Infants and toddlers in out of home care* (pp. 7–48). Baltimore, MD: Brookes.

31. Skeels, H. M., & Dye, H. B. (1939). *A study of the effects of differential stimulation on mentally retarded children. Proceedings. American Association on Mental Deficiency, 44*(1), 114–136.

32. Spitz, R. A. (1945). Hospitalism: An inquiry into the genesis of psychiatric conditions of early childhood. *Psychoanalytic Study of the Child, 1,* 53–74.

33. Perry, B. (1999, July–August). Time is precious in early childhood development. *Good Health Magazine, 1.*

34. National Scientific Council on the Developing Child. (2010). *Early experiences can alter gene expression and affect long-term development: Working paper 10.* Retrieved from *http://www.developingchild.harvard.edu*

35. Shonkoff, J. P., Garner, A. S., & the Committee on Psychosocial Aspects of Child and Family Health, Committee on Early Childhood, Adoption, and Dependent Care, and Section on Developmental and Behavioral Pediatrics. (2012). The lifelong effects of early childhood adversity and toxic stress. *Pediatrics, 129*(1), e232–246. Retrieved from *www.ncbi.nlm.nih.gov/pubmed/22201156*

36. Child Welfare Information Gateway. (2015). *Understanding the effects of maltreatment on early brain development.* Retrieved from *https://www.childwelfare.gov/pubPDFs/brain_development.pdf*

37. National Scientific Council on the Developing Child. (2014). *Excessive stress disrupts the architecture of the developing brain: Working paper 3.* Updated Edition. Retrieved from *www.developingchild.harvard.edu.*

38. Roth, T. L., & Sweatt, J. D. (2011). Epigenetic mechanisms and environmental shaping of the brain during sensitive periods of development. *Journal of Child Psychology and Psychiatry, and Allied Disciplines, 52*(4), 398–408. Retrieved from *http://www.ncbi.nlm.nih.gov/pmc/articles/PMC2965301/*

39. Gunnar, M., Herrera, A., and Hostinar, C. (2009). Stress and early brain development. In R. Tremblay, R. Barr, R. Peters, & M. Boivin (Eds.), *Encyclopedia on early childhood* (pp. 1–8). Montreal, Quebec: Centre of Excellence for Early Childhood Development.

40. ZERO TO THREE. (2014). *What are the most important changes in the brain after birth?* Retrieved from *http://www.zerotothree.org/child-development/brain-development/faqs-on-the-brain.html#changes*

41. Hart, B., & Risley, T. R. (1995). *Meaningful differences in the everyday experience of young American children.* Baltimore, MD: Brookes.

42. Shonkoff, J. P., & Phillips, D. A. (Eds.). (2000). *From neurons to neighborhoods: The science of early development.* Washington, DC: National Academy Press.

43. KidsHealth. (2009). *A primer on preemies.* Retrieved from *health.msn.com/kids-health/articlepage.aspx?cp-documentid=100151172*

44. March of Dimes. (2009). *Multiples: Twins, triplets, and beyond.* Retrieved from *search.marchofdimes.com*

45. March of Dimes. (2009). *Preterm births rise 36 percent since early 1980s.* Retrieved from *www.marchofdimes.com*

Chapter 6

1. Lally, R. (1992) Plenary on infant learning and development. Head Start Child Development Institute. Washington, D.C.

2. Thomas, A., Chess, S., Birch, H. G., Hertzig, M. E., & Korn, S. (1963). *Behavioral individuality in early childhood.* New York: New York University Press.

3. Rothbart, M. K. (1989). Biological processes of temperament. In G. Kohnstamm, J. Bates, & M. K. Rothbart, (Eds.), *Temperament in childhood* (pp. 77-110). Chichester, UK: Wiley.

4. Robinson, J. L., & Acevedo, M. C. (2001). Infant reactivity and reliance on mother during emotion challenges: Prediction of cognition and language skills in a low-income sample. *Child Development, 72*(2), 402–416.

5. Porter, C. L., & Jones, B. L. (2011). Does brief bradycardia at the onset of arm-restraint predict infants' emotional reactivity during restraint? *Infancy, 16*(2), 166–179.

6. Phillips, D. A., Fox, N. A., & Gunnar, M. R. (2011). Same place, different experiences: Bringing individual differences to research in child care. *Child Development Perspectives, 5*(1), 44–49. doi:10.1111/j.1750-8606.2010.00155.x

7. Hostinar, C. E. & Gunnar, M. R. (2013). The developmental psychobiology of stress and emotion in childhood. In I. B. Weiner, D. K. Freedheim, & R. M. Lerner (Eds.), *Handbook of Psychology* (2nd edition, pp. 121-141). Hoboken, NJ: Wiley.

8. Thomas, A., Chess, S., Birch, H. G., Hertzig, M. E., & Korn, S. (1963). Behavioral individuality in early childhood. New York: New York University Press.

9. Chaplin, T. & Aldeo, A. (2013). Gender differences in emotion expression in children: A meta-analytic review. *Psychological Bulletin, 139*(4), 735–765.

10. Ibid.

11. Warber, K. M., & Emmers-Sommer, T. M. (2012). The relationships among sex, gender and attachment. *Language and Communication Quarterly, 1*, 60–81. Retrieved from *http://www.untestedideas.com/uploads/3/1/1/6/3116134/sex_gender_and_attachment.pdf.*

12. David, D. H., & Lyons-Ruth, K. (2005). Differential attachment responses of male and female infants to frightening maternal behavior: Tend or befriend versus fight or flight? *Infant Mental Health Journal, 21*(1), 1–18. Retrieved from *http://www.ncbi.nlm.nih.gov/pmc/articles/PMC1857276/*

13. Frankel, L. A., Hughes, S. O., O'Connor, T. M., Power, T. G., Fisher, J. O., & Hazen, N. L. (2012). Parental influences on children's self-regulation of energy intake: Insights from developmental literature on emotion regulation. *Journal of Obesity,* 327259. doi:10.1155/2012/327259. Epub March 28, 2012. Retrieved from *www.hindawi.com/journals/jobes/2012/327259/*

14. MacLean, P. C., Rynes, K. N., Aragón, C., Caprihan, A., Phillips, J. P., & Lowe, J. R. (2014). Mother-infant mutual eye gaze supports emotion regulation in infancy during the still-face paradigm. *Infant Behavior and Development. 37*(4), 512–22. Retrieved from *http://www.researchgate.net/publication/263968605_Motherinfant_mutual_eye_gaze_supports_emotion_regulation_in_infancy_during_the_Still-Face_paradigm*

15. Moracsch, K., & Bell, M. A. (2012). Self-regulation of negative affect at 5 and 10 months. *Developmental Psychobiology, 54*(2), 215–221.

16. Als, H., Lester, B., Tronick, E. Z., & Brazelton, T. B. (1982). Towards a research instrument for the assessment of preterm infants' behavior (A.P.I.B.). In H. E. Fitzgerald, B. M. Lester, & M. W. Yogman (Eds.), *Theory and research in behavioral pediatrics* (Vol. 1, pp. 85–132). New York: Plenum.

17. Ibid

18. Ibid

19. Robinson, J. L., & Acevedo, M. C. (2001). Infant reactivity and reliance on mother during emotion challenges: Prediction of cognition and language skills in a low-income sample. *Child Development, 72*(2), 402–416.

20. Ibid

21. Butterworth, G. (1992) Origins of self-perception in infancy. *Psychological Inquiry, 3*, 103–111

22. Mahler, M. S. (1975). *The psychological birth of the human infant.* New York: Basic Books Stern (2000).

23. Stern, D. (2000). *The interpersonal world of the infant.* New York: Basic Books.

24. Brown, J. (1998). *The self.* New York: Taylor & Francis Group.

25. Damasio, A. (2003). *Looking for Spinoza: Joy, sorrow, and the feeling brain.* Orlando, FL: Harcourt.

26. Centers for Disease Control and Prevention. (2015). *Autism spectrum disorder.* Retrieved from *http://www.cdc.gov/ncbddd/autism/facts.html*

27. Mind Institute, U-C Davis. Autism. (n.d.) *Autism early signs in infants.* Retrieved from *http://www.ucdmc.ucdavis.edu//news/pdf/autism-in-infants.pdf*

28. Lartseva, A., Dijkstra, T., & Buitelaar, J. K. (2014). Emotional language processing in autism spectrum disorders: a systematic review. *Frontiers in Human Neuroscience, 8*, 991 Retrieved from *http://www.ncbi.nlm.nih.gov/pmc/articles/PMC4285104/*

29. Rogers, S., Vismara, L., Wagner, A., McCormick, C., Young, G., & Ozonoff, S. (2014). Autism treatment in the first year of life: A pilot study of infant start, a parent-implemented intervention for symptomatic infants. *Journal of Autism & Developmental Disorders, 44*(12), 2981-2995. Retrieved from *http://www.autismsciencefoundation.org/sites/default/files/Rogers%20Infant%20Start%20outcome%20paper%20JADD%202014.pdf*

30. Bowlby, J. (1982). *Attachment.* New York: Basic Books

31. Ainsworth, M. D. S., Blehar, M. C., Waters, E., & Wall, S. (1978). *Patterns of attachment: A psychological study of the strange situation.* Hillsdale, NJ: Erlbaum.

32. Ibid.

33. Main, M., & Cassidy, J. (1988). Categories of response with the parent at age 6: Predicted from infant attachment classifications and stable over a one-month period. *Developmental Psychology, 24,* 415–426.

34. Schore, A. (2001). Effects of a secure attachment relationship on right brain development, affect regulation, and infant mental health. *Infant Mental Health Journal, 22*(1–2) 7–66.

35. Drake, K., Pasco Fearon, R. M., & Belsky, J. (2014). From early attachment to engagement with learning in school: The role of self-regulation and persistence. *Developmental Psychology, 50*(5), 1350–1361.

36. Troy, M., & Sroufe, L. A. (1987). Victimization among preschoolers: Role of attachment relationship history. *Journal of the American Academy of Child & Adolescent Psychiatry, 26*(2), 166–172.

37. Main, M., & Goldwyn, R. (1994). Adult attachment rating and classification systems. In M. Main (Ed.), *A typology of human attachment organization assessed in discourse, drawings, and interviews.* New York: Cambridge University Press.

38. Main, M. (2000). The organized categories of infant, child, and adult attachment: Flexible vs. inflexible attention under attachment-related stress. *Journal of the American Psychoanalytic Association, 48,* 1055–1096.

39. Keller, H., & Otto, H. (2009). The cultural socialization of emotion regulation during infancy. *Journal of Cross-Cultural Psychology, 40*(6), 996–1011. doi:10.1177/0022022109348576

40. Greenspan, S. I., & Greenspan, N. T. (1994). *First feelings: Milestones in the emotional development of your baby and child.* New York: Penguin. (Original work published 1985)

41. Stern, D. (2000). *The interpersonal world of the infant.* New York: Basic Books.

42. Klinnert, M., Emde, R. N., Butterfield, P., & Campos, J. J. (1986). Social referencing: The infant's use of emotional signals from a friendly adult with mother present. *Developmental Psychology, 22*(4), 427–432.

43. Ibid

44. Repacholi, B. M. (1998). Infants' use of attentional cues to identify the referent of another person's emotional expression. *Developmental Psychology, 33*(5), 1017–1025.

45. Repacholi, B., Meltzoff, A.N. Rowe, H. & Spiewak Toub, T. (2014) Infant, control thyself: Infants' integration of multiple social cues to regulate their imitative behavior. *Cognitive Development, 32,* 46–57

46. Gottman, J. M., Katz, L. F., & Hooven, C. (1997). *Meta-emotion: How families communicate emotionally.* Mahwah, NJ: Erlbaum.

47. National Scientific Council on the Developing Child (2005/2014). Excessive Stress Disrupts the Architecture of the Developing Brain: Working Paper No. 3. Updated Edition. Retrieved from *www.developingchild.harvard.edu.*

48. Early Head Start Research and Evaluation Project. (2006). *Research to practice: Depression in the lives of early head start families.* Retrieved from *www.acf.hhs.gov/programs/opre/resource/depression-in-the-lives-of-early-head-start-families-research-to-practice*

49. Wickramaratne, P., Gameroff, M. J., Pilowsky, D. J., Hughes, C. W., Garber, J., Malloy, E., King, C., . . . Weissman, M. M. (2011). Children of depressed mothers 1 year after remission of maternal depression: findings from the STAR*D-Child study. *The American Journal of Psychiatry, 168*(6), 593–602. doi:10.1176/appi.ajp.2010.10010032

50. Hospital for Sick Children Toronto. (2012). *Infant mental health promotion.* Retrieved from *http://www.imhpromotion.ca/HOME.aspx*

51. Maternal, Infant, and Early Childhood Home Visiting. Retrieved from *http://mchb.hrsa.gov/programs/homevisiting/*

52. Fraiberg, S. (1996). *The magic years: Understanding and handling the problems of childhood* (Reissue ed.). New York: Fireside

53. Pawl, J. H. (1995). The therapeutic relationship as human connectedness: Being held in another's mind. *ZERO TO THREE, 15*(4), 1–5.

54. Weatherston, D. (2001). Infant mental health: A review of relevant literature. *Psychoanalytic Social Work, 8*(1), 39–69.

Chapter 7

1. Wittmer, D. S. (2008). Focusing on peers: The importance of relationships in the early years. Washington, DC: ZERO TO THREE.

2. Rubin, K. H., Coplan, R. J., & Bowker, J. C. (2009). Social withdrawal in childhood. *Annual Review of Psychology, 60,* 141–171.

3. Rubin, K. H., & Coplan, R. J. (2004). Paying attention to and not neglecting social withdrawal and social isolation. *Merrill-Palmer Quarterly, 50*(4), 506–535.

4. Rubin, K. H., Coplan, R. J., & Bowker, J. C. (2009). Social withdrawal in childhood. *Annual Review of Psychology, 60,* 141–171.

5. Rubin, K. H., Burgess, K., & Hastings, P. (2002). Stability and social-behavioral consequences of toddlers' inhibited temperament and parenting behaviors. *Child Development, 73*(2), 483–496.

6. Ibid.

7. Moller, L., & Serbin, L. (1996). Antecedents of toddler gender segregation: Cognitive consonance, gender-typed toy preferences, and behavioral compatibility. *Sex Roles: A Journal of Research, 34*(7–8), 445–461.

8. Fabes, R. A., Martin, C. L., & Hanish, L. D. (2004). The next 50 years: Considering gender as a context for understanding young children's peer relationships. *Merrill-Palmer Quarterly, 50*(3), 260–274.

9. Maccoby, E. E. (1998). *The two sexes: Growing up apart, coming together.* Cambridge, MA: Belknap.Press.

10. Chrisman, K., & Couchenour, D. (2003). Developing concepts of gender roles. In C. Copple (Ed.), *A world of difference* (pp. 116–117). Washington, DC: NAEYC.

11. McCabe, J., Fairchild, E., Grauerholz, L., Pescosolido, B. A., & Tope, D. (2011). Gender in twentieth-century children's books: Patterns of disparity in titles and central characters. *Gender & Society, 25,* 197–226.

12. Pines, M. (1984). Children's winning ways. *Psychology Today, 18,* 59–65

13. Ibid.

14. Ødegaard, E. E. (2006). What's worth talking about? Meaning-making in toddler-initiated conarratives in preschool. *Early Years, 26*(1), 79–92.

15. Parten, M. B. (1932). Social participation among preschool children. *Journal of Abnormal and Social Psychology, 27,* 243–269.

16. Howes, C. (1988). Peer interaction in young children. *Monographs of the Society for Research in Child Development, 53*(1), 1–92.

17. Howes, C., & Hamilton, C. E. (1992). Children's relationships with caregivers: Mothers and childcare teachers. *Child Development, 63,* 859–866.

18. Murphy, L. B. (1936). Sympathetic behavior in young children. *Journal of Experimental Education, 5,* 79–90.

19. Zahn-Waxler, C., Radke-Yarrow, R., & King, R. A. (1979). Child rearing and children's prosocial initiations toward victims of distress. *Child Development, 50*(2), 319–330.

20. Ibid.

21. Hamlin, J. K., & Wynn, K. (2011). Young infants prefer prosocial to antisocial others. *Cognitive Development, 26*(1), 30–39. doi:10.1016/j.cogdev.2010.09.001

22. Hamlin, J. K., Wynn, K., & Bloom, P. (2007). Social evaluation by preverbal infants. *Nature, 450*(7169), 557.

23. Warneken, F., & Tomasello, M. (2008). Extrinsic rewards undermine altruistic tendencies in 20-month-olds. *Developmental Psychology, 44*(6), 1785–1788.

24. Brownell, C. A., Ramani, G. B., & Zerwas, S. (2006). Becoming a social partner with peers: Cooperation and social understanding in one- and two-year-olds. *Child Development, 77*(4), 803–821.

25. Lokken, G. (2004). Greetings and welcomes among toddler peers in a Norwegian barnehage. *International Journal of Early Childhood, 36*(2), 43–58.

26. Howes, C. (2000). Social development, family, and attachment relationships. In D. Cryer & T. Harms (Eds.), *Infants and toddlers in out-of-home care* (pp. 87–113). Baltimore, MD: Brookes.

27. Shin, M. (2010). Peeking at the relationship world of infant friends and caregivers. *Journal of Early Childhood Research, 8*(3), 294–302.

28. Hawley, P., & Little, T. (1999). On winning some and losing some: A social relations approach to social dominance in toddlers. *Merrill-Palmer Quarterly, 45*(2), 185–214.

29. Capatides, J., Collins, C. C., & Bennett, L. (1996). *Peer interaction in toddlers: Parallel play revisited.* Paper presented at the conference "Ask the Child: Why, When, and How?" New York: Teachers College Press.

30. DaRos, D., & Kovach, B. (1998). Assisting toddlers and caregivers during conflict resolutions: Interactions that promote socialization. *Childhood Education, 75*(1), 25.

31. Wittmer, D., & Petersen, S. (1992). Social development and interaction: Facilitating the prosocial development of typical and exceptional infants and toddlers in group settings. *ZERO TO THREE, 12*(4), 52–60.

32. Gandini, L., & Edwards, C. (Eds.). (2001). *Bambini: The Italian approach to infant/toddler care.* New York: Teachers College Press.

33. McElwain, N. L., Cox, M. J., Burchinal, M. R., & Macfie, J. (2003). Differentiating among insecure mother-infant attachment classifications: A focus on child-friend interaction and exploration during solitary play at 36 months. *Attachment & Human Development, 5*(2), 136–164.

34. Belsky, J., & Fearon, R. M. P. (2002). Early attachment security, subsequent maternal sensitivity, and later child development: Does continuity in development depend upon continuity of caregiving? *Attachment and Human Development, 4,* 361–387.

35. Howes, C. (1988). Peer interaction in young children. *Monographs of the Society for Research in Child Development, 53*(1), 1–92.

36. de Groot Kim, S. (2010). There's Elly, It must be Tuesday: Discontinuity in child care programs and its impact on the development of peer relationships in young children. *Early Childhood Education Journal, 38*(2), 153–164. doi:10.1007/s10643-010-0400-6

37. Ibid.

38. Howes, C., Hamilton, C. E., & Matheson, C. (1994). Children's relationship with peers: Differential associations with aspects of the teacher-child relationship. *Child Development, 65*(5), 253–263.

39. NICHD Early Child Care Research Network. (2001). Nonmaternal care and family factors in early development: An overview of the NICHD study of early child care. *Journal of Applied Developmental Psychology, 22,* 457–492.

Chapter 8

1. Spelke, E. S., & Kinzler, K. D. (2007). Core knowledge. *Developmental Science, 10*(1), 89–96.

2. Meltzoff, A. N., Kuhl, P. K., Movellan, J., & Sejnowski, T. J. (2009). Foundations for a new science of learning. *Science, 325,* 284–288. doi:10.1126/science.1175626

3. Piaget, J. (1954). *The construction of reality in the child*. New York: Basic Books.

4. Lamb, M. E., Bornstein, M. H., & Teti, D. (2002). *Development in infancy* (4th ed.). Hillsdale, NJ: Erlbaum.

5. ZERO TO THREE. (2009). *Brain development*. Retrieved from www.zerotothree.org

6. Haith, M. M. (1980). *Rules that babies look by: The organization of newborn visual activity*. Hillsdale, NJ: Erlbaum

7. Lamb, M. E., Bornstein, M. H., & Teti, D. (2002). *Development in infancy* (4th ed.). Hillsdale, NJ: Erlbaum.

8. Spelke, E. S., Breinlinger, K., Jacobson, K., & Phillips, A. (1993). Gestalt relations and object perception: A developmental study. *Perception, 22*, 1483–1501.

9. DeCasper, A., & Spence, M. J. (1986). Prenatal maternal speech influences newborns' perception of speech sounds. *Infant Behavior and Development, 9*, 133–150.

10. Spelke, E. S., & Kinzler, K. D. (2007). Core knowledge. *Developmental Science, 10*(1), 89–96.

11. Mehler, J., Jusczyk, P., Lambertz, G., Halsted, N., Bertoncini, J., & Ameil-Tison, C. (1988). A precurser of language acquisition in young infants. *Cognition, 29*, 143–178.

12. Moon, C., Lagercrantz, H., & Kuhl, P. K. (2013). Language experienced in utero affects vowel perception after birth: A two-country study. *Acta Pediatrica, 102*, 156-160.

13. Spitz, R. A. (1945). Hospitalism: An inquiry into the genesis of psychiatric conditions of early childhood. *Psychoanalytic Study of the Child, 1*, 53–74.

14. Perry, B. (1996). *Maltreated children: Experience, brain development, and the next generation*. New York: Norton.

15. Field, T. (2010). Touch for socioemotional and physical well-being: A review. *Developmental Review, 30*(4), 367–383.

16. Richardson, H. (1997). Kangaroo care: Why does it work? *Midwifery Today, 44*, 50–51.

17. Field, T., & Brazelton, T. B. (1990). *Advances in touch*. Skillman, NJ: Johnson & Johnson

18. McFarlane, J. (1975). Olfaction in the development of social preferences in the human neonate. In M. Hofer (Ed.), *Parent-infant interaction* (Ciba Foundation Symposium 33; pp. 103–113). Amsterdam: Elsevier.

19. Meltzoff, A. N., & Moore, M. K. (1977). Imitation of facial and manual gestures by human neonates. *Science, 198*, 75–78.

20. Spelke, E. S., & Owlsley, C. (1979). Infants' intermodal perception of events. *Infant Behavior and Development, 2*, 13–17.

21. Spelke, E. S., & Kinzler, K. D. (2007). Core knowledge. *Developmental Science, 10*(1), 89–96.

22. Meltzoff, A. N., Kuhl, P. K., Movellan, J., & Sejnowski, T. J. (2009). Foundations for a new science of learning. *Science, 325*, 284–288. doi:10.1126/science.1175626

23. Posner, M.I., Rothbart, M.K. & Tang, Yiyuan. (2013) Developing self-regulation in early childhood. *Trends in Neuroscience Education. 2*(3-4) 107–110. Retrieved from http://www.ncbi.nlm.nih.gov/pmc/articles/PMC3927309/

24. Center on the Developing Child at Harvard University. (2011). *Building the brain's "air Traffic control" system: How early experiences shape the development of executive function. Working Paper No. 11*. Retrieved from www.developingchild.harvard.edu

25. Rothbart, M. K., Sheese, B. E., Rueda, M. R., & Posner, M. I. (2011). Developing mechanisms of self-regulation in early life. *Emotion Review, 3*(2), 207–213.

26. Bauer, P. J., Evren Güler, O., Starr, R. M., & Pathman, T. (2011). Equal learning does not result in equal remembering: The importance of post-encoding processes. *Infancy, 16*(6), 557–586. doi:10.1111/j.1532-7078.2010.00057.x

27. Bowlby, J. (1982). *Attachment*. New York: Basic Books.

28. Stephens, K. (2007) *Teaching children to resolve conflict respectfully*. Retrieved from: http://www.easternflorida.edu/community-resources/child-development-centers/parent-resource-library/documents/teaching-kids-to-resolve-conflicts-respectfully.pdf

29. Sparks, T. A., Hunter, S. K., Backman, T. L., Morgan, G. A., & Ross, R. G. (2012). Maternal parenting stress and mothers' reports of their infants' mastery motivation. *Infant Behavior & Development, 35*(1), 167–173. doi:10.1016/j.infbeh.2011.07.002

30. Shonkoff, J. P., & Phillips, D. A. (Eds.). (2000). *From neurons to neighborhoods: The science of early development*. Washington, DC: National Academy Press.

31. Mulligan, S. (1997). Group activities: One child at a time. *Child Care Plus, 8*(1), 1.

32. Meltzoff, A. N., Williamson, R. A., & Marshall, P. J. (2013). Developmental perspectives on action science: Lessons from infant imitation and cognitive neuroscience. In W. Prinz, M. Beisert, & A. Herwig (Eds.), *Action science: Foundations of an emerging discipline* (pp. 281–306). Cambridge, MA: MIT Press.

33. Vygotsky, L. S. (1978). *Mind in society: The development of higher mental processes*. Cambridge, MA: Harvard University Press.

34. Meltzoff, A. N., & Moore, M. K. (1977). Imitation of facial and manual gestures by human neonates. *Science, 198*, 75–78.

35. Vygotsky, L. S. (1978). *Mind in society: The development of higher mental processes*. Cambridge, MA: Harvard University Press.

36. Super, C. M., & Harkness, S. (1997). The cultural structuring of child development. In J. W. Berry, P. R. Dasen, & T. S. Saraswathi (Eds.), *Handbook of cross-cultural psychology. Basic processes and human development* (Vol 2, pp. 1–39). Boston: Allyn & Bacon.

37. Uzgiris, I. C., & Hunt, J. M. (1975). *Assessment in infancy: Ordinal scales of psychological development.* Urbana, IL: University of Illinois Press.

38. NCTM (National Council of Teachers of Mathematics). (2000). *Principles and standards for school mathematics.* Washington, DC: Author.

39. Xu, F., & Carey, S. (1996). Infants' metaphysics: The case of numerical identity. *Cognitive Psychology, 30*(2), 111–153.

40. Greenspan, S. I. (1997). *The growth of the mind and the endangered origins of intelligence.* Reading, MA: Perseus Books.

41. DeLoache, J. S., Strauss, M. S., & Maynard, J. (1979). Picture perception in infancy. *Infant Behavior and Development, 2*, 77–89.

42. DeLoache, J. S., Pierroutsakos, S. L., Troseth, G. L., Uttah, D. H., Rosengren, K. S., & Gottlieb, A. (1998). Grasping the nature of pictures. *Psychological Science, 9*, 205–210.

43. Howes, C., Unger, O., & Seidner, L. (1989). Social pretend play in toddlers: Parallels with social play and with solitary pretend. *Child Development, 60*, 77–84.

44. Westby, C. (1980). Assessment of cognitive and language abilities through play. *Language, Speech, and Hearing Sciences in Schools, 11*, 154–168.

45. Office of Head Start. (2015). *Head start early learning outcome framework: Ages birth to five.* Retrieved from *http://eclkc .ohs.acf.hhs.gov/hslc/hs/sr/approach/pdf/ohs-framework.pdf*

46. National Infant and Toddler Child Care Initiative. (2010). *Infant/toddler curriculum and individualization.* Retrieved from *http://www.zerotothree.org/public-policy/state-community-policy/ nitcci/multidisciplinary-consultant-module-3.pdf.* p.9

47. Rinaldi, C. (2001). Reggio Emilia: The image of the child and the child's environment as a fundamental principle. In L. Gandini & C. Edwards (Eds.), *Bambini: The Italian approach to infant care* (pp. 49–55). New York: Teachers College Press

48. NICHD Early Child Care Research Network. (2000). Characteristics and quality of child care for toddlers and preschoolers. *Applied Developmental Science, 4*(3), 116-135

Chapter 9

1. Damasio, A., & Damasio, H. (1999). Brain and language. In Scientific American Magazine (Eds.), *The scientific American book of the brain* (pp. 29-42). Guilford, CT: Lyons.

2. Özçalşkan, Ş., & Goldin-Meadow, S. (2010). Sex differences in language first appear in gesture. *Developmental Science, 13*(5), 752-760. doi:10.1111/j.1467-7687.2009.00933.x

3. Sung, J., Fausto-Sterling, A., Garcia Coll, C., & Seifer, R. (2013). The dynamics of age and sex in the development of mother-infant vocal communication between 3 and 11 months. *Infancy, 18*(6), 1135-1158. doi:10.1111/ infa.12019

4. Eriksson, M., Marschik, P. B., Tulviste, T., Almgren, M., Pérez Pereira, M., Wehberg, S., . . . Gallego, C. (2012). Differences between girls and boys in emerging language skills: Evidence from 10 language communities. *British Journal of Developmental Psychology, 30*(2), 326–343.

5. Berglund, E., & Eriksson, M. (2000). Communicative development in Swedish children 16–28 months old. The Swedish early communicative development inventory— words and sentences. *Scandinavian Journal of Psychology, 41*(2), 133–144.

6. Sung, J., Fausto-Sterling, A., Garcia Coll, C., & Seifer, R. (2013). The dynamics of age and sex in the development of mother-infant vocal communication between 3 and 11 months. *Infancy, 18*(6), 1135–1158. doi:10.1111/infa.12019

7. Vallotton, C., & Ayoub, C. (2011). Use your words: The role of language in the development of toddlers' self-regulation. *Early Childhood Research Quarterly, 26*(2), 169–181. doi:10.1016/j.ecresq.2010.09.002

8. Kubicek, L. F., & Emde, R. N. (2012). Emotional expression and language: A longitudinal study of typically developing earlier and later talkers from 15 to 30 months. *Infant Mental Health Journal, 33*(6), 553–584. doi:10.1002/imhj.21364

9. Ibid.

10. Salley, B. J., & Dixon Jr., W. E. (2007). Temperamental and joint attentional predictors of language development. *Merrill-Palmer Quarterly, 53*(1), 131-154.

11. Derauf, C., LaGasse, L., Smith, L., Newman, E., Shah, R., Arria, A., . . . Lester, B. (2011). Infant temperament and high-risk environment relate to behavior problems and language in toddlers. *Journal of Developmental Behavioral Pediatrics, 32*(2), 125–135.

12. Buss, K. A., Davis, E. L., Kiel, E. J., Brooker, R. J., Beekman, C., & Early, M. C. (2013). Dysregulated fear predicts social wariness and social anxiety symptoms during kindergarten. *Journal of Clinical Child & Adolescent Psychology, 42*(5), 603–616. doi:10.1080/15374416.2013.769170

13. Papoušek, M. (2012). From the start: Integration of affect and language in parent-infant interactions. *Infant Mental Health Journal, 33*(6), 585–589. doi:10.1002/imhj.21371

14. DeCasper, A., & Fifer, W. (1980). Of human bonding: Newborns prefer their mothers' voices. *Science, 208*, 1174–1176.

15. DeCasper, A., & Spence, M. J. (1986). Prenatal maternal speech influences newborns' perception of speech sounds. *Infant Behavior and Development, 9*, 133–150.

16. de Boer, B., & Kuhl, P. K. (2003). Investigating the role of infant-directed speech with a computer model. *Acoustics Research Letters Online (ARLO), 4*(4), 129–134.

17. Soderstrom, M. (2007). Beyond babytalk: Re-evaluating the nature and content of speech input to preverbal infants. *Developmental Review, 27*, 501–532.

18. Kuhl, P. K., Tsao, F. M., & Liu, H. M. (2003). Foreign-language experience in infancy: Effects of short-term exposure and social interaction on phonetic learning. *Proceedings of the National Academy of Science, U.S.A., 100*(15), 9096–9101.

19. Ibid.

20. Saffran, J. R., Loman, M. M., & Robertson, R. W. (2000). Infant memory for musical experiences. *Cognition, 77*(1), B15–B23.

21. Swingley, D. (2008). The roots of the early vocabulary in infants' learning from speech. *Current Directions in Psychological Science, 17*(5), 308–312.

22. Saffran, J. R. (2002). Constraints on statistical language learning. *Journal of Memory and Language, 47*, 172–196.

23. Seidl, A. (2007). Infants' use and weighting of prosodic cues in clause segmentation. *Journal of Memory and Language, 57*(1), 24–48. doi:10.1016/j.jml.2006.10.004

24. Pruden, S. M., Hirsh-Pasek, K., Golinkoff, R. M., & Hennon, E. A. (2006). The birth of words: Ten-month-olds learn words through perceptual salience. *Child Development, 77*(2), 266–280. doi:10.1111/j.1467-8624.2006.00869.x

25. Brooks, R., & Meltzoff, A. N. (2005). The development of gaze following and its relation to language. *Developmental Science, 8*(6), 535–543.

26. Ibid.

27. Twomey, K. E., Ranson, S. L., & Horst, J. S. (2014). That's more like it: Multiple exemplars facilitate word learning. *Infant & Child Development, 23*(2), 105–122. doi:10.1002/icd.1824

28. Wilbourn, M. P., & Sims, J. P. (2013). Get by with a little help from a word: Multimodal input facilitates 26-month-olds' ability to map and generalize arbitrary gestural labels. *Journal of Cognition & Development, 14*(2), 250–269. doi:10.1080/15248372.2012.658930

29. Brady, K. W., & Goodman, J. C. (2014). The type, but not the amount, of information available influences toddlers' fast mapping and retention of new words. *American Journal of Speech-Language Pathology, 23*(2), 120–133. doi:10.1044/2013_AJSLP-13-0013

30. Peredo, T. N., Owen, M. T., Rojas, R., & Caughy, M. O. (2015). Child vocabulary, maternal behavior, and inhibitory control development among Spanish-speaking children. *Early Education and Development, 26*(5-6), 749–769.

31. Morgan, P. L., Farkas, G., Hillemeier, M. M, Hammer, C. S., & Maczuga, S. (2015). 24-month-old children with larger oral vocabularies display greater academic and behavioral functioning at Kindergarten entry. *Child Development, 86*(5), 1351–1370.

32. Pagani, L. S., Fitzpatrick, C., & Barnett, T. A. (2013). Early childhood television viewing and kindergarten entry readiness. *Pediatric Research*, doi:10.1038/pr.2013.105

33. Roseberry, S., Hirsh-Pasek, K., & Golinkoff, R. M. (2014). Skype me! socially contingent interactions help toddlers learn language. *Child Development, 85*(3), 956–970. doi:10.1111/cdev.12166

34. Katz, J., & Snow, C. (2000). Language development in early childhood: The role of social interaction. In D. H. Cryer, (Ed.) *Infants and toddlers in out of home care* (pp. 49–86). Baltimore, MD: Brookes Publishing Co., Inc.

35. Lee, S., Davis, B. L., & MacNeilage, P. F. (2009). Universal production patterns and ambient language influences in babbling: A cross-linguistic study of Korean- and English-learning infants. *Journal of Child Language, 35*, 591–617.

36. Esteve-Gibert, N., & Prieto P. (2013). Prosody signals the emergence of intentional communication in the first year of life: evidence from Catalan-babbling infants. *Journal of Child Language, 40*(5), 919–944. doi:10.1017/S0305000912000359.

37. Goldstein, M. H., & Schwade, J. A. (2008). Social feedback to infants' babbling facilitates rapid phonological learning. *Psychological Science (Wiley-Blackwell), 19*(5), 515–523. doi:10.1111/j.1467-9280.2008.02117.x

38. Legerstee, M., & Barillas, Y. (2003). Sharing attention and pointing to objects at 12 months: Is the intentional stance implied? *Cognitive Development, 18*(1), 91110.

39. Ibid.

40. Begus, K., & Southgate, V. (2012). Infant pointing serves an interrogative function. *Developmental Science, 15*(5), 611–617.

41. Acredolo, L., & Goodwyn, S. (1985). Symbolic gesturing in language development: A case study. *Human Development, 28*, 40–49.

42. Carey, S. (1978). The child as word learner. In M. Halle, J. Bresnan, & G. A. Miller (Eds.), *Linguistic theory and psychological reality* (pp. 264–293). Cambridge, MA: MIT Press.

43. Brown, R. (1973). *A first language: The early stages.* London: Allen & Unwin.

44. Crais, E. R., Watson, L. R., & Baranek, G. T. (2009). Use of gesture development in profiling children's prelinguistic communication skills. *American Journal of Speech-Language Pathology, 18*(1), 95–108.

45. NICHD Early Child Care Research Network. (2005). Pathways to reading: The role of oral language in the transition to reading. *Developmental Psychology, 41*, 428–442.

46. Roberts, M. Y., & Kaiser, A. P. (2015). Early intervention for toddlers with language delays: A randomized controlled trial. *Pediatrics, 135*(4), 686–693. doi:10.1542/peds.2014-2134

47. Healthy Children.Org. (2015). *Hearing loss.* Retrieved from *https://www.healthychildren.org/English/health-issues/conditions/ear-nose-throat/Pages/Hearing-Loss.aspx*

48. American Academy of Otolaryngology-Head and neck surgery. (2016). *The necessity of early intervention in hearing.* Retrieved from *www.entnet.org/content/necessity-early-intervention-hearing*

49. Yoshinaga-Itano, C., Sedey, A., Coulter, D. K., & Mehl, A. L. (1998). Language of early and later identified children with hearing loss. *Pediatrics, 102*, 1161–1171

50. Tamis-LeMonda, C., Kuchirko, Y., & Song, L. (2014). Why is infant language learning facilitated by parental responsiveness? *Current Directions in Psychological Science (Sage Publications Inc.)*, 23(2), 121–126. doi:10.1177/0963721414522813

51. Hart, B., & Risley, T. R. (1999). *The social world of children learning to talk.* Baltimore, MD: Brookes.

52. Honig, H. S., & Brophy, H. E. (1996). *Talking with your baby: Family as a first school.* Syracuse, NY: Syracuse University Press.

53. Ibid.

54. Ibid.

55. Adamson, L. B., Bakeman, R., & Deckner, D. J. (2004). The development of symbol-infused joint engagement. *Child Development*, 75(4), 1171–1189.

56. Dunham, P., & Dunham, F. (1996). The semantically reciprocating robot: Adult influences on children's early conversational skills. *Social Development, 5,* 261–274.

57. Newman, R., & Hussain, I. (2006). Changes in preference for infant-directed speech in low and moderate noise by 4.5- to 13-month-olds. Infancy, 10, 61–76.

58. Hart, B., & Risley, T. R. (1992). American parenting of language-learning children: Persisting differences in family-child interactions observed in natural home environments. *Developmental Psychology, 28,* 1096–1105.

59. Ibid.

60. Barrera, I., & Kramer, L. (1997). From monologues to skilled dialogues: Teaching the process of crafting culturally competent early childhood environments. In P. Winton, J. McCollum, & C. Catlett (Eds.), *Reforming personnel preparation in early intervention: Issues, models, and practical strategies* (pp. 217–252). Baltimore, MD: Brookes.

61. Goffman, E. (1976). Replies and responses. *Language and Society, 5*(3), 257–313.

62. Shonkoff, J. P., & Phillips, D. A. (Eds.). (2000). *From neurons to neighborhoods: The science of early development.* Washington, DC: National Academy Press.

63. Shneidman, L.A., & Goldin-Meadow, S. (2012). Language input and acquisition in a Mayan village: How important is directed speech? *Developmental Science*, 15(5), 659–673.

64. Reese, E., & Fivush, R. (1993). Parental styles of talking about the past. *Developmental Psychology*, 29(3), 596–606.

65. Pham, L. (1994). Infant dual language acquisition revisited. *Journal of Educational Issues of Language Minority Students, 14,* 185–210.

66. Byers-Heinlein, K., Burns, T. C., & Werker, J. F. (2010). The roots of bilingualism in newborns. *Psychological Science*, 21(3), 343–348. doi:10.1177/0956797609360758

67. Office of Head Start Department of Health and Human Services. (2008). *What does it take? Head Start dual language report.* Retrieved from http://eclkc.ohs.acf.hhs.gov/hslc/tta-system/teaching/eecd/Dual%20Language%20Learners%20and%20Their%20Families/Learning%20in%20Two%20Languages/DLANA_final_2009%5B1%5D.pdf

68. Singh, L., Fu, C. S. L., Rahman, A. A., Hameed, W. B., Sanmugam, S., Agarwal, P., . . . Rifkin-Graboi, A. (2015). Back to basics: A bilingual advantage in infant visual habituation. *Child Development*, 86(1), 294–302. doi:10.1111/cdev.12271

69. Poulin-Dubois, D., Blaye, A., Coutya, J., & Bialystok, E. (2011). The effects of bilingualism on toddlers' executive functioning. *Journal of Experimental Child Psychology*, 108(3), 567–579.

70. Engel de Abreu, P. M. J., Cruz-Santos, A., Tourinho, C. J., Martin, R., & Bialystok, E. (2012). Bilingualism enriches the poor: Enhanced cognitive control in low-income minority children. *Psychological Science, 23*(11), 1364–1371. doi:10.1177/0956797612443836

71. Garcia-Sierra, A., Rivera-Gaxiola, M., Percaccio, C. R., Conboy, B. T., Romo, H., Klarman, L., . . . Kuhl, P. K. (2011). Bilingual language learning: An ERP study relating early brain responses to speech, language input, and later word production. *Journal of Phonetics*, 39(4), 546–557.

72. Poulin-Dubois, D., Bialystok, E., Blaye, A., Polonia, A., & Yott, J. (2013). Lexical access and vocabulary development in very young bilinguals, *International Journal of Bilingualism, 17*(1), 57–70.

73. DeHouwer, A. (1999, July). Two or more languages in early childhood: Some general points and practical recommendations. *ERIC Digest* (ED433697). District of Columbia: ERIC Clearinghouse on Languages and Linguistics.

74. Sánchez, S. Y., & Thorp, E. K. (1998b). Policies on linguistic continuity: A family's right, a practitioner's choice, or an opportunity to create shared meaning and a more equitable relationship? In E. Fenichel (Ed.), *Bulletin of Zero to Three: National Center for Infants, Toddlers, and Families, 18*(6), 12–20.

75. DeHouwer, A. (1999, July). Two or more languages in early childhood: Some general points and practical recommendations. *ERIC Digest* (ED433697). District of Columbia: ERIC Clearinghouse on Languages and Linguistics.

76. Kirk, E., Howlett, N., Pine, K. J., & Fletcher, B. (2013). To sign or not to sign? The impact of encouraging infants to gesture on infant language and maternal mind-mindedness. *Child Development*, 84(2), 574–590. doi:10.1111/j.1467-8624.2012.01874.x

77. Vallotton, C. (2011). Babies open our minds to their minds: How 'listening' to infant signs complements and extends our knowledge of infants and their development. *Infant Mental Health Journal, 32*(1), 115–133. doi:10.1002/imhj.20286

78. Kirk, E., Howlett, N., Pine, K. J., & Fletcher, B. (2013). To sign or not to sign? The impact of encouraging infants to gesture on infant language and maternal mind-mindedness. *Child Development*, 84(2), 574–590. doi:10.1111/j.1467-8624.2012.01874.x

79. Vallotton, C. (2011). Babies open our minds to their minds: How 'listening' to infant signs complements and

extends our knowledge of infants and their development. *Infant Mental Health Journal, 32*(1), 115–133. doi:10.1002/imhj.20286

80. DeHouwer, A. (1999, July). Two or more languages in early childhood: Some general points and practical recommendations. *ERIC Digest* (ED433697). District of Columbia: ERIC Clearinghouse on Languages and Linguistics.

81. NICHD Early Child Care Research Network. (2000). The relation of child care to cognitive and language development. *Child Development, 71*(4), 960–980.

82. Vallotton, C. D., Harewood, T., Ayoub, C. A., Pan, B., Mastergeorge, A. M., & Brophy-Herb, H. (2012). Buffering boys and boosting girls: The protective and promotive effects of early head start for children's expressive language in the context of parenting stress. *Early Childhood Research Quarterly, 27*(4), 695–707. doi:10.1016/j.ecresq.2011.03.001

Chapter 10

1. Hussey-Gardner, B. (2003). *Parenting to make a difference.* Palo Alto, CA: Vort.

2. Bornstein, M. H., Hahn, C., & Suwalsky, J. T. D. (2013). Physically developed and exploratory young infants contribute to their own long-term academic achievement. *Psychological Science, 10,* 1906–1917. Retrieved from *www.ncbi.nlm.nih.gov/pmc/articles/PMC4151610/*

3. Saccani, R., Valentini, N. C., Pereira, K., Müller, A., & Gabbard, C. (2013). Associations of biological factors and affordances in the home with infant motor development. *Pediatrics International, 55,* 197–203.

4. Hines, M. (2011). Gender development and the human brain. *Annual Review of Neuroscience, 34,* 69–88. doi:10.1146/annurev-neuro-061010-113654

5. Mondschein, E. R., Adolph, K. E., & Tamis-LeMonda, C. S. (2000). Gender bias in mothers' expectations about infant crawling. *Journal of Experimental Child Psychology, 77,* 304–316.

6. Eaton, W. O. (2009). Motor activity level. Retrieved from *http://home.cc.umanitoba.ca/~eaton/child-development-motor-activity-level.html*

7. Malina, R. M. (2004). Motor development during infancy and early childhood: Overview and suggested directions for research. *International Journal of Sport and Health Medicine, 2,* 50–66.

8. Liu, C. H., & Tronick, E. (2011). Neurobehavioural development in infancy. In D. Skuse, H. Bruce, L. Dowdney, & D. Mrazek (Eds.), *Child psychology and psychiatry: Frameworks for practice,* (2nd ed., pp. 18–22). Chichester, UK: John Wiley & Sons.

9. Adolph, K. E. (2008). Learning to move. *Current Directions in Psychological Science, 17,* 213–218.

10. Thelen, E., & Smith, L. B. (1996). *A dynamic systems approach to the development of cognition and action.* Cambridge, MA: MIT Press.

11. Adolph, K. E., & Eppler, M. A. (2002). Flexibility and specificity in infant motor skill acquisition. In J. Fagan (Ed.), *Progress in infancy research* (Vol. 2, pp. 121–167). Mahwah, NJ: Erlbaum.

12. Caçola, P., Gabbard, C., Santos, D. C., & Batistela, A. C. (2011). Development of the affordances in the home environment for motor development-infant scale. *Pediatrics International, 53*(6), 820–825.

13. Miquelote, A. F., Santos, D. C. C., Caçola, P. M., Montebelo, M. I. de L., & Gabbard, C. (2012). Effect of the home environment on motor and cognitive behavior of infants. *Infant Behavior & Development, 35*(3), 329–334. doi:10.1016/j.infbeh.2012.02.002

14. Karasik, L. B., Adolph, K. E., Tamis-LeMonda, C. S., & Zuckerman, A. L. (2012). Carry on: Spontaneous object carrying in 13-month-old crawling and walking infants. *Developmental Psychology, 48*(2), 389–397.

15. Murphy, L. B. (1994). Hopping, jumping, leaping, skipping, and loping: Savoring the possibilities of locomotion. *ZERO TO THREE, 15*(1), 27.

16. Adolph, K. A., & Tamis-LaMonda, C. (2014). The costs and benefits of development: The transition from crawling to walking. *Child Development Perspectives, 8*(4), 187–192.

17. Ibid.

18. Adolph, K. E., & Kretch, K. S. (2015). Gibson's theory of perceptual learning. In H. Keller (Ed.), *International encyclopedia of the social and behavioral sciences,* (2nd ed., Vol.10, pp. 127–134). New York: Elsevier.

19. Clifton, R. K., Rochat, P., Robin, D., & Berthier, N. E. (1994). Multimodal perception in the control of infant reaching. *Journal of Experimental Psychology: Human Perception and Performance, 20*(4), 876–886.

20. Robin, D. J., Berthier, N. E., & Clifton, R. K. (1996). Infants' predictive reaching for moving objects in the dark. *Developmental Psychology, 32,* 824–835.

21. Brownell, C. A., Nichols, S. R., Svetlova, M., Zerwas, S., & Ramani, G. (2010). The head bone's connected to the neck bone: When do toddlers represent their own body topography? *Child Development, 81*(3), 797–810. doi:10.1111/j.1467-8624.2010.01434.x

22. Marshall, P., & Meltzoff, A. N. (2015). Body maps in the infant brain. *Trends in Cognitive Sciences, 19*(9), 499–505.

23. Marshall, P. J., Saby, J. N., & Meltzoff, A. N. (2013). Imitation and the developing social brain: Infants' somatotopic EEG patterns for acts of self and other. *International Journal of Psychological Research, 6,* 22–29. Retrieved from *http://www.ncbi.nlm.nih.gov/pmc/articles/PMC3923378/*

24. UCP (United Cerebral Palsy). (2013). *About Cerebral Palsy.* Retrieved from *www.ucp.org/*

25. MOD (March of Dimes). (2014). *Cerebral palsy. Quick reference: fact sheets.* Retrieved from *www.marchofdimes.com*

26. RIE (Resources for Infant Educators. (n.d.) *RIE basic principles.* Retrieved from *https://www.rie.org/educaring/ries-basic-principles/*

27. Ohio State University & US Department of Defense. (n.d.) *Supporting Physical Development: Environments and Experiences. Virtual Lab School.* Retrieved from *www.virtuallabschool.org/infants-toddlers/physical-development/lesson-3*

28. American Academy of Pediatrics (AAP). (2004). *U.S. government should ban baby walkers.* Retrieved from *http://www.aap.org*

29. Consumer Products Safety Commission. (2009). *Nursery product-related safety injuries and deaths among children under five.* Retrieved from *www.cpsc.gov/library/nursery08.pdf*

30. Siegel, A. C., & Burton, R. V. (1999). Effects of baby walkers on motor and mental development in human infants. *Journal of Developmental and Behavioral Pediatrics, 20,* 355–361.

31. Brazelton, T. B. (1972). Implications of infant development among the Mayan Indians of Mexico. *Human Development, 15*(2), 90–111.

32. Kaplan, H., & Dove, H. (1987). Infant development among the Ache of eastern Paraguay. *Developmental Psychology, 23*(2), 190–198.

33. Konner, M. (1977). Infancy among the Kalihari Desert San. In P. H. Liederman, S. R. Tulin, & A. Rosenfeld (Eds.), *Culture and infancy: Variations in the human experience* (pp. 287–327). New York: Academic Press.

34. Thompson-Rangel, T. (1994). The Hispanic child and family: Developmental disabilities and occupational therapy intervention. *Developmental Disabilities Special Interest Newsletter.*

35. Louv, R. (2013). *Last child in the woods: Saving our children from nature deficit disorder.* Chapel Hill, NC: Algonquin Books.

36. Matthews, D. M., & Jenks, S. M. (2013). Ingestion of Mycobacterium vaccae decreases anxiety-related behavior and improves learning in mice. *Behavioural Processes, 96,* 27–35.

37. Aamodt, S., & Wang, S. (2011). *Welcome to your child's mind: How the mind grows from conception to college.* New York: Bloomsbury, USA.

38. Wells, N. M., & Evans, G. W. (2003). Nearby nature: A buffer of life stress among rural children. *Environment and Behavior, 35,* 311–330

39. Taylor, A. F., & Ming-Kuo, F. E. (2011). Could exposure to everyday green spaces help treat ADHD? Evidence from children's play settings. *Applied Psychology: Health and Well-Being, 3*(3), 281–303.

40. Spencer, K. M., & Wright, P. H. (2014). Quality outdoor play spaces for young children. *Young Children, 69*(5), 28–34.

41. American Academy of Pediatrics, American Public Health Association, National Resource Center for Health and Safety in Child Care. (2011). *Caring for our children: National health and safety performance standards for out-of-home child care programs* (3rd ed.). Elk Grove Village, IL: American. Retrieved from nrckids.org/CFOC3/

42. Ibid.

43. Early Head Start National Resource Center. (2012). *EHS TA paper no. 14: Supporting outdoor play and exploration for infants and toddlers.* Author: Washington, D.C. Retrieved from *http://eclkc.ohs.acf.hhs.gov/hslc/tta-system/ehsnrc/docs/ehs-ta-paper-14-outdoor-play.pdf*

44. Ibid.

Chapter 11

1. U.S. Census Bureau. (2011). *Who's minding the kids? Child care arrangements.* Retrieved from *www.naccrra.org/about-child-care/child-demographics*

2. Ruzek E., Burchinal, M., Farkas, G., Duncan, G., Dang, T., & Lee, W. (2011, March). *Does high quality childcare narrow the achievement gap at two years of age?* Presented at Society for Research on Educational Effectiveness: Washington, DC.

3. NICHD Early Child Care Research Network. (2002a). Child care structure, process, outcome: Direct and indirect effects of child care quality on young children's development. *Psychological Science. 13,* 199–206.

4. NICHD Early Child Care Research Network. (2000). Characteristics and quality of child care for toddlers and preschoolers. *Applied Developmental Science, 4*(3), 116–135.

5. Emde, R. N., Biringen, Z., Clyman, R. B., & Oppenheim, D. (1991). The moral self of infancy: Affective core and procedural knowledge. *Developmental Review, 11,* 251–270.

6. Emde, R. N. (1994). Individuality, context, and the search for meaning. *Child Development, 65,* 719–737.

7. Zahn-Waxler, C., & Radke-Yarrow, R. (1990). The origins of empathic concern. *Motivation and Emotion, 14,* 107–130.

8. Recchia, S. L. (2012). Caregiver-child relationships as a context for continuity in child care. *Early Years: An International Journal of Research and Development, 32*(2), 143–157.

9. Snyder, C. (2011, Spring). It's good to see you again! Continuity of care in infant and toddler program. *ReSource,* 11–15. Retrieved from *www.highscope.org*

10. Ruzek, E., Burchinal, M., Farkas, G., Duncan, G., Dang, T., & Lee, W. (2011, March). *Does high quality childcare narrow the achievement gap at two years of age?* Presented at Society for Research on Educational Effectiveness, Washington, DC.

11. Ibid.

12. Snyder, C. (2011, Spring). It's good to see you again! Continuity of care in infant and toddler program. *ReSource,* 11–15. Retrieved from *www.highscope.org*

13. Institute of Medicine (IOM) and National Research Council (NRC). (2015). *Transforming the workforce for children birth through age 8: A unifying foundation.* Washington, DC: The National Academies Press.

14. Snow, K. (2013, November 13). *Who is the early child care and education workforce?* Retrieved from *.naeyc.org/blogs/gclarke/2013/11/who-early-care-and-education-workforce-0*

15. Flagler, B. (2010). Quality child care vital. *Atlanta Constitution.*

16. Office of Program Research and Evaluation. (2013). *Number and characteristics of early care and education (ECE) teachers and caregivers: Initial findings from the national survey of early care and education (NSECE)*. Retrieved from *acf.hhs.gov/sites/default/files/opre/nsece_wf_brief_102913_0.pdf*

17. Clarke-Stewart, K. A., Vandell, D. L., Burchinal, M., O'Brien, M., & McCartney, K. (2002). Do regulable features of child-care homes affect children's development? *Early Child Research Quarterly, 17*(1), 52–86.

18. Arnett, J. (1989). Caregivers in child care centers. Does training matter? *Journal of Applied Developmental Psychology, 10(4)*, 541–552.

19. Bureau of Labor Statistics. (2015). Occupational employment statistics. Child care workers. Retrieved from *bls.gov/oes/current/oes399011.htm*

20. Suttle, R. (2014). *The average annual income for in-home childcare*. Retrieved from *work.chron.com/average-annual-income-inhome-childcare-23472.html*

21. Jacobs, E., & Adrien, E. (2012). Canadian child care regulations regarding training and curriculum. In N. Howe & L. Prochner (eds.). *Recent Perspectives on Early Childhood Education in Canada.* University of Toronto Press: Toronto.

22. Lally, J. R. (2001). The art and science of child care. *Program for Infant Toddler Care.* Retrieved from *pitc.org/cs/pitclib/query/q/2915?author=Lally&search_year=2001&name=Art%20and%20Science%20of%20Child%20Care&x-template=pitclib.search.form*

23. American Academy of Pediatrics, American Public Health Association, National Resource Center for Health and Safety in Child Care and Early Education. (2011). *Caring for our children: National health and safety performance standards; Guidelines for early care and education programs. 3rd Edition.* Elk Grove Village, IL: American Academy of Pediatrics; Washington, DC: American Public Health Association.

24. Ibid.

25. WebMD. (2015). *Overview of breastfeeding.* Retrieved from *http://www.webmd.com/parenting/baby/nursing-basics?page=1*

26. American Academy of Pediatrics, American Public Health Association, National Resource Center for Health and Safety in Child Care and Early Education. (2011). *Caring for our children: National health and safety performance standards; Guidelines for early care and education programs. 3rd Edition.* Elk Grove Village, IL: American Academy of Pediatrics; Washington, DC: American Public Health Association.

27. Ibid.

28. Ibid.

29. Ibid.

30. Ibid.

31. Ibid.

32. eXtension. (2015*). Preventing injuries in child care*. Retrieved from *articles.extension.org/pages/25767/preventing-injuries-in-child-care*

33. American Academy of Pediatrics. (2011). Policy Statement—SIDS and other sleep-related deaths: expansion of recommendations for a safe infant sleep environment. *Pediatrics, 128*(5), 1030–1039.

34. Administration for Children and Families. (2010). *Child Abuse Prevention and Treatment Act. Reauthorization Act of 2010 (P.L. 111-320), § 3.* Retrieved from *https://www.acf.hhs.gov/sites/default/files/cb/capta2010.pdf*

35. Child Welfare Information Gateway. (2014). *Definitions of child abuse and neglect.* Retrieved from *www.childwelfare.gov/pubPDFs/define.pdf*

36. Clermont County, Ohio Children's Protective Services. (n.d.) *Detecting child abuse.* Retrieved from *cps.clermontcountyohio.gov/IdentifyingAbuse.aspx*

37. Lazarov, M., & Evans, A. (2000). Breastfeeding: Encouraging the best for low-income women. *ZERO TO THREE, 21*(1), 15–23.

38. Meyers, A., & Chawla, N. (2000). Nutrition and the social, emotional, and cognitive development of infants and young children. *ZERO TO THREE, 21*(1), 5–11.

39. American Academy of Pediatrics. (2012). Breastfeeding and the use of human milk. *Pediatrics, 129*(3). Retrieved from *http://pediatrics.aappublications.org/content/129/3/e827*

40. WebMD. (2015). *What are the benefits of breastfeeding for your baby?* Retrieved from *http://www.webmd.com/parenting/baby/nursing-basics#1*

41. American Academy of Pediatrics, American Public Health Association, National Resource Center for Health and Safety in Child Care and Early Education. (2011). *Caring for our children: National health and safety performance standards; Guidelines for early care and education programs.* 3rd Edition. Elk Grove Village, IL: American Academy of Pediatrics; Washington, DC: American Public Health Association.

42. Beard, J. L., Connor, J. D., & Jones, B. C. (1997). Brain iron: Location and function. *Progress in Food and Nutrition Science, 17*, 183–221.

43. KidsHealth.(2014). *Iron deficiency anemia.* Retrieved from *kidshealth.org/en/parents/ida.html#*

44. Whiteman, H. (2015, February 2). CDC: most commercial foods for infants, toddlers contain too much salt, sugar. *Medical News Today.* Retrieved from *medicalnewstoday.com/articles/288837.php*

45. KidsHealth. (2014). *Nutrition guide for toddlers.* Retrieved from *kidshealth.org/en/parents/toddler-food.html#*

46. healthychildren.org. (2015). *Unsafe foods for toddlers.* Retrieved from *healthychildren.org/English/ages-stages/toddler/nutrition/Pages/Unsafe-Foods-for-Toddlers.aspx*

47. American Academy of Pediatrics, American Public Health Association, National Resource Center for Health and Safety in Child Care and Early Education. (2011). *Caring for our children: National health and safety performance standards; Guidelines for early care and education programs.* 3rd Edition.

Elk Grove Village, IL: American Academy of Pediatrics; Washington, DC: American Public Health Association.

48. Ibid.

49. Ibid.

50. Ibid.

51. Child and Adult Care Food Program. (2015). *Child and adult care food program.* Retrieved from *fns.usda.gov/cacfp/child-and-adult-care-food-program*

52. Harmes, T., Cryer, D., & Clifford, R. M. (2006). *Infant/toddler environment rating scale.* New York: Teachers College Press.

53. Administration for Children and Families. (2011). *Head Start program performance standards.* Retrieved from *eclkc.ohs.acf.hhs.gov/hslc/standards/hspps/45-cfr-chapter-xiii*

54. Child Trends. (2010). *The compendium of quality rating systems and evaluations.* Author: Washington, DC.

55. National Association for the Education of Young Children. (2012). *Accreditation.* Retrieved from *naeyc.org/accreditation*

56. National Association for Family Child Care. (2013). *Accreditation updates.* Retrieved from *http://nafcc.org/*

Chapter 12

1. National Association for the Education of Young Children (NAEYC). (2009). *Developmentally appropriate practice in early childhood programs serving children from birth through age 8.* Retrieved from *https://www.naeyc.org/files/naeyc/file/positions/PSDAP.pdf*

2. Weil, J. L. (1993). *Early deprivation of empathic care.* Madison, CT: International Universities Press.

3. Meins, E. (1997). Security of attachment and maternal tutoring strategies: Interaction within the zone of proximal development. *British Journal of Developmental Psychology, 15,* 129–144.

4. Meins, E., Fernyhough, C., Wainwright, R., Clark-Carter, D., Gupta, M. D., . . . Tuckey, M. (2003). Pathways to understanding mind: Construct validity and predictive validity of maternal mind-mindedness. *Child Development, 74,* 1194–1211.

5. Meins, E., Fernyhough, C., de Rosnay, M., Arnott, B., Leekam, S. R., & Turner, M. (2012). Mind-mindedness as a multidimensional construct: Appropriate and nonattuned mind-related comments independently predict infant—mother attachment in a socially diverse sample. *Infancy, 17*(4), 393–415.

6. UNICEF. (2009). *Convention on the rights of the child.* Retrieved from *www.unicef.org/crc/*

7. Bruner, J. (1996). *The culture of education.* Cambridge, MA: Harvard University Press.

8. Honig, A. (1993). Mental health for babies: What do theory and research tell us? *Young Children, 48*(3), 69–76.

9. Shonkoff, J. P., & Phillips, D. A. (Eds.). (2000). *From neurons to neighborhoods: The science of early development.* Washington, DC: National Academy Press.

10. Bronfenbrenner, U. (1994). Who cares for the children. In H. Nuba, M. Searson, & D. L. Sheiman (Eds.), *Resources for early childhood: A handbook* (pp. 113–129) New York: Garland.

11. Gonzalez-Mena, J., & Eyer, D. W. (2001). *Infants, toddlers, and caregivers* (5th ed.). Mountain View, CA: Mayfield.

12. Lally, J. R., Torres, Y., & Phelps, P. (1994). Caring for infants and toddlers in groups: Necessary considerations for emotional, social, and cognitive development. *ZERO TO THREE, 14*(5), 1–8.

13. Howes, C., Phillips, D., & Whitebook, M. (1992). Thresholds of quality: Implications for the social development of children in center-based child care. *Child Development, 63,* 449–460.

14. Shonkoff, J. P., & Phillips, D. A. (Eds.). (2000). *From neurons to neighborhoods: The science of early development.* Washington, DC: National Academy Press.

15. NICHD Early Child Care Research Network. (2000). The relation of child care to cognitive and language development. *Child Development, 71*(4), 960–980.

16. Gandini, L., & Edwards, C. (Eds.). (2001). *Bambini: The Italian approach to infant/toddler care.* New York: Teachers College Press.

17. Lally, J. R. (1995). The impact of child care policies and practices on infant/toddler identity formation. *Young Children, 51*(1), 58–67.

18. Honig, A. S. (2001). *Secure relationships: Nurturing infant-toddler attachment in child care settings.* Washington, DC: NAEYC.

19. Honig, A. S. (2014). *The BEST for Babies.* Lewisville, NC: Gryphon House.

20. Parlakian, R. (2003). *Before the ABCs: Promoting school readiness in infants and toddlers.* Washington, DC: ZERO TO THREE.

21. NAEYC (2016). *DAP with infants and toddlers.* Retrieved from *http://www.naeyc.org/dap/infants-and-toddlers*

22. Early Childhood Research and Practice (ECRP). (2009). Spend your whole life learning and giving. An interview with Alice Sterling Honig. *ECRP, 11*(2), Retrieved from *http://ecrp.uiuc.edu/v11n2/interview-honig.html*

23. Cawlfield, M. E. (1992). Velcro time: The language connection. *Young Children, 47*(4), 26–30.

24. Lerner, C., & Dombro, A. (2000). *Learning and growing together: Understanding and supporting your child's development.* Washington, DC: ZERO TO THREE.

25. Goncu, A., & Gaskins, S. (Eds.). (2007). *Play and development: Evolutionary, sociocultural, and functional perspectives.* Mahwah, NJ: Erlbaum.

26. Hirsh-Pasek, K., Golinkoff, R. M., Berk, L. E., & Singer, D. G. (2009). *A mandate for playful learning in preschool: Presenting the evidence.* New York: Oxford University Press.

27. Smith, P. K., & Pellegrini, A. (2008). Learning through play. In R. E. Tremblay, R. G. Barr, R. deV Peters, & M. Boivin (Eds.), *Encyclopedia on early childhood development* (pp. 1–6). Montreal, Quebec: Centre of Excellence for Early Childhood Development.

28. Bettelheim, B. (1987, March). The importance of play. *Atlantic,* 35–46.

29. Perry, B. (2001, April). The importance of pleasure in play. *Scholastic Early Childhood Today,* 24–25.

30. Smilansky, S., & Shefatya, L. (1990). *Facilitating play: A medium for promoting cognitive, socioemotional, and academic development in young children.* Gaithersburg, MD: Psychosocial and Educational Publications.

31. Caruso, D. A. (1988). Play and learning in infancy: Research and implications. *Young Children, 43*(6), 63–70.

32. Howes, C., & Phillipsen, L. (1998). Continuity in children's relations with peers. *Social Development, 7*(3), 340–349.

33. Carter, M., & Curtis, D. (1998). *The visionary director: A handbook for dreaming, organizing, and improvising in your center.* St. Paul, MN: Redleaf.

34. Greenman, J., Stonehouse, A., & Schweikert, G. (2008). *Prime times: A handbook for excellence in infant and toddler programs* (2nd ed.). Minneapolis, MN: Redleaf Press.

35. Honig, A. (2002). Playing it out: The aftermath of September 11th in early care and education. *ZERO TO THREE, 22*(3), 52.

36. Zanolli, K. M., Saudargas, R. A., & Twardosz, S. (1997). The development of toddlers' responses to affectionate teacher behavior. *Early Childhood Research Quarterly, 12*(1), 99–116.

37. Honig, A. (2002). *Secure relationships: Nurturing infant toddler attachment in early care settings.* Washington, DC: NAEYC.

38. Mangione, P. L., Lally, R. J., & Signer, S. (1990). The ages of infancy: Caring for young, mobile, and older infants [Video magazine]. Sacramento, CA: CDE Press.

39. Sears, W., & Sears, M. (2001). *Attachment parenting: A commonsense guide to understanding and nurturing your baby.* New York: Little, Brown.

40. Honig, A. (2003, September). Helping babies feel secure. *Scholastic Early Childhood Today, 18*(1), 27–29.

41. Honig, A. (personal communication January 6, 2005)

42. Honig, A. (2002c). *Secure relationships: Nurturing infant toddler attachment in early care settings.* Washington, DC: NAEYC.

43. Lerner, C., & Dombro, A. (2000). Learning and growing together: Understanding and supporting your child's development. Washington, DC: ZERO TO THREE.

44. Copple, C. (Ed.). (2003). *A world of difference: Readings on teaching young children in a diverse society.* Washington, DC: NAEYC.

45. Gonzalez-Mena, J. (2008). *Diversity in early care and education: Honoring differences* (5th ed.). Washington, DC: NAEYC.

46. Barrera, I., Kramer, L., Macpherson, D. (2012). *Skilled Dialogue. Strategies for responding to cultural diversity in early childhood* (2nd ed.). Baltimore, MD: Brookes Publishing.

47. Gonzalez-Mena, J. (2001). *Multicultural issues in child care* (3rd ed.). Mountain View, CA: Mayfield Publishing Co.

48. Ibid.

49. Barrera, I., Kramer, L., Macpherson, D. (2012). *Skilled Dialogue. Strategies for responding to cultural diversity in early childhood* (2nd ed.). Baltimore, MD: Brookes Publishing.

50. Derman-Sparks, L., LeeKeenan, D., & Nimmo, J. (2015). *Leading anti-bias early childhood programs—A guide for change.* Washington, DC: NAEYC.

51. Emde, R. N. (2001). Preface. In L. Gandini & C. Edwards (Eds.), *Bambini: The Italian approach to infant/toddler care* (pp. vii–xiv). New York: Teachers College Press.

52. Meisels, S. J., Dombro, A., Marsden, D. B., Weston, D. R., & Jewkes, A. M. (2003). *The Ounce Scale.* New York: Pearson Early Learning.

Chapter 13

1. Pawl, J. H., & St. John, M. (1998). *How you are is as important as what you do . . . in making a positive difference for infants, toddlers, and their families.* Washington, DC: ZERO TO THREE.

2. Griffin, A. (1998). Infant/toddler sleep in the child care context: Patterns, problems, and relationships. *ZERO TO THREE, 19*(2), 24–29.

3. Butterfield, P. (2002). Child care is rich in routines. *ZERO TO THREE, 22*(4), 29–32.

4. Carter, M., & Curtis, D. (1998). *The visionary director: A handbook for dreaming, organizing, and improvising in your center.* St. Paul, MN: Redleaf.

5. Greenman, J. (1988). *Caring spaces, learning places: Children's environments that work.* Redmond, WA: Exchange.

6. Miller, K. (1999). *Simple steps: Developmental activities for infants, toddlers, and two-year-olds.* Beltsville, MD: Gryphon House.

7. Vernon, F. (2003, Spring). Sink play. *Focus on Infants and Toddlers, 15*(1), 5.

8. Honig, A. (2003). Beauty for babies. *Scholastic Early Childhood Today, 17*(7), 22–25.

9. Hirsch, E. S. (1996). *The block book* (3rd ed.). Washington, DC: NAEYC.

10. Stroud, J. E. (1995). Block play: A foundation for literacy. *Early Childhood Education Journal, 23*(1), 9–13.

11. Im, J. H., Osborn, C. A., Sánchez, S. Y., & Thorp, E. K. (2007). *Cradling literacy: Building teachers' skills to nurture early language and literacy from birth to 5.* Washington, DC: ZERO TO THREE.

12. Geist, E. (2003). Infants and toddlers exploring mathematics. *Young Children, 58*(1), 10–12.

13. Miller, K. (1999). *Simple steps: Developmental activities for infants, toddlers, and two-year-olds.* Beltsville, MD: Gryphon House.

14. Teaching Strategies, LLC (2016). *The Creative Curriculum*® *for Infants, Toddlers & Twos* (3rd Ed.) Retrieved from *https:// shop.teachingstrategies.com/page/76108-Creative-Curriculum-Infants-Toddlers-Twos.cfm*

15. Gandini, L., & Edwards, C. (Eds.). (2001). *Bambini: The Italian approach to infant/toddler care.* New York: Teachers College Press.

16. Rinaldi, C. (2001). Reggio Emilia: The image of the child and the child's environment as a fundamental principle. In L. Gandini & C. Edwards (Eds.), *Bambini: The Italian approach to infant care* (pp. 49–55). New York: Teachers College Press.

17. Gandini, L., & Edwards, C. (Eds.). (2001). *Bambini: The Italian approach to infant/toddler care.* New York: Teachers College Press.

Chapter 14

1. Phillips, D., Crowell, N. A., Sussman, A. L., Gunnar, M., Fox, N., Hane, A., & Bisgaier, J. (2012). Reactive temperament and sensitivity to context in childcare. *Social Development, 21*(3), 628–643. doi:10.1111/j.1467-9507.2011.00649.x

2. Deynoot-Schaub, M., & Riksen-Walraven, J. (2006). Peer contacts of 15-month-olds in childcare: Links with child temperament, parent-child interaction and quality of childcare. *Social Development, 15*(4), 709–729. doi:10.1111/j.1467-9507.2006.00366.x

3. Gonzalez-Mena, J. (2006). *50 early childhood strategies for working and communicating with diverse families.* Upper Saddle River, NJ: Merrill/Prentice Hall.

4. Gonzalez-Mena, J. (2008). *Diversity in early care and education: Honoring differences* (5th ed.). Washington, DC: NAEYC.

5. Vallotton, C. D. (2009). Do infants influence their quality of care? Infants' communicative gestures predict caregivers' responsiveness. *Infant Behavior and Development, 32,* 351–365.

6. Irwin, J., Carter, A. S., & Briggs-Gowan, M. I. (2002). The social-emotional development of "late-talking" toddlers. *Journal of the American Academy of Child and Adolescent Psychiatry, 41*(11), 1324–1332.

7. Van De Zande, I. (1995). *1, 2, 3 . . . The toddler years: A practical guide for parents and caregivers.* Santa Cruz, CA: Santa Cruz Toddler Care Center.

8. Brook, J. S., Zheng, L., Whiteman, M., & Brook, D. (2001). Aggression in toddlers: Associations with parenting and marital relations. *Journal of Genetic Psychology, 162*(2), 228–241.

9. Brazelton, T. B. (1992). *Touchpoints: Your child's emotional and behavioral development.* Reading, MA: Perseus.

10. Bromwich, R. (1997). *Working with families and their infants at risk.* Austin, TX: Pro-Ed.

11. Honig, A.S., & Lally, R.J. (1981). *Infant caregiving: A design for training.* Syracuse, NY: Syracuse University Press.

12. de Hann, D., & Singer, E. (2003). Use your words: A sociocultural approach to the teacher's role in the transition from physical to verbal strategies of resolving peer conflicts among toddlers. *Journal of Early Childhood Research, 1*(1), 95–109.

13. Vallotton, C., & Ayoub, C. (2011). Use your words: The role of language in the development of toddlers' self-regulation. *Early Childhood Research Quarterly, 26*(2), 169–181. doi:10.1016/j.ecresq.2010.09.002

14. Laible, D. J., & Thompson, R. A. (2002). Mother-child conflict in the toddler years: Lessons in emotion, morality, and relationships. *Child Development, 73*(4), 1187–1203.

15. Batya, L., Simoni, H., & Perrig-Chiello, P. (2008). Conflict between peers in infancy and toddler age: What do they fight about? *Early Years: Journal of International Research & Development, 28*(3), 235–249.

16. Gloeckler, L., & Cassell, J. (2012). Teacher practices with toddlers during social problem solving opportunities. *Early Childhood Education Journal, 40*(4), 251–257. doi:10.1007/s10643-011-0495-4

17. Singer, E., & Hannikainen, M. (2002). The teacher's role in territorial conflicts of 2- to 3-year-old children. *Journal of Research in Early Childhood Education, 17*(1), 5–18.

18. Lieberman, A. (1993). *The emotional life of a toddler.* New York: Free Press.

19. Stephens, K. (1999). Toilet training: Children step up to independence. *Child Care Information Exchange,* 76–80.

20. Ibid.

21. Brazelton, T. B., & Sparrow, J. D. (2004). *Toilet training: The Brazelton way.* Cambridge, MA: Da Capo.

22. Stephens, K. (1999). Toilet training: Children step up to independence. *Child Care Information Exchange,* 76–80.

23. Lieberman, A. (1993). *The emotional life of a toddler.* New York: Free Press.

24. Crockenberg, S., Leerkes, E., & Lekka, S. K. (2007). Pathways from marital aggression to infant emotion regulation: The development of withdrawal in infancy. *Infant Behavior and Development, 30*(1), 97–113.

25. Baillargeon, R. H., Normand, C. L., Séguin, J. R., Zoccolillo, M., Japel, C., . . . Tremblay, R. E. (2007). The evolution of problem and social competence behaviors during toddlerhood: A prospective population-based cohort survey. *Infant Mental Health Journal, 28,* 12–38.

26. Baillargeon, R. H., Sward, G. D., Keenan, K., & Cao, G. (2011). Opposition-defiance in the second year of life: A population-based cohort study: Opposition-defiance in the second year of life. *Infancy, 16*(4), 418–434.

27. Crick, N. R., Ostrov, J. M., & Kawabata. Y. (2007). Relational aggression and gender: An overview. In D. J. Flannery & A. Vazsonyi (Eds.), *The Cambridge handbook of violent behavior and aggression* (pp. 243–260). New York: Cambridge University Press.

28. Séguin, J. R., Parent, S., Tremblay, R. E., & Zelazo, P. D. (2009). Different neurocognitive functions regulating physical aggression and hyperactivity in early childhood. *Journal of Child Psychology & Psychiatry, 50*(6), 679–687. doi:10.1111/j.1469-7610.2008.02030.x

29. Tremblay, R. E. (2004). Decade of behavior distinguished lecture: Development of physical aggression during infancy. *Infant Mental Health Journal, 25*(5), 399–407. doi:10.1002/imhj.20015

30. Benzies, K., Keown, L., & Magill-Evans, J. (2009). Immediate and sustained effects of parenting on physical aggression in Canadian children aged 6 years and younger. *Canadian Journal of Psychiatry, 54*(1), 55–64.

31. Cote, S. M., Vaillancourt, T., LeBlanc, J. C., Nagin, D. S., & Tremblay, R. E. (2006). The development of physical aggression from toddlerhood to pre-adolescence: A nationwide longitudinal study of Canadian children (Clinical report). *Journal of Abnormal Child Psychology, 34*(1), 71–86.

32. Lorber, M. F., & Egeland, B. (2011). Parenting and infant difficulty: Testing a mutual exacerbation hypothesis to predict early onset conduct problems. *Child Development, 82*(6), 2006–2020. doi:10.1111/j.1467-8624.2011.01652.x

33. Mesman, J., Stoel, R., Bakermans-Kranenburg, M. J., van IJzendoorn, M.H., Juffer, F., . . . Alink, L. R. A. (2009). Predicting growth curves of early childhood externalizing problems: Differential susceptibility of children with difficult temperaments. *Journal of Abnormal Child Psychology, 37*, 625–636.

34. LeCuyer, E., & Houck, G. M. (2006). Maternal limit-setting in toddlerhood: Socialization strategies for the development of self-regulation. *Infant Mental Health Journal, 27*(4), 344–370. doi:10.1002/imhj.20096

35. Lee, S. J., Taylor, C. A., Altschul, I., & Rice, J. C. (2013). Parental spanking and subsequent risk for child aggression in father-involved families of young children. *Children & Youth Services Review, 35*(9), 1476–1485. doi:10.1016/j.childyouth.2013.05.016

36. Gromoske, A. N., & Maguire-Jack, K. (2012). Transactional and cascading relations between early spanking and children's social-emotional development. *Journal of Marriage & Family, 74*(5), 1054–1068. doi:10.1111/j.1741-3737.2012.01013.x

37. Holden, G. W., Williamson, P. A., & Holland, G. W. O. (2014). Eavesdropping on the family: A pilot investigation of corporal punishment in the home. *Journal of Family Psychology, 28*(3), 401–406. doi:10.1037/a0036370

38. Holden, G. W., Brown, A. S., Baldwin, A. S., & Croft Caderao, K. (2014). Research findings can change attitudes about corporal punishment. *Child Abuse & Neglect, 38*(5), 902–908. doi:10.1016/j.chiabu.2013.10.013

39. Jabaley, J., Lutzker, J., Whitaker, D., & Self-Brown, S. (2011). Using iPhones™ to enhance and reduce face-to-face home safety sessions within SafeCare®: An evidence-based child maltreatment prevention program. *Journal of Family Violence, 26*(5), 377–385. doi:10.1007/s10896-011-9372-6

40. Baillargeon, R. H., Normand, C. L., Séguin, J. R., Zoccolillo, M., Japel, C., . . . Tremblay, R. E. (2007). The evolution of problem and social competence behaviors during toddlerhood: A prospective population-based cohort survey. *Infant Mental Health Journal, 28*, 12–38.

41. Gaensbauer, T. (2004). Telling their stories: Representation and reenactment of traumatic experiences occurring in the first year of life. *ZERO TO THREE, 24*(5), 25–31.

42. Lieberman, A. (1993). *The emotional life of a toddler.* New York: Free Press.

Chapter 15

1. Center for Parent Information and Resources. (2014). *Providing early intervention services in natural environments.* Retrieved from *http://www.parentcenterhub.org/repository/naturalenvironments/*

2. Faddiman, A. (1998) *The spirit catches you and you fall down: A Hmong child, her American doctors, and the collision of two cultures.* New York: Noonday Press

3. Human Genome Project. (2011). *Human genome project information.* Retrieved from *www.ornl.gov/sci/techresources/Human_Genome/home.shtml*

4. National Down Syndrome Society (NDSS). (2012). *What is Down syndrome?* Retrieved from *http://www.ndss.org/Down-Syndrome/What-Is-Down-Syndrome/*

5. Down Syndrome Education International. (2014). *Different early interventions have different outcomes: Responsive teaching.* Retrieved from *http://www.dseinternational.org/en-us/education21/12/*

6. Centers for Disease Control and Prevention. (2015). *Facts about fragile X syndrome.* Retrieved from *http://www.cdc.gov/ncbddd/fxs/facts.html*

7. Cassels, C. (2008). *Widespread newborn screening for fragile X under way.* Retrieved from *http://www.medscapre.com/viewarticle/579468*

8. Mayo Clinic. (2015). *Cystic fibrosis.* Retrieved from *http://www.mayoclinic.org/diseases-conditions/cystic-fibrosis/basics/definition/con-20013731*

9. National Heart, Lung, and Blood Institute. (2012). *What is sickle cell anemia?* Retrieved from *www.nhlbi.nih.gov/health/health-topics/topics/sca/*

10. Sensory Processing Disorder (SPD) Resource Center. (2015). *Tactile defensiveness . . . So that's why he acts that way!* Retrieved from *http://www.sensory-processing-disorder.com/tactile-defensiveness.html*

11. March of Dimes. (2013). *PKU (phenylketonuria) in your baby.* Retrieved from *http://www.marchofdimes.org/complications/phenylketonuria-in-your-baby.aspx*

12. Genetics Home Reference. (2016). *Tay-Sachs disease*. Retrieved from *http://ghr.nlm.nih.gov/condition/tay-sachs-disease*

13. UCP (United Cerebral Palsy). (2013). *Cerebral palsy—Facts & figures*. Retrieved from *www.ucp.org/ucp_generaldoc.cfm/1/9/37/37-37/447*

14. Spina Bifida Association. (2012). *Important message on folic acid*. Retrieved from *http://www.spinabifidaassociation.org/site/c.evKRI7OXIoJ8H/b.8029669/k.9884/Lower_the_Risk.html*

15. KidsHealth. (2015). *Abusive head trauma (shaken baby syndrome)*. Retrieved from *http://kidshealth.org/parent/medical/brain/shaken.html*

16. Associated Press. (2016). *Court cases challenge 'shaken baby' diagnosis*. Retrieved from *http://abcnews.go.com/US/wireStory/court-cases-challenge-shaken-baby-diagnosis-36916005*

17. MedlinePlus. (2012). *TORCH screen*. Retrieved from *http://www.nlm.nih.gov/medlineplus/ency/article/003350.html*

18. National Early Childhood Technical Assistance Center (NECTAC). (2012). *Early intervention program for infants and toddlers with disabilities (Part C of IDEA)*. Retrieved from *http://www.nectac.org/partc/partc.asp*

19. Division for Early Childhood. (2011). *Individuals with disabilities education act Part C: Early intervention program for infants and toddlers with disabilities*. Retrieved from *http://www.cec.sped.org/~/media/Files/Policy/Early%20Learning/Finished%20Part%20C%20Regs.pdf*

20. The Early Childhood Technical Assistance Center. (2015). *Early identification: Screening, evaluation and assessment*. Retrieved from *http://ectacenter.org/topics/earlyid/screeneval.asp*

21. Center for Parent Information and Resources. (2014). *Writing the IFSP for your child*. Retrieved from *http://www.parentcenterhub.org/repository/ifsp/#contents*

22. American Speech, Hearing, and Language Association. (2011). *IDEA Part C issue brief: Service coordination*. Retrieved from *http://www.asha.org/Advocacy/federal/idea/IDEA-Part-C-Issue-Brief-Service-Coordination/*

23. Ibid.

24. Kontos, S. (1988). Family day care as an integrated early intervention setting. *Topics in Early Childhood Special Education, 8*(2), 1–4.

25. Buell, M. J., Gamel-McCormick, M., & Hallam, R. A. (1999, December). Inclusion in a child development and education context: Experiences and attitudes of family child development and education providers. *Topics in Early Childhood Special Education, 19*, 217–224.

26. eXtension. (2015). *What is inclusive child care?* Retrieved from *http://articles.extension.org/pages/61602/what-is-inclusive-child-care*

27. Cross, A. F., Traub, E. K., Hutter-Pishagi, L., & Shelton, G. (2004). Elements of successful inclusion for children with significant disabilities. *Topics in Early Childhood Special Education, 24*(3), 169–184.

28. O'Brien, M. (1997). *Inclusive child care for infants and toddlers: Meeting individual and special needs*. Baltimore, MD: Brookes.

29. California Department of Education. (2009). *Inclusion works! Creating child care programs that promote belonging for children with special needs*. Retrieved from *http://www.cde.ca.gov/sp/cd/re/documents/inclusionworks.pdf*

30. Meisels, S. J., Marsden, D., Dombro, A. L., Weston, D. R., & Jewkes, A. M. (2003). *The Ounce Scale*. New York: Pearson Early Learning

31. Child Care Law Center. (2014). *Know the law about The Americans with Disabilities Act and child care in California*. Retrieved from *http://childcarelaw.org/wp-content/uploads/2014/06/Know-the-Law-About-The-Americans-with-Disabilities-Act-and-Child-Care.pdf*

32. U.S. Department of Health and Human Services and U.S. Department of Education. (2015). *Policy statement on inclusion of children with disabilities in early childhood programs*. Retrieved from *http://www2.ed.gov/policy/speced/guid/earlylearning/joint-statement-full-text.pdf*

33. DEC/NAEYC. (2009). *Early childhood inclusion: A joint position statement of the Division for Early Childhood (DEC) and the National Association for the Education of Young Children (NAEYC)*. Chapel Hill, NC: The University of North Carolina, FPG Child Development Institute.

Chapter 16

1. Katz, L. G. (1987). The nature of professions: Where is early childhood education? In L. G. Katz (Ed.), *Current topics in early childhood education* (Vol. 7). Norwood, NJ: Ablex.

2. Feeney, S. (2012) *Professionalism in early childhood education: Doing our best for young children*. Upper Saddle River, N.J.: Pearson.

3. National Association for the Education of Young Children (NAEYC). (2009). *NAEYC standards for early childhood professional preparation*. Washington, DC: NAEYC. Retrieved from *www.naeyc.org/files/naeyc/files/2009%20Professional%20Prep%20stdsRevised%204_12.pdf*

4. Council for Exceptional Children (CEC). (2009). *What every special educator must know—Ethics, standards, and guidelines for special educators* (6th ed.). Arlington, VA: Author.

5. The National Association for Family Child Care (NAFCC).(2013). *Quality standards for NAFCC accreditation*. Retrieved from *https://www.nafcc.org/file/35a7fee9-1ccf-4557-89d4-973daf84a052*

6. Dean, A., LeMoine, S., & Mayoral, M. (2015). *Critical competencies for infant toddler educators™*. Washington, DC: ZERO TO THREE.

7. Allen, L., & Kelly, B. B. (Eds). (2015). Committee on the Science of Children Birth to Age Deepening and Broadening the Foundation for Success; Board on Children, Youth, and Families; Institute of Medicine; National Research

Council. *Transforming the workforce for children birth through age 8: A unifying foundation*. Washington, DC: Author.

8. National Association for the Education of Young Children (NAEYC). (2005). *Code of ethical conduct and statement of commitment*. Retrieved from *www.naeyc.org/files/naeyc/file/positions/PSETH05.pdf*

9. Division for Early Childhood. (2009). *Code of ethics*. Arlington, VA: Author. Retrieved from *http://dec.membership-software.org/files/Position%20Statement%20and%20Papers/Member%20Code%20of%20Ethics.pdf*

10. Honig, A. (2013). Infants & toddlers: Building intimacy. *Early Childhood Today*. Retrieved from *www.scholastic.com/teachers/article/infants-toddlers-building-intimacy*

11. Feeney, S. (2012). *Professionalism in early childhood education: Doing our best for young children*. Upper Saddle River, N.J.: Pearson.

12. Honig, A. (1986). Tuning in to toddlers: A communication challenge. *Early Child Development and Care, 25,* 207–219.

13. Parlakian, R., & Seibel, N. (2001). *Being in charge: Reflective leadership in infant/family programs*. Washington, DC: ZERO TO THREE.

14. Allen, L. & Kelly, B. B. (Eds). (2015). Committee on the Science of Children Birth to Age Deepening and Broadening the Foundation for Success; Board on Children, Youth, and Families; Institute of Medicine; National Research Council. *Transforming the workforce for children birth through age 8: A unifying foundation*. Washington, DC: Author.

15. NAEYC. (2015). *Early childhood educators: Advancing the profession*. Washington, DC: Author. Retrieved from *https://www.naeyc.org/files/naeyc/Executive%20Summary.pdf*

16. Pianta, R. (2008). *Classroom assessment scoring system*™ *(CLASS)*. Baltimore, MD: Brookes Publishing.

17. Lally, J. R. (2003). Infant-toddler child care in the United States: Where has it been? Where is it now? Where is it going? *ZERO TO THREE, 24*(1), 29–34.

18. Carter, M., & Curtis, D. (1998). *The visionary director: A handbook for dreaming, organizing, and improvising in your center*. St. Paul, MN: Redleaf.

19. Zoglio, S. (1997). *Training program for teams at work*. Doylestown, PA: Tower Hill.

20. Ibid.

21. Ibid.

22. Carter, M. (1992). Honoring diversity: Problems and possibilities for staff and organization. In B. Neugebauer (Ed.), *Alike and different: Exploring our humanity with young children* (Rev. ed.). Washington, DC: NAEYC.

23. Shamoon-Shanok, R. (2009). What is reflective supervision? In S.S. Heller & L. Gilkerson (Eds.) *A practical guide to reflective supervision* (pp. 1–22). Washington, DC: ZERO TO THREE.

24. Eggbeer, L., Mann, T., & Seibel, N. (2007). Reflective supervision: Past, present, and future. *ZERO TO THREE, 28*(2), 5–9.

25. Heller, S., & Gilkerson, L. (Eds). (2009). *A practical guide to reflective supervision*. Washington DC: ZERO TO THREE.

26. Early Head Start National Resource Center. (2015). *Tips on becoming a reflective supervisor and a reflective supervisee*. Washington, DC: Author. Retrieved from *http://eclkc.ohs.acf.hhs.gov/hslc/tta-system/ehsnrc/comp/program-design/tips-reflective-supervisor-supervisee.html*

27. Bellm, D., Whitebook, M., & Hnatiuk, P. (1997). *The early childhood mentoring curriculum: A handbook for mentors*. Washington, DC: National Center for the Early Childhood Work Force.

28. Ibid.

29. Bellm, D., Whitebook, M., & Hnatiuk, P. (1997). *The early childhood mentoring curriculum: A handbook for mentors*. Washington, DC: National Center for the Early Childhood Work Force.

30. Chu, M. (2014). *Developing mentoring and coaching relationships in early care and education: A reflective approach*. Upper Saddle River, NJ: Pearson

31. Parlakian, R., & Seibel, N. (2001). *Being in charge: Reflective leadership in infant/family programs*. Washington, DC: ZERO TO THREE.

Name Index

*Go to References for a list of names of authors referred to in the chapters with numerals.

Subject Index